# FIELDS OF APPLIED PSYCHOLOGY

**ANNE ANASTASI**

*Professor of Psychology*
*Graduate School, Fordham University*

# *Fields of*
# *Applied Psychology*

**McGRAW-HILL BOOK COMPANY**

*New York*
*San Francisco*
*Toronto*
*London*

6789101112–BP–9876

FIELDS OF APPLIED PSYCHOLOGY

01606

# PREFACE

The primary aim of this book is to bring together what the well-educated person needs to know about the professional activities of psychologists in business, industry, advertising and marketing, education, clinical practice, law, government, and the military services. The book does not presume to give advice on how to treat neuroses, bring up children, handle employees, or live one's life. It seeks rather to give a comprehensive view of the work of applied psychologists, that is, all psychologists other than those engaged primarily in teaching or basic research within an academic setting. Although directed principally to the college student, the book is also appropriate for beginning graduate students in psychology, as well as for students in schools of business and possibly in schools of law and medicine. It should likewise be of special interest to personnel workers, advertisers, and businessmen in general who want an overview of what psychology has to offer in practical contexts.

Throughout the book, attention is focused on the specialized research methodologies which represent the psychologist's most distinctive contribution to each field. To this end, each area of professional activity is illustrated with one or more major research projects that provide the scientific foundation for the particular professional applications. What the student can most profitably learn from science is method, and this is especially true in a young and rapidly changing science like psychology. By focusing on method, moreover, the book provides the reader with the needed skills for critical evaluation of psychological findings, conclusions, and practices encountered in daily life. A special effort has been made to alert the reader to the types of methodological loopholes, fallacies, and misinterpretations likely to occur in popular writings on applied psychology and in the claims of charlatans and inadequately trained practitioners.

Another major aim of the book is to present an integrated and comprehensive picture of applied psychology. Combining such disparate fields as clinical, engineering, and consumer psychology within a single book makes it possible to perceive relations among their findings that have previously gone unnoticed. Fresh insights often emerge from the juxtaposition of similar problems that have been studied in different contexts by investigators with diverse points of view. For this reason, cross references have been used liberally throughout the book, and every effort has been made to note connections and unify the various areas.

Still another aim has been to give the reader a sense of the historical continuity of the field. Although applied psychology has undergone explosive development during and since World War II, it did not originate at that time. A deliberate effort has been made to include outstanding early experiments and to give the antecedents of certain characteristic modern developments, such as teaching machines, human-factors research in equipment design, or the psychosomatic approach to physical disorders.

Mention should also be made of the way in which references are utilized. Throughout the book, references are given, not only to identify sources of data and ideas, but also to suggest further readings for anyone interested in delving more deeply into a topic. The extensive bibliographies at the end of each chapter have been selected partly with this objective in mind. In the text itself, references are cited only by number in order not to clutter the page with names and dates of little intrinsic interest to the college student.

The author is indebted to many colleagues for their contributions to the preparation of this book. The following psychologists read one or more chapters and made many constructive suggestions: Edwin A. Fleishman, Joseph D. Matarazzo, Arthur W. Melton, Charles K. Ramond II, E. J. Shoben, Jr., S. D. S. Spragg, J. Wayne Wrightstone, and Joseph Zubin. Among the many persons who graciously provided relevant material in the form of unpublished reports, reprints, illustrations, or extensive correspondence, special mention should be made of the following: Leslie J. Briggs, Brant Clark, Lee J. Cronbach, Theodore W. Forbes, Robert M. Gagné, James J. Gallagher, Mary Agnes Gordon, Louis M. Heil, Jane D. Hildreth, Arthur Koponen, Milton Levine, Joseph P. Loftus, Jr., Bernard Lubin, Arthur A. Lumsdaine, John M. McKee, Mildred B. Mitchel, Norman L. Munn, D. Morgan Neu, Charles K. Ramond II, James J. Regan, Horacio J. A. Rimoldi, Sol M. Roshal, Morton A. Seidenfeld, Karl U. Smith, Lawrence N. Solomon, Julius Wishner, J. Wayne Wrightstone, and Joseph Zubin.

To my colleagues in the Fordham University Psychology Department I am grateful for their continued interest in the progress of the book and their readiness to discuss questions and provide pertinent materials; special thanks are extended to Joseph F. Kubis, William G. Lawlor, S. J., Dorothea McCarthy, and Henryk Misiak. I am happy to acknowledge the contribution of my husband, John P. Foley, Jr., to the solution of countless problems at all stages in the preparation of the book. Finally, I am indebted to Margaret Tighe of the Fordham University library staff, for her competence and dedication in tracking down elusive references and providing other bibliographic services, to Josephine McMahon for her skillful assistance in indexing, and to Kathleen Gentile, whose handling of typing and proofreading tasks transformed what might have been routine chores into a responsible and constructive performance.

*Anne Anastasi*

# CONTENTS

# PART V  CLINICAL PSYCHOLOGY

# PART VI  COUNSELING PSYCHOLOGY

# I

## *Introduction*

# 1

## What Is
## Applied Psychology?

Applied psychology is coming to play a vital role in more and more facets of modern society. Prior to World War II, the majority of psychologists were engaged in university teaching and basic research. Today over half of the members of the American Psychological Association are working in business, industry, clinics, hospitals, schools, community agencies, government, or the military services. It is the object of this book to provide an over-all view of the types of functions performed by such applied psychologists. Within each field, attention will be focused upon what psychologists as such can contribute to the solution of problems that are the joint concern of many different specialists.

### FIELDS OF APPLIED PSYCHOLOGY

The varied and growing activities of psychologists cannot be readily classified into neat and exclusive categories. The multiplicity of ways in which psychologists perceive themselves is well illustrated by the more than twenty divisions of the American Psychological Association (see Appendix A). Some of these, like the Divisions of General and of Experimental Psychology and the Division on the Teaching of Psychology, clearly draw most of their members from university faculties. Others, like the Divisions of Industrial, Consumer, Clinical, Counseling, Consulting, and Military Psychology, the Division of Psychologists in Public Service, and the Division of School Psychologists, are composed chiefly of applied psychologists. Still other divisions represent interest areas that cut across teaching or basic research and professional applications.

The fact that many APA members belong to more than one division is in part a reflection of the overlapping and changing roles played by contemporary psychologists. A few years ago a concerted effort was made to simplify the divisional structure of the APA. Several classifications were proposed that were simpler and logically more elegant than the existing one. But the project was abandoned when it was recognized that a set of coordinate, well-balanced, and mutually exclusive categories was neither realistic nor practicable.

Traditionally, the term "applied psychology" has been most closely identified with the applications of psychology in business and industry. The *Journal of Applied Psychology*, established in 1917, is still concerned largely with industrial and business psychology. Early textbooks, as well as college courses entitled "Applied Psychology," which began to appear at the time of World War I, usually covered problems of personnel selection, efficiency of work, and advertising. The first two of these areas were included in 1913 in a book on *Psychology and Industrial Efficiency* (30)[1] by Hugo Münsterberg, a Harvard professor who has been called the first all-round applied psychologist in America. Münsterberg did much to define the field of applied psychology and to outline the possible uses of psychology in business and industry, as well as in other areas.

Another pioneer in applied psychology was Walter Dill Scott, whose book on *Psychology of Advertising* (37) appeared in 1908. With his appointment as professor of applied psychology at Carnegie Institute of Technology in 1915, he became the first psychologist to hold such a title in an American university. Scott initiated research in several areas of personnel selection and in 1919 founded The Scott Company, the first consulting firm in this country devoted to industrial psychology. The reader interested in historical perspectives can find a comprehensive list of landmarks of professional psychology, from 1860 to 1939, in a handbook edited by Fryer and Henry (16, pp. vii–x). These landmarks include antecedent developments in general psychology that contributed to the rise of applied psychology, as well as noteworthy events within the entire area of applied psychology itself. A very detailed account of the rise and growth of industrial psychology in America, with special reference to the contributions of the Carnegie Institute group, is given in a 12-volume survey by Ferguson (14).

Within industrial psychology, later developments led to the differentiation of three major areas. These areas grew out of three corresponding traditions within general psychology. The area of personnel selection evolved from psychological testing and differential psychology; that of human engineering, from experimental psychology; and that of employee relations, from research on personality and social psychology (21).

*Personnel psychology,* covered in the first major division of this book (Part II), includes personnel selection and classification procedures, the closely related area of training,[2] and employee relations. Although some psychologists specialize in one or another of these areas, most psychologists qualified to work in one of them can and frequently do work in the others. There is considerable similarity in the interests, training, and experience of personnel psychologists concerned with any of these areas.

A distinctly different group, however, is engaged in *engineering psychology,* treated in Part III. Such psychologists deal with problems of work and fatigue, the improvement of work methods, conditions in the working environment—such as illumination, ventilation, and noise—and the design of equipment for more effective use by the human operator. Some psychologists identify the field of engineering psychology wholly with equipment design; others use the term more broadly to cover the other areas mentioned. Engineering psychology, whether in the broader or more restricted sense, has also been called by several other names, including "human engineering," "applied experimental psychology," "biomechanics," "biotechnology," "human-factors research," and "ergo-

[1] Throughout the book, the numbers in parentheses correspond to the numbers of the references listed at the end of each chapter.
[2] The application of learning principles and experimental techniques to industrial training has lagged far behind the development of the three major areas cited above, although many experimental psychologists participated in research on military training during and after World War II.

nomics." The term "engineering psychology," however, has been most widely accepted, especially in America. As can be surmised, psychologists in this field work in close collaboration with engineers.

In industry, the activities of both personnel and engineering psychologists have been traditionally sponsored by management. More recently, increasing interest has been evidenced in the possible roles of psychologists in trade unions (see, e.g., 12). Working either under joint union-management auspices or directly for labor unions, psychologists could conduct investigations in such familiar areas as employee attitudes, placement, work methods, working environment, and equipment design. They could study internal organizational and administrative problems within the unions themselves. And they could conduct research on the process of collective bargaining and labor-management negotiations. So far only meager beginnings have been made in any of these directions.

*Advertising and consumer psychology*, discussed in Part IV, also started as a part of business and industrial psychology but now represents a distinct field. Beginning at the turn of the century in laboratory studies of individual features of advertisements, this field has broadened to include extensive research on consumer characteristics, wants, and preferences. Such research merges into studies of economic behavior on the one hand and product design on the other. With regard to methodology, consumer surveys also have much in common with public opinion polling. Psychological work in these areas has many points of contact with economics and sociology.

In Part V, the reader is introduced to *clinical psychology*. One chapter considers techniques for the diagnosis of emotional and intellectual disorders; another, therapeutic procedures; and a third, research in clinical psychology. Although the first psychological clinic in America was established by Lightner Witmer at the University of Pennsylvania as early as 1896, the practice of clinical psychology dates largely from World War II. Prior to that time, clinical psychologists were chiefly mental testers, and most of their clients were children. The years since World War II have witnessed a phenomenal rise in the number of psychologists working in the clinical area, as well as an expansion of their activities to include more work with adults and more psychotherapy at all age levels. Research on clinical problems has also increased sharply both in quantity and in methodological sophistication.

That the work of psychologists often defies classification is well illustrated by the distinction between clinical psychology and *counseling psychology* (Part VI). In general, the counseling psychologist is concerned with milder forms of maladjustment than is the clinical psychologist. He deals, too, with a variety of problems encountered by essentially normal persons. Nevertheless, the functions of many individual clinical and counseling psychologists undoubtedly overlap.

Since vocational counseling constitutes a major part of the functions of many counseling psychologists, special attention will be given in Part VI to the nature of vocational choices, the factors affecting them, and their significance in the life of the individual. It is noteworthy, too, that the field of counseling psychology, although now much broader, originated in the vocational-guidance movement (see 6). The first vocational-guidance bureau was opened in Boston in 1908 by Frank Parsons, whose book on *Choosing a Vocation* (32) was published the following year. The National Vocational Guidance Association was organized in 1913. And in 1914 the first vocational-guidance unit in a public school system was established in Cincinnati. In its subsequent growth, the vocational-guidance movement itself was greatly influenced by the development of psychological testing. Still later, the emerging and broader field of counseling psychology incorporated many concepts and procedures originating within clinical psychology.

Part VII, covering *psychology and other professions,* is concerned with areas in which psychologists function chiefly as consultants to other professional personnel. These areas include education, medicine, and law. Psychologists also contribute indirectly to these fields through the training of professional personnel, particularly in education. It is characteristic of these fields that, although potentially they provide many opportunities for the application of psychology, their contacts with psychology have remained relatively undeveloped. But this situation is changing. Today there are many indications of a growing interest in the fuller utilization of psychology in all these fields.

## THE SCIENCE AND PROFESSION OF PSYCHOLOGY

Applied psychology does not differ in any fundamental way from the rest of psychology. In terms of training and orientation, every applied psychologist is a psychologist first and an applied specialist secondarily. This point of view was reaffirmed in a conference on graduate education in psychology held in 1958 under the auspices of the American Psychological Association (19). Psychology is probably alone in its status of "professional science" or "scientific profession," and *that,* the conference concluded, is the way psychology should remain if it is to be maximally effective. Psychologists are not sharply separated into basic scientists and professional practitioners. All have had essentially the same types of courses; specialization occurs chiefly at the level of practicum training and on-the-job experience. The clinical, counseling, or personnel psychologist, for example, has received training in experimental psychology, and the experimental psychologist in his research utilizes concepts or hypotheses that may have originated in the clinic or factory.

The unique contribution that the psychologist can make in business, industry, government, hospitals, clinics, schools, and other practical settings stems principally from his research approach to problems of human behavior. When the psychologist goes to work in an applied context, he brings with him, not a set of rules or specific facts, but a *method* for attacking problems. This is essentially the scientific method, common to all sciences. The applied psychologist has been trained in the many techniques for utilizing this basic method in the study of human behavior. It is for this reason that the major emphasis in the present book will be placed on the specific methodologies appropriate to each field of applied psychology.

What, specifically, is meant by the statement that the applied psychologist uses the scientific method? First, like his colleagues in all fields of psychology, he relies on *empirical observation* rather than subjective opinion. His choice of a personnel selection test, training method, or type of therapy is *not* based on his "superior wisdom" as a psychologist, nor on the recommendation of leading authorities, standard texts, or "hundreds of satisfied clients." Instead, the psychologist gathers data to evaluate empirically the effectiveness of different tests, training methods, or forms of therapy. He will, of course, draw upon his previous knowledge and whatever wisdom he possesses to choose promising procedures and to formulate testable hypotheses. His familiarity with psychological facts and principles and his prior experience in similar practical situations will greatly facilitate the selection or development of effective procedures. But their effectiveness cannot be assumed—it always needs to be demonstrated.

It is also characteristic of the scientific method that full *records* of observations are made without delay, with the aid of mechanical devices when feasible. Even when relying on his unaided observation, however, the psychologist does not trust to memory for his facts. As a psychologist, he is particularly aware of the selectivity of attention and memory. We tend to notice and to recall just those observations that support our preconceived expectations or biases and to forget contradictory facts. Or we may recall the most dramatic instances, which are likely to be atypical and less representative than the more readily forgotten ordinary cases.

Another prerequisite of scientific observation is *replication*. Observations must be repeated. Generalizing from a single observation or from a few cases is especially hazardous in psychology because of the extensive individual differences in behavior, as well as the variability in the responses of the same individual on different occasions. Many repetitions are needed to establish a conclusion with adequate certainty.

But numbers are not enough. Statistics *may* lie when improperly employed. The cases observed must be *representative* of the groups about which conclusions are to be drawn. The samples utilized must be carefully scrutinized for possible selective bias. Perhaps the most vivid demonstration of the effect of such selective bias is provided by public opinion polls that "went wrong" in their predictions because certain income levels or other categories of persons happened to be either overrepresented or underrepresented in the samples interviewed.

One of the chief distinguishing features of the scientifically trained applied psychologist is that he never fails to specify the *margin of error* of his procedures. No technique is perfect; and the extent of error inherent in each must be taken into account in any administrative decisions based upon its application. Such error itself must be empirically determined before the technique is ready for operational use. An example of the type of chance errors that affect psychological measurement is provided by temporal fluctuation. Thus a job applicant might score lower on a test on one day because he is sleepy and depressed, and higher on another day when he feels alert and confident. Or he might perform better on one form of the test and poorer on another because of the particular choice of items in the two forms, thereby illustrating another type of measurement error.

Still another example is to be found in the use of personnel selection tests to predict an applicant's job performance. Since so many factors influence an employee's achievement on the job, it is obvious that no test could make such a prediction with perfect accuracy. Some variation between the predicted and actual outcome is inevitable. Through follow-up studies, it is possible to determine the magnitude of such prediction errors for any given test and any given job.

A different kind of chance error can be seen in an attitude survey, when one sample of 50 employees reports more dissatisfaction with management policies than another sample of 50. Even though both samples were chosen with equal care to represent a cross section of the company's employees in all important characteristics, the first sample happened to include more disgruntled individuals than the second. Any statistical measure, such as an average, percentage, or correlation, should be accompanied by some indication of the fluctuation in its value to be expected from sample to sample. With such a sampling error, we are able to estimate the limits within which results in other samples are likely to fall. Thus we might be able to predict that the percentage of dissatisfied employees in the company falls between 24 and 32, even though we cannot say definitely whether it is 27, 31, or some other specific figure.

Although all of the above procedures are characteristic of the scientific method, the very heart of the method is to be found in the design of experiments that permit observations under *controlled conditions*. Only under such circumstances can we identify cause-and-effect relations. To establish the effectiveness of a particular form of therapy, it is not enough to report that 63 per cent of the patients recovered. We must also know what percentage recovered in an untreated control group equated in all relevant respects with the treated group. As long as the two groups differed in only one respect, namely, the presence or absence of a given treatment, then differences in outcome can be attributed to the treatment.

It should not be inferred, however, that the scientific method is limited to the study of a single variable at a time. With more complex experimental designs, it is possible to investigate simultaneously the effects of two or more variables, as well as the interaction between them. In Table 1 is a hypothetical example of an experimental design in which two methods of teaching arithmetic are employed systematically with three groups of children differing in IQ. Of the 40 subjects in Group I, with IQ's between 120 and 140, 20 are taught by method A and 20 by method B. The 40 subjects in Group II are similarly

**TABLE 1**  *Schematic Illustration of Interaction between Teaching Method and Ability Level*

| Group | Method A | Method B |
|---|---|---|
| I. IQ 120–140 | $N_1 = 20$<br>$M_1 = 41$ | $N_2 = 20$<br>$M_2 = 59$ |
| II. IQ 90–110 | $N_3 = 20$<br>$M_3 = 38$ | $N_4 = 20$<br>$M_4 = 22$ |
| III. IQ 60–80 | $N_5 = 20$<br>$M_5 = 21$ | $N_6 = 20$<br>$M_6 = 8$ |

assigned to the two teaching methods, and the same procedure is followed with Group III. The mean scores obtained by the six subgroups, showing amount of improvement following the course, indicate that method B is more effective than method A with the brighter subjects (Group I), while the reverse is true of the less able groups. If the appropriate statistical analyses reveal that these differences exceed those expected by chance, we can conclude that there is a significant *interaction* between teaching method and ability level.[3] The joint analysis of both variables thus permits the discovery of relationships that would have gone undetected if either variable had been investigated separately.

Since applied psychologists follow the same fundamental procedures as their laboratory colleagues in solving problems, how can they be differentiated? When the applied psychologist is engaged in research—as is true much of the time for many applied psychologists—the distinction hinges on the difference between basic and applied research. This difference is one of degree. Although examples can be found that fall clearly into the basic or applied categories, some research could be classified in either. One determining factor is how the problem is chosen: to help in theory construction or in making administrative decisions. For instance, is the investigation concerned primarily with the nature of learning or with the most effective method for training airplane pilots?

A closely related difference pertains to the specificity or generality of the results. The findings of basic research can usually be generalized more widely than those of applied research. The latter characteristically yields results pertaining only to narrowly limited situations. Similarly, applied research permits less analysis of causal relationships, since situations are likely to be compared in their totality, rather than being broken down into more elementary components. For instance, applied research may demonstrate that one of two training procedures, in all their operational complexities, yields better results than the other within a particular context. But it may not be possible, under these circumstances, to specify *why* the one method was superior. It should be added that the sponsorship or setting of a research project does not necessarily indicate its nature. Some research conducted under industrial or government auspices, or in hospitals or clinics, is clearly basic rather than applied.

Some applied psychologists spend all or most of their time in service rather than research functions. How does such a psychologist use scientific method when engaged, for example, in psychotherapy with a neurotic patient, in testing a child with a reading disability, in interviewing an applicant for an executive position, or in planning a consumer survey for a toothpaste manufacturer? He does so in at least two ways. First, he evaluates and chooses his procedures, not on the basis of subjective opinion, but in the light of available published research conducted in comparable situations. Being unable under the circumstances to carry out his own empirical evaluations, he nevertheless is guided by whatever empirical data are available regarding tests, questionnaire techniques, types of psychotherapy, or any other procedure he plans to use.

In a still more general way, the psychologist's scientific training influences his approach to every problem he encounters in his service functions. Through such training, he has formed habits of accurate and objective observation and recording of facts and has learned to guard against preconceived notions and premature acceptance of conclusions. He has learned to reserve judgment and to modify or discard conclusions as fresh facts become available. In his service

[3] The statistical procedure required for this purpose is *analysis of variance*. Introductions to it can be found in any recent text on statistics, such as Edwards (10), Ferguson (13), Garrett (17), Guilford (20), and McNemar (28). More detailed treatment of experimental design is provided by Edwards (9) and Ray (34).

functions as in his research, the applied psychologist often needs to formulate hypotheses and verify them against subsequent data. In trying to discover the sources of a patient's neurotic fear, the causes of a child's reading difficulty, or the leadership potential of a job applicant, the psychologist forms a succession of tentative hypotheses. Each hypothesis suggests what further facts must be elicited and is in turn either confirmed or disconfirmed by such facts.[4]

To be sure, not all applied psychologists have profited so fully from their scientific training. But it is the goal of such training to foster this type of problem-solving attitude. Such an attitude represents an important difference between the professional psychologist and either the well-meaning but untrained "psychologizer" or the deliberate impostor.

## THE PROBLEM OF CHARLATANISM

Some of the areas in which applied psychologists work have traditionally proved attractive to charlatans, pseudoscientists, and self-styled experts. In this flourishing psychological underworld are found phrenologists, physiognomists, and others who try to diagnose your aptitude and personality traits or prescribe a specific career by examining the shape of your skull, the angle of your jaw, or the color of your eyes. Here, too, are the many systems for improving your personality, developing your memory or your selling ability, overcoming your fears and other emotional problems, and generally attaining health-wealth-and-happiness for the payment of a small fee (see 40). On the borderland are the practitioners who assume a semblance of scientific respectability by administering tests. They may, however, rely on a single test of unknown validity for which extravagant claims are made. Or they may send a batch of tests by mail, which are taken under uncontrolled conditions and interpreted without any other knowledge about the individual. All these practices represent flagrant misuses of tests and yield meaningless results.

Charlatanism is against the public interest under whatever guise it is practiced. But charlatans have often called themselves psychologists, thus further confounding the public and undermining its confidence in psychology. When the glowing promises go unfulfilled and the anticipated benefits fail to materialize, psychology gets the blame. Some charlatans hold "degrees" from diploma mills and dubious correspondence schools offering bizarre or token curricula. Several of these schools grant a degree called "Doctor of Psychology," which to the unsuspecting public may sound even more convincing than the "Doctor of Philosophy in Psychology" held by genuine psychologists. The Ph.D. title itself is used by a still larger number of these questionable institutions (7, 25), thus increasing the confusion with the legitimate Ph.D. degree granted by accredited universities.

The prevalence of charlatanism in psychology arises partly from the widespread misconceptions and lack of knowledge about the nature of psychology itself (see, e.g., 39). Psychology is one of the youngest of the sciences. Modern experimental psychology dates from about 1875; and until quite recently few psychologists worked outside of universities. Consequently, the general public

---

[4] For a provocative discussion of the relationship between the psychologist's service and research roles, see Rychlak (36).

is still vague about the functions of psychologists and is thus more receptive to the claims of the charlatans.

Even more important in accounting for the spread of charlatanism is people's strong desire for the sort of help the charlatans offer them. People believe the claims—however fantastic—because they want to believe them. And the charlatan, unhampered by facts, promises easier and more satisfying solutions to life's problems than does the reputable psychologist. The charlatan offers shortcuts to self-evaluation, quick cures for your neuroses, a new personality in ten easy lessons, and decisive vocational advice in a neat package —all with the bland assurance of 99½ per cent accuracy. The hard realities of science look unattractive against such prospects.

Still another reason for the spread of pseudopsychology is to be found in the lack of adequate legal controls for the title of psychologist. This condition, however, is rapidly being remedied. Since World War II, nearly a half of the states have enacted certification or licensing laws for psychologists, and the number is steadily increasing (see 24 and Appendix B).

Among their clients, charlatans include not only individuals seeking personal help but business organizations as well. In fact, certain consulting firms using highly questionable procedures specialize in personnel selection for business and industry. Even the more obvious forms of quackery, such as phrenology and physiognomy, have not been without adherents among business executives (e.g., 5). Such gullibility is not so prevalent today as it was early in the century, when psychology was largely unknown to the layman. But it is still encountered. As recently as 1953, for instance, *Fortune,* a magazine read widely by businessmen, published a serious and sympathetic account of a personnel selection system based on facial characteristics (41). The article refers to the use of this system by a number of high-level business executives as an aid in personnel decisions. The personnel and industrial-relations director of one large manufacturing company, for instance, is quoted as saying that this system "is one of the greatest contributions ever made to the field of executive selection and development" (41, p. 146).

Efforts to judge personality and aptitudes from physical appearance date back to antiquity. Today this accumulated folklore survives, not only in the organized systems of charlatanry, but also in common social stereotypes. Literature and art have done much to perpetuate these stereotypes. And our very language makes it difficult to escape them. Thus we associate "highbrow" or "egghead" with the intellectual, red hair with a fiery temper, and a square jaw with firmness of character. These familiar examples illustrate one source of popular stereotypes, namely, analogy and superficial resemblance. Red is the color of fire, and a square jaw looks more solid and firm than a receding chin. Similarly, the association between head size or shape and intelligence is bolstered by the vague knowledge that the brain plays an important part in behavior.

A little knowledge about the brain was also the basis for the doctrine of phrenology, formulated by the eighteenth- and early nineteenth-century anatomist Franz Gall. Going far beyond the meager data then available on the localization of cortical functions, Gall proposed that different areas of the brain control specific and complex traits, such as mechanical ingenuity, conscientiousness, and combativeness. He maintained further that over- or under-development of these traits could be diagnosed by examining the protuberances on the skull. The identification of a particular "bump" was taken to mean that the function allegedly controlled by the corresponding cortical area was highly developed in the individual. In the hands of its later exponents, Gall's theoretical formulation degenerated into a popular system for quick personality assessment and vocational guidance (15).

An examination of the rationale underlying phrenology will serve to illustrate the sort of fallacious reasoning prevalent in such pseudoscientific systems. First, the assumed correspondence between skull shape and brain shape ignores the cerebrospinal fluid and the several layers of membrane that intervene between brain and skull. Second, size is not a dependable index of the degree of development of different parts of the brain. Efficiency of function is more likely to be related to complexity of interrelations among neurones and other microscopical characteristics of nerve matter. Third, the type of trait that phrenologists ascribe to different brain areas is quite unlike the functions identified through research on cortical localization. Connections have been demonstrated between certain muscle groups or sense organs and specific brain areas, the very areas where phrenologists localize such traits as veneration and parental love.

Fourth, and probably most important, is the nature of the evidence cited by phrenologists in support of their doctrine (15). Such evidence vividly illustrates the popular fallacy of citing selected cases. In their published writings, phrenologists amassed examples of eminent men whose cranial protuberances corresponded to the alleged cerebral location of their special talents. Similarly, they cited cases of intellectual leaders who had unusually large skulls. A favorite example is Daniel Webster, whose massive skull measured over 24½ inches in circumference and who had a cranial protuberance in the exact spot where phrenologists locate literary talent. But of course the phrenologists ignore all the other eminent men with average or small skulls and with bumps in the wrong places. Phrenologists also refer to microcephalic idiots, who have abnormally small skulls and very low intelligence. But they overlook the other clinical varieties of mental deficiency with normal skulls or with characteristically large skulls. Investigations conducted by psychologists on large, unselected samples of children and adults have revealed very low correlations between cranial capacity and intelligence (4, ch. 5; 33, ch. 3). Similarly, precise measurements of head shape have shown no consistent relationships with either general intellectual level or special aptitudes (4, ch. 5; 22, ch. 4; 33, ch. 3).

Closely related to phrenology is the doctrine of physiognomy, under which are loosely grouped a number of characteristics pertaining to facial structure, hand shape, skin texture, and hair and eye color. Drawing partly from ancient lore and partly from selected examples of the physiognomies of famous men, Johann Lavater wrote extensively on this system in the eighteenth century. Early in the present century, Katherine Blackford (5) elaborated certain aspects of it with special reference to its use in personnel selection. In this form, the system enjoyed considerable vogue for a number of years.

In this area, too, psychologists have conducted several investigations designed to check on various alleged associations between physical and psychological traits (22, ch. 4; 33, ch. 7). Carefully measured facial dimensions and indices were correlated with aptitudes and personality characteristics as determined by tests or associates' ratings. Among the physical traits investigated were convexity of profile, height of forehead, blondness, and a variety of other facial measures chosen to test traditional claims of physiognomists. All the relationships investigated yielded insignificant correlations. It might be added that when psychologists invited practicing physiognomists or phrenologists to participate in controlled investigations, they repeatedly met with refusal (see, e.g., 22, p. 121).

## WHO IS AN APPLIED PSYCHOLOGIST?

The prevalence of charlatanism provides one reason for inquiring into ways of identifying genuine psychologists. In addition, the phenomenal growth of applied psychology since World War II means that more and more psychologists are working with laymen or with members of other professions who may lack the technical knowledge to evaluate the psychologist's qualifications. Hence it has become increasingly important to set up standard procedures for identifying psychologists and judging their special competencies.

Typically, the psychologist holds the Ph.D. degree in psychology from the graduate school of an accredited university. He should not be confused with a psychiatrist or psychoanalyst. The *psychiatrist* is trained in medicine. After receiving the M.D. degree, he undergoes several years of supervised experience in the diagnosis and treatment of mental disorders. His preparation thus parallels that of other medical specialists, such as the surgeon or pediatrician. The *psychoanalyst* may be either a psychiatrist or a psychologist who utilizes a particular approach to the treatment of emotional disorders, an approach originating in the psychoanalytic theories of Sigmund Freud. The *clinical psychologist*, like psychologists in other fields, has earned a Ph.D. degree in psychology, with additional experience in working with maladjusted persons. More will be said in Part V of this book regarding the functions of clinical psychologists and their relations with psychiatry.

Some psychologists in all fields have only the M.A. degree. But the proportion of psychologists at this training level is decreasing as standards improve and become more formalized. Persons with the M.A. degree in psychology are often qualified to function as psychological technicians, in a limited area or under supervision, rather than as professional psychologists (19).

A significant step, both in raising professional standards and in helping the general public to determine who is a psychologist, has been the enactment of licensing and certification laws for psychologists. Before World War II, there was virtually no legal control over either the practice of psychology or the use of the title "Psychologist." Today, most of the states in which large numbers of psychologists are employed either have such laws or are in the process of enacting them (see 24). In such states, psychologists may be identified by the possession of a certificate indicating that certain standards have been met. In New York State, for example, the requirements include the Ph.D. degree in psychology from an accredited university, two years of relevant experience, and the passing of a written qualifying examination. The law is administered by the State Education Department, with the assistance of a committee of psychologists.

At a still higher level, specialty certification is handled by the American Board of Examiners in Professional Psychology (ABEPP), established in 1946.

Requiring the Ph.D. degree, five years of experience, and intensive written and practical examinations, this board issues diplomas in three specialties: clinical, counseling, and industrial psychology. ABEPP publishes a directory of diplomates in each specialty, which is available in libraries and may also be obtained by interested individuals or organizations (see Appendix B). The function of ABEPP is essentially to provide information on qualified psychologists. As a privately constituted board within the profession, it has no legal authority for enforcement. The various state laws pertaining to psychology, on the other hand, do carry such authority. In a state having such laws, a person without the appropriate certificate who holds himself forth as a psychologist is subject to legal penalties.

ABEPP was originally established by the American Psychological Association (APA), the national association to which most psychologists belong (see Appendix B). Membership in this association does not imply that the psychologist is certified for the performance of any service functions—only state certificates and ABEPP diplomas serve that purpose. Nevertheless, the annual directory of the APA is a source of considerable information about the location, training, and professional functions of its members. The APA has also undertaken many other activities designed to improve and systematize training standards, raise the level of professional practice, work out effective relations with other professions, and clarify the public image of psychology. An example is the participation of an APA committee in the preparation of a booklet, *Psychologists in Action* (31), designed to introduce the layman to the work of psychologists. Another booklet prepared under APA auspices is *The Psychologist in Industry* (2), dealing with one major area of applied psychology.

Of particular importance was the formulation of a professional code of ethics, *Ethical Standards of Psychologists* (11). First published by the American Psychological Association in 1953 and revised in 1963, this code is especially relevant to the problems encountered by applied psychologists in their relations with the public. The abridged, 1963 revision is reproduced in Appendix C.

A final question that may be asked about applied psychologists is where they work. Through what channels do they bring their specialized techniques to the public? Many industrial psychologists operate through consulting firms staffed largely by psychologists. Most of these organizations were established after World War II, often by groups of psychologists who had been engaged in psychological work in the Armed Forces. Some consulting firms are broader in scope, having been formed by business consultants or engineers but employing a number of full-time psychologists. All perform services for industry or government on a contract basis as needed. It has been estimated that in 1959 approximately one-third of all full-time industrial psychologists in the United States were employed by consulting firms (27, p. 707).

Other psychologists are employed directly by business and industry. They can now be found in practically every type of business, including manufacturing, retailing, transportation, advertising, insurance, and many others. An example of an industry-wide cooperative organization that has been using the services of psychologists for many years is the Life Insurance Agency Management Association (LIAMA). With a psychologist as its research director, this association develops and evaluates personnel selection techniques for life insurance salesmen, conducts employee attitude surveys, and performs other personnel research functions.

Many clinical or counseling psychologists are employed by hospitals, clinics, and counseling bureaus. State institutions for mental defectives or for emotionally disturbed patients, Veterans Administration hospitals, out-patient clinics, and community counseling centers are examples of such organizations. A much smaller number of psychologists work in prisons or in schools for juvenile delinquents (8, 38). In most of these correctional institutions, psychological services are hampered by serious understaffing. A recently defined and growing specialty area is that of the school psychologist, employed by public school systems and by some private schools. In addition, a considerable number of counseling psychologists and some clinical psychologists work in school systems.

Full-time private practice claims a small proportion of psychologists. In a 1960 survey (3), slightly less than 10 per cent of all psychologists were classified as self-employed. Among the clinical psychologists, approximately 14 per cent were in private practice. A one-third random sample of the Division of Clinical Psychology of the American Psychological Association, also surveyed in 1960, yielded a somewhat larger percentage (26). In this group, 17 per cent reported that they were engaged in full-time private practice, and an additional 12 per cent that they had part-time private practices. Because the private practitioner works without the systematic and close contacts with other professional personnel that are provided in an institutional setting, he should meet especially high standards of qualification (see 1). Preferably, he should hold an ABEPP diploma in his specialty.

A thriving area of applied psychology is represented by military psychology. In 1957, it was estimated that about 5 per cent of all APA members were working for the Army, Navy, or Air Force as full-time military or civilian personnel (29). The functions of these psychologists resemble most closely those of industrial psychologists. They include chiefly personnel selection and classification, training, military management and morale, and human engineering (18, 29). Some basic research is conducted by military psychologists, especially in connection with human engineering problems. Certain units in the military services also include clinical psychologists.

A particularly large group of psychologists is employed by civilian government agencies, such as the United States Civil Service Commission, United States Employment Service, United States Public Health Service, Department of Health, Education, and Welfare, Department of Agriculture, and Veterans Administration. Beginning in 1922, when the first government psychologist, L. J. O'Rourke, was appointed director of research in the United States Civil Service Commission (23), the employment of psychologists in public service has shown prodigious growth. In a spot check conducted in 1955, it was estimated that approximately 33 per cent of all psychologists in the APA were employed by government agencies (35). This estimate includes several previously mentioned categories, such as military services, state hospitals, and public school systems.[5] Within the total government service group, about 14.5 per cent were employed by the Federal

___

[5] Not included, however, are psychologists teaching in state universities or city colleges. Were this group to be added, the total number of APA members employed by the government would rise to 48 per cent (35).

government, 11.4 per cent by cities and counties, and 7.4 per cent by state governments.

Finally, mention should be made of the place of applied psychology in universities. Most universities have counseling centers where counseling and sometimes clinical psychologists provide service for the university's own students. Where an active clinical training program is under way, the university may also have hospital facilities, clinics, and counseling centers that serve the public. Some universities have bureaus of industrial psychology which operate much like a consulting firm, carrying out contract research and development programs for industry or government. To this should be added the contract research conducted by individual faculty members, usually under government sponsorship. Although many of these individual research grants are for basic research, some clearly belong in applied psychology.

## SUMMARY

Before World War II, psychology was primarily an academic discipline. Today, over half of America's psychologists work outside of universities. Employed largely by government agencies, industry, school systems, hospitals, clinics, and counseling centers, these applied psychologists are contributing in such areas as personnel selection and training, employee relations and management practices, the improvement of work methods and of the working environment, equipment design, advertising and consumer research, the diagnosis and treatment of personality disorders, and vocational and other types of personal counseling. Some psychologists work with members of other professions, as consultants or in the training of other professional personnel. This relationship is currently illustrated in the fields of education, law, and medicine.

Like all psychologists, the applied psychologist is trained in the basic science of psychology. His unique contribution stems from his application of the scientific method to problems of human behavior. The experimental method common to all the sciences consists essentially in the empirical observation and recording of facts under systematically controlled conditions. It requires replication, the use of representative samples, and a determination of the margin of error inherent in its procedures. The distinction between basic and applied research is one of degree. In his service functions, the applied psychologist is influenced in many ways by his training in scientific method. In this regard he differs from the charlatan, who has traditionally invaded several areas of applied psychology. Such professional developments as state certification of psychologists, the establishment of the American Board of Examiners in Professional Psychology, and the formulation of *Ethical Standards of Psychologists* represent significant steps in combating charlatanism and in clarifying the public image of psychology.

## REFERENCES

1. American Psychological Association, Board of Professional Affairs, Committee on Private Practice. Standards for APA *Directory* listings of private practice. *Amer. Psychologist,* 1960, **15,** 827–828.

2. American Psychological Association, Division of Industrial Psychology. *The psychologist in industry.* New York: Res. Inst. Amer., 1959.

3. *American science manpower, 1960.* Washington: Nat. Sci. Found., 1962.

4. Anastasi, Anne. *Differential psychology.* (3rd ed.) New York: Macmillan, 1958.

5. Blackford, Katherine M. H., and Newcomb, A. *The job, the man, the boss.* Garden City, N.Y.: Doubleday, 1919.

6. Brewer, J. M., et al. *History of vocational guidance: Origins and early development.* New York: Harper & Row, 1942.

7. Brophy, A. L., and Durfee, R. A. Mail-order training in psychotherapy. *Amer. Psychologist,* 1960, **15**, 356–360.

8. Corsini, R. J., and Miller, G. A. Psychology in prisons, 1952. *Amer. Psychologist,* 1954, **9**, 184–185.

9. Edwards, A. L. *Experimental design in psychological research.* New York: Holt, Rinehart and Winston, 1950.

10. Edwards, A. L. *Statistical analysis.* (Rev. ed.) New York: Holt, Rinehart and Winston, 1958.

11. Ethical standards of psychologists. *Amer. Psychologist,* 1963, **18**, 56–60.

12. Feinberg, M. R. et al. Implications of psychology in labor-management relations (A symposium). *Personnel Psychol.,* 1961, **14**, 239–284.

13. Ferguson, G. A. *Statistical analysis in psychology and education.* New York: McGraw-Hill, 1959.

14. Ferguson, L. W. *The heritage of industrial psychology.* (12 vols.) Hartford, Conn.: Finlay, 1963. Vol. 1.

15. Fowler, O. S. *Human science or phrenology.* Philadelphia: Nat. Publ. Co., 1873.

16. Fryer, D. H., and Henry, E. R. (Eds.) *Handbook of applied psychology.* (2 vols.) New York: Holt, Rinehart and Winston, 1950.

17. Garrett, H. E. *Statistics in psychology and education.* (5th ed.) New York: Longmans, Green, 1958.

18. Geldard, F. A. The first international symposium on military psychology. *Amer. Psychologist,* 1957, **12**, 737–739.

19. *Graduate education in psychology.* Washington: Amer. Psychol. Assoc., 1959.

20. Guilford, J. P. *Fundamental statistics in psychology and education.* (3rd ed.) New York: McGraw-Hill, 1956.

21. Haire, M. Psychological problems relevant to business and industry. *Psychol. Bull.,* 1959, **56**, 169–194.

22. Hull, C. L. *Aptitude testing.* Yonkers, N.Y.: World Book Co., 1928.

23. Kavruck, S. Thirty-three years of test research: A short history of test development in the U.S. Civil Service Commission. *Amer. Psychologist,* 1956, **11**, 329–333.

24. Kayton, I. Statutory regulation of psychologists: Its scope and constitutionality. *St. John's Law Rev.,* 1959, **33**, 249–279.

25. Lebo, D. Degrees for charlatans. *Amer. Psychologist,* 1953, **8**, 231–234.

26. Lubin, B. Survey of psychotherapy training and activities of psychologists. *J. clin. Psychol.,* 1962, **18**, 252–256.

27. McCollom, I. N. Psychologists in industry in the United States. *Amer. Psychologist,* 1959, **14**, 704–708.

28. McNemar, Q. *Psychological statistics.* (3rd ed.) New York: Wiley, 1962.

29. Melton, A. W. Military psychology in the United States of America. *Amer. Psychologist,* 1957, **12**, 740–746.

30. Münsterberg, H. *Psychology and industrial efficiency.* Boston: Houghton Mifflin, 1913.

31. Ogg, Elizabeth. *Psychologists in action.* New York: Public Affairs Comm., 1955.

32. Parsons, F. A. *Choosing a vocation.* Boston: Houghton Mifflin, 1909.

33. Paterson, D. G. *Physique and intellect.* New York: Century, 1930.

34. Ray, W. S. *An introduction to experimental design.* New York: Macmillan, 1960.

35. Rogers, L. S. Psychologists in public service and the public. *Amer. Psychologist,* 1956, **11**, 307–313.

36. Rychlak, J. F. Clinical psychology and the nature of evidence. *Amer. Psychologist,* 1959, **14**, 642–648.

37. Scott, W. D. *Psychology of advertising.* Boston: Small, Maynard, 1908.

38. Shelley, E. L. V. Psychological services in state schools for delinquent boys. *Amer. Psychologist,* 1954, **9,** 186–187.
39. Sherman, A. W., Jr. The image of psychology: Some implications for teaching. *Amer. Psychologist,* 1960, **15,** 465.
40. Steiner, Lee R. *Where do people take their troubles?* Boston: Houghton Mifflin, 1945.
41. Stryker, P. Is there an executive face? *Fortune,* 1953, **48,** 145–147, 162–168.

# II

*Personnel Psychology*

# 2

# *Developing a Personnel Selection Program*

Concerned with the general area of personnel psychology, Part II of this book deals with the application of psychology to the selection and training of personnel, as well as to problems of employee relations and management practices. The first three chapters of this part are devoted to personnel selection, covering in turn: (1) basic problems and procedures in developing a selection program; (2) the place of psychological tests in selection; and (3) selection procedures based on personal interactions and biographical data. In industry, the techniques of personnel selection are used not only in the hiring of new employees but also in connection with promotions, discharges, transfers, and other personnel decisions.

Nor are such techniques limited to industrial psychology. Essentially the same procedures are applicable to the selection and classification of military personnel, the admission of students to colleges and professional schools, or the identification of patients most likely to benefit from a particular form of therapy. Although first discussed in this section within the context of industrial psychology, these techniques provide an introduction to methodology that is of basic importance in most fields of applied psychology. For this reason, they will be examined more fully than more specialized procedures of limited application.

## JOB ANALYSIS

The development of a personnel selection program illustrates the basic problem-solving approach followed by the applied psychologist. Essentially, this approach includes four steps: (1) gathering information to define the problem; (2) formulating hypotheses; (3) testing hypotheses; and (4) translating the findings of the preceding step into administrative procedures. In the development of personnel selection techniques, definition of the problem is achieved through a *job analysis*. The purpose of such a job analysis is to provide a description of what workers do on the job for which selection procedures are being developed. The description should cover operations performed, equipment used, conditions of work, hazards and other special characteristics of the job, rate of pay, nature and amount of training required, opportunities for promotion or transfer, relation to other jobs, and any other pertinent information. The information included varies somewhat with the job, the company, and the use that is to be made of the job analysis. In selection research, the job description provides the basis for the job specification, or list of worker qualifications for which tests or other selection devices must be prepared. An example of a job description prepared by the United States Employment Service for a relatively simple job, that of hand dry cleaner, is given in Appendix D.

To be effective, a job analysis must be specific to the job being described. A description in terms of vague generalities that would be equally applicable to many jobs is of little use for purposes of personnel selection. Viteles (49), a pioneer in the development of job analysis techniques, highlighted this point by citing the following description of a librarian: "A love of reading is not a major qualification since a librarian has little time for reading. She needs accuracy, quickness, neatness, a pleasing appearance and the application necessary to do much routine work. All these qualities must be founded upon a sincere and active enthusiasm for library work" (49, p. 76). Commenting upon this superficial description, Viteles noted that it would be just as accurate if in place of librarian we were to substitute other job titles, such as cashier, file clerk, or dressmaker. Yet the requirements of these jobs are actually quite different. The job analyst must focus on specific requirements that differentiate the particular job from other jobs.

An even more important characteristic of an effective job analysis is that it indicate those aspects of performance that differentiate most sharply between the better and the poorer workers. In many jobs, workers of different levels of proficiency may differ little in the way they carry out most parts of their jobs—only certain features of the job may bring out the important differences between successes and failures. In his classic book on *Aptitude Testing*, Hull stressed the importance of these differentiating aspects of job performance, which he called "critical part-activities" (30, p. 286). More recently, this concept has been reemphasized by Flanagan (19, 20) under the name of "critical requirements."

Although for the present purpose we are considering job analysis as the first step in developing a personnel selection program, it should be noted that it has other important uses in industry. It can serve as a basis for setting up or modifying training programs, improving operating procedures, reducing accident hazards, and redesigning equipment. Job analyses also help in arriving at job evaluations for adjusting pay rates. For this purpose, different jobs are rated with regard to certain major factors, such as training and experience required, physical and psychological demands, degree of responsibility, and working conditions. By assigning weights to these factors, one can obtain an over-all evaluation for each job, which is then used in setting up the wage scale.[1] Still another application of job analysis is to be found in the preparation of job descriptions and classifications used in vocational counseling. More will be said about such sources of occupational information in Part VI.

For whatever purpose conducted, job analysis requires systematic data-gathering techniques if it is to yield usable information. When job information is sought in order to develop selection procedures, the available sources can be classified into seven types. First, the job analyst may consult *published analyses* of similar jobs. This procedure corresponds to the literature survey that customarily precedes any research project. When available, published job analyses may provide promising leads and suggestions, but their

[1] For a discussion of different systems of job evaluation, see Otis and Leukart (38), Patton and Littlefield (39), and Tiffin and McCormick (47, ch. 17).

limitations are obvious. Although possibly similar, the previously analyzed jobs are rarely identical with the one under consideration. Moreover, the same title may connote very different jobs. Well-known examples are the job titles of "secretary" and "engineer," each of which covers a multiplicity of widely varying jobs. Another difficulty is that verbal descriptions of job activities may have little meaning for the job analyst unless supplemented by more direct contacts with the job.

A second source of job-analysis data is to be found in *manuals and records* that may be available for the particular job. These include instructional and operating manuals specifying the procedures to be followed by the worker in various phases of the job. Among the performance records that would be useful are those containing qualitative descriptions of common errors, learning difficulties, or reasons for failure. Similarly, clues as to characteristics conducive to failure on the job can be obtained from an analysis of exit interview reports. Held regularly with employees who are leaving the company, these interviews often cover the reasons for job termination, whether initiated by the employer or employee. Records of customer complaints provide still another source of information about the problems encountered on a particular job.

A third and very common type of job-analysis technique involves *interviews* with workers, supervisors, or job instructors. Interviews with successful and unsuccessful workers, with employees having different amounts of job experience, and with learners at different stages of training are especially fruitful. Foremen, instructors, and other supervisors can often provide still other kinds of information. Such interviews have a number of advantages as job-analysis techniques. It is obvious that persons who have been carrying on the job are in a good position to report what occurs on such a job. Moreover, the participation of workers and supervisors in the job analysis gives them a better understanding of what the psychologist is trying to do and increases their ultimate acceptance of the results of the project. On the other hand, the worker, however experienced in job activities, may have little insight into the reasons for his own or other workers' success or failure. Nor can he readily translate job activities into worker qualifications. Semantic problems may also interfere with communication. Such terms as "good judgment," "sense of humor," or "dependability" may have very different connotations for different persons. For all these reasons, such interviews should cover objective facts as much as possible, focusing on what workers do and what happens.

An attempt to introduce more objectivity into workers' reports is illustrated by a fourth technique, which may be described as a *systematic activity log*. Rather than relying on memory during an interview, the worker is required to keep a running record of all the tasks he performs during a specified period of time. Such a procedure reveals many activities that may be overlooked when one relies on the recollections of a small sample of workers, as was demonstrated in an early analysis of the job of secretary (11). First, the members of the research staff together with six secretaries recorded all the secretarial duties they could recall. The list they compiled contained 166 items. Next a chart was prepared covering one working week, each day being divided into smaller time units. Copies of this chart were distributed to 125 secretaries with the instructions to record each activity in the appropriate space as it was performed. The resulting list revealed 871 different duties, in contrast to the 166 on the first list.

Forgetting undoubtedly accounts for part of this difference. That variation in duties on different secretarial jobs may also contribute to the difference, however, was suggested by a third part of the study. A survey of 715 secretaries with the complete checklist of 871 duties showed that only 3 per cent of the duties were common to the reports of three-fourths or more of the secretaries. Systematic performance logs kept by a large sample of workers can undoubtedly reveal job information not readily obtainable in other ways. There are many jobs, however, in which the keeping of such records would not be practicable.

A procedure that utilizes some of the features of the systematic activity log is the *critical-incident technique* described by Flanagan (20). Essentially, this technique calls for factual descriptions of specific instances of job behavior that are especially characteristic of either satisfactory or unsatisfactory workers. It thus centers attention on the previously discussed critical job requirements, leaving out of consideration job behavior that does not differentiate successful from unsuccessful workers. Depending on the nature of the job and other circumstances, the incidents may be reported by supervisors, co-workers, subordinates, or other associates. To ensure frankness in reporting, anonymity of the data should be preserved. The information is frequently obtained in an interview or in group-administered or mailed questionnaires. To avoid memory errors, the incidents may be recorded as they occur over a designated period, such as two weeks. Growing out of Air Force research during World War II, the critical-incident technique has been employed with such varied groups as commercial airline pilots, research personnel in physical science laboratories, factory workers, dentists, and department store salesclerks.

A sixth technique that is always desirable—even if only to supplement other procedures—is *direct observation* by the job analyst. This technique may involve no more than unaided personal observation, as when the job analyst accompanies a house-to-house salesman or a credit investigator on his rounds. When applicable, sound recordings, motion pictures, and other objective performance records may be utilized. In the analysis of manual operations, the job analyst may use the techniques of time-and-motion study, to be discussed in Part III. To be sure, the mere presence of an observer may affect performance somewhat in many types of jobs. Nevertheless, this type of observation provides the job analyst with a fuller and more vivid picture of job activities than could be obtained through more indirect sources.

For the same reason, a seventh source of information is sometimes utilized, namely, *performance of the job* by the analyst. Obviously, the job analyst can spend only a short time working on any one job. Moreover, this technique is not feasible with certain kinds of jobs, such as those requiring special skills or long training periods or those involving risk from an inexperienced operator. Early examples of job analyses based on extensive job performance include studies of department store salesclerks (6), taxi drivers, streetcar motormen, and assembly-line operators (see 30, p. 286). Today, a limited amount of job performance is occasionally used to supplement other sources of job information.

## PREPARATION AND PRELIMINARY
## TRYOUT OF PREDICTORS

Job analysis enables the personnel psychologist to define the problem by specifying the critical worker requirements for success in the given job. Such an analysis may suggest, for example, that the job demands finger dexterity, perceptual speed, computational accuracy, and the ability to work effectively under confusing and distracting conditions. The next step is to prepare tests, questions, rating scales, or other selection devices designed to assess the applicant's standing in these traits. All such selection instruments are known as *predictors*, since they are used to predict each individual's subsequent job performance.

The predictors assembled at this stage may include previously available published tests, instruments developed specially for this project, or a combination of the two. In choosing a predictor or in preparing a new one, the psychologist is in effect formulating a series of hypotheses, namely, that the score on each test or the answer to each question on an application or recommendation form is significantly related to eventual success on the given job. The correctness of these hypotheses depends upon several factors, such as the effectiveness of the job analysis in bringing out important job requirements, the proper utilization of previous research data obtained with available instruments in similar job situations, the psychologist's ingenuity in devising new instruments, and his general familiarity with psychological facts and principles. But although much can be done in advance to increase the chances that correct hypotheses will be formulated, it is only by an empirical follow-up that their correctness can be demonstrated.

Before embarking on a full-scale follow-up of the predictors, however, the psychologist will usually submit them to preliminary tryouts. Some predictors may be discarded and others modified as a result of such tryouts. Using groups similar to the applicant population for which the predictors are designed, we can check on time required, clarity of instructions, suitability of vocabulary and reading level, layout of printed matter, and similar questions.

Selection programs usually include some aptitude tests. In the preliminary tryout of such tests, it is particularly important to obtain information regarding their dispersion, difficulty level, reliability, and specificity. The first two characteristics can be checked by examining the distribution of scores obtained by a representative sample of persons. Obviously, if everyone achieves the same or nearly the same score, the test is of little use. The object of a test is to discriminate among individuals. Thus, the wider the variability or dispersion of scores, the better is the test fulfilling its function. Similarly, if the difficulty level of the test is suitable for the group, the scores will tend to fall into a symmetrical distribution, with the largest number near the center of the range and a decreasing number as the extremes are approached. With large samples, the distribution approximates the bell-shaped normal probability curve (see Figure 2, p. 30). If, however, the test is too difficult for the group, the scores will pile up at the low end; if it is too easy, they will pile up at the high end. In either case, the distributions will be appreciably skewed rather than normal.

The reliability of a test refers to its consistency. Will individuals retain the same relative position in the group if examined on two occasions with the same finger dexterity test? Obviously, if there were broad shifts in position, so that the person who was best in the group on one day scored near the bottom when retested on another day, the test could have no value as a predictor of subsequent job performance. As suggested by the above example, the temporal stability of a test can be determined by comparing the scores obtained by the same subjects on two administrations of the test.

Another aspect of test reliability pertains to consistency of scores on parallel forms of the test. Although designed to measure the same ability, such parallel forms are composed of different items. For example, two forms of a vocabulary test might yield slightly different scores because some individuals happen to know more words on one list, while others know more words on the other list. This type of reliability can be measured by comparing the scores obtained by the same persons on two forms of a test. When two forms are not available, the reliability is often estimated by comparing scores on two halves of a single form, such as the scores on odd and even items.

In the event that the test cannot be objectively scored but requires evaluation or interpretation of responses by the examiner, a further type of reliability that should be checked is scorer reliability. This can be done by having a sample of papers independently scored by two examiners and computing the degree of scorer agreement between the two sets of scores. Scorer reliability is more likely to represent a problem in certain types of personality tests than in aptitude tests, although it needs to be considered in some of the latter too.

Whatever the type of reliability under consideration, it can be expressed in terms of a *correlation coefficient*.[2] This statistical technique, which is used for many purposes in psychological research, shows the degree of relationship or correspondence between two sets of scores. The correlation coefficient, conventionally designated by the symbol $r$, provides a single index of the closeness and direction of relationship within the whole group. It can vary from $+1.00$ (a perfect positive correlation), through 0, to $-1.00$ (a perfect negative, or inverse, correlation). A $+1.00$ correlation means that the individual receiving the highest score in one variable also receives the highest score in the other, the one who is second best in the first is second best in the second, etc., each person falling just as far above or below the mean in one variable as he does in the other. A $-1.00$ correlation, on the other hand, indicates that the highest score in one variable is paired off with the lowest in the other, a corresponding perfect reversal occurring throughout the group. A zero correlation signifies no relationship at all between the two sets of scores, or the sort of arrangement that would result if the scores were shuffled and paired off at random.

The correlations found in actual practice are almost never equal to $+1.00$ or $-1.00$, but fall on some intermediate value. The numerical size of the coefficient represents the closeness of relationship, in either a positive or negative direction. An example of high positive correlation is given in Figure 1. This figure shows a "bivariate distribution," indicating the scores obtained by each of 100 persons on Forms A and B of a test. Each tally mark shows the score of one subject on both forms. It can be seen, for example, that seven

[2] Procedures for computing correlation coefficients can be found in any elementary statistics book, such as those cited in Chapter 1 (p. 9). For further discussion of test reliability, see any recent text on psychological testing, such as Anastasi (2) or Cronbach (12).

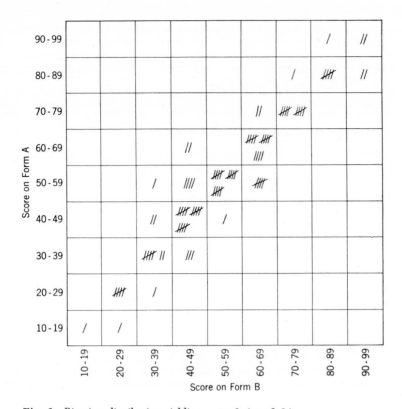

**Fig. 1** Bivariate distribution yielding a correlation of .94.

persons obtained scores between 30 and 39 on both forms, while three scored between 30 and 39 on Form A but between 40 and 49 on Form B. When computed, the correlation between the two forms proves to be .94. Such a correlation indicates a strong tendency for individuals to maintain the same relative standing on the two forms, although it can be seen that the correspondence is not perfect.

Correlation is also useful in checking the specificity of different tests. "Specificity" refers to the fact that the tests used in a selection program should measure separate and independent abilities in order to avoid wasteful duplication. Each test should be chosen to cover a different aspect of the job performance that is to be predicted. A test yielding a single score based on a combination of several aptitudes would be less useful than a set of separate tests measuring relatively pure and independent functions. The latter arrangement permits a more efficient and flexible use of data.

Specificity can be checked by correlating the scores obtained by a group of persons on the different tests. When two or more tests correlate too highly among themselves, one of them can be chosen on the basis of other considerations, such as dispersion, difficulty level, and reliability. To be sure, two or even more tests covering the same function may be included at this stage if the object is to see which will prove best in the subsequent follow-up. The choice among them would then be postponed until the next step. In any event, more predictors of all sorts should be included at the outset than we ultimately plan to retain, so that we may adopt for operational use those that prove most effective in the follow-up.

## VALIDATION OF PREDICTORS

It is apparent that the preliminary tryouts discussed in the preceding section involve the testing of several hypotheses regarding difficulty level, reliability, and other features of the predictive instruments. The major task of hypothesis testing, however, is concerned with the relationship between predictors and job performance. All other hypotheses regarding predictors are secondary. The job performance that we set out to predict is known as the *criterion*. The validity of a predictor is its correlation with the criterion. Validation consists essentially in the administration of the predictors to a representative sample of job applicants or newly hired employees and the checking of each individual's initial scores against his subsequent criterion status. The intervening period may be six months, a year, or several years, depending upon the nature of the job and available facilities. Although several types of validity are recognized in test construction, *predictive validity* is the most relevant to personnel selection (see 2, ch. 6; 45).

When limitations of time or other circumstances make a longitudinal study impracticable, validity may be determined by administering the predictors to present employees and checking scores against current criterion status. This procedure, yielding a measure of *concurrent validity,* is not so satisfactory for the validation of personnel selection instruments and must be regarded as a makeshift. Since unsatisfactory employees tend to leave, a group of present employees is not a representative sample of the applicant population on which the instruments are to be used. Moreover, present employees have had varying amounts of experience on the job, and such experience may affect their test performance.

**The Criterion.**   A selection program can be no better than the criterion against which it is validated. Industrial psychologists regard the criterion problem as of prime importance, at the same time recognizing that criterion measures employed in most personnel research leave much to be desired. Job success is a complex concept, and it can be assessed in many ways. Production records provide a criterion measure available for many kinds of jobs. Quantity and quality of output, waste through spoilage of materials, amount of sales, and merchandise returned are among the records that can be used for this purpose. Length of time the individual remains on the job represents a more comprehensive criterion measure, especially important in jobs having rapid turnover. Whether an employee is discharged for incompetence or whether he leaves spontaneously, he contributes to turnover costs. In certain jobs, performance in training provides useful criterion data. Other sources include records of accidents, absenteeism, tardiness, and disciplinary actions.

Regardless of how much objective information may be available, it is always desirable to include ratings among criterion measures. Depending upon the nature of the job, such ratings may be procured from supervisors, co-workers, subordinates, instructors, or other personnel. Many companies have merit rating programs as part of their administrative procedures. In other companies, ratings may have to be secured specially for criterion purposes. If obtained under satisfactory conditions, ratings represent a particularly good source of criterion data. Specific rating techniques, as well as ways of reducing common judgment errors, will be discussed in Chapter 4.

With any type of criterion data, we must guard against *criterion contamination*. Production records, for instance, may be influenced by extraneous factors. Thus one factory worker may turn out fewer articles than another because he has poorer equipment, or one salesman may sell more life insurance than another because he operates in a higher-income territory. Either the criterion measures should be obtained solely from individuals working under similar conditions, or they should be adjusted in some way for existing inequalities.

Criterion contamination may also occur through the influence of the predictors themselves upon the criterion. For example, if a foreman knows that one employee scored low and another high on an aptitude test, this knowledge may affect the ratings he assigns them for job performance. Such influences will artificially inflate the correlation between test scores and criterion. It is therefore imperative that anyone who participates in the assignment of criterion ratings have no access to test scores or other predictor data. While the predictors are being validated, they must not be used for operational purposes in selecting or evaluating personnel.

For a realistic and comprehensive picture of each employee's job performance, several sources of criterion data should be combined. The simplest way to do so is to express all criterion scores in comparable units and add them to find an over-all criterion index for each person. In this way, for instance, we could combine information about quantity of output, number of rejects, absenteeism, and foreman's ratings. To convert scores into comparable units, we may express them as *standard scores*, so called because they use as their unit the standard deviation of the group. The standard deviation is a measure of variability or extent of individual differences within the group. It is computed by finding each person's deviation from the group mean and squaring it. The standard deviation (SD) is the square root of the mean of these squared deviations.[3]

Standard scores express each individual's standing in the group as so many SD's above or below the group mean. Thus, if the mean is 30 and the SD 5, an individual with a score of 35 falls 1 SD above the mean and receives a standard score of +1.00. Figure 2 shows where these successive SD units fall in a normal curve. Reference to this figure indicates, for instance, that an individual with a standard score of +1.00 exceeds the lower 84.13 per cent of the group (50 per cent below mean plus 34.13 per cent between mean and 1 SD). Similarly, by consulting tables of normal curve frequencies, we may find the percentage of cases exceeded by standard scores of +1.5, −0.8, +2.1, or any other given value. These positions will be equivalent in different distributions, provided the distributions approximate the normal curve.

Different criteria usually vary in importance with reference to the objectives

---

[3] $SD = \sqrt{\dfrac{\Sigma (X - M)^2}{N}}$. SD is also symbolized by the Greek letter sigma $(\sigma)$.

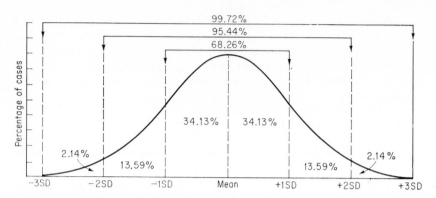

**Fig. 2**  Standard scores in a normal curve.

of the job. Accordingly, weights may be assigned to each standard score by multiplying it by a constant before adding. Still another way of combining criterion scores is in terms of their estimated dollar value—the so-called "dollar criterion" (9). This procedure applies cost accounting techniques to criterion measures. For example, rate of production, amount of material wasted, and time lost by absences can each be expressed in terms of cost to the company and these dollar values added. A difficulty arises in assigning dollar values to such factors as customer goodwill or departmental morale. But in trying to assess these intangible effects of an employee's behavior, the dollar estimates may be no more subjective than ratings expressed in other quantitative terms.

   *Determining Validity.*   The validity of each predictor may be determined by analyzing the relationship between predictor scores and criterion scores. Suppose the validation sample includes two contrasted groups of life insurance salesmen, one composed of highly successful salesmen, the other of near failures. With such a dichotomous, or twofold, criterion, we may compare the mean predictor scores obtained by the two groups. If the successful salesmen achieve higher predictor scores than the unsuccessful, then the predictor has some validity for this criterion.

   To answer the question conclusively, we need to determine the *significance of the difference* between the means of the two groups. Measures of statistical significance are widely used in psychological research, being required in nearly all types of investigations. Statistical significance refers essentially to the chances that similar results will be obtained if the investigation is repeated. How likely is it that the successful salesmen would again score higher than the unsuccessful if another sample were tested and followed up? A certain amount of variation in results will always occur through *sampling error,* as well as through the unreliability of measuring instruments discussed in an earlier section. Every investigation utilizes only a sample of the total relevant population. In personnel selection research, for instance, the sample on which validity is determined is never the same as the groups on whom the predictors will be used operationally. How far, then, can we generalize from the validation sample to other samples?

   To find the statistical significance of a mean difference, we need to know

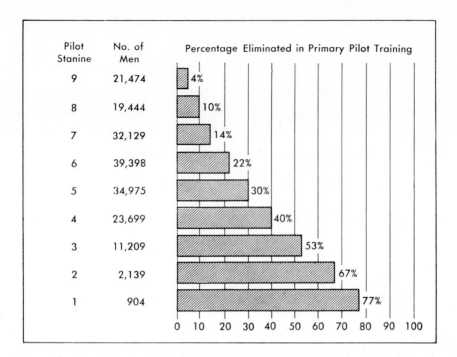

| Pilot Stanine | No. of Men | Percentage Eliminated in Primary Pilot Training |
|:---:|:---:|:---|
| 9 | 21,474 | 4% |
| 8 | 19,444 | 10% |
| 7 | 32,129 | 14% |
| 6 | 39,398 | 22% |
| 5 | 34,975 | 30% |
| 4 | 23,699 | 40% |
| 3 | 11,209 | 53% |
| 2 | 2,139 | 67% |
| 1 | 904 | 77% |

**Fig. 3**   Expectancy table showing relation between pilot stanine and elimination from primary flight training. (*From Flanagan, 18, p. 58.*)

the obtained difference and the SD's of the two groups compared. From these data we can compute the sampling fluctuation to be expected for each mean separately, as well as for the difference between them. The end product of these computations is usually a ratio (critical ratio, or *t* ratio) between the difference and the standard error of the difference. With such a ratio, we can look up the probability (P) that the difference is small enough to have resulted from chance errors. If this probability is less than 1 out of 100 (P < .01), we generally conclude that the difference is large enough to be significant. In other words, we conclude that in other samples the difference would still favor the same group (e.g., the successful salesmen). The chances of such a conclusion being wrong are less than 1 out of 100. It might be added that a lower level of significance, such as .05, is sometimes accepted. In every investigation, however, the level used is specified.

A finer breakdown of the relation between predictor and criterion may be presented in the form of an *expectancy table,* illustrated in Figure 3. This chart shows the percentages of student pilots who failed primary flight training within each stanine on the pilot selection battery developed by the Air Force. A stanine (contraction of "standard nine") is essentially a standard score expressed on a nine-point scale. In such a scale, the mean is 5, and the SD is approximately 2. Figure 3 shows that 77 per cent of the men with the lowest stanine score (1) were eliminated, while only 4 per cent of those receiving the highest stanine (9) failed to complete the course satisfactorily. The percentage of failures decreases consistently over the intervening stanines. The percentages given in Figure 3 provide an estimate of the probability that student pilots tested subsequently would pass or fail. For example, it can be predicted that approximately 40 per cent of candidates scoring 4 will fail and 60 per cent will pass. Similar statements can be made about the expectancy of success or failure on the part of individuals. Thus an individual with a pilot stanine of 4 has a 60:40, or 3:2, chance of completing primary flight training.

The most precise expression of the relation between predictor and criterion is provided by a *validity coefficient*. Such a coefficient is customarily computed when both predictor and criterion scores are in the form of continuous variables. In that case, the relation can be represented in a bivariate distribution such as that illustrated in Figure 1 and the correlation computed by the same method. Other types of correlations, however, can be employed when predictor, criterion, or both are in the form of dichotomies or of multiple categories. These techniques are described in standard statistics texts. Like all statistical measures, validity coefficients must be evaluated for significance. If we find that a validity coefficient is significant at the .01 level, we conclude that it is too high to have resulted from chance errors and we accept it as evidence of genuine validity.

The higher the validity coefficient, of course, the more valid the predictor. The practical implications of a validity coefficient may be expressed in several ways. For example, we may want to know what effect the use of a selection test will have on the percentage of employees who exceed a minimum standard of job success. Suppose that the percentage of successful employees prior to the use of the test was 60, that the supply and demand is such that we must hire 30 per cent of all applicants for the job (selection ratio = 30), and that the validity coefficient of the test is .45. By reference to the appropriate table (see 2, pp. 162–164; 44), we find that under these conditions the percentage of successful employees following the use of the test should rise from 60 to 80. Techniques are also available for estimating what effect the use of a predictor of given validity will have on the over-all output level of the selected workers (see 2, pp. 164–166; 10). It has been demonstrated that the expected increase in output is directly proportional to the validity of the test (7). Thus the improvement resulting from the use of a test whose validity coefficient is .45 will be approximately 45 per cent as great as the improvement expected from a test of perfect validity.

*Cross Validation.* When a set of predictors has been selected on the basis of their individual validities, the validity of the set as a whole should be checked in a new sample. Such an independent determination of validity in a second comparable sample is known as "cross validation" (37). This step is especially important when we start with a large number of predictors, such as individual items for an application form, and retain a small proportion for final use. Cross validation is also advisable in making up a battery of tests, especially if a relatively large number of the original tests are discarded because of low validities. The validity of the composite—be it test battery, application form, or total test whose items were individually validated—should not be computed on the same sample used for choosing the individual predictors. If it were so computed, the validity coefficient would capitalize on chance errors within the original sample and would consequently be spuriously high. In fact, a high validity coefficient will result under these circumstances, even when the set of predictors has no validity at all for the particular criterion.

Let us suppose that, out of a sample of 100 salesclerks, the 30 with the highest and the 30 with the lowest sales records are chosen to represent contrasted criterion groups. If, now, these two groups are compared in a number of traits actually irrelevant to success in selling, certain chance differences will undoubtedly be found. Thus there might be an excess of urban-born and of red-haired salesclerks within the upper criterion group. If we were to assign each individual a "score" by crediting him with one point for urban residence and one point for red hair, the mean of such scores would undoubtedly be higher in the upper than in the lower criterion group. This is not evidence for the validity of the predictors, however, since such a validation process is based upon a circular argument. The two predictors were chosen in the first place on the basis of the chance variation that occurred in this particular sample. And the same chance differences operate to produce the mean differences in total score. When tested in another sample, the chance differences in frequency of urban residence and red hair are likely to disappear or be reversed. Consequently, the validity of the scores will collapse.

A specific illustration of the need for cross validation is provided by an investigation of the Rorschach inkblot test (31). In an attempt to determine whether the Rorschach could be of any help in selecting sales managers for life insurance agencies, this test was administered to 80 managers, including an upper criterion group of 42 considered very satisfactory by their companies and a lower criterion group of 38 considered unsatisfactory. The 80 test records were studied by a Rorschach expert, who selected 32 signs, or response characteristics, occurring more frequently in one criterion group than in the other. A scoring key was developed in which signs occurring more often in the upper group were scored $+1$, those more frequent in the lower group $-1$. When this scoring key was reapplied to the original 80 managers, 79 of the 80 were correctly classified in the upper or lower group. The correlation between test score and criterion would thus have been close to 1.00. However, when the test was cross-validated on a second comparable sample of 41 managers, 21 in the upper and 20 in the lower group, the validity coefficient dropped to a negligible .02.

That such results can be obtained under pure-chance conditions was demonstrated by Cureton (14), who determined the "scores" of 29 students on each of 85 nonexistent test items by shaking 85 numbered tags and letting them fall, once for each student. If a tag fell numbered side up, the item was scored right; if blank side up, it was scored wrong. An item analysis conducted with these chance scores against the students' grade-point averages yielded a 24-item "test." Total scores on this test correlated .82 with the criterion of college grades in the original group of 29 students. This correlation, of course, does not demonstrate validity, but the operation of pure chance—or, to use Cureton's more vivid term, "baloney."

**Synthetic Validity.**  The same test may have high validity for office clerks or machinists in one company and low or negligible validity for jobs bearing the same title in another company. Surveys of validity coefficients against occupational criteria reveal wide variations. In one of the most comprehensive of these surveys, Ghiselli (22) reports, for example, that intelligence tests correlated from −.40 to +.80 with proficiency criteria for general clerks; and spatial relations tests correlated from −.55 to +.65 with job performance of machine tenders. Of course, some of this variation is to be expected because of differences among tests designed to measure intelligence or spatial relations, as well as differences in the composition of the samples tested. But the range of validity coefficients found is far greater than could be explained in these terms. Differences in the criteria themselves are undoubtedly a major factor in the variation observed among validity coefficients. Thus the duties of office clerks or of mechanics may differ widely among companies or among departments in the same company.

Test validities also vary when checked against different criteria of success in a single job. For example, the tests that predict performance in training may fail to predict subsequent job proficiency, or vice versa (22). Similarly, a test may fail to correlate significantly with supervisors' ratings and yet show appreciable validity in predicting who will resign and who will be promoted at a later date (1). When different types of criteria are compared for the same individuals, moreover, their intercorrelations are often quite low. For instance, accident records or absenteeism may show virtually no relation to productivity or error data (41). It is abundantly clear that: (1) job criteria are complex; (2) various types of criterion data, or subcriteria, for any one job may have little relation to each other; and (3) different jobs bearing the same name often represent a different combination of subcriteria.

It is largely for these reasons that industrial psychologists find it necessary to develop custom-made tests or selection programs within each company. Although clearly desirable, however, this practice is often inapplicable in small companies or in jobs having few employees. The latter would be true, for instance, for certain executive and other high-level jobs. Even when adequate facilities and a sufficient number of validation cases are available, the validation of each predictor against a composite criterion of job success may be of questionable value. If different subcriteria are relatively independent, then a more effective procedure would be to validate each predictor against that aspect of the criterion it was designed to measure.

The concept of synthetic validity was introduced by Lawshe (32, 33) as one possible approach to these problems (see also 3). In finding synthetic validity, each predictor is validated, not against a composite criterion, but against job elements identified through job analyses. The validity of any predictor or battery of predictors is then computed synthetically for a given job on the basis of the job elements entering into that job and their relative weights. Thus, if a test has a high validity in predicting performance in delicate manipulative tasks, and if such tasks loom large in a particular job, then the test will have high synthetic validity for that job. A statistical technique known as the "J coefficient" (for "job coefficient") has been developed for estimating the synthetic validity of a test from a knowledge of the weights of job elements in the job and in the test (3, 40). This technique offers a promising tool for generalizing validity data from one job to another without actually conducting a separate validation study for each job. How effective the technique will eventually prove in practice can be determined only by further research.

**Subgroup Analysis and Moderator Variables.** Validity may also vary among subgroups differing in personal characteristics. Thus a test may be a better predictor of criterion performance for men than for women or for applicants from a lower than for applicants from a higher socioeconomic level. In such examples, sex and socioeconomic level are known as "moderator variables," since they modify the predictive validity of the test. Even when a test is equally valid for all subgroups, the same score may have a different predictive significance when obtained by members of different subgroups. For example, if a student who has had poor schooling obtains the same score on a college aptitude test as one who has had excellent schooling, the former is likely to earn better grades than the latter if they are both admitted to the same college. In such a situation, the same test score would lead to a different prediction for persons in different subgroups.

Interests and motivation often function as moderator variables in individual cases. Thus, if an applicant has little interest in a job, he will probably do poorly regardless of his scores on relevant aptitude tests. Among such persons, the correlation between aptitude test scores and job performance would be low. For individuals who are interested and highly motivated, on the other hand, the correlation between aptitude test score and job success may be quite high.

A moderator variable may itself be a test score, in terms of which individuals are sorted into subgroups. There have been some promising attempts to identify such moderator variables in test scores (4, 21, 23, 24). In a study of taxi drivers, for example, the correlation between an aptitude test and a criterion of job performance in a total applicant sample was only .220 (23). The group was then sorted into thirds, on the basis of scores on an occupational interest test. When the validity of the aptitude test was recomputed within the third whose occupational interest level was most appropriate for the job, it rose to .664. Such findings suggest that one test might first be used to screen out individuals for whom the second test is likely to have low validity; then, from among the remaining cases, those scoring high on the second test are selected. In many ways, the analysis of validity data for subgroups of the validation population may enhance the usefulness of available predictors.

## FORMULATING A STRATEGY FOR PERSONNEL DECISIONS

Having determined the validity of various predictors for a given job criterion and having on that basis chosen the predictors to be retained for operational purposes, the personnel psychologist must now formulate an appropriate strategy for using these predictors in making personnel decisions. In the terminology of decision theory, a strategy is a technique for utilizing information in order to reach a decision about the individual (13, ch. 3). The simplest kind of strategy involves the use of a single predictor. If circumstances of supply and demand determine the selection ratio, then all that is required is to start selecting individuals from the top of the predictor distribution and continue downward until the required number of persons has been hired. If only persons likely to fall above a minimum criterion level are acceptable, then a cutoff point in predictor scores can be established by examining the bivariate distribution of criterion and predictor scores. How high a test score should applicants have, for example, to ensure that 90 per cent of those hired will reach or exceed a specified standard of job performance?

Most selection programs, however, are not so simple as this. Since criteria are complex, several predictors are usually required for adequate criterion coverage. With multiple predictors, the question arises as to how they are to be combined in reaching a decision about the individual. Given five scores earned by an individual on tests or other selection devices, how are they to be used in deciding whether to accept or reject the applicant?

*Clinical Judgment.* When tests or other predictors are employed in the intensive study of individual cases, as in selection of high-level personnel, executive evaluation, clinical diagnosis, or counseling, it is a common practice for scores to be interpreted by the examiner in arriving at a decision without further statistical manipulation (see, e.g., 48). To be sure, the individual's scores are evaluated with reference to any available general or local norms. But no statistical formula or other automatic procedure is applied in combining scores from different predictors or in interpreting the individual's score pattern. Through a relatively subjective process, the examiner interprets the individual's scores in terms of his own past experience with similar cases, his familiarity with particular job requirements, or his knowledge of psychological theory and relevant published research. The results are usually presented in the form of a detailed description of personality dynamics and aptitudes, supplemented by specific predictions such as "Mr. Greenwald will make a good executive vice-president for this company" or "Miss Adams will not respond well to psychotherapy."

Research has been under way to try to discover just what the clinician or interviewer does when evaluating and combining data to reach a decision (15, 27, 28, 34, 35, 43, 48). Some investigators have also tried to compare the relative effectiveness of clinical and statistical methods of combining data in situations where both are applicable (see 35). But, in practice, both are rarely applicable to the same situation. We may lack either the extensive quantitative data needed to develop statistical prediction formulas or the time and personnel needed for clinical prediction.[4]

*Multiple Cutoff Scores.* A simple statistical strategy for combining scores utilizes multiple cutoff points. This procedure requires the establishment of a minimum score on *each* predictor. Every applicant who falls below the minimum score on any one of the predictors is rejected; only those reaching or exceeding the cutoff scores on all predictors are accepted. This is the technique followed, for example, in the General Aptitude Test Battery (GATB) developed by the United States Employment Service for use in the occupational counseling program of its State Employment Service offices (17, 25). This battery yields nine aptitude scores, only some of which are considered for any one occupation. For example, accounting was found to require a minimum score of 105 in intelligence and 115 in numerical aptitude; plumbing called for a minimum of 85 in intelligence and 80 in numerical aptitude, in spatial aptitude, and in manual dexterity. These are standard scores on a scale having a mean of 100 and an SD of 20.

The multiple cutoff strategy is readily applicable to predictors that are not linearly related to the criterion. Up to a certain point, for example, speed of

[4] Further discussion of clinical judgment will be found in Chapter 13.

hand movement may be closely related to output in an assembly-line job. But, beyond that point, greater speed may be of no avail because of the mechanical limitations of the operation. The relevance of speed to performance in such a job would be reflected in the failure of persons below a certain speed. Yet the correlation between speed and performance level among employed workers may be low and negligible. The multiple cutoff technique is also especially suitable for jobs in which superior ability along one line cannot compensate for a deficiency in an essential skill. Operators of sound-detection devices, for example, need good auditory discrimination. Anyone incapable of making the necessary discriminations will fail in such a job, regardless of how well qualified he may be in other respects.

*Multiple Regression Equation.* The most precise strategy for combining predictor scores is that using the multiple regression equation. This equation yields a predicted criterion score for each individual. Specific techniques for computing regression equations can be found in many texts on psychological statistics (e.g., 26). In such an equation, each predictor is weighted in direct proportion to its criterion correlation and in inverse proportion to its correlation with other predictors in the battery. Thus a test that overlaps other tests in the battery receives less weight than one that measures a unique aspect of the criterion, even if their validity coefficients are equally high. The weights employed are also such as to translate all predictor scores into the same units, so that they may be added. Finally, a constant is added to the total so as to express the predicted criterion score in terms of some convenient scale, usually the same scale employed in reporting the original criterion scores.

In the process of computing a regression equation, it is also possible to select from the original set of predictors those that will yield the highest multiple correlation ($R$) with the criterion. The multiple correlation itself should be corrected for "shrinkage." When the predictor battery is applied to a new sample, the multiple correlation will drop somewhat, because the weights derived in the first sample are optimum for that sample only. Because of chance errors in the original correlation coefficients, the weights will vary somewhat from sample to sample. The amount of shrinkage in $R$ can be estimated by applying a shrinkage formula, or it can be determined empirically by cross-validating the battery.

The use of a multiple regression equation in predicting an applicant's job performance can be illustrated with the following equation:

$$X'_c = .23X_1 + .32X_2 + .18X_3 + .39X_4 + 46$$

Let us suppose that an applicant, Henry Barclay, earns the following scores on four predictors, in the order listed in the above equation: 15, 8, 11, and 13. His predicted criterion score ($X'_c$) is then computed by substituting these values in the equation, as follows:

$$X'_c = (.23)(15) + (.32)(8) + (.18)(11) + (.39)(13) + 46 = 59.06$$

Rounding the total to two significant figures, we would report Mr. Barclay's estimated criterion score, or index of expected job performance, as 59. This score can then be evaluated either in reference to the scores of other applicants or in reference to an empirically established cutoff score.

It can be seen that, unlike the multiple cutoff strategy, the multiple regression equation makes it possible for high scores in some predictors to compensate for low scores in others. For this reason, this technique should not be used when deficiencies in key skills ought to disqualify an applicant. With such jobs, a combination of multiple cutoff and regression equation may be employed, whereby applicants are first screened on key skills and then the regression equation is applied to the remaining cases. An advantage of the regression equation is that it provides an index of each individual's predicted job performance, permitting a comparison of the relative qualifications of applicants. With multiple cutoff procedures, individuals are simply classified as accepted or rejected.

*Classification Decisions.*   So far we have considered only selection decisions, in which each individual is either accepted or rejected. Deciding whether or not to hire a job applicant, admit a student to medical school, or accept a candidate for officer training are examples of selection. In classification decisions, on the other hand, every individual must be utilized. The question is where to assign each person so as to maximize the effectiveness of the total organization. Classification always involves more than one criterion—be it jobs, military specialties, courses of study, or clinical treatments.

In the military services, classification is a major problem. After preliminary screening, everyone in the remaining manpower pool must be assigned to the military specialty where he can serve most effectively. An example of a classification battery is that developed by the Air Force during World War II for assigning men to training programs for pilot, navigator, bombardier, or other aircrew specialties. Similar batteries are now used by all branches of the armed services. Another example of classification decisions is provided by the choice of a field of concentration by a college student. Vocational counseling, too, is based essentially on classification, since the client is told his chances of succeeding in different kinds of work. Clinical diagnosis is likewise a classification problem, the major purpose of each diagnosis being a decision regarding the appropriate type of therapy.

In industry, classification decisions are required when new employees are assigned to different training programs or different jobs within the company. With rising employment and with a gradual shift from the limited goal of filling a particular job to the broader goal of utilizing every individual in the work he is best qualified to perform, classification assumes increasing importance.

For classification purposes, predictors must have *differential validity*. Such validity is higher, the larger the difference between the correlations of the predictor with the separate criteria to be predicted. In a two-criterion classification problem, for example, the ideal test would have a high correlation with one criterion and a zero correlation (or preferably a negative correlation) with the other criterion. General intelligence tests are of little use for classification decisions, since they predict success about equally well in most fields. Hence their correlations with the criteria to be differentiated would be too similar. An individual scoring high on such a test would be classified as successful for either assignment, and it would be impossible to predict in which he would do better. In a classification battery, we need some tests that are good predictors of criterion A and poor predictors of criterion B and other tests that are poor predictors of A and good predictors of B. Statistical procedures have been developed for selecting predictors so as to maximize the differential validity of a classification battery (8, 13, 29, 36, 46). When the number of criteria is greater than two, such procedures become quite complex.

## THE ILLUSION OF SUBJECTIVE VALIDATION

A favorite sales appeal of charlatans and borderline "consultants" is to invite the business executive to undergo their particular brand of personality analysis so that he may "judge it for himself." The sort of personality description that they provide consists of vague generalities applicable to most people. When confronted with such a description of himself, the recipient is impressed with its apparent accuracy and insight and concludes that the method will work equally well with his employees. This illusory validation has been called the "Barnum effect" (see 5, p. 47; 16, p. 223), after Phineas T. Barnum, the famous showman who is credited with the remark that there's a fool born every minute.

The readiness with which these general personality descriptions are accepted as true was demonstrated at a conference of personnel managers (42). A standard personality inventory was administered to the group, and the papers were then collected for scoring. Before getting the actual scores, each participant received an identical copy of a fake "personality analysis." The analysis consisted of a list of descriptive statements, in which the same 13 had been marked for each person. These 13 statements had been chosen because they were assertions applicable to the large majority of people; most were flattering, thus increasing their acceptability. Examples include:

You have a great need for other people to like and admire you.
You have a tendency to be critical of yourself.
You have a great deal of unused capacity which you have not turned to your advantage.
You pride yourself as an independent thinker and do not accept others' statements without satisfactory proof.

The unmarked statements, interspersed among the others, were generally unfavorable comments about the personality being tested.

After examining his own report, each man was asked to rate the accuracy of the description on the following five-point scale: amazingly accurate, rather good, about half and half, more wrong than right, almost entirely wrong. Of the 68 personnel managers in the group, 50 per cent marked the description "amazingly accurate," 40 per cent "rather good," and 10 per cent "about half and half." When given the genuine test scores and told about the hoax, the personnel managers were quite vocal in their surprise. Apparently none had doubted the authenticity of the original reports.

Similar results have been obtained with other groups, including college students and industrial managers (see 42, p. 350). Not only were the personality descriptions as a whole accepted as accurate by the large majority of all these groups, but most of the individual statements marked for each person were also classified as predominantly correct. It will be recognized that this Barnum effect also accounts for much of the success of fortune tellers, astrologers, and similar charlatans. All these systems provide only random assortments of universally applicable generalities and fail to indicate how one person actually differs from another. And it is this differentiation of individuals that is the primary function of personnel selection and evaluation.

## SUMMARY

Developing a personnel selection program involves four major steps: (1) job analysis, (2) preparation and preliminary tryout of predictors, (3) validation of predictors, and (4) formulating a strategy for personnel decisions. Job analysis defines the problem by specifying worker qualifications for which predictors are needed. Job descriptions should be specific to the job and should concentrate on critical worker requirements.

The predictors assembled or prepared on the basis of the job analysis should be checked for such characteristics as dispersion, difficulty level, reliability, and specificity before they are administered to the validation sample. Predictive or concurrent validity is found by comparing predictor scores with criterion scores. Criterion contamination should be avoided. Different criterion indices may be combined in terms of weighted standard scores or by the dollar-criterion technique. Among the techniques for expressing the relationship between predictor and criterion are significance of mean differences, expectancy tables, and correlation coefficients. Cross validation in a new sample is advisable, especially when only a small proportion of the original predictors survive initial validation. Synthetic validity provides for the validation of predictors against separate job elements, whence their validity for a total job can be estimated.

When predictors are used in making personnel decisions, they may be combined through clinical judgment, multiple cutoff scores, or regression equations. For classification decisions, predictors need differential validity with regard to the separate criteria. An illusory validation based on subjective, anecdotal observations has been described as the Barnum effect.

## REFERENCES

1. Albright, L. E., Smith, W. J., and Glennon, J. R. A follow-up on some "invalid" tests for selecting salesmen. *Personnel Psychol.*, 1959, **12**, 105–112.
2. Anastasi, Anne. *Psychological testing.* (2nd ed.) New York: Macmillan, 1961.
3. Balma, M. J., *et al.* The development of processes for indirect or synthetic validity —a symposium. *Personnel Psychol.*, 1959, **12**, 395–420.
4. Berdie, R. F. Intra-individual variability and predictability. *Educ. psychol. Measmt,* 1961, **21**, 663–676.
5. Blum, M. L., and Balinsky, B. *Counseling and psychology.* Englewood Cliffs, N.J.: Prentice-Hall, 1951.
6. Bregman, Elsie O. Studies in industrial psychology. *Arch. Psychol.*, 1922, No. 59.
7. Brogden, H. E. On the interpretation of the correlation coefficient as a measure of predictive efficiency. *J. educ. Psychol.*, 1946, **37**, 65–76.
8. Brogden, H. E. Increased efficiency of selection resulting from replacement of a single predictor with several differential predictors. *Educ. psychol. Measmt,* 1951, **11**, 173–196.
9. Brogden, H. E., and Taylor, E. K. The dollar criterion—applying the cost accounting concept to criterion construction. *Personnel Psychol.*, 1950, **3**, 133–154.

10. Brown, C. W., and Ghiselli, E. E. Per cent increase in proficiency resulting from use of selective devices. *J. appl. Psychol.*, 1953, **37**, 341–345.
11. Charters, W. W., and Whitley, I. B. *Analysis of secretarial duties and traits.* Baltimore: Williams & Wilkins, 1924.
12. Cronbach, L. J. *Essentials of psychological testing.* (2nd ed.) New York: Harper & Row, 1960.
13. Cronbach, L. J., and Gleser, Goldine C. *Psychological tests and personnel decisions.* Urbana, Ill.: Univer. Illinois Press, 1957.
14. Cureton, E. E. Validity, reliability, and baloney. *Educ. psychol. Measmt,* 1950, **10**, 94–96.
15. Donahoe, J. W. A dimensional analysis of clinical judgment. *J. consult. Psychol.,* 1960, **24**, 96.
16. Dunnette, M. D. Use of the sugar pill by industrial psychologists. *Amer. Psychologist,* 1957, **12**, 223–225.
17. Dvorak, Beatrice J. The General Aptitude Test Battery. *Personnel Guid. J.,* 1956, **35**, 145–154.
18. Flanagan, J. C. Scientific development of the use of human resources: Progress in the Army Air Forces. *Science,* 1947, **105**, 57–60.
19. Flanagan, J. C. Critical requirements: A new approach to employee evaluation. *Personnel Psychol.,* 1949, **2**, 419–425.
20. Flanagan, J. C. The critical incident technique. *Psychol. Bull.,* 1954, **51**, 327–358.
21. Fulkerson, S. C. Individual differences in response validity. *J. clin. Psychol.,* 1959, **15**, 169–173.
22. Ghiselli, E. E. *Measurement of occupational aptitude.* Berkeley, Calif.: Univer. Calif. Press, 1955.
23. Ghiselli, E. E. Differentiation of individuals in terms of their predictability. *J. appl. Psychol.,* 1956, **40**, 374–377.
24. Ghiselli, E. E. Moderating effects and differential reliability and validity. *J. appl. Psychol.,* 1963, **47**, 81–86.
25. *Guide to the use of the General Aptitude Test Battery: Section III. Development.* Washington: Govt. Printing Office, 1962.
26. Guilford, J. P. *Fundamental statistics in psychology and education.* (3rd ed.) New York: McGraw-Hill, 1956.
27. Hoffman, P. J. The paramorphic representation of clinical judgment. *Psychol. Bull.,* 1960, **57**, 116–131.
28. Holt, R. R. Clinical *and* statistical prediction: A reformulation and some new data. *J. abnorm. soc. Psychol.,* 1958, **56**, 1–12.
29. Horst, P. A technique for the development of a differential prediction battery. *Psychol. Monogr.,* 1954, **68**, No. 9.
30. Hull, C. L. *Aptitude testing.* Yonkers, N.Y.: World Book Co., 1928.
31. Kurtz, A. K. A research test of the Rorschach test. *Personnel Psychol.,* 1948, **1**, 41–51.
32. Lawshe, C. H. Employee selection. *Personnel Psychol.,* 1952, **5**, 31–34.
33. Lawshe, C. H., and Steinberg, M. D. Studies in synthetic validity. 1. An exploratory investigation of clerical jobs. *Personnel Psychol.,* 1955, **8**, 291–301.
34. McArthur, C. Analyzing the clinical process. *J. counsel. Psychol.,* 1954, **1**, 203–207.
35. Meehl, P. E. *Clinical versus statistical prediction: A theoretical analysis and a review of the evidence.* Minneapolis: Univer. Minn. Press, 1954.
36. Mollenkopf, W. G. Predicted differences and differences between predictions. *Psychometrika,* 1950, **15**, 409–417.
37. Mosier, C. I., Cureton, E. E., Katzell, R. A., and Wherry, R. J. Symposium: The need and means of cross-validation. *Educ. psychol. Measmt,* 1951, **11**, 5–28.
38. Otis, L., and Leukart, R. H. *Job evaluation.* (2nd ed.) Englewood Cliffs, N.J.: Prentice-Hall, 1954.
39. Patton, J. A., and Littlefield, C. L. *Job evaluation: Text and cases.* (Rev. ed.) Homewood, Ill.: Irwin, 1957.
40. Primoff, E. S. The J-coefficient approach to jobs and tests. *Personnel Admin.,* 1957, **20**, 34–40.
41. Seashore, S. E., Indik, B. P., and Georgopoulos, B. S. Relationships among criteria of job performance. *J. appl. Psychol.,* 1960, **44**, 195–202.

42. Stagner, R. The gullibility of personnel managers. *Personnel Psychol.*, 1958, **11**, 347–352.
43. Sydiaha, D. On the equivalence of clinical and statistical methods. *J. appl. Psychol.*, 1959, **43**, 395–401.
44. Taylor, H. C., and Russell, J. T. The relationship of validity coefficients to the practical effectiveness of tests in selection: Discussion and tables. *J. appl. Psychol.*, 1939, **23**, 565–578.
45. *Technical recommendations for psychological tests and diagnostic techniques.* Washington: Amer. Psychol. Assoc., 1954. (Also in *Psychol. Bull.*, 1954, **51**, No. 2, pt. 2.)
46. Thorndike, R. L. *Personnel selection: Test and measurement techniques.* New York: Wiley, 1949.
47. Tiffin, J., and McCormick, E. J. *Industrial psychology.* (4th ed.) Englewood Cliffs, N.J.: Prentice-Hall, 1958.
48. Trankell, A. The psychologist as an instrument of prediction. *J. appl. Psychol.*, 1959, **43**, 170–175.
49. Viteles, M. S. *The science of work.* New York: Norton, 1934.

# 3

## Psychological Tests in Personnel Selection

In developing a personnel selection program, the industrial psychologist generally includes tests among the predictors. Over the past three decades, personnel selection in general has come to rely more and more upon tests (76). As might be expected, however, tests are more likely to be employed by the larger companies. In a survey conducted in 1954, the use of employment tests was reported by 53 per cent of the companies with 5,000 or more employees, in contrast to only 15 per cent of those with fewer than 250 employees (67). It should be noted that there is hardly a job for which just one test is an adequate predictor. This is understandable in view of the complexity of job criteria, discussed in the preceding chapter. The fact that validity coefficients of single tests are rarely larger than .40 and often fall below this value suggests that at best each test measures only some of the prerequisites for any particular job. For this reason, the common practice is to use a combination of tests. Moreover, test scores should be supplemented with information derived from other sources, such as application forms, recommendations, and interviews, to be discussed in Chapter 4.

In the present chapter, the major kinds of tests used in personnel selection will be examined and illustrated with a few examples. In accordance with common usage, these instruments have been grouped into five categories: intelligence tests, special aptitude tests, multiple aptitude batteries, achievement tests, and personality tests.

A more comprehensive coverage of available tests can be found in textbooks on psychological testing, such as Anastasi (3) and Cronbach (21). Some books on industrial psychology devote several chapters to the use of tests in industry (see, e.g., 93, chs. 5–7). Of particular interest are surveys of tests validated against industrial criteria. A handbook by Dorcus and Jones (23), published in 1950, summarizes information about each test for which validation data against an industrial criterion are available. Ghiselli (35) prepared a comprehensive survey of validity coefficients of various types of tests against occupational criteria, although validities are not given separately for individual tests. Patterson (66) reports validities of specific tests in predicting performance in trade and vocational courses.

Current information on tests can be obtained from several psychological journals, such as *Psychological Abstracts, Journal of Applied Psychology,* and *Educational and Psychological Measurement;* the last-named contains a special "Validity Studies Section." Similarly, *Personnel Psychology* includes a section entitled "Validity Information Exchange" which summarizes new data on the validity of specific tests. A most important source of information about tests is the series of *Mental Measurements Yearbooks,* edited by Buros (18). Published every few years, these yearbooks cover nearly all commercially available tests developed in English-speaking countries. Besides routine information about each test, they contain one or more critical reviews of most tests, prepared by test experts in the appropriate area. Direct information about specific tests can also be found in the catalogues of test publishers and in the manual that accompanies each test. The names and addresses of some of the larger American publishers and distributors of tests are listed in Appendix E.

## INTELLIGENCE TESTS

*Nature of Intelligence Tests.* Intelligence tests were first developed in the attempt to measure the individual's general intellectual level. It was hoped that the score on such a test would reflect a sort of over-all average of what the individual could do with different intellectual tasks. The tasks were chosen so as to sample a wide variety of abilities. In actual practice, however, intelligence tests do not sample all abilities equally. They are overweighted with some abilities and may omit or scarcely touch upon others. Most intelligence tests measure chiefly verbal comprehension, a fact that is illustrated by the very high correlations found between total scores on intelligence tests and scores on vocabulary tests. Arithmetic reasoning and numerical computation are also frequently included. This combination of abilities will be recognized as being of prime importance in schoolwork at all levels. In fact, intelligence tests have frequently been validated against academic achievement as a criterion. Many intelligence tests correlate nearly as highly with tests of school achievement as they do with each other. For these reasons intelligence tests are often more accurately designated as tests of "scholastic aptitude."

It should also be borne in mind that different intelligence tests may cover a somewhat different combination of abilities. Thus performance and nonlanguage tests often stress spatial and perceptual rather than verbal and numerical aptitudes. And as might be anticipated, their correlations with school achievement are somewhat lower. Partly for this reason and partly for other reasons pertaining to the construction of the tests, the same score may have quite different meanings when obtained on different intelligence tests. The "IQ" is not a property of the organism, but a score on a particular test. It cannot be interpreted without knowledge about the test from which it was derived.

The IQ, it might be added, is not a very satisfactory way of expressing scores, especially for adults. Other types of scores, such as standard scores or percentiles, are technically preferable and more widely applicable. Standard scores, it will be recalled, express the individual's position as so many standard deviations above or below the mean of the normative group (see Chapter 2). The so-called "deviation IQ," now used with several tests, is actually a standard score with a mean of 100 and an SD equal to 15 or to some other specified value close to it. For instance, a person with a deviation IQ of 115 falls 1 SD above the mean. Percentile scores report the percentage of persons in the normative group who scored below the individual. Thus, if an examinee's score is at the 64th percentile, his performance excelled 64 per cent of the normative sample.

In interpreting intelligence test scores, we should also bear in mind that such scores are influenced by the individual's past experience. Hence they should not be evaluated in the absence of background information about the individual. The same score obtained by persons varying widely in education, socioeconomic level, or cultural milieu may have different connotations in the prediction of subsequent performance in training, on a job, or in other criterion situations.

Since intelligence tests are often used in industry for a rough, preliminary screening of applicants, several tests have been specially developed for this purpose. These tests are short, usually requiring between 10 and 30 minutes; they are easy to administer; and they can be objectively scored by a clerk or by machine. It should be recognized that, while such tests may have fair validity for some jobs, they may have little or no validity for others. The aptitudes sampled by intelligence tests are undoubtedly far more relevant to some types of jobs than to others. Jobs cannot simply be put into a hierarchy in terms of the amount of "intelligence" they require, because the type of "intelligence" needed for different jobs varies. For many occupations, especially those requiring mechanical skills, tests of special aptitudes will serve as better predictors of achievement than will the so-called general intelligence tests.

An early test that has been widely employed in personnel screening is the Otis Self-Administering Test of Mental Ability (62), which later served as the basis for developing the highest level of the Otis Quick-Scoring Mental Ability Tests (63). The earlier test has been used in screening applicants for such varied jobs as those of clerks, calculating-machine operators, assembly-line workers, and foremen and other supervisory personnel. Dorcus and Jones (23) cite 36 validation studies in which the Otis test was checked against an industrial criterion. Not all these studies yielded significant validity coefficients, of course, but many of them did. In semiskilled jobs, for example, the Otis test correlated moderately well with success in learning the job and ease of initial adaptation, but not with subsequent job achievement (85). This would be expected for jobs that are largely routine, once they are learned. Among high-level professional personnel, who represent a select group in terms of academic achievement, correlations between Otis score and criteria of job success are usually negligible, since this test does not discriminate adequately at the upper levels.

The Wonderlic Personnel Test (103) is an adaptation and abridgment of the Otis Self-Administering Test. Despite its time limit of only 12 minutes, it yields correlations of .81 to .87 with the original, longer Otis test. Correlations with industrial criteria vary widely with the nature of the job, the sample tested, and the type of criterion measure employed (23). The test appears to have its highest validity in the selection of clerical workers. Another example is the Adaptability Test (92). In approximately 20 minutes, this test yields a single score based on a wide variety of verbal, numerical, and spatial items. It has been used in many kinds of industrial and office jobs, with fair evidence of validity.

A more recently developed test is the Wesman Personnel Classification Test (98). Like most current intelligence tests, it yields separate Verbal and

Numerical scores, as well as a Total score. The Verbal score is derived from an 18-minute verbal analogies test, in which each item contains two blanks, as illustrated in Figure 4. The Numerical score is based on a 10-minute arithmetic computation test whose items were designed so as to put a premium on ingenuity and ability to perceive numerical relations. Correlations of Total scores with criteria of job success, usually consisting of supervisors' ratings, range from .29 to .62. From the nature of the items, as well as from the distribution of scores reported for various educational and occupational groups, this test appears to be better suited for higher-level than for lower-level personnel.

Another rapid screening test is the Oral Directions Test (55), a 15-minute test in which both directions and test items are presented on sound recordings. This procedure ensures more uniformity than would be possible through oral administration by different examiners. The test is rather heavily weighted with perceptual and spatial items and also depends to a considerable extent upon immediate memory for auditory instructions. Available data suggest that it discriminates somewhat better at the lower intellectual levels and may be particularly useful in screening applicants for such jobs as general laborer, maintenance and service worker, and messenger. The Oral Directions Test is part of a short battery, called Personnel Tests for Industry, which also includes a 5-minute Verbal Test (99) and a 20-minute Numerical Test (22).

Mention may also be made of nonlanguage tests, designed for use with illiterates, the foreign-speaking, or persons with widely different cultural backgrounds (see 3, ch. 10). Some of these tests can be administered without either spoken or written language, the instructions being conveyed by gesture, pantomime, and demonstration. Others require simple oral instructions that can be readily translated into different languages. Figure 5 shows two sample items from such a nonlanguage test, the Progressive Matrices (69). Each of the 60 items in this test consists of a matrix, or design, from which a piece has been removed. The subject must choose the correct insert from the given options. The earlier items in the series require primarily accuracy of discrimination, as in the first item in Figure 5. Later, more difficult items involve analogies, permutation and alternation of pattern, and other logical relations, as illustrated in the second item in Figure 5.

*Some Industrial Applications.*  Since intelligence tests—especially those

---

*Fig. 4*  Sample verbal item from Wesman Personnel Classification Test.
(*Reproduced by permission. Copyright 1946, The Psychological Corporation.*)

---

**Example 3.**      ..... is to night as breakfast is to .....      _____

1. flow          2. gentle          3. supper          4. door
A. include       B. morning         C. enjoy           D. corner

**Supper** is to night as breakfast is to **morning**. So you should have written **3B** on the line at the right.

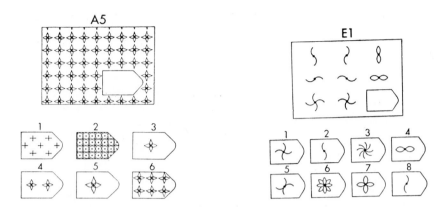

**Fig. 5** Sample items from Progressive Matrices. (*Reproduced by permission of J. C. Raven.*)

of the more common, verbal type—are largely measures of scholastic aptitudes, we should expect them also to predict performance in occupational *training*. Most investigations do in fact support this expectation, although the correlations with industrial training criteria are somewhat lower than those with academic criteria. In the extensive survey by Ghiselli (35, p. 134), the validity coefficients of intelligence tests with industrial training criteria averaged about .35, in contrast with the correlations of .50 or .60 commonly found with academic achievement.

On the other hand, intelligence tests generally predict training performance somewhat better than they predict subsequent job performance. This undoubtedly results in part from the greater similarity of training criteria to the educational criteria which intelligence tests were originally designed to predict. Another reason is that samples of employed workers tend to be more homogeneous than training groups, because of the sequential dropping out of unsuccessful employees. Available measures of training criteria are also likely to be more reliable than measures of job criteria. Similarly, personality characteristics and fortuitous circumstances more often affect job performance than performance in training. All these factors would tend to make for higher correlations with training than with job criteria.

When intelligence tests are correlated with criteria of *job proficiency* among employed personnel, the correlations vary widely with the nature of the job. In jobs requiring a high degree of the abstract verbal and numerical aptitudes covered by these tests, the correlation is likely to be high. In other jobs, however, the correlation may be low or negligible, *once the required minimum is exceeded.* Thus in certain jobs the relation between job proficiency and intelligence may be nonlinear. This might be the case, for instance, when job success depends chiefly upon traits not measured by intelligence tests, such as mechanical aptitude, artistic sensitivity, manual skills, or personality factors. Even in such jobs, of course, persons falling below a certain minimum in academic intelligence would fail.

Another example of nonlinear relation is provided by routine and monotonous jobs, for which individuals may have too much as well as too little intelligence. Maximum proficiency in such jobs may be achieved by persons falling within an optimal range. This would also be true, of course, of any other relevant job skills, besides those measured by intelligence tests (14). The worker who is overqualified for such a routine job is likely to become bored, disinterested, inattentive, and dissatisfied—attitudes that may decrease job proficiency. Or he may become a chronic complainer and troublemaker, thus adversely affecting the morale of his co-workers.

Intelligence tests may also serve to reduce *job turnover*. When employees are discharged because of inability to perform a job or when they leave voluntarily for a variety of reasons, the resulting disruption of operations and the hiring and training of replacements are often costly. Several investigations have shown a significant relation between intelligence test scores and job turnover. This relation is frequently nonlinear, indicating the greatest job stability for persons within an optimal intellectual range. In an early study on groups of cashiers and inspector-wrappers, average length of service in days was at its peak (142 days) for persons scoring between 40 and 49 points on an intelligence test (96). As scores rose, length of service declined steadily to a low of 35 days for those scoring 90 or above. Length of service likewise fell off as intelligence test scores decreased, reaching a mean of only 3 days for those scoring between 10 and 19.

In another study (12), clerical jobs were classified into levels, from the easiest (A) to the hardest (E). As can be seen in Table 2, among employees scoring above 110 on an intelligence test, turnover rate was greater the easier the job, this rate reaching 100 per cent for the two lowest levels. Those scoring below 80, on the other hand, showed high turnover when put in the harder jobs and minimal turnover at the easiest job level. Obviously proper

**TABLE 2**   *Relationship of Labor Turnover*
*to Intelligence Test Score and Job Level*
(*Data from Bills, 12, p. 155*)

| Level of Work | Percentage Turnover among Employees Scoring | |
|---|---|---|
| | Above 110 | Below 80 |
| A (easiest) | 100 | 37 |
| B | 100 | 62 |
| C | 72 | 50 |
| D | 53 | 58 |
| E (hardest) | 41 | 66 |

job placement on the basis of intelligence test scores would have markedly reduced turnover in this company.

When promotional opportunities are available within a company, intelligence tests are often used to help determine an individual's *promotion potential*. This is especially important when employees are hired at one job level with the definite expectation that they will be upgraded to a higher level within a specified interval. Some data relevant to this application of intelligence tests are provided by a follow-up study of 120 clerical workers (68). Table 3 shows the relation between the intelligence test scores of these employees at the time they were hired and the job level they subsequently attained within a seven-year period. It is evident that persons with high initial scores tended to be promoted to the higher-level jobs, while those with lower scores tended to remain in lower-level jobs. For example, of those scoring above 100, only 15 per cent remained in a low-level job, 30 per cent were in middle-level jobs, and 55 per cent in high-level jobs. In contrast, of those scoring below 81, 64 per cent remained in low-level jobs, 24 per cent were in middle-level jobs, and 12 per cent in high-level jobs.

**T A B L E  3**   *Relationship between Initial Intelligence Test Score of Clerical Workers and Job Level Subsequently Attained* (*Data from Pond and Bills, 68, p. 46*)

| Intelligence Test Score | Percentage of Employees in | | |
|---|---|---|---|
| | Low Job | Middle Job | High Job |
| Above 100 | 15 | 30 | 55 |
| 81–100 | 40 | 48 | 12 |
| Below 81 | 64 | 24 | 12 |

Another example is provided by an investigation of supervisors (93, p. 118). Within one company, 70 operators were promoted to supervisory jobs. On the first day of their supervisory training classes, they were given an intelligence test, and the scores were filed for future research use. Six months later, about one-fourth of the 70 supervisors were no longer on their jobs, having left or been demoted, dismissed, or transferred. Figure 6 shows a rather striking relation between intelligence test score and the proportion remaining in their supervisory jobs.

**Job Placement of Mental Defectives.** It has long been recognized that many industrial jobs can be filled by persons of subnormal intelligence. In several investigations, individuals of known mental age[1] have been placed on jobs on a trial basis and then followed up long enough to ascertain whether or not they could carry out their duties satisfactorily (7, 8, 19). Through such empirical procedures, lists of jobs have been drawn up for which persons of each mental age level from 5 to 14 could meet required performance standards. A mental age of 5, for instance, proved adequate for such jobs as sandpapering furniture, washing dishes, or making nets; a mental age of 6, for mowing lawns, handling freight, or mixing cement; and a mental age of 7, for rough painting, simple shoe repairing, or simple carpentry. More highly skilled crafts, as well as the operation of machinery, required somewhat higher mental ages.

It is a well-established practice, of course, for institutionalized mental defectives to perform jobs such as these under supervision in the institution itself. Since World War II, however, rehabilitation programs have been actively under way to enable high-grade mental defectives to return to the community. Several factors have contributed to this development. First, labor

[1] Such mental ages are generally determined through the administration of individual intelligence tests, such as the Stanford-Binet or Wechsler scales (see 3, chs. 8 and 12).

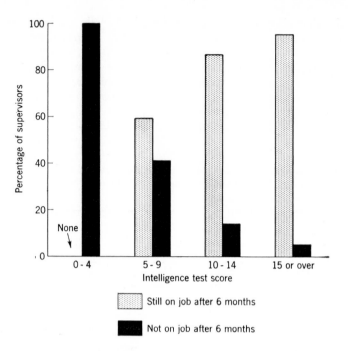

**Fig. 6**   Relationship between intelligence test score and supervisory job tenure. (*From Tiffin and McCormick, 93, p. 119.*)

shortages make it desirable to tap one more potential source of manpower in the trainable mental defective. Second, rehabilitation and discharge provide one way to help "depopulate" overcrowded institutions for mental defectives. The greatest impetus to such rehabilitation programs undoubtedly came from legislation enacted in 1943 that made it possible to include mental defectives in vocational rehabilitation programs for the handicapped and made Federal funds available to the states for this purpose.

Since that time, several states have initiated vocational rehabilitation programs for institutionalized mental defectives. The success of such programs depends upon several conditions, including selection of promising cases, institutional training in self-care and in vocational skills, proper job placement, and availability of counseling facilities during the adjustment period as well as after discharge when needed (28). Follow-up investigations covering intervals of several years have yielded consistently encouraging results (20, 45, 52). Although some mental defectives must be returned to institutions and a few get into difficulties, the majority make satisfactory social and vocational adjustments.

**Identifying Creative Talent.**   At the opposite end of the intelligence scale, rising demands for scientists and engineers have stimulated intensive research on the identification and maximal utilization of high-level creative talent. Most of the recent investigations have been concerned with scientific creativity, as manifested in industrial and governmental laboratories, the military services, or the contributions of individual eminent scientists (86–88). Some attention, however, has also been given to creative productivity in the arts (e.g., 24, 39). Research has focused on three major aspects of the problem: (1) formulation of suitable criterion measures for creative behavior (5, 17, 87); (2) investigation of conditions conducive to the development and manifestation of creative talent (70–72, 86–88); and (3) the development of predictors of creative achievement (40, 86–88).

Studies of the characteristics of gifted persons, with which predictor development logically begins, have stressed the importance of personality as well as intellectual factors. Examples of the former include: liking for manipulation of ideas or "toying with ideas" for its own sake, need for independence and autonomy, intellectual persistence, and a strong drive for the activity of intellectual ordering (86). With regard to intellectual qualities, it is generally recognized that creative talent is not synonymous with academic intelligence as measured by traditional intelligence tests. Several investigations have been concerned with identifying the abilities that constitute creative talent, as well as developing new kinds of tests for measuring these abilities. The most comprehensive of these studies is that of Guilford and his associates, who set out to explore four areas of thinking, namely, reasoning, creativity, planning, and evaluation. For the present purpose, interest centers on the various fluency, flexibility, and originality factors found to be most closely associated with creativity (101). These factors come under the heading of "divergent thinking," which Guilford describes as "the kind that goes off in different directions" (40, p. 381). Such thinking permits changes of approach in problem solving and leads to a diversity of answers. In contrast, "convergent thinking" leads to a single right answer determined by the given facts.

The divergent-thinking factors identified in Guilford's studies can be illustrated by examining some of the tests found to be heavily loaded with each factor (40, pp. 381–390). Some of these tests have been published; others will become available in the near future. Until more data are gathered with these tests, however, all should be regarded as research instruments only. A test of *word fluency* requires the subject to write words containing a given letter. In this, as in all fluency tests, the score is simply the total number of acceptable responses written in the time allowed. In one *ideational fluency* test, the task is to name things that belong in a certain class, such as fluids that will burn. In another, the subject lists different uses for a common object, such as a brick or pencil. *Associational fluency* can be illustrated by a test calling for all words similar in meaning to a given word, such as "hard." Words for this test were chosen because each has a variety of meanings. Another test requires the insertion of an adjective to complete each simile (e.g., "As _____ as a fish"). *Expressional fluency* can be measured by a test of four-word combinations, in which the subject writes four connected words, the first letters of which are given. For example, if given "Y_____ c_____ t_____ d_____," the subject could write "You can throw dice." The subject continues to write different sentences for each set until time is called.

Among the tests having high loadings in *flexibility* factors may be mentioned Hidden Figures and Match Problems. In the first of these tests, illustrated in Figure 7, the subject must identify a simple geometric figure embedded in a more complex figure. The Match Problems test requires the removal of a specified number of matchsticks to leave a given number of squares

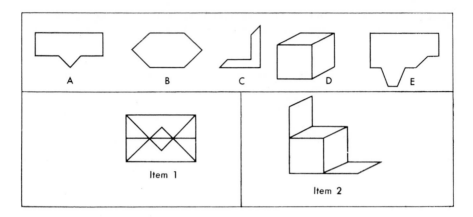

**Fig. 7** Sample items from the Hidden Figures test. Which of the five figures at the top is concealed in each of the item figures? Answers: 1, A; 2, D. (*From Guilford, 40, p. 386.*)

or triangles. An example from this test is reproduced in Figure 8. In all these tests, a good performance requires freedom from persistence of approaches, permitting a restructuring of the given stimuli.

*Originality* can be measured by an adaptation of the familiar free association test, in which the subject must respond rapidly to each stimulus word by giving the first word that occurs to him. In scoring this test, each response is weighted in inverse proportion to its commonness in the general population. There is some evidence that such groups as scientists, engineers, artists, musicians, and writers tend to give less common associations than executives, salesmen, teachers, and politicians. Another example is the Consequences test, which provides separate scores in ideational fluency and originality. In this test, the subject is told to list as many different consequences of some hypothetical event as he can. For example, "What would be the results if

**Fig. 8** Sample item from the Match Problems test. If each line is a match, can you take away four matches from A, leaving three squares and nothing more? If the subject works under the assumption that all squares must be of the same size, he will be unable to reach the correct solution, shown in B. (*From Guilford, 40, p. 387.*)

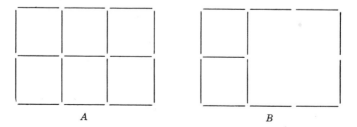

people no longer needed or wanted sleep?" Responses are classified as obvious or remote according to rules given in the manual. The number of obvious
responses provides the ideational fluency score; the number of remote responses, the originality score.

That research on creativity is beginning to influence the very concept of
intelligence in our culture is illustrated by Guilford's later discussions of the
broader implications of his project (38, 41). In a comprehensive reexamination
of his own results and those of other investigators, Guilford proposed a revised
and expanded definition of intelligence. In contrast to earlier definitions, this
formulation gives more weight to nonverbal and to creative processes. In the
light of such developments, intelligence tests of the future will probably include more spatial and other nonverbal content and will tap more reasoning
and creative functions, in addition to the traditional functions of comprehension
and retention.

## SPECIAL APTITUDE TESTS

In the selection of personnel for most jobs, intelligence tests must be
supplemented with tests of special aptitudes. Frequently, such aptitude tests
are custom-made to fit the demands of a particular job. For certain aptitudes
common to many jobs, however, published tests are available. Most of these
standardized tests for general use are in the areas of vision, hearing, simple
motor skills, mechanical aptitude, and clerical aptitude.

Many industrial jobs call for minimum standards in vision or hearing. Considerable research is available showing the effects of sensory capacities upon
quantity and quality of output, spoilage and waste of materials, job turnover, and accidents (93, chs. 5 and 14). Many types of military specialties
likewise make heavy demands upon visual or auditory capacities.

Both visual and auditory sensitivity include not one but many functions.
Among the *visual* characteristics found to be of greatest practical importance
may be mentioned: near acuity at "reading distance" (13 to 16 inches), far
acuity (usually measured at 20 feet), perception of distance or depth, muscular balance of the eyes (phoria), and color discrimination. Composite instruments have been developed for measuring all these aspects of vision. An
example is the Ortho-Rater, illustrated in Figure 9. Providing measures of
each of the above characteristics, the Ortho-Rater is widely used in industry.

In *hearing,* the aspect of most general concern is auditory acuity, measured
by finding the faintest sound that the individual can just barely hear. Both
individual and group audiometers are available for measuring such acuity
(47). Other hearing characteristics important for certain industrial and military functions include discrimination of pitch and of loudness of different
sounds.

Tests of *motor skills* are used widely in the selection of industrial and military personnel. Usually, however, such tests are tailored to meet specific job
requirements. The United States Air Force, for instance, developed many
motor coordination tests for its classification program (31, 57). An example
is the Complex Coordination Test, illustrated in Figure 10. In this test, the
examinee operates three controls similar to the rudder and stick controls used

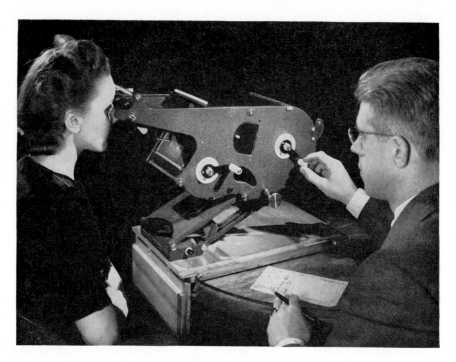

**Fig. 9**  Ortho-Rater for testing visual functions. (*Courtesy of Bausch &*
*Lomb Optical Company.*)

in an airplane. The stimuli consist of different patterns of signal lights on the
vertical panel.

Most commercially available tests of motor skills call for very simple types
of movement. Often they require the manipulation of small objects, as in the
Purdue Pegboard (90), illustrated in Figure 11. In one part of this test, the
subject inserts a pin in each hole, using the right hand, the left hand, and
both hands simultaneously in successive trials. In another part of the test,
pins, collars, and washers are assembled and fitted into each hole, the subject employing both hands in a prescribed procedure. Tests such as these are
utilized in selecting workers for assembling, packing, routine machine operations, and similar jobs. Their validity should be checked for each job, however, since motor skills have proved to be highly specific (see 3, pp. 383–386).
Even for the same job, moreover, different tests may be required to predict
quantity and quality of output, as illustrated in a study of power-sewing-
machine operators (64).

Tests commonly classified under the heading of *mechanical aptitude* cover
a variety of functions. Motor skills enter into some of these tests, either because the test may call for rapid manipulation of materials or because special
subtests designed to measure motor dexterity are included. Perceptual speed
and accuracy also play a part in certain tests. The major factors measured by
mechanical aptitude tests, however, are spatial visualization and mechanical
comprehension.

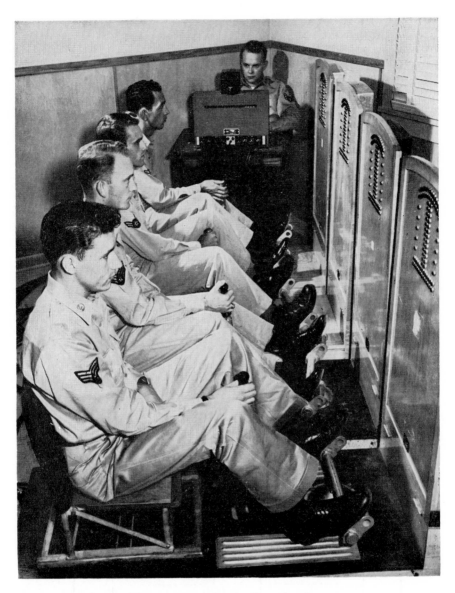

*Fig. 10* Complex Coordination Test used in Air Force classification
program during World War II. (*Courtesy of U.S. Air Force; for
description of test, see Melton, 57.*)

A test designed to measure the first of these abilities is the Minnesota
Paper Form Board. This is one of a series of tests originally developed in an
extensive investigation of mechanical aptitude conducted at the University
of Minnesota (65). Its current revision (56) is illustrated in Figure 12. Each
item consists of a geometric figure cut into two or more parts. The subject

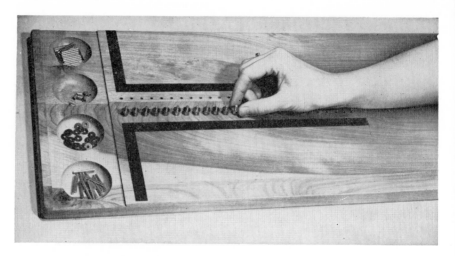

**Fig. 11**   Purdue Pegboard. (*Courtesy of Science Research Associates.*)

must visualize how the pieces fit together and choose the drawing that shows the correct arrangement. A large number of studies conducted with this test indicate that it is one of the most valid available instruments for measuring the ability to visualize and manipulate objects in space (56). Among the criteria employed in this research were performance in shop courses, grades in engineering and in other technical and mechanical courses, supervisors'

**Fig. 12**   Sample items from the Revised Minnesota Paper Form Board. (*Reproduced by permission of The Psychological Corporation. Copyright 1941, Rensis Likert and W. H. Quasha.*)

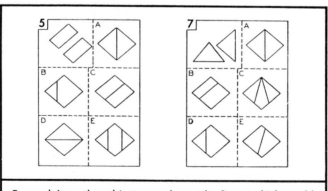

For each item, the subject must choose the figure which would result if the pieces in the first section were assembled.

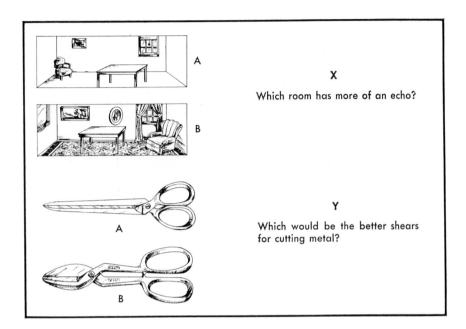

*Fig. 13*  Sample items from the Test of Mechanical Comprehension,
Form AA. (*Reproduced by permission. Copyright 1940, The
Psychological Corporation.*)

ratings, and objective production records. The test has also shown some
validity in predicting the achievement of dentistry and art students.

Another test that has been widely employed for both civilian and military
purposes is the Bennett Test of Mechanical Comprehension (9), illustrated in
Figure 13. Several published studies of this test provide evidence of both
concurrent and predictive validity for mechanical trades and engineering.
Correlations between .30 and .60 have been found with either training
or job-proficiency criteria in many kinds of mechanical jobs (35, 66). During
World War II, this test proved to be one of the best predictors of pilot success (42). Its validity for this criterion seems to have resulted chiefly from
the contribution of a mechanical information factor and a spatial visualization
factor, which together accounted for about 60 per cent of the variance of its
scores.

Tests designed to measure *clerical aptitude* are primarily concerned with
perceptual speed and accuracy. A well-known example is the Minnesota
Clerical Test (4), illustrated in Figure 14. In the two parts of this test, the
subject compares pairs of numbers and names, respectively, to determine
whether they are the same or different. Although a deduction is made for
errors, the scores depend predominantly upon speed. Moderately high correlations have been reported between scores on this test and ratings by office
supervisors or by commercial teachers, as well as performance records in
courses and in various kinds of clerical jobs (4, 23). Several studies compared

When the two numbers or names in a pair are <u>exactly the same</u>, make a check mark on the line between them.

66273894_____66273984

527384578_____527384578

New York World_____New York World

Cargill Grain Co._____Cargil Grain Co.

**Fig. 14**   Sample items from the Minnesota Clerical Test. (*Reproduced by permission. Copyright 1933, The Psychological Corporation.*)

the scores obtained by different levels of clerks, by clerks and by persons in other occupations, and by employed and unemployed clerks. All these comparisons yielded significant mean differences in the expected directions.

It is apparent that such a relatively homogeneous instrument as the Minnesota Clerical Test measures only one aspect of clerical work. Clerical jobs cover a multiplicity of functions. Moreover, the number and particular combination of duties vary tremendously with the type and level of job. Even specific jobs designated by the same name, such as typist, filing clerk, or shipping clerk, may differ considerably from one company to another. Despite this diversity of activities, however, job analyses of general clerical work indicate that a relatively large proportion of time is spent in such tasks as classifying, sorting, checking, collating and stapling, stuffing and sealing envelopes, and the like (10). Speed and accuracy in perceiving details are thus of primary importance for the clerical worker, especially in the lower-level, routine clerical jobs (44). For higher-level clerical jobs, the verbal and numerical abilities measured by intelligence tests are undoubtedly more relevant. Several clerical aptitude tests combine verbal and numerical tests with tests of perceptual speed and accuracy in a single battery (see 3, pp. 395–396). Such composite tests are useful provided they yield separate scores for each part, since the relative weights of these abilities may vary widely from one clerical job to another (see, e.g., 77).

## MULTIPLE APTITUDE BATTERIES

Special aptitude tests in such fields as the mechanical and the clerical were originally developed to supplement general intelligence tests. Particularly in vocational testing, it soon became evident that intelligence tests did not cover all requisite intellectual functions. Concurrently, analyses of intelligence test performance revealed conspicuous intraindividual differences from one intelligence test to another or among different parts of the same test. A person might do well on a written test but poorly on a performance test requiring spatial orientation; or, in the traditional written test, he might be consistently better on the numerical than on the verbal items. It thus appeared that the intelligence tests themselves might be measuring a small number of relatively independent aptitudes in which the same individual could vary appreciably.

A parallel development in basic research was the study of the nature and organization of intelligence by the techniques of *factor analysis* (see 3, pp. 338–348). Essentially such techniques involve the administration of a large number of tests to the same persons. The scores on all the tests are then intercorrelated and the correlations subjected to further statistical analyses in order to determine which tests tend to cluster together and which are relatively independent. Examples of the separate abilities, or "factors," thus identified include verbal comprehension, numerical computation, quantitative reasoning, perceptual speed, spatial visualization, and mechanical comprehension. Through factor analysis, what had formerly been called intelligence could now be subdivided into relatively independent abilities, and these abilities could be combined with those underlying the special aptitude tests to provide a more comprehensive picture of intelligence.

The construction of *multiple aptitude batteries* was the direct outcome of factorial research. Rather than yielding a single global score, such as an IQ, these batteries provide a profile of scores on separate tests, most of which correspond more or less closely to traits identified through factor analysis. Several batteries of this sort are now commercially available (see 3, ch. 13; 84). An example is the Differential Aptitude Tests (DAT), for which the largest amount of validity information is available (11). The DAT yields scores in eight abilities: Verbal Reasoning, Numerical Ability, Abstract Reasoning, Clerical Speed and Accuracy, Mechanical Reasoning, Space Relations, Spelling, and Grammar. Sample items from each of these tests can be found in Chapter 16 (Fig. 107, pp. 436–437). Figure 15 is a profile chart showing the DAT scores obtained by a young man whose greatest strengths are in Verbal Reasoning and Numerical Ability. The score in the third column, based on the sum of these two scores, provides a single index of scholastic aptitude similar to that obtained from most intelligence tests.

Another multiple aptitude battery is the more recently published Flanagan Aptitude Classification Tests, or FACT (30). Oriented principally toward vocational counseling and employee selection, this battery comprises 21 tests, each designed to measure a "critical job element" identified through job analyses. Examples of these tests include: *Assembly* (ability to visualize the appearance of an object assembled from a number of separate parts); *Planning* (ability to plan, organize, and schedule; ability to foresee problems that may arise and to anticipate the best order for carrying out the various steps); *Ingenuity* (creative or inventive skill; ability to devise ingenious procedures, equipment, or presentations). Sample items from the Assembly and Ingenuity tests are illustrated in Figure 16.

On the basis of the initial job analyses, scores from the FACT battery were combined into "occupational aptitude scores" for over three dozen jobs ranging from humanities teacher to plumber. The predictive validity of these occupational scores is being investigated by following up the educational and

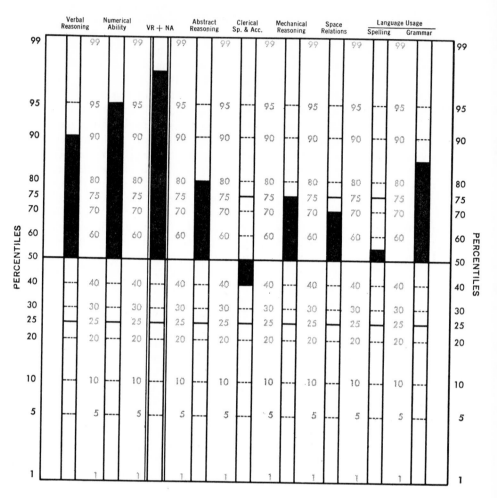

**Fig. 15**  Profile of scores on the Differential Aptitude Tests. Vertical
bars show distance above or below norm on each test. Percentiles are
spaced so as to correspond to equal distances in a normal distribution.
(*Reproduced by permission. Copyright 1963, The Psychological Corporation.*)

vocational careers of high school students tested in the standardization sample.
Preliminary findings suggest moderately promising validity, but a definitive
evaluation of this battery must await the accumulation of many more research
data.

Mention should also be made of the classification batteries developed for
use in the military services and of the General Aptitude Test Battery (GATB)
prepared by the United States Employment Service (26). The latter consists
of 12 tests yielding the following nine scores: Intelligence, Verbal Aptitude,
Numerical Aptitude, Spatial Aptitude, Form Perception, Clerical Perception,
Motor Coordination, Finger Dexterity, and Manual Dexterity. The Intelligence

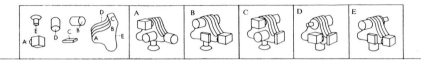

*Assembly:* In each figure, parts are to be assembled so that places having the same letter are put together. Which of the five assemblies below shows the parts put together correctly?

*Ingenuity:* Think of a word or words that will complete a clever and ingenious solution to the stated problem. Then choose the alternative having the same first and last letters and the same number of letter spaces as your answer.

> S1. A hostess for a children's party wanted to serve ice cream in an interesting manner, and she decided to make a clown for each child. She placed a ball of ice cream to represent the clown's head on a round cookie which served for a collar, and on top of this she inverted a
>
> A. t __ __ e.
> B. u __ __ i.
> C. r __ __ s.
> D. c __ __ e.
> E. t __ __ r.

Answers:      Assembly, C                               Ingenuity, D (cone)

**Fig. 16**  Sample items from Flanagan Aptitude Classification Tests. (*Reproduced by permission of John C. Flanagan.*)

score is a factorially complex but practically useful measure based on performance in vocabulary, arithmetic reasoning, and spatial visualization tests. The other scores correspond more nearly to independent abilities identified through factor analysis.

So far, multiple aptitude batteries have been used more extensively for vocational counseling of individuals than for personnel selection or placement. With the growing emphasis on classification programs, however, such batteries may come to play a more prominent part in industrial personnel programs. When selecting applicants for a single job, most personnel psychologists rely on a general intelligence test plus very specific aptitude tests chosen to fit the particular job. But when the problem is that of maximum utilization of an available manpower pool, a multiple aptitude battery measuring a few broad abilities that cut across many different jobs is more effective. A major weakness of current multiple aptitude batteries, however, is their disappointing performance with regard to *differential validity* (see Chapter 2). It is possible that with an increasing utilization of vocational proficiency criteria—in contrast to academic or vocational training criteria—more differentiating batteries can be developed. Further research is undoubtedly needed to explore the potential contribution of this type of testing instrument.

## ACHIEVEMENT TESTS

Achievement tests are designed to assess the proficiency level currently attained by an individual. An end-of-term school examination is an achievement test, as are the many standardized tests employed in educational settings, from the elementary grades to graduate and professional schools. When used in industrial situations, achievement tests are often called *trade tests*. It is customary to contrast achievement tests with aptitude tests, the latter including intelligence tests, special aptitude tests, and multiple aptitude batteries. From one point of view, the distinction is one of *degree of uniformity of assumed antecedent experience*. Achievement tests measure the effects of relatively uniform sets of experiences, such as a course in Spanish, in speed writing, or in TV repairing. Aptitude test performance, on the other hand, reflects the cumulative influence of a multiplicity of experiences in daily living, including nature and extent of general education, home environment, and a myriad other influences. We might say that aptitude tests measure the effects of learning under relatively uncontrolled and unknown conditions, while achievement tests measure the effects of learning under partially known and controlled conditions.

A second distinction between aptitude and achievement tests pertains to their *uses*. Aptitude tests serve to predict subsequent performance. They are employed to estimate the extent to which the individual will profit from training or to forecast his performance in a new situation. Achievement tests, on the other hand, generally provide a terminal evaluation of the individual's status upon the completion of training. The emphasis in such tests is upon what the individual can do at the time. Neither distinction, however, can be rigidly applied. Some aptitude tests may presuppose fairly specific and uniform prior training, while some achievement tests cover relatively broad and unstandardized educational experiences. Similarly, *any achievement test may be used as a predictor of future learning*. As such it serves the same purpose as an aptitude test.

When used in personnel selection, achievement tests play the same role as aptitude tests. In such situations, they should be validated against criteria of subsequent job proficiency, as is done for any other predictor. Examples of this use of achievement tests can be found in the hiring of typists, engineers, apprentices in skilled trades, or any other job for which specialized vocational training is a prerequisite. Achievement tests may also be used to assess the effectiveness of a training program, to determine when individuals have attained the required proficiency level in a training course, to identify present employees in need of special training, and to help in selecting employees for transfers or promotions.

Some achievement tests are concerned with technical information, others with job skills. Information may be tested by a set of standardized oral questions or by written tests, the latter permitting either group or individual administration. Examples of commercially available *written tests* developed for general use are provided by the Purdue Vocational Tests,[2] which cover such jobs as those of machinist, engine-lathe operator, electrician, or carpenter.

Another technique for appraising vocational training and experience involves the use of *oral trade tests,* or short series of questions about specialized trade knowledge. The items of information are chosen so as to be fairly easy for anyone who has actually worked in a particular trade but rarely familiar to others. For this reason, oral trade questions are often used as a check on the reported job experience of an applicant. The United States Employment Service has developed standardized sets of oral trade questions for well over a hundred jobs (79, ch. 3 and pp. 156–162). Each set consists of 15 questions, such as the following taken from the bricklayer's test:

Question: What do you mean by building up a lead?
Answer: Building up a section (corner) of wall.

For each occupation, the questions that had been formulated on the basis of extensive job analyses and preliminary tryouts were administered to three groups of workers: experts, beginners, and workers in related occupations. Items were chosen for the final sets in terms of the significance and magnitude of the differences between the percentage of workers in each of these groups who answered the question correctly. The differences were so large that little overlapping in total scores remained when the three groups were compared.

In the large majority of jobs, information is a necessary but not a sufficient condition for satisfactory performance. Information tests thus need to be supplemented by tests of *job skills.* These skills are usually measured through standardized work samples which closely reproduce actual job processes. Tests administered before the granting of a driver's license or a pilot's license illustrate the work sample technique. Another example is the Miniature Punch Press Test, reproduced in Figure 17. More complex work-sample tests have been developed for the evaluation of technical military personnel (see, e.g., 13). Among the best-known work-sample tests available for general use are those designed for clerical jobs, especially typewriting, stenography, and bookkeeping (e.g., 74, 95). Stenographic tests usually employ sound recordings to ensure uniformity in speed and clarity of dictation.

Of particular interest is a recent attempt to devise a work-sample test for certain aspects of executive work. Known as the In-Basket Test, this technique has been adapted for testing Air Force officers in administrative positions (34), business executives (49), and school principals (33, 46). Simulating the familiar "in-basket" found on the administrator's desk, this test provides a carefully prepared set of incoming letters, memoranda, reports, papers to be signed, and similar items. Before taking the test, the subject has an opportunity to study background materials for orientation and information regarding the hypothetical job. During the test proper, his task is to handle all the matters in his in-basket as he would on the job. All actions must be recorded in writing but may include letters, memos, decisions, plans, directives, information to be obtained or transmitted by telephone, agenda for meetings, or any other notes.

2 Distributed partly by Science Research Associates and partly by University Book Store, West Lafayette, Ind.

**Fig. 17** Miniature Punch Press Test. (*From Tiffin and Greenly, 91, p. 451.*)

## PERSONALITY TESTS

It is now widely recognized that many job failures result from personality deficiencies. Having the required intellectual level, knowledge, and skills does not ensure that the individual will be an effective producer, a satisfied employee, or a well-liked co-worker. Personality characteristics may determine success or failure on *any* kind of job. Nevertheless, it is obvious that they play a particularly important part in jobs requiring extensive interpersonal contacts, such as selling and supervisory work. Understandably enough, the possible contributions of available personality tests to personnel selection have been somewhat more fully explored in these fields than elsewhere.

Several attempts have also been made to develop special tests for salesmen (15, 16, 53) and for managerial personnel (29, 32, 59, 73). The construction of objective testing instruments for such traits as empathy, social sensitivity, or supervisory attitudes presents many difficulties. Frequently the resulting tests measure mostly intelligence or familiarity with acceptable human-relations practices and may show little relation to criteria of actual interpersonal behavior. The earlier instruments have proved disappointing; the later ones, although more promising, are still largely untried. But the continuing research program in this area, coupled with improved techniques of test construction, may yield fruitful results before too long.

Of considerable relevance, too, is the extensive research concerned with executive job analyses and criteria of executive success (see 36, 75, 78, 89). Much has been learned about the relative amount of time executives spend in different duties, the traits considered important in an executive, causes of executive failure and success, differences between executives at various levels or between industrial and military executives, and similar questions. It has been found, for instance, that all executives spend a large proportion of their time in interpersonal contacts and that public relations, or "representative," functions assume increasing importance at the higher executive levels. Similarly, inter-personal traits are frequently cited to account for the success or failure of individual executives.

The increasing use of personality tests in executive selection has certainly not been without its critics, as exemplified by the vituperative treatment given this topic by Whyte in *The Organization Man* (100). A thorough and lucid analysis of Whyte's criticisms can be found in a paper by Stark (78). For the present purpose, it will suffice to note two points about Whyte's discussion. First, many of Whyte's criticisms are directed against *misuses* of tests, such as excessive reliance on personality test scores in the absence of other information or the administration of inadequately validated instruments. These are ob-jectionable practices that reputable psychologists themselves have vigorously condemned.

In the second place, Whyte argues that personality tests are generally used in industry to select executives who are conformists and lacking in indi-viduality (i.e., typical "organization men"). Insofar as this criticism may be true, it is an indictment, not of the tests, but of the criteria of executive success against which they must be validated. It would apply just as much—if not more so—to the relatively subjective and unstandardized predictors advocated by Whyte, such as previous job history and interviewing techniques. The underlying social philosophy that Whyte so eloquently attacks is a matter for debate in its own right. But it has no intrinsic relation to psychological tests or to their use in personnel selection.

In the rest of this section, we shall consider the major types of personality tests used in personnel selection in general. These include measures of in-terests, personality inventories, projective techniques, and situational tests. Each type of test will be illustrated with two or three examples.

**Measurement of Interests.**  An early instrument that has stood the test of time unusually well is the Vocational Interest Blank (VIB). First developed by Strong in 1928, this test has undergone continuing revision, extension, and research—including long-term longitudinal validation (80–83). In this test, the individual records his liking or dislike for a wide variety of activities, objects, or types of people commonly encountered in daily living. He is not required to judge in advance his interest in occupations about which he may have inadequate knowledge or which he may perceive in terms of misleading popular stereotypes. Preliminary research demonstrated that persons engaged in a given occupation tend to have common interests, not only in job activities, but also in school subjects, hobbies, sports, types of plays or books, social relations, and the like. It thus proved feasible to question the individual about his interests in familiar things and thereby determine how closely his interests resemble those of persons successfully engaged in each occupation.

The Strong VIB is scored with a different key for each occupation. The items to be included in each key, as well as the weights assigned to each response, were found empirically by comparing the percentage of persons in the particular occupation giving each answer with the percentage of "men in general" who gave it. Responses occurring significantly more often, let us say, among lawyers than among men in general received positive weights in the lawyer's key; those occurring significantly less often among lawyers received negative weights. By such empirical criterion keying, about fifty occupational keys have been developed for the men's form and about thirty for the women's form. New keys are constructed as the need and opportunity arise.

Other tests, such as the Kuder Preference Record (54), report interest scores, not in terms of specific occupations, but in terms of broad areas, such as mechanical, scientific, persuasive, and artistic areas. Similarly, the Study of Values (1) assesses the relative strength of six basic interests, motives, or evaluative attitudes, designated as theoretical, economic, aesthetic, social, political, and religious. From a different angle, the more recently developed Survey of Interpersonal Values (37) determines the relative importance the individual places on six aspects of his relationships with others: support, conformity, recognition, independence, benevolence, and leadership.

With all these tests, the score pattern desirable for any occupation needs to be empirically established by the usual validation procedures. As in any test, scores cannot be interpreted at face value on the basis of the trait names ascribed to them. To some extent this is also true of the Strong VIB, especially for certain occupations. Different types of salesmen, for instance, show different response patterns on this test, so that separate keys had to be developed for them (e.g., 48, 102). It should be added that interest tests are used more extensively in vocational counseling than in personnel selection and will therefore be discussed further in Chapter 16.

***Personality Inventories.*** This type of personality test originated in the attempt to identify emotional maladjustment and neurotic behavior. A number of current personality inventories—especially those designed for use in clinical contexts—still focus primarily on emotional abnormality. Most of the newer inventories, however, are concerned with individual differences in emotional, motivational, and social traits among essentially normal persons. Moreover, such inventories typically provide a profile of scores in a number of traits, rather than a single score. The norms on such tests generally fall near the center of the score range. Deviations in either direction from such a norm need to be interpreted in terms of particular job requirements. Desirable score patterns for each type of job may be empirically established by the usual follow-up procedures described in the preceding chapter.

An example of a personality inventory is the Guilford-Zimmerman Temperament Survey (43), which yields separate scores on the following 10 traits: general activity, restraint, ascendance, sociability, emotional stability, objectivity, friendliness, thoughtfulness, personal relations, and masculinity. The items measuring these traits are presented in random order and not identified as such to the subject. Three typical items are:

You start work on a new project with a great
    deal of enthusiasm.............................. YES    ?    NO
You are often low in spirits........................... YES    ?    NO
Most people use politeness to cover up what is
    really "cutthroat" competition...................... YES    ?    NO

A common difficulty limiting the usefulness of personality inventories in personnel selection is their susceptibility to *faking.* Many investigations have demonstrated that, on self-report inventories, subjects can frequently identify the socially desirable answers and will mark such answers instead of those corresponding to their own habitual behavior (see 3, pp. 59–60). The motivation to create a favorable impression is of course stronger in a selection than in a counseling situation, although not totally absent even in the latter. Several techniques have been devised for reducing or at least detecting such faking. The Guilford-Zimmerman, for example, provides three *verification keys,* based on the responses to certain items, to detect falsification and carelessness in responses. A procedure designed to reduce the tendency to fake is known as the *forced-choice technique.* In a forced-choice item, the subject must choose between answers that appear equally acceptable (or unacceptable) but differ in validity for a specific criterion.

The first commercially available inventory to use the forced-choice technique was the Jurgensen Classification Inventory (51). Designed specifically for industrial application, this inventory provides no general norms or scoring key. Test users are expected to develop scoring keys by empirical tryout against local criteria. Sample items from this inventory are reproduced below, together with abridged instructions to subjects:

Mark the one that you think is MOST irritating and the one that you think is
    LEAST irritating.
        People who are
            Bluffers ........................................... M     L
            Complainers ....................................... M     L
            Interrupters ....................................... M     L
Decide which reputation you would MOST prefer to have and which you would
    LEAST prefer to have.
        Considered
            Calm ............................................. M     L
            Alert ............................................. M     L
            Friendly .......................................... M     L
Mark the item you prefer, using XX if your preference is strong and X if it is weak.
    Have interesting work with moderate pay _____
    Have uninteresting work with high pay _____

Another personality inventory utilizing the forced-choice technique is the Edwards Personal Preference Schedule (EPPS) (27). Based on the personality theory of Murray (61), this inventory was designed to measure the relative strength of 15 needs, described as follows: Achievement, Deference, Order, Exhibition, Autonomy, Affiliation, Intraception, Succorance, Dominance, Abasement, Nurturance, Change, Endurance, Heterosexuality, Aggression. In the inventory, items from each of these needs are paired off with items from the other 14. Within each pair, the two items were matched in their previously determined social desirability. A sample profile of scores on the EPPS is shown in Figure 18. The EPPS has not been available long enough to permit an adequate evaluation of its potential industrial contribution. Some promising results are provided by recent research with this test on the personality patterns of engineers (50) and of industrial and retail salesmen (25). It should be noted, however, that the forced-choice technique reduces but does not eliminate faking, especially by the applicant for a specific job. Even when items are equated for general social desirability, the individual may recognize that certain responses are more relevant to the particular job.

**Projective Techniques.** It is principally in clinical psychology that projective techniques have enjoyed their greatest popularity. Hence they will be

**Fig. 18**  Profile on the Edwards Personal Preference Schedule.
(*Reproduced by permission. Copyright 1959, The Psychological Corporation.*)

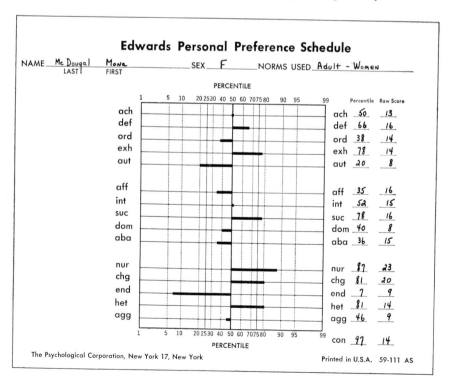

discussed more fully in Chapter 13. These techniques, however, are also used to a limited extent in industry, especially for intensive individual evaluation of executives and other high-level personnel. Typically in a projective test the subject is assigned an *unstructured* task, which permits an almost unlimited variety of possible responses. The test stimuli are usually vague and equivocal and the instructions brief and general. Such tests are based on the hypothesis that the way the individual perceives and interprets the test material, or "structures" the situation, reflects basic characteristics of his personality. The test stimuli thus serve as a sort of screen on which the subject "projects" his own ideas. Since the subject is generally unaware of the way his responses will be scored or evaluated, projective techniques are less susceptible to faking than are self-report inventories, but they are not entirely immune to it (e.g., 97).

A widely used projective technique, which has also served as a model for the development of many later instruments, is the Thematic Apperception Test (TAT). First developed by Murray and his associates (60, 61), this test consists of a set of pictures, for each of which the subject is to make up a story. As in most projective tests, there is no objective scoring procedure, the stories being interpreted by the examiner in terms of Murray's theory of needs and of environmental forces that either facilitate or interfere with the satisfaction of these needs. Several adaptations of the TAT have been developed for special purposes. One of these, prepared for use in assessing managerial potential, provides a semiobjective scoring system (see 89, p. 392).

Pictures are employed in a different way in the Tomkins-Horn Picture

*Fig. 19*   Sample item from the Tomkins-Horn Picture Arrangement Test. The subject indicates the sequence that makes the best sense for the three pictures and writes three sentences explaining them. (*Reproduction by permission of Springer Publishing Company, Inc.*)

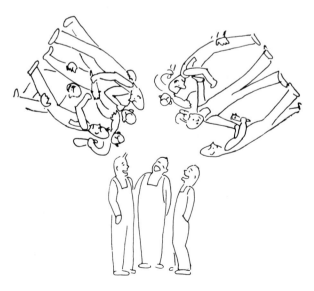

Arrangement Test (PAT), a projective technique originally designed for the selection and guidance of industrial personnel (94). Each item of the PAT consists of three sketches presented in a round-robin arrangement so as to minimize positional set (see Figure 19). The subject's task is to indicate the order of the three pictures "which makes the best sense" and to write a sentence for each of the three pictures to tell the story. Most items deal with interpersonal relations, more than half of them portraying work situations in an industrial setting. Advantages of this test are that it can be group-administered and machine-scored. The norms are also unusually good for a projective test, having been obtained on a large, representative sample of the United States population. Subjective interpretation has not been entirely eliminated, however. After the objective score pattern is found for each subject, it must be interpreted by a clinical psychologist, who may also refer to the subject's written material at this stage. Like many other personality tests, the PAT has been used in exploratory research on the executive personality (58).

In the light of available knowledge regarding their reliability, validity, and other technical characteristics, projective techniques in general must still be regarded as research instruments. None is ready for operational use, especially in personnel selection. In some situations, these techniques are employed in a relatively subjective manner, as aids to the interviewer. When so used, however, they do not function as tests and cannot be evaluated as such.

**Situational Tests.** Although the term "situational test" first came into prominence during World War II, tests of this type had been developed before that time. Essentially a situational test is one that closely resembles or simulates a "real-life" criterion situation. In this respect such tests are similar to the work-sample trade tests discussed earlier in this chapter. In situational tests, however, the criterion behavior that is sampled is more varied and complex. Moreover, interest is centered, not on aptitude or achievement, but on emotional, social, attitudinal, and other personality traits.

Several kinds of situational tests have been developed for military use to assess the leadership behavior and human-relations skills of officers. Most involve the sort of face-to-face problem situations encountered by administrators in any setting. An example of such a problem situation is briefly described below:

The examinee is evaluated as the commanding officer of a small ship. He must discuss with Ensign Baker, the ship's engineering officer, an unsatisfactory performance report he is about to submit. Although Baker is highly qualified in the technical skills required, he lacks experience. He has allowed the enlisted men to run his department. This has led to no specific incident in which his department has interfered with the ship's operating efficiency, but his behavior has set a bad example for the men and the other officers on board (2, p. 2).

The subject is instructed to assume the given role and carry out the interview with "Ensign Baker," whose part is played by a trained actor. The examiner observes and evaluates the subject's performance with the aid of a previously developed checklist of effective and ineffective behaviors. Examples of such behaviors include: Gives reason for meeting; Allows Baker to direct conversation; Vacillates in, or changes position on, unsatisfactory Report; Mentions Baker's fine engineering background; Mentions constructive nature of Fitness Report (2, p. 2).

A promising type of situational test is the Leaderless Group Discussion (LGD). Requiring a minimum of equipment and time, this technique has been widely used in the selection of such personnel as military officers, civil service supervisors and administrators, industrial executives, management trainees, sales trainees, teachers, and social workers (see 3, pp. 610–612; 6; 40, pp. 260–263). In this test, a group of examinees is assigned a topic for discussion during a specified period. Examiners observe and rate each person's performance but do not participate in the discussion. Although often used under informal and unstandardized conditions, the LGD has been subjected to considerable research and some objective scoring procedures have been worked out for it.

Validity studies suggest that LGD techniques are among the most effective applications of situational tests. Many significant and sizable correlations have been reported between ratings from LGD performance and follow-up or concurrent ratings obtained in military, industrial, and social settings. Some of these correlations are as high as .60. Neither LGD nor other, more elaborate situational tests, however, have proved valid as devices for assessing broad personality traits. All such tests appear to be most effective when they approximate actual work samples of the criterion behavior they are designed to predict. The LGD tests in particular have some validity in predicting performance in jobs requiring a certain amount of verbal communication, verbal problem solving, and acceptance by peers. Another factor that seems to increase the predictive validity of situational tests is job familiarity on the part of the raters. Such a finding again suggests that situational tests work best when the subject's performance is interpreted as a work sample rather than in terms of underlying personality variables.

## SUMMARY

Personnel selection may utilize tests of intelligence, special aptitudes, achievement, or personality. Classification programs are making increasing use of multiple aptitude batteries, which combine the traits measured by intelligence tests with some of the broader abilities traditionally covered by special aptitude tests. Designed to assess the individual's general intellectual level, intelligence tests actually measure largely verbal comprehension and other abstract functions required for scholastic achievement. Several short intelligence tests have been developed for screening industrial personnel. Intelligence tests may be used to predict performance in training, job proficiency, job turnover, and promotion potential. A special contribution of such tests is in the job placement of mental defectives. At the other end of the scale, research on creative talent has produced many new testing techniques, some of which may find their way into the intelligence tests of the future.

Special aptitudes are often measured by custom-made tests designed for a particular job. Among the most common standardized tests for general use are tests of vision, hearing, simple motor skills, spatial aptitude, mechanical comprehension, and clerical aptitude. Achievement tests measure current proficiency following relatively uniform training or experience. However, they may also serve as predictors of subsequent performance. They include written or oral information tests and tests of job skills. Many of the latter are standardized work samples, such as taking dictation, operating a punch press, or handling the matters in an executive's in-basket.

Personality tests may be used with any type of worker but have found their greatest application in jobs requiring extensive interpersonal contacts, such as selling and executive work. It is especially important in this area to guard against common misuses of tests, such as undue reliance on test scores in the absence of other information or the use of inadequately validated instruments. The major types of personality tests used in personnel selection include interest tests, personality inventories, projective techniques, and situational tests. Being among the most successful of all personality tests, interest tests rely chiefly on the empirical criterion keying of reported interests in a variety of familiar experiences. The readiness with which personality inventories can be faked has led to the development of such techniques as verification keys and forced-choice items. While less subject to faking, projective techniques are still largely unvalidated. Some situational tests have promise, especially when they closely approximate actual work samples.

# REFERENCES

1. Allport, G. W., Vernon, P. E., and Lindzey, G. *A Study of Values.* (3rd ed.) Boston: Houghton Mifflin, 1960.
2. American Institute for Research. Situational tests for evaluating supervisory skills. *AIR Res. Notes,* 1957, No. 14.
3. Anastasi, Anne. *Psychological testing.* (2nd ed.) New York: Macmillan, 1961.
4. Andrew, Dorothy M., and Paterson, D. G. *Minnesota Clerical Test.* New York: Psychol. Corp., 1933–1959.
5. Barron, F. The disposition toward originality. *J. abnorm. soc. Psychol.,* 1955, **51,** 478–485.
6. Bass, B. M. The leaderless group discussion. *Psychol. Bull.,* 1954, **51,** 465–492.
7. Beckham, A. S. Minimum intelligence levels for several occupations. *Personnel J.,* 1930, **9,** 309–313.
8. Bell, H. M. *Matching youth and jobs.* Washington: Amer. Coun. Educ., 1940.
9. Bennett, G. K. *Test of Mechanical Comprehension: Form AA.* New York: Psychol. Corp., 1940–1954.
10. Bennett, G. K., and Cruikshank, Ruth M. *A summary of clerical tests.* New York: Psychol. Corp., 1949.
11. Bennett, G. K., Seashore, H. G., and Wesman, A. G. *Differential Aptitude Tests (1963 Edition), Forms L and M.* New York: Psychol. Corp., 1963.
12. Bills, Marion A. Relation of mental alertness test score to positions and permanency in company. *J. appl. Psychol.,* 1923, **7,** 154–156.
13. Bresnard, G. G., and Briggs, L. J. A system simulator for measuring job proficiency. In E. A. Fleishman (Ed.), *Studies in personnel and industrial psychology.* Homewood, Ill.: Dorsey, 1961. Pp. 85–95.
14. Brown, C. W., and Ghiselli, E. E. Prediction of labor turnover by aptitude tests. *J. appl. Psychol.,* 1953, **37,** 9–12.
15. Bruce, M. M. *Sales Motivation Inventory.* New Rochelle, N.Y.: Author, 1953.
16. Bruce, M. M. *Sales Comprehension Test.* New Rochelle, N.Y.: Author, 1953–1957. (See also *J. appl. Psychol.,* 1954, **38,** 302–304.)
17. Buel, W. D. The validity of behavioral rating scale items for the assessment of individual creativity. *J. appl. Psychol.,* 1960, **44,** 407–412.
18. Buros, O. K. (Ed.) *The fifth mental measurements yearbook.* Highland Park, N.J.: Gryphon Press, 1959. (See also preceding volumes in series.)

19. Burr, Emily T. Minimum intellectual levels of accomplishment in industry. *J. Personnel Res.*, 1924, **3**, 207–212.
20. Charles, D. C. Ability and accomplishment of persons earlier judged mentally deficient. *Genet. Psychol. Monogr.*, 1953, **47**, 3–71.
21. Cronbach, L. J. *Essentials of psychological testing.* (2nd ed.) New York: Harper & Row, 1960.
22. Doppelt, J. E. *PTI—Numerical Test.* New York: Psychol. Corp., 1952–1954.
23. Dorcus, R. M., and Jones, Margaret H. *Handbook of employee selection.* New York: McGraw-Hill, 1950.
24. Drevdahl, J. E., and Cattell, R. B. Personality and creativity in artists and writers. *J. clin. Psychol.*, 1958, **14**, 107–111.
25. Dunnette, M. D., and Kirchner, W. K. Psychological test differences between industrial salesmen and retail salesmen. *J. appl. Psychol.*, 1960, **44**, 121–125.
26. Dvorak, Beatrice J. The General Aptitude Test Battery. *Personnel Guid. J.*, 1956, **35**, 145–154.
27. Edwards, A. L. *Edwards Personal Preference Schedule.* New York: Psychol. Corp., 1953–1959.
28. Engel, Anna M. Employment of the mentally retarded. *Amer. J. ment. Defic.*, 1952, **57**, 243–267.
29. File, Q. W., and Remmers, H. H. *How Supervise?* New York: Psychol. Corp., 1948.
30. Flanagan, J. C. *Flanagan Aptitude Classification Tests.* Chicago: Sci. Res. Assoc., 1953–1959.
31. Fleishman, E. A. Psychomotor selection tests: Research and application in the United States Air Force. *Personnel Psychol.*, 1956, **9**, 449–467.
32. Fleishman, E. A. *Leadership Opinion Questionnaire.* Chicago: Sci. Res. Assoc., 1960.
33. Frederiksen, N. In-basket tests and factors in administrative performance. *Proc. 1960 invit. Conf. test. Probl., Educ. Test. Serv.*, 1961, 21–37.
34. Frederiksen, N., Saunders, D. R., and Wand, Barbara. The In-Basket Test. *Psychol. Monogr.*, 1957, **71**, No. 9.
35. Ghiselli, E. E. The measurement of occupational aptitude. Berkeley, Calif.: Univer. Calif. Press, 1955.
36. Gilmer, B. von H. Industrial psychology. *Ann. Rev. Psychol.*, 1960, **11**, 323–350.
37. Gordon, L. V. *Survey of Interpersonal Values.* Chicago: Sci. Res. Assoc., 1960.
38. Guilford, J. P. The structure of intellect. *Psychol. Bull.*, 1956, **53**, 267–293.
39. Guilford, J. P. Creative abilities in the arts. *Psychol. Rev.*, 1957, **64**, 110–118.
40. Guilford, J. P. *Personality.* New York: McGraw-Hill, 1959.
41. Guilford, J. P. Three faces of intellect. *Amer. Psychologist*, 1959, **14**, 469–479.
42. Guilford, J. P., and Lacey, J. I. (Eds.) *Printed classification tests.* (AAF Aviation Psychology Program, Research Reports, Rep. No. 5.) Washington: Govt. Printing Office, 1947.
43. Guilford, J. P., and Zimmerman, W. S. *The Guilford-Zimmerman Temperament Survey.* Beverly Hills, Calif.: Sheridan Supply Co., 1949–1955.
44. Hay, E. N. Comparative validities in clerical testing. *J. appl. Psychol.*, 1954, **38**, 299–301.
45. Hegge, T. G. The occupational status of higher-grade mental defectives in the present emergency. *Amer. J. ment. Defic.*, 1944, **49**, 86–98.
46. Hemphill, J., Griffiths, D., and Frederiksen, N. *Administrative performance and personality.* New York: Teach. Coll., Columbia Univer., Bur. Publ., 1962.
47. Hirsh, I. J. *The measurement of hearing.* New York: McGraw-Hill, 1961.
48. Hughes, J. L., and McNamara, W. J. Limitations on the use of Strong sales keys for selection and counseling. *J. appl. Psychol.*, 1958, **42**, 93–96.
49. *The in-basket technique: Proceedings of the Conference on the Executive Study.* Princeton, N.J.: Educ. Test. Serv., 1961.
50. Izard, C. E. Personality characteristics of engineers as measured by the Edwards Personal Preference Schedule. *J. appl. Psychol.*, 1960, **44**, 332–335.
51. Jurgensen, C. E. Report on the "classification inventory," a personality test for industrial use. *J. appl. Psychol.*, 1944, **28**, 445–460.

52. Kennedy, Ruby J. R. *The social adjustment of morons in a Connecticut city.*
    Hartford, Conn.: Mansfield-Southbury Soc. Serv., 1948.
53. Kerr, W. A., and Speroff, B. J. *The Empathy Test.* Chicago: Psychometric
    Affiliates, 1947–1955.
54. Kuder, G. F. *Kuder Preference Record—Vocational.* Chicago: Sci. Res. Assoc.,
    1934–1956.
55. Langmuir, C. R. *PTI Oral Directions Test.* New York: Psychol. Corp., 1954.
56. Likert, R., and Quasha, W. H. *Revised Minnesota Paper Form Board.* New York:
    Psychol. Corp., 1941–1948.
57. Melton, A. W. (Ed.) *Apparatus tests.* (AAF Aviation Psychology Program, Re-
    search Reports, Rep. No. 4.) Washington: Govt. Printing Office, 1947.
58. Miner, J. B., and Culver, J. E. Some aspects of the executive personality. *J. appl.
    Psychol.,* 1955, **39**, 348–353.
59. Mowry, H. W. A measure of supervisory quality. *J. appl. Psychol.,* 1957, **41**,
    405–408.
60. Murray, H. A. *Thematic Apperception Test.* Cambridge, Mass.: Harvard Univer.
    Press, 1943.
61. Murray, H. A., et al. *Explorations in personality.* New York: Oxford Univer.
    Press, 1938.
62. Otis, A. S. *Otis Self-Administering Tests of Mental Ability: Higher Examination.*
    New York: Harcourt, Brace & World, 1922–1929.
63. Otis, A. S. *Otis Quick-Scoring Mental Ability Tests: New Edition.* New York:
    Harcourt, Brace & World, 1954.
64. Otis, J. L. The prediction of success in power sewing machine operating. *J. appl.
    Psychol.,* 1938, **22**, 350–366.
65. Paterson, D. G., et al. *Minnesota mechanical ability tests.* Minneapolis: Univer.
    Minn. Press, 1930.
66. Patterson, C. H. Predicting success in trade and vocational courses: Review of the
    literature. *Educ. psychol. Measmt,* 1956, **16**, 352–400.
67. Personnel practices in factory and office. *Studies in Personnel Policy,* No. 145.
    New York: Nat. Industr. Conf. Bd, 1954.
68. Pond, Millicent, and Bills, Marion A. Intelligence and clerical jobs. *Personnel J.,*
    1933, **12**, 41–56.
69. Raven, J. C. *Progressive Matrices* (1938), *1956 Revision.* London: Lewis, 1956.
    (U.S. distributor: Psychol. Corp.)
70. Roe, Anne. A psychological study of eminent biologists. *Psychol. Monogr.,* 1951,
    **65**, No. 14.
71. Roe, Anne. A psychological study of physical scientists. *Genet. Psychol. Monogr.,*
    1951, **43**, 121–235.
72. Roe, Anne. A psychological study of eminent psychologists and anthropologists,
    and a comparison with biological and physical scientists. *Psychol. Monogr.,* 1953,
    **67**, No. 2.
73. Schwartz, S. L., and Gekoski, N. The supervisory inventory: A forced-choice
    measure of human relations attitude and technique. *J. appl. Psychol.,* 1960, **44**,
    233–240.
74. Seashore, H., and Bennett, G. K. *The Seashore-Bennett Stenographic Proficiency
    Test: A Standard Recorded Stenographic Worksample.* New York: Psychol. Corp.,
    1946–1956.
75. Sparks, C. P. Differential characteristics of executives. *Amer. Psychologist,* 1960,
    **15**, 477.
76. Spriegel, W. R., and James, V. A. Trends in recruitment and selection practices.
    *Personnel,* 1958, **35**, 42–48.
77. Staff, Adjutant General's Office. Validation of the General Clerical Abilities Test
    for selection and placement of War Department civilian personnel. *Amer. Psy-
    chologist,* 1947, **2**, 141–144.
78. Stark, S. Executive personality and psychological testing. *Curr. econ. Comment,*
    1958, **20**, (2), 15–32.
79. Stead, W. H., Shartle, C. L., et al. *Occupational counseling techniques.* New
    York: Amer. Book Co., 1940.

80. Strong, E. K., Jr. *Vocational Interest Blank for Men, Revised.* Palo Alto, Calif.: Consulting Psychol. Press, 1959.
81. Strong, E. K., Jr. *Vocational interests of men and women.* Stanford, Calif.: Stanford Univer. Press, 1943.
82. Strong, E. K., Jr. *Vocational Interest Blank for Women, Revised.* Palo Alto, Calif.: Consulting Psychol. Press, 1959.
83. Strong, E. K., Jr. *Vocational interests 18 years after college.* Minneapolis: Univer. Minn. Press, 1955.
84. Super, D. E. (Ed.) *The use of multifactor tests in guidance.* Washington: Amer. Personnel Guid. Assoc., 1959. (Reprinted from *Personnel Guid. J.,* 1956–1957.)
85. Super, D. E., and Crites, J. O. *Appraising vocational fitness by means of psychological tests.* (Rev. ed.) New York: Harper & Row, 1962.
86. Taylor, C. W. The 1955 and 1957 research conferences: The identification of creative scientific talent. *Amer. Psychologist,* 1959, **14**, 100–102.
87. Taylor, C. W. (Ed.) *The third (1959) University of Utah research conference on the identification of creative scientific talent.* Salt Lake City, Utah: Univer. Utah Press, 1959.
88. Taylor, C. W., and Barron, F. *Scientific creativity: Its recognition and development.* New York: Wiley, 1963.
89. Taylor, E. K., and Nevis, E. C. Personnel selection. *Ann. Rev. Psychol.,* 1961, **12**, 389–412.
90. Tiffin, J. *Purdue Pegboard.* Chicago: Sci. Res. Assoc., 1941–1948.
91. Tiffin, J., and Greenly, R. J. Experiments in the operation of a punch press. *J. appl. Psychol.,* 1939, **23**, 450–460.
92. Tiffin, J., and Lawshe, C. H. *Adaptability Test.* Chicago: Sci. Res. Assoc., 1942–1954.
93. Tiffin, J., and McCormick, E. J. *Industrial psychology.* (4th ed.) Englewood Cliffs, N.J.: Prentice-Hall, 1958.
94. Tomkins, S. S., Horn, D., and Miner, J. B. *The Tomkins-Horn Picture Arrangement Test.* New York: Springer, 1944–1957.
95. Tydlaska, Mary, and White, C. *SRA Typing Adaptability Test.* Chicago: Sci. Res. Assoc., 1956.
96. Viteles, M. S. Selection of cashiers and predicting length of service. *Personnel Res.,* 1924, **2**, 467–473.
97. Weisskopf, Edith A., and Dieppa, J. Experimentally induced faking of TAT responses. *J. consult. Psychol.,* 1951, **15**, 469–474.
98. Wesman, A. G. *Wesman Personnel Classification Test.* New York: Psychol. Corp., 1946–1951.
99. Wesman, A. G. *PTI—Verbal Test.* New York: Psychol. Corp., 1952–1954.
100. Whyte, W. H., Jr. *The organization man.* New York: Simon and Schuster, 1956.
101. Wilson, R. C., Guilford, J. P., *et al.* A factor-analytic study of creative-thinking abilities. *Psychometrika,* 1954, **19**, 297–311.
102. Witkin, A. A. Differential interest patterns in salesmen. *J. appl. Psychol.,* 1956, **40**, 338–340.
103. Wonderlic, E. F. *Wonderlic Personnel Test.* Glencoe, Ill.: Author, 1939–1945.

# 4

## Personal Appraisal and Biographical Data in Personnel Selection

Long before the appearance of the first psychological test, job applicants were being selected through letters of application, references from past employers, and personal interviews. Tests have by no means replaced these traditional procedures of personnel selection. In fact, as was pointed out in the preceding chapter, no reputable industrial psychologist would evaluate an applicant on the basis of tests alone. Test scores must be interpreted in the light of other information about the individual's background. Moreover, good tests are not available for all traits, especially in the area of personality. A rating obtained from a well-conducted interview, or from persons who have observed the applicant adequately in previous relevant situations, is preferable to a poor test or a test of unknown validity. It is also likely that for certain interpersonal traits, involving as they do the reactions of the individual to other persons, ratings will always provide the most valid predictors.

Application forms, references, and interviews may all be used to obtain *biographical data* pertaining to education, special training, job history, and other relevant facts of past experience. When properly interpreted, an accurate record of what the individual has done in the past is an effective predictor of what he will do in the future. Interviews and references also provide *interpersonal data* based on the interaction of the applicant with the interviewer and with previous acquaintances, respectively. The present chapter is concerned with available ways of improving application forms, reference reports, and interviews and with an evaluation of the effectiveness of these techniques. But first we shall consider rating procedures in general, since they underlie both reference reports and interviewing, besides having other important uses in personnel psychology.

## RATING PROCEDURES

In Chapter 2 we have already seen that ratings constitute an important source of criterion data for most jobs. The evaluation of on-the-job performance against which predictors can be validated represents one application of rating procedures in personnel psychology. An important operational use of rating is to be found in the merit rating systems regularly employed by many companies. Such periodic performance ratings serve as an aid in administrative decisions regarding promotions, salary increments, transfers, or discharges. They also provide information needed for the improvement of worker performance through conferences or additional training. In personnel selection, rating procedures can be effectively incorporated into reference forms and interview reports. Although many rating procedures have been developed in the effort to make judgments more objective and precise, they can be conveniently classified under seven types: order-of-merit comparisons, rating scales, scaled checklists, forced-choice technique, sociometric or nominating techniques, critical incidents, and field review method.

**Order-of-merit Comparisons.**   In order-of-merit procedures, the rating is done by ranking, comparing, or classifying people. Thus a supervisor may be asked to *rank* the 27 employees in his department in order of merit for over-all job performance or for any specified trait. A more precise but time-consuming procedure is that of *paired comparisons,* in which each individual is paired in turn with every other and the judge merely indicates which is the better in each pair.

Even order-of-merit ranking becomes laborious when the group is large. As a result, it may be done carelessly and inaccurately by the busy rater. A less demanding variant, which nevertheless yields results of sufficient accuracy for most purposes, is the *forced distribution.* In this procedure, the rater may be given a rating scale similar to those to be discussed shortly, but the number of persons to be placed in each category is specified—either rigidly or, more often, approximately.

An example of a forced distribution with 40 cases is given in Table 4. The numbers in each category are derived from normal curve frequencies, on the assumption that the trait under consideration is normally distributed in the group.

**T A B L E   4   *A Forced Distribution with 40 Cases***

| Rating | A | B | C | D | E |
|---|---|---|---|---|---|
| Number of persons to be assigned each rating | 3 | 10 | 14 | 10 | 3 |

If this assumption is correct, the trait categories in the scale can be treated as equal units of amount. In fact, they have the mathematical properties of the previously described standard scores (Chapter 2). Such equality of units is a further advantage of the forced distribution as compared with ordinary ranking. Ranks cannot be treated as equal units. The difference in job proficiency between two employees ranked first and second in a group of 27 is likely to be much greater than the differences between those ranked thirteenth and fourteenth in the same group. This follows from the fact that in a normal distribution individuals cluster more closely in the center and are more widely scattered as the extremes are approached.[1]

All order-of-merit techniques presuppose that the same judge evaluates all members of the group on a single occasion. Such a procedure is feasible in certain situations, as when a supervisor rates the employees in his department. But there are obviously other situations to which this procedure is inapplica-

[1] For a discussion of the statistical problems and procedures pertaining to the use of ranks and rating scales, see Guilford (29, ch. 11).

ble, notably reference forms submitted on individual applicants and interview reports prepared as each applicant is interviewed. Another limitation of order-of-merit techniques is that they provide information only on the relative position of each individual within a group; they do not permit evaluation in terms of absolute standards. Thus from order-of-merit data alone it would be impossible to determine which individuals if any fall below minimum proficiency standards required for a job or to compare different groups that have been independently rated.

**Rating Scales.**   To obtain a record of absolute judgments in terms of an external standard, various types of rating scales have been developed. With such scales, each individual is independently evaluated. In the preparation of all rating scales, the basic problem pertains to the choice of units for expressing degrees of the trait to be rated. These units must be easily understood and uniformly interpreted by all raters.

An early attempt to achieve such intelligibility of units by an ingenious adaptation of ranking procedures resulted in the *man-to-man rating scale*. First developed by Walter Dill Scott for use in salesman selection, this device was later adapted for rating army officers during World War I. The man-to-man scale requires a common reference group with which all raters are acquainted. From this group, the raters choose "scale men" to represent equally spaced degrees of the trait, such as lowest, low, average, high, and highest. The names of the individual scale men are then used to define these five steps. In applying the scale to any individual, the rater simply chooses the scale man whom that individual resembles most closely in the trait and assigns him the corresponding rating. For instance, if in his leadership behavior the individual resembles Henry Brown more closely than he does any of the other four scale men, and if Henry Brown was the "high" scale man, then this individual is given a rating of "high."

The units in a man-to-man scale are the men selected to define the scale positions. Such units provide objective and readily comprehensible anchor points for the judgment scale. A major difficulty with this technique, however, is that the different raters must not only be acquainted with a common reference group but must also agree in their choice of scale men from that group.

A common type of rating scale utilizes *descriptive adjectives* as its units. For example, an individual's punctuality, accuracy, or sense of humor might be rated as very inferior, inferior, average, superior, or very superior. In the effort to make the units more meaningful, different sets of adjectives may be substituted to fit each trait. Thus in the rating of general ability level, the adjectives might be: stupid, dull, mediocre, clever, brilliant. Although still frequently encountered, the descriptive-adjective rating scale is one of the least satisfactory. Whether general or specific adjectives are employed, different raters are likely to interpret them with considerable variation. Not only are the terms themselves vague, but each rater may also apply a somewhat different standard in his judgments. Because of differences in their previous experiences with employee groups, one rater may describe as mediocre the same job behavior that another rater considers clever.

Nor should we be misled by the false impression of objectivity and quantification created by *numerical rating scales*. Substituting the numbers 1 to 5 for the previously cited descriptive terms in no way clarifies the meaning

| Dependa-bility Punctuality Attendance Application Industry | ☐ Seldom on time. Absent often. Loafs on job. Will not apply self. | ☐ Occasionally late. Attendance record not too good. Needs constant supervision to keep busy. Could work harder. | ☐ Attendance record good. May be late on occasion. Steady work-er but could show more industry. Needs nor-mal supervision. | ☐ Rarely late or absent. Works hard without driving. Turns out work on time. Requires less than average super-vision. | ☐ Never late or absent without good excuse. Needs very little super-vision. Always gets job done on time. |

*Fig. 20*  A rating-scale item using graded behavioral descriptions. The rating is recorded by checking the proper box. (*From Dooher and Marquis, 15, fig. 10; reproduced by permission of American Management Association.*)

of the units. To rate a person "4" in sense of humor is just as vague and subjective as to say he is "superior" in this regard. Both types of ratings are subject to the same misunderstandings and judgment errors. The use of finer units in a numerical scale, moreover, does not necessarily increase the precision of the ratings. To rate sense of humor on a 100-point scale is probably no more accurate than to rate it on a 10-point scale. Raters cannot reliably discriminate between, let us say, ratings of 73 and 74 in such a trait. Hence either they will not use the intervening values or they will use them in a haphazard and nondiscriminating manner.

A more effective way to make the scale units meaningful is to utilize *graded behavioral descriptions* for the scale units. An example of such a scale is given in Figure 20. In this scale, the worker's dependability is rated by checking the specific description that most nearly represents his typical behavior. If it is desired to combine ratings on several traits, numerical values can be assigned to the different units in this scale. Unlike the units of the numerical rating scale, however, these numbers are given concrete and uniform meaning by the behavioral descriptions that define them.

Since human traits are continuous variables, any assignment of individuals to discrete categories is artificial. Raters often report difficulty in placing an individual into any one of the given categories, objecting that he seems to fall between two categories. This difficulty is obviated in *graphic rating scales,* in which the individual's trait rating may be indicated by checking any position along a continuous line. To ensure uniformity of interpretation by different raters, it is desirable to "anchor" the graphic rating scale at several points by giving behavioral descriptions, as illustrated in Figure 21. The raters are told, however, that these behavioral descriptions do not represent separate categories but indicate only the direction of the line. This type of rating scale thus combines the continuity of graphic ratings with the interpretive clarity of graded behavioral descriptions. For most purposes, it is the most satisfactory type of rating scale. In recording or combining ratings from such a scale, it is customary to employ a stencil that divides the line into sections. The number of sections is usually between 5 and 10. While leaving the rater free to check anywhere he chooses, such a procedure recognizes the fact that very small differences in the position of the checkmarks are of no significance because of limitations in the discriminative ability of the raters.

**Scaled Checklists.**  In another type of rating procedure, the rater checks

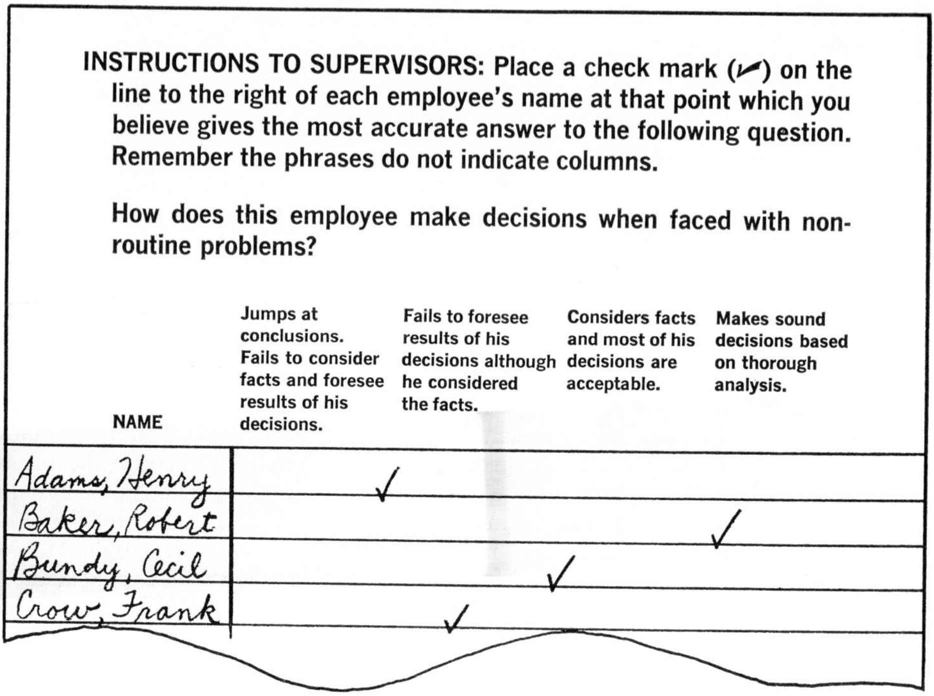

---

**INSTRUCTIONS TO SUPERVISORS:** Place a check mark (✔) on the line to the right of each employee's name at that point which you believe gives the most accurate answer to the following question. Remember the phrases do not indicate columns.

**How does this employee make decisions when faced with non-routine problems?**

| NAME | Jumps at conclusions. Fails to consider facts and foresee results of his decisions. | Fails to foresee results of his decisions although he considered the facts. | Considers facts and most of his decisions are acceptable. | Makes sound decisions based on thorough analysis. |
|---|---|---|---|---|
| *Adams, Henry* | ✔ | | | |
| *Baker, Robert* | | | | ✔ |
| *Bundy, Cecil* | | | ✔ | |
| *Crow, Frank* | | ✔ | | |

*Fig. 21* A graphic rating scale. (*From Dooher and Marquis, 15, p. 110; reproduced by permission of American Management Association.*)

all statements in a given list that characterize the individual. Although presented in random order, these statements range from very favorable to very unfavorable and cover a variety of traits. To find the individual's over-all rating, the scale values of all statements checked for him are averaged. These scale values, which do not appear on the rating form, are derived during the construction of the checklist by a procedure first employed by Thurstone and his co-workers (75) in developing attitude scales. First, a large number of descriptive statements about workers are assembled. These statements are then presented one at a time to individual judges, who sort them into piles (usually 11), from least to most favorable. The scale value given to each statement is the mean position assigned to that statement by all the judges.

It has been found that different groups of judges, such as foremen, personnel men, college professors, and students, agree closely in the mean position assigned to such statements (76). Within each group, any statement showing too wide a variability in the positions assigned to it by individual judges is discarded as ambiguous. The final list of statements is selected so as to cover a wide range of favorableness and to comprise statements spaced by approximately equal distances in scale values. In Table 5 will be found some typical checklist statements, together with their scale values and variability measures.

**TABLE 5**  *Illustrative Statements from a Scaled Checklist*
*for Rating Workers*
*(Data from Uhrbrock, 76)*

| Statement | Scale Value[a] | SD[b] |
|---|---|---|
| Is seriously lacking in judgment | 13 | 8.45 |
| Is poor at following instructions | 25 | 6.12 |
| Is a steady worker | 69 | 8.57 |
| Occasionally develops new ideas | 74 | 12.23 |
| Effectively coordinates departmental activities | 89 | 12.18 |
| Is dynamic leader who stimulates enthusiasm | 109 | 2.42 |

[a] Statements were sorted into 11 piles by 16 judges. Scale values are mean positions multiplied by 10 to eliminate decimals.
[b] Standard deviation of positions assigned by 16 judges, also multiplied by 10.

**Forced-choice Technique.**  In Chapter 3, the forced-choice technique was described as a procedure for reducing faking on personality inventories. The same technique has been employed for rating purposes in the effort to minimize certain rater biases, such as the tendency to rate an individual too high or too low (62). Figure 22 shows two typical forced-choice items from a scale for rating supervisors and executives. These items are in pentad form, each containing five statements. The rater is instructed to mark the statement most descriptive and the one least descriptive of the person. As in all forced-choice items, the unfavorable statements in each pentad are approximately equated in undesirability, and the favorable statements are approximately equated in desirability. These matched statements, however, differ markedly in validity for the job under consideration.

The statements checked for each individual are scored by recording their empirically established weights, which are based on their criterion correlations. Such weights, of course, never appear on the rating forms. But insofar

*Fig. 22*  Two items from a forced-choice rating report. *(Reproduced by permission of Richardson, Bellows, Henry & Co., Inc.)*

Read each block carefully.  Decide which of the statements is **Most Descriptive** of the man as he carries on his job.  Then, in the column headed **Most,** place an X over the letter which goes with the statement you choose.  Next, decide which statement is **Least Descriptive** of the man and his job performance, and, in the column headed **Least,** place an X over the letter which goes with that statement.  If you have any comments about your choices, write them on the line provided in each block.  Answer every block.  Only one **Most** and one **Least** should be marked in any block.

MOST LEAST
A  A  Doing everything possible to keep costs down.
B  B  Knows when to exercise his authority and when not to.
C  C  Unable to relax after a hard day's work.
D  D  People do not like to work for him.
E  E  Cannot handle several details of his job at the same time.

MOST LEAST
A  A  Sometimes says the right thing at the wrong time.
B  B  Studies work closely for possible improvements.
C  C  Confidently relies on his memory which is not always accurate.
D  D  Gets good results from his people.
E  E  Quick to grasp information passed on to him.

as a rater can detect the difference in job relevance between two equally desirable statements, he can still deliberately slant his evaluation of a given individual in either a favorable or an unfavorable direction. For this reason, the forced-choice technique cannot entirely eliminate rater bias, although it can probably reduce it in most situations.

*Nominating Technique.* A promising approach to rating is based on the nominating technique. Originally developed in sociometry for investigating group structure, this technique is generally used in obtaining peer ratings, as when a group of co-workers, students, or officer candidates rate each other (48). Such ratings are used regularly in the armed services, where they are known as "buddy ratings" (21, 81). They are also being employed increasingly in industry. The nominating technique can be applied in any group whose members have been together long enough to ensure a necessary minimum of acquaintance, as in a factory, office, class, or military unit. Each person is asked to choose or nominate the group member with whom he would most like to work, eat lunch, spend his free time, or carry out any other specified activity. Or he may be asked who would make the best fore-man, district manager, officer, or group leader. The total number of nomina-tions received by each person represents his rating. A separate rating may be found for each question, or all nominations may be added to provide a single over-all rating.

Peer ratings apparently reflect much more than mere popularity. There is considerable evidence from military studies indicating that these ratings may be more reliable and valid than supervisors' ratings on the same individ-uals. Their superiority is particularly evident in ratings of interpersonal traits, such as leadership (81). Validity studies of peer nominations in industry have also yielded promising results. Life insurance agents in one company, for example, submitted peer nominations on a 14-item questionnaire, from which an over-all rating was computed for each individual (80). Without any knowledge of these ratings, the company subsequently promoted 100 of the agents to supervisory jobs. Performance ratings of these men after six months on their supervisory jobs were significantly and substantially related to their initial peer ratings, as shown in Table 6. The performance ratings were as-signed by supervisors who had no access to the original peer nominations. Other studies of the validity of the nominating technique have shown it to be a good predictor of several practical criteria dependent upon interpersonal relations (see 48).

TABLE 6   *Relation between Peer Nomination Ratings and Subsequent Supervisory Performance*
(*Data from Weitz, 80*)

| Peer Nomination Score | Number of Men | Percentage Rated Good or Ex-cellent in Supervisory Performance[a] |
|---|---|---|
| 10–14 | 33 | 76 |
| 4–9 | 28 | 54 |
| 0–3 | 39 | 39 |

[a] The significance of the relationship is indicated by a $\chi^2$ of 10.08, P < .01.

Although only applicable to certain types of situations, the nominating technique has proved to be one of the most dependable of rating techniques. These findings are not surprising when we consider some of the features of peer nominations. First, the number of raters is large, including all group members. Second, an individual's peers are often in a particularly favorable position to observe his typical behavior. They may be better judges of certain interpersonal traits than foremen, superior officers, instructors, or other outside observers. Third, and probably most important, is the fact that the opinions of group members—right or wrong—influence their actions and hence partly determine the nature of the individual's subsequent interactions with the group. Other comparable groups may be expected to react in a similar way toward the individual. Peer ratings thus have the same kind of validity as work samples.

**Critical Incidents.** The critical-incident technique, discussed in Chapter 2 as a means of gathering job-analysis data, has also been adapted for the rating of individual workers. A specific example of this use of critical incidents is provided by The Performance Record, developed by Flanagan and his associates (22, 23). Separate forms are available for evaluating the performance of hourly workers, nonsupervisory salaried employees, and foremen and supervisors. In each case, the supervisor records on a specially prepared record sheet all actions by the employee that represent either satisfactory or unsatisfactory critical job behavior. Categories are provided for classifying these actions under such headings as Judgment and Comprehension, Improving Equipment and Showing Inventiveness, Dependability, Accepting Supervision and Organizational Procedures, and Getting Along with Others.

Although no total score or over-all rating is obtained from The Performance Record, the number of good and bad incidents under each category may be separately counted and these figures, together with specific incidents, used as a basis for employee conferences. Evaluation of this rating technique must await the gathering of reliability, validity, and other research data, which are almost entirely lacking at present. It undoubtedly has practical advantages in providing a fairly objective and systematic foundation for qualitative evaluation of employee performance.

**Field Review Method.** Another procedure designed chiefly to improve qualitative evaluations of employee performance is the field review method (15, pp. 164–165). In this method, a consulting psychologist or a member of the personnel department interviews each supervisor regarding the performance of employees in his department. Although the discussion is kept informal, the interviewer sees to it that certain points are covered and adequately followed up in the course of the interview. Special efforts are made to elicit supporting facts for each statement, such as the specific ways in which one employee's performance is outstanding, the particular weaknesses another has exhibited in his relations with co-workers, and the like.

On the basis of such an interview, the personnel worker may rate the over-all job effectiveness of the employee into rough categories, such as definitely outstanding, satisfactory, or definitely a problem. These ratings, for example, could serve as a criterion measure if more precise quantitative ratings are unobtainable. Frequently, however, the object of the field review method is merely to stimulate the supervisor to evaluate the employee more objectively and to plan appropriate action.

## FACTORS INFLUENCING THE
## ACCURACY OF RATINGS

Like other predictors, ratings can be evaluated in terms of reliability and validity. Reliability of ratings covers temporal stability as well as interrater agreement. The former may be found by comparing the ratings assigned by a single judge to the same individuals on different occasions, the latter by comparing the ratings assigned by different judges to the same individuals.

The validity of ratings has been investigated much less frequently than their reliability, probably because of the difficulty of finding adequate criterion measures. It cannot be assumed, however, that high rating reliability implies high validity. Raters may be highly consistent over time and may agree closely with each other while subject to common errors and biases which reduce validity. For the same reason, the use of a consensus or average rating by a group of judges as a criterion does not provide conclusive evidence of validity, except for such traits as popularity or leadership, which are defined largely in terms of social interaction. For most traits, follow-up data on the subject's behavior in relevant situations represent the most satisfactory criteria against which to validate ratings. This is particularly true when ratings are used as predictors of future proficiency, in connection with selection or classification decisions.

**Constant Errors of Judgment.** Unlike variable errors, which tend to cancel out when the number of observers is increased, constant errors tend to occur in the same direction for all observers. One of the most common sources of rating errors is the *halo effect,* first empirically demonstrated and named by Thorndike (73) in 1920. The name was suggested by the fact that a single trait in which an individual is conspicuously superior or inferior may cast a "halo" over his other traits and thus raise or lower the ratings assigned to him on all traits. As a result the intercorrelations of ratings on all traits tend to be uniformly high. For example, in an analysis of the ratings assigned to over one thousand employees in a single plant, intercorrelations of ratings for such traits as health, personality, versatility, and accuracy ranged from .50 to .84 (18). When objective measures are available, such as test scores, production figures, or accident records, the intercorrelations of these measures are generally much lower than the intercorrelations of the ratings for the corresponding traits.

One way to reduce the halo effect is to define traits very specifically, in terms of concrete behavior rather than vague general concepts. In graphic rating scales, it is advisable to reverse the favorable and unfavorable ends of the line in random order for different traits (12, 26). This device serves to emphasize the distinctness of each trait and forces the rater to read the descriptive statements under each line rather than marking a similar position indiscriminately for all traits. When several subjects are to be rated by the same judge, a recommended procedure is to rate all subjects in a single trait before rating anyone on the next trait. Thus all subjects are first rated in cooperativeness, then all are rated in punctuality, and so on. This procedure tends to focus the rater's attention on each trait separately rather than on his general impression of each individual. Although experimental evidence for the effectiveness of this technique is meager and inconclusive (see 40), more thorough empirical investigation of its possible usefulness in reducing halo effect would be desirable.

Another constant error, known as the *error of central tendency*, refers to judges' avoidance of extreme scale positions and their tendency to place an excessive number of persons in the center of the scale. This error is eliminated in forced-distribution and other order-of-merit procedures. Explaining the purpose of the rating so that judges are motivated to identify rather than to conceal individual differences helps to reduce the error. It should be noted, however, that, if judges do not have an adequate basis for making the required discriminations, encouraging them to use the ends of the scale leads to overdifferentiation and increases the over-all amount of judgment error. In such a situation, reduction in range is desirable and corresponds to the regression toward the mean that occurs in statistical prediction.

The *leniency error* denotes the reluctance of many raters to assign unfavorable ratings, especially when ratings are used for administrative purposes. The ratings actually given may thus range from average to excellent, or they may even cluster entirely near the upper end of the scale. Like the error of central tendency, the leniency error reduces the effective size of the scale and makes ratings less discriminative. It, too, can be eliminated through the use of a forced distribution. Providing more favorable than unfavorable terms in the scale is another way to reduce this error. Judges may be less reluctant to characterize an individual as "only slightly cooperative" than to call him "uncooperative"! The forced-choice technique and some of the other special rating procedures described in the preceding section were designed partly to avoid the leniency error. There is evidence that the forced-choice technique reduces but does not entirely eliminate this error (30, p. 145; 72). Under certain conditions, moreover, graphic rating scales may be just as satisfactory as forced-choice procedures in this regard (7).

Constant errors of judgment may also arise from *social stereotypes*. Controlled experiments have demonstrated, for instance, that ratings for such traits as intelligence, dependability, industriousness, talkativeness, and conscientiousness may be influenced by the wearing of spectacles or lipstick (49, 74). Other stereotypes stemming from folklore or from the pseudoscientific systems of phrenology and physiognomy may also affect ratings in many psychological traits (64). The association of a high forehead with intelligence, a square jaw with determination, or a steady look with honesty are familiar examples. Such stereotypes may influence ratings even when the rater is unaware of their operation. What the rater accepts as a hunch or general impression may in fact stem from an unrecognized response to some irrelevant physical cue. Judgment errors resulting from social stereotypes tend to be most prevalent in ratings based on a brief interview or other initial contact. The less behavioral information the rater has about the individual, the more likely is he to rely upon stereotypes and snap judgments.

**Amount of Acquaintance.** It is obvious that a certain minimum of acquaintance with the person to be rated is an essential prerequisite for accurate rating. In the absence of concrete knowledge about the subject's behavior, the rater tends to be misled by irrelevant characteristics and to invoke clichés, generalities, and stereotypes. That increasing amount of acquaintance improves both reliability and validity of ratings was illustrated by an analysis of the ratings assigned to 1,597 assistant managers in an insurance company by traveling field representatives (20). Studies of buddy ratings obtained during officer candidate training, on the other hand, suggest that beyond a certain point longer acquaintance may have little value (37, 81). Peer nominations made early in the training period closely approximated later ratings obtained by the same procedure. Under these conditions, the close and extensive contacts among the subjects and their many opportunities to observe relevant behavior undoubtedly contributed to the accuracy of early ratings.

A useful distinction between personal acquaintance and "trait acquaintance" was proposed as early as 1922 by Slawson (65). It is not how long the rater has known the subject that matters so much as the opportunities he has had to observe the trait being rated. A rater, for example, may have known an individual for ten years and yet may never have seen him in situations where ability to work with a group could be manifested. In an investigation of ratings assigned to teachers by their supervisors, Slawson (65) found higher interrater reliability for those traits for which more extensive objective evidence was available to the raters. Moreover, the relative rater reliability of different traits varied from school to school, depending upon the opportunities for observation provided by local circumstances. A more recent illustration is to be found in a study of supervisory ratings of clerical employees, which revealed higher rater agreement and less leniency error in the ratings of such "job" traits as amount of work done and ability to do complicated jobs than in the ratings of less readily observable "personal" traits such as conscientiousness and ability to work with others (71). When these personal traits were more fully defined in terms of concrete job behavior, the difference in rater reliability between the two sets of traits disappeared.

Increase in duration of personal acquaintance, without a corresponding increase in opportunities to observe the trait rated, may actually reduce the accuracy of ratings. Both halo effect and leniency error, for instance, tend to increase with very long acquaintance (45, 65). An effective technique to ensure that the judge will rate only traits for which he has trait acquaintance with the ratee is to include after each trait a space to be marked when there was no opportunity to observe, as illustrated in Figure 23. Apparently, when raters have inadequate information, they are more willing to mark such a designated space than to leave the trait unmarked. A request for supporting evidence or specific examples of behavior is a further way of encouraging judges to rate only those traits they have actually observed.

**Rater Characteristics.** Ratings may vary in a number of ways as a function of the rater himself. Some raters are characteristically "hard," others characteristically "easy." Thus the same group of subjects may cluster at different parts of the scale when evaluated by different judges, even if the relative position assigned to each subject remains approximately the same. Raters may also differ in the spread, or variability, of their ratings, some utilizing only a narrow portion of the scale, others spreading their ratings over a much wider range.

Rater biases in mean and variability can be eliminated by converting all ratings to standard scores (see Chapter 2). This procedure will have the effect of expressing the ratings by all judges in terms of a common mean and SD. Such a conversion is needed when we wish to average the ratings assigned by different judges to the same individuals. If the various judges have rated

---

DIRECTIONS: Place a check mark (✓) on the line under each of the following traits. Note that each trait is defined, and it is this definition that should be used in rating rather than your own idea of what the terms mean. Choose the point on each line most nearly fitting the student. If you have had no opportunity to observe a particular trait, check the section marked "not observed."

SELF-EXPRESSION (Skill in Communication): Ability to manipulate language symbols and to formulate thought for effective communication.

| Expresses self extremely well. Formulates and communicates thoughts clearly. | Good self-expression. Usually gets his ideas across. | Average ability to express ideas. Partly lacking in effective communication. | Poor self-expression. Has difficulty in making himself understood. | Noticeably poor in ability to communicate ideas. | Not observed |

INDUSTRY: Application to work and responsibility; effort expended to get work done.

| Applies himself thoroughly and energetically to all tasks. | Applies himself to the extent necessary. Diligent worker. | Average industry. Sometimes shirks work. | Poor attitude toward responsibilities. | Never does today what he can put off till tomorrow. | Not observed |

**Fig. 23** Two items from a graphic rating scale with provision for lack of trait acquaintance. (*Adapted from Student Rating Scale, Fordham College.*)

different groups, however, it should be borne in mind that the use of standard scores will serve to eliminate any real differences in level or variability from one group to another. The operation of rater biases can be somewhat reduced during the rating process itself by defining the traits to be rated fully and concretely and by specifying the standards in terms of which subjects are to be rated.

Raters also vary in the relative positions they assign to particular individuals. Rater A may regard John Brown as much more dominant than Elmer Green, while Rater B holds the opposite view with equal conviction. To some extent these differences may reflect idiosyncracies of the raters, arising from their past experience, their differing concepts of the traits, and similar factors. Some of the variation, however, may result from the fact that the subjects have been observed in different situations by the two raters. Even in similar situations, the raters' own manner, appearance, reputation, and other characteristics may evoke different behavior from the same individual. Thus some of the variation among the ratings assigned by different judges may reflect genuine differences in the behavior of the subject under different circumstances.

The relation between raters' characteristics and their ability to judge others has been extensively investigated (see 30, pp. 149–152; 69). Accuracy of judgment is positively related to intelligence and academic ability. Satisfactory emotional adjustment is likewise associated with good judging ability, probably because the poorly adjusted rater allows emotional biases to affect his judgments. The good judge also tends to be more tough-minded, impersonal, and socially detached. It is partly for this reason, perhaps, that some studies have found physical scientists and experimental psychologists to excel clinical psychologists in judging others. A clinical, counseling, or social service orientation may be a handicap in the objective evaluation of an individual's assets and liabilities.

While much more research is needed to spell out all the qualifications of a good rater and the reasons for such qualifications, it is clear that differences among raters are large and significant. A number of experiments using a variety of rating procedures agree in one conclusion: Who does the rating makes more difference in the ratings received than do the characteristics of the rating scale, the rating technique employed, or the conditions under which ratings are made (4, 6, 21).

*Training.* Much of what has been said regarding factors that influence the accuracy of ratings suggests the desirability of training raters. Research in both industrial and military settings has demonstrated the effectiveness of training in increasing the validity of ratings and in reducing such judgment errors as halo effect and leniency error (10). Training programs are especially appropriate for supervisors who must assign periodic merit ratings as part of their regular duties. They are also helpful for selection interviewers who must rate applicants and for anyone who is asked to provide criterion ratings.

Rater training programs vary in duration and thoroughness depending upon their purposes and the available facilities (10, 16). Even a relatively simple orientation session lasting only an hour or two will produce noticeable results. In general, such a training program should explain the aims and purposes of the ratings, provide information on common judgment errors such as halo effect and stereotypes, stress the importance of obtaining maximal differentiation and avoiding both leniency and central tendency errors, clarify and illustrate the meaning of the traits to be rated and of the scale units, and give supervised practice in the assignment of ratings.

## APPLICATION FORMS

One of the best-known procedures of personnel selection is the evaluation of candidates through letters of application or application forms. The traditional *letter of application* stating the applicant's availability and qualifications for the job is subject to many errors. Owing to inadequate knowledge of job requirements, the applicant may be unable to determine what personal characteristics or background facts are most relevant to the job. Moreover, adverse factors are not likely to be included and qualifications may be deliberately falsified. Characteristics of the letter itself, such as neatness, handwriting, grammatical or spelling errors, organization of content, and effectiveness of expression may influence the reader in many ways. Of course, when the job duties include extensive letter writing, the letter of application may be regarded as a job sample. But in many jobs, such skills are quite irrelevant. If a photograph is included for jobs in which appearance is of little relevance, physical stereotypes may further distort judgment.

*Application forms,* or biographical inventories, ensure more uniformity in the facts ascertained, since the employer determines what items are to be included. The information requested generally deals with age, marital status, number of dependents, previous job history, and education. Club memberships, hobbies, and other social and recreational activities are often covered. Also relevant for many jobs are data on present and previous financial position, home-ownership, and amount of insurance carried. The last-mentioned item, for instance, has been found to be specifically related to success in selling life insurance (3). It was shown that this relation could not be attributed simply to differences in income level among salesmen. Apparently the salesman who believes strongly enough in the value of what he is selling to buy it himself is better able to convince clients of its merits. Much of the information regarding domestic and financial condition is obtained because of the clues it may provide to the applicant's stability, responsibility, and maturity of judgment. Similarly, social and recreational activities may be related to personality characteristics.

Because of the high correlation between educational achievement and intelligence test scores (see Chapter 3), educational data are effective predictors of performance in many jobs, especially when promotion potential is of interest. In addition, extracurricular activities may furnish information about the individual's leadership qualifications and other social traits. A study of the relation between salary and academic grades, conducted on nearly four thousand employees of a large company, provides relevant data (13). Not only was salary positively related to average grade earned in college, but this relationship was higher the longer the employees had been out of college. Thus college grades made relatively little difference in entry salary, but they were substantially related to advancement in the company and ultimate job level. A similar though less pronounced relation was found when salary was compared with extent and level of extracurricular participation in college.

That both extracurricular activities and scholastic achievement in college are significantly related to later job success was also demonstrated in another investigation, based on a questionnaire survey of a college class 30 years after graduation (39). Those who had excelled as undergraduates, whether in grades, sports, student government, or other college activities, had achieved far beyond average success at middle age. These relationships were found in both directions, i.e., by examining the subsequent vocational status of outstanding undergraduates or by checking the undergraduate performance of vocationally successful men.

It is evident that application forms, by providing information about relevant biographical data, can serve as effective aids in personnel selection. But the relevance of items and the significance of specific responses must be empirically determined. Otherwise, the application form may prove wasteful and misleading. In developing an application form, the personnel psychologist is guided in his original choice of items by available research on the relationships between biographical data and job criteria, as illustrated by the studies cited above. A further, more specific guide is provided by a job analysis of the job under consideration. The final selection of items, however, can be done only through an empirical validation of specific responses against a criterion of job success. This process is similar to test validation. It includes the selection and weighting of items in one group of employees and a cross validation of the complete application form in another group (see Chapter 2). However relevant a biographical item may seem for a particular job, its validity cannot be assumed without such empirical verification.

The procedure followed in developing a *weighted application blank* is illustrated in Table 7, which gives some of the items from an application blank used at Yale University for selecting clerical and secretarial employees (24, pp. 30–36; 25). In an effort to reduce turnover, items were chosen against a criterion of job stability. The subjects were 120 women, all of whom had been hired as permanent employees. Half of these employees had been on the job from two to four years and were still on it ("long-term group"); the other half had remained on the job less than two years, most of them having left within their first year ("short-term group"). Weights were assigned on the basis of the percentages of long-term and short-term employees who gave each response. It will be seen in Table 7, for instance, that living within the city was much more frequent in the long-tenure than in the short-tenure group. Accordingly, this response received a weight of +2, while living in the outlying suburbs received a weight of −2. Similarly, the long-tenure employee in this particular group of jobs was more likely to be in the older age brackets; if she had children, they were of high school age or older. Previous salary, on the other hand, failed to differentiate between the two tenure groups and thus received zero weights (i.e., it was omitted from scoring).

All other items on the blank were evaluated in the same way. An applicant's score on the entire blank is the algebraic sum of all item weights. Cross validation of this weighted application form in a second sample of 85 employees yielded a correlation of +.51 with job tenure. In this sample, the average score of the short-tenure group was −0.7, that of the long-tenure group 6.3.

Although for most purposes the above procedure for finding item weights is probably adequate, more refined techniques can be used when the amount and nature of available data justify them. Each item response, for example, may be correlated with the criterion. The weights are then assigned according to the size and statistical significance of these correlations. Another procedure, known as the "horizontal per cent method," uses as the weight the percentage of employees giving each answer who are in the successful category (68, pp. 256–257). Suppose, for example, that 80 employees report high school graduation and that within this group 48 are successful and 32 unsuccessful on the job. The percentage of successful employees giving this answer is thus 60 $\left(\dfrac{48}{80} \times 100 = 60\right)$. Rounded to one digit, the weight assigned to high school graduation is +6.

**T A B L E  7**   *Determining Item Weights for a Weighted Application Blank*
*(From Fleishman and Berniger, 25, p. 65. Reproduced by permission
of American Management Association and Personnel)*

| Application-blank Items | Percentage of | | Weight Assigned to Response |
| --- | --- | --- | --- |
| | Short-tenure Group | Long-tenure Group | |
| *Local address* | | | |
| Within city | 39 | 62 | +2 |
| Outlying suburbs | 50 | 36 | −2 |
| *Age* | | | |
| Under 20 | 35 | 8 | −3 |
| 21–25 | 38 | 32 | −1 |
| 26–30 | 8 | 2 | −1 |
| 31–35 | 7 | 10 | 0 |
| 35 and over | 11 | 48 | +3 |
| *Previous salary* | | | |
| Under $2,000 | 31 | 30 | 0 |
| $2,000–3,000 | 41 | 38 | 0 |
| $3,000–4,000 | 13 | 12 | 0 |
| Over $4,000 | 4 | 4 | 0 |
| *Age of children* | | | |
| Preschool | 12 | 4 | −3 |
| Public school | 53 | 33 | −3 |
| High school or older | 35 | 63 | +3 |

Beginning in the early 1920s with a form for the selection of salesmen (28), weighted application blanks have been developed for many types of jobs. One of the most extensive current users of this technique is the Life Insurance Agency Management Association, which has developed a system of scoring weights for evaluating biographical data of life insurance salesmen. Among the jobs for which weighted application blanks have proved valid are those of salesmen, salesclerks, and sales managers (34, 42, 47, 53, 57, 63); clerical, secretarial, and other office workers (25, 43, 46, 52, 78); chemists and engineers (36); seasonal production workers (17); service station dealers (67); and high-level executives (44). The technique has yielded promising results in the identification of research competence and scientific creativity (66, 70). It has been effectively employed during and after World War II in the selection of army officers, air force pilots, and other military personnel (31, 61). Exploratory studies have also been conducted on its possible uses with college students (1, 9) and with ROTC cadets (35).

While the weighted application blank, or biographical inventory, has proved successful in a wide variety of situations, certain cautions should be observed in its development and use. First, the validity of items is *specific to the job*. A personal or background characteristic that is favorable for one job may be irrelevant or unfavorable for another. Such specificity may extend to very similar jobs, such as selling different products. It may also hold for different criteria within the same job. For example, different scoring weights may be required to predict earnings, turnover, accident rate, or promotion potential for the same job.

It is also important to check for possible *nonlinear relationships* between items and criterion. In some jobs, for instance, maximal proficiency may be associated with the intermediate ages or educational levels. In such cases, lower or negative weights would be assigned to both extremes, while the intermediate values would receive the highest positive weights. This relationship is similar to that found between intelligence or aptitude test scores and success in certain jobs, as discussed in Chapter 3. Still another point to check is *preselection*. If applicants have already been screened on the basis of any of the characteristics included in the blank, a comparison of successful and unsuccessful workers among those hired may fail to reveal any validity for this characteristic (58). For example, when only high school graduates are hired, amount of education may show no relation to later job success of employees. But if education is in fact related to success on this job, dropping this item will worsen rather than improve the selection process. There are several ways of handling preselection, depending upon specific circumstances. But in no case can we *assume* either the absence of preselection or the irrelevance of preselection items.

## REFERENCE REPORTS

Another common selection procedure is to investigate the applicant's "references." This involves essentially the obtaining of information about the applicant from persons acquainted with him. Such persons are usually former employers, although teachers, co-workers, and personal acquaintances may also be included. A major use of references is to verify the job experience claimed by the applicant. It is also expected that the applicant's performance in previous jobs or other situations will be predictive of his performance in the prospective job. Since this second objective requires the identification and appraisal of relevant behavior, it presents a much more difficult task.

The reference may be in the form of a *letter of recommendation,* in which the writer is left free to choose the content. It has been aptly said of such letters that "they are often sealed with a shrug and opened with a smile. The letter may be only one way of speeding the parting guest. The enthusiasm of the writer may indicate only his joy over a separation long overdue."[2] This criticism is particularly applicable to the open letter given to the applicant upon termination. Not being confidential, it is likely to contain only favorable statements. It will also tend to be vague and general, since the writer has no knowledge of the specific jobs for which it will eventually be used.

A letter mailed directly to the prospective employer has the advantage of confidentiality. It can also be made more relevant to the prospective job, since at least the job title and the company are known to the writer. Even under these conditions, however, the writer may have little familiarity with actual job requirements. A still better type of letter is one written in response to an inquiry from the prospective employer. In such an inquiry, the nature of the job can be further specified and relevant items of information can be requested.

From the third type of letter it is a short step to an *employment recommendation questionnaire* (ERQ). This type of questionnaire is coming to be used more

[2] Quoted by Poffenberger (59, p. 238).

and more in place of the open-ended testimonial letter and narrative recommendation (54). Recommendation questionnaires can be developed by the same procedures as weighted application blanks. Items can be chosen on the basis of their empirical validities in predicting any desired criterion. The responses can be scored in terms of empirically established weights, and a total score on the entire form can be computed. Insofar as certain items may call for the rating of the applicant's previous job performance, abilities, or personality traits, rating procedures can be incorporated into the form. The previously discussed graphic rating scale and the forced-choice technique are especially suitable for this purpose.

Unlike application blanks, however, recommendation forms have so far been subjected to little research. Although widely used, they usually consist of subjectively chosen items of unverified validity. Either the responses are examined qualitatively, or crude scoring weights are assigned to them in terms of their "face value." Under these conditions, it is not surprising that follow-up studies have revealed little or no validity for the personnel evaluations based on such forms.

Among the few research publications dealing with recommendation forms is a series of studies conducted in the Federal civil service (27, 55, 56). In one of these studies (55), the ERQs of 1,193 employees in 12 skilled trades were analyzed. Standard recommendation forms had been mailed prior to employment to the references listed on each man's application blank. An average of about four ERQs were sent out for each applicant. Of these, 56 per cent returned completed, 23 per cent returned incomplete, 18 per cent failed to return, and 3 per cent returned unopened. These figures are described as typical of the return rate of Federal ERQs. Total scores for each applicant, found by applying "rational" rather than empirical weights to the ERQ items, yielded low and generally insignificant correlations with a criterion of subsequent job performance based on supervisory ratings. An analysis of separate items on the ERQ showed poor discriminative power, with heavy concentration of responses on the favorable answers.

Another technique for investigating references is the *telephone checkup*. This procedure has several practical advantages over mailed questionnaires. It is likely to yield a much larger proportion of completed inquiries. Respondents are generally less reluctant to give a frank and full evaluation of the applicant orally than in writing. Through skillfully worded questions, proper sequence of items, and other devices, the trained telephone interviewer can do much to reduce suggestion, halo effect, and other judgment errors. Frequently he can also pick up clues in the respondent's remarks, tone of voice, inflection, hesitation, or other expressive behavior that suggest the need for further probing. As a result, he may elicit important facts that would not have been provided spontaneously or in answer to routine questions.

A more time-consuming but effective procedure is the full-scale *field investigation*. Relying on face-to-face interviews with several persons who know the applicant, these investigations can provide the most comprehensive and unbiased record of past performance. They generally cover not only job proficiency but also other information bearing on abilities, personality, and character. In one of the previously cited civil service studies (56), field investigation findings on 109 applicants for three professional positions (economist, budget examiner, and training officer) were compared with the ERQ scores for the same persons. Although significant correlations were obtained for two of the three positions, none of the correlations was high. In several cases, moreover, the ERQ failed to detect extremely disqualifying features revealed by the field investigation. This failure may have resulted in part from a selective bias in ERQ returns. Persons who have adverse information about an applicant and cannot recommend him favorably often fail to respond at all to a written inquiry. To determine how much confidence can be placed in field investigation data, however, the investigator should also evaluate the respondent in the course of the interview, checking on his accuracy and dependability as well as on any possible biases toward the applicant.

# INTERVIEWING

Interviewing techniques are used for many purposes in journalism, law, medicine, social work, clinical psychology, counseling, public opinion polling, and market research. Within personnel psychology, interviews are commonly employed not only as selection procedures but also in conducting employee attitude surveys, as a means of communication between management and workers, in handling grievances, and in other supervisory functions. A special application is provided by the exit interview, held with employees who are leaving the company. Apart from dealing with the routine details of termination, such an interview can serve a public relations function by ensuring that workers leave with a more favorable attitude toward the company. It can also yield valuable data on the causes of turnover as found both in worker characteristics and in conditions within the company. Still another type of personnel interview is that used for employee development. Related both to merit rating and to training programs, this type of interview is designed to let the employee know how well he is doing on the job and to help him improve. It is used especially with supervisory and executive personnel in so-called "management development programs."

Psychological discussions of the interview can be found in a number of books. Some cover all types of interviews (8, 41); others concentrate on personnel selection interviews (5, 19); and one focuses entirely on the employee development interview (51). Some include a survey of published research on the interview (5, 8, 41); others are essentially how-to-do-it books on interviewing procedures (19, 51). Within the present chapter, we shall be concerned only with the interview as a personnel selection tool. Much of what is said about interviewing in this context, however, will also apply to other uses of interviews.

*Nature of the Selection Interview.* Through face-to-face conversation with the applicant, the selection interview provides two major sources of information, namely, a behavior sample and a reactional biography. As a behavior sample, the interview permits the direct observation of certain traits such as voice, speech, use of language, nervous mannerisms, and general appearance. Since the interview is a dynamic interaction between two persons, it may also yield clues to certain complex social traits, such as poise, dominance, emotional control, tact, and egocentrism.

The second source of interview information is the biographical data reported by the applicant in response to questioning. Such data should pertain not only to job experiences but to the complete life history. Moreover, they should cover not only what has happened to the individual but also how he reacted to it and how he now perceives it. To have been fired because of a fight with the supervisor may have a different significance if the individual perceives it as an instance of his own emotional immaturity, as plain tough luck, or as systematic persecution. Similarly, we want to find out not only what grades he received in school but also what subjects he liked and disliked, and why.

On the interviewer's part, the interview requires skill in data gathering and in data interpreting. An interview may lead to wrong decisions because important data were not elicited or because given data were inadequately or incorrectly interpreted. An important qualification of the successful interviewer is sensitivity in picking up clues in the subject's behavior or in facts he reports. Such clues then lead to further probing for other facts that may either verify or contradict the original hypothesis. Thus the interviewer engages in the cycle of hypothesis formation and hypothesis testing discussed in Chapter 1.

The chief potential contributions of the interview to the selection process include, first, the assessment of traits for which no satisfactory tests are available. It would be foolish to try to gauge intelligence or mechanical aptitude, for instance, through an interview, since tests can do the job quicker and better. For many social, emotional, and motivational traits, however, an intensive interview provides the best source of information. A second advantage of the interview is that it permits fuller coverage of biographical data than is possible through application blanks. Through selective probing, the interview makes it possible to explore a particular area more intensively as the individual's own responses point the way. This individual adaptability of procedure, of course, is impossible with such mass techniques as the application blank.

A third contribution of the interview concerns the combining of data to arrive at final evaluations or decisions. Characteristically, the interviewer utilizes a clinical approach in combining both interview data and information obtained from tests and other sources (see Chapter 2). Such a procedure permits the qualitative interpretation of trait patterns, of the interaction of different factors, and of rare circumstances that may be important in individual cases but unsuitable to statistical treatment.

**Form of the Interview.** The *traditional* personnel selection interview is haphazard, unsystematic, and impressionistic. It is generally brief and unplanned. As such it is likely to vary at random from one applicant to another and to elicit as much irrelevant as relevant information. At the other extreme is the completely *standardized* interview, which may be little more than an orally administered questionnaire. Because of its rigid and artificial nature, such a procedure sacrifices the opportunity for personal interaction and flexibility that an interview can provide, while requiring more staff time than the administration of a written questionnaire.

Between these two extremes is the *patterned* interview. Also known as "guided," "semistructured," and "systematic," this type of interview covers certain specified areas, such as work history, education, early home background, present domestic and financial condition, and social and recreational activities (19, 38, 50). The sequence of areas is usually uniform, and each is introduced with a comprehensive standardized question. Within these limits, however, the interviewer has considerable latitude. His role is to steer the conversation into relevant channels and make sure that all areas are adequately explored. Through follow-up questions, he checks on any points that may have been omitted by the applicant or that seem unclear or suspect.

*Sources of Error in Interviewing.* Interpretation of interview data is subject to the various judgment errors discussed in connection with rating. Since evaluations must be made on the basis of a brief contact, halo effect and social stereotypes are especially likely to operate. The interviewer's "hunches" and "intuitions" often arise from just such judgment errors. Some hunches may result from a chance resemblance to a former acquaintance. If a previous employee who embezzled company funds happened to have widely spaced eyes which gave him a distinctive appearance, the interviewer may respond with a vague feeling of distrust when he encounters an applicant with the same facial peculiarity. This feeling may be aroused without the interviewer's awareness of the basis of his response—hence the mysterious and awesome nature of many hunches.

Hunches as such should not be summarily dismissed in the course of the interview. Rather, they should be examined. First, we should try to identify the basis of the hunch. Recognizing the underlying cue will in itself go far toward showing whether the hunch was based on a stereotype or chance resemblance, or whether it occurred in response to a relevant fact in the applicant's behavior or past record. Second, the hunch should be regarded, not as conclusive in itself, but as a hypothesis to be tested by further probing.

Another type of error that may affect interview findings has been called *contagious bias.* This error refers to the effect that the interviewer's own beliefs, expectations, or preconceived notions may have upon the subject's responses. The term contagious bias was first used by Rice (60) in an early analysis of sociological survey data. Twelve investigators interviewed a total of 2,000 homeless men applying for lodging at a municipal lodging house. One of the items dealt with the men's own explanations of their destitution. Although the men were assigned at random to each interviewer, certain subgroups differed significantly from others in their answers to this question. Among those interviewed by an ardent prohibitionist, 34 per cent cited liquor as the cause of their difficulties, while 42.5 per cent cited industrial conditions. In contrast, among those interviewed by an investigator with a socialist bias the following results were obtained: 11 per cent, liquor; 60 per cent, industrial conditions.

More recent studies, some of which used tape recordings, have repeatedly corroborated the effect of interviewer bias and have thrown some light on its operation (see 41, ch. 7). Significant differences in the findings of different interviewers may occur through incorrect recording of data, misunderstanding of ambiguous answers, or actual differences in the subjects' responses. The interviewer may inadvertently inject his ideas into the conversation by his wording of questions, by reacting to the respondent's answers in ways that differentially reinforce certain types of answers, or by suggesting appropriate answers when the respondent hesitates. He may also slant the results by accepting some ambiguous answers while following up others by further probing. Insofar as the respondent perceives the interviewer's bias, he tends to follow the lead. This reaction may be regarded as a special instance of the "social desirability" factor that affects both interview replies and personality inventory

responses (see Chapter 3). In both situations, the respondent tends to give replies that are "acceptable" to the recipient (79).[3]

*Interviewer Training.* Since the interviewer himself is an important element in the interviewing process, the most effective way to improve the interview is by better selection and training of interviewers. In all too many companies, however, personnel interviewers are still chosen because of their "interest in people" and clean-cut appearance. Often they are persons lacking special qualifications who cannot be fitted into any other job. Actually, interviewers should be selected like any other technical personnel, in terms of relevant abilities, personality traits, educational level, and specialized training.

Intensive training courses in interviewing itself, usually conducted by an outside consulting psychologist, have proved successful in many companies. Such courses should include an introductory orientation in interviewing principles, followed by skill training. The latter may utilize any convenient combination of direct observation of interviews, tape recordings, transcripts, role playing in which trainees assume in turn the roles of interviewer and applicant, and supervised practice in interviewing genuine applicants (41, ch. 9).

In the course of such training, the interviewer is alerted to the operation of various judgment errors and biasing effects. He is also introduced to other practices designed to improve the effectiveness of interviewing, such as recording of facts promptly rather than trusting to memory, citing supporting evidence for judgments, and preparing for each interview by studying both the job specifications and any available information about the applicant from tests, application blank, telephone checkups, and other sources. Such preparation ensures that the interviewer focus on relevant qualifications and provides hypotheses to be checked in the course of the interview.

The importance of establishing good rapport and putting the applicant at ease at the opening of the interview should also be recognized. Most applicants are inclined to be tense on first contact with the interviewer, especially if they are eager to get the job. In fact, unusual freedom from tension in such a situation may indicate either lack of interest in the job or extensive interview experience because of frequent job changes. In both instances, the attitude would be an unfavorable sign, although it may, of course, have other explanations that would emerge in individual cases.

Training programs often employ interviewing manuals and forms specially developed for the particular company. Much of the orientation material, as well as areas to be covered, opening questions, and other interviewing aids, can be succinctly presented in such fashion.

*Interview Research.* In contrast to the extensive use of the interview as a selection device, relatively little research has been done on it. Among available published studies, some are concerned with *factors influencing interview results,* such as characteristics of the interviewer and of the interviewing methods employed (41, ch. 7). Much of this research is relevant to the question of interviewer biases, discussed in an earlier section.

Another group of studies deals with the *interviewing process* itself. Several provide only descriptive accounts of what occurs during the interview. They may cover such features as total duration of interviews, proportion of time

[3] Further discussion of interviewer bias will be found in Chapter 10.

taken up with interviewer talking, respondent talking, and silent pauses; mean length of individual exchanges; and time spent on different kinds of questions and answers by interviewer and respondent (14). A suggestive finding of one study was that the interviewer tends to talk proportionately more with applicants he accepts than with those he rejects, more time being spent in empty pauses with the rejected cases (2). Of course, such relationships may well vary with interviewing methods and other circumstances.

The total time covered by the interview is also an important consideration. A survey of 65 companies showed the most frequent total duration of selection interviews to be 15 minutes for unskilled workers, 30 for skilled workers and for clerical workers, and 45 for technical workers (see 5, p. 17). The entire range extended from 1 or 2 minutes to several hours per interview. When lasting only a few minutes, the interview can provide little more than a general impression of appearance and a few superficial behavioral characteristics. Stereotypes and other judgment errors are also likely to play a major part in such brief interviews. For intensive evaluation of high-level personnel, two or more hours are generally required.

A recent well-controlled investigation utilized synthetic protocols of interview information, assembled so that favorable and unfavorable items could be matched in number and strength and could be presented in predetermined orders (11). An initial set to accept or reject the applicant was established by providing the interviewer with a preliminary test score. Figure 24 shows the effect of successively presented favorable items (in protocol A) and unfavorable items (in protocol C) in shifting the interviewers' ratings away from the initial position. Each graph is based on mean ratings of 16 interviewers. It can be seen that an average of 8.8 favorable items was required in protocol A to shift the ratings from "reject" to "accept." In contrast, an average of only 3.8 unfavorable items was sufficient to shift ratings from "accept" to "reject" in protocol C. These results suggest that trained interviewers may develop a differential sensitivity to unfavorable items, probably because such items are less likely to be revealed by interviewees and hence are more significant than favorable items when they do emerge. Position of items in the protocol also affected interviewer response. The earlier items produced larger shifts than did the later items.

A third type of interview research centers on the basic questions of *reliability* and *validity*. Reliability of interviews includes both intrarater and interrater consistency. Intrarater reliability may be studied by having the same interviewer either reinterview the same persons at different times or independently reappraise the applicants from sound recordings of the identical interviews after a time interval. When an over-all interview rating is computed from the ratings on individual items, odd-even correlations can also be found for each interview. Interrater consistency can be measured either by comparing the results of interviews of the same persons by different interviewers or by having different interviewers evaluate the applicants from sound recordings of single interviews. All of these procedures provide somewhat different information. Differences in the applicant's own behavior at different times or with different interviewers, for example, are eliminated as a source of variation when recordings of single interviews are used.

Validity is sometimes determined globally, by checking final interview prediction against a composite criterion of job success. Other investigators analyze

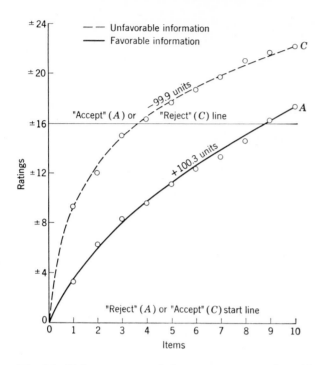

**Fig. 24**  Shift in interviewer judgment in response to favorable and unfavorable items. Units noted on each curve represent total item weight of the 10 items in each protocol. (*From Bolster and Springbett, 11, p. 99.*)

the validity of individual trait evaluations in terms of subsequent manifestations of the same traits. It must be recognized that any general statements about reliability or validity of *the* interview are bound to be misleading. Interviews vary widely in both reliability and validity depending upon many factors, such as the form of the interview (traditional, standardized, or patterned), its duration and thoroughness, and the qualifications of the interviewer. Since the interviewer, like the clinician, is an integral part of the process, research designs on the reliability and validity of interviewing should take into account individual differences among interviewers (32).

In the light of the above considerations, it is not surprising to find marked variations in the reliabilities and validities of interviews reported in published surveys (30, pp. 162–168; 50; 77). In general, early studies of "experienced" but untrained interviewers (usually sales managers) using the traditional, unplanned type of interview reveal very poor interrater agreement. Thus, in a group of 57 applicants for a sales position, the same applicant might be rated first by one interviewer and fifty-seventh by another! More recent studies of patterned interviews conducted by trained interviewers yield much more promising evidence of reliability and validity (33, 38, 50, 82). In one such study, for example, significant correlations ranging from .43 to .68 were found between interview ratings of predicted job success and subsequent

criterion measures (50). These validity coefficients were obtained on groups comprising from 84 to 587 employees in three companies; the criteria included foremen's ratings and turnover data.

## SUMMARY

Application blanks, references, and personal interviews utilize combinations of biographical and interpersonal data. What the individual has done in the past is an effective predictor of future performance. Interpersonal evaluations provide appropriate indices for many social traits. Rating procedures, utilized for many personnel purposes, include order-of-merit comparisons, rating scales, scaled checklists, forced-choice technique, nominating technique, critical incidents, and field review method. Ratings are susceptible to halo effect, leniency and central tendency errors, and social stereotypes. They are influenced by amount and kind of acquaintance and by many rater characteristics.

Letters of application and traditional application blanks are being replaced by weighted application blanks, found to be valid for a wide variety of jobs. Letters of recommendation are often too general and insufficiently discriminative. Employment recommendation questionnaires are a potentially useful selection device but have been inadequately developed. Telephone checkups and field investigations provide fuller and more dependable information.

Interviews are used not only for personnel selection but also for a number of supervisory and employee-relations functions. The selection interview provides a behavior sample and a reactional biography. With regard to form, interviews include the traditional, standardized, and patterned. Common interviewing errors, besides those shared with other rating procedures, include hunches based on irrelevant cues and contagious bias. Patterned interviews conducted by trained interviewers have yielded promising evidence of reliability and validity.

## REFERENCES

1. Anastasi, Anne, Meade, M. J., and Schneiders, A. A. *The validation of a biographical inventory as a predictor of college success.* New York: Coll. Entr. Exam. Bd, 1960. (Distributed by Educ. Test. Serv., Princeton, N.J.)
2. Anderson, C. W. The relation between speaking times and decision in the employment interview. *J. appl. Psychol.,* 1960, **44**, 267–268.
3. Baier, D. E., and Dugab, R. D. Factors in sales success. *J. appl. Psychol.,* 1957, **41**, 37–40.
4. Bayroff, A. G., Haggerty, Helen R., and Rundquist, E. A. Validity of ratings as related to rating techniques and conditions. *Personnel Psychol.,* 1954, **7**, 93–113.
5. Bellows, R. M., and Estep, M. Frances. *Employment psychology: The interview.* New York: Holt, Rinehart and Winston, 1954.
6. Bendig, A. W. Rater reliability and the heterogeneity of the scale anchors. *J. appl. Psychol.,* 1955, **39**, 37–39.
7. Berkshire, J. R., and Highland, R. W. Forced-choice performance rating—a methodological study. *Personnel Psychol.,* 1953, **6**, 355–378.
8. Bingham, W. V., Moore, B. V., and Gustad, J. W. *How to interview.* (4th ed.) New York: Harper & Row, 1959.
9. Bittner, R. H. Quantitative prediction from qualitative data: Predicting college entrance from biographical information. *J. Psychol.,* 1945, **19**, 97–108.

10. Bittner, R. H. Developing an industrial merit rating procedure. *Personnel Psychol.*, 1948, **4**, 403–432.
11. Bolster, B. I., and Springbett, B. M. The reaction of interviewers to favorable and unfavorable information. *J. appl. Psychol.*, 1961, **45**, 97–103.
12. Bradshaw, F. F. The American Council on Education Rating Scale: Its reliability, validity, and use. *Arch. Psychol.*, 1930, No. 119.
13. Bridgman, D. S. Success in college and business. *Personnel J.*, 1930, **9**, 1–19.
14. Daniels, H. W., and Otis, J. L. A method for analyzing employment interviews. *Personnel Psychol.*, 1950, **3**, 425–444.
15. Dooher, M. J., and Marquis, Vivienne (Eds.) *Rating employee and supervisory performance: A manual of merit-rating techniques.* New York: Amer. Mgmt Assoc., 1950.
16. Driver, R. S. Training as a means of improving employee performance rating. *Personnel*, 1942, **18**, 364–370.
17. Dunnette, M. D., and Maetzold, J. Use of a weighted application blank in hiring seasonal employees. *J. appl. Psychol.*, 1955, **39**, 308–310.
18. Ewart, E., Seashore, S. E., and Tiffin, J. A factor analysis of an industrial merit rating scale. *J. appl. Psychol.*, 1941, **25**, 481–486.
19. Fear, R. A. *The evaluation interview: Predicting job performance in business and industry.* New York: McGraw-Hill, 1958.
20. Ferguson, L. W. The value of acquaintance ratings in criterion research. *Personnel Psychol.*, 1949, **2**, 93–102.
21. Fiske, D. W., and Cox, J. A., Jr. The consistency of ratings by peers. *J. appl. Psychol.*, 1960, **44**, 11–17.
22. Flanagan, J. C., and Burns, R. K. The employee performance record: A new appraisal and development tool. *Harvard Bus. Rev.*, 1955, **33**, 95–102.
23. Flanagan, J. C., and Miller, R. B. *The Performance Record.* Chicago: Sci. Res. Assoc., 1955.
24. Fleishman, E. A. (Ed.) *Studies in personnel and industrial psychology.* Homewood, Ill.: Dorsey, 1961.
25. Fleishman, E. A., and Berniger, J. One way to reduce office turnover. *Personnel*, 1960, **37** (3), 63–69.
26. Freyd, M. The graphic rating scale. *J. educ. Psychol.*, 1923, **14**, 83–102.
27. Goheen, H. W., and Mosel, J. N. Validity of the employment recommendation questionnaire: II. Comparison with field investigations. *Personnel Psychol.*, 1959, **12**, 297–301.
28. Goldsmith, D. B. The use of the personal history blank as a salesmanship test. *J. appl. Psychol.*, 1922, **6**, 149–155.
29. Guilford, J. P. *Psychometric methods.* (2nd ed.) New York: McGraw-Hill, 1954.
30. Guilford, J. P. *Personality.* New York: McGraw-Hill, 1959.
31. Guilford, J. P., and Lacey, J. I. *Printed classification tests.* (AAF Aviation Psychology Program, Research Reports, Rep. No. 5). Washington: Govt. Printing Office, 1947.
32. Hammond, K. R. Representative vs. systematic design in clinical psychology. *Psychol. Bull.*, 1954, **51**, 150–159.
33. Handyside, J. D., and Duncan, D. C. Four years later: A follow-up of an experiment in selecting supervisors. *Occup. Psychol. (London)*, 1954, **28**, 9–23.
34. Harrell, T. W. The validity of biographical data items for food company salesmen. *J. appl. Psychol.*, 1960, **44**, 31–33.
35. Himelstein, P., and Blaskovics, T. L. Prediction of an intermediate criterion of combat effectiveness with a biographical inventory. *J. appl. Psychol.*, 1960, **44**, 166–168.
36. Hinrichs, J. R. Technical selection: How to improve your batting average. *Personnel*, 1960, **37** (2), 56–60.
37. Hollander, E. P. Interpersonal exposure time as a determinant of the predictive utility of peer ratings. *Psychol. Rep.*, 1956, **2**, 445–448.
38. Hovland, C. I., and Wonderlic, E. F. Prediction of success from a standardized interview. *J. appl. Psychol.*, 1939, **23**, 537–546.
39. Husband, R. W. What do college grades predict? *Fortune*, 1957, **55** (6), 157–158.

40. Johnson, D. M. Reanalysis of experimental halo effects. *J. appl. Psychol.*, 1963, **47**, 46–47.
41. Kahn, R. L., and Cannell, C. F. *The dynamics of interviewing: Theory, technique, and cases.* New York: Wiley, 1957.
42. Kennedy, J. E. A general device versus more specific devices for selecting car salesmen. *J. appl. Psychol.*, 1958, **42**, 206–209.
43. Kirchner, W. K., and Dunnette, M. D. Applying the weighted application blank technique to a variety of office jobs. *J. appl. Psychol.*, 1957, **41**, 206–208.
44. Kirkpatrick, J. J. Background history factors that lead to executive success. *Amer. Psychologist*, 1960, **15**, 477.
45. Knight, F. B. The effect of the "acquaintance factor" upon personal judgments. *J. educ. Psychol.*, 1923, **14**, 129–142.
46. Kreidt, P. H. and Gadel, Marguerite S. Prediction of turnover among clerical workers. *J. appl. Psychol.*, 1953, **37**, 338–340.
47. Kurtz, A. K. Recent research in the selection of life insurance salesmen. *J. appl. Psychol.*, 1941, **25**, 11–17.
48. Lindzey, G., and Borgatta, E. F. Sociometric measurement. In G. Lindzey (Ed.), *Handbook of social psychology.* Reading, Mass.: Addison-Wesley, 1954. Vol. 1, ch. 11.
49. McKeachie, W. J. Lipstick as a determiner of first impression of personality: An experiment for the general psychology course. *J. soc. Psychol.*, 1952, **36**, 241–244.
50. McMurry, R. N. Validating the patterned interview. *Personnel*, 1947, **23**, 263–272.
51. Maier, N. R. F. *The appraisal interview: Objectives, methods, and skills.* New York: Wiley, 1958.
52. Minor, F. J. The prediction of turnover of clerical employees. *Personnel Psychol.*, 1958, **11**, 393–402.
53. Mosel, J. N. Prediction of department store sales performance from personal data. *J. appl. Psychol.*, 1952, **36**, 8–10.
54. Mosel, J. N., and Goheen, H. W. Use of the "ERQ" in hiring. *Personnel J.*, 1958, **36**, 338–340.
55. Mosel, J. N., and Goheen, H. W. The validity of the employment recommendation questionnaire in personnel selection. I. Skilled traders. *Personnel Psychol.*, 1958, **11**, 481–490.
56. Mosel, J. N., and Goheen, H. W. The employment recommendation questionnaire: III. Validity of different types of references. *Personnel Psychol.*, 1959, **12**, 469–477.
57. Mosel, J. N., and Wade, R. R. A weighted application blank for reduction of turnover in department store salesclerks. *Personnel Psychol.*, 1951, **4**, 177–184.
58. Myers, J. H., and Errett, W. The problem of preselection in weighted application blank studies. *J. appl. Psychol.*, 1959, **43**, 94–95.
59. Poffenberger, A. T. *Principles of applied psychology.* (2nd ed.) New York: Appleton-Century-Crofts, 1942.
60. Rice, S. A. Contagious bias in the interview. *Amer. J. Sociol.*, 1929, **35**, 420–423.
61. Richardson, M. W. Selection of army officers. In G. A. Kelly (Ed.), *New methods in applied psychology.* College Park, Md.: Univer. Maryland, 1947. Pp. 79–85, 86–89.
62. Richardson, M. W. Forced-choice performance reports, a modern merit rating method. *Personnel*, 1949, **26**, 205–212.
63. Scollay, R. W. Personal history data as a predictor of success. *Personnel Psychol.*, 1957, **10**, 23–26.
64. Secord, P. F., and Muthard, J. E. Personalities in faces. IV. A descriptive analysis of the perception of women's faces and the identification of some physiognomic determinants. *J. Psychol.*, 1955, **39**, 269–278.
65. Slawson, J. The reliability of judgments of personal traits. *J. appl. Psychol.*, 1922, **6**, 161–171.
66. Smith, W. J., Albright, L. E., Glennon, J. R., and Owens, W. A. The prediction of research competence and creativity from personal history. *J. appl. Psychol.*, 1961, **45**, 59–62.
67. Soar, R. S. Personal history data as a predictor of success in service station management. *J. appl. Psychol.*, 1956, **40**, 383–385.

68. Stead, W. H., Shartle, C. L., *et al. Occupational counseling techniques.* New York: Amer. Book Co., 1940.
69. Taft, R. The ability to judge people. *Psychol. Bull.,* 1955, **68**, 1–23.
70. Taylor, C. W. The 1955 and 1957 research conferences: The identification of creative scientific talent. *Amer. Psychologist,* 1959, **14**, 100–102.
71. Taylor, E. K., *et al.* Rating scale content: II. Effect of rating on individual scales. *Personnel Psychol.,* 1958, **11** 519–533.
72. Taylor, E. K., and Wherry, R. J. A study of leniency in two rating systems. *Personnel Psychol.,* 1951, **4**, 39–47.
73. Thorndike, E. L. A constant error in psychological ratings. *J. appl. Psychol.,* 1920, **4**, 25–29.
74. Thornton, G. R. The effect of wearing glasses upon judgments of personality traits of persons seen briefly. *J. appl. Psychol.,* 1944, **28**, 203–207.
75. Thurstone, L. L., and Chave, E. J. *The measurement of attitude.* Chicago: Univer. Chicago Press, 1929.
76. Uhrbrock, R. S. 2000 scaled items. *Personnel Psychol.,* 1961, **14**, 375–420.
77. Wagner, R. The employment interview: A critical summary. *Personnel Psychol.,* 1949, **2**, 17–46.
78. Walther, R. H. Self-description as a predictor of success or failure in foreign service clerical jobs. *J. appl. Psychol.,* 1961, **45**, 16–21.
79. Weiss, D. J., and Dawis, R. W. An objective validation of factual interview data. *J. appl. Psychol.,* 1960, **44**, 381–385.
80. Weitz, J. Selecting supervisors with peer ratings. *Personnel Psychol.,* 1958, **11**, 25–35.
81. Wherry, R. J., and Fryer, D. H. Buddy ratings: Popularity contest or leadership criteria? *Personnel Psychol.,* 1949, **2**, 147–159.
82. Yonge, K. A. The value of the interview: An orientation and a pilot study. *J. appl. Psychol.,* 1956, **40**, 25–31.

# 5

## Personnel Development and Training

Selection and classification do not provide industry with all the skills it requires. Many of these skills must be learned by employees after they are hired. The emergence of new industries and the rapid changes in industrial operations characteristic of modern society create especially heavy demands for training. When there is a manpower shortage in any field, moreover, improved and augmented training programs must make up for the necessary lowering of selection standards. The relative weight placed on selection and training also varies with the nature of the job. Typists, for instance, have generally learned to type before they are employed, while assembly-line operators are usually trained on the job.

That psychology has much to contribute to training programs is apparent when we realize that the psychology of training is the applied psychology of learning. Learning theory is at the very core of the science of psychology and has been especially productive of well-designed research. Yet psychologists have not been so widely involved in industrial training as they have in personnel selection. The missing link was a dearth of applied research in this area. Such applied research was needed to bridge the gap between the wealth of available basic research on learning and the vast number of practical situations where training was going on. It is only since World War II that psychologists have come to play a major part in training programs. The significant contributions of psychologists to military training during the war undoubtedly did much to demonstrate their potential contribution to training problems in general (5, 81). Although the necessary applied research is now being conducted in industrial contexts as well, much of it is still done under military sponsorship.

## THE SCOPE OF INDUSTRIAL TRAINING

Traditionally, training is differentiated from education in terms of breadth of goals. The primary objective of training is the acquisition of specific skills and information, as in learning to drive a truck, operate a lathe, or fill out a sales slip. Education is concerned with the development of more widely applicable skills, knowledge, and attitudes, as in reading, solving arithmetic problems, understanding modern society, or enjoying music. Industrial training, however, is being increasingly directed toward broader, long-range goals and is thus taking on more and more of the earmarks of education. This trend is exemplified by the increasing use of the term "development" in connection with industrial training programs. The term "training" itself is coming to be used in a more comprehensive sense, to include development. Particular emphasis is now placed on the role of training programs in the development of attitudes, especially with regard to interpersonal relations. However broadened in scope, though, industrial training is necessarily job-oriented. While recognizing that the development of the "whole person" may in the long run be the best way to train more effective workers, industry is still primarily concerned with improving job performance.

**Who Is to Be Trained?**    Training is not limited to the new employee. It is a continuing process from which old as well as new workers can benefit. Apart from the orientation and skill training provided for the incoming worker, training is a means of preparing promising workers for promotion to a higher job level. Such training is particularly important for promotion to a supervisory post, in which the employee must assume functions not covered by his present job. Training may take the form of refresher courses for experienced workers, to ensure the continuance of effective work methods or to update information and procedures.

A comprehensive and continuing training program is one way to maintain and improve operating procedures throughout the company. An important function of the training department is to make periodic surveys of training needs through analyses of production, accident, turnover, and other records; interviews and conferences with supervisors; questionnaire surveys of employees; and other appropriate techniques (see 20, ch. 3; 45, chs. 2–4; 47; 75, pp. 252–261). Checklists have been developed to help training specialists to carry out such surveys. These procedures serve to locate departments or areas of operation in which training is particularly desirable. Similarly, the examination of merit ratings and other individual evaluation techniques help to identify workers most in need of training. With regard to job level, the area of training is coextensive with the full range of jobs, from unskilled labor to top management. Widespread adoption of management development programs is, in fact, one of the chief characteristics of modern industrial training.

**Kinds of Training.**    The number and variety of training programs that may be found within a single company are very great. In duration, the training may range from a one-hour orientation lecture to a four-year course in a company school. In large companies, each of the major functions (i.e., marketing, finance, manufacturing, engineering, and employee relations) often has its own training program. And, within each function, separate programs are available for many different activities. In employee relations, for example, there might be training programs on merit rating, interviewing, safety, wage and salary administration, and labor relations.

Most training programs for manual and clerical jobs are concerned chiefly with *job skills*. Training programs in *technical and professional* areas deal with many specialized techniques, from drafting to job evaluation. Cutting across training in the different company functions are *management development* programs for supervisory and executive personnel. Human-relations training plays a particularly important part in such management development programs, although it also enters into more specialized programs, as in the training of sales and employee-relations personnel. Because of the growing interest in management development, this type of training will be discussed more fully in a separate section of the chapter.

Another company-wide type of training is *orientation*. Also known as "induction" or "indoctrination," orientation training is designed to acquaint new employees with company practices, policies, and regulations. It should also provide information about the company and its products or services in such a way as to increase the employee's identification with the company and to foster desirable attitudes toward the job. Although traditionally associated with incoming employees, orientation training is now regarded as a continuing process. Keeping *all* employees informed about the company through lectures, conferences, handbooks, employee magazines, and more informal personal contacts is the comprehensive aim of modern orientation programs. There is also an increasing emphasis on the development of attitudes, as contrasted with the imparting of routine facts.

Some companies also provide *general education* in practically any field in which there is enough employee interest. As a service to employees, courses of a purely cultural or recreational nature—from sociology or ancient history to choral singing or contract bridge—may be offered in company schools. Certain employees may also be sent under company auspices to colleges or universities to complete educational requirements for promotion to higher-level jobs or possibly just to obtain the broad perspectives of a liberal education.

**Training Media.**   In view of the wide diversity of trainees, objectives, and content, it is to be expected that industrial training programs utilize many different media. Although two or more media are frequently combined and the distinctions among media are not at all sharply drawn, the most common training media may be considered under seven headings: (1) lectures, (2) training manuals and other printed materials, (3) films and television. (4) training devices, (5) job performance, (6) group-discussion and social-interaction methods, and (7) problem-solving interviews.

A *lecture* consists essentially of a single oral presentation of verbal material. Although usually given in person, it can also be presented through recordings, sound films, or television. In itself, the lecture does not provide for active participation by the learner, nor for repeated practice. Frequently it is used for preliminary explanation of procedure, which is then followed up with demonstration, practice, discussion, or other techniques. The lecture itself can also be supplemented with such training aids as charts, slides, or models. Lectures are often employed in orientation training to provide simple factual information such as plant organization or safety rules. Under certain conditions, lectures can be effective in modifying attitudes (31).

*Training manuals,* handbooks, and other printed materials also present information in verbal terms and—like the lecture—may include pictures and diagrams. Such printed materials are likewise suitable for orientation purposes. Unlike the lecture, however, they permit repeated exposure, since the trainee may consult the printed instructions as often as necessary. For this reason, this instructional medium is appropriate for the learning of long sequences or complicated procedures which could not be acquired in a single oral presentation. Training manuals are often combined with lectures and with practice in actual job performance. A training manual should be much more than a list of steps to be followed. Much can be done to make such a manual interesting to read and easy to understand. Learning principles can be utilized in its preparation, as in the development of any training procedure.

*Films,* as well as closed-circuit *television,* may be used as a substitute for the formal lecture and demonstration. When so employed, they share the advantages and limitations of the personally delivered lecture. They do, nevertheless, provide uniformity of presentation in a large-scale program. And they permit maximal utilization of the best qualified instructors. Short films are frequently combined with ordinary lectures, as a training aid.

Certain intrinsic features of the motion-picture medium make it particularly suitable for training purposes. Since they permit the controlled presentation of visual stimuli in motion, films can be used in discrimination training, as in learning to recognize aircraft or read a radar scope. They are well adapted to learning a sequence of movements. The fact that the operation can be slowed down without altering its nature gives the film an added advantage over a live demonstration, where this is often impossible. The editing of a film by cutting and splicing may also increase its training effectiveness through focusing attention on important details, eliminating irrelevant material, altering sequences for increased comprehension, and similar modifications.

Films can present a situation realistically, while avoiding the hazards of direct experience. For instance, a film can show the consequences of incorrect procedures, as in an automobile or airplane crash. Still another intrinsic advantage of films arises from the use of the camera in the "subjective" point of view, i.e., showing objects and movements as seen by the participant rather than by an external observer. This difference can be readily demonstrated if we try to teach someone how to tie knots, as illustrated in Figure 25. The picture on the left shows how the observer's own hands would look in tying the knot, while the picture on the right shows the instructor facing the observer. In experiments with naval trainees (65), the proportion who could correctly tie three kinds of knots after a single presentation of different training films was compared. The results showed a significant difference in favor

*Fig. 25*   Single frames from two training films on knot tying, illustrating the "subjective" (left) and "objective" (right) point of view of camera. (*See Roshal, 65; photographs by courtesy of S. M. Roshal.*)

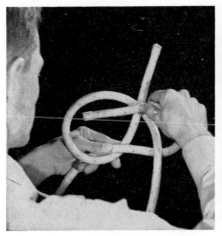 

of the subjective over the objective camera angle. In the same study, films portraying continuous motion led to significantly better learning than those showing static shots of successive stages in the knot-tying process.

In a still different connection, films have proved effective in the dramatic presentation of facts or events to aid understanding of abstract ideas and to modify attitudes. During World War II, for example, films were employed in the army's orientation program on "Why We Fight" (31).

In contrast to the previously discussed, "passive" training procedures, *training devices* provide learner participation and repeated practice in actual job skills. They may be employed as a substitute for real equipment when use of the latter by an inexperienced operator might entail risk to materials or personnel. Training devices may also isolate or recombine different job functions, so that the learner may spend more time on the more difficult or critical part activities. On the other hand, when operating equipment is relatively inexpensive and readily available and can be used without risk, it would be uneconomical to develop special training devices. There would be no justification, for instance, in preparing a training device for learning to type.

Although training devices call for the manipulation of equipment, they are by no means limited to the teaching of motor skills. Many deal with the understanding of operating principles and their application to problem solving. Sensory discrimination, tracking skills, and complex sequences of motor responses may likewise be required. Because of the importance and growing utilization of training devices, they will be discussed in a separate section of this chapter, devoted to automated training. In that section will also be included the so-called "teaching machines," which provide automated, programmed instruction with verbally presented materials.

Even more direct than training devices is actual *job performance*. By this method, the new employee learns while actually working under the guidance of an experienced worker, a supervisor, or an instructor. *On-the-job training* is an age-old method for transmitting job skills. All too often it provides little more than unguided experience, including the learner's own trial and error, his undirected observation of experienced workers, and some casual, unsystematic instruction. Supervisors and experienced workers often lack the time, motivation, and teaching skills to provide the necessary instruction. It is well known that a successful performer is often a poor teacher. Traditional on-the-job training has been described as "sitting by Nellie," since it involves little more than assigning the novice a place near an experienced worker (80).

On-the-job training can be improved by training supervisors or other selected employees in effective instructional methods and by ensuring that they have enough time for training new workers. The substitution of systematic on-the-job training for traditional haphazard procedures has regularly led to marked improvements in speed of learning and quality of performance. There is considerable research demonstrating that "experience" is *not* the best teacher, when it is in the form of unguided exposure to the task. Individuals do not work out the most effective procedures when left to their own devices. The conspicuous rises in production often found when experienced workers are put through a systematic training program demonstrate the same point.

The *vestibule school* represents one way of increasing the effectiveness of job-performance training. Such a school may use regular job equipment, as well as training devices and other instructional procedures. It provides training in a separate room, free from the distractions and pressures of the working environment. Instruction is conducted by a training-oriented instructor rather than by a production-oriented supervisor. Depending upon the skills to be taught, vestibule training may last from a few days to several months.

Systematic job-performance training is also provided in *apprenticeship programs*. Developed for the preparation of skilled craftsmen, such programs combine classroom instruction with directed shop practice. Detailed specifications have been worked out for apprentice programs in different crafts, such as machinist or toolmaker, which may require as much as four years. Unlike the vestibule school, whose goal is the rapid teaching of one or more semi-skilled operations, the apprenticeship provides training for a total skilled job covering many different activities.

Several related training procedures involving *group discussion and social interaction* have come into prominence with increasing interest in the development of human-relations skills. Like training devices and job-performance methods, they are characterized by active learner participation. The training activities involve many of the interpersonal skills required in supervisory and executive jobs, such as solving problems by group discussion, effective conference leadership, and face-to-face contacts with individuals in handling realistic supervisory problems. Because they are used chiefly in management development, these training methods will be discussed in the later section on that topic.

Still another training medium is the *problem-solving interview*. Closely related to both merit rating and employee counseling, such interviews are held periodically by supervisors or training officers as a means of improving the job effectiveness of individual workers. Although applicable to all types of employees, this technique is most widely employed in management development and will be discussed further in that connection.

## DEVELOPING A TRAINING PROGRAM

As in many other personnel functions, the principal role of the psychologist in industrial training is that of consultant. His major contribution is in the development, installation, and evaluation of training programs. He may also carry out applied research on training problems. And he may conduct specialized training courses in such functions as interviewing, merit rating, or the human-relations aspects of supervision. Frequently, too, he "trains the trainers," who then carry out the bulk of the company's training in all areas.

Like the development of personnel selection programs described in Chapter 2, the development of training programs illustrates the fundamental scientific procedures of defining the problem, formulating hypotheses, and testing hypotheses under controlled conditions. What is actually done in carrying out such a program can be summarized under three major headings: (1) task analysis, (2) development of training procedures, and (3) evaluation of training program.

**Task Analysis.** The purpose of the task analysis is to determine the content of the training program. This step tells us *what* must be learned.

Such a task analysis is similar to the job analysis conducted for selection programs, in that both emphasize the skills needed to perform the job. Both begin with a full listing of operations to be performed and indicate which are the critical part activities (see Chapter 2). In task analysis, however, the operations to be performed are generally broken down into finer units. Through task analysis, it should be possible to determine whether some activities require little training because they are already in the learner's behavior repertory, which activities require the most intensive training, what is the most effective sequence for learning different tasks, and similar points useful in planning the training program.

Many of the procedures followed in task analysis are similar to those described in Chapter 2 for use in job analysis (see 20, ch. 3; 23, ch. 7; 45, ch. 3; 75, ch. 9). Observation of the job by the analyst and consultation with workers and supervisors are common procedures. Previously prepared checklists and questionnaires are often used to facilitate task description. These techniques may be supplemented by examination of operating manuals and of available records and reports that might indicate causes of job failure and special sources of difficulty. The critical-incident technique has also been used in this connection (see, e.g., 25).

Factor analysis can help in identifying the skills that are of primary importance in different stages of learning a task. The value of this approach was demonstrated in an investigation of a complex sensorimotor task similar to that required in flying an interceptor aircraft (61). Factorial analyses of this training task had shown that performance in early practice sessions depended largely on spatial orientation, while performance in later sessions depended increasingly on multilimb coordination. On this basis, an experimental training program was devised in which the oral instructions to trainees focused on different aspects of the operation at different learning stages. Performance records showed that the group taught by this method learned significantly better than a group taught by conventional methods. This investigation illustrates the sort of contribution that task analysis can make to training procedures themselves.

**Development of Training Procedures.** Once we know *what* must be learned, the next step is to determine *how* it should be taught. This question concerns not only the choice of training media but also decisions regarding many other aspects of training procedure, such as how to motivate the learner, how to distribute learning over time, how to inform the learner regarding his performance and progress, and how to ensure maximal transfer of training to job performance. The answers to all these questions depend in part on the content of learning. They also depend upon learner characteristics. Training research should be so designed as to permit an analysis of the interaction of method with both content and subject variables (11, 16). The relative effectiveness of different training methods may vary with the age, education, job experience, and intellectual level of the persons to be trained. It may also vary more specifically with the individual's aptitude pattern. Thus some persons may learn better through techniques requiring primarily spatial visualization, others through techniques relying chiefly on verbal comprehension. The qualifications of the available instructors who will conduct the training may also be a determining factor in choosing procedures.

In his development of training procedures, the psychologist is also guided by certain learning principles. Derived from basic learning theory, these principles are supported by applied research conducted in industry and the armed services (see 23, ch. 7; 44; 45, chs. 5 and 6; 81). It is well established, for example, that *motivation* helps learning. Such motivation may be in the form of higher pay, security, promotion, other forms of recognition or status, or even the satisfaction of succeeding on the job. To be effective, the anticipated reward must be one that is significant for the particular learner. In addition, the training itself may provide intrinsic motivation through definite and realistic goals. If the learning is broken down into units and if performance standards are set neither too high nor too low, the individual's feeling of accomplishment as he achieves each goal motivates him to continue learning. Unrealistic goals, on the other hand, may produce frustration and resentment and retard learning.

Learning is also hindered by *stress,* which may result from anxiety, embarassment, distraction, or confusion. Stress is especially detrimental in the learning of complex functions requiring discrimination, problem solving, and flexibility of approach (35). Freedom from stress is one of the advantages of the vestibule school as compared with training on the job. After essential skills have been mastered, the worker is better able to cope with the more stressful working environment.

The familiar adage, "Practice makes perfect," is well grounded in learning theory and has several implications for the management of training. *Active participation* by the learner is a prerequisite for effective learning. Elaborate visual aids and impressive demonstrations may be of little use unless they lead to some action on the part of the learner. Moreover, the task should be practiced as it will eventually be performed. Verbal description of a sequence of movements, for instance, is no substitute for carrying them out. At the same time, the learner should have sufficient guidance, especially in the early stages of training, to prevent the practicing of errors. Practicing the wrong response makes it necessary to unlearn it later on. It is for this reason that correctness and accuracy are generally emphasized in the early stages of training, speed in the later stages. This approach is effective except when reduction of speed alters the nature of the responses. In that case, the learner would not be practicing the responses he ultimately needs to make.

One of the best-established learning principles pertains to *feedback,* or knowledge of results (58, 81). Letting the learner know how well he is doing serves the dual function of motivating him and of identifying and thus differentially reinforcing the correct responses. Such reinforcement is more effective if it is immediate and specific. With increasing delay, the effect of the reinforcement drops off rapidly. Precise information about nature and extent of errors produces faster improvement than being simply told whether a response is right or wrong.

The relative merits of *part versus whole* learning have been repeatedly investigated. Performing the whole task during each trial has the advantage of affording practice in the activity that is ultimately required. In many situations, whole learning also makes the task more meaningful and permits the proper establishment of relations among parts. In many industrial tasks, however, some operations or units are more difficult to learn than others. Hence uniform practice by the whole method would lead to overlearning of some parts and underlearning of others. Under such conditions, some combination of part and whole methods usually proves best (40, 71).

To be of practical use, industrial training must *transfer* to job performance. A trainee may become highly proficient in the use of a training device; a supervisor may exhibit sophisticated human-relations attitudes and skills in the course of group-discussion training; but if these newly learned responses are not manifested in improved job performance, the training has failed. Learning research suggests that transfer of training is more likely to occur between situations that have many identical elements in common. This again highlights the desirability of making the training tasks as similar as possible to the job task. Another way of increasing transfer is to provide a variety of tasks in the learning situation. Such variation helps the individual to generalize his learning to new situations. Variation in the irrelevant parts of the stimulus situation forces the learner to respond to its critical aspects. Finally, giving the learner an understanding of principles facilitates transfer. But merely stating a principle is not enough. A more effective way is to have the learner work out the principle for himself by observing its application in a number of different situations. The relative merits of these different techniques for achieving transfer depend to some extent on the nature of the task (see, e.g., 69).

The above discussion is not intended as an exhaustive survey of the ways in which available learning research may guide the development of training procedures. It merely illustrates how the psychology of learning can be applied to industrial training. The list of principles could readily be expanded; and many more detailed findings could be cited regarding the application of any of the given principles (21, 44, 81). Moreover, the usefulness of any of these principles in a specific training situation cannot be assumed but must be determined through task analysis and through applied research within the particular context. Practicing the final task, for example, is not always the most effective learning technique. Thus in learning a procedural sequence, such as is required for routine maintenance operations, the individual activities of turning dials, throwing switches, and the like are already in the learner's repertory. What must be learned is the identification of parts to be manipulated and the sequence of acts to be performed (21). Other operations, such as "troubleshooting," or diagnosis of malfunction, require the learning of rules and concepts, rather than the practice of a given set of tasks.

**Evaluation of Training Program.** Like selection programs, training programs should be objectively and systematically evaluated. We cannot *assume* that training improves job performance. Nor can we rely on expressions of opinion, as is done in many companies (47). Workers and supervisors may believe they have benefited from training without manifesting any genuine improvement. To evaluate a training program, we need to compare the job performance of the same group before and after training, or the performance of a trained group with that of a control group, or the performance of two or more groups trained by different methods. Like the content of training, the criteria for evaluating its effectiveness must be derived from a job analysis. Whether or not training was successful can be determined only in the light of the specific objectives of the training program.

Several sources of criterion data are available for evaluating the effectiveness of training (20, ch. 8; 37; 75, ch. 9). For many jobs, a major criterion

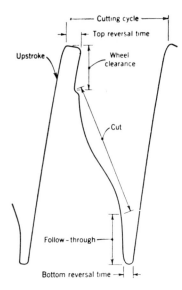

**Fig. 26**   Graphic record of foot action in disk-cutting cycle used as a training standard. (*From Lindahl, 40, p. 423.*)

is increase in productivity, as indicated by average hourly output, time required per unit task, total amount of sales, and other indices of amount or quality of work. Breakage and use of consumable supplies may also be an important criterion in some types of jobs.

A combination of these criteria was employed by Lindahl (40) in evaluating a specially developed training program. The job was that of cutting small tungsten disks with a machine whose successful operation depends upon the speed, form, rhythm, and pressure pattern of the operator's hand and foot action. Through a careful task analysis with specially devised recording equipment, Lindahl was able to get a graphic record of the proper pattern of foot movement. This pattern, reproduced in Figure 26, was then used as a standard in training operators. The recording instrument, which provided continuous knowledge of results, served as a training device. The progress made by one trainee is illustrated in Figure 27. It will be seen that after 239 hours the trainee's foot action closely approximated the standard pattern.

Weekly production records showed the effectiveness of this systematic training as compared with unguided job experience. After 11 weeks of training, the new employees reached the production level of untrained employees who had been on the job 5 months. Training also brought about considerable saving in costs by reducing the breakage of abrasive cutting wheels. As can be seen in Figure 28, after only 5 weeks of training, the trained group was breaking fewer wheels than did untrained employees with 5 months of job experience; by the tenth week, the trainees excelled the workers with 9 months of job experience.

Other criteria of training effectiveness include number of accidents, absenteeism, and labor turnover. In a follow-up study reported by Lawshe (37), 70

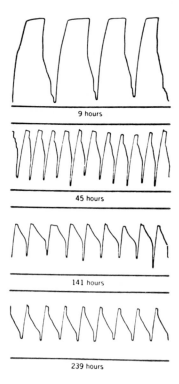

9 hours

45 hours

141 hours

239 hours

*Fig. 27*  Disk-cutting foot-action patterns of a trainee after 9, 45, 141, and 239 hours of supervised operation. (*From Lindahl, 40, p. 425.*)

operators who had attended a vestibule school were compared with 70 trained "on the floor." During the first 30 days on the job, the vestibule-school group had 19 per cent fewer accidents, 51 per cent fewer absences, and 55 per cent less turnover than the control group.

Certain types of criterion data may be obtained in the course of training. Thus different training procedures may be compared with regard to rate of learning or percentage of operators who meet specified performance standards within the training period. During World War II, Keller (33) developed an improved method for teaching Morse code to radio operators. The new method provided immediate knowledge of results and utilized "whole learning" of the complete set of letters and digits. The superiority of this training method over the previously used army method was indicated by two training measures. The average amount of training time required to reach the standard of five words per minute was reduced from between 35 and 40 hours to 27 hours. Similarly, only 3.4 per cent of the trainees taught by the new method failed to attain the required speed, in contrast to 15 per cent of those taught by the old method (see, 81, p. 1269).

Training criteria were also employed in evaluating a program developed in England for training shoe machinists (71). The training was conducted in separate schools by trained instructors. Effective work methods were first developed through a careful task analysis. Target times and quality standards were also empirically established for different training stages. The training was conducted by a progressive-part method, which involves the independent learning of different units and their subsequent practice in combination with previously learned units. Films, filmstrips, and training devices were employed. Through these various improvements, the required training period was reduced from one year to between six and eight weeks. Moreover, the new trainees earned more when first employed on piece rate than did experienced workers trained by unsystematic on-the-job procedures.

Objective written examinations administered upon the completion of training are a further source of criterion data. Such measures are appropriate when the objective of training is to impart technical information or other factual content such as details of company policy, union contracts, and labor regulations (see, e.g., 64). Insofar as such factual knowledge may be one prerequisite for success as a foreman, for example, performance on the examination is an index of training effectiveness.

Other aspects of job performance, however, may bear little or no relation to performance in training or to the acquisition of factual knowledge. In the application of human-relations skills, for instance, it is particularly important to obtain follow-up data on actual job performance. The effectiveness of supervisory training in general may be evaluated through the job performance of the men who work under the supervisor. Since the foreman "works through people," the ultimate success of his training should be manifested in improved

**Fig. 28**   Decrease in breakage rate of trainees, in comparsion with average breakage rates of present employees after 2, 5, and 9 months of job experience. (*From Lindahl, 40, p. 430.*)

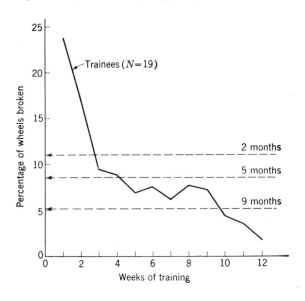

job performance by his subordinates. Any of the previously mentioned indices of job performance could be utilized for this purpose.

An approximation of such ultimate criterion data of supervisory success may be obtained through questionnaires filled out by the men in each supervisor's work group. This procedure was followed in a well-designed longitudinal investigation conducted at the International Harvester Company by Harris and Fleishman (30). A random sample of workers in each foreman's group completed a Supervisory Behavior Description on two occasions, 11 months apart. During this period, 39 of the foremen had attended a two-week course in leadership training conducted at a central company school; the remaining 59, who had received no such training, constituted the control group. On the Supervisory Behavior Description, each worker indicated how often his foremen did what the item described, such as planning each day's activities in detail, insisting that everything be done his way, or helping his men with their personal problems. These questionnaires were scored for two independent leadership dimensions, which had been identified through factor analyses in earlier research. One of these dimensions was described as "Consideration," representing a friendly, warm, and considerate supervisory relation, as contrasted with an impersonal and authoritarian relation. The other dimension, designated as "Initiating Structure," concerned the extent to which the supervisor actively plans and directs group activities oriented toward goal attainment.

A comparison of the mean scores obtained by the foremen in both leadership dimensions on the two occasions revealed no significant change in supervisory behavior in either the trained or the control group. In an earlier study conducted in the same company, on the other hand, significant differences had been found in the foremen's supervisory attitudes as reported in a questionnaire filled out by the foremen themselves at the beginning and end of training (17). However, a comparison of matched groups of foremen who had been back on the job for varying periods showed no significant mean differences between trained and untrained groups in either attitudes or behavior. These findings suggest that what was learned in training did not transfer to the plant situation.

Through an ingenious set of additional questionnaires designed to elicit the attitudes and expectations of the foreman's own supervisor, as well as the foreman's description of his supervisor's behavior and his perception of what his supervisor expects, Fleishman was able to demonstrate that the "leadership climate" in which the foreman operates is a major determinant of his own attitudes and behavior. Moreover, the effect of training varied for individual foremen, probably as a function of the foreman's pretraining characteristics and of the leadership climate under which he worked. Although training did not produce significant group differences in job behavior, it led to greater shifts in the attitudes and behavior of individual foremen than were found in the untrained control group. It thus appears that training may have made lasting changes in attitudes and job behavior but that the interaction of training effects with other variables prevented the identification of such changes in group means. One practical implication of these findings is the importance of conducting supervisory training from the top down. To train foremen who will then resume their duties in a leadership climate inconsistent with their training may be worse than useless.

# AUTOMATED TRAINING

An automated trainer usually represents a whole training program, in which the instructor's role is minimized. In this regard, such trainers differ from training aids and other equipment used by the instructor for demonstration purposes. The design of an automatic trainer should incorporate principles of efficient learning, such as those discussed in the preceding section. Among the chief advantages of available trainers are their provision for active learner participation and for immediate feedback. On the other hand, insofar as a trainer may differ from the job itself either in the operations required or in the surrounding working conditions, transfer of training to the job situation may be reduced. Even tasks that are superficially alike may not be interchangeable for training purposes. In an investigation of typing, for instance, transfer of training from electric to manual typewriters averaged only 58 per cent (1). The extent of transfer needs to be empirically demonstrated for each trainer.

Available automatic trainers are of three major types: training devices, simulators, and teaching machines. Each will be briefly discussed and illustrated in the following sections.

**Training Devices.**    Designed to develop essential job skills, training devices may isolate operations and alter their sequence to increase training effectiveness. Training devices vary in their complexity, degree of dependence upon an instructor, and closeness with which they reproduce the job situation. They also differ in the type of functions in which they afford training. Among the best-known training devices are those providing practice in *motor skills*. An example is the flight trainer used to train student pilots in instrument flying. One model of flight trainer is illustrated in Figure 29. Without leaving the ground, the student performs all necessary operations for specified flight maneuvers and receives immediate feedback on the effects of each action as though he were in actual flight. Several investigations have shown that such ground training transfers well to aircraft flying and can effect considerable saving in costly aircraft training time (15, 78). There is also evidence to suggest that simple types of trainers are about as effective for basic training as complex trainers that reproduce aircraft features more fully (77).

A more specialized type of trainer, providing practice in visual tracking, is the flexible gunnery trainer (27). This device was used by the Air Force during World War II in training gunners to fire from a bomber at an attacking fighter aircraft. The trainer includes an actual sighting and gunnery station, which is used by the trainee in tracking and triggering. Attacking airplanes are shown by projection on a screen. As the trainee operates the equipment, he receives immediate knowledge of results regarding hits. A score based on time-on-target during each attack can also be obtained. Other trainers have been designed for bombardiers, navigators, radar operators, submarine crews, and other military specialists. Some utilize techniques that are applicable to civilian jobs. Research on these devices is thus of more general interest than their military uses suggest.

Training devices may also be used for *conceptual training*. This application can be best illustrated by the devices developed for training technicians in the maintenance of complex electronic equipment (22, ch. 12). Job analyses indicate that such a technician needs to learn a variety of facts, procedures, and concepts. He must be able to identify and locate many objects and parts

***Fig. 29*** A flight trainer used to provide basic training in instrument flying. (*Courtesy of Link Division, General Precision Inc.*)

in the equipment. He must also learn to follow many fixed sequences of operations. In some of these identifications and actions, he must rely on memory; in others, he uses charts, guides, and checklists with which he must be familiar. Even more important is his mastery of concepts and rules, which provide a basis for problem-solving activities that cannot be specified in advance. In the same connection, he must acquire some understanding of the principles and functioning of electronic circuits, as well as a knowledge of what the specific equipment is designed to do.

Figure 30 shows one training device developed by the Air Force to train technicians in troubleshooting electronic equipment (19). On the front panel are reproduced in miniature the various components, controls, and check points of a complex electronic system. A typical malfunction can be set into the system by operating one of the many switches on the side panel. The trainee must then manipulate controls and carry out various checking operations to trace the source of the malfunction. Use of this trainer requires an instructor to inform and guide the student when he makes illogical or unnecessary checks.

The combination of equipment illustrated in Figure 31 includes both an equipment-component mock-up (on the left) to be manipulated by the trainee and a microfilm projector (on the right) which provides instructions (41). By presenting problems and auxiliary information in this form, such a trainer permits greater flexibility than is possible with the type of trainer illustrated in Figure 30. A single device can thus be used to provide training for a wide

***Fig. 30***   A training device for training technicians in troubleshooting
electronic equipment. (*See French and Martin, 19; photograph by
Maintenance Laboratory, Air Force Personnel and Training Research Center.*)

scope of operations. The results of the trainee's manipulations may also be
fed back into the programming of the microfilm projector. Hence the instructions can be varied in accordance with the trainee's own previous responses.

A high degree of automation may also be achieved by constructing the
training device itself so that it provides performance guidance, feedback, and
recording (6; 8; 22, ch. 12). Written instructions may be presented by means
of a roll chart. The system may be so designed that it "freezes" when the
trainee makes an error and will not "unfreeze" until the correct move is made.
Similarly, signal lights may flash on to inform the trainee that he has followed
an incorrect or illogical procedure.

***Simulators.***   The distinction between trainers and simulators is not a sharp
one. Some of the training devices discussed in the preceding section could be
classified as simulators. Essentially simulators reproduce job characteristics
more closely than do trainers. Their design emphasizes realism in equipment
and operations. As a result, simulators are highly specific. For example, flight
simulators such as that illustrated in Figure 32 are usually built for each new
major aircraft. These simulators reproduce with a high degree of fidelity the
instrument panels in the cockpit, the "feel" of the controls, the sound of the
engines, cockpit motion, and any other characteristics perceptible to the
trainees. In the simulator shown in Figure 32, the runway is reproduced on

***Fig. 31*** Troubleshooting trainer with microfilm projection device for presenting instructions. (*See Lumsdaine, 41, p. 86; photograph by Maintenance Laboratory, Air Force Personnel and Training Research Center.*)

closed-circuit television in order to provide realistic practice in takeoffs and landings. The appropriate visual cues can be seen through the cockpit window.

Simulators are generally utilized for "proficiency training," that is, for advanced stages of training or for the maintenance of a high level of job performance in experienced operators. Flight simulators are regularly employed by major commercial airlines as well as by the Air Force. One function of these simulators is to give experienced pilots periodic practice in handling emergencies which would rarely be encountered during ordinary operations. Another function is to introduce the pilot to a new type of airplane. Before practicing in the air, the experienced pilot may spend several hours operating the simulator for the new airplane. This simulator practice enables him to transfer the skills and concepts he has acquired in previous flight training and experience to the operation of the unfamiliar airplane.

Simulators are available for several other types of jobs, although their use has been limited largely to the armed services. In industry, they have so far found little application outside of aviation. Unquestionably, their greatest value is in jobs where use of regular equipment for training purposes would be hazardous. Both simulators and training devices have proved especially

*Fig. 32*  A flight simulator for advanced proficiency training. (*Courtesy of Link Division, General Precision Inc.*)

useful in the preparation of astronauts for space flight (59). The procedures trainer illustrated in Figure 33 was employed in training astronaut crew members with actual spacecraft controls and displays in normal and emergency operating procedures. It is a fixed-base trainer providing instrument environment only. The instructor's console permits the insertion of different problems and the simulation of ground facilities such as the launch control center and remote sites.

**Teaching Machines.**  Although any automatic instructional device could logically be called a teaching machine, the latter term has come to be associated with verbal learning (22, 42, 70). Such learning may range from rote learning, as in spelling or foreign vocabulary, to complex conceptual learning, as in mathematics or psychology. The teaching machine need not be a machine in the popular sense of "hardware." Some do use apparatus to present stimuli and record responses. But others require only printed materials, such as a specially prepared book or even a set of mimeographed sheets.

An important feature shared by different types of teaching machines is commonly known as *programmed learning*. Programming involves essentially the preparation of a series of teaching steps through which the learner is guided in a systematically established sequence. The sequence may be uniform for all learners, or it may follow different routes, depending upon the learner's own responses. Once the program, or instructional content, has been prepared, it can be presented to the learner through various media, ranging from programmed textbooks, through films or specially developed mechanical gadgets, to electronic computers. Although the mechanics of the process have

**Fig. 33**   Astronaut John H. Glenn, Jr., using procedures trainer. (*Courtesy of National Aeronautics and Space Administration.*)

received extensive publicity, it is the program that is of prime importance. Unfortunately, the development of programs has lagged far behind the development of hardware devices.

From the standpoint of the psychology of learning, teaching machines have much in common with the previously discussed training devices. Both require active learner participation and provide immediate feedback after each response. Both allow for individual differences insofar as the individual may progress at his own pace. Because they deal with verbal learning, however, teaching machines usually present far greater complexities of programming than do training devices.

The possibilities of automated teaching have received widespread attention in education, where programs have already been developed in many areas of instruction from the preschool to the college level. Such automated teaching programs will be discussed more fully and illustrated in Chapter 18, dealing with the contributions of psychology to education. That industry is interested in the potentialities of teaching machines is suggested by the many conferences, seminars, institutes, and workshops on teaching machines conducted by various organizations, including the American Management Association. A discussion of teaching machines from the standpoint of industrial training directors can be found in the articles by Levine and Silvern (39) and in the book edited by Margulies and Eigen (52). Current bibliographies on the whole area of automated learning are published in each monthly issue of the journal *AID* (*Auto-Instructional Devices*), founded in April, 1961.

Teaching machines have been incorporated into the ongoing training programs of a number of companies in such varied fields as manufacturing, life insurance, public utilities, and retail selling. Little research has been done, however, to test the effectiveness of such procedures. One of the few published studies on this question compared the use of a programmed text with conventional classroom instruction in a course on a data-processing system given to IBM computer servicemen (32). The classes that used the programmed text required 24 per cent less classroom teaching time, reported less time spent in home study, and obtained significantly higher scores on a terminal examination than did the control classes.

The armed services have also been making increasing use of teaching machines, along with other types of auto-instructional devices (42). In connection with the previously cited training procedures for electronic maintenance technicians, for example, two simple devices for verbal training were developed (7; 9; 22, ch. 12). Both employed a multiple-choice technique for teaching factual elements and for "verbal pretraining" in the memorizing of short series of operations. Of particular interest is the possibility of combining several media into an instructorless and programmed course for group instruction. This approach is illustrated in a combined tape-recording, film, and workbook package designed by the Air Force to teach English to aviation personnel in foreign countries (22, ch. 13). Although suitable for group instruction, this course provided active learner participation through individual workbooks. The instructional materials were programmed as in other teaching machines. By demonstrating the adaptability of the teaching machine to group instruction, this project opens up possibilities for the wider utilization of teaching-machine principles.

## MANAGEMENT DEVELOPMENT

Management development takes many forms, from personal counseling to subsidized university courses (20, chs. 7 and 9; 55). In content it may range from reading skills to interpersonal attitudes. The manager needs thorough and continuing orientation regarding company policies; he needs supervisory skills in handling the many face-to-face situations encountered in his daily work; he needs knowledge of scientific management principles for effective planning and organizing; in some departments, such as engineering, he obviously needs to keep up with the latest technical and scientific developments in his field; and he needs the imagination and breadth to take a comprehensive and long-range view of company functions. Not all these needs are equally strong at all levels. In general, supervisory functions assume more importance at the lower management levels. They play a particularly important part in the job of foreman, or first-line supervisor. At the higher or executive levels, planning, organizing, and creativity become increasingly more important.

Among the many types of management training programs, three are of special interest. These are concerned with human-relations training, management games, and creativity training. The first has been chosen for discussion because it covers a major portion of current management training. More has undoubtedly been written about human-relations training than about any other phase of management development. The other two, on the other hand, represent no more than promising ventures into relatively unexplored territory.

**Human-relations Training.** Employee opinion surveys indicate that the greatest felt need for supervisory training is in the area of human-relations skills and interpersonal attitudes (4, 14). Such results were obtained when workers were questioned about the training they believed their supervisor should have, as well as when foremen were queried about their own training needs. The principal techniques currently employed for human-relations training include individual interviews, as well as various group procedures. Whatever the training technique, however, its effectiveness depends upon the leadership climate in which the supervisor must function. In other words, the supervisor's behavior toward his subordinates is itself affected by the behavior of his own supervisor toward him. The importance of this factor was demonstrated by the previously cited International Harvester study (17, 30). Similar results have been obtained in other industrial research in which leadership climate was investigated (see 47).

The use of the *problem-solving interview* as an instrument of human-relations training has been fully described by Maier (49). If the individual seeks help because of a personal problem or job difficulty, the interview or series of interviews conducted to solve the problem would usually be considered counseling. The appraisal interview, on the other hand, is either initiated by the individual's supervisor because of a perceived job difficulty or is held periodically as a regular supervisory procedure. Essentially, the object of all such interviews is to give the individual an opportunity to bring up, talk about, and work out solutions for his own problems. The interviewer serves chiefly as an "active listener." His function is to create a permissive climate conducive to free discussion and constructive problem solving and to help clarify the individual's own feelings. Since this type of interview is patterned closely after the "nondirective interview" developed in clinical psychology, it will be discussed more fully in Chapter 14. Illustrations of its use in industrial contexts can be found in Maier's book (49). Problem-solving interviews with top executives represent one of the growing functions of the consulting psychologist in industry (see, e.g., 24).

In the course of solving his problems in the interview, the supervisor also learns how to use the interview as a supervisory tool with his own subordinates. This dual function runs through much of human-relations training. Such training is designed to give the individual, not a set of ready-made solutions or rules, but a *method* for solving interpersonal problems. It is also designed to induce the individual to become active in his own self-training. Another important objective is the development of sensitivity to the feelings and attitudes of others. Thus the supervisor must learn to respond to slight cues in the behavior of others which may suggest underlying reasons for what they say and do.

All of these objectives are illustrated in the various supervisory training techniques that utilize *group discussion and social interaction* (20, ch. 7; 50; 51). As used in this context, "discussion" means active individual participation and group interaction in reaching decisions. It does *not* refer to the question-and-answer type of discussion that often follows a formal lecture. The discussion methods used in human-relations training provide direct practice in interpersonal relations, group problem solving, conference leadership, and other skills needed in a supervisory job. The participant has a chance to observe feelings and attitudes as manifested in his own and his associates' behavior. He may discover that the same objective events are differently perceived by different persons. And he should learn to recognize and avoid snap judgments, pat solutions, and stereotypes in solving human-relations problems.

Several special techniques and training aids have been developed to increase the effectiveness of discussion methods for these purposes. One is the *case method,* whereby the group is given specific cases to discuss. Each case provides a description of a realistic human-relations problem for which the group undertakes to work out a solution. The many collections of cases that have been published for this purpose bear witness to the popularity of the method (e.g., 10, 12, 18, 26, 29, 34, 36, 46, 50, 63, 67). A variant of the case method, designed to increase active participation by discussants, has been described as the "incident process" (63). In this method, the case is introduced by reporting a specific incident, about which the discussants then ask questions to elicit background facts. When sufficient information has been accumulated, the discussants proceed to summarize the case, identify the problem, propose courses of action, and evaluate the relative merits of the proposals.

A much less structured approach is illustrated by a technique commonly designated as *sensitivity training* (56, 66). A group of about a dozen trainees spend a short period (usually a week) living in a relatively isolated place, with a minimum of outside contacts and distractions. The group leader undertakes in a variety of ways to induce an atmosphere of frank and uninhibited airing of problems and feelings in group sessions. In this context, the participants are encouraged to study their own reactions and those of other group members as they occur. Having much in common with group psychotherapy (to be considered in Chapter 14), sensitivity training is designed to increase insight into oneself and others, promote acceptance of self and associates, and improve interpersonal behavior.

Some sensitivity training groups include only a single person from each organization, on the assumption that greater freedom of expression is likely to be achieved among strangers. Under these conditions, however, the single participant may find it difficult to apply his newly learned approaches upon returning to his company. Moreover, important interpersonal issues may not emerge in a group of strangers and there is little opportunity for coming to grips with existing conflicts and interpersonal problems within each organization. For these reasons, an increasing number of practitioners of sensitivity training prefer to work with a "family group," that is, a group of persons who actually work together in a particular company.

Another technique, which can be combined with either the case method or sensitivity training, is *role playing.* First developed by Moreno (57) as a clinical and counseling procedure, role playing has been extensively employed in management development by Maier and others (50, 51). In its basic form, role playing requires individuals to assume designated roles and enact a human-relations incident. A typical case may be presented orally, in written instructions, on a film, or through a dramatized version with prepared script and dialogue. The prepared material stops at the point where the problem has fully developed. Beyond that point, the trainees must carry on in their own way, assuming the roles of workers, foreman, or whatever the case requires.

Each individual, however, is instructed always to play himself, that is, to act as *he* would if placed in that situation. Other group members serve as observers. Following the role playing, the entire group discusses what was done. The number of role players in different cases may vary from two to a dozen or more. Trainees take turns in assuming the roles of employees, supervisors, and observers.

Another form of role playing worked out by Maier and his associates (50, 51) is *multiple role playing* (MRP). This technique is suitable for use with large groups. First, the group is subdivided into subgroups of six persons, by requesting that every three persons in alternate rows turn around and meet with the three persons directly behind them.[1] By means of written instructions, the six members of each group are then assigned roles to play in an ensuing decision-making discussion. Each group receives identical instructions. Besides affording every individual in a large group an opportunity at role playing, this method has the further advantage of generating data of intrinsic interest to the group. Thus at the end of the discussion the solutions reached by each subgroup can be tabulated and compared. Such solutions will usually vary because of differences in the personalities of group members.

The MRP technique also lends itself to research on the effect of various factors on group decision making. One investigator, for example, wanted to see how training in discussion leadership would affect group behavior (48). About half of the MRP groups in this study consisted of persons who had attended a short, intensive course in discussion leadership; the other half consisted of persons who had received no such training. An analysis of outcomes showed that 50 per cent of the untrained groups, as compared with only 4½ per cent of the trained, had failed to reach a decision that was acceptable to all group members. Differences in the nature of the solutions also reflected the influence of the preceding training.

Other studies evaluating the effectiveness of human-relations training procedures generally report significant improvement in attitudes, sensitivity, and problem-solving behavior when the trainees are tested in the training situation itself (e.g., 38, 72). Few studies have obtained any evidence of transfer of training to the job situation. As noted in an earlier section of this chapter, such follow-ups as have been conducted have failed to reveal any significant over-all change in job behavior. Situational factors, such as leadership climate, apparently determine the direction and extent of changes resulting from human-relations training.

*Management Games.* Not all management decisions deal with interpersonal relations. It is in handling personnel problems that the previously described group problem-solving methods are likely to prove most effective. Decisions reached jointly by all persons concerned are more likely to fit all the idiosyncrasies of those particular individuals than would decisions reached by a single person. Such a joint decision will also tend to be more acceptable to the group than would a decision imposed from without, however reasonable the latter decision may be when evaluated objectively. Executives, however, are called upon to make many other kinds of decisions, concerning other matters besides personnel relations. Often these decisions require specialized knowledge and

[1] This procedure resembles in several ways a method known as "Phillips 66," whereby a large group is divided into committees of six, each of which discusses some assigned question for six minutes (62).

skills that only a few members of the organization may possess. Reaching a correct decision in such areas is not merely a matter of choosing a course of action that satisfies all group members. Other procedures are required to enable the executive to balance different company objectives, to secure and evaluate relevant information, and to predict the probability of different outcomes. Special mathematical techniques, designated as "operations research," have been developed to systematize many aspects of this decision-making process.

In training executives to make this type of decision, the previously mentioned *case method* has again proved useful. Several published collections of "cases" deal not only with personnel problems but also with many other types of management decisions in such areas as production, research, distribution, advertising, and financing (12, 46, 68). A more specialized technique that has aroused considerable interest utilizes *management games,* or *simulation* (3, 13, 43). Gaming as a training procedure is not new, having been used for a long time by the armed services in their "war games." The application of this concept to business, however, is more recent, dating from the late 1950s. In a management decision game, one or more teams, each representing a business firm, make a series of decisions controlling the operations of their firm during a specified period. The simulated time period may be as short as a week or as long as a year or more. A mathematical model of how the industry operates is then used to calculate the outcomes of each team's decisions. With simple models, such calculations can be performed manually (2, 28); with more complex models, a computer is required. The management game thus provides immediate feedback to the trainees.

The first management game was developed by the American Management Association for use in its executive training seminars (3, 43). Several other games have subsequently been developed for use in schools of business and in company training programs (see 13, 45, 79). They have even been played by mail or leased telephone wires by teams in different cities.

In contrast to earlier, simpler games requiring 15 to 30 minutes for each move, a more complex game was developed in 1960 at the Carnegie Institute of Technology (13). The Carnegie game is played at the rate of one or two moves a week over a full academic year. Each move requires from two to three hours on the part of a 7- to 10-man team. Between 100 and 300 decisions must be made for each simulated month of company time. Many require long-range plans with regard to production, marketing, or financing. Decisions might have to be reached about such matters as conducting research to develop new products, obtaining funds by issuing debentures or common stock, or putting up a new plant building. Information is provided by a variety of regular monthly and quarterly reports, as well as by other special reports requested by the team as needed. It is the object of this game not only to give the players an awareness of the complexity of the economic environment in which they must operate and the interdependence of company decisions but also to train them to cope with such complexity through systematic analysis and effective problem-solving procedures.

**Creativity Training.**    Industry is constantly clamoring for new ideas—from a catchy trade name to the complex creations of modern engineering. In today's rapidly changing world, industry needs creative and imaginative management more than ever before. It is therefore not surprising to find that the development and facilitation of creative thinking have received some attention in management development programs, as well as in the training of scientists and engineers.

Psychological research on creativity has concentrated chiefly on ways of identifying creative persons. It is being increasingly recognized, however, that creative talent should be not only identified but also developed. There is growing interest in the conditions conducive to creative achievement, in the work methods followed by creative producers, and in procedures for developing creative productivity (73).

A widely publicized technique designed to favor original and creative thinking is known as "brainstorming" (60). By this method, the individual segregates in time the production of ideas from their evaluation. It is argued that an evaluative set makes the individual too critical and inhibits the development of new ideas. Hence the instructions emphasize quantity rather than quality of ideas. Subjects are told to express any idea that occurs to them, however foolish or unsatisfactory it may seem. Any form of criticism is strictly taboo. Selection and evaluation of ideas occur in a completely separate, later stage. The hypothesis is that brainstorming will produce not only more ideas in general but also more ideas of high quality than will the more critical traditional procedure.

Research on the effectiveness of brainstorming is still meager, but it tends to confirm this hypothesis (53, 54). The advantages of brainstorming may disappear, however, when the quality criterion gives little weight to originality (76). On the basis of rather casual evidence, it has been commonly accepted that brainstorming is more effective when carried out in groups than individually (60). In a well-designed experiment, on the other hand, individual performance was found to excel group performance significantly in mean number of ideas produced, mean number of unique ideas, and quality of solutions (74). It is possible that group interaction may contribute more to the subsequent evaluation of ideas than to their initial production. The relative effectiveness of individual and group procedures may also vary with the nature of the problem. There are still many unanswered questions about brainstorming. With further research, moreover, other techniques to facilitate creative thinking will undoubtedly emerge.

## SUMMARY

Personnel development and training are closely related to personnel selection in the effective utilization of manpower. Although the psychology of learning has much to contribute to the improvement of training procedures, well-designed applied research in this area is still rare. Industrial training is a continuing process that can benefit all employees, from beginner to experienced worker and from unskilled labor to top management. Training programs in industry serve a variety of functions, including orientation, development of job skills, technical and professional training, management development, and general education. Among the principal training media employed for these purposes are lectures, training manuals and other printed materials, films and television, training devices, job performance, group-discussion and social-interaction methods, and problem-solving interviews.

The development of a training program should include task analysis to determine what must be learned, development of training procedures, and objective evaluation of the program. The choice of training media and procedures depends in part on what is to be taught and to whom. In developing training procedures, one should also be guided by the results of available training research, in connection with such questions as motivation, stress, practice, feedback, part versus whole learning, and transfer of training. The effectiveness of a training program should be evaluated in terms of job criteria as well as training criteria.

Recent developments in the automation of training procedures are illustrated by training devices, simulators, and teaching machines (or programmed learning). The rapidly growing area of management development covers many types of training and utilizes a diversity of training techniques. Much of it is concerned with the development of human-relation skills and attitudes through such techniques as problem-solving interviews, group discussion, the case method, and role playing. In other aspects of management development, two techniques of special interest are management games (or simulation) and creativity training.

# REFERENCES

1. Adams, H. L. The comparative effectiveness of electric and manual typewriters in the acquisition of typing skill in a Navy Radioman School. *J. appl. Psychol.*, 1957, **41**, 227–230.
2. Andlinger, G. R. Business games—play one! *Harvard Bus. Rev.*, 1958, **36** (2), 115–125.
3. Appley, L. A. Executive decision making: A new strategy. *Think*, 1957, **23** (10), 2–6.
4. Biggane, R. J. How we determined training needs. *Personnel J.*, 1950, **29**, 13–16.
5. Bray, C. W. *Psychology and military proficiency*. Princeton, N.J.: Princeton Univer. Press, 1948.
6. Briggs, L. J. Design of maintenance training equipment for fighter-interceptor fire control systems. *Lowry Air Force Base, Colo.: Mainten. Lab. AFPTRC, Tech. Mem.* ML-TM-57-16, 1957.
7. Briggs, L. J. Two self-instructional devices. *Psychol. Rep.*, 1958, **4**, 671–676.
8. Briggs, L. J., and Du Vall, W. E. Design of two fire control system maintenance training devices. *Lackland Air Force Base, Tex.: AFPTRC, Tech. Rep.* TR-57-7, 1957. (ASTIA Document No. 134242.)
9. Briggs, L. J., and Besnard, G. G. Experimental procedures for increasing reenforced practice in training Air Force mechanics for an electronic system. In G. Finch and F. Cameron (Eds.), *Symposium on Air Force human engineering, personnel, and training research*. Washington: Nat. Acad. Sci–Nat. Res. Coun., 1956. (Publ. No. 455). Pp. 48–58.
10. Calhoon, R. P., Noland, E. W., and Whitehill, A. M., Jr. *Cases on human relations in management*. New York: McGraw-Hill, 1958.
11. Cronbach, L. J. The two disciplines of scientific psychology. *Amer. Psychologist*, 1957, **12**, 671–684.
12. Cruickshank, H. M., and Davis, K. *Cases in management*. (Rev. ed.) Homewood, Ill.: Irwin, 1958.
13. Dill, W. R. Management games for training decision makers. In E. A. Fleishman (Ed.), *Studies in personnel and industrial psychology*. Homewood, Ill.: Dorsey, 1961. Pp. 219–238.
14. Dominick, W. B., and Crawford, J. E. The foreman expresses his training needs. *Personnel*, 1944, **21**, 19–30.
15. Dougherty, Dora J., Houston, R. C., and Nicklas, D. R. Transfer of training in flight procedures from selected ground training devices to the aircraft. *U.S. Naval Train. Device Center, Tech. Rep.: NAVTRADEVCEN* 71-16-16, 1957.

16. Edgerton, H. A. Some needs in training research. *Personnel Psychol.*, 1955, **8**, 19–25.
17. Fleishman, E. A. Leadership climate, human relations training, and supervisory behavior. *Personnel Psychol.*, 1953, **6**, 205–222.
18. Flippo, E. B. *Principles of personnel management.* New York: McGraw-Hill, 1961.
19. French, R. S., and Martin, L. B. A flight-line troubleshooting trainer for a complex electronic system: The MAC-2 Trainer. *Lackland Air Force Base, Tex.: AFPTRC -TN-57-106*, 1957. (ASTIA Document No. 134227.)
20. Fryer, D. H., Feinberg, M. R., and Zalkind, S. S. *Developing people in industry: Principles and methods of training.* New York: Harper & Row, 1956.
21. Gagné, R. M. Military training and principles of learning. *Amer. Psychologist*, 1962, **17**, 83–91.
22. Galanter, E. (Ed.) *Automatic teaching: The state of the art.* New York: Wiley, 1959.
23. Gilmer, B. von H., *et al. Industrial psychology.* New York: McGraw-Hill, 1961.
24. Glaser, E. M. Psychological consultation with executives: A clinical approach. *Amer. Psychologist*, 1958, **13**, 486–489.
25. Glickman, A. S., and Vallance, T. R. Curriculum assessment with critical incidents. *J. appl. Psychol.*, 1958, **42**, 329–335.
26. Glover, J. D., and Hower, R. M. *The administrator: Cases on human relations in business.* (3rd ed.) Homewood, Ill.: Irwin, 1957.
27. Goldstein, M., and Ellis, D. S. Pedestal sight gunnery skills: A review of research. *Lackland Air Force Base, Tex.: AFPTRC-TN-56-31*, 1956.
28. Greene, J. R., and Sisson, R. L. *Dynamic management decision games.* New York: Wiley, 1959.
29. Harrell, T. W., and Rusmore, J. T. *A casebook in industrial and personnel psychology.* New York: Holt, Rinehart and Winston, 1958.
30. Harris, E. F., and Fleishman, E. A. Human relations training and the stability of leadership patterns. *J. appl. Psychol.*, 1955, **39**, 20–25.
31. Hovland, C. I., Lumsdaine, A. A., and Sheffield, F. D. *Studies in social psychology in World War II.* Vol. III. *Experiments on mass communication.* Princeton, N.J.: Princeton Univer. Press, 1949.
32. Hughes, J. L., and McNamara, W. J. A comparative study of programed and conventional study in industry. *J. appl. Psychol.*, 1961, **45**, 225–231.
33. Keller, F. S. Studies in International Morse Code. I. A new method of teaching code reception. *J. appl. Psychol.*, 1943, **27**, 407–415.
34. Kindall, A. F. *Personnel administration: Principles and cases.* Homewood, Ill.: Irwin, 1961.
35. Klier, S., and Linskey, J. W. Selected abstracts from the literature on stress. *U.S. Naval Train. Device Center, Tech. Rep.: NAVTRADEVCEN 565-1*, 1960.
36. Lawrence, P. R., *et al. Organizational behavior and administration: Cases, concepts, and research findings.* Homewood, Ill.: Irwin, 1961.
37. Lawshe, C. H. Eight ways to check the value of a training program. *Factory Mgmt Mainten.*, 1945, **103** (5), 117–120.
38. Lawshe, C. H., Bolda, R. A., and Brune, R. L. Studies in management training evaluation: II. The effects of exposure in role playing. *J. appl. Psychol.*, 1959, **43**, 287–292.
39. Levine, S. L., and Silvern, L. C. The evolution and revolution of the teaching machine. Parts 1 and 2. *J. Amer. Soc. train. Dir.*, 1960, **14** (12), 4–16; 1961, **15** (1), 14–26.
40. Lindahl, L. G. Movement analysis as an industrial training method. *J. appl. Psychol.*, 1945, **29**, 420–436.
41. Lumsdaine, A. A. Graphic aids, models, and mockups as tools for individual and classroom instruction. In G. Finch (Ed.), *Educational and training media: A symposium.* Washington: Nat. Acad. Sci.–Nat. Res. Coun., 1960. (Publ. No. 789) Pp. 69–113.
42. Lumsdaine, A. A., and Glaser, R. (Eds.) *Teaching machines and programmed learning.* Washington: Nat. Educ. Assoc., 1960.
43. McDonald, J., and Ricciardi, F. The business decision game. *Fortune*, 1958, **57** (3), 140–142, 208, 213.

44. McGehee, W. Are we using what we know about training?—Learning theory and training. *Personnel Psychol.*, 1958, **11**, 1–12.
45. McGehee, W., and Thayer, P. W. *Training in business and industry.* New York: Wiley, 1961.
46. McLarney, W. J. *Management training: Cases and principles.* Homewood, Ill.: Irwin, 1959.
47. Mahler, W. R., and Monroe, W. H. How industry determines the need for and effectiveness of training. *Pers. Res. Sect., Dept. of the Army, PRS Rep. No. 929,* 1952.
48. Maier, N. R. F. An experimental test of the effect of training on discussion leadership. *Hum. Relat.*, 1953, **6**, 161–173.
49. Maier, N. R. F. *The appraisal interview: Objectives, methods, and skills.* New York: Wiley, 1958.
50. Maier, N. R. F., Solem, A. R., and Maier, A. A. *Supervisory and executive development: A manual for role playing.* New York: Wiley, 1957.
51. Maier, N. R. F., and Zerfoss, L. F. MRP: A technique for training large groups of supervisors and its potential use in social research. *Hum. Relat.*, 1952, **5**, 177–186.
52. Margulies, S., and Eigen, L. D. (Eds.) *Programed instruction: Uses in industry and the armed services.* New York: Wiley, 1962.
53. Meadow, A., and Parnes, S. J. Evaluation of training in creative problem solving. *J. appl. Psychol.*, 1959, **43**, 189–194.
54. Meadow, A., Parnes, S. J., and Reese, H. Influence of brainstorming instructions and problem sequence on a creative problem solving test. *J. appl. Psychol.*, 1959, **43**, 413–416.
55. Merrill, H. F., and Marting, Elizabeth (Eds.) *Developing executive skills: New patterns for management growth.* New York: Amer. Mgmt Assoc., 1958.
56. Miles, M. B. Human relations training: Processes and outcomes. *J. counsel. Psychol.*, 1960, **7**, 301–306.
57. Moreno, J. L. *Who shall survive? Foundations of sociometry, group psychotherapy, and sociodrama.* (2nd ed.) Beacon, N. Y.: Beacon House, 1953.
58. Mosel, J. N. How to feed back performance results to trainees. In E. A. Fleishman (Ed.), *Studies in personnel and industrial psychology.* Homewood, Ill.: Dorsey, 1961. Pp. 173–181.
59. National Aeronautics and Space Administration, Manned Spacecraft Center. *Results of the first United States manned orbital space flight, February 20, 1962.* Washington: Govt. Printing Office, 1962.
60. Osborn, A. F. *Applied imagination: Principles and procedures of creative thinking.* (Rev. ed.) New York: Scribner, 1957.
61. Parker, J. F., Jr., and Fleishman, E. A. Use of analytical information concerning task requirements to increase the effectiveness of skill training. *J. appl. Psychol.*, 1961, **45**, 295–302.
62. Phillips, J. D. Report on Discussion 66. *Adult Educ. J.*, 1948, **7**, 181–182.
63. Pigors, P., and Pigors, Faith. *Case method in human relations: The incident process.* New York: McGraw-Hill, 1961.
64. Pond, S. A., and O'Keefe, R. W. The contract questionnaire. *Personnel*, 1950, **26**, 304–306.
65. Roshal, S. M. Film-mediated learning with varying representation of the task. In A. A. Lumsdaine (Ed.), *Student response in programmed instruction.* Washington: Nat. Acad. Sci.–Nat. Res. Coun., 1962. Pp. 155–175.
66. Roth, C., et al. Sensitivity training for industrial supervisors. Symposium held at N. Y. State Psychol. Assoc., New York City, May 1963.
67. Saltonstall, R. *Human relations in administration: Text and cases.* New York: McGraw-Hill, 1959.
68. Seimer, S. J. *Cases in industrial management.* Homewood, Ill.: Irwin, 1961.
69. Siegel, A. I., Richlin, M., and Federman, P. A comparative study of "transfer through generalization" and "transfer through identical elements" in technical training. *J. appl. Psychol.*, 1960, **44**, 27–30.
70. Silverman, R. E. Automated teaching: A review of theory and research. *U.S. Naval Train. Device Center, Tech. Rep.: NAVTRADEVCEN 507-2,* 1960.

71. Singleton, W. T. Symposium on training: The training of shoe machinists. *Ergonomics*, 1959, **2**, 125–132.
72. Smith, E. E., and Kight, S. S. Effects of feedback on insight and problem solving efficiency in training groups. *J. appl. Psychol.*, 1959, **43**, 209–211.
73. Taylor, C. W. (Ed.) *The third (1959) University of Utah research conference on the identification of creative scientific talent.* Salt Lake City, Utah: Univer. Utah Press, 1959.
74. Taylor, D. W., Berry, P. C., and Block, C. H. Does group participation when using brainstorming facilitate or inhibit creative thinking? *Admin. Sci. Quart.*, 1958, **3**, 23–47.
75. Tiffin, J., and McCormick, E. J. *Industrial psychology.* (4th ed.) Englewood Cliffs, N.J.: Prentice-Hall, 1958.
76. Weisskopf-Joelson, Edith, and Eliseo, T. S. An experimental study of the effectiveness of brainstorming. *J. appl. Psychol.*, 1961, **45**, 45–49.
77. Wilcoxon, H. C., Davy, E., and Webster, J. C. Evaluation of the SNJ operational flight trainer. *U.S. Navy Spec. Devices Center, Tech. Rep.: SPECDEVCEN* 999-2-1, 1954.
78. Williams, A. C., Jr., and Flexman, R. E. An evaluation of the Link SNJ operational trainer as an aid in contact flight training. *U.S. Navy Spec. Devices Center, Tech. Rep.: SDC* 71-16-5, 1949.
79. Williams, E. H. Business games: Their use for the training of managers. *Personnel Mgmt,* 1961, **43**, 239–244.
80. Wilson, P. H. St. J. Symposium on training: Introductory address. *Ergonomics,* 1959, **2**, 125–132.
81. Wolfle, D. Training. In S. S. Stevens (Ed.), *Handbook of experimental psychology.* New York: Wiley, 1951. Pp. 1267–1286.

# 6

## Motivation and Morale

Selection and training provide qualified personnel to do each job. But to get the job done, the individual must also *want* to work. The motives that impel people to work are complex, and the incentives for which they strive include more than the paycheck. Within the limits set by his qualifications, what the individual actually accomplishes may vary widely as a function of his attitudes toward the company, toward his immediate superior, toward his fellow work ers, and toward other aspects of the job. Low morale can make a brilliant worker totally unproductive; high morale can lead ordinary men to well-nigh incredible feats.

To be sure, employee selection is concerned not only with abilities but also with attitudinal and motivational factors. Similarly, training programs contribute to the development of attitudes. Nevertheless, the nature of the work and the conditions under which it is performed may substantially affect employee motivation. It is chiefly in terms of these job variables that employee motivation will be considered in the present chapter.

Today's widespread concern with problems of industrial motivation and morale dates from the classic Hawthorne Studies, which first focused attention on the part played by employee attitudes in productivity. Following an examination of these studies, we shall consider procedures for investigating employee attitudes, together with typical findings. Since interpersonal relations are a major factor determining employee attitudes, the study of industrial motivation and morale is almost co-extensive with what some writers call "industrial social psychology" (24, 76). Three broad topics in this field are supervision, communication, and organization theory. Each will be treated in a separate section of this chapter.

## THE HAWTHORNE STUDIES

The series of investigations that have come to be known as the "Hawthorne Studies" began in 1924 at the Hawthorne Works of the Western Electric Company, in Chicago, and extended over 15 years (54, 57). The focus of these studies shifted toward human relations in 1927, when the research came under the general direction of Elton Mayo of the Harvard Business School. This change in viewpoint, however, was gradual and was not fully effected until several years later. The first studies were designed to investigate the effects of illumination, rest pauses, length of working days, and pay rates on productivity. It soon became apparent, however, that output did not bear a simple relation to these factors. Some of the studies yielded apparently haphazard results that defied interpretation. In others, productivity rose steadily, regardless of what experimental changes were introduced. Even when poorer conditions were reinstated in the course of some experiments, worker performance continued to improve instead of dropping back to the earlier level.

An examination of the actual procedures followed in the course of these experiments reveals what would now be recognized as an astounding number of uncontrolled factors. In their efforts to secure cooperation, the investigators had made conditions as pleasant as possible for their subjects. Thus, in addition to their exposure to the systematically controlled experimental variables, the subjects were released from their customary close supervision, worked in a small group of congenial co-workers of their own choice, were assigned to a more cheerful and comfortable workroom, were allowed to converse more freely during work, received considerable attention from the experimenter and other company personnel, and were consulted about the changes that were introduced.

Following their recognition of the role of supervisory practices and other factors influencing employee attitudes, the Hawthorne investigators embarked upon an intensive attitude survey through interviews of over 21,000 workers. These interviews began as highly structured inquiries into what each employee liked and what he disliked about working conditions, supervision, and the job itself. It was soon discovered, however, that employees often talked about "irrelevant" topics which were usually of interest in their own right. As a result, the structured interviews were replaced by longer, unguided interviews in which the employee was allowed to bring up any problem he considered important. This survey served several purposes. It was noted that most employees welcomed the opportunity to express their views and exhibited more favorable attitudes as a result of it. Specific complaints registered during the interviews were studied by management with a view to correcting the conditions that evoked them. Principally, however, the results of the interviews were used as a basis for the discussion of human-relations problems in the company's supervisory training program.

The interview survey also suggested other problems for investigation. It was found that the expressed satisfaction or dissatisfaction often bore little relation to the actual condition cited. One employee might be satisfied and another dissatisfied with the same condition, such as wages, hours of work, or specific features of the working environment. The meaning of these items for the individual seemed to depend in part upon their value as status symbols, and this in turn often depended upon the attitudes of the group in which he worked. There was also evidence of voluntary restriction of output as a result of pressures from the work group. The formation of informal social groups within the organization and the influence they exert upon individuals' attitudes and job performance thus became the subject of the next phase of the Hawthorne Studies.

Accordingly, an intensive observational study was initiated with a small group of workers assigned to a special room. Data were gathered over a six-month period by two investigators: an observer stationed in the room who recorded verbal and other overt behavior; and an interviewer who explored individual attitudes, meanings, and values and sought information on the individual's personal history and his life outside the plant. Special attention was given to the existence of informal groupings among the men, the relation of these groupings to the formal supervisory organization of the department, and the types of social pressures whereby the group controlled individual work performance.

The last stage of the Hawthorne Studies is represented by the installation of a plant-wide program of employee counseling. This program provided professional counselors for problem-solving interviews with any employee having a problem to discuss. Its objectives were to help employees in the solution of their personal problems and to provide management with general guides for improving employee-relations and supervisory procedures.

All this research activity, together with the original demonstration that employee attitudes can counteract the effects of such factors as illumination and work schedules, did much to launch the "human-relations" movement in management. Today it is widely recognized that employee attitudes are an important determiner of job performance and that interpersonal relations with supervisors and co-workers play a major part in the development of these attitudes.

The Hawthorne Studies also served to highlight the need for controlling attitudinal variables in the design of psychological experiments. The term "Hawthorne effect" is now commonly used to refer to the influence that participation in an experiment may have upon the subject's behavior. Insofar as being a subject in a particular experiment may in itself involve certain interpersonal relations with the research personnel, as well as associated changes in status, self concept, or environmental milieu, a control group should be exposed to the same conditions in order to separate their effects from those of the experimental variable.

## MEASUREMENT OF EMPLOYEE ATTITUDES AND MORALE

Systematic surveys of employee attitudes are now an accepted management practice. Some of the uses of these surveys were already suggested by the Hawthorne Studies: to indicate needed changes in policies, procedures, or facilities; to provide a realistic basis for supervisory selection and training programs; and to help in evaluating the effect of different factors upon job performance. Attitude surveys have also been utilized in more general research on employee motivation, to find out what people want in a job and how these wants vary in relation to age, sex, education, occupational level, or other worker characteristics. In such research, data are often gathered on a community-wide or nationwide basis, rather than being limited to a single company or plant.

**Methods for Measuring Attitudes.** The major procedures for gathering data on employee attitudes and morale include interviewing, opinion questionnaires, attitude scales, projective and other indirect techniques, observational methods, and nominating techniques. A combination of two or more of these techniques is often desirable. To ensure frankness, the respondent's anonymity and the confidentiality of the data should be preserved, whatever technique is employed.

*Interviews* may be conducted with every member of a small unit or with a representative sample of a larger unit, such as a plant or company. A special form is the exit interview, held with employees who are about to leave the company. Although ranging from highly standardized to completely unstructured, most attitude-survey interviews are of the guided, or patterned, type (see Chapter 4).

While more superficial than interviewing techniques, *opinion question-naires* make it possible to reach a large number of employees in a short time. Anonymity can be easily provided by having employees drop the question-naires in a ballot box or mail them directly to an outside survey agency. Typi-cally, opinion questionnaires include questions on specific items within such areas as working conditions, relation to fellow workers, supervisory relations, company policies, pay, employee benefits, and opportunity for advancement. Responses may be analyzed so as to identify major areas of dissatisfaction; to single out specific items, such as employee cafeteria or vacation policy, about which opinions may be outstandingly favorable or unfavorable; to compare the frequency of dissatisfaction in different departments or different kinds of jobs within the company; or to answer other questions pertinent to the local cir-cumstances.

Like opinion questionnaires, *attitude scales* are suitable for mass administra-tion in written form. Rather than surveying attitudes toward a wide variety of specific items, however, such scales concentrate on measuring intensity of atti-tude in a single broad area, such as attitude toward the company or over-all job satisfaction. They consist of a series of statements whose scale values have been determined by procedures similar to those described in Chapter 4 for the construction of scaled checklists. Typical items for use in employee attitude measurement are given in Table 8. The statements are presented in random

**T A B L E  8**  *Illustrative Statements for Use in an Employee Attitude Scale* (*Selected from Uhrbrock, 73*)

| Scale Value | Statement |
|---|---|
| 10.4 | I think this company treats its employees better than any other company does. |
| 8.9 | A man can get ahead in this company if he tries. |
| 7.4 | On the whole, the company treats us about as well as we deserve. |
| 5.1 | The workers put as much over on the company as the company puts over on them. |
| 2.1 | You've got to have "pull" with certain people around here to get ahead. |
| 0.8 | An honest man fails in this company. |

order and without the accompanying scale values. The respondent's attitude score is found by taking the mean scale value of all the statements he en-dorses.

In a variant of this technique (5), the statements are still selected in terms of scale values, but the individual is required to respond to each statement by marking one of five terms: Strongly Agree, Agree, Undecided, Disagree, Strongly Disagree. He thus obtains a score of 1 to 5 on each statement, and the sum of these values is taken as his total job-satisfaction index. This procedure has the effect of providing finer differentiation of attitudes and raising reliability (5).

*Projective and other indirect techniques* for investigating attitudes are relatively unstructured, allowing the respondent considerable freedom of expression. Insofar as they are indirect, these techniques are believed to be less subject to rationalization and other face-saving devices and hence more likely to reveal genuine attitudes. Several familiar projective techniques, such as word association, sentence completion, or picture interpretation, have been adapted for attitude measurement. Another example is provided by a survey conducted at General Motors and known as "My Job Contest" (16). Employees were invited to participate in a letter-writing contest on the topic, "My Job and Why I Like It," for which 5,000 prizes were awarded. The content of the letters, which totaled nearly 150,000, was analyzed with reference to 58 "themes," or factors associated with favorable job attitudes.

*Observational methods* for investigating employee attitudes and morale have already been illustrated in the description of the Hawthorne Studies. Such techniques require the services of a trained observer, who may spend several months in a department. While maintaining friendly relations with the employees, he should serve only as an observer. It should be made clear to the employees that he has no administrative functions or authority. Although at first the presence of a stranger creates a strained and unnatural situation, these difficulties can usually be overcome with time. The technique is used especially in studying group structure and interpersonal reactions among employees. Qualitative data pertaining to attitudes toward company policies, supervisors, and other aspects of the job situation can also be obtained from the comments and general behavior of the employees.

Another procedure for investigating group structure is the *nominating technique* derived from sociometry (see Chapter 4). Each employee is asked to name the person in his group whom he would choose as the best worker, the most fair-minded, the one who would make the best supervisor, or the one who fits some other given designation. The results can then be plotted in a "sociogram," as illustrated in Figure 34. Each circle in these diagrams represents a

*Fig. 34* Sociograms of three groups. (*Figures 6.3, 6.4, and 6.5 from Industrial psychology and its social foundations by Milton L. Blum. Harper & Row, Publishers, Incorporated, 1956.*)

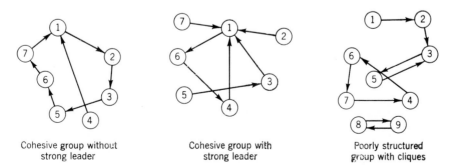

Cohesive group without strong leader      Cohesive group with strong leader      Poorly structured group with cliques

person. If individual 1 names individual 2 as his choice, an arrow is drawn from circle 1 to circle 2. Mutual choices are indicated by two arrows pointing in opposite directions. Sociograms are useful in identifying informal leaders, cliques which may disrupt group unity, and other characteristics of group structure.

**Factors in Job Satisfaction.** A number of attitude surveys have been concerned with what workers want from their jobs. An example is an opinion survey of about 3,700 men and women applying for jobs with the Minneapolis Gas Company (37). Each applicant was given a list of 10 factors and was asked to rank them in order of their importance to him, a rank of 1 representing the most important. The average ranks assigned by men and women are shown in Table 9. It will be noted that the men gave the highest ranks to security, advancement (opportunity for promotion), and type of work (interesting work that they like). Company (feeling of pride in the company), pay, congenial co-workers, and a considerate and fair supervisor received intermediate ratings. Hours, working conditions, and employee benefits were regarded as least important.

**TABLE 9**  *Mean Ranks Assigned to Job Factors by Applicants*
(*From Jurgensen, 37, p. 353*)

| Job Factor | 3,345 Men | 378 Women |
|---|---|---|
| Security | 3.3 | 4.6 |
| Advancement | 3.6 | 4.8 |
| Type of work | 3.7 | 2.8 |
| Company | 5.0 | 5.4 |
| Pay | 6.0 | 6.4 |
| Co-workers | 6.0 | 5.4 |
| Supervisor | 6.1 | 5.4 |
| Hours | 6.9 | 6.1 |
| Working conditions | 7.1 | 5.8 |
| Benefits | 7.4 | 8.2 |

With minor exceptions, this rank order agrees with those found in several other similar surveys (30, 75). It has been frequently pointed out that such rank orders differ in a number of ways from those obtained when executives are asked what they believe the workers want. As a rule, executives rank pay much higher than the workers do themselves[1] (3, ch. 4; 75, ch. 15). The interpretation of reported order of importance, however, is not entirely clear. For one thing, people may give rationalizations because they sound more acceptable than their actual preferences. Some may not be fully aware of their own motives. It is interesting to note that, in a study of 40 retail-grocery-store workers, a projective technique (story completion) revealed greater emphasis on pay than did direct questioning of workers about their current sources of job satisfaction (26).

Another approach to the question of job satisfaction is to have employees rate their attitudes toward different aspects of their present job, as well as their

[1] Much effort has been expended, too, in working out elaborate financial incentive plans. For surveys and critical evaluations of such plans, see Blum (3, ch. 3), Rothe (61), and Viteles (75, ch. 2).

over-all job satisfaction (e.g., 1). Those factors that correlate highly with over-all job satisfaction can then be regarded as the most important for the workers, those that correlate low as the least important. For example, if attitude toward employee benefits correlates negligibly with over-all job satisfaction, it means that an individual's satisfaction or dissatisfaction with his company's policies in this regard contributes little or nothing to his job satisfaction.

The relative importance assigned to job factors has been found to vary somewhat with the characteristics of the workers. In Table 9, certain differences can be seen between the mean ranks given by men and women. For the women, type of work stands out as the most important factor, benefits as the least important, and all other factors are fairly close to each other. A number of surveys have likewise found differences associated with age, education, type of work, and job level.

With regard to job level, lower-level workers tend to stress factors extrinsic to the work, such as security and pleasant relations with co-workers and supervisor, while higher-level workers put more emphasis on the opportunities for self-expression, interesting work, and leadership that the job itself provides (8; 12; 75, ch. 20). Several investigators have interpreted these findings in terms of a theory of "need hierarchy," first proposed by Maslow (52, 53). According to this theory, needs fall into a hierarchy of prepotency, beginning with basic physiological needs for air, food, and water and proceeding through such needs as those for safety (or security), belongingness, self-esteem, and independence, to the need for self-actualization (i.e., using one's capacities to the fullest extent). When a need is satisfied, it no longer serves to motivate behavior, and the next higher need in the hierarchy emerges. Although this theory is consistent with observed job-level differences in sources of job satisfaction, it should be noted that the nature of the job itself may also account for some of these differences. If a job is so organized as to allow the worker little or no self-expression, he must seek satisfaction in factors extrinsic to the work. This situation can be seen in semiskilled factory jobs as well as in the more routine types of clerical work.

**Relation of Attitudes to Job Performance.** The relation between attitudes and job performance is not a simple one. To be sure, absenteeism, tardiness, accident rate, and turnover tend to be consistently higher the poorer the reported job attitudes (4, 30, 60). Studies of productivity, however, have yielded inconsistent results (4, 30). Some of these discrepancies may arise from methodological differences among investigations. But there are other factors that complicate the relationship itself.

To understand the relationship between employee attitudes and productivity, we must find out how productivity is related to the employee's own goals (4). For example, an individual strongly motivated to advance to a higher level in the company may produce more for this reason and at the same time be dissatisfied with his present job. Or acceptance by his co-workers may be of prime importance to an employee, and such acceptance may be contingent upon restriction of output to conform to a norm set by his group. This would be especially true in a cohesive group with high morale and strong feelings of loyalty. Under some circumstances, quantity and quality of output may bear a different relation to the individual's goals, as when a skilled craftsman resists efforts to increase speed if he believes the quality of his work will suffer. For some persons, a high degree of expressed job satisfaction may mean no more than complacency, a condition not especially conducive to the exertion of great effort.

It is apparent that a proper interpretation of the relation between employee attitudes and productivity requires complex experimental designs, comprising more variables than have usually been investigated. An example is provided by a study conducted by Katzell and his associates (10, 41,) in 72 wholesale warehouses of a pharmaceutical company. Comparison of the different warehouses showed that both productivity and average job satisfaction were related to such situational variables as plant size, community size, proportion of women workers, and unionization. The positive correlation between productivity and job satisfaction found in this study could be explained in terms of plant differences in these situational variables.

An investigation by Herzberg and his co-workers (31) sheds further light upon the sources and effects of employee attitudes. Data were gathered through intensive interviews of about two hundred engineers and accountants employed by nine industrial plants in the vicinity of Pittsburgh. In each interview, the employee was asked to think of a time when he felt exceptionally good or exceptionally bad about his job and to describe what happened. An account of both a "good" and a "bad" situation was obtained from each person. The interviewer also inquired into the duration of the situation itself and of the attitudes it engendered, the factors leading to the satisfaction or dissatisfaction (including both objective events and the individual's perception of them), and the effects of the situation on the individual's feelings, health, job performance, interpersonal relations, and other behavior.

An analysis of the content of these interviews yielded a wealth of specific data. In interpreting their findings, the authors differentiate between "satisfiers" and "dissatisfiers." Their results show that the satisfiers, producing favorable job attitudes, usually pertain to the *job itself*. Predominant among such factors, in order of their frequency, were achievement, recognition, characteristics of the work, responsibility, and advancement. These factors center around opportunities for self-actualization and growth. Recognition was most effective when related to genuine achievement and progress. Otherwise, its effects tended to be trivial and short-lived. The dissatisfiers, on the other hand, more often referred to *job context*, as illustrated by ineffective or unfair company policies, incompetence of supervisor, poor interpersonal relations with supervisor, and unsatisfactory working conditions. Furthermore, dissatisfaction could be aroused by a wider variety of factors than could satisfaction.

It might be noted, too, that salary appeared with intermediate frequency among both satisfiers and dissatisfiers. However, mention of salary nearly always pertained to obtaining raises or failure to receive an expected raise. Thus salary was perceived either as an instance of unfairness in supervision and company policy or as tangible recognition for achievement and as a sign of progress.

With regard to the effects of attitudes, the authors conclude that dissatisfiers (contextual factors) influence principally emotional adjustment, job turnover, absenteeism, and the like. But only the satisfiers (intrinsic job factors) can provide the positive motivation to greater productivity. Thus human-relations programs and fringe benefits can at best eliminate dissatisfaction, but they cannot provide motivation for better job performance, especially of a creative nature. This is a provocative hypothesis, which should be tested further, particularly with other kinds of work and other job levels. It would be interesting, for instance, to repeat the study with such groups as salesmen, executives, office clerks, and assembly-line operators. There is evidence from other sources to suggest that persons who enter different occupations vary systematically in interests and other personality traits (see Chapter 17). These differences may very well be reflected in sources of job satisfaction and dissatisfaction.

## SUPERVISION

Despite the many complexities that beset the study of employee attitudes, one fact that emerges clearly is the importance of supervisory practices. Attention has been focused particularly on the key role of the foreman or first-line supervisor in shaping employee attitudes (see, e.g., 21, 29). In the previously cited "My Job Contest," for example, supervision ranked first in frequency among the 58 themes mentioned in the letters (16). Surveys of the sources of job dissatisfaction have repeatedly shown the behavior of the immediate supervisor to be a major factor (30, 31, 75). Supervisory behavior has also been found to be significantly related to absenteeism, accidents, grievances, and turnover in different departments (20). It is interesting to note, too, that some invesigators have found group productivity to be more closely related to the supervisor's attitudes and behavior than to employee attitudes (39, 40, 47). Measures of employee attitudes may reflect attitudes on a variety of matters, some of which may be unrelated to productivity. Supervisory behavior, on the other hand, is more likely to have a direct bearing on productivity and to influence those employee attitudes that are more relevant to effective job performance.

A series of investigations conducted at the Institute for Social Research of the University of Michigan has been concerned with the characteristics of successful supervisors (47). Over 70 studies were carried out in many different industries, as well as in hospitals, government agencies, and voluntary organizations. Data were gathered at all management levels and on workers in a wide variety of jobs, from unskilled labor and clerical work to scientific research. The general design of these studies involved essentially a comparison of the supervisory practices followed in the "best" and "poorest" units of an organization. The criteria of administrative effectiveness used in identifying these units included productivity; job satisfaction; turnover, absenteeism, and similar indices; costs; scrap loss; and employee and managerial motivation.

A major finding of the Michigan studies was that supervisors of the high-producing units were more often "employee-centered," while supervisors of low-producing units were more often "job-centered" (Figure 35). By "employee-centered" the investigators mean specifically that the supervisor places the primary emphasis on the human problems of the workers; he is friendly and supportive toward the worker, trying to build and maintain the individual's sense of personal worth; and he provides only general supervision, allowing considerable individual freedom in carrying out the job. In contrast, the job-centered supervisor places primary emphasis on production itself, seeing that the workers use the prescribed methods and overseeing their work closely. The more effective supervisors were also found to play a more differentiated role. They spent less time performing the same functions as the workers and more time in motivating their subordinates, in keeping them informed about policies, and in long-range planning (38).

*Fig. 35*  Relation between supervisory practices and group productivity.
(*From Likert, 47, p. 7.*)

The investigators recognized, of course, that such comparative studies do not in themselves permit an analysis of cause-and-effect relations. It is conceivable, for example, that low group productivity leads to closer supervision and more pressure on the part of the supervisor, rather than vice versa. Although most of the research in the Michigan series utilized a cross-sectional approach, there are some longitudinal data to support the hypothesis that supervisory practices influence productivity. In one company, managers of high-producing and of low-producing divisions were shifted. Regardless of the initial productivity level of the new division, these managers tended to retain their former orientation toward the employees. Productivity itself changed after the shift, the low-producing divisions improving and the high-producing divisions slipping under the new supervisors. Moreover, the favorable change occurred more rapidly than the unfavorable (47, p. 12).

Another approach to supervision is illustrated by the Ohio State Leadership Studies, most of which were concerned with descriptive analyses of organizational structure, executive functions, and supervisory behavior in many different settings (64). One of these studies, already cited in Chapter 5 in connection with the evaluation of human-relations training, identified two major dimensions of supervisory behavior: "Consideration," characterized by a friendly, warm, considerate supervisory relationship, as contrasted with an impersonal and authoritarian relationship; and "Initiating Structure," pertaining to the extent to which the supervisor actively plans and directs group activities oriented toward goal attainment (17, 67).

These two dimensions will be recognized as bearing a general resemblance to the employee-centered and job-centered orientations identified by the Michigan group. In the Ohio State research, however, the two characteristics were found to be independent dimensions. In other words, an individual's rating on one is unrelated to his rating on the other. It was found further that supervisors rating low on both traits proved to be weak and ineffective leaders, who were often bypassed by their own subordinates (20). Although the results varied somewhat with the situation, in general the most effective leaders were above average in both Consideration and Initiating Structure (67). Supervisors emphasizing either dimension at the expense of the other tended to be less effective. It might be added that the Michigan investigators, too, observed that the foremen in charge of high-producing units tended to be *both* employee-centered and oriented toward high production goals (47, p. 8). But this relationship is not clearly demonstrated or emphasized in the published accounts of the Michigan research.

Further research on the dimensions of Consideration and Initiating Structure indicated that the relation between these supervisory characteristics and certain indices of employee morale may be curvilinear (19). Thus both employee grievances and turnover within different units of a manufacturing plant were related to supervisors' ratings in these dimensions only at the extremes of low Consideration and high Structure. Beyond certain critical levels, increasing Consideration or decreasing Structure had no effect on grievance and turnover rates. The same investigation revealed interaction effects between the two supervisory dimensions. Specifically, the relation between Structure and grievance or turnover rate differed among foremen who rated high, medium, or low in Consideration.

It will be recalled from Chapter 5 that a follow-up study of the effects of supervisory training, conducted at the International Harvester Company, revealed the importance of "leadership climate" as represented by the behavior, attitudes, and expectations of the foreman's own supervisor. In a still later follow-up, it was found that management rated as most proficient those foremen whose scores (unknown to the raters), were high in Initiating Structure and low in Consideration (18, p. 312). This occurred despite the fact that foremen with this trait pattern had work groups with higher rates of accidents, absenteeism, and turnover than did those with other patterns. Apparently these foremen received high ratings because they fitted the stereotype of effective leadership. The merit ratings were thus reinforcing supervisory practices that were inconsistent with those taught in the supervisory training course.

Several other studies have demonstrated that supervisory practices must be viewed against the management context in which the supervisor operates. One relevant factor, for instance, is the amount of influence the supervisor can wield with his own superiors. A study (56) conducted in a large public utility showed that such supervisory behavior as "siding with employees" and "social closeness to employees" tended to be positively correlated with employee satisfaction if the supervisor had enough influence to have his recommendations accepted by higher management. For supervisors lacking such influence, however, the correlations tended to be zero or negative. In such cases, the supervisory behavior probably served only to arouse in the employee expectations that remained unfulfilled and thus increased their feelings of frustration.

It is evident that there is no one simple formula for improving supervision. Here as in all situations involving interpersonal relations, there is no set of rules for "getting along with people." As Likert (46) has pointed out, effective supervision must be adaptive and relative. Procedures that work for one person or in one situation may be useless or harmful with another person or in a different situation. Because of differences in past experiences, workers vary in the way they perceive the same behavior on the part of a supervisor. Employees also vary in their values, goals, and expectations. Personality differences, too, may make one worker welcome additional responsibility and freedom from supervision, whereas another feels lost and insecure in the same situation.

A second important factor is the personality and habitual behavior of the supervisor himself. Any sudden change in the supervisor's manner or procedures, such as might occur after a supervisory training program, may be viewed with suspicion and distrust by his subordinates. Moreover, supervisory practices that are inconsistent with the supervisor's personality and run counter to his deep-rooted behavior patterns are likely to be superficial and insincere. In this lies one of the chief fallacies of the popular books and high-pressure courses on how to get along with people. Such an approach to interpersonal relations leads to behavior that is contrived and deliberate, rather than spontaneous and forthright. Not only is such behavior likely to repel one's associates, but it is also questionable from the standpoint of the individual's own mental health (36).

A third factor is the leadership climate or managerial context within which the supervisor must function. Important as his job is, the first-line supervisor cannot operate in a vacuum. His over-all success as a supervisor, as well as the relative effectiveness of specific supervisory practices, depends upon the company's organizational structure, the attitudes of higher management, and other situational conditions.

Finally, it must be recognized that for effective supervision an employee-centered, human-relations point of view is not enough. This limitation has been noted by some of the Michigan investigators, more clearly demonstrated in some of the Ohio State studies, and vigorously expounded by Herzberg and his associates in the report of their previously cited investigation of employee attitudes (31). These investigators emphasized the importance of the sense of achievement that can be provided only by the work itself. Part of the supervisor's role in this connection is to recognize good work and to reward it selectively—rather than praising indiscriminately just because to do so is "good human relations"! The supervisor can also help by structuring and assigning jobs so as to give the individual more opportunity for creativity and self-actualization. What the supervisor can accomplish in this regard, of course, is limited by the organizational system within which he must work. This is just another example of the fact that supervisory practices must be integrated with organizational structure. We shall take a closer look at some of the problems of organizational structure in a later section of this chapter.


## COMMUNICATION

*Nature and Scope of Industrial Communication.* With the increasing size of industrial organizations, communication assumes more and more importance as a means of linking the various parts together, channeling incoming information to the appropriate outlets, and ensuring coordinated action. Industrial communication may take many forms. It can be as personal as a luncheon conversation between two vice-presidents or as impersonal as an announcement over the plant's public address system. It can be as succinct as a one-sentence bulletin-board notice or as detailed as a 100-page report, as formal as a stockholders' meeting or as informal as the transmission of a rumor over the grapevine. A common and effective medium of communication is the face-to-face interview in all its forms, such as performance-appraisal, problem-solving, and counseling interviews. Group meetings are among the most widely used communication techniques in all types of organizations. Company training programs serve a communication function, as do employee attitude surveys.

Suggestion systems are a traditional means of routing employee ideas to management.

Within an organization, communication may flow downward, as when policy statements, operating procedures, and the like, are transmitted from management to employees; upward, as illustrated by employee suggestions and grievances; and horizontally, or across units at the same level. The mere presentation of material in oral or written form does not assure communication. The complete communication process comprises transmission, reception, comprehension, and acceptance or rejection. What is communicated includes not only cognitive material, such as facts, procedures, policies, and ideas, but also emotional climate, feelings, and attitudes.

We must bear in mind, too, that actions speak louder than words and are thus a part of the communication system. A raise, a promotion, or a reduction in job responsibility are likely to be perceived by the employee as evaluations of his job performance—and as such they will carry more weight than a verbal communication. When supervisors in a large public utility were asked, "On what basis do you judge your standing with your immediate superior?" many more of their replies referred to actions than to verbal appraisals (47, p. 54). Figure 36 shows the percentage who checked each answer.

That communication has an important influence on employee attitudes and morale is quite generally recognized (62). Empirical demonstrations of this influence, however, are more difficult to find. Some suggestive data are reproduced in Figure 37. Based on a survey of white-collar workers in a large public utility, this graph shows a consistent relation between freedom of communication and absenteeism in different departments (50). Apparently those departments in which employees felt free to discuss their problems with the supervisor had fewer absences than those in which the atmosphere was less conducive to

*Fig. 36* Replies of supervisors to the question: "On what basis do you judge your standing with your immediate superior?" (*From Likert, 47, p. 54.*)

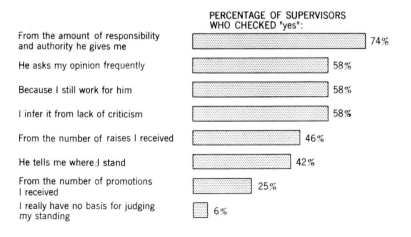

PERCENTAGE OF SUPERVISORS
WHO CHECKED "yes":

| | |
|---|---|
| From the amount of responsibility and authority he gives me | 74% |
| He asks my opinion frequently | 58% |
| Because I still work for him | 58% |
| I infer it from lack of criticism | 58% |
| From the number of raises I received | 46% |
| He tells me where I stand | 42% |
| From the number of promotions I received | 25% |
| I really have no basis for judging my standing | 6% |

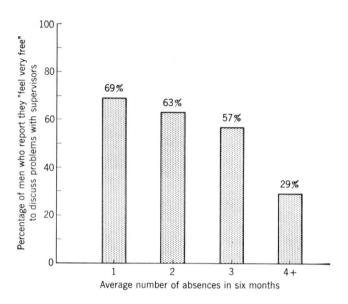

**Fig. 37**   Relationship between absenteeism and supervisory communication in different departments. (*From Likert, 47, p. 18.*)

free communication. Similar results were obtained with blue-collar workers in the same company.

**The Communication Process.**   Industrial psychologists have investigated the communication process from many angles. Some have been concerned with the relative effectiveness of different media. In one such study (11), information was transmitted by five different methods in various departments of an industrial plant. Later, tests were administered to determine how much the individual employees had actually received and retained. The results are shown in Table 10. It will be noted that the combination of oral and written communication gave the best results but that oral only was more effective than written only. Bulletin board and grapevine yielded the poorest results.

**TABLE 10**   *Mean Information Test Scores of Employees Receiving Communication through Different Media* (*From Dahle, 11, p. 245*)

| Medium | Number of Employees | Mean Test Score* |
|---|---|---|
| Combined oral and written | 102 | 7.70 |
| Oral only | 94 | 6.17 |
| Written only | 109 | 4.91 |
| Bulletin board | 115 | 3.72 |
| Grapevine only (control group) | 108 | 3.56 |

* All differences are significant at the 5 per cent level or better except that between the last two means in the column.

Written and oral communications each have certain intrinsic advantages that make them suitable for different purposes. Written communications are more accurate and provide a permanent record. They permit fuller coverage of detail and can be cited as an official, authoritative reference. Oral communications, on the other hand, are more personal, permit the give-and-take of two-way communication, can be adapted to the individual listener, and can be reinforced by the appropriate tone of voice, facial expressions, and gestures.

With regard to written communication, extensive early research is available on the legibility of printed matter as a function of such typographical characteristics as style and size of type, amount of space between letters, color of print and of background, and length of lines (see 55). A number of studies have been more specifically concerned with the content and readability of such employee publications as handbooks, plant magazines, and company bulletins (6, 62). Using a measure known as the Flesch Index, to be discussed in Chapter 12, these studies have demonstrated that the large majority of employee publications are too difficult for employees to read. Rewriting them in a style better suited to the educational level of their readers would increase their effectiveness as communication media. The same techniques have been applied to checking the readability of union-management agreements, with similar results (42, 70).

Another approach has focused on the improvement of communication skills, including both the transmitting and the receiving of information. There has been considerable interest, for example, in the development of reading improvement programs for executives (43). A more comprehensive and individualized type of training is represented by the "communication clinic," which has been successfully employed in a number of organizations (63). Concerned with both psychological and linguistic aspects of communication, this approach provides whatever remedial procedures are needed to increase the individual's effectiveness in reading, writing, and speech.

Considerable basic research has been done on the role of communication in modifying beliefs and attitudes (33–35, 59). Several studies have been concerned with factors influencing the persuasiveness of communication, such as order of presenting ideas, prestige of the communicator, and various characteristics of recipients. Other studies have investigated changes in both retention and acceptance of the communicated material over a period of time. Such research has broad implications, tying in with learning principles on the one hand and with the social psychology of propaganda and mass communication on the other.

*Communication Barriers and Breakdowns.* Special attention has been given to the factors associated with communication failures (27; 47, ch. 4). Certain supervisory practices and attitudes may reduce the effectiveness of upward communication, as illustrated in Figure 38. It will be seen that, in those departments where the men felt the greatest "unreasonable pressure" for better performance, only a small percentage said they would take grievances and complaints first to their superiors. The less the pressure, the greater the percentage of men who reported that they would communicate first with their superiors in these matters. Similarly, a correlation of .73 was found between the extent of unreasonable pressure felt by the men and the difficulty they reported in trying to communicate ideas for improving operations to higher management levels (47, p. 45).

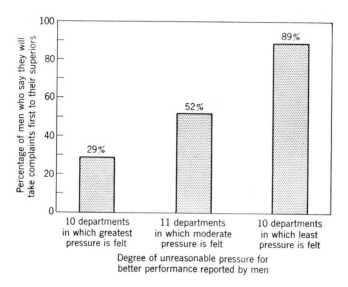

**Fig. 38**   Relationship between supervisory practices and freedom of upward communication. (*From Likert, 47, p. 45.*)

Attitudes of hostility and distrust not only may reduce the flow and acceptance of information but also may lead to deliberate distortion of communication at all organizational levels. Status relationships and organizational climate may likewise hamper the upward flow of communication (32). In some organizations, superiors are told only what subordinates think they want to hear.

A common cause of communication failures is to be found in the different frames of reference against which individuals may perceive a situation. It is well known that perception is selective and that each person tends to perceive what fits in with his own experiences, interests, and needs. This fact was demonstrated when 23 middle-management executives participating in a company training program were requested to identify the major problem facing a company about which they had read (15). Although the instructions asked for the problem that should be dealt with first by a newly appointed company president—and thus emphasized a broad, company-wide perspective—the executives tended to perceive chiefly problems in their own areas, such as sales, organizational structure and policy, or human relations.

Differences in the way the same situation is perceived by persons at different organizational levels are revealed when superiors and subordinates are questioned about the effectiveness of their intercommunications. Table 11 summarizes results obtained at two management levels and with regard to both downward and upward communication. The differences are conspicuous. Whereas 100 per cent of the top staff believed they always or nearly always told foremen in advance about changes, only 63 per cent of the foremen thought so. Similarly, 92 per cent of the foremen reported that they always or nearly always informed their men in advance about changes, but only 47 per cent of the men were of the opinion that the foremen did so. The same

**TABLE 11** *Effectiveness of Communication as Perceived by Superiors and Subordinates*
(*Adapted from Likert, 47, pp. 52, 53*)

| Do superiors tell subordinates in advance about changes that will affect them or their work? | Top staff says as to own behavior | Foremen say about top staff's behavior | Foremen say as to own behavior | Men say about foremen's behavior |
|---|---|---|---|---|
| Always | 70% | 27% | 40% | 22% |
| Nearly always | 30 | 36 | 52 | 25 |
| More often than not | – | 18 | 2 | 13 |
| Occasionally | – | 15 | 5 | 28 |
| Seldom | – | 4 | 1 | 12 |

| Do superiors get subordinates' ideas and opinions in solving job problems? | Top staff says as to own behavior | Foremen say about top staff's behavior | Foremen say as to own behavior | Men say about foremen's behavior |
|---|---|---|---|---|
| Always or almost always | 70% | 52% | 73% | 16% |
| Often | 25 | 17 | 23 | 23 |
| Sometimes or seldom | 5 | 31 | 4 | 61 |

trends can be seen when the question deals with the frequency with which subordinates' ideas and opinions are obtained by superiors in solving job problems.

Communication breakdowns often result from preconceived notions, prejudices, stereotypes, and strong emotional associations with certain words (see 27). A tendency to overgeneralize or to jump to conclusions may also seriously retard communication. The "evaluative tendency" has been described as another barrier to effective communication (58). When we hear or read a statement made by another person, often our first reaction is to express agreement or disagreement with it, i.e., to evaluate it within our own frame of reference, rather than trying to understand it from the other person's point of view. The attempt to remove this communication barrier underlies the nondirective or client-centered techniques developed by Carl R. Rogers and his associates for use in counseling and psychotherapy (see Chapter 14). These techniques are now being applied to more and more areas of interpersonal relations.

**Communication Networks.** The typical organization chart, showing who reports to whom, may be regarded as a map of the organization's formal communication channels. That information often flows through other, informal channels even in a relatively rigid military organization is illustrated in Figure 39. The routing of information through an organization has important implications for decision making. The decisions made by a top executive depend upon the information he receives. The larger the organization, the more likely it is that information is highly screened, condensed, and interpreted before it reaches the top management levels. Persons at lower organizational levels may thus influence decisions by their selective filtering of information. Of particular interest is the type of communication network illustrated in Figure 40, in which all information going to a top executive must filter through an assistant. As a result, the assistant may become the one who really makes the decisions and runs the organization. Such a situation may not only limit organizational effectiveness but may also disrupt morale.

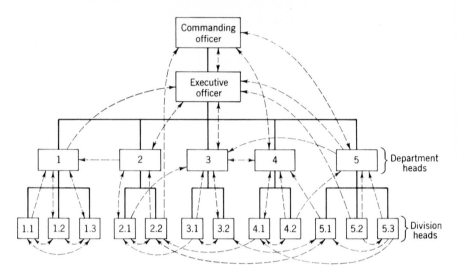

*Fig. 39*  Formal and informal organization of a military unit. The broken
lines show with whom each person spent the most time in getting work
done. (*From Stodgill, R. M., The sociometry of working relationships
in formal organizations, Sociometry, Vol. XII, 1949, page 282, J. L.
Moreno, M.D., Editor, Beacon House, publishers.*)

A number of techniques have been employed to analyze the flow of communication in both large organizations and small groups (13). Asking individuals with whom they spend their time during working hours is one approach.
Having a trained observer stationed in a workroom, as in the Hawthorne
Studies, is another. Other techniques study the communications more directly.
Thus in a "duty study" a record is made of all communications passing a particular spot, such as a given executive's desk, throughout the day. In a "cross-
sectional analysis" each person is asked what communication (if any) was in
progress at a specified point in time.

Another technique, known as "ecco analysis" (episodic communication
channels in organization), follows a specific unit of information throughout the
communication network (13). In applying this method, for example, the investigator might ask each individual whether he knows some particular item
of information. If so, the respondent is further asked from whom and through
what medium he learned of it and in what respects, if any, the information he
received differed from that presented by the investigator. This method is especially well suited for the study of grapevine and other informal communication channels. Data can be analyzed in various ways to show, for instance, extent and direction of information flow, distortion of facts in the process of
transmission, and relative use of different media.

Still another approach is represented by laboratory studies of communication
nets in small task-oriented groups (2, 44, 65, 72). Figure 41 shows some of the
communication nets investigated in these studies. Subjects are seated around a
table but are separated by radial partitions so that they cannot see each other
and must communicate by passing notes through slots in the partitions. Each

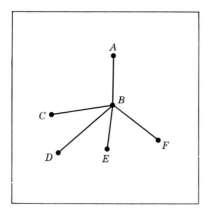

**Fig. 40** A communication network in which B plays an important filtering role. (*Adapted from Leavitt, 45, p. 201.*)

group is assigned problems whose solution requires the pooling of information by all group members. The experimenter sets up different communication nets by opening some slots and closing others.

In the star pattern (Figure 41), all information must be sent to a central person C, who transmits the answers back to each individual member. In the chain, information is sent by the two peripheral members P, through the middle men M, to C. In the circle, there is no centralized organization, information traveling back and forth among all members. With regard to speed and accuracy of problem solving, the star yielded the best results and the circle the poorest. However, circle nets had better morale and were better able to adapt to sudden and confusing changes of task. A leader and a stable form of organization emerged most readily with the star pattern, more slowly with the chain, and failed to emerge with the circle. It is quite likely that different kinds of communication nets may be most effective for different purposes. The chief contribution of this series of studies was to point the way for future research on the effect of communication patterns on group performance and morale.

**Fig. 41**   Three types of communication nets. (*Adapted from Leavitt, 44.*)

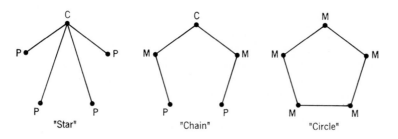

## ORGANIZATION THEORY

Supervision, communication, and other specific managerial practices must be viewed against the broader framework of organizational structure. Essentially, the structure of an organization refers to the nature and interrelations of its units, that is, of the individuals and groups assigned to carry out its various functions. The links in an organizational chart indicate not only formal channels of communication but also other organizational relations, such as lines of authority and influence, relative status, promotion ladders, work flow, and functional dependencies integrating the organization's division of labor. Organization theory is concerned with the characteristics of organizational structure and their relation to organizational effectiveness. In a broader sense, the term is also used to encompass all managerial practices, since these are so intimately bound up with organizational structure.

Organizations have been described from many points of view and by representatives of diverse disciplines, including business administration, engineering, economics, sociology, and psychology (25, 64). Some psychologists have utilized biological models to conceptualize the growth of organizations (23) or mathematical models to analyze their linkage systems (7). Others have focused on qualitative descriptions of the "psychological climate" of organizations, using such concepts as permissiveness versus rigidity, cooperativeness versus competitiveness, autocratic versus democratic leadership, group conformity versus individual freedom, and the like. Still others have employed the statistical techniques of item analysis to identify such organizational dimensions as degree of control exerted over members' behavior, flexibility or informality of procedures, pleasantness of hedonic tone accompanying group membership, homogeneity of members in socially relevant characteristics, and extent of stratification into status hierarchies (28).

This diversity of approaches is reflected in the varied proposals for improving organizational effectiveness. Among those of particular interest to psychology are employee participation in decision making, sociometry in work-group assignments, and job design to maximize opportunities for individual responsibility and initiative.

*Participation.* One of the chief results of the human-relations movement in management has been a growing emphasis on employee participation in decision making (47–49, 69). There is some variation, however, in the nature and extent of participation that is advocated, the mechanics for implementing it, and the extent to which it involves group or individual responsibility. Some writers have pointed out that the optimum degree of employee partcipation is a function of the characteristics of the employees, the supervisor, and the situation (68).

Likert (47) typifies the group-dynamics approach in his advocacy of group-decision processes at all levels. To this end, he proposes a type of organizational structure consisting of many overlapping groups that extend across adjacent management levels. Each foreman, for example, would participate in decision-making conferences with the men in his work unit and would also participate with other foremen and their supervisor in similar conferences at the next level. Thus the supervisor in one group is a subordinate in the next, and so on at successive levels. Horizontal as well as vertical linkages are built into this system. The emphasis on groups rather than on individuals is quite evident in this approach, as illustrated by Likert's statement that "an organization will function best when its personnel function not as individuals but as members of highly effective work groups with high performance goals" (47, p. 105).

On the basis of one of the Michigan studies, Likert presents some evidence that participation of employees in decision making does not reduce the influence exerted by superiors but actually increases the total amount of influence exerted by all members of the organization (47, pp. 179–181). This, he argues, follows from the fact that decisions in which subordinates participate are more likely to be effectively implemented. When superiors have the sole authority for making decisions, they exert more influence on the decision making itself but exert less influence on what actually goes on than when subordinates participate in the decisions.

One of the most widely quoted studies of employee participation was conducted at the Harwood Manufacturing Company, a pajama factory (9). Certain necessary changes in the design of the garments required new work assignments for the operators. As is usually the case, the workers had reacted with considerable resistance to previous changes. Even when their earnings are protected, workers resent having to learn new work methods. As a result, production drops, and grievances, absenteeism, and turnover increase. At the time of the investigation, four equated work groups were formed. One group of 13 served as a control, being merely informed of the change in the usual way. Two groups of 7 and 8 workers actively participated with management in planning the changes. A fourth group of 18 was represented by two members, who participated with management in making the changes and discussed developments with the rest of the group.

The results with regard to productivity are shown in Figure 42. The two groups with full participation (whose results have been averaged in the graph) showed less drop after the changeover, faster recovery, and higher ultimate level of output than the control group. The group with limited participation yielded intermediate results. The control group also had more grievances and turnover after the change than did the experimental groups. Several months after the original experiment, the control group was given full participation before undergoing another change of procedure. On this occasion, its productivity record equaled that of the experimental groups. A much later report from the same company shows the successful introduction of extensive changes in production methods with the help of a company-wide program of employee participation (22).

Although the results of the Harwood studies are impressive, it should be noted that in such field investigations, as in much applied research, it is difficult to identify causal factors with certainty. It is possible that at least some of the group differences in productivity in the first study may have resulted from other differences between the groups, such as the nature of the training received (see 75, pp. 168–169). Nevertheless, the findings of these studies are in line with those of other research indicating that participation in decision making tends to improve employee morale and job performance (47, ch. 3; 75, ch. 9).

*Sociometry.* Sociometric methods have been used in industry to assign individuals to work groups, as well as in the military services to assemble crews and combat teams. The effect of sociometric work assignments on job per-

**Fig. 42**  Group participation and productivity. (*Adapted from Coch and French, 9, p. 522.*)

formance was demonstrated in a study of 74 carpenters and bricklayers who had been working on a housing project for a period of 5 months or more (74). Each man was asked for his first, second, and third choice of work mates, and teams were formed on the basis of these preferences. Comparison of records for an 11-month period when these teams were in operation with the records for the preceding 9-month period showed statistically significant reductions in labor and material costs, as well as in turnover rate. The total saving in production costs amounted to 5 per cent.

In this connection it might be noted that studies conducted both in industry and in the armed services have found high peer-group loyalty to be associated with better job attitudes, less tension and anxiety at work, and less absenteeism (47, ch. 3). The relation of group loyalty and cohesiveness to productivity is more complex. When the objectives of the group conflict with those of the organization, then productivity is likely to be lower the more cohesive the group. Voluntary restriction of output is a familiar example of this situation. But when supervisory relations and other organizational practices are such as to motivate the group toward high productivity, then group cohesiveness is positively related to productivity (47, ch. 3).

Studies on the "geography of production" (24), or the spatial arrangement of workers in groups, are also relevant. In an intensive investigation of assembly-line workers, for example, the number of contacts a worker had with his associates at work was found to be related to his expressed job satisfaction, as well as to turnover, grievances, and other indices of job adjustment (78). By its very nature, the assembly line tends to minimize such contacts.

Further evidence of the importance of relations with co-workers was provided by a study of coal miners in England (71). When technological a.

vances led to certain changes in mining procedures, separate shifts of men performing one function at a time replaced the small teams that had previously done the whole job. This change was followed by an increase in accidents, a decrease in production, and other indications of weakened group morale. Gradually, other means were found to restore the work-group structure. Where this was done, it was observed that accidents declined and production rose. Findings such as these suggest the effectiveness of organizational procedures that facilitate work contacts with congenial co-workers and encourage identification with a work group.

**Job Design.**   The process of job designing includes three phases: identification of individual tasks to be performed; specification of the method for performing each task; and combination of tasks into jobs to be assigned to individual workers. In the effort to reduce operating costs, industrial engineers have relied chiefly on the principle of *specialization* in job design. The objects of specialization are to minimize skill requirements and learning time for each job and to limit the number and variety of tasks to be performed by each worker. At the same time, there has been growing recognition of the adverse effects of such specialization on the worker, notably through the increase in monotony and the loss of a sense of personal achievement. Traditionally, however, industrial psychlogists have accepted the content of each job as fixed by the production process and have tried to improve worker satisfaction through interpersonal relations and other factors extrinsic to the work.

Today there is evidence of a growing interest in modifying job content itself so as to provide greater work satisfaction (14, 31). It might be added that with the increasing automation of industrial processes there is less and less need for human operators to perform routine tasks and more and more need for skilled personnel to carry on the varied and demanding jobs of maintenance, troubleshooting, and equipment development.

Several specific attempts to reverse the trend toward job specialization have proved promising. At a very simple level, *job rotation* may reduce monotony by having each worker perform different operations in a rotated order, rather than performing a single operation all the time. In *group planning*, a team of workers participates in specifying the content of various jobs to be performed by members of the group. This procedure will be recognized as typical of the previously discussed group-dynamics approach. *Job enlargement* tackles the problem more directly by designing the job in such a way that the individual performs a longer sequence and wider variety of operations. He may also be responsible for testing the quality of his work, setting up and maintaining equipment, and carrying out other related functions. And he may have control over the way the job is done.

Some relevant data are provided by an investigation conducted in a company manufacturing a hospital appliance (51). The subjects were 29 unskilled women workers. Performance was compared under four conditions: (*a*) line design, in which a single operation was performed at each work station, production rate was paced by the conveyor line, and workers rotated among work stations every two hours; (*b*) group job design, in which the conveyor was eliminated and the workers set their own pace, but the job was otherwise unchanged; (*c*) individual job design No. 1, in which each worker performed all operations at her own station, controlled the sequence of assembly, procured supplies, and inspected her own product; and (*d*) individual job design

No. 2, in which the procedure was the same as in individual job design No. 1, but the workers were back in the main production area—in parts *b* and *c,* the workers had been in an adjacent room.

The principal effect of these changes in job design was an improvement in quality of work. This can be seen in Figure 43, showing the percentage of defective assemblies in successive lots under the four job conditions. Both of the two individual job designs yielded significantly fewer defective assemblies than did the original line job design. Quantity of output dropped at first, when conveyor pacing was eliminated, but after a few days of practice under conditions of individual job design, it rose to the line job level. It is interesting to note, too, that with individual job design individual differences in rate of work increased markedly, the better workers producing 30 to 40 per cent more than under line design. Workers' attitudes were also found to be more favorable with individual job design, in which each individual was personally responsible for quality and quantity of production.

These findings appear promising and are in line with the results of other studies on job enlargement (77, 79). In this particular experiment, however, one wonders to what extent a Hawthorne effect may have operated. It would have been desirable, for example, to observe the performance of the same workers during a fifth period in which they returned to a line job design.

In their previously cited study on employee attitudes, Herzberg and his associates (31) emphasized the importance of structuring jobs so as to give the individual more control over the way he does his work and hence a stronger sense of personal achievement. Other spokesmen for the individual have urged—in their various ways—that he be protected against organizational pressures for conformity, against the anonymity and depersonalization of the assembly line, and even against an exaggerated emphasis on teamwork and group thinking. Undoubtedly many persons can function effectively and happily on

**Fig. 43** Relation of job design to quality of production. (*Adapted from Marks, 51, p. 87.*)

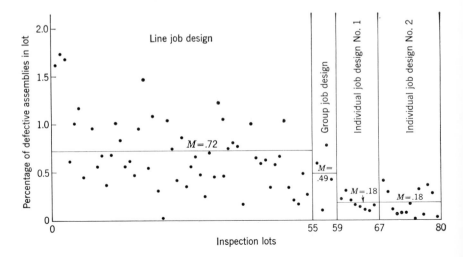

the job as members of a closely knit team. But others function better as individual contributors.

Is the individual to be rescued from the anonymity of the assembly line only to be plunged into the more intimate anonymity of the team? It need not be so. Job designing can be sufficiently comprehensive in its approach to encompass individual differences with respect to teamwork too. Some jobs can be performed better by a team, others by an individual. Some phases of the same job can be handled more effectively on a group basis, others on an individual basis. Some kinds of decisions can be made more judiciously by groups, others by individuals. Job designing should capitalize on these differences, not obliterate them. And personnel selection should take this aspect of jobs into account in matching persons with jobs.

## SUMMARY

The current concern with human relations in industrial management dates from the classic Hawthorne Studies, which focused attention upon the relation of job performance to employee attitudes and morale. These studies also highlighted the importance of controlling attitudinal factors in the design of psychological experiments.

The principal procedures used in gathering data on employee motivation, attitudes, and morale include interviews, opinion questionnaires, attitude scales, projective and other indirect techniques, observational methods, and nominating techniques. Among the factors making for job satisfaction, workers generally rate security, opportunities for advancement, interest in the work, feeling of pride in the company, and relations with co-workers and supervisors as high as pay or higher. The relative weight given to these factors, however, varies somewhat with the age, sex, and education of the workers, as well as with type of work and job level. Favorable employee attitudes are associated with a lower accident rate and with less absenteeism, tardiness, and job turnover. The relation between attitudes and productivity, however, is more complex and depends upon other individual and situational variables. There is also some evidence to suggest that favorable job attitudes more often arise from characteristics of the work itself, while unfavorable job attitudes more often arise from the job context, and that the former bear a more direct relation to productivity than do the latter.

The attitudes and morale of any group are deeply influenced by the supervisory practices, communication system, and organizational structure under which it operates. Research on supervisory and leadership behavior has identified the independent factors of Consideration and Initiating Structure, both of which are related to employee attitudes and productivity.

Industrial communication takes many forms. It may be written or oral, formal or informal, individual or group, factual or attitudinal. It may flow upward, downward, or horizontally. Research has been concerned with such problems as the relative merits of different media; legibility, content, and readability of written communications; the development of communication skills; factors influencing the persuasiveness of communication; sources of communication barriers and breakdowns; and the nature and effectiveness of communication networks.

Organizational structures have been analyzed from many points of view, and this diversity is reflected in the proposals for improving organizational effectiveness. Although controlled experiments pertaining to organizational theory are few, some research is available on the effectiveness of such organizational practices as employee participation in decision making, sociometric work-group assignments, and the redesign of jobs with reference to attitudinal factors. While all these approaches are promising, it must be borne in mind that there is no single organizational formula, management procedure, or supervisory practice that fits all jobs and all individuals.

# REFERENCES

1. Ash, P. The SRA Employee Inventory: A statistical analysis. *Personnel Psychol.,* 1954, **7**, 337–364.
2. Bavelas, A., and Barrett, D. An experimental approach to organizational communication. *Personnel,* 1951, **27**, 367–371.
3. Blum, M. L. *Industrial psychology and its social foundations.* (Rev. ed.) New York: Harper & Row, 1956.
4. Brayfield, A. H., and Crockett, W. H. Employee attitudes and employee performance. *Psychol. Bull.,* 1955, **52**, 396–424.
5. Brayfield, A. H., and Rothe, H. F. An index of job satisfaction. *J. appl. Psychol.,* 1951, **35**, 307–311.
6. Carlucci, C., and Crissy, W. J. E. How readable are employee handbooks? *Personnel Psychol.,* 1951, **4**, 383–395.
7. Cartwright, D. The potential contribution of graph theory to organization theory. In M. Haire (Ed.), *Modern organization theory.* New York: Wiley, 1959. Ch. 9.
8. Centers, R. Motivational aspects of occupational stratification. *J. soc. Psychol.,* 1948, **28**, 187–217.
9. Coch, L., and French, J. R. P., Jr. Overcoming resistance to change. *Hum. Relat.,* 1948, **1**, 512–532.
10. Cureton, E. E., and Katzell, R. A. A further analysis of the relations among job performance and situational variables. *J. appl. Psychol.,* 1962, **46**, 230.
11. Dahle, T. L. Transmitting information to employees: A study of five methods. *Personnel,* 1954, **31**, 243–246.
12. Darley, J. G., and Hagenah, Theda. *Vocational interest measurement: Theory and practice.* Minneapolis: Univer. Minn. Press, 1955.
13. Davis, K. A method of studying communication patterns in organizations. *Personnel Psychol.,* 1953, **6**, 301–312.
14. Davis, L. E. Job design and productivity: A new approach. *Personnel,* 1957, **33**, 418–430.
15. Dearborn, D. C., and Simon, H. A. Selective perception: A note on the departmental identifications of executives. *Sociometry,* 1958, **21**, 140–144.
16. Evans, C. E., and Laseau, L. N. My Job Contest—an experiment in new employee relations methods. Parts I—IV. *Personnel Psychol.,* 1949, **2**, 1–16; 185–227; 311–367; 461–474. (Also publ. as *Personnel Monogr. Ser.,* No. 1, 1950.)
17. Fleishman, E. A. The description of supervisory behavior. *J. appl. Psychol.,* 1953, **37**, 1–6.
18. Fleishman, E. A. (Ed.) *Studies in personnel and industrial psychology.* Homewood, Ill.: Dorsey, 1961.
19. Fleishman, E. A., and Harris, E. F. Patterns of leadership behavior related to employee grievances and turnover. *Personnel Psychol.,* 1962, **15**, 43–56.
20. Fleishman, E. A., Harris, E. F., and Burtt, H. E. *Leadership and supervision in industry.* Columbus, Ohio: Ohio State Univer., Bur. Educ. Res., 1955.
21. Foley, J. P., Jr., and Anastasi, Anne. *"Human relations" and the foreman.* New London, Conn.: Nat. Foremen's Inst., 1951.
22. French, J. R. P., Jr., *et al.* Employee participation in a program of industrial change. *Personnel,* 1958, **35**, 16–29.
23. Haire, M. Biological models and empirical histories of the growth of organiza-

tions. In M. Haire (Ed.), *Modern organization theory.* New York: Wiley, 1959. Ch. 10.

24. Haire, M. Psychological problems relevant to business and industry. *Psychol. Bull.*, 1959, **56**, 169–194.
25. Haire, M. (Ed.) *Modern organization theory.* New York: Wiley, 1959.
26. Haire, M., and Gottsdanker, Josephine S. Factors influencing industrial morale. *Personnel*, 1951, **27**, 445–454.
27. Haney, W. V. *Communication patterns and incidents.* Homewood, Ill.: Irwin, 1960.
28. Hemphill, J. K., and Westie, C. M. The measurement of group dimensions. *J. Psychol.*, 1950, **29**, 325–342.
29. Hersey, R. B. *Better foremanship.* Philadelphia: Clinton, 1955.
30. Herzberg, F., Mausner, B., Peterson, R. O., and Capwell, Dora F. *Job attitudes; review of research and opinion.* Pittsburgh: Psychol. Serv. Pittsburgh, 1957.
31. Herzberg, F., Mausner, B., and Snyderman, Barbara B. *The motivation to work.* (2nd ed.) New York: Wiley, 1959.
32. Hoslett, S. D. Barriers to communication. *Personnel*, 1951, **28**, 108–114.
33. Hovland, C. I., *et al. Communication and persuasion.* New Haven, Conn.: Yale Univer. Press, 1953.
34. Hovland, C. I., *et al. The order of presentation in persuasion.* (Yale studies in attitude and communication, vol. 1.) New Haven, Conn.: Yale Univer. Press, 1957.
35. Janis, I. L., Hovland, C. I., *et al. Personality and persuasibility.* (Yale studies in attitude and communication, vol. 2.) New Haven, Conn.: Yale Univer. Press, 1959.
36. Jourard, S. M. *Personal adjustment: An approach through the study of healthy personality.* (Rev. ed.) New York: Macmillan, 1963.
37. Jurgensen, C. E. What do job applicants want? *Personnel*, 1949, **25**, 352–355.
38. Kahn, R. L., and Katz, D. Leadership practices in relation to productivity and morale. In D. Cartwright and A. Zander (Eds.), *Group dynamics.* New York: Harper & Row, 1953. Pp. 612–628.
39. Katz, D., Maccoby, N., Gurin, G., and Floor, L. G. *Productivity, supervision and morale among railroad workers.* Ann Arbor, Mich.: Inst. Soc. Res., 1951.
40. Katz, D., Maccoby, N., and Morse, Nancy. *Productivity, supervision and morale in an office situation.* Ann Arbor, Mich.: Inst. Soc. Res., 1950.
41. Katzell, R. A., Barrett, R. S., and Parker, T. C. Job satisfaction, job performance, and situational characteristics. *J. appl. Psychol.*, 1961, **45**, 65–72.
42. Lauer, Jeanne, and Paterson, D. G. Readability of union contracts. *Personnel*, 1951, **28**, 36–40.
43. Lawshe, C. H., and Chandler, R. E. How to get going with a reading improvement program. *Personnel*, 1955, **34**, 15–19.
44. Leavitt, H. J. Some effects of certain communication patterns on group performance. *J. abnorm. soc. Psychol.*, 1951, **46**, 38–50.
45. Leavitt, H. J. *Managerial psychology: An introduction to individuals, pairs, and groups in organizations.* Chicago: Univer. Chicago Press, 1958.
46. Likert, R. Effective supervision: An adaptive and relative process. *Personnel Psychol.*, 1958, **11**, 317–332.
47. Likert, R. *New patterns of management.* New York: McGraw-Hill, 1961.
48. McGregor, D. *The human side of enterprise.* New York: McGraw-Hill, 1960.
49. Maier, N. R. F. *Principles of human relations.* New York: Wiley, 1952.
50. Mann, F. C., and Baumgartel, H. J. *Absences and employee attitudes in an electric power company.* Ann Arbor, Mich.: Inst. Soc. Res., 1953.
51. Marks, A. R. An investigation of modifications of job design in an industrial situation and their effects on some measures of economic productivity. Unpublished doctoral dissertation, Univer. Calif., Berkeley, Calif., 1954.
52. Maslow, A. H. A theory of motivation. *Psychol. Rev.*, 1943, **50**, 370–396.
53. Maslow, A. H. *Motivation and personality.* New York: Harper & Row, 1954.
54. Mayo, E. *The human problems of an industrial civilization.* New York: Macmillan, 1933.
55. Paterson, D. G., and Tinker, M. A. *How to make type readable.* New York: Harper & Row, 1940.
56. Pelz, D. C. Influence: A key to effective leadership in the first-line supervisor *Personnel*, 1952, **29**, 209–217.

57. Roethlisberger, F. J., and Dickson, W. J. *Management and the worker.* Cambridge, Mass.: Harvard Univer. Press, 1939.
58. Rogers, C. R., and Roethlisberger, F. J. Barriers and gateways to communication. *Harvard Bus. Rev.,* 1952, **30** (4), 46–52.
59. Rosenberg, M. J., Hovland, C. I., *et al. Attitude organization and change.* (Yale studies in attitude and communication, vol. 3.) New Haven, Conn.: Yale Univer. Press, 1960.
60. Ross, I. C., and Zander, A. F. Need satisfactions and employee turnover. *Personnel Psychol.,* 1957, **10**, 327–338.
61. Rothe, H. F. Does higher pay bring higher productivity? *Personnel,* 1960, **37**, 20–27.
62. Sexton, R., and Staudt, Virginia. Business communication: A survey of the literature. *J. soc. Psychol.,* 1959, **50**, 101–118.
63. Sexton, R., and Staudt, Virginia. The communication clinic: A proposed solution to the business communication problem. *J. gen. Psychol.,* 1959, **60**, 57–62.
64. Shartle, C. L. *Executive performance and leadership.* Englewood Cliffs, N.J.: Prentice-Hall, 1956.
65. Shaw, M. E. Some effects of unequal distribution of information upon group performance in various communication nets. *J. abnorm. soc. Psychol.,* 1954, **49**, 547–553.
66. Stodgill, R. M. The sociometry of working relationships in formal organizations. *Sociometry,* 1949, **12**, 276–286.
67. Stodgill, R. M., and Coons, A. E. *Leader behavior: Its description and measurement.* Columbus, Ohio: Ohio State Univer., Bur Bus. Res., 1957.
68. Tannenbaum, R., and Schmidt, W. H. How to choose a leadership pattern. *Harvard Bus. Rev.,* 1958, **36** (2), 95–101.
69. Tannenbaum, R., Weschler, I. R., and Massarik, F. *Leadership and organization.* New York: McGraw-Hill, 1961.
70. Tiffin, J., and Walsh, F. X. Readability of union-management agreements. *Personnel Psychol.,* 1951, **4**, 327–337.
71. Trist, E. L., and Bamforth, V. Some social and psychological consequences of the longwall method of coal-getting. *Hum. Relat.,* 1951, **4**, 3–38.
72. Trow, D. B. Autonomy and job satisfaction in task-oriented groups. *J. abnorm. soc. Psychol.,* 1957, **54**, 204–209.
73. Uhrbrock, R. S. Attitudes of 4430 employees. *J. soc. Psychol.,* 1934, **5**, 365–377.
74. Van Zelst, R. H. Sociometrically selected work teams increase production. *Personnel Psychol.,* 1952, **5**, 175–185.
75. Viteles, M. S. *Motivation and morale in industry.* New York: Norton, 1953.
76. Vroom, V. H., and Maier, N. R. F. Industrial social psychology. *Ann. Rev. Psychol.,* 1961, **12**, 413–446.
77. Walker, C. R. The problem of the repetitive job. *Harvard Bus. Rev.,* 1950, **28** (3), 54–58.
78. Walker, C. R., and Guest, R. H. *The man on the assembly line.* Cambridge, Mass.: Harvard Univer. Press, 1952.
79. Worthy, J. R. Factors influencing employee morale. *Harvard Bus. Rev.,* 1950, **28** (1), 61–73.

# III

*Engineering Psychology*

# 7

# *Work Methods*

In a broad sense, engineering psychology utilizes knowledge of human behavior in the development of effective working procedures and equipment. The three chapters dealing with this topic will consider in turn *how* the work is done, *where* it is done, and *with what*. The present chapter, concerned with work methods, will begin with an examination of the nature of work and fatigue and the problem of monotony in industrial work. We shall then inquire into work schedules, or the distribution of work in time. This will be followed by a discussion of time-and-motion study and of the more comprehensive approach represented by methods improvement. Finally, we shall discuss accident prevention and industrial safety as one aspect of methods improvement, as well as in their broader research implications.

The second chapter in this section is concerned with the working environment. In it will be considered the effects of such factors as illumination, ventilation, and noise. The third chapter deals with the design and arrangement of equipment and with the more inclusive problem of developing effective man-machine systems.

## WORK AND FATIGUE

The principles of efficient work apply to any situation involving human performance. Although usually associated with industrial work, they are equally relevant to activities performed in offices, classrooms, homes, or military situations. Basically, the concept of efficiency refers to the ratio of output to input. A machine that requires 50 units of power to produce 10 units of work is more efficient than one requiring 70 units of power to produce the same 10 units of work. When the concept is extended to human work, many more factors need to be considered, both on the input and on the output side. Thus, in addition to the time required to perform a job, we must take into account the worker's energy expenditure, his feelings of strain and effort, and the emotional costs of persistent worries, disagreeable obligations, or unpleasant interpersonal contacts. Similarly, a long-range comprehensive measure of output would include not only immediate quantity of production but also quality of original contributions and other creative achievements, errors and wastage, accidents, absenteeism, turnover, grievances, labor unrest and strife, physical and mental health of workers, and many other indirect or remote consequences of job performance.

It is customary to portray changes in output in the course of work by means of a work curve. This curve usually shows quantity of production, but it may also be plotted in terms of errors or other measures of performance. Figure 44 illustrates some of the concepts commonly used in describing work curves.

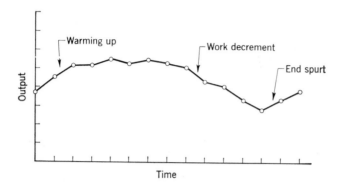

**Fig. 44**  A hypothetical work curve, illustrating concepts used to describe performance changes.

These include the initial "warming up" before peak productivity is reached, the eventual work decrement presumably indicating the onset of fatigue, and a possible "end spurt" as the end of the work period is anticipated. Random, momentary fluctuations are also characteristic of work curves. Not all the features shown in Figure 44, of course, need be found in any individual work curve.

A major goal of human efficiency is the reduction of fatigue. Everyone "knows" what fatigue is, but definitions of it reveal widespread confusion (see 7, 8). Sometimes the term is used to refer to feelings of tiredness, sometimes to a reduction in output, and sometimes to the physiological conditions resulting from continued activity. It might be argued that these three classes of phenomena are just different manifestations of the same general state of the organism. But the difficulty is that they often disagree. Pronounced feelings of tiredness may be accompanied by no drop in output; output may decline in the absence of corresponding physiological changes; and output and feelings may remain unchanged for some time after the physiological onset of fatigue.

Feelings of fatigue, moreover, may take many forms, depending upon the type of activity that evoked them. They may range from muscular soreness, localized stiffness, and aches to sleepiness, mental confusion, muscular tensions, and general weariness (74). Sometimes such feelings are difficult to distinguish from sheer boredom and loss of interest. The decline in output, too, may take different forms, such as decrease in speed of performance, deterioration of quality, loss in originality, increase in errors and spoilage, rise in accident frequency, and greater variability of performance. Several of these output changes may occur together, of course. But, under certain circumstances, output may continue unchanged in some respects while showing marked deterioration in others.

It should likewise be noted that feelings of tiredness as well as output indices of fatigue are highly specific to the task. Transfer of fatigue to other tasks declines rapidly as task similarity decreases (9, 10). Even with very similar tasks, a sharp drop in output from continued performance of the one task is unlikely to produce an equally pronounced drop in the other. Change of activity, even though slight, will usually decrease the effects of fatigue.

In the light of much that was said in the preceding chapter, it should be apparent that both feelings of fatigue and output decrement depend in part upon motivation and attitude. Everyone has undoubtedly had the experience of tiring quickly when performing a job he disliked but working for long stretches with no noticeable change in output or feelings at something that fired his enthusiasm. It is partly for this reason that many investigators have turned to physiological indices of fatigue. Among the measures used for this purpose are heart rate, blood pressure, oxygen consumption, blood composition, and electrical resistance of the skin. The increase in oxygen consumption occurring during continuous work is the basis of the *respiration calorimeter* used in many early studies of work methods. This technique requires the subject to wear a breathing mask and a bag to collect the expired air. Chemical analyses of samples of such air show the amount of oxygen consumed, which can be readily translated into calories of heat production (75).

Another index that has been investigated quite extensively is the *heart-rate recovery curve* (16). The more strenuous the work, the longer the time required for the heart rate to return to a normal level. Figure 45 illustrates the difference in heart recovery rate following performance of a heavy manual job before and after it had been partially mechanized. The difference in physiological cost to the worker is evident in this graph.

For many years psychologists have been trying to find behavioral indices of the onset of fatigue that would not be susceptible to the many extraneous variables affecting output. Performance on tests that are relatively neutral with regard to motivational factors and that are not a part of the task at which the

**Fig. 45**   Heart-rate recovery curves for a heavy manual job before and after partial mechanization. (*From Brouha, 16, p. 15.*)

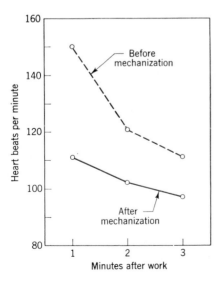

individual has been working should provide a fairly "pure" index of behavioral impairment. It has generally been found, however, that short tests of any sort revealed little or no performance loss. Even when very tired, a person can usually muster his resources sufficiently to give a normal momentary performance.

Among the most promising behavioral indices of fatigue are tests of *vigilance,* which call for continued alertness (37, 65). Typically in such tests the individual must respond to irregularly appearing signals. Although he is required to react only to very infrequent stimuli, he must watch for them over long periods. Fatigue is manifested chiefly in an increase in variability of performance. By this method it was shown, for instance, that, after a 4- to 6-hour flight, most experienced pilots show no appreciable fatigue but, after an 8- to 10-hour flight, there is significant evidence of fatigue (37). Suggestive differences were also found in the fatigue effects of flying jet as compared with piston-engined aircraft and in the effects of day and night flights. This research indicated that continued work may affect high-grade performance, which requires precise timing and coordination of various activities, *before* the appearance of any physiological signs of fatigue. The behavioral signs of fatigue, furthermore, may be too slight to be manifested in gross output measures. They may show up only in an occasional slip, a brief confusion of similar signals, or a slight interruption of the smooth rhythm of a skilled performance. These minor lapses, however, may have serious consequences in certain tasks, such as piloting a high-speed airplane.

From all the research that has been conducted on fatigue, one point emerges clearly: Fatigue is not one but many things, and each should be investigated in its own right. Different indices, whether they be introspective reports, physiological changes, output measures, or special behavioral tests, all have their place and should be chosen with reference to the specific problem under investigation.

A frequent question pertains to the nature of "mental fatigue," such as might result from solving mathematical problems or reading a difficult textbook. First it should be noted that the physiological effects of intellectual activity are very slight but of the same kind as those following physical work (see 8). It is likely that these slight changes are the result of the muscular responses that always accompany even the most "purely intellectual" work. For example, there are contractions of the eye muscles in reading; subvocal contractions of speech muscles during silent thought; postural reactions in the head and neck, as well as in the rest of the body; hand and arm movements in writing; and various muscular tensions from such tangential acts as gripping the pencil hard, setting the jaw, and frowning while trying to concentrate. Measures of muscle-action potentials taken while children or adults solve arithmetic problems without the use of paper and pencil show evidence of muscle activity which increases as the difficulty of the problems increases (22, 43, 78).

Among the other components of what is commonly called mental fatigue are general feelings of strain and effort. Boredom, drowsiness, and sleepiness are often included. Emotional reactions to frustration and conflict may also be an integral part of the experience. Frustration may arise from failure to solve a problem, indecision, inability to comprehend a difficult idea, and other stressful experiences accompanying mental work.

## MONOTONY AND BOREDOM

In the preceding discussion of fatigue, frequent reference was made to monotony and boredom. These feelings are difficult to differentiate from fatigue, although they can be distinguished under certain circumstances. Thus an individual may become appreciably tired from a long spell of interesting and absorbing work which he at no time found boring. Or he may find a light, repetitive task highly boring but not feel tired from it. Nevertheless, boredom and fatigue are frequently associated. In a monotonous task we generally find greater output decrement and more energy expenditure than in a varied and absorbing task. Like feelings of fatigue, boredom is an unpleasant experience, often characterized by difficulty in keeping attention fixed on the task at hand. Part of the unpleasant emotional tone comes from a conflict between wanting to turn away to more attractive activities and realizing that one must continue with the dull task.

Variability of performance has been found to be associated with the experience of boredom. In one of the early investigations of monotony conducted by British psychologists for the Industrial Fatigue Research Board, output showed wider fluctuation for workers who reported they were bored than for those performing the same operations but reporting that they were not bored (93). This difference was observed both in the work curves of individual workers and in the standard deviations computed for individual productivity during short time units, such as 10-minute intervals throughout the day. Such variability, which is also characteristic of fatigue in general, may result from lapses of attention. It may also arise from a feedback process. As the worker becomes aware that production is dropping off, he may put forth more effort and thereby raise output until the next letdown starts another cycle.

The research conducted by the Industrial Fatigue Research Board also suggested that monotony produces a U-shaped work curve, with a production drop in the center of the total work period and an "end spurt" (see Figure 44) occurring as the period draws to a close (93, 94). It is reasonable to expect end spurts to be more common when output drops because of boredom than when it drops because of physical exhaustion. Nevertheless, it cannot be assumed that all monotonous work will produce a characteristic U-shaped curve, nor that all such curves indicate the presence of boredom. Many other factors affect the rate of production. Workers reporting severe feelings of boredom may show no appreciable output trend throughout the day. And the work curves of those who are bored may be indistinguishable from the work curves of those who are not (79).

In industrial work, voluntary pacing of output during the day supersedes other factors that might influence the shape of the work curve. Not only is restriction of output for fear of rate cutting quite prevalent, but also, when no such fear exists, workers tend to form a concept of a proper day's work and adjust their pace accordingly as the end of the day approaches. The findings of the early British studies regarding monotony curves in industrial work, which have been widely quoted, are questionable owing to failure to control certain conditions and other methodological difficulties (see 79).

There is some evidence to suggest that the effects of monotony may be greatest for tasks requiring an intermediate degree of attention (76, 93). With completely routine tasks demanding a minimum of attention, the individual is free to engage in reverie or, if the situation permits it, to talk with his co-workers. At the other extreme, a complex and varied task tends to hold the attention because of its intrinsic features. It is the semiautomatic task, requiring constant attention but providing little intrinsic interest, that is likely to produce the greatest strain. When performing such a task, the worker must repeatedly resist the tendency to attend to other stimuli or to pursue other thoughts that have greater pulling power than the work at hand.

It is apparent too that monotony cannot be understood solely in terms of task characteristics. The identical task may be boring in one set of circumstances and not boring in another. Monotony depends upon the relation of task, surroundings, and individual. Other things being equal, of course, the more uniform and repetitive the task, the more monotonous it will be. In an intensive interview study of assembly-line operators in an automobile factory, the percentage of men who reported their work to be boring was 67 for those engaged in single-operation jobs, 56 for those whose jobs involved two to four operations, and only 30 for those whose jobs involved five or more operations (90).

Nevertheless, the role of situational and individual variables has been repeatedly demonstrated. Work may become more boring when performed under distracting conditions, because of the strain of fighting off the pull of competing stimuli. The distracting stimuli may be of many sorts, from other people talking or moving about to thoughts about last night's date or tomorrow's holiday. On the other hand, with highly routine types of work, giving the individual an opportunity to converse with his neighbors may reduce monotony. In the next chapter we shall see that under certain circumstances even the introduction of noise may help to reduce monotony. Incentives also affect the degree of boredom experienced on a job, higher motivation tending to reduce monotony.

Individuals differ widely in their susceptibility to monotony when performing the same job. To some, even a highly repetitive job such as packing light bulbs is interesting; to others, a varied and complex job may be boring. Some relevant data, taken from one of the early British studies of industrial workers, are reproduced in Table 12. It will be noted that individuals differ not only in the absolute level of monotony reported but also in the relative monotony of different tasks. For worker C, for example, "staying boxes" is the least mo-

TABLE 12   *Individual Differences in Extent of Boredom Experienced When Performing Five Industrial Tasks*[a]
(*From Wyatt, Langdon, and Stock, 94, p. 15. By permission of the Controller of Her Britannic Majesty's Stationery Office.*)

| Task | Worker | | | | | | | | | |
|------|------|------|------|------|------|------|------|------|------|------|
|  | A | B | C | D | E | F | G | H | I | J |
| Packing (14 lb) | 0.4 | 0.7 | 3.5 | 1.4 | 1.0 | 1.1 | 0.9 | 3.2 | 0.8 | 3.6 |
| Packing (4 lb) | 1.5 | 1.1 | 4.0 | 2.5 | 0.3 | 1.9 | 0.5 | 2.6 | 1.5 | 1.0 |
| Staying boxes | 1.9 | 2.0 | 1.1 | 1.8 | 2.1 | 4.7 | 3.2 | 3.0 | 1.6 | 1.5 |
| Making crackers | 4.0 | 4.8 | 1.8 | 3.7 | 3.4 | 1.0 | 0.3 | 1.2 | 2.0 | 1.9 |
| Bundling chocolates | 4.2 | 4.6 | 4.3 | 4.8 | 3.2 | 4.4 | 4.1 | 4.5 | 3.8 | 4.0 |

[a] Scale extends from 0 to 5; higher ratings indicate more boredom. Each entry is the mean of the ratings assigned to the individual's replies to 13 questions.

notonous of the five tasks; for worker F, it is the most monotonous. Similar discrepancies can be found with regard to the other tasks. As these data suggest, susceptibility to monotony cannot be regarded wholly as a general trait but may exhibit considerable task specificity.

On the other hand, it is likely that some common variance could be identified in individual susceptibility to monotony, especially in a more heterogeneous sample than that employed in the above study. In a sample of workers engaged in routine, repetitive jobs, a certain amount of selection has occurred, since persons highly susceptible to monotony would tend to leave or not to enter such jobs in the first place. It has been suggested, for instance, that more intelligent persons are more likely to find a repetitive task boring. This may be true when a sufficiently wide range of intelligence is considered. Among individuals employed on a particular job, however, most investigators have found no relation between intelligence and reported feelings of boredom (see 80). Within such groups, individual differences in susceptibility to boredom appear to be more closely associated with personality characteristics.

In an investigation of 72 women sewing-machine operators, for instance, susceptibility to monotony was found to be significantly related to certain other indications of discontent and restlessness (80). The workers reporting stronger feelings of boredom more often preferred active leisure activities, disliked regularity of daily routine, and indicated dissatisfaction with their personal and home life as well as their factory life than did those reporting less boredom. The former also tended more often to be under twenty years of age. The investigator describes those less susceptible to boredom as being relatively placid, contented with the existing state of affairs, and possibly rigid in their behavior. This type of investigation needs to be repeated with many different kinds of jobs and a wide variety of workers. It is possible that the personality correlates of susceptibility to monotony differ with the job.

Many remedies have been proposed for monotony in industry. Each undoubtedly has something to contribute in specific situations. The findings on individual differences in susceptibility to monotony suggest the importance of personnel selection and placement, with reference to relevant personality characteristics as well as job aptitudes. The study of sewing-machine operators cited above opens up the possibility of identifying the more susceptible individuals in terms of biographical and interview data.

Changes in the working conditions and working environment may also serve to reduce monotony. The introduction of rest pauses often relieves monotony as well as fatigue. Eliminating distractions in the case of work requiring constant attention reduces conflict and strain. With more automatic jobs demanding little attention, on the other hand, such activities as conversation with co-workers or listening to music often help.

A third approach concentrates on making the work itself more varied or interesting. Grouping repetitive work into broad units tends to give the worker a sense of accomplishment as each unit is completed. Work done in batches is usually less monotonous than work done with a continuous—and endless—succession of items. Films or plant tours showing where the individual's work fits into the total production picture or giving information about uses and characteristics of the product are also sometimes employed to increase interest. Finally, job rotation and job enlargement, discussed in the preceding chapter, represent more basic attacks on the problem of industrial monotony.

## WORK SCHEDULES

Among the many conditions affecting efficiency of work is the distribution of working time. Several questions can be asked in this connection. What is the effect of introducing rest pauses during the work period, and what is the best way to distribute and utilize these rest pauses? How is productivity related to total length of workday and work week? Does the time of day when work is done affect output?

**Rest Pauses.** Investigations conducted in industry have quite consistently demonstrated an increase in output following the introduction of regularly scheduled rest pauses. In the early studies of the Industrial Fatigue Research Board, relevant data were gathered on many kinds of industrial operations ranging from light to heavy work (61, 89). The results showed a rise in average daily output, even though the employees spent less time working after the introduction of scheduled rest pauses. For example, in a group of women assembling bicycle chains, the introduction of a 5-minute rest at the end of each hour reduced total working time by 7 per cent while increasing average output by 13 per cent (89). Among the factors leading to such gains in productivity are an increase in rate of work, reduction in errors, decrease in unauthorized rest pauses, and improved employee attitudes.

An investigation of a group of women comptometer operators in a United States government office provided systematic data on performance before and after the introduction of authorized rest periods (64). The rest schedule consisted of an 8-minute pause in the morning and a 7-minute pause in the afternoon. Owing to government regulations, the working day had to be lengthened by 15 minutes to make up for the time spent in scheduled rest periods. Thus, in this study, total working time remained unchanged. Records kept during two-week observation periods showed a significant decrease in time spent in unauthorized rest pauses and a significant rise in output following the introduction of the scheduled rest pauses.

The superiority of scheduled over unscheduled rest pauses probably results in part from better placement within the work period. For maximum effectiveness, rest pauses should usually be introduced just before output begins to drop appreciably. If introduced too late, the rest period may be insufficient to overcome the accumulated fatigue. If introduced too soon, on the other hand, the rest may simply interrupt performance at its peak of efficiency. Following such a rest period, the worker must go through another warming-up period (see Figure 44) before he again attains his previous efficiency level.

The optimum distribution of rest pauses, as well as their individual duration, varies with the nature of the work and with the skill and experience of the worker. Heavy work or tasks demanding close concentration generally require more rest than lighter or more automatic work. Similarly the novice, who may be using less efficient procedures, tends to become fatigued more readily than does the skilled performer. The former may therefore require more frequent rest pauses than the latter. The optimal distribution of work and rest should be established by empirical tryouts in the particular situation. Daily output curves and data on the frequency of errors and accidents at different hours, as well as interviews with workers, help to determine the effective placement of rest pauses. With regard to method of using the rest periods, change of posture, as well as change of activity in general, is most beneficial. Refreshments and conversation with fellow workers improve attitude and relieve monotony, even if they serve no other functions.

It should be noted that the improvement resulting from the introduction of scheduled rest pauses may not be immediately evident. In the previously cited study of bicycle-chain assemblers, for example, it was not until the new schedule had been in effect for six months that output manifested its full improvement (89). Similar delays have been observed in other industrial studies. It may require several months for the previously established work habits and pacing of performance to respond to improved working conditions of any sort. Such findings suggest the need for continued observations in industrial research. Conclusions based on short-range follow-ups may be misleading.

When any change is made in working conditions, moreover, it is important to take into consideration its possible effects on employee attitudes. The Hawthorne Studies discussed in Chapter 6 bear witness to this fact. On the one hand, the introduction of rest pauses without adequate communication regarding the purpose of the change and without employee participation in planning it may arouse suspicion and antagonism. The result may be a decline rather than a rise in output. On the other hand, rest pauses that are welcomed by the employees may lead to better job performance only because the employees feel that management is taking an interest in their welfare. Under such conditions, a rise in output cannot be attributed to rest pauses as such, since any other expression of interest might have served equally well. It is undoubtedly true that a judicious distribution of work and rest will improve working efficiency for anyone, in any situation. But, in industrial studies, it is often difficult to isolate the effect of this factor because of the operation of other uncontrollable variables.

**Length of Work Week.** Lengthening or shortening the workday and work week also affects productivity. A survey of about thirty-five hundred men and women workers in 34 industrial plants in the United States showed maximal efficiency with an 8-hour day and a 40-hour week (54). With longer hours, output rate declined and absenteeism and accident rate increased.

During periods of national emergency, as in World Wars I and II, unusually long work weeks were instituted in some plants to meet critical shortages. It thus became possible to study the effect of major changes in work periods on job performance. A series of studies conducted during World War I by the Industrial Fatigue Research Board of Great Britain represents a particularly rich source of data on this question. The most striking finding of this research was that, beyond certain limits, total output was less the longer the work week. As this fact was recognized and the work week was again shortened, output rose. In one large munitions plant, for example, shortening the work week from 66 to 47.5 hours increased *total* weekly output by 13 per cent (87).

Part of the explanation for these results is to be found in a comparison of the nominal with the actual number of hours worked. With longer work weeks, much more time is lost through absenteeism, tardiness, and unauthorized rest pauses. The rate of work is also slower during longer work periods; and it takes longer to reach the production peak at the beginning of the day. The tendency for workers to adjust their effort automatically to length of work period has been observed in laboratory experiments as well as in industrial investigations. It is a natural tendency to conserve one's energy in various ways as one faces the prospect of a long period of activity and to increase one's energy expenditure when a short period of activity is anticipated.

There may be considerable lag in the effects of a shortened work week, just as there is after the introduction of rest pauses. In the previously cited study of munitions workers, two reductions in average number of working hours occurred, the first from 66 to 54.4 and the second from 54.4 to 47.5. On each occasion, no change in output was evident for a month. At that time, output began to improve gradually, but did not reach its maximal level until four or five months after the reduction of hours. In other similar follow-ups, the lag in effect varied from 3 weeks to over a year, being longer for the heavier work (88).

It should not be assumed that the beneficial effects of shortening the work period continue indefinitely. Beyond a certain limit, further reduction may result in wasted effort. Thus with shorter periods a greater proportion of the total working time is spent in warming up to peak daily production. Similarly, a larger proportion of time is needed for preparatory and terminal activities, such as obtaining supplies and adjusting equipment at the beginning of the day or cleaning up and putting away tools at the end of the day. Since these activities require the same amount of time regardless of length of work period, they occupy a greater proportion of time in the shorter work periods. The optimum length undoubtedly varies with the nature of the work and with situational and personal conditions. Little systematic research has been done on this question since the early studies of the Industrial Fatigue Research Board.

**Shift Work.**   The nature of many functions performed both in the military services and in modern industry has created an increasing need for round-the-clock, seven-days-a-week operation. The demand for shift workers is thus steadily expanding. Shift work must be evaluated not only in terms of productivity but also in terms of its long-range effects upon the worker's health and well-being. The problem is twofold, involving, first, the relative effectiveness of day and night work and, second, the effect of adapting to periodic changes in work cycle.

By following socially established schedules of work, recreation, meals, and sleep, man has developed a daily rhythm in physiological activities as well as in efficiency of work (see 52, 53). Body temperature, for example, reaches a low point between 2 and 5 A.M. and a high point in mid-afternoon. Similar cycles have been observed in blood pressure, pulse rate, chemical composition of the blood, activity of endocrine glands, and other physiological functions. With regard to behavioral indices, corresponding cycles have been found in laboratory studies using tests of sensory, motor, and intellectual functions, as well as in investigations of the output of industrial workers (see 12). It should be noted that by altering living schedules all these cycles can be shifted forward or backward by several hours or completely reversed with regard to day and night. It is more difficult, however, to lengthen or shorten the basic 24-hour cycle, at least in some physiological processes, even when subjects live under experimentally controlled conditions (52, 58).

Vernon (88) surveyed the output of shift workers performing a wide variety of jobs in British munitions plants during World War I. Among workers on a rotating shift, with rotation periods ranging from a week to a month, average hourly output was approximately the same on day and night shifts. It is likely that the disruption of daily cycles resulting from changing shifts affected both the day and night performance of these workers. When continuous night work was compared with continuous day work in different groups, the night workers averaged 8 per cent lower in output than the day workers.

In a survey of more recent investigations conducted in several countries, Bloom (12) notes a number of difficulties encountered by shift workers. With regard to night work as such, the most common problem is inability to get enough sleep in the daytime. In a military setting, this may be less serious than in a civilian community, because there is no conflict with the living habits of family and friends. In all situations, however, daytime noise, light, and heat tend to interfere with sleep.

Even more disturbing, however, is adaptation to changing cycles. Studies of workers on rotating shifts report high frequency of errors, high accident rate, disturbances in eating and sleeping, and adverse effects on general health. In one survey, gastric ulcers were eight times as common among shift workers as among day workers (see 12). Because of these adaptive difficulties, Bloom proposes that fixed shifts may be preferable to rotating shifts. If rotation is unavoidable, the periods between shift changes should be long enough to permit adaptation. Workers should also have several days off between changes. It has been noted, for instance, that a flight across the Atlantic, with its five-hour change in daily schedule, requires about a week for complete adjustment. More extensive changes, as from day to night shifts, may require longer adjustment periods. Much more research is needed, however, to determine the effects of different shift systems and the course of adaptation to shift changes. Insofar as there seem to be individual differences in adaptability to change in daily cycles, selection of personnel for shift work should take such differences into account.

## TIME-AND-MOTION STUDY

*Contributions of Taylor and Gilbreth.* In 1881 Frederick W. Taylor (21; 67, pp. 67–113; 83), a mechanical engineer, began his observations of steelworkers which led to the development of *time study*. His aim was to increase productivity by improving the performance of the workers. This approach represented a radical departure from engineering practices prevailing at the time, since it shifted attention from the machines to the worker. Even in the simplest unskilled operation, Taylor argued, the way in which the worker carries out the job can make a big difference in productivity. Time study was essentially a process of analyzing an operation into its component parts and noting the time required by the best workers to perform each part. Although Taylor defined time study to include the elimination of useless movements and the selection of the best way to perform each of the remaining movements (21, vol. 1, p. 227), little was done along these lines prior to the work of Gilbreth, to be discussed below. Taylor himself concentrated on establishing optimal times for different operations and setting pay rates in accordance with such times.

Taylor was also a strong advocate of the selection and training of workers and of the introduction of rest pauses. In a widely quoted demonstration, he increased the output of a pig-iron handler from 12½ to 47½ tons per day. This increase was effected by instituting a schedule of rest pauses that required the

worker to spend 58 per cent of the working day at rest (83, p. 60). The interpretation of these findings, however, is complicated by the influence of motivational factors, since the worker was also offered a higher rate of pay for
meeting the prescribed production standard.

Taylor's time-study procedures were incorporated into the more elaborate
and refined techniques of *motion study* developed by Frank B. Gilbreth (39–
41; 67, pp. 245–291). Like Taylor, Gilbreth was an engineer; his wife, who
collaborated in much of his work, is a psychologist.[1] Gilbreth's observations of
many kinds of workers convinced him of the prevalence of wasted effort.
When left to their own resources, he noted, most workers use many unnecessary and inefficient movements. It was chiefly through the elimination of unnecessary movements that Gilbreth believed output could be increased and
fatigue decreased at the same time. In one of his most famous investigations,
he was able to reduce the number of separate movements required in bricklaying from 18 to 5. He thereby increased the average number of bricks that
could be laid in an hour from 120 to 350.

In motion study, movements are broken down into much smaller elements
than was done in the earlier time study of Taylor. In mapping out the path of
motion followed by the hand of the operator, Gilbreth utilized many special
observational aids, such as photographs, moving pictures, stereoscopic slides,
and three-dimensional wire models. The motion-picture camera is now standard equipment in time-and-motion analysis. To assist further in the description
and recording of industrial operations, Gilbreth devised a set of 17 units in
terms of which any work cycle can be analyzed. These units are called "therbligs," which is "Gilbreth" spelled backward but with the "th" unreversed.
Figure 46 lists the 17 therbligs, together with abbreviations and symbols employed in rapid recording. A standard color code was also developed for use in
the graphic representation of sequence and duration of each elementary movement. Through an examination of the films and charts showing exactly what
is done by each hand of the operator and the time spent in each activity, the
time-and-motion analyst eliminates unnecessary movements and rearranges the
remaining movements in what appears to be the quickest and easiest pattern.

In working out an improved method for performing an industrial operation,
the time-and-motion analyst is guided by certain commonly accepted rules, or
"principles." Lists of such principles can be found in standard contemporary
works on time-and-motion analysis (e.g., 4, 11, 70). One of the most important
rules is to minimize the number of motions by eliminating unnecessary movements. Another is to minimize the length of motions, as illustrated by reducing
the distance that the worker must reach in obtaining tools or materials or in
operating machinery. Other common objectives are to utilize rhythmic motions whenever feasible and to employ continuous, curved movements in preference to straight-line movements involving sudden and sharp changes of direction. Still another example is the principle of bimanual symmetry, providing
for the use of both hands simultaneously in opposite and symmetrical movements.

**Critique of Traditional Time-and-Motion Study.**   When first introduced,
time-and-motion study did not prove to be the boon that its enthusiastic ex-

---

[1] This couple and their 12 children were the subject of a popular book and a motion
picture entitled *Cheaper by the Dozen* (42).

| Therblig | Abbreviation | Symbol | Explanation of symbol | Color |
|---|---|---|---|---|
| Search | Sh | ⌒ | Eye turned as if searching | Black |
| Select | St | → | Reaching for object | Gray, light |
| Grasp | G | ∩ | Hand open for grasping object | Lake red |
| Transport empty | TE | ⌣ | Empty hand | Olive green |
| Transport loaded | TL | ⌣ | A hand with something in it | Green |
| Hold | H | ⨅ | Magnet holding iron bar | Gold ochre |
| Release load | RL | ⌢ | Dropping content out of hand | Carmine red |
| Position | P | ⌐ | Object being placed by hand | Blue |
| Pre-position | PP | ⴷ | A nine-pin which is set up in a bowling alley | Sky-blue |
| Inspect | I | ◯ | Magnifying lens | Burnt ochre |
| Assemble | A | ⊞ | Several things put together | Violet, heavy |
| Disassemble | DA | ╫ | One part of an assembly removed | Violet, light |
| Use | U | U | Word "Use" | Purple |
| Unavoidable delay | UD | 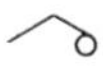 ⌒₀ | Man bumping his nose, unintentionally | Yellow ochre |
| Avoidable delay | AD | 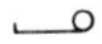 ⌐₀ | Man lying down on job voluntarily | Lemon yellow |
| Plan | Pn | ϱ | Man with his fingers at his brow thinking | Brown |
| Rest for overcoming fatigue | R | ρ | Man seated as if resting | Orange |

**Fig. 46** The therbligs used in time-and-motion study. (*Adapted from Barnes, 4, p. 117.*)

ponents had anticipated. As we view it in retrospect from the vantage point of industrial psychology, we can recognize many weaknesses in its original approach. The atomistic treatment of movements overlooked the fact that the speed of a given movement is influenced by the other movements that precede and follow it. The identical element of motion may require appreciably more time when performed in one context than when performed in another (5, 45, 91). A related objection is that a movement pattern that looks simple on a chart may be awkward and fatiguing to the human operator. Today more emphasis is put on the anatomic and behavioral characteristics of the human operator and less on the geometry of the path of motion.

From the psychologist's viewpoint, a fundamental weakness in the approach of the early time-and-motion analysts was their failure to recognize individual differences in work methods. They were firmly convinced that there is "one best way" for performing each job. We now know that there may be an interaction between work methods and individual variables. As a result of differences in physical or psychological characteristics among workers, one method may be best for individual A and another method for individual B (2, 25). An interesting illustration is provided by research on the performance of older workers (92), showing that older persons tend to modify their method of performing a task so as to compensate for any decline in perceptual skills and other minor disabilities. When a task permitted a variety of approaches and the method was largely under the subject's control, compensatory changes occurred and performance showed no age decrement. In tasks whose performance was rigidly set by the conditions of the experiment, on the other hand, performance declined with age.

In time-and-motion analysis, the pattern of movement and the time for each part movement are generally derived from observation of a small number of workers. Usually the most successful performers are chosen for this purpose. It cannot be assumed that the method so derived will be the most effective for other individuals, who may differ in degrees of skill, experience, and other characteristics.

A fourth criticism pertains to the criterion of efficiency used in traditional time-and-motion analysis, namely, speed of production. More attention needs to be given to other effects of work methods, such as energy expenditure and fatigue, errors and other qualitative aspects of output, accidents, and employee attitudes.

An even more important factor is the workers' misunderstanding and suspiciousness regarding the objectives of time-and-motion study. Employees often fear that the result may be simply a speedup of production, to be followed by a drop in pay rate and the dismissal of some workers. The fact that time-and-motion study did sometimes lead to these consequences in the past has done much to delay its acceptance by workers. In addition, there may be a general distrust of the "outsider," the time-and-motion analyst who introduces the change. Here, too, it might be noted that an outsider *can* go wrong. Not being as close to the job as the workers themselves, he may overlook important points and make impracticable recommendations.

The following passages are taken from a parody of what an outsider might do if he tried to increase the operating efficiency of a symphony orchestra. They are part of a report prepared by a mythical work-study engineer after attending a concert.

For considerable periods the four oboe players had nothing to do. The number should be reduced and the work spread more evenly over the whole of the concert, thus eliminating peaks of activity. All the twelve violins were playing identical notes; this seems unnecessary duplication. The staff of this section should be drastically cut. If a larger volume of sound is required, it could be obtained by means of electronic apparatus. . . .

There seems to be too much repetition of some musical passages. Scores should be drastically pruned. No useful purpose is served by repeating on the horns a passage which has already been handled by the strings. It is estimated that if all redundant passages were eliminated the whole concert time of two hours could be reduced to 20 minutes and there would be no need for an interval. . . .

There were excessive reaches for some notes on the piano and it is probable that redesign of the keyboard to bring all notes within the normal working area would be of advantage to this operator. In many cases the operators were using one hand for holding the instrument, whereas the use of a fixture would have rendered the idle hand available for other work. It was noted that excessive effort was being used occasionally by the players of wind instruments, whereas one air compressor could supply adequate air for all instruments under more accurately controlled conditions (47).

Finally, the principles of time-and-motion study need to be more fully checked in well-controlled research. Some are based only on "common sense" and are essentially hypotheses to be tested. Others are based on early studies with many uncontrolled variables. The advantages of using both hands simultaneously, for example, has been questioned by the findings of at least two well-controlled studies. One investigation was concerned with a routine manual operation, in which the subjects had to pick up screw nuts from a bin and drop them into a receiver hole (6). For this task, a single-handed operation proved to be faster than a simultaneous bimanual operation. The other study compared a bricklaying method involving the use of only one hand at a time with Gilbreth's method involving bimanual symmetry of movement (57). By means of a specially devised instrument, it was shown that Gilbreth's bimanual method requires more physical effort on the part of the worker than does the new method that departs from this motion principle. These results should not be interpreted to mean that the principle of bimanual symmetry ought to be discarded. In most situations, it may still be effective to use both hands in symmetric movements. But the principle cannot be applied indiscriminately, without due regard for other concomitant circumstances.

## MODERN APPROACHES TO METHODS IMPROVEMENT

Early misuses and abuses of time-and-motion study should not obscure the intrinsic merits and potential contributions of this technique. Today time-and-motion study is used widely. Although its current applications do not always meet all the objections cited above, the more serious faults have been corrected.

*Worker Participation.* In line with present recognition of the importance of employee attitudes, there is a growing tendency to have workers participate in any methods-improvement program. With good two-way communication, many suggestions for improving work methods will originate with the workers themselves. If workers become "motion-minded," moreover, they can readily discover ways of eliminating waste motion and increasing operating efficiency. It has been proposed that workers and supervisors should be trained in the basic techniques of work simplification, so that they may themselves apply these procedures, with technical assistance and advice from experts when needed (see 59). Under these conditions, work methods can remain sufficiently flexible to allow for individual differences. No longer need the "one best way" be imposed upon all individuals by an outside expert.

*Broad Scope.* A second characteristic of current methods-improvement procedures is their breadth. Time-and-motion study is only one of the techniques used. But work methods include more than movements. Attention must also be given to the improvement of the perceptual and intellectual aspects of work processes (77). Any activity could probably be performed more efficiently if persons habitually engaged in it were to examine it systematically from this point of view.

Methods-improvement programs merge imperceptibly with equipment design and layout, to be discussed in Chapter 9, as well as with ways of improving the working environment, to be discussed in Chapter 8. Some are concerned with work performed by a group of persons functioning as an integrated team. In this respect they border on some of the organizational and supervisory problems considered in Chapter 6.

The broader scope of the present approach is also evidenced in the utilization of more comprehensive criteria for evaluating efficiency of work methods. More use is now made of qualitative indices of output, such as errors, rejects, and spoilage, in addition to measures of sheer quantity. Safety has also become a major goal in the improvement of work methods.

*Basic Research.* Still another feature of the present approach is to be found in the growing body of basic research on psychomotor performance. This is reflected in the very categories used to classify human movements. In contrast to the task-oriented therbligs of traditional time-and-motion study, increasing use is being made of categories that focus upon the nature of the motor responses themselves. Thus we now speak of positioning, repetitive, continuous, serial, and static responses—the last involving the use of muscular exertion to maintain a required position. From a still different angle, factor analysis has been used to identify basic motor skills, such as reaction time, manual dexterity, finger dexterity, and arm-hand steadiness.[2]

The close collaboration of psychologists and engineers in the newly emerging field of engineering psychology has done much to stimulate such basic research. The interest of the military services in these problems has been another important contributing factor. A survey of much of this research can be found in books on engineering psychology (e.g., 62). Only three examples will be cited here.

As one illustration, we may consider research on methods of *carrying loads* (see 84). Despite the development of mechanical devices, loads are still being carried by many kinds of workers, from construction laborers to restaurant waitresses—not to mention students who carry books! Experimental studies in this area have used several measures of energy cost to the organism, such as pulse rate and oxygen consumption. Output indices have also been employed, as illustrated by time required to carry a standard load over a prescribed course by different methods. By these procedures it has been established that the optimal weight of load is about 35 per cent of the carrier's body weight and the optimal rate is from 85 to 95 yards per minute. Faster rates and heavier loads result in greater energy expenditure. The best position in

---

[2] For a brief summary of this factor-analytic research, as well as references, see Anastasi (1, pp. 383–385).

carrying loads is the one that interferes least with the carrier's normal balance and center of gravity. This optimal position varies somewhat with the weight of the load. High positions, as on a tray, are better for lighter loads, while low positions are better for heavier loads. Similarly, the shape of the load may affect the carrier's posture and hence the efficiency of operation.

The second example concerns the accuracy of *blind positioning movements*. This is the type of movement required when a person operates some control device without looking at it, usually because he must look at something else at the time. When landing an airplane, for example, the pilot is unable to look at the lever that lowers the flaps but must reach for it blindly. In an experiment on this problem (26), the subjects wore blindfolds and were required to touch various targets with a sharp-pointed marker, as shown in Figure 47. There were three tiers of targets, the middle one being at approximately shoulder level and the others at about 45° above and below. Horizontally, the targets extended from front to 135° to the subject's right and left. The relative accuracy of movement in the different directions is shown in Figure 48. Mean error scores for each target position were found by assigning 0 to a mark on the bull's-eye, the scores 1 to 5 to marks in successive concentric circles, and a score of 6 to any mark falling outside the outermost circle. It

*Fig. 47*   View of left side of target stand used in study of blind positioning movements. (*From Fitts, 26; photograph by courtesy of Aerospace Medical Research Laboratories, United States Air Force.*)

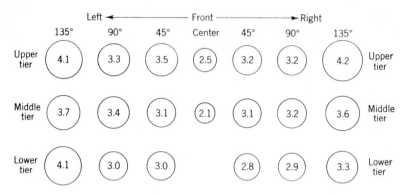

**Fig. 48**  Accuracy of blind positioning movements in different directions. Each circle represents the location of a target. Size of circle is proportional to average error score, which is also given within circle. (*Adapted from Fitts, 26, p. 214.*)

will be seen that accuracy is greatest for the front positions and least for the extreme lateral positions. With regard to level, accuracy tends to be higher for the lowest tier and lowest for the highest tier.

A final example is provided by a set of experiments dealing with *serial movements*.[3] For this research, the investigators designed a type of apparatus which they called the Universal Motion Analyzer, illustrated in Figure 49. The principal feature of this apparatus is that different elements of the movement sequence can be separately timed by electric clocks that are started and stopped by the subject's own responses. Several different response panels were used in different experiments.

The experiment illustrated in Figure 49 was designed to determine the effect of complexity of movement pattern on speed of movement. The panel provides 34 switches that can be turned on by the subject. In this experiment (73), only 5 were used in each of four movement patterns. The first pattern consisted of a single row of 5 switches, to be turned on successively. The second pattern required one change of direction, from horizontal to vertical; the third required two changes, and the fourth required three. Contrary to expectation, it was found that speed of movement was not affected by pattern complexity. Neither travel time from one switch to another nor manipulation time in turning on each switch was any longer when direction of the subject's hand movement changed than when it did not change.

Of particular interest for time-and-motion study are two experiments in this series showing that the time required to perform the *same* movement varies with the context. In one of these experiments, manipulation time required to turn on switches was longer, the longer the distance traveled by the hand from one switch to another (91). In the other, the distance traveled remained constant, but the type of manipulation required to turn on the switches was systematically varied (45). The manipulations included, among others, pulling, pushing, turning, and dial setting. The most noteworthy finding was that travel

[3] Conducted under the direction of K. U. Smith, these experiments are reported in a series of articles appearing in the *Journal of Applied Psychology* from 1951 to 1959

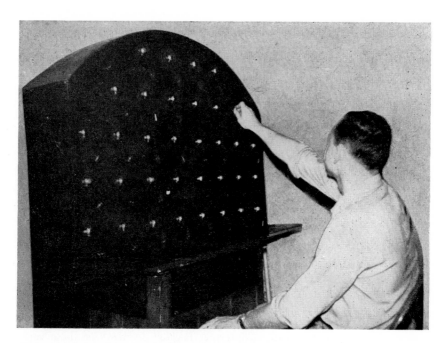

**Fig. 49**   Universal Motion Analyzer used in experiments on effect of
complexity of movement pattern upon speed of movement. (*From
Rubin, Von Trebra, and Smith, 73, p. 273.*)

time varied significantly as a function of manipulation. When the subject had
to perform a more time-consuming manipulation, as in setting dials, his hand
also moved more slowly from one position to the next than it did when he
performed quicker manipulations. It thus appears that, when the subject is set
for more precise and slower movement, this set carries over to all components
of the movement sequence. For this reason, it is necessary for the time-and-
motion analyst to check the times of the total movement sequence in its final
form, rather than relying on estimates obtained for separate components or for
these components observed in a different sequence.

## ACCIDENT PREVENTION

Considerable effort is now devoted to the problem of industrial safety. The
procedures employed in safety programs vary widely, from the development of
safety devices and protective clothing to safety campaigns and competitions.
One of the recognized objectives of methods improvement is to increase operational safety. Studies of fatigue, rest pauses, length of work week, and shift
work have frequently employed accident rate as a criterion. In fact, accident
prevention is related to nearly every topic in industrial psychology, including
selection, training, and employee attitudes. For several types of jobs, screening
out individuals likely to have many accidents is an important aspect of personnel selection. Training employees to follow safe operating procedures is a

significant part of many training programs. And the role of employee attitudes in the observance of safety rules and in other behavior related to accidents is widely recognized. Characteristics of the working environment and equipment design have also been investigated with reference to safety.

Psychology's contribution to industrial safety consists chiefly in research on the causes of accidents. Some typical approaches will be examined below. They have been chosen because they either illustrate important methodological problems or concern some explanatory concept that has been used widely in accident research.

*Accidents and Personal Characteristics.* It has been estimated that about 88 per cent of industrial accidents are caused by human factors, that is, by something that a person does or fails to do (46, p. 21). Such causes include not only unsafe operating procedures but also faulty or inadequate inspection of equipment or materials. Thus even accidents attributed to equipment failure may in many cases be traceable to human errors. It is therefore understandable that many investigators have looked for a relationship between accident rate and personal characteristics. A large number of variables have been studied in this connection, including intelligence, educational level, special job-related aptitudes, emotional and social traits, attitudes, sensory deficiencies, health and physical characteristics, job experience, age, sex, and socioeconomic background factors. Although a few clear-cut relationships have been established, results are often difficult to interpret because so many of these variables are interrelated.

Some of the methodological problems involved in isolating the contribution of different factors are illustrated in a well-designed study of the relation of age and experience to accident rate (86). A frequent difficulty in evaluating the relation of job experience to accident rate stems from selective turnover. Since workers with the worst accident records tend to be separated from the company, the longer an employee remains on a job the more highly selected is he likely to be with regard to safety. This progressive selection could bring about a spurious negative relation between length of job experience and accident rate. In the above study, monthly accident records were plotted separately for 1,237 employees who remained with the company during a five-year period and for 1,317 employees who were hired at the same time but who had left or been discharged during that period. Figure 50 shows the results. It can be seen that accident rate drops sharply for both groups during the first five months on the job. Beyond that point, however, there is a general leveling off in both groups. Of particular interest is the finding that, after the initial adjustment period, accident rate is consistently higher for the turnover than for the non-turnover group.

In the same study, accident records were similarly plotted for 387 workers hired after a systematic training program had been installed in the company. These men thus had the benefit of formal training in correct job procedures and safety methods. The result was a lower initial accident rate and a more rapid drop than in the untrained group. The trained group required only three months of job experience to reach the safety level achieved by the untrained group after five months.

In still another part of the same study, age was found to be significantly associated with accident rate, when the effect of job experience is ruled out. Figure 51 gives the average monthly accident rates for three groups of work-

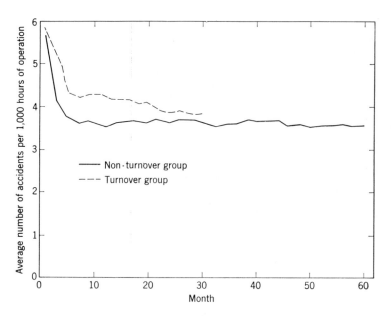

**Fig. 50** Relationship between job experience and average monthly accident rate for a non-turnover and a turnover group. (*From Van Zelst, 86, p. 315.*)

ers. Groups A and B were equated in job experience, each having spent an average of three years on their present job. Group A, however, was younger than Group B, their mean ages being 29 and 41 years. It can be seen that the younger group had a consistently higher accident rate throughout the experimental period. Group C was in the same general age bracket as Group B (mean age 39 years) but unlike the first two groups had no job experience. It is interesting to note that after the usual adjustment period this group's accident rate dropped to a level that practically coincided with that of Group B.

In studies of the relation between frequency of traffic accidents and personal characteristics of drivers, it is necessary to control mileage and exposure hazard. Thus, if drivers in certain age ranges drive more miles per year than those in other age brackets, or if they drive under more dangerous conditions with regard to weather, illumination, or traffic volume, they are more likely to have accidents. Yet only a few studies of the characteristics of "safe" and "unsafe" drivers have adequately controlled these factors. The sort of procedure needed for this purpose is illustrated by an investigation of 482 street-car operators in a large Middle Western transit company (55). Individual accident expectancy was computed in terms of vehicle mileage operated and variations in accident frequency among routes, seasons, days, and hours. An accident index was then found for each operator by dividing the actual number of accidents over a three-year period by the expected number. Comparison of this index with each of 76 medical and personal items yielded low correlations, of which only about a third reached statistical significance. Although many of these characteristics may have contributed to accident causation in individual

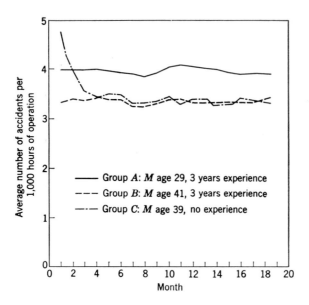

***Fig. 51***  Relationship between age of employee and average monthly accident rate. (*From Van Zelst, 86, p. 316.*)

cases, none exhibited a sufficiently close relation to accident rate to permit adequate prediction.

Surveys of automobile drivers have generally failed to reveal any close association between personal characteristics and accident frequency, although measures of attitudes and personality factors appear somewhat more promising than other variables investigated (13, 15, 17, 18, 44, 82). Even in the case of personality characteristics, however, it seems likely that different response patterns account for accidents on the part of different individuals. For example, some may have accidents because of habitual unconcern with the rights of others, some because of a manic tendency to hurry at all times, some because of strong feelings of hostility and competitiveness toward other drivers, and so on (17). It is also interesting to note that two studies of young automobile drivers found no significant relation between accident frequency and either habitual driving speed or number of traffic violations (20, 81). All these results suggest that the type of behavior that produces accidents may be quite specific and cannot be identified in terms of broad personality traits or general driving habits.

***Accident-proneness.***   The interpretation of accident statistics is beset with pitfalls. An example is provided by the concept of "accident-proneness," which has been defined as the tendency of an individual to retain his relative accident liability over a long period of time. Often this concept has been used with the further implications of generality and causality. Thus it is assumed that a highly accident-prone person will tend to incur many accidents in all situations, from opening a can to driving a car, and that his accident liability is a reflection of personal characteristics leading to unsafe behavior. The distribution of

accidents within a group has often been cited as evidence of accident-proneness. For example, if 10 per cent of the group have 50 per cent of the accidents, these individuals are identified as accident-prone. It would then seem
that, if we could either remove these persons from hazardous jobs or possibly
retrain them, we should be able to cut the accident rate in half.

The fallacy in this reasoning stems from the assumption that by chance
everyone should have the same number of accidents. Hence any marked deviation from the average accident rate is regarded as accident-proneness. Actually
the distribution of accidents obtained in most groups closely approximates the
distribution expected by chance (69). With rare events, such as serious accidents, this distribution is highly skewed, since most persons will have no accidents during the period covered.[4] Suppose a total of 10 accidents occur in a
group of 100 persons. Obviously at least 90 persons will have had no accident.
In fact, since some will have two or even more accidents by chance, more than
90 will have had no accident. As the total number of accidents in the group
increases, the distribution becomes less skewed and approaches a symmetrical
curve. This is illustrated in Figure 52, which shows the distributions of accidents among 59 streetcar motormen over increasingly longer periods, ranging
from 1 to 13 months (38, pp. 343–344). The longer the observation period,
the larger the total number of accidents and hence the more nearly symmetrical the curve.

The only sure test of accident-proneness is to compare the accident records
of the same individuals for two periods of time (66). In this way we can
ascertain whether the *same* individuals have high accident records during both
observation periods. The correlations that have been found between accident
records for two periods vary widely, averaging about .40 (38, p. 344; 51; 69).
When viewed as a reliability coefficient, such a correlation does not appear

[4] When the number of events (e.g., accidents) is quite small compared with the number of persons to whom such events can happen, the appropriate chance distribution is
the Poisson distribution (see 66, 68, 69).

**Fig. 52**   Distribution of accidents among 59 streetcar motormen for
various periods of time. (*Adapted from Ghiselli and Brown, 38, p. 343.*)

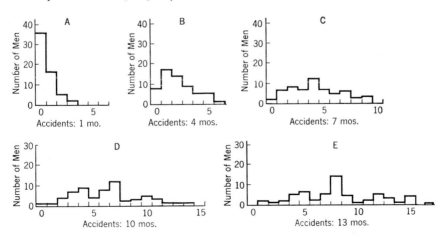

very high. It suggests that an individual's past accident record, taken by itself, is a poor predictor of his subsequent accident liability. It should be added that even lower correlations are found when the frequencies of different kinds of accidents are correlated. Moreover, the correlations obtained undoubtedly reflect in part stable environmental conditions, which contribute to the consistency of individual accident records. For example, individuals performing relatively hazardous jobs will be doing so during both observation periods and will thus tend to have higher accident rates in both periods than will workers in safer jobs.

A striking demonstration of the inadequacy of accident-proneness to account for traffic accidents is provided by a re-analysis of the accident records of about 29,500 Connecticut drivers over a six-year period (27). The original survey in which these data were gathered showed that 3.9 per cent of the drivers accounted for 36.4 per cent of the accidents during the six-year period (23, p. 196; 85). This finding was widely quoted in support of the concept of accident-proneness. Re-analysis of the same data with regard to the first and second three-year intervals, however, revealed that the high-accident records during the two periods were obtained largely by *different individuals*. As a result, if those drivers having two or more accidents during the first three-year period had been prevented from driving during the second period, the total number of accidents during the second period would have been reduced by only 3.7 per cent. To put it differently, those identified as "safe drivers" during the first three years (because they had either one accident or none) accounted for 96.3 per cent of all the accidents during the next three years. When properly interpreted, the findings on accident-proneness suggest that lasting personal characteristics play a relatively minor part in the over-all occurrence of accidents and that situational factors play a relatively large part.

***Accidents and Psychological Climate.*** Among the situational variables investigated in relation to accident rate are various working conditions subsumed under the concept of "psychological climate" (50, 51). One group of investigators (50) analyzed all lost-time accidents of 7,103 employees of a tractor factory over a five-year period. Mean accident rate per person was computed for each of 44 shop departments. The same departments were also rated on a number of situational variables by a panel of eight raters from the company's managerial personnel. The mean accident rate for departments was then correlated with each of these rated situational variables. Partial correlation technique was employed in the effort to tease out the effects of variables that were themselves intercorrelated.

One of the closest relationships found in this study was that between accident rate and physical discomfort of the shop environment, as from excessive heat, noise, vibration, or dust. The investigators concluded that the annoyance and distraction occasioned by these conditions increase accident liability. It was also interesting to note that the presence of an obvious danger, such as glowing molten metal, increased the likelihood of unrelated accidents that did not involve the particular hazard. It may be that the presence of an obvious danger reduces the attention given to other, less conspicuous accident hazards. Another finding of special interest was that amount of crew work was positively correlated with accident rate. Crew work calls for coordination and synchronization of the actions of crew members; it also requires more vigilance in accepting and relinquishing responsibility in the performance of a group task than is needed in individual work. These conditions may increase the accident risk in crew work.

In a survey of published findings pertaining to psychological climate and accident rate, Kerr (51) proposes two major explanatory mechanisms, based upon alertness and stress. First he argues that accidents are simply one kind of low-quality work behavior, similar to errors or spoilage. Conditions that improve the quality of work tend also to reduce accident rate. One of these is alertness; another is freedom from distracting negative stresses. With regard to alertness, Kerr maintains that a psychological climate that encourages passive compliance and discourages individual initiative is likely to reduce alertness and thereby increase accident frequency. One survey of different factory departments, for instance, found a correlation of −.40 between promotion possibilities and accident rate. In the same survey, departments with the best suggestion records tended to have the fewest accidents.

Among stress factors, Kerr includes internal as well as external conditions. The former can be illustrated by disease, alcohol, and worry; the latter, by temperature excesses, poor illumination, and disturbing noise level. Unlike the constitutional factors implicit in some accident-proneness theories, such stress factors need not be permanent. It is apparent that psychological-climate theories of accidents link the problem of industrial safety with questions of organizational structure and supervisory practices discussed in Chapter 6.

*Task Variables.* With the growing realization that accident-proneness and personal characteristics account for relatively few accidents, attention has turned more and more to the contribution of task variables. Any conditions that increase the complexity or difficulty of the operator's task will lengthen response time and raise the likelihood of error (28). When a driver becomes confused because of inadequate road marking, for example, he is likely to slow down or stop abruptly, make an improper turn, get on a one-way lane in the wrong direction, or engage in other unsafe and hazardous behavior.

Psychologists first approached the problem of traffic accidents by developing tests for the selection of drivers (23, 56). A later development was the establishment of "drivers' clinics" for rehabilitating accident-prone drivers by making them aware of deficiencies and of faulty operating habits (23, 49, 56). More recently, interest has shifted to the application of human engineering to the design of highways and equipment (28, 29, 31). For example, research has been conducted on the dimensions and placement of controls, displays, seats, and windows in buses and trucks (63). A number of studies have been concerned with characteristics of highway signs, such as position, size, color, and lettering (33; 35; 62, pp. 113–114). Others have dealt with the relative perceptibility of stop signs and blinker lights (48), the interpretability of traffic symbols (14, 32), and driver reactions to various highway markings and illumination systems at a cloverleaf interchange (24).

Drivers' responses to the amber phase of traffic signals (71) and drivers' judgments of the speeds of their own and of other cars on the highway (3, 72) have also been investigated. It has been noted, for example, that on superhighways the absence of reference objects on the roadside makes it more difficult to estimate the speed of other cars (28). Research has also been conducted on the conditions affecting the rate of flow of both highway and tunnel traffic (30, 36). These conditions may produce accident hazards as well as traffic stoppages and delays.

Much of the research on traffic problems cited in this section deals with the designing of equipment and with man-machine systems, to be discussed in Chapter 9. Other studies have investigated the effects of fatigue, loss of sleep, and alcohol on driving behavior (see 23, 29, 34, 56, 60). These conditions create serious accident hazards by reducing vigilance, alertness, sensorimotor coordination, and speed of response. It is apparent that the study of accidents has been approached from so many different angles that it cuts across several fields of applied psychology.

*Near Accidents.*    In many situations, the accumulation of data on a sufficient number of accidents to permit adequate statistical analysis takes a long time. To obtain enough cases, the investigator may have to combine different types of accidents or accidents occurring under different conditions, thereby increasing the difficulty of interpreting results. Partly for these reasons, some investigators have turned to the study of near accidents, or "close calls" (see 19, ch. 3). Another advantage of studying near accidents is that people are usually less reluctant to report near accidents than full-fledged accidents in which they were involved. Since the potentially dangerous situations leading to near accidents are often similar to those producing actual damage, near accidents provide a fruitful field of research.

Systematic studies of near accidents have been conducted with Air Force flight personnel and with long-haul truck drivers, among others (19, ch. 3). Data can be gathered in various ways, as by having an observer ride in the truck with the driver, by having individuals record their own near accidents as they occur, or by means of a critical-incident technique. In one Air Force study, for example, a large number of pilots were asked whether they had ever made or seen anyone else make "an error in reading or interpreting an aircraft instrument, detecting a signal, or understanding instructions" (19, p. 89). If they had, they were requested to describe the incident. Tabulation of replies revealed that the two most common errors were reversal errors (e.g., in interpreting direction from compasses) and errors in interpreting multirevolution instruments (e.g., in reading an instrument having more than one pointer or one with a pointer and a rotating dial). Such findings helped to pinpoint potential sources of danger and led to research on the redesign of these instruments.

In view of the many difficulties encountered in the analysis of accident records, the investigation of near accidents represents a distinct methodological improvement. More general research on driver behavior and driving skills is also relevant to the problem of accident prevention. Such research can be conducted under realistic driving conditions in the field or through the use of simulators in the laboratory. This positive approach holds more promise than that of waiting for accidents (or near accidents) to happen.

## SUMMARY

Engineering psychology uses research on human behavior in the design of work methods, working environment, and equipment. Minimizing fatigue is an important goal of human efficiency. Fatigue has been variously defined in terms of feelings of tiredness, changes in output, and physiological conditions. Studies with the respiration calorimeter and with the heart-rate recovery curve illustrate the physiological concept of fatigue. Vigilance tests provide a promising behavioral index of fatigue. Feelings of monotony and boredom are difficult to differentiate from fatigue, and especially from so-called mental fatigue. Monotony depends upon the relationship of task, surroundings, and worker. Among the proposed remedies for industrial monotony are personnel selection and placement, changes in the working environment, rest pauses, broad work units, orientation regarding product and total production process, job rotation, and job enlargement.

Human efficiency can be increased through the effective distribution of working time. Properly scheduled rest pauses generally increase total output, although the effects may not be immediately apparent. Lengthening the work week beyond an optimal number of hours has usually lowered rather than raised total output. Shift work involves a disruption of daily physiological rhythms, especially for workers on rotating shifts. Individual differences in adjusting to changing activity cycles have been noted.

Beginning with the early contributions of Taylor and Gilbreth, time-and-motion study has now become a part of more comprehensive methods-improvement programs. The latter are characterized by an increasing emphasis upon worker participation, broadened scope, and the accumulation of basic research on principles of human performance.

Accident prevention is a recognized objective of modern methods improvement, besides being related to nearly every other aspect of industrial psychology. Psychologists' contributions to this problem consist largely in research on the causes of accidents. Studies on the relation of accident rate to personal characteristics must take into account the interrelation of many personal variables. Accident-proneness can be conclusively demonstrated only through the correlation of individual accident records over different time periods. Studies of psychological climate have shown accident rate to be significantly related to several situational variables. With the recognition of the importance of task variables as causes of traffic accidents, the methods of engineering psychology are being used increasingly to improve the layout, illumination, and marking of highways. Research on near accidents, as well as the direct study of driver behavior and driving skills, provides a promising technique for investigating potential sources of danger in operating procedures or in equipment.

## REFERENCES

1. Anastasi, Anne. *Psychological testing.* (2nd ed.) New York: Macmillan, 1961.
2. Balchin, N. Movement study in packing. *J. nat. Inst. industr. Psychol.,* 1931, **5,** 274–275.
3. Barch, A. M. Judgments of speed on the open highway. *J. appl. Psychol.,* 1958, **42,** 362–366.
4. Barnes, R. M. *Motion and time study.* (4th ed.) New York: Wiley, 1958.
5. Barnes, R. M., and Mundel, M. E. Studies of hand motions and rhythm appearing in factory work. *Univer. Iowa Stud. Engng,* No. 12, 1938.
6. Barnes, R. M., Mundel, M. E., and MacKenzie, J. M. Studies of one- and two-handed work. *Univer. Iowa Stud. Engng,* No. 21, 1940.
7. Bartley, S. H. Fatigue and inadequacy. *Physiol. Rev.,* 1957, **36,** 301–324.
8. Bartley, S. H., and Chute, Eloise. *Fatigue and impairment in man.* New York: McGraw-Hill, 1947.
9. Bills, A. G. *The psychology of efficiency.* New York: Harper & Row, 1943.
10. Bills, A. G., and McTeer, W. Transfer of fatigue and identical elements. *J. exp. Psychol.,* 1932, **15,** 23–36.

11. Blair, R. N. A fresh look at the principles of motion economy. *J. industr. Engng,* 1958, **9**, 3–5.
12. Bloom, W. Shift work and the sleep-wakefulness cycle. *Personnel,* 1961, **38**, 24–31.
13. Boek, Jean K. Automobile accidents and driver behavior. *Traffic Safety Res. Rev.,* 1958, **2** (4), 2–12.
14. Brainard, R. W., Campbell, R. J., and Elkin, E. H. Design and interpretability of road signs. *J. appl. Psychol.,* 1961, **45**, 130–136.
15. Brody, L. Personal characteristics of chronic violators and accident repeaters. *Bull. Highw. Res. Bd,* 1957, No. 152, 1–2.
16. Brouha, L. Fatigue—measuring and reducing it. *Advanced Mgmt,* 1954, **19** (1), 9–19.
17. Brown, P. L., and Berdie, R. F. Driver behavior and scores on the MMPI. *J. appl. Psychol.,* 1960, **44**, 18–21.
18. Case, H. W., and Stewart, R. G. Some personal and social attitudes of habitual traffic violators. *J. appl. Psychol.,* 1957, **41**, 46–50.
19. Chapanis, A. *Research techniques in human engineering.* Baltimore: Johns Hopkins Press, 1959.
20. Comrey, A. L. A factor analysis of variables related to driver training. *J. appl. Psychol.,* 1958, **42**, 218–221.
21. Copley, F. B. *Frederick W. Taylor, father of scientific management.* New York: Harper, 1923. 2 vols.
22. Davis, R. C. The relation of muscle action potentials to difficulty and frustration. *J. exp. Psychol.,* 1938, **23**, 141–158.
23. DeSilva, H. R. *Why we have automobile accidents.* New York: Wiley, 1942.
24. Dunnette, M. D. Driver opinions and reported performance under various interchange marking and nighttime visibility conditions. *J. appl. Psychol.,* 1961, **45**, 170–174.
25. Farmer, E. Time and motion study. *Industr. Fat. Res. Bd, Rep. No.* 14, 1923.
26. Fitts, P. M. A study of location discrimination ability. In P. M. Fitts (Ed.), *Psychological research on equipment design.* (AAF Aviation Psychology Program, Research Reports, Rep. No. 19.) Washington: Govt. Printing Office, 1947. Pp. 207–217.
27. Forbes, T. W. The normal automobile driver as a traffic problem. *J. gen. Psychol.,* 1939, **20**, 471–474.
28. Forbes, T. W. Driver characteristics and highway operation. *Traffic Engng,* 1953, **24**, 49–51.
29. Forbes, T. W. Psychological factors in traffic accidents on freeways. *Traffic Safety Res. Rev.,* 1958, **2** (4), 24–26.
30. Forbes, T. W. Human factors in highway design, operation and safety problems. *Hum. Factors,* 1960, **2** (1), 1–8.
31. Forbes, T. W. Some factors affecting driver efficiency at night. *Bull. Highw. Res. Bd,* 1960, No. 255, 61–71.
32. Forbes, T. W., Gervais, E., and Allen, T. Effectiveness of symbols for lane control signals. *Bull. Highw. Res. Bd,* 1960, No. 244, 16–29.
33. Forbes, T. W., and Holmes, R. S. Legibility distances of highway destination signs in relation to letter height, letter width, and reflectorization. *Proc. Highw. Res. Bd,* 1939, **19**, 321–335.
34. Forbes, T. W., Katz, M. S., Cullen, J. W., and Deterline, W. A. Sleep deprivation effects on components of driving behavior. *Highw. Res. Abstr.,* 1958, **28** (1), 21–26.
35. Forbes, T. W., and Moscowitz, K. A comparison of lower case and capital letters for highway signs. *Proc. Highw. Res. Bd,* 1950, **30**, 355–373.
36. Forbes, T. W., Zagorski, H. J., Holshouser, E. L., and Deterline, W. A. Measurement of driver reaction to tunnel conditions. *Proc. Highw. Res. Bd,* 1958, **37**, 345–357.
37. Fraser, D. C. Recent experimental work in the study of fatigue. *Occup. Psychol.,* 1958, **32**, 258–263.
38. Ghiselli, E. E., and Brown, C. W. *Personnel and industrial psychology.* (2nd ed.) New York: McGraw-Hill, 1955.
39. Gilbreth, F. B. *Bricklaying system.* New York: Clark, 1909.

40. Gilbreth, F. B. *Motion study.* New York: Van Nostrand, 1911.
41. Gilbreth, F. B., and Gilbreth, Lillian M. *Applied motion study.* New York: Sturgis & Walton, 1917.
42. Gilbreth, F. B., Jr., and Carey, Ernestine Gilbreth. *Cheaper by the dozen.* New York: Crowell, 1948.
43. Hadley, J. M. Some relationships between electrical signs of central and peripheral activity: II. During "mental work." *J. exp. Psychol.,* 1941, **28**, 53–62.
44. Haner, C. F. Use of psychometric instruments in the prediction of automobile accidents. *Amer. Psychologist,* 1961, **16**, 455.
45. Hecker, D., Green, D., and Smith, K. U. Dimensional analysis of motion: X. Experimental evaluation of a time-study problem. *J. appl. Psychol.,* 1956, **40**, 220–227.
46. Heinrich, H. W. *Industrial accident prevention.* (4th ed.) New York: McGraw-Hill, 1959.
47. How to be efficient with fewer violins. *Amer. Assoc. Univer. Prof. Bull.,* 1955, **41**, 454–455.
48. Hummel, C. F., and Schmeidler, Gertrude R. Driver behavior at dangerous intersections marked by stop signs or by red blinker lights. *J. appl. Psychol.,* 1955, **39**, 17–19.
49. Johnson, H. M., and Cobb, P. W. The educational value of "drivers' clinics." *Psychol. Bull.,* 1938, **35**, 758–766.
50. Keenan, V., Kerr, W., and Sherman, W. Psychological climate and accidents. *J. appl. Psychol.,* 1951, **35**, 108–111.
51. Kerr, W. Complementary theories of safety psychology. *J. soc. Psychol.,* 1957, **45**, 3–9.
52. Kleitman, N. *Sleep and wakefulness as alternating phases in the cycle of existence.* Chicago: Univer. Chicago Press, 1939.
53. Kleitman, N. The sleep-wakefulness cycle of submarine personnel. In National Research Council, Committee on Undersea Warfare, Panel on Psychology and Physiology, *A survey report on human factors in undersea warfare.* Washington: Nat. Res. Coun., 1949. Pp. 329–341.
54. Kossoris, M. D., and Kohler, R. F. Hours of work and output. *U.S. Bur. Labor Statist. Bull.,* No. 917, 1947.
55. Kraft, M. A., and Forbes, T. W. Evaluating the influence of personal characteristics on the traffic accident experience of transit operators. *Proc. Highw. Res. Bd,* 1944, **24**, 278–291.
56. Lauer, A. R. *The psychology of driving: Factors of traffic enforcement.* Springfield, Ill.: Thomas, 1960.
57. Lauru, L. The measurement of fatigue, Parts 1 and 2. *Manager,* 1954, **22**, 299–304, 369–375.
58. Lewis, P. R., and Lobban, M. C. Dissociation of diurnal rhythms in human subjects living on abnormal time routines. *Quart. J. exp. Physiol.,* 1957, **42**, 371–386.
59. Likert, R. *New patterns of management.* New York: McGraw-Hill, 1961.
60. Loomis, T. A., and West, T. C. The influence of alcohol on automobile driving ability. *Quart. J. Stud. Alcohol,* 1958, **19**, 30–46.
61. Loveday, J., and Munroe, S. H. Preliminary notes on the boot and shoe industry. *Industr. Fat. Res. Bd, Rep. No.* 10, 1920.
62. McCormick, E. J. *Human engineering.* New York: McGraw-Hill, 1957.
63. McFarland, R. A., and Moseley, A. L. *Human factors in highway transport safety.* Boston: Harvard Sch. Publ. Hlth, 1954.
64. McGehee, W., and Owen, E. B. Authorized and unauthorized rest pauses in clerical work. *J. appl. Psychol.,* 1940, **24**, 605–614.
65. Mackworth, N. H. The breakdown of vigilance during prolonged visual search. *Quart. J. exp. Psychol.,* 1948, **1**, 6–21.
66. Maritz, J. S. On the validity of inference drawn from the fitting of Poisson and negative binomial distributions to observed accident data. *Psychol. Bull.,* 1950, **47**, 434–443.
67. Merrill, H. F., (Ed.) *Classics in management.* New York: Amer. Mgmt Assoc., 1960.
68. Mintz, A. The inference of accident liability from the accident record. *J. appl. Psychol.,* 1954, **38**, 41–46.

69. Mintz, A., and Blum, M. L. A re-examination of the accident proneness concept. *J. appl. Psychol.*, 1949, **33**, 195–211.

70. Niebel, B. W. *Motion and time study.* (Rev. ed.) Homewood, Ill.: Irwin, 1958.

71. Olson, P. L., and Rothery, R. Driver response to the amber phase of traffic signals. *Amer. Psychologist*, 1961, **16**, 439.

72. Olson, P. L., Wachsler, R. A., and Bauer, H. J. Driver judgments of relative car velocities. *J. appl. Psychol.*, 1961, **45**, 161–164.

73. Rubin, G., Von Trebra, Patricia, and Smith, K. U. Dimensional analysis of motion: III. Complexity of movement pattern. *J. appl. Psychol.*, 1952, **36**, 272–276.

74. Ryan, T. A. Varieties of fatigue. *Amer. J. Psychol.*, 1944, **57**, 565–569.

75. Ryan, T. A. *Work and effort.* New York: Ronald, 1947.

76. Schachter, S., *et al.* Emotional disruption and industrial productivity. *J. appl. Psychol.*, 1961, **45**, 201–213.

77. Seashore, R. H. Work and motor performance. In S. S. Stevens (Ed.), *Handbook of experimental psychology.* New York: Wiley, 1951. Pp. 1341–1362.

78. Shaw, W. A., and Kline, L. H. A study of muscle action potentials during the attempted solution by children of problems of increasing difficulty. *J. exp. Psychol.*, 1947, **37**, 146–158.

79. Smith, Patricia C. The curve of output as a criterion of boredom. *J. appl. Psychol.*, 1953, **37**, 69–74.

80. Smith, Patricia C. The prediction of individual differences in susceptibility to industrial monotony. *J. appl. Psychol.*, 1955, **39**, 322–329.

81. Stewart, R. G. Reported driving speeds and previous accidents. *J. appl. Psychol.*, 1957, **41**, 292–296.

82. Stewart, R. G. Can psychologists measure driving attitudes? *Educ. psychol. Measmt*, 1958, **18**, 63–73.

83. Taylor, F. W. *The principles of scientific management.* New York: Harper, 1911.

84. Teeple, J. B. Work of carrying loads. *Percept. mot. Skills*, 1957, **7**, 60.

85. U.S. Bureau of Public Roads. *Motor vehicle traffic conditions in the United States: The accident-prone driver.* Washington: Govt. Printing Office, 1938.

86. Van Zelst, R. H. The effect of age and experience upon accident rate. *J. appl. Psychol.*, 1954, **38**, 313–317.

87. Vernon, H. M. The speed of adaptation of output to altered hours of work. *Industr. Fat. Res. Bd, Rep. No. 6*, 1920.

88. Vernon, H. M. *Industrial fatigue and efficiency.* London: Routledge, 1921.

89. Vernon, H. M., and Bedford, T. The influence of rest pauses on light industrial work. *Industr. Fat. Res. Bd, Rep. No. 25*, 1924.

90. Walker, C. R., and Guest, R. H. *The man on the assembly line.* Cambridge, Mass.: Harvard Univer. Press, 1952.

91. Wehrkamp, R., and Smith, K. U. Dimensional analysis of motion: II. Travel-distance effects. *J. appl. Psychol.*, 1952, **36**, 201–206.

92. Welford, A. T., *et al. Skill and age; an experimental approach.* London: Oxford Univer. Press, 1951.

93. Wyatt, S., Fraser, J. A., and Stock, F. G. L. The effects of monotony in work. *Industr. Fat. Res. Bd, Rep. No. 56*, 1929.

94. Wyatt, S., Langdon, J. N., and Stock, F. G. L. Fatigue and boredom in repetitive work. *Industr. Fat. Res. Bd, Rep. No. 77*, 1937.

# 8

# *The Working Environment*

It has long been recognized that working efficiency depends in part upon the characteristics of the working environment. Engineers have been concerned with the establishment of illumination standards for different types of work, the maintenance of suitable temperature and other atmospheric conditions, the reduction of noise, and similar problems. Considerable interest has been aroused, too, by the possible uses of music to relieve monotony, improve employee morale, and facilitate certain kinds of work. It is apparent that such problems pertain not only to factories and offices but also to schools, libraries, homes, waiting rooms, and any other environments designed for prolonged human use. From a different angle, recent developments in space travel have stimulated intensive research on the effects of certain extreme environmental conditions upon human performance.

The principal contributions of psychologists to all these problems have been methodological. Research in this field has been advanced by the introduction of experimental designs that control for such factors as suggestion and attitude changes. The Hawthorne Studies, one of which was originally concerned with the effects of illumination, focused attention on the need to control these more subtle variables. Psychology has also stimulated the investigation of individual differences in the effects of environmental variables. It is now recognized that in the working environment, as in work methods, certain individual characteristics must be considered in setting optimum standards.

## ILLUMINATION

*Amount of Light.* To determine optimal illumination levels for different types of work, we need some criterion of visual efficiency. Shall we use measures of output, subjective reports of comfort, or some physiological index of energy expenditure and fatigue? The use of different criteria accounts in part for the discrepancies in the results obtained by different investigators and for a controversy that began in the 1930s and is not yet completely resolved. In general, the research of lighting engineers led to higher recommended levels of illumination than did the research of psychologists. The former is represented chiefly by the work of Luckiesh and his associates (45), the latter by that of Tinker (74, 75).

In a series of studies, Luckiesh and his co-workers compared the effectiveness of different illumination levels in terms of such criteria as visual acuity, blink rate, heart rate, muscular tension, and expressed preferences (see 45; 47, ch. 3). Tinker (74, 75) and others have criticized these studies on several grounds. First, the Luckiesh experiments employed too few illumination levels to permit a precise determination of optimal amounts of light. In most of the studies, only 1, 10, and 100 footcandles[1] were investigated, and in some only 1 and 100. As Tinker points out, the improvement observed in these studies from 10 ft-c to 100 ft-c was generally slight; investigation of intermediate intensities might have revealed a leveling off in significant change not far above 10 ft-c.

The specific criteria of visual efficiency employed in these studies have also been called into question. *Visual acuity* is undoubtedly the most satisfactory among them, since it is most closely related to the visual functions to be performed. Nevertheless, it should be noted that higher illumination is needed to make fine discriminations close to the acuity threshold than would be required for the suprathreshold discriminations involved in most visual tasks. Hence visual acuity is likely to show continued improvement with increasing illumination beyond the point where the performance of many ordinary visual tasks would exhibit appreciable gains (75, p. 438).

The results obtained with *heart rate* are difficult to interpret because of some ambiguity regarding the implications of a drop in heart rate. Luckiesh found that during continuous reading heart rate declined, the decline being greater under 1 ft-c than under 100 ft-c. From this he concluded that reading under the dimmer light was more difficult for the subjects. It could be argued with greater justification, however, that the greater drop (obtained under 1 ft-c) is the more desirable physiological condition and indicates less expenditure of effort (4).

*Blink rate* and *muscular tension* have proved equally unsatisfactory as criteria. Studies of the frequency of involuntary blinking while the subject is performing a visual task under different levels of illumination have yielded negative or conflicting results (see 75). Measures of muscle-action potentials in various body parts not directly involved in task performance have likewise revealed no consistent relation to intensity or other qualities of illumination (66).

In some investigations, these negative findings may result from the subject's tendency to reduce output rate and decrease the work-rest ratio under more difficult working conditions, as when illumination is poorer. There is some evidence to suggest that subjects do in fact adjust their work-rest ratio to the difficulty level of the visual task performed (85, p. 133). When work rate is controlled by the experimenter, the subjects may make more errors when working under more stressful conditions. Measures of effort or energy expenditure unaccompanied by measures of output may thus provide an inadequate picture of the effects of working conditions.

On the other hand, measures of output taken by themselves may also be misleading, because of the opposite tendency to maintain a "normal" pace of work and adjust effort accordingly. This tendency is most likely to affect results when observation periods are short. It is apparent that the factors influencing both effort and output are complex, and their contribution varies with the specific circumstances. Reliance upon any single criterion of visual efficiency may thus be misleading, especially when such a criterion is applied without due consideration of situational factors.

In view of all these difficulties encountered in applying objective criteria of visual efficiency, it might seem that subjective *expressions of preference*

---

[1] A footcandle (ft-c) is the amount of light from a 1-candlepower source falling on a surface 1 foot away. For a simple explanation of the units employed in the measurement of light, see McCormick (47, ch. 2).

for different illumination levels might be the best index after all. Unfortunately the solution is not that simple. In a well-designed series of experiments, Tinker (77) demonstrated that subjects' choices of illumination levels depend to a large extent upon visual adaptation. In one of these experiments, 53 students read individually under direct light for six successive 5-minute periods. The reading was preceded by 20 minutes of adaptation to a general illumination of 4 ft-c. This general illumination was turned off when the local light was turned on. Before starting to read, as well as after every 5 minutes of reading, the subject was asked to adjust the local light to his preferred level. In one series, the subjects began with 1 ft-c and increased the intensity to the chosen level; in the other, they began with 50 ft-c and decreased the intensity to the desired level.

The effect of the starting level was revealed both in the initial choice made during the first 5-minute period and in the mean level chosen throughout the series. When the subjects started with 1 ft-c, their mean initial choice was 14.4; when they started with 50 ft-c, it was 29.2. The over-all preference averaged 21.5 in the former series and 28.9 in the latter.

In another experiment, Tinker (77) controlled visual adaptation more thoroughly. A total of 144 students participated. Working under diffuse, indirect lighting, each subject read for two 50-minute sessions, following an initial 15-minute adaptation period. At one session, the subjects were adapted to 8 ft-c; at the other, to 52 ft-c. Half of the subjects began with the 8 ft-c session, the other half with the 52 ft-c session. During the 50-minute reading period, the same light intensity (8 or 52 ft-c) was used as a standard with which the subject was asked to compare lights ranging from 1 to 26 ft-c in the one series and from 18 to 100 ft-c in the other. Before each comparison, the subjects were readapted to the standard light for 4 minutes. In each series, the comparison lights were presented in random order.

TABLE 13    *Effect of Visual Adaptation upon Intensity of Light Preferred for Reading under Diffuse General Illumination*[a] (*From Tinker, 77, p. 63*)

| | Adapted to 8 ft-c (Standard) | | | | | | | | |
|---|---|---|---|---|---|---|---|---|---|
| Footcandles | 1 | 2 | 3 | 5 | 8 | 12 | 18 | 26 | 41 |
| Percentage of times preferred | 0.0 | 1.2 | 1.5 | 4.4 | 26.2 | 24.0 | 17.1 | 13.9 | 11.7 |
| | Adapted to 52 ft-c (Standard) | | | | | | | | |
| Footcandles | 18 | 30 | 41 | 46 | 52 | 59 | 62 | 71 | 100 |
| Percentage of times preferred | 5.4 | 8.0 | 11.4 | 14.0 | 21.0 | 11.6 | 11.9 | 9.1 | 7.6 |

[a] $N = 144$; total number of judgments = 1,152. The number of preferences for the standard lights were divided by 8 before computing percentages, in order to adjust for the reappearance of standard in each of the 8 comparisons.

The results are summarized in Table 13. It will be seen that in both series the largest percentage of subjects chose the light to which they had been adapted, the frequency of choice declining gradually for higher and lower intensity levels. In the 8 ft-c series, the median preference fell roughly at 12 ft-c; in the 52 ft-c series, it fell approximately at 52 ft-c. It is also noteworthy that individual differences in these preferences were very large. With the exception of 1 ft-c, every given level of illumination was chosen by some subjects. The principal implication of these experiments, however, is that expressed preferences based on short observation periods are highly susceptible to prior visual adaptation.

Several laboratory investigations have utilized *output* criteria for various tasks performed under different levels of illumination. In a typical study, 27 male college students took the Purdue Hand Precision Test under 5, 50, and 150 ft-c illumination (48). This test was chosen because it calls for a combination of visual and motor skills required in a number of industrial jobs. The subject must insert a stylus successively into three holes that are uncovered by a rotating shutter. Each hole is ½ inch in diameter. An error is automatically recorded whenever the stylus touches the side of a hole, the disk in which the holes are located, or the rotating shutter. In this experiment, the three illumination levels were presented to different subjects in a counterbalanced order so as to control the effects of practice, fatigue, motivation, and other cumulative factors. As can be seen in Figure 53, the average error scores decreased with increasing illumination. The differences between the mean scores at 5 ft-c and those at the other two levels were significant; the difference between mean scores at 50 ft-c and at 150 ft-c was not.

Tinker (74–76) has summarized the findings of similar investigations conducted by himself and others with a variety of tasks, such as reading different sizes of print. He reports the results in terms of *critical levels of illumination*, which he defines as the intensity above which there is no appreciable improvement in performance. To these critical levels he adds a certain "margin of safety" to provide for individual differences and other unpredictable factors. Thus he arrives at recommended levels of illumination for different functions. For reading good-sized print (10- to 11-point), for instance, 10 to 15 ft-c

*Fig. 53*  Errors in Purdue Hand Precision Test under three levels of illumination. (*From McCormick, 47, p. 60; data from McCormick and Niven, 48.*)

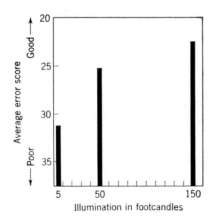

is considered adequate.[2] For sorting mail and other tasks requiring the reading of handwriting, 20 to 30 ft-c is recommended. For the most demanding visual tasks encountered in work situations, such as bookkeeping and drafting, 40 to 50 ft-c is regarded as desirable. These recommended levels run generally lower than those given in standard sources by illuminating engineers (see 47, pp. 64–67).

The amount of light needed for clear seeing varies with characteristics of the task and of the person. Thus, the less the contrast between objects to be discriminated, the higher the illumination required. Identifying black objects against a gray background calls for a brighter light than does identifying the same objects against a white background. Individual characteristics also affect light requirements. Persons with subnormal visual acuity or other visual deficiencies can improve their performance through the use of brighter illumination (20, 41). Similarly, older persons need more light than younger persons. The acuity of older workers can often be brought up to that of younger workers by increasing illumination to the proper level (21).

A number of studies conducted in industrial settings show the relation between changes in illumination and work performance (see 47, pp. 61–63; 74). Most of these merely compared performance records before and after the introduction of some improvement in illumination, usually an increase in the amount of available light. Many operations were covered by these studies, including letter sorting, weaving, machine-shop work, inspection, assembly, and various other skilled or semiskilled manufacturing operations. Initial illumination was generally quite low, varying from less than 1 ft-c to slightly over 13 ft-c for different types of work. When illumination was raised to levels ranging from about 5 to 29 ft-c, output improved by amounts varying from 4 to 35 per cent. Other, similar studies have shown a decrease in errors and spoilage or a sharp drop in accident rate following improvements in lighting conditions.

This type of experimental design, of course, is subject to the Hawthorne effect. Rises in output may have resulted partly or wholly from better employee attitudes. On the other hand, if employee attitudes *can* be improved by slight increases in illumination, such changes may be fully justified on those grounds alone. Perhaps some of the illumination changes did increase visibility, while others only made the surroundings more cheerful and attractive. From a practical standpoint, anything that increases job satisfaction or productivity is desirable. From a scientific standpoint, however, we would like to identify just what factors led to improved job performance and to learn how they operated. This information is needed if we want to be able to generalize beyond the immediate situation in which data were gathered.

An example of the type of experimental design required for the identification of cause-effect relations is provided by a study of nine card-punch operators in the Bureau of the Census (see 47, pp. 62–63). Three card-punch machines were set up in each of three work zones. In Zone I, the original incandescent-lighting conditions were continued unchanged. In Zone II, illumination on work surfaces was increased by painting walls, ceiling, and equipment; re-covering floor; and cleaning light fixtures and furnishing new

---

[2] It might be noted that 15 ft-c corresponds roughly to the light falling on a working surface 12 inches from a frosted 25-watt bulb or 21 inches from a frosted 50-watt bulb (74, p. 13).

bulbs. In Zone III, luminous indirect fluorescent fixtures were installed, in addition to making the general renovations described for Zone II. The illumination levels at the machines averaged 28, 38, and 49 ft-c in Zones I, II, and III, respectively. Performance records were kept for nine weeks. During this period, each employee worked for one week at each machine in a random sequence. Mean production indices for Zones I, II, and III over the nine-week period were 43.7, 46.0, and 50.4. The difference between Zones I and II was not statistically significant, but that between Zones I and III was. From these results, the investigators concluded that for card-punch operation an illumination level of about 50 ft-c is desirable.

Some industrial situations present special lighting problems. An example is the airplane cockpit during night flying, when it is desirable to preserve as much dark adaptation as possible to facilitate the pilot's perception of stimuli outside the airplane. Thus the question is: How far can illumination be reduced and still permit accurate reading of dials? In a laboratory experiment designed to help answer this question, 20 subjects with normal vision were tested individually with photographic reproductions of a bank of 12 dials (72). After a 10-minute period of dark adaptation, the subject was instructed to read each dial orally as rapidly and accurately as possible. The subject read 10 cards at each of five brightness levels, corresponding to .005, .018, .022, .296, and 6.0 foot-lamberts.[3] The sequences of illumination levels were rotated for different subjects to balance practice and fatigue effects.

Performance records showed considerable improvement in speed and accuracy up to .022 ft-L, with no significant change above that level. At lower levels of illumination, both frequency and magnitude of errors increased. When smaller dials were substituted in a second experiment, performance continued to improve at higher illumination levels, the critical region for accuracy falling between .02 and .05 ft-L. The principal contribution of this investigation was to demonstrate that fairly low levels of illumination are adequate for accurate performance of a task such as dial reading, which calls for visual discriminations well above threshold value.

**Distribution of Light.**   Other characteristics of light besides its intensity affect visual efficiency. Of particular importance is the degree of uniformity of illumination. Poor distribution of light is likely to produce glare, which may cause discomfort, visual fatigue, poor performance, and accidents. Glare may result from the presence of direct light sources in the visual field, from marked brightness contrast between two surfaces, or from surfaces that concentrate the light in one direction instead of diffusing it (e.g., shiny metal, glossy paper).

Any bright object tends to attract the eyes away from the work surface. Muscular effort is expended in turning the eyes back and forth between fixation points, as well as in the accompanying convergence and accommodation changes. The presence of bright spots in the visual field thus heightens visual fatigue, which is largely fatigue of the eye muscles. To maintain fixation on

---

[3] The foot-lambert (ft-L) is a unit for expressing the brightness *reflected from* a surface. Depending not only upon the intensity and distance of the light source but also upon the reflecting properties of the work surface, it is the most appropriate unit to use in studies of the effect of illumination on visual efficiency. One foot-lambert is the brightness of a perfectly reflecting surface illuminated by 1 ft-c. Since even white paper ordinarily reflects only about 80 per cent of the light, the foot-lamberts reflected by a work surface are less than the footcandles falling upon it.

the work surface with a minimum of strain, the surroundings should be some-what darker than the work area. At the same time, the contrast should not be so great as to require shifts from light to dark adaptation. It has been generally recommended (although without much empirical verification) that the bright-ness ratio should be no greater than 3:1 between work area and immediate sur-roundings and no greater than 10:1 between work area and more remote parts of the room (47, p. 71). Excessive uniformity of light may also be undesirable, because of its emotional effect on the worker. Such lighting may produce boredom and sleepiness (85). In most practical situations, satisfactory results can be obtained through a combination of diffuse general illumination of fairly low intensity and local light units near the work surface.

As examples of laboratory investigations that have demonstrated the advan-tages of diffuse lighting and glare reduction, we may consider the pioneer ex-periments of Ferree and Rand[4] (19). In these experiments, as in most of their research on various aspects of illumination, Ferree and Rand administered visual acuity tests before and after a three-hour period of continuous reading under each kind of illumination. Recognizing that momentary tests of per-formance may fail to reveal fatigue, they required the subject to observe two points continuously for three minutes and to indicate when they blurred and when they were seen as separate. The percentage of time during which the two points appeared separate was taken as an index of the subject's visual efficiency at the time. These percentages were compared in the two acuity tests to determine what loss, if any, had occurred as a result of the three hours of reading.

In one experiment, Ferree and Rand (19) compared three types of illumina-tion differing in diffuseness. With indirect lighting, which provides the most diffuse illumination, they found little loss in visual acuity in the course of three hours of continuous reading. With semi-indirect and especially with direct lighting, the drop in acuity was much sharper. This loss could be minimized, however, by reducing the number of lighting fixtures within the subject's visual field. Each light source visible to the subject represents a pos-sible glare spot that might attract the eyes away from the work surface. Visual efficiency showed the least loss when no light fixture was visible to the subject; the loss increased progressively when two, four, and six fixtures were visible.

*Color of Light.* On theoretical grounds, pure, or monochromatic, light should give a clearer image than light that is a mixture of several colors, or wavelengths. The different wavelengths are refracted differently in passing through the lens of the eye and hence come to a focus at slightly different points. This phenomenon, known as "chromatic aberration," produces a slightly blurred image. Daylight, as well as light from common artificial sources, is a mixture of different wavelengths. Certain types of artificial illuminants, such as sodium-vapor lamps, have been specially developed to provide nearly monochromatic light, from a narrow spectral band. Contrary to expectation, however, empirical studies show little or no significant differences between visual performance under such lights and under ordinary illumination (47, ch. 3; 74).

Nor have appreciable differences in visual efficiency been found from one

---

[4] Like the Gilbreths, whose work was cited in Chapter 7, Ferree and Rand were a husband-and-wife team that collaborated in a long series of research projects. In this case, however, both were psychologists.

color of light to another, except possibly for tasks at or near threshold level. In tasks requiring color discrimination, of course, colored lights that alter the surface color of objects should be avoided. Another relevant consideration is the affective responses of persons to differently colored lights. A greenish light that gives a sickly cast to the complexion has been known to make some workers ill!

Still another factor that may influence the choice of illuminant color in special situations is dark adaptation. This is illustrated by the previously cited example of cockpit illumination for night flying. Light from the red end of the spectrum permits the human eye to dark-adapt faster and more completely and to maintain dark adaptation better than does light from other parts of the spectrum. Accordingly, an experiment was conducted to determine the effect of color on the ability to read dials in dim light (73). The general procedure was similar to that followed in the previously reported study on dial reading under different levels of illumination. Four colors, including yellow-green, yellow-orange, orange-red, and deep red, were investigated at each of two illumination levels (.01 and .1 ft-L).

Although at .01 ft-L red light tended to be inferior to the other colors in terms of accuracy and speed of dial reading,[5] at .1 ft-L it was equal or superior to them. It was also found that all four colored lights (which were relatively monochromatic) yielded better performance than did the white light used in the earlier experiment. The practical implication of this experiment is that red light, with its advantages for dark adaptation, may be used in cockpit illumination without loss in speed or accuracy of dial reading.


## ATMOSPHERIC CONDITIONS

**Regulation of Body Heat.**   In the process of metabolism, the body generates heat. When the organism is at rest, metabolic rate is slower and less heat is generated than when the organism is engaged in physical activity. The more strenuous the activity, the greater the amount of heat generated. To maintain its normal temperature, the body must give off excess heat. If body heat is dissipated too slowly, one feels uncomfortably warm; if it is dissipated too fast, one feels chilled. Body heat is dissipated chiefly through *evaporation* of perspiration, *radiation* of thermal energy from the body to cooler surfaces in its environment, and *convection* of heat by the air around the body.

The cooling power of a particular environment depends upon other characteristics besides its temperature. There is a sound factual basis for the popular cliché that "It's not the heat, it's the humidity" which often causes discomfort. High humidity reduces the rate of evaporation of perspiration and thus decreases the effectiveness of an important mechanism for the dissipation of bodily heat. The role of humidity can be illustrated by the reactions of a group of men exposed for one hour to different combinations of temperature and humidity (see 47, pp. 232–233). When the humidity was only 10 per cent, temperatures as high as 140° Fahrenheit were judged to be tolerable. On the other hand, when the humidity reached 80 per cent, a temperature of 110° proved intolerable. Similar interactions of temperature and humidity

---

[5] .01 ft-L falls below the critical illumination level identified in the earlier study (72).

have been found when the ability to carry on physical work was the criterion (47, pp. 233–234).

Circulation of the air also affects its cooling power. The effectiveness of fans derives from this principle. Dissipation of bodily heat is accelerated if the blanket of warm air that surrounds the body is carried away and cooler air replaces it. However, if air temperature is near or above body temperature and humidity is high, fans will be of no avail.

At one time it was believed that the discomfort and other ill effects of poor ventilation resulted from changes in the chemical composition of the air we breathe. Under ordinary circumstances, however, changes in the proportion of oxygen, carbon dioxide, and other chemicals in the air are too slight to affect the organism (see 47, p. 243). Even if a crowd of people remains for several hours in an unventilated room, the proportion of oxygen will still be well above the minimum requirement and the proportion of carbon dioxide well below the safe maximum. The discomfort experienced under these circumstances arises from the body's inability to dissipate heat properly. This fact was demonstrated in a classic experiment in which subjects in an ill-ventilated room breathed fresh air conveyed through a tube (see 80, pp. 9–12). Under these conditions, they experienced the same discomfort and showed all the physiological symptoms associated with poor ventilation. When the situation was reversed and they breathed stale air while sitting in a well-ventilated room, they experienced no discomfort and showed no physiological changes.

Laboratory studies (80) have also shown that output in physical work declines sharply under conditions of poor ventilation but that mental work is relatively unaffected. Such findings are understandable when we consider that much more heat is produced during physical than during mental work. When subjects feel uncomfortable because of poor ventilation, however, they are less *willing* to carry on mental work. Hence, when motivation is not very high, or when work continues over long periods of time, output may slacken off in mental tasks too.

**Ventilation Studies in Industry.** Several early investigations by the Industrial Fatigue Research Board of Great Britain were concerned with atmospheric conditions in factories and mines (see 1). Some of these studies used the *kata thermometer,* an instrument that records the cooling power of the air resulting from the combined effects of temperature, humidity, and rate of air motion. By this method, the cooling power of the air in different coal mines or at different depths within a mine was determined. The results showed that, as the cooling power decreased, the number and severity of accidents rose, the duration of voluntary rest pauses increased, and output decreased (82). In another study conducted in coal mines, absenteeism was found to be related to temperature (83). As temperature rose above 70°F, the percentage of working time lost on account of employee illness increased.

In still another investigation (63), the frequency of minor accidents in three munitions plants was plotted against daily temperature over a period of about ten months. The minimum number of accidents occurred at a temperature of 67.5°F. As the temperature rose to a high of about 78°F or dropped to a low of about 48°F, accident rate increased by as much as 30 per cent. The physical discomfort resulting from any pronounced deviation from the optimum temperature is likely to distract workers and hence lead to accidents. In addition, at high temperatures perspiration makes it more difficult to grasp tools properly; and, at low temperatures, stiffness of the hands interferes with coordination of movement.

The effect of installing fans was investigated in a textile mill, where temperature and humidity had to be kept fairly high to prevent breakage of thread (88). Fans were operated on alternate days over a period of six weeks. Analysis of output records showed that on the days when the fans were in operation productivity was significantly higher and waste lower than on the other days.

A more recent study (54) was concerned with the performance of telegraph operators under extreme climatic conditions. The average number of errors made by 11 operators in receiving Morse code was compared under different combinations of temperature and humidity. The operators had been acclimatized to the atmospheric conditions under investigation for periods of 7 to 11 weeks prior to the experiment. Results were reported in terms of *effective temperature,* a commonly used index combining into a single value the effects of temperature, humidity, and air velocity on the sensation of warmth felt by the human body (34). Any given effective temperature (ET) corresponds to the temperature of still, saturated air (100 per cent humidity) that would give the same perceived warmth. Thus an ET of 80° is equivalent to a temperature of 80°F with 100 per cent humidity and completely stagnant air. It follows that 80°ET would be considerably more uncomfortable than a temperature of 80° experienced under ordinary conditions of humidity and air movement encountered in everyday life.

Figure 54 shows average number of errors per man-hour with effective temperatures of 79° and above. It can be seen that when ET exceeds 95° there is a sharp rise in errors. It is also noteworthy that the increase in errors

**Fig. 54**  Relation between effective temperature and average number of errors in Morse code receiving. (*Data from Mackworth, 54, p. 148.*)

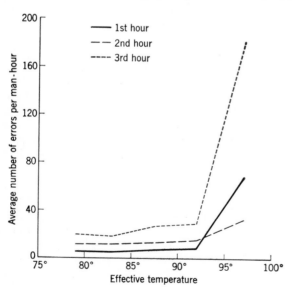

is greater during the third hour than during the first hour of work, indicating the cumulative effects of working for long periods of time under such uncomfortable conditions. Analysis of individual records showed that deterioration under adverse atmospheric conditions was greater for operators who were initially less skilled than for the more highly skilled.

**Weather and Related Conditions.**   The various atmospheric variables considered in connection with ventilation are obviously related also to the broader and more pervasive conditions subsumed under weather, seasons, and climate. Theories regarding the effects of climate upon human behavior and upon the development of civilizations date back to Aristotle and probably earlier. During the first quarter of the present century, Huntington (38) wrote extensively on this subject and conducted several field surveys to test his hypotheses. Of paricular interest were his analyses of seasonal variations in the output of piece-rate workers in different latitudes (38, ch. 4). For example, 410 operatives in three Connecticut hardware factories, surveyed over a period of four years, showed production peaks in the spring and fall, with a steep production drop in midwinter and a smaller drop in midsummer. One year when the summer was exceptionally cool, the midsummer drop in output failed to appear. These factories were chosen because working conditions were unusually uniform throughout the year and there seemed to be no major external constraints affecting production.

When the output curves of 120 workers in South Carolina cotton factories were similarly analyzed, the spring and fall peaks were found to be farther apart, both falling closer to the winter months than was true in the Connecticut survey. Moreover, the midsummer production drop was now steeper than the midwinter drop. These trends became more pronounced in the output curve of 2,300 cigar makers in Tampa, Florida. In this group, there was a single output peak in midwinter, as well as a steep midsummer drop. In this connection, it is also relevant to note that, in a study of tinplate mills conducted by the Great Britain Industrial Fatigue Research Board (81), a 13 per cent summer drop in output was found in a plant with no artificial ventilation and poor natural ventilation, while the summer drop was only 3 per cent in another plant with artificial ventilation that provided good air circulation.

In another early study, Dexter (14) compiled a mass of statistical data on the relationship between daily weather conditions and the frequency of such occurrences as natural deaths, crimes of violence, suicides, absences from school, and clerical errors of bank clerks. Dexter interpreted the various relationships he found as suggesting that one's general vitality increases on moderately warm, clear days and decreases on cold, cloudy, and rainy days. If weather does have any significant effects upon human behavior, it is unlikely that they can be summed up as simply as this. The interpretation of survey data of this sort is difficult because of the large number of uncontrolled factors that may influence the results.

Recently there has been a revival of interest in the relation between weather conditions and human behavior. A research group established in Germany, for example, has been gathering data on the effects of many different meteorological variables on the human organism (60). These investigators differentiate between periodical meteorological variations, corresponding to daily and seasonal cycles, and aperiodical rhythm-changing processes, which they believe to be more stressful for the organism. The effects of storms would be an example of the latter changes. Surveys of large groups conducted by these investigators showed that such aperiodic weather changes tended to be associated with a rise in frequency of industrial accidents, an increase in number of visits to plant dispensaries for medical aid, a lengthening of reaction time, and a lowering of critical flicker frequency.[6] Studies of "tropical fatigue," conducted during and after World War II, represent another area of research in psychoclimatology (see 16, 18). Still further evidence of interest may be seen in the fact that the American Institute of Medical Climatology, established in 1958, contains a section on psychology.

Mention may also be made of recent research on the possible biological and behavioral effects of atmospheric ions (25). "Ionization" refers to the state of electric charge of the atmosphere. All atmospheric particles can be described as either neutral or positively or negatively charged. The concentration of positive or negative ions in the air can be radically altered through such factors as heat sources, operating electronic equipment, or storms. In a number of experiments conducted by biologists, certain behavioral effects of ion concentration have been observed incidentally. None of the behavioral effects, however, has as yet been demonstrated under adequately controlled conditions.

One psychological study designed specifically to test alleged effects of ion concentration on reaction time obtained negative results (65). A number of commercially available ion generators, or "ionizers," have been marketed on the supposition that an increase in negative-ion concentration is conducive to improved vitality and feelings of well-being. The previously cited study (65) also lent no support to such claims, since subjects were unable to identify increased concentration of positive or negative ions and their reported feelings during experimental and control sessions were indistinguishable. Any conclusions regarding the effects of atmospheric ions on behavior must await further research.

**Extreme Conditions.**    Although relatively restricted in its applications, considerable research has been done on more extreme atmospheric conditions than those discussed in the preceding sections (see 47, ch. 9). Among the factors investigated are extreme cold, as found in arctic regions; toxic gases, radioactive material, and other impurities in the atmosphere; rapid changes in barometric pressure, such as might be encountered during escape from a submarine or in a sudden emergency loss of pressure in high-altitude pressurized aircraft; and oxygen deficiency, or anoxia, as found at high altitudes.

Of all these conditions, the one whose psychological effects have been most thoroughly investigated is anoxia[7] (47, ch. 9; 49; 50; 51, ch. 3). By placing subjects in experimental chambers, it is possible to expose them to atmospheric conditions corresponding to different altitudes, to present these conditions in random sequence, and to intersperse them with control sea-level sessions in order to rule out the effects of suggestion. Although individuals differ widely in their responses to oxygen deficit, behavioral effects of anoxia usually begin at an altitude of approximately 10,000 feet and increase in extent and severity

---

[6] Critical flicker frequency (CFF) is the rate at which a flickering light is first seen to fuse. It is believed that CFF may serve as an index of the efficiency of functioning of the nervous system.

[7] Strictly speaking, "anoxia" means oxygen lack, and the correct term for oxygen deficit is "hypoxia." In common usage, however, anoxia designates any degree of oxygen deficit, and it is so employed in this text because of its greater familiarity.

with increasing altitude. Loss of consciousness and collapse generally occur at about 20,000 feet.[8]

The individual is usually unaware of the onset of anoxia, a fact that makes it all the more important that persons who may be exposed to oxygen deficit take proper precautions in advance. The first symptoms are often emotional: the individual may become irritable and belligerent or—more often—euphoric and jolly. These initial changes are not unlike the effects of mild doses of alcohol. With increasing altitude, there is progressive loss of sensory and motor functions. Night vision may be impaired even below 10,000 feet in some persons. Visual acuity, color discrimination, and other visual functions are among the first to decline. Hearing is affected later. Complex motor processes are disrupted earlier than simpler activities. Handwriting deteriorates, and speech becomes slurred and unintelligible. At higher altitudes reaction time is lengthened. Intellectual functions are likewise affected in the order of their complexity. The more complex functions requiring memory, reasoning, and judgment are lost first; at higher altitudes, even such simple functions as canceling letters deteriorate.

Rapid ascent to very high mountains, as in a railroad, produces anoxic effects similar to those described above. Slower ascent, as in ordinary mountain climbing, produces a rather different set of symptoms, which may include illness and depression (50). Persons reared at high altitudes show considerable physiological adaptation to such altitudes. This is true of the residents of certain villages in the Andes, who normally live at altitudes close to 15,000 feet. Such persons also exhibit much greater tolerance to acute and severe anoxia when experimentally exposed to simulated altitudes beyond 30,000 feet (79).

## ENVIRONMENTAL FACTORS IN SPACE TRAVEL

In their approach to problems of space travel, psychologists have been able to apply well-established research methodologies and other procedures previously developed in other contexts. Personnel selection and training are an important aspect of the space program and one to which psychologists have made major contributions (see 30; 68, ch. 8). The advantages of training devices and simulators are especially evident in the preparation of astronauts for both routine and emergency tasks that they may have to perform in the space vehicle. Research on human factors in equipment design and the development of effective man-machine systems, to be discussed in the next chapter, are basic to the successful operation of manned spacecraft. Within the context of the present chapter, it is the extreme environmental conditions encountered in space travel that are of primary interest. Although several environmental factors have been investigated in this connection, those that have stimulated the greatest amount of research are weightlessness and isolation.

*Weightlessness and Related Gravitational Phenomena.* The experience of *weightlessness*, resulting from zero gravity, is one of the most spectacular problems with which the space traveler must cope (see 2, pp. 422–434; 26; 30; 33; 44; 68). Human posture and locomotion are adapted to the earth's normal gravitational pull. Under highly reduced or zero gravity, locomotion is

[8] Modern high-altitude aircraft are regularly equipped with pressurized cabins that reproduce the atmospheric conditions pevailing at low altitudes. Under such conditions, of course, the symptoms of anoxia do not occur.

extremely difficult, movements are erratic and uncoordinated, and perception becomes disoriented. Circulatory changes, nausea, and other physiological disturbances may also occur. Prolonged exposure may lead to muscular weakening from disuse. Return to normal gravity conditions may be accompanied by marked debility and gross disruption of psychomotor performance.

In short space flights in which the operator is strapped to the seat, weightlessness does not significantly impair performance. Any initial disorientation occurring under these conditions can be overcome with practice, especially if visual cues are available. In the first United States manned orbital space flight, for example, in which the pilot remained weightless for approximately 4½ hours, manipulation of controls was unaffected and no adverse physiological or psychological effects were observed (61, pp. 99, 119, 136). In a longer flight, one of the Russian astronauts did report symptoms of motion sickness, but others experienced no such ill effects during even longer periods of weightlessness. The problem of weightlessness with a free-floating subject, however, has not yet been satisfactorily solved (30, 69). Empirical data on the effects of prolonged weightlessness are also very meager.

For experimental purposes, weightlessness can be produced by flying an aircraft in a parabolic trajectory so that centrifugal force exactly balances the pull of gravity. This technique has been utilized in most of the research on the effects of zero gravity with both animal and human subjects. By this method, however, weightlessness can be maintained only for periods of a minute or less. Because of this limitation, some investigators have experimented with other situations that simulate at least some aspects of weightlessness. For instance, subjects have been floated in water-filled tanks for several hours at a time while the effects on both physiological condition and task performance were measured (28, 33, 44).

Still another approach to the problem has been concerned with the effects of slow *rotation* upon human performance (13, 29). This sort of experiment is of interest because artificial gravity can be produced by rotating the spacecraft or space platform around its own gravitational center. The difficulties of weightlessness might thus be overcome, provided the rotation itself did not introduce new disturbances. Preliminary results suggest that with adaptation any initial deleterious effects of such rotation tend to disappear.

A related problem pertains to the high *accelerative forces* experienced during launch and reentry. In a sense, this condition is the opposite of weightlessness, since the gravitational force acting upon the body is increased many times (see 47, ch. 8). High acceleration can be simulated in a human centrifuge. This device has been used experimentally to determine the amount of accelerative force that can be safely tolerated for different periods of time, the optimal body position and other conditions that affect such tolerance, and the effect of different amounts of force upon the subject's ability to operate controls and perform other tasks (2, pp. 464–477; 57; 84). Figure 55 shows an astronaut preparing to enter the gondola of the human centrifuge. Within this gondola were installed the display and control panels of the Mercury space capsule, thus permitting direct observation of the effects of these environmental stresses upon performance in space flight. The centrifuge has also been effectively employed for purposes of adaptation and training in preparation for actual space flight.

It should be noted that many of the psychological problems investigated

*Fig. 55* Human centrifuge used to simulate accelerative stresses encountered during lift-off and reentry in space flight. (*Courtesy of National Aeronautics and Space Administration.*)

with reference to propeller and jet aircraft are also relevant to space travel. An example is to be found in the research on *pilot disorientation* (10, 12). In the flight situation, familiar sensory cues are often encountered in unfamiliar contexts and hence misperceived. As a result, the position and motion of the aircraft may be misjudged. The gravity receptors (otolith organs) located in the inner ear play an important part in our spatial orientation. In the absence of suitable visual cues, these gravity receptors may lead to disorientation because of the unusual conditions of gravity and acceleration encountered in flight. Some accidents attributed to "pilot error" have probably resulted from such spatial disorientation.

When in flight, the human organism is subject to a number of illusions not occurring in earthbound conditions. For example, a fixed visual target viewed in the dark will appear to rotate as a function of the acceleration or deceleration of the airplane (9). The best safeguards against illusions and spatial disorientation are provided by knowledge regarding the occurrence of these phenomena and by adequate training in the use of instruments and other dependable checks.

**Isolation.** The conditions discussed in the preceding section illustrate several kinds of physiological stress that may arise in space travel. In addition, psychological stress may be induced by various aspects of the situation, such as unfamiliarity, danger, and isolation. Considerable research has been conducted on the effects of isolation (see 2, pp. 409–421; 86). The problem of isolation is of concern not only in space travel but also in long-submerged submarine cruises, assignments to arctic bases, and a number of similar situations. Isolation may involve several factors, chief among which are confinement, detachment or separation, and sensory deprivation. Although these factors are interrelated and often occur together, they can be considered independently for purposes of analysis.

The effects of *confinement* on the individual's psychological condition and on his performance have been studied in both laboratory and field situations (7, 17, 30, 31, 33, 62, 64). The psychological stress induced by confinement arises partly from restriction of movement and partly from being enclosed in a small space, a condition which some persons find intrinsically oppressive. When several persons are confined together, as in the case of a work crew, there are additional problems of interpersonal relations. Lack of privacy and inability to escape from an unpleasant social situation are potential sources of stress.

In certain types of isolation, the individual may experience feelings of *detachment,* separation, and aloneness. Such feelings are illustrated by the "break-off" phenomenon described by some high-altitude fliers (see 11; 71, pp. 159–173). In an investigation of this experience, 137 military jet pilots were interviewed (11). Of this group, 35 per cent reported that they had experienced the break-off effect, and an additional 12 per cent said they had heard others describe it. Those who experienced it characterized the break-off effect as a feeling of being isolated or separated physically from the earth. Feelings of loneliness often accompanied this experience. Some pilots reported exhilaration and a sense of power; others, anxiety and insecurity. The break-off effect occurred most often when the pilot was flying alone, at a high altitude, and with little to keep him busy. It appeared to be unrelated to the pilot's flight experience but seemed to be influenced by personality characteristics.

*Sensory deprivation* refers to a reduction in the absolute level, variability, or patterning of sensory stimulation. In milder forms it produces boredom and restlessness; in more severe forms it may lead to hallucinations and other serious aberrations. Although research on the effects of sensory deprivation is of recent origin, its implications have aroused interest in many connections, from child development to psychotherapy, and from "brainwashing" to space travel (see 22, 71). From a theoretical standpoint, it has been suggested that variety of stimulation contributes to the activation level, or "alertness," of the organism and that activation level is in turn related to the effectiveness of behavior. Underlying neurological mechanisms have been proposed to explain this phenomenon (35, 71).

Under certain circumstances, highly repetitive visual tasks may induce sleep or mild hypnosis. Similarly, when driving on a superhighway with little to do and few objects to see along the roadside, some drivers become drowsy and sleepy. In long-distance truck driving, hallucinations are a recognized accident hazard (52, pp. 124–125). In experimental studies of sensory deprivation, adult volunteers have usually been confined individually in a small enclosure providing a minimum of visual, auditory, and touch stimuli for periods ranging from a few hours to several days (15, 23, 58, 67, 71, 87, 90). Among the observed effects are perceptual distortions and cognitive disorientations, major disturbances of time estimation, hallucinations, inability to concentrate, decline in test performance, and unpleasant emotional states. Some subjects voluntarily terminate the experiment ahead of schedule because they find it intolerable. It is noteworthy, too, that subjects in such isolation experiments characteristically show an abnormal concern with time (58).

Mention should also be made of the autokinetic illusion, long familiar in the psychological laboratory. When an observer gazes steadily at a small, dim light in an otherwise dark room, the light soon appears to move in an irregular path. This illusory movement has practical importance in night flying and may account for some aircraft accidents (27).

Individuals vary widely in their reactions to all aspects of isolation. Such individual differences are especially marked with regard to emotional responses. In general, persons who adjust well to the psychological stresses of isolation are those who adjust well in other everyday-life situations. Motivation is an important factor in counteracting the adverse effects of isolation. Personnel selection is thus a major way to prevent isolation effects. Habituation and training, including a knowledge of expected phenomena and specific ways of circumventing them, are also effective. Isolation stress may be further reduced by maintaining communication and by providing activity and stimulation for the operator.[9] When a crew must work together in prolonged confinement, the use of sociometric techniques in assigning members to the group may be helpful (see ch. 6).

## NOISE

In discussions of the effects of noise on human behavior, the term "noise" has commonly been used to mean "unwanted sound" (3; 47, ch. 8). Regardless of its physical properties, noise in this context customarily refers to sounds that are injurious, disruptive, distracting, or annoying.

***Noise and Hearing Loss.*** There is abundant evidence that exposure to loud noises produces hearing loss, although many of the details regarding the characteristics of the sound stimuli and the nature of the effect are still to be worked out (3; 47, ch. 8). It is well established that several years' exposure to a high noise level, as in the work of boilermakers, riveters, and train crewmen, may result in permanently impaired hearing. The frequency and severity of such impairment varies with the loudness of the sounds in the work environment, as illustrated by the data from different departments of an aircraft plant, shown in Figure 56.

Some of the hearing loss resulting from noise is temporary. Partial or total recovery may occur within periods varying from a few hours to several months. The extent and rate of recovery probably depend upon the individual, the nature of the sound, and the duration of exposure. Estimates of the lower bounds of harmful noise level vary widely, but the majority cluster at or slightly above 100 decibels (db) for continuous exposure (47, p. 191). This intensity corresponds roughly to the maximum noise obtained from riveting or

[9] As an illustration of the successful application of all these procedures, it is noteworthy that no evidence of sensory deprivation or break-off phenomenon was observed by the astronaut John H. Glenn, Jr. during the first American manned orbital space flight (61, p. 99).

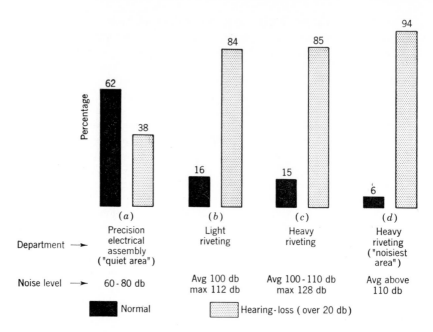

*Fig. 56* Percentage of workers in four departments of an aircraft plant with "normal" hearing versus those with hearing loss. (*Data from MacLaren and Chaney, 55, p. 112.*)

from a New York subway train (8, p. 112). Intermittent loud noises, as from gun blasts, may also cause either temporary or permanent hearing loss.

**Noise and Auditory Communication.** In work requiring the proper response to auditory cues, noise may interfere directly with task performance. Considerable research has been done on the *masking* of sounds by different kinds of noise (47, pp. 147–152). The effect of such masking is to raise the auditory threshold for various sounds. We can thus determine how much the loudness of a sound signal or other auditory stimulus must be increased for the stimulus to be just barely audible against the given noise. The task may call for *discrimination* of two or more auditory signals, as in underwater sonar operations or in certain kinds of blind flying (47, pp. 174–177). In this connection, it has been found that the smallest noticeable difference between the signals depends upon the ratio between signal intensity and noise intensity.

A problem of widespread practical importance concerns the *intelligibility of speech* under different noise conditions. Whether in face-to-face contacts, over the telephone, or in an "intercom" system, many situations demand accurate voice communication. Accordingly, extensive research has been devoted to testing the effects of noise on the understanding of speech under different circumstances. Attention has also been given to ways of improving communications that must be carried out under adverse noise conditions (47, ch. 7). For example, the substitution of a set of easily identifiable words (like "Roger") for letters improves the intelligibility of the message itself. Training personnel in communication techniques that have proved effective also helps. It has been found, for instance, that under noisy conditions intelligibility improves if the pauses between syllables and words are shortened and the speech sounds themselves are prolonged.

**Noise as Distraction.**   Consider the following statements:

"I can study much better with the radio going full blast—commercials and all."

"I never turn the radio on myself when I want to work, but it doesn't bother me if my roommate turns it on. I just ignore it."

"I simply can't work in the library. With people walking around or whispering, it's impossible to concentrate."

"How can New Yorkers ever get any work done? Trucks rumbling past, sirens screaming, buildings going up or coming down, streets periodically torn up—you can't hear yourself think!"

These represent a few of the many opinions people express about the effect of distraction on work. What do the facts show?

Any attention-arousing stimulus that is irrelevant to the task at hand may serve as a distractor. Besides noise, common sources of distraction include the presence of other persons, anything in motion, bright lights or vivid colors, internal sensations of pain or discomfort, excesses of temperature, pleasant thoughts, and worries. In industrial settings, offices, and other work situations, however, noise is probably the most common distractor. Hence investigations of distraction have usually been concerned with noise. The results would probably be quite similar if other distractors were used.

Research on the effects of noise on performance has yielded many apparently inconsistent results. This does not mean that the question is unanswerable, but rather that the answer is complex. Let us begin by noting the fact that laboratory experiments often show no decline in gross output measures, even when fairly drastic noise distractions are introduced. In one experiment, two groups of students took an intelligence test under normal conditions and were retested after six weeks with a parallel form of the test. While the control group took the retest also under normal conditions, the experimental group was subjected to a variety of distractions, including phonograph records, whistles, bells, buzzers, shop machinery, a spotlight, and students performing stunts in the room or marching in step on the floor above (36). With all this disturbance, the experimental group showed only a little less improvement on the retest than did the control group, the difference failing to reach statistical significance.

One of the first clues to an understanding of such findings was provided by an early laboratory study (59). While subjects were engaged in translating coded material on a typewriter, several loud noises were introduced unexpectedly. Although output did not differ significantly during quiet and noisy periods, what did differ was the amount of pressure the subjects exerted on the typewriter keys. This pressure was recorded through a device attached to each key. When working under noisy conditions, the subjects pressed harder on the keys than when working under quiet conditions. When working against distraction, they also tended to read the numbers and letters aloud or at least move their lips. Such accessory reactions probably helped them to concentrate upon the task, much as one might do when trying to read while people are talking nearby. In their efforts to compensate for the distraction, subjects sometimes overcompensate and actually perform better under the more stressful conditions. In so doing, however, they use more energy. Hence work under distracting conditions may be more costly to the organism.

This hypothesis was supported by later experiments providing more direct measures of energy cost (24, 32, 42). In one study (24), subjects added columns of figures under quiet and noisy conditions. A system of rotation was used to balance out practice and other cumulative effects. Although the introduction of noise caused a temporary drop in number of correct additions per work period, output gradually reached the same level observed during quiet periods. During noisy periods, however, the subjects used more energy, as indicated both by a respiration calorimeter and by measures of muscle-action potentials. Figure 57 gives the average results for action potentials from the four limbs. The graph shows that muscular tension was greater under noisy than under quiet conditions. Over the 12-day period, however, muscle-action potentials decreased until they reached approximately the level of the quiet periods. Essentially the same results were obtained with regard to oxygen consumption.

The above experiment thus demonstrates a further point, namely, physiological adaptation to noise with continued exposure (47, p. 199). It seems that, when unfamiliar noises are first introduced, they produce a startle re-

**Fig. 57**   Average magnitude of muscle-action potentials on successive days of work under quiet and noisy conditions. (*Adapted from Freeman, 24, p. 358.*)

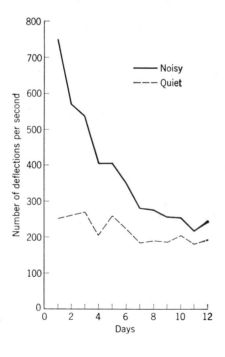

action that may interfere with work. When well motivated, subjects quickly bring output up to their normal level by exerting more effort. With time, however, the noise is no longer distracting, and energy expenditure itself drops back toward a normal rate. Whether such adaptation is partial or complete cannot be ascertained without more evidence. It may be that work under noisy conditions will always remain at least a little more costly than work under quiet conditions. Moreover, the amount and rate of adaptation undoubtedly vary with the intensity of the distraction, the nature of the task, and the intellectual and emotional characteristics of the individual.

The degree of annoyance engendered by a noise, as well as its effects on output, depends upon several characteristics besides its loudness. Intermittent or irregular noises are more disturbing than steady noises; and higher pitches are more disturbing than those in the middle or lower ranges (3, pp. 156–157; 43; 47, pp. 202–203). In many situations, the disruptive effects of a distraction result not so much from the intrinsic properties of the stimulus as from the individual's emotional response to it. This is particularly true when the distraction is caused by some inconsiderate action on the part of another person, such as supervisor, co-worker, fellow student, or neighbor.

It should also be noted that, even when subjects are not working on any assigned task, mere exposure to noise produces an increase in muscle tension and other physiological changes similar to those occurring during emotional excitement (see 3, pp. 154–155; 47, p. 199). Under these conditions, too, adaptation effects have been observed.

That the effects of distraction on output depend upon the nature of the task has been repeatedly demonstrated. Noise has little or no effect upon the performance of highly automatic tasks requiring a minimum of attention (3, 5). The effects of noise likewise depend upon the amount of previous experience the individual has had with the task (39; 56, p. 74). Like extremes of temperature and other environmental stresses, noise is less disruptive the more thoroughly learned the performance.

Research with vigilance tests suggests that the detrimental effects of noise are most pronounced in tasks requiring flexibility of attention, as when a single operator monitors several indicators (see 56, p. 74). Laboratory experiments in general indicate that the principal effect of noise is to increase the frequency of momentary lapses of efficiency (5). While output rate and other gross indices of performance may remain unaffected, errors and accidents are thus likely to increase. It will be recalled that fatigue has a similar effect on the performance of tasks demanding a high level of attention (Chapter 7). All such stressful conditions probably affect behavior in a similar way.

A different approach is exemplified by McBain's recent application of the concept of *arousal* to the noise problem (46). Considering the joint effects of environmental noise and task uniformity, McBain attributes monotony to a total work situation that offers little variation and hence little opportunity for arousal. This hypothesis was suggested in part by the research on sensory deprivation discussed in the preceding section. For maximal effectiveness of performance, McBain argues, the degree of arousal should be at an optimum level, which probably varies with the individual. Either too little or too much arousal will have deleterious effects on performance. He also observes, however, that noise external to the task at hand should have a minimum of "intelligibility" for the individual, in order to minimize its distracting power. In other words, it should have little meaning for the individual. Parenthetically, it might be added that this concept of intelligibility would help to explain why the student whispering across the library table may prove more distracting than the drilling, pounding, and crashing noises from the construction job across the street or why a political speech on the radio is more distracting than music.

In an experiment to test the arousal hypothesis, McBain chose a uniform but attention-demanding task, requiring the subjects to hand-print seven pairs of letters in a continuous sequence at a mechanically paced rate. Each work session lasted 42 minutes. A series of unintelligible noises varying widely in intensity and content was employed during the noisy sessions. McBain notes that, in many laboratory studies of noise, highly homogeneous noises have been employed. Such noises may simply increase the total monotony of the work situation. A variable noise, he maintained, should *improve* the performance of an intrinsically monotonous task. The subjects were 26 members of the Canadian Air Force. A counterbalanced order of quiet and noisy sessions was followed with two equated subgroups.

Although this experiment included several parts, only one will be reported here. This part yielded the most clear-cut results and is also the most relevant to the present topic. The interested reader is urged to examine the original article. For the present purpose it will suffice to note that the subjects made significantly fewer errors under the noisy than under the quiet conditions, thus supporting McBain's hypothesis. These findings should be borne in mind in considering the use of music in industry, to be discussed in the next section.

But first let us inquire briefly into the findings of industrial studies on noise and distraction. Unlike some of the laboratory studies cited by McBain, these investigations deal with complex and generally varying noise back-grounds. In this respect they would be expected to yield results similar to those of McBain's study. However, the "quiet sessions" in the industrial studies in-volve, not a cessation of noise stimuli, but rather an over-all reduction in their intensity through the use of soundproofing, sound baffles, or earplugs. Hence it can be argued that the "arousal" effect of the varied noise background re-mains relatively unaltered.

The interpretation of results from most industrial studies is questionable because of many uncontrolled variables, such as amount of job experience, fi-nancial incentives, and the ever-present specter of the Hawthorne effect (3; 6; 47, pp. 200–201). It has been suggested that the ideal experimental design for this problem would require that all workers be issued earplugs, some of which are defective and hence function like the placebos used in drug studies (see 6). Only in this way could we clearly separate the effects of noise reduc-tion as such from the attitudinal effects of merely introducing a change de-signed to improve employee comfort.

The next best type of control involves having the same employees working under noisy and quiet conditions in a balanced or random sequence. Under these circumstances, improvement attributable to morale effects would tend to be more general, while that attributable directly to noise reduction would tend to be limited to the quiet periods. Such an investigation was conducted with a group of workers tending machines that insert the perforations in motion-picture film (6). The operators thread the film on one machine while the film is running through another machine. Payment is based on rate of work as well as film breakage and other operational breakdowns. The task is described as being sensitive to momentary lapses of attention and hence well suited to the investigation of distraction. All operators normally shifted from room to room in a six-week cycle. Some of these rooms remained at their original noise levels, while others were treated for noise reduction by placing absorbent materials on walls and ceilings and absorbent baffles between the rows of machines. The sound level in the treated rooms was reduced from about 99 db to about 90 db.

Performance data were gathered for several six-week periods distributed over two years. Following noise reduction, output rose and absenteeism declined throughout, with no significant differences between treated and untreated areas. Such changes can thus be attributed to improved morale and other general factors. Errors, on the other hand, declined significantly more in treated than in untreated areas. These findings are consistent with those of laboratory studies in that they indicate fewer momentary lapses of attention when environmental stress is reduced.

## MUSIC IN INDUSTRY

Industrial music had its origins in early work songs, which served chiefly to pace the rhythm of motor activities but undoubtedly helped also to relieve monotony and improve morale. Although music is now used widely in American industry, there are few controlled studies of its effects and results are inconclusive (78). Investigations of simple assembly operations and other repetitive jobs have reported slight increases in output, reduction in scrappage rate, and no change in accident frequency following the introduction of music during work (37, 40, 70, 89).

On the other hand, a well-controlled study of a somewhat more complex industrial job yielded negative results (53). The subjects were 142 women employed in the manufacturing of rugs. Their particular job required a high level of mental and manipulative skill, good visual memory and color discrimination, and the ability to attend to a variety of job demands. Two to four years of experience are generally required to become a skilled operator. During each week of the five-week experimental period, music was played for 80 minutes on each of four days and not played on one day. The programs on the four days were the same with respect to type of music but differed in the time of day when music was played. These programs as well as the no-music day were rotated during the five-week period. Output records for music and no-music days showed no significant changes that could be attributed to music. As an explanation of these negative findings, the authors suggested that over the long periods of prior job experience these workers had developed stable patterns of work and work tempo that remained uninfluenced by relatively mild changes in the working environment.

Surveys of employee attitudes, however, have consistently revealed predominantly favorable reactions to the introduction of music during work. When the workers in the above study were asked, "Do you want us to continue playing music in this department?" 84.5 per cent answered affirmatively,

14.5 per cent said it made no difference, and only 1 per cent answered in the negative (53). Among the most frequently cited effects of music on work were that it reduces monotony, makes time pass more quickly, makes work easier, and gives you a lift. It is also interesting to note that 59 per cent of the workers reported that they got more work done with music, despite the fact that objective output records showed that they did not.

It is entirely possible that, at least in some jobs, music serves to improve attitudes and job satisfaction without appreciably affecting output. Such a finding would be quite consistent with the results of research on employee attitudes discussed in Chapter 6.

At this point it may be of interest for the reader to turn back to the four opinions cited on page 211 and reexamine them in the light of experimental findings on noise and music.

## SUMMARY

Research on the working environment has been concerned with the effects of such factors as illumination, ventilation, noise, and music upon job performance and employee well-being. Discrepant findings and controversy are common in this area because of the use of different criteria of efficiency as well as inadequate experimental designs. With regard to illumination, research has concentrated on the establishment of minimum standards of intensity for different types of work, determination of the optimum distribution of light to minimize visual fatigue, and a comparison of vision under different colors of light.

The primary object of ventilation is to enable the body to give off excess heat through evaporation, radiation, and convection. Industrial studies have shown the relation of ventilating conditions to quantity and quality of production, accident rate, and absenteeism. Suggestive results on the behavioral effects of weather, seasons, and climate were obtained in a number of early studies. In recent years, there has been a revival of interest in these problems. Research is also being conducted on the psychological consequences of exposure to extreme atmospheric conditions, among which oxygen deprivation has received the greatest attention from psychologists.

Chief among the special psychological problems of space travel are those arising from extreme and stressful environmental conditions. The physical conditions investigated in this connection include weightlessness, rotation, high accelerative forces, and the conflicting sensory cues leading to spatial disorientation. A major source of psychological stress is isolation, comprising the factors of confinement, detachment, and sensory deprivation.

Noise has been investigated as a cause of temporary or permanent hearing impairment, as a source of interference with auditory communication, and as a major form of distraction. The effects of noise distraction on behavior are complex. Their proper understanding requires data, not only on output, but also on energy expenditure, adaptation, and emotional response to the source of distraction. The results depend upon the interaction of various characteristics of the distracting stimuli, the task, and the individual. With regard to the use of music in industry, the few well-controlled studies of its effects suggest that it tends to improve output in simple routine jobs but may have little or no effect on more complex operations performed by experienced workers. Employee opinions, however, are predominantly in favor of music during work.

# REFERENCES

1. Bedford, T. Thermal factors in the environment which influence fatigue. In W. F. Floyd and A. T. Welford (Eds.), *Symposium on fatigue.* London: Lewis, 1953. Pp. 7–17.
2. Benson, O. O., Jr., and Strughold, H. (Eds.) *Physics and medicine of the atmosphere and space.* New York: Wiley, 1960.
3. Berrien, F. K. The effects of noise. *Psychol. Bull.,* 1946, **43**, 141–161.
4. Bitterman, M. E. Lighting and visual efficiency: The present status of research. *Illum. Engng,* 1948, **43**, 906–922.
5. Broadbent, D. E. Effects of noise on behavior. In C. M. Harris (Ed.), *Handbook of noise control.* New York: McGraw-Hill, 1957. Ch. 10.
6. Broadbent, D. E., and Little, E. A. J. Effects of noise reduction in a work situation. *Occup. Psychol.,* 1960, **34**, 133–140.
7. Burns, N. M. Knowledge of results and ego involvement as determining variables in long term confinement. *Amer. Psychologist,* 1961, **16**, 451.
8. *City noise.* New York: Noise Abatement Commission, Dept. of Health, 1930.
9. Clark, B., and Graybiel, A. Apparent motion of a fixed target associated with linear acceleration in flight. *Amer. J. Ophthalm.,* 1949, **32**, 549–557.
10. Clark, B., and Graybiel, A. Disorientation: A cause of pilot error. *USN Sch. Aviat. Med., Res. Rep. No.* NM 001 110 100.39, 1955.
11. Clark, B., and Graybiel, A. The break-off phenomenon: A feeling of separation from the earth experienced by pilots at high altitude. *J. Aviat. Med.,* 1957, **28**, 121–126.
12. Clark, B., and Graybiel, A. Vertigo as a cause of pilot error in jet aircraft. *J. Aviat. Med.,* 1957, **28**, 469–478.
13. Clark, B., and Graybiel, A. Human performance during adaptation to stress in the Pensacola slow rotation room. *Aerospace Med.,* 1961, **32**, 93–106.
14. Dexter, E. G. *Weather influences.* New York: Macmillan, 1904.
15. Doane, B. K., Mahatoo, W., Heron, W., and Scott, T. H. Changes in perceptual function after isolation. *Canad. J. Psychol.,* 1959, **13**, 210–219.
16. Edholm, O. G. Tropical fatigue. In W. F. Floyd and A. T. Welford (Eds.), *Symposium on fatigue.* London: Lewis, 1953. Pp. 19–20.
17. Eilbert, L. R., and Glaser, R. Differences between well and poorly adjusted groups in an isolated environment. *J. appl. Psychol.,* 1959, **43**, 271–274.
18. Ellis, F. P. Tropical fatigue. In W. F. Floyd and A. T. Welford (Eds.), *Symposium on fatigue.* London: Lewis, 1953. Pp. 21–39.
19. Ferree, C. E., and Rand, Gertrude. The power of the eye to sustain clear seeing under different conditions of lighting. *J. educ. Psychol.,* 1917, **8**, 451–468.
20. Ferree, C. E., and Rand, Gertrude. Care needed in lighting. *Personnel J.,* 1936, **14**, 323–326.
21. Ferree, C. E., Rand, Gertrude, and Lewis, E. F. Sight and intensity of light. *Personnel J.,* 1935, **14**, 18–25.
22. Fiske, D. W., and Maddi, S. R. (Eds.) *Functions of varied experience.* Homewood, Ill.: Dorsey, 1961.
23. Freedman, S. J., and Greenblatt, M. Studies in human isolation. *USAF WADC tech. Rep.,* 1959, No. 59–266.
24. Freeman, G. L. Changes in tension-pattern and total energy expenditure during adaptation to "distracting" stimuli. *Amer. J. Psychol.,* 1939, **52**, 354–360.
25. Frey, A. H. Human behavior and atmospheric ions. *Psychol. Rev.,* 1961, **68**, 225–228.
26. Gerathewohl, S. J. The peculiar state of weightlessness. In E. L. Hartley and Ruth E. Hartley (Eds.), *Outside readings in psychology.* New York: Crowell, 1957. Pp. 64–71.

27. Graybiel, A., and Clark, B. The autokinetic illusion and its significance in night flying. *J. Aviat. Med.*, 1945, **16**, 111–151.
28. Graybiel, A., and Clark, B. Symptoms resulting from prolonged immersion in water: The problem of G asthenia. *Aerospace Med.*, 1961, **32**, 181–196.
29. Graybiel, A., Clark, B., and Zarriello, J. J. Observations on human subjects living in a "slow rotation room" for periods of two days. *Arch. Neurol.*, 1960, **3**, 55–73.
30. Grether, W. F. Psychology and the space frontier. *Amer. Psychologist*, 1962, **17**, 92–101.
31. Hanna, T. D., and Gaito, J. Performance and habitability aspects of extended confinement in sealed cabins. *Aerospace Med.*, 1960, **31**, 399–406.
32. Harmon, F. L. The effects of noise upon certain psychological and physiological processes. *Arch. Psychol.*, 1933, No. 147.
33. Hartman, B. O. Experimental approaches to the psychophysiological problems of manned space flight. *Lectures in Aerospace Med.*, USAF Aerospace Med. Center (*ATC*), Brooks AFB, Tex., 1961, No. 14.
34. *Heating, ventilating, air conditioning guide.* New York: Amer. Soc. Heating Ventilating Engrs, 1955.
35. Hebb, D. O. Drives and the C.N.S. (conceptual nervous system). *Psychol. Rev.*, 1955, **62**, 243–254.
36. Hovey, H. B. Effects of general distraction on the higher thought processes. *Amer. J. Psychol.*, 1928, **40**, 585–591.
37. Humes, J. F. The effect of occupational music in the manufacture of radio tubes. *J. appl. Psychol.*, 1941, **24**, 573–587.
38. Huntington, E. *Civilization and climate.* (3rd ed.) New Haven, Conn.: Yale Univer. Press, 1924.
39. Jerison, H. J. Effects of noise on human performance. *J. appl. Psychol.*, 1959, **43**, 96–101.
40. Kerr, W. A. Effects of music on factory production. *Appl. Psychol. Monogr.*, 1945, No. 5.
41. Kuntz, J. E., and Sleight, R. B. Effect of target brightness on "normal" and "subnormal" visual acuity. *J. appl. Psychol.*, 1949, **33**, 83–91.
42. Laird, D. A. Experiments on the physical cost of noise. *J. nat. Inst. industr. Psychol.*, 1929, **4**, 251–258.
43. Laird, D. A. Influence of noise on production and fatigue, as related to pitch, sensation level and steadiness of noise. *J. appl. Psychol.*, 1933, **17**, 320–330.
44. Loftus, J. P., and Hammer, Lois R. Weightlessness and performance: A review of the literature. *USAF Aeronaut. Sys. Div. tech. Rep.*, 1961, No. 61–166.
45. Luckiesh, M., and Moss, F. K. *The science of seeing.* Princeton, N.J.: Van Nostrand, 1937.
46. McBain, W. N. Noise, the "arousal hypothesis," and monotonous work. *J. appl. Psychol.*, 1961, **45**, 309–317.
47. McCormick, E. J. *Human engineering.* New York: McGraw-Hill, 1957.
48. McCormick, E. J., and Niven, J. R. The effect of varying intensities of illumination upon performance on a motor task. *J. appl. Psychol.*, 1952, **36**, 193–195.
49. McFarland, R. A. The psychological effects of oxygen deprivation on human behavior. *Arch. Psychol.*, 1932, No. 145.
50. McFarland, R. A. Psycho-physiological studies at high altitude in the Andes. Parts I to IV. *J. comp. Psychol.*, 1937, **23**, 191–225, 227–258; **24**, 147–188, 189–220.
51. McFarland, R. A. *Human factors in air transport design.* New York: McGraw-Hill, 1946.
52. McFarland, R. A., and Moseley, A. L. *Human factors in highway transport safety.* Boston: Harvard Sch. Publ. Hlth, 1954.
53. McGehee, W., and Gardner, J. E. Music in a complex industrial job. *Personnel Psychol.*, 1949, **2**, 405–417.
54. Mackworth, N. H. Effects of heat on wireless operators hearing and recording Morse messages. *Brit. J. industr. Med.*, 1946, **3**, 143–158.
55. MacLaren, W. P., and Chaney, A. L. An evaluation of some factors in the development of occupational deafness. *Industr. Med.*, 1947, **16**, 109–115.
56. Melton, A. W. Engineering psychology. *Ann. Rev. Psychol.*, 1960, **11**, 71–98.
57. Miller, I., Simon, G. B., and Cohen, E. Evaluating intellectual abilities of man undergoing acceleration. *Amer. Psychologist*, 1960, **15**, 481.

58. Mitchell, Mildred B. Time disorientation and estimation in isolation. *USAF ASD-TDR* 62-277, 1962.
59. Morgan, J. J. B. The overcoming of distraction and other resistances. *Arch. Psychol.*, 1916, No. 35.
60. Muecher, H., and Ungeheuer, H. Meteorological influence on reaction time, flicker fusion frequency, job accidents, and use of medical treatments. *Percept. mot. Skills,* 1961, **12**, 163–168.
61. National Aeronautics and Space Administration, Manned Spacecraft Center. *Results of the first United States manned orbital space flight, February 20, 1962.* Washington: Govt. Printing Office, 1962.
62. Ormiston, D. W. Intellectual and perceptual functioning during confinement. *Amer. Psychologist,* 1960, **15**, 481.
63. Osborne, Ethel E., and Vernon, H. M. The influence of temperature and other conditions on the frequency of industrial accidents. *Industr. Fat. Res. Bd, Rep. No.* 19, 1922.
64. Ruff, G. E., Levy, E. Z., and Thaler, V. H. Studies of isolation and confinement. *Aerospace Med.,* 1959, **30**, 599–604.
65. Ruocco, J. N. Effect of ionized air on human reaction time. Unpublished doctoral dissertation, Fordham Univer., 1962.
66. Ryan, T. A. Muscular potentials as indicators of effort in visual tasks. In W. F. Floyd and A. T. Welford (Eds.), *Symposium on fatigue.* London: Lewis, 1953. Pp. 109–116.
67. Scott, T. H., Bexton, W. H., Heron, W., and Doane, B. K. Cognitive effects of perceptual isolation. *Canad. J. Psychol.,* 1959, **13**, 200–209.
68. Sells, S. B., and Berry, C. A. (Eds.) *Human factors in jet and space travel: A medical-psychological analysis.* New York: Ronald, 1961.
69. Simons, J. C. Walking under zero-gravity conditions. *USAF WADC tech. Note,* 1959, No. 59-327.
70. Smith, H. C. Music in relation to employee attitudes, piece-work production, and industrial accidents. *Appl. Psychol. Monogr.,* 1947, No. 14.
71. Solomon, P., et. al. (Eds.) *Sensory deprivation: A symposium held at Harvard Medical School.* Cambridge, Mass.: Harvard Univer. Press, 1961.
72. Spragg, S. D. S., and Rock, M. L. Dial reading performance as a function of brightness. *J. appl. Psychol.,* 1952, **36**, 128–137.
73. Spragg, S. D. S., and Rock, M. L. Dial reading performance as a function of color of illumination. *J. appl. Psychol.,* 1952, **36**, 196–200.
74. Tinker, M. A. Illumination standards for effective and comfortable vision. *J. consult. Psychol.,* 1939, 3, 11–19.
75. Tinker, M. A. Illumination standards for effective and easy seeing. *Psychol. Bull.,* 1947, **44**, 435–450.
76. Tinker, M. A. Trends in illumination standards. *Illum. Engng,* 1948, **43**, 866–881.
77. Tinker, M. A. Light intensities preferred for reading. *Amer. J. Optom.,* 1954, **31**, 55–66.
78. Uhrbrock, R. S. Music on the job: Its influence on worker morale and production. *Personnel Psychol.,* 1961, **14**, 9–38.
79. Velasquez, T. Correlation between altitude and consciousness time in high-altitude natives. *USAF Sch. Aviat. Med. Rep. No.* 60-8, 1959.
80. *Ventilation: Report of the New York State Commission on Ventilation.* New York: Dutton, 1923.
81. Vernon, H. M. The influence of hours of work and of ventilation on output in tin plate manufacture. *Industr. Fat. Res. Bd, Rep. No.* 1, 1919.
82. Vernon, H. M., and Bedford, T. The relation of atmospheric conditions to the working capacity and the accident rate of coal miners. *Industr. Fat. Res. Bd, Rep. No.* 39, 1927.
83. Vernon, H. M., and Bedford, T. A study of absenteeism in a group of ten collieries. *Industr. Fat. Res. Bd, Rep. No.* 51, 1928.
84. Von Beckh, H. J. Human reactions during flight to acceleration preceded by or followed by weightlessness. *Aerospace Med.,* 1959, **30**, 391–409.
85. Weston, H. C. Visual fatigue, with special reference to lighting. In W. F. Floyd and A. T. Welford (Eds.), *Symposium on fatigue.* London: Lewis, 1953. Pp. 117–135.

86. Weybrew, B. B., and Parker, J. W. Bibliography of sensory deprivation, isolation, and confinement. *USN Med. Res. Lab. memo. Rep.,* 1960, No. 60–1.
87. Wheaton, J. L. Fact and fancy in sensory deprivation studies. *Aeromed. Rev.,* 1959, No. 5–59.
88. Wyatt, S., Fraser, J. A., and Stock, F. G. L. Fan ventilation in a humid weaving shed. *Industr. Fat. Res. Bd, Rep. No.* 37, 1926.
89. Wyatt, S., Langdon, J. N., and Stock, F. G. L. Fatigue and boredom in repetitive work. *Industr. Hlth Res. Bd, Rep. No.* 77, 1937.
90. Zuckerman, M., Albright, R. J., Marks, C. S., and Miller, G. L. Stress and hallucinatory effects of perceptual isolation and confinement. *Psychol. Monogr.,* 1962, **76**, No. 30.

# 9

# *Equipment Design*

In current usage, "engineering psychology" is a rather flexible term. This flexibility also characterizes its many synonyms, such as "human engineering," "human-factors research," and "ergonomics." All these terms are sometimes used in a broad sense to cover practically every topic in industrial psychology, including selection, training, motivation, work methods, working environment, and equipment design. A more common usage restricts the coverage to the last three topics, as has been done in this book. A still narrower usage identifies engineering psychology with equipment design. The present chapter thus deals with engineering psychology in this last and most restricted sense.

From another angle, equipment design extends beyond industrial psychology into some of the fields covered in other parts of this book. The techniques of engineering psychology are now being applied more and more to the designing of consumer goods. Psychologists are contributing, not only to the designing of industrial machinery, military equipment, and space vehicles, but also to the designing of such products as kitchen stoves, radios, and telephone dials. The latter type of research will be considered in Chapter 10, in connection with consumer psychology. Still another application is provided by improvements in highway design, road signs, traffic lights, and other matters that concern the general motorist, which were discussed in Chapter 7. The basic methodology and principles considered in the present chapter are equally relevant to these other applications.

## HUMAN FACTORS IN EQUIPMENT DESIGN

Although engineering psychology has only recently attained the status of a fully developed field of applied psychology, its antecedents can be traced to the earliest beginnings of industrial psychology. As early as 1898, Frederick W. Taylor, whose time study was discussed in Chapter 7, applied systematic observation of worker performance to the designing of shovels (7, vol. II, ch. 5). Taylor found that, owing to the haphazard selection of shovel shapes and sizes, shovelers in a steel plant were lifting loads varying from 3½ to 38 pounds. Through empirical tryout of different loads, he ascertained that 21½ pounds constituted an optimal load for men working regularly as shovelers. When either heavier or lighter loads were tried, total daily output declined. Accordingly, he designed different sizes of shovels for different materials, so as to yield approximately this load. Thus a small spade-shovel was provided for handling heavy iron ore, and a large scoop for shoveling ashes.

Frank B. Gilbreth, of motion-study fame, also devoted considerable effort to designing special chairs for different types of work, in order to minimize strain and fatigue (27). One of these was a high chair with a footrest, to be used with a tall desk or worktable. With such an arrangement, the operator could work equally well while either sitting or standing and could thus shift body posture to relieve muscular strain. Among his classic "rules" for motion economy, Gilbreth included several dealing with the arrangement of the workplace, the position of tools, and the design of equipment. His writings include many observations and recommendations on all these ways of improving worker efficiency (e.g., 26, ch. 3).

Two investigations (38, 48) conducted in Germany in the 1920s on the relative effectiveness of different sizes and shapes of handles for cranks and screwdrivers anticipated some of the later research on tool designing. During the same decade, the Great Britain Industrial Fatigue Research Board was concerned with ways of altering existing machines to facilitate their use by the human operator (39, 63). In one survey sponsored by this board, the focus of interest was described as "a large class of machines requiring frequent manipulation of a release or control or some other manual operation in which . . . the worker and the machine form a single system" (39, p. iii). This statement has a remarkably modern ring to it and could have been taken from a current publication on engineering psychology. The survey led to recommended improvements in several types of laundry and leatherworking machines, as well as in certain machines used in the manufacture of textiles, shoes, and brushes, in sheet-metal work, and in tobacco processing.

As a final point of historical interest, it might be noted that, in a report on psychologists' activities during World War I, Raymond Dodge referred to "the new problems of human engineering which modern warfare occasioned" (see 54). Dodge's own contributions during World War I include a pioneer attempt to design a wearable gas mask, as well as the development of selection tests and training devices.

It was during World War II, however, that engineering psychology rose into prominence as a separate discipline. The immediate impetus for its emergence came from the increasing complexity of the machines that men were called upon to operate. High-speed aircraft, rockets, and radar were among the many new instruments whose operation taxed human capacities to unprecedented degrees. It soon became apparent that selection and training were inadequate to provide a sufficient number of operators who could function at the required level of proficiency. The solution was to redesign the equipment so as to make the operator's job simpler, less confusing, less demanding, or in other ways more manageable. This might be accomplished by improving the displays (such as dials) through which information is received, by making the controls easier to operate, or by having the machine take over some of the complicated intervening processes formerly carried out by the human operator.

The same techniques of equipment design, of course, can be applied to improving productivity in any type of job, regardless of its initial complexity or difficulty. The improvement that can be effected by such procedures is usually far greater than that ordinarily obtained through the selection or training of operators or the introduction of more efficient work methods (57). Moreover, equipment redesign permits a fuller utilization of available manpower by reducing the ability requirements of the job or by making provision for special disabilities. For instance, some research has been done to identify ways in which industrial equipment might be modified for more effective use by older workers (31).

Present-day engineering psychology differs in a number of ways from earlier work in the design of equipment. The most conspicuous difference is in its magnitude. Since its formal beginnings in World War II, engineering psychology has been expanding at a prodigious rate. Its bibliographies run into many thousands of titles (6, 13, 42, 45, 47). Much of this research is conducted under military sponsorship, but industrial participation is increasing steadily. In contrast to early, scattered efforts, modern engineering psychology approaches the problems of equipment design more systematically. This can be illustrated by the many interrelated studies exploring the variables affecting tracking performance, to be discussed in a later section. Another example is provided by the publication of several handbooks summarizing normative data on sensory, motor, and other relevant human capacities for use by engineers in the design of equipment (43, 47, 59, 62).

Another differentiating characteristic of engineering psychology is its strong research orientation. Earlier work on equipment design was often based on superficial observation of workers followed by "commonsense" recommendations. Although the more glaring equipment deficiencies could be corrected in this fashion, the "commonsense" approach is quite limited and may at times lead to false conclusions (4, pp. 5–10). Today the relative effectiveness of different types of equipment is investigated empirically under controlled conditions.

A major feature of current engineering psychology is its comprehensive approach. Beginning as "knob-and-dial" research, which dealt with rather specialized equipment problems, engineering psychology is becoming increasingly concerned with man-machine systems (19, 55, 57). The latter involve a composite analysis of all that is done by the machines and by the operator or team of operators required to carry out a complex task. It is in such systems research that the most spectacular progress is being made today. Moreover, it is chiefly through this research that the applied field of engineering psychology is in turn beginning to make contributions to basic psychological knowledge.

## SPATIAL LAYOUT OF WORK

Among the earliest recommendations of time-and-motion analysts were those pertaining to the spatial arrangement of the workplace, tools, and supplies. Materials should be arranged in the order in which they are to be used, so that the worker need not cross and recross his path of motion. Moreover, having a regular place for each article eliminates search. Further savings are effected by *pre-positioning* tools in holders in such a way that they are grasped in the position in which they will be used. Holders for pens provide a simple and familiar example of this principle. Several holders have been devised for pre-positioning screwdrivers and other small tools (2, pp. 288–290).

The application of knowledge regarding human dimensions and movement characteristics to the designing of work layout is illustrated by the *semicircular work space*. In an assembly job, for example, the bins containing the parts to be assembled should be arranged, not in a straight line, but in a semicircle in front of the worker, as illustrated in Figure 58. Such an arrangement eliminates the excessive reaching required for the end bins in a linear arrangement. Figure 58 also shows the outer dimensions of the so-called "normal" and

*Fig. 58* Arrangement of bins for an assembly operation. Normal and maximal semicircular areas have been superimposed. (*From Barnes, 2, p. 250.*)

"maximum" working areas. The former is determined by sweeping the fore-arm across the table, with the upper arm hanging against the body and with the elbow as a pivot. The latter is found in the same fashion, except that the whole arm is now rotated, with the shoulder as a pivot. The area where the semicircles defined by the right and left hands overlap represents a zone where two-handed work can be performed most conveniently.

The semicircular work space is appropriate for any situation where the operator must reach for a number of items in a repetitive sequence. The collating of papers and the stuffing of envelopes by a clerk represent familiar examples. It might appear that the saving in time and energy effected by the semicircular work space are trivial. This is true if we consider the collating of a single set of papers or the assembly of a single article. But in a repetitive job the savings mount up to impressive figures. In one large radio-manufacturing company, for instance, it was estimated that, by shortening the reach to each supply bin by 6 inches, the total saving in time was 34,000 hours a year and the saving in distance traveled by the operators' hands was 98,500 miles a year! (See 2, p. 254.)

For most purposes, the semicircular pattern provides a sufficiently accurate guide for defining the most effective work space. Human movements, however, rarely fit into such simple geometric forms. A detailed empirical study recently conducted under Navy auspices demonstrated that the normal working area is more limited in extent and is defined by a more complex figure, known in mathematics as a "prolate epicycloid" (53). This figure—which does not look quite so complicated as it sounds—is shown in heavy solid line in Figure 59. The traditional semicircular areas corresponding to normal and maximum working space have been superimposed for comparative purposes. The deviation from a semicircle results chiefly from the fact that, when the forearm moves outward, the elbow does not remain in a fixed position but moves out and away from the body. Consequently, the figure is somewhat flattened, and the right and left corners are chopped off. This type of curve is useful not only in designing a flat working surface but also as a guide for the construction of control panels and other vertical working areas. For the latter purpose, the vertical surface is erected perpendicularly along the outer contour of the figure, which is first flattened out at the center as shown by the dotted line in Figure 59.

Another illustration of research on work layout is provided by the *typewriter keyboard* (8, 9, 34). The arrangement of characters on the standard keyboard makes insufficient use of the more efficient fingers, while overloading the less efficient. Empirical surveys provide a count of the frequency of occurrence of the 26 letters of the alphabet in the most commonly used English words, as well as the frequency of punctuation marks, capitals, and other characters in large samples of business letters. The relative ability of the eight fingers used for typewriting has been investigated by means of tapping tests and by analyses of the number of errors made by each finger (9, 34).

**Fig. 59**  Modified normal working area, with traditional semicircular areas superimposed. Dimensions shown are in inches. (*Adapted from Squires, 53, p. 2.*)

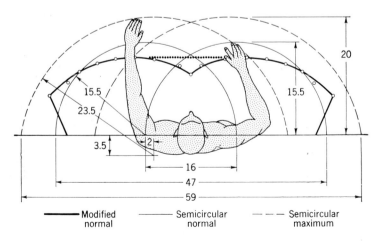

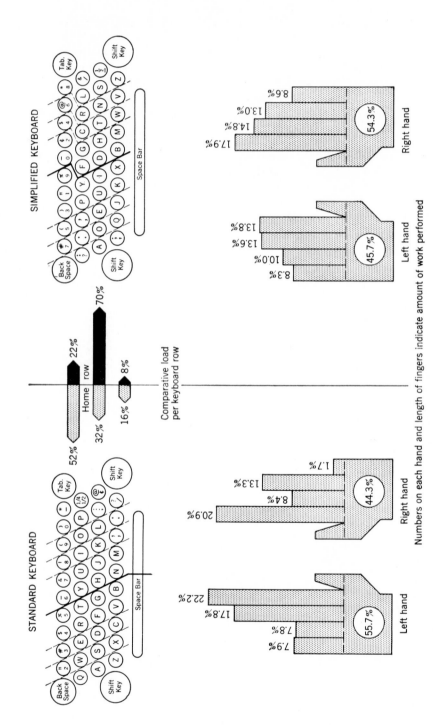

**Fig. 60** Distribution of load with standard and simplified typewriter keyboards. (*Data from Dvorak et al., 9, p. 218; simplified keyboard reproduced by permission of A. Dvorak.*)

On the basis of all this information, the "simplified" keyboard reproduced in the right-hand portion of Figure 60 was developed. The load carried by each finger of the right and left hands is also shown in Figure 60. This distribution of load can be contrasted with that obtained with the standard keyboard, given in the left half of Figure 60. It will be seen that with the standard keyboard the less efficient left hand carries more than half of the typing load, insufficient use is made of the relatively efficient right middle finger, and the second, or "home," row is used less frequently than the less accessible third row. Research conducted with high school and college students and with schoolchildren over a period of several years indicated that the simplified keyboard requires less learning time, increases typing speed, decreases errors, and produces less fatigue than the standard keyboard (8). A major obstacle in the way of introducing an innovation of this sort, of course, is the resistance of typists who have become expert with the old keyboard.

## DISPLAY PROBLEMS

In the terminology of engineering psychology, a display is a device used to present information indirectly by symbolic or pictorial means. Examples of common displays include speedometers, thermometers, pressure gauges, gas meters, altimeters, doorbells, and fire gongs. With advancing automation, there is an increase in the number and complexity of displays to which the human operator must successfully respond. Research has shown that improvements in the design of displays can lead to substantial savings in time and energy and a marked reduction in accident risk.

*Visual Displays.* By far the most common types of displays are visual. Such displays may become very complex, as illustrated by the instrument panels of modern aircraft. Engineering psychologists have studied many aspects of visual displays, such as dial size and shape, length of scale units, number and spacing of scale markers, direction of pointer movements, size and style of letters and numerals, and position of displays in relation to the normal position of the operator's head and eyes (see 43, chs. 4 and 14). Some experimental findings indicate an interaction of different variables in the subject's performance. For example, certain dial characteristics are more effective in situations calling for rapid reading, while others are more effective when the operator can take as much time as he needs for careful reading. Thus, in rapid reading, greater accuracy is usually achieved with a dial having fewer scale markers and hence requiring some interpolation. On the other hand, a dial with individual markers corresponding to each scale unit yields better results when adequate reading time is available (43, ch. 4).

Several experiments have been concerned with dial design. One experiment with 60 male college students compared the five types of dials reproduced in Figure 61, including vertical, horizontal, semicircular, round, and open-window (50). In the first four dial types, the pointer moves along the dial scale; in the open-window types, the pointer remains fixed, and the dial scale moves. Seventeen settings were presented with each dial, each setting falling on one of the scale markers (i.e., either a whole number or a half number). Exposure time for each setting was 0.12 second. An error was scored when the subject either gave an incorrect reading or was unable to give a reading during the

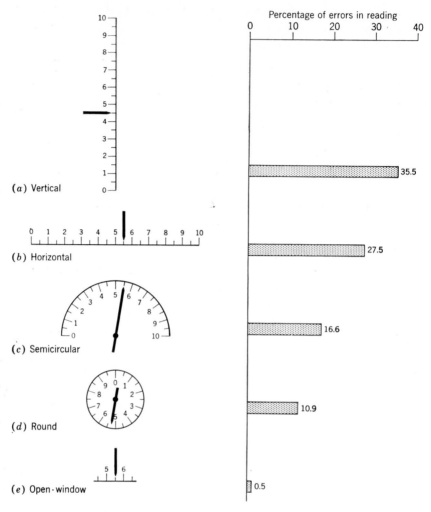

**Fig. 61**   Percentage of errors in reading five types of dials.
(*Adapted from Sleight, 50, pp. 177, 181.*)

brief exposure. As can be seen in Figure 61, the smallest percentage of errors
(0.5) was obtained with the open-window design, the largest with the vertical
dial (35.5).

One factor determining the relative accuracy of reading different types of
dials seems to be the area that the observer must scan in order to make a
reading. In the above experiment, the greater the area, the higher was the
error frequency. The open-window type provides the most compact design,
the circular the next most compact. The semicircular and horizontal scales
require the eye to cover increasingly more ground. It is also relevant to note
in this connection that with semicircular and horizontal scales errors were
more common at the extreme positions. The difference between horizontal and

vertical scales, on the other hand, is undoubtedly related to the fact that horizontal eye movements are easier and faster than vertical eye movements. Customary reading habits, involving the horizontal scanning of the page, would also tend to favor the horizontal type of scale. It is noteworthy that the advantage of horizontal as compared with vertical scales persists when longer exposure times are used (29).

Another variable that affects the results of dial-reading experiments is the type of reading required. The above experiment called for quantitative reading, in which the actual numerical value must be determined. In such dial reading, the open-window and moving-tape design has generally yielded the greatest speed and accuracy. In qualitative or check-reading, on the other hand, the purpose may be simply to determine whether the indicator is within a normal or safe range or whether the equipment is or is not functioning properly. Moreover, qualitative reading may be concerned with the direction and rate of movement of an indicator, as well as with its position. For this type of reading, the dial and moving-pointer display is superior to the open-window type (11). Such findings again illustrate the importance of considering the interaction of different variables in drawing conclusions from applied research. It should also be noted that engineering considerations may make the use of the psychologically optimal display impracticable in certain situations. Under such circumstances the compromise solution must utilize both physical and psychological facts in the best possible way.

One experiment on check-readings was concerned with the simultaneous monitoring of groups of dials (49). The subject's task was to identify in each panel the one dial whose pointer was not in the normal position. As illustrated

**Fig. 62**   Speed of check-reading dials with normal pointer positions aligned and not aligned in panel. (*Data from Senders, 49, p. 21; chart prepared by Aero Medical Laboratory, United States Air Force.*)

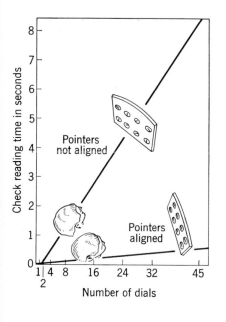

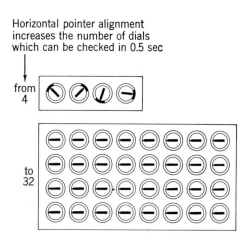

Horizontal pointer alignment increases the number of dials which can be checked in 0.5 sec

in Figure 62, two arrangements were used for the normal pointer positions. In one arrangement, the normal position varied from dial to dial, being defined by the location of a small red arc on the circumference of the dial. In the other, the normal position was the same in all dials, the pointers being in a horizontal "nine o'clock" position. Various numbers of dials up to 45 were employed with each arrangement.

Reference to the graph in Figure 62 shows that the time required by the subjects to identify the deviant dial increases with the number of dials in the panel, as would be expected. The increase is much steeper, however, when the normal pointer positions are not aligned than when they are aligned on the different dials. In 0.5 second, for instance, subjects could check-read as many as 32 aligned dials, but only 4 nonaligned dials. Even the largest number of dials employed in the experiment, 45, could be check-read in less than 1 second when pointers were uniformly aligned. Increasing the number of dials makes little practical difference under these conditions.

A final example of research on visual displays is provided by studies on airplane-attitude indicators. The "attitude" of an airplane refers to its relationship to the earth, that is, whether the airplane is climbing, diving, or banking and the amount of its tilt from the horizontal. Two ways of showing this relationship on an indicator are illustrated in Figure 63. In the left-hand indicator, the position of the airplane is fixed, while the horizon turns; in the right-hand indicator, the horizon is fixed, while the airplane turns. Both of the indicators in Figure 63 show a left roll of the airplane.

The left-hand indicator corresponds to what one would see if he looked out the window, since when the airplane rolls the horizon appears to turn. This is also the way attitude indicators were originally designed. Nevertheless, it was the right-hand indicator with fixed horizon and turning airplane that gave the more accurate results and required less training time (3, 20, 21, 41). It was this arrangement, too, that was preferred by most subjects, including experienced pilots who had been using the old type of indicator. Apparently in this situation intellectual realism, based upon the knowledge that the airplane tilts and the horizon remains fixed, is more important than visual realism.

*Fig. 63*   Two types of airplane-attitude indicators. (*From McCormick, 43, p.* 388.)

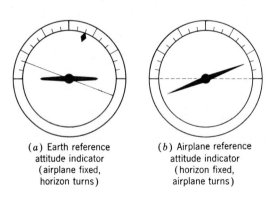

(*a*) Earth reference
attitude indicator
(airplane fixed,
horizon turns)

(*b*) Airplane reference
attitude indicator
(horizon fixed,
airplane turns)

*Auditory Displays.* Although relatively little use has been made of auditory displays, their potentialities are being explored in more and more situations. Because of their attention-compelling nature, auditory signals are especially suitable for reporting emergencies. While the observer might be looking elsewhere or might close his eyes, his ears are always "open" to stimuli. Auditory displays are also useful in situations where heavy demands are made upon visual attention. The substitution of auditory displays for one or more of the visual displays in these situations would remove some of the overload from the visual modality. Such is the case, for instance, in "blind flying," when the number of instruments to be monitored is very large.

As an aid in blind flying, or instrument flying, the military services have experimented with a system of auditory signals known as "Flybar" (Flying by auditory reference). In this system, sound signals are employed to provide information regarding airspeed, turn movements, and banking movements. Although Flybar has not been used operationally, it has yielded some research data having broad implications for the use of auditory displays in general (18). For example, auditory signals should be as realistic as possible and should tie in with habitual associations. Thus air speed may be indicated by varying the rate of a continuous series of "putt-putt-putts," commonly associated with the sound of a motor. It was also found that a three-in-one signal, in which different characteristics of the sound stand for different types of information, was better than three separate signals. In the latter case, one signal was likely to catch and hold the attention for a time, to the neglect of the others. Combining the information into a single signal permitted the operator to attend to all three kinds of data.

Another example of auditory displays is provided by the radio-range signals employed in aerial navigation. These signals are produced by using two directional radio beams at right angles to each other. One beam transmits the letter A by Morse code (dot-dash); the other beam transmits the letter N (dash-dot). The signals are so generated that if the aircraft is "on the beam," or flying just between the two crossed beams, a steady tone results. If the airplane veers too far to the left or right, the A or N will be heard instead. Still another illustration of auditory displays is to be found in sonar, a technique for identifying underwater objects and for determining the direction of their movement. Pitch discrimination is crucial in this operation.

To all these examples of auditory displays we must of course add the very important medium of speech communication. Some reference to research on speech intelligibility was made in Chapter 8. In that chapter we also considered investigations on the effects of noise on all forms of auditory communication, an area of research that also constitutes a major part of the present topic.

*Other Sense Modalities.* In recent years, some exploratory research has been conducted on the communication possibilities offered by still other sense modalities, notably the kinesthetic and the tactual. Thus the "feel," or amount of resistance encountered in operating a stick, lever, or other control, may convey relevant information to the operator. The distance over which a control is moved may also be perceived through kinesthetic cues. And different controls may be identified tactually by the shape of their knobs. Some illustrative research on the shape coding of knobs will be cited in the following section, dealing with control problems. The skin senses have also been investigated as a more general medium of communication, through the use of either electrical (28, 33) or mechanical (24, 25) stimulation.

A dramatic demonstration of "tactile literacy" has been provided by Geldard and his students (24, 25). By applying a vibratory stimulus to any one of five chosen areas on the chest and employing three durations (0.1, 0.3, and 0.5 second) and three intensity levels, Geldard was able to produce an "alphabet" of 45 discriminable tactual sensations (5×3×3). Years of psychophysical research on tactual sensitivity preceded the development of this system. For purposes of communication, the 26 letters, 10 digits, and a few common short words were assigned to the elements of this "vibratese language." The apparatus for sending messages is operated by means of a typewriter. It was found that subjects can learn this alphabet about as quickly as they can learn Morse code. The receiving speed attained, moreover, was substantially higher than that of experienced Morse code operators.

## CONTROL PROBLEMS

A control is a device for utilizing human effort in activating or directing a machine. Controls include a wide variety of handles, levers, handwheels, cranks, foot pedals, and the like. The steering wheel of an automobile is a familiar example. In designing controls, the engineering psychologist draws upon much of the basic research on human motor activities, such as the studies cited in Chapter 7. He might, for example, take into account the relative accuracy, speed, or strength of hand movements in different directions, the accuracy of blind positioning movements at various points, or the conditions that affect the speed of serial movements. In addition, a considerable body of applied research has dealt more specifically with the operation of controls.

*Tracking.*    A task that has been extensively studied by engineering psychologists is that of tracking a moving target. Tracking is basic to several military operations, such as those involved in radar, gunnery, and fire control. It is also required in certain industrial tasks and other civilian activities, such as driving a car. When the driver turns the steering wheel to keep the car moving within the proper lane, he is carrying out a tracking operation.

In tracking experiments, the subject must make continuous adjustments with a crank, wheel, or other control device in order to maintain alignment between a "target" and a "cursor," or indicator (Figure 64). Tracking may be of the pursuit or the compensatory variety. In *pursuit tracking*, the target moves, and the subject must follow this movement with the cursor, which he controls. In *compensatory tracking*, there is a fixed center reference mark, and the operation of the control counteracts the target movement so as to keep the target aligned with this fixed mark. In compensatory tracking the subject does not directly observe either the experimentally controlled stimulus movement or the response movement, which he himself controls. What he does observe is the error, or difference, between the two movements. Under most conditions, compensatory tracking is more difficult than pursuit tracking.

In several hundred experiments, engineering psychologists have investigated the effects of a variety of task variables upon tracking performance (see 1; 40; 43, ch. 11). Examples of these variables include characteristics of the target, such as its rate of movement and size; characteristics of the control,

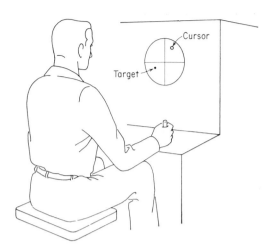

*Fig. 64*   A typical tracking task.

such as its position, size, plane of rotation, rate of motion, friction, and inertia; ratio between rate of motion of control and of cursor; and type of control exerted, namely, position, velocity, or acceleration. Some studies have employed two-handed tracking, in which one hand controls right-left movement of the cursor and the other hand controls front-back or up-down movement.

The possibility of carrying out two separate tracking tasks with the two hands has also been explored (see 1). Such experiments may use two visual sources or a visual and an auditory source. This line of research is related to the theoretical question of whether man is a "one-channel system" or whether he can actually handle two simultaneous operations. Available data on exactly what occurs when the subject carries out multiple tasks are as yet insufficient to answer this question.

Relatively few tracking experiments have dealt with procedural variables, such as amount and distribution of practice and nature of instructions to subjects (1). It is important to know how task characteristics interact with such subject conditions as fatigue, motivation, and degree of learning. It is also important to know more about the subject's behavior in carrying out a tracking operation. Some research suggests, for example, that the subject's motor responses in tracking are essentially intermittent rather than continuous, even when they may appear to be proceeding smoothly and without interruption. Other research has been concerned with the subject's ability to anticipate target movements and the extent to which he may learn to do so with practice (1).

*Display-Control Compatibility.*    The spatial relationships between display and control affect the speed and accuracy with which the control is operated. *Isomorphism,* or similarity in pattern of displays and controls, facilitates response (15, 16, 22). For example, if the operator must push a button corresponding to the particular light that flashes on a panel, he can do so faster and with fewer errors if lights and buttons follow the same pattern. If the lights are arranged in a square, the buttons should also form a square; if the lights are in a column, the buttons should also be in a column, and so on. And of course, within such a pattern, the light and button that belong together should occupy corresponding positions. The greater the display-control compatibility, the less "translating," or data processing, will be required of the operator.

As the correspondence between display and control patterns decreases, not only does the difficulty of the task increase, but there are also changes in the number and nature of the abilities required by the task. These effects were demonstrated in an experiment with the task illustrated in Figure 65 (17). When a stimulus light flashed on the vertical display panel, the subject was to push the corresponding button on the response panel as quickly as possible. The position of the arrow on display and control panels served as a reference point. Thus, if the light that flashed on was the third to the left of the arrow, the subject was to push the third button to the left of the arrow. The first illustration in Figure 65 shows the two arrows in identical positions on both panels. Seven other positions were investigated, in which the display panel was rotated by different amounts. The 90° position is shown in the right-hand half of Figure 65.

The effect of such rotations on accuracy of performance can be seen in Figure 66. It is evident that a 0° display rotation, representing complete iso-morphism of display and control panels, yields a far greater number of correct responses than do any of the other arrangements. The subjects in this study had also taken several tests chosen so as to measure a number of abilities previously identified through factor analysis. Performance on the easiest task, with 0° rotation, correlated .47 with perceptual speed and had negligible correlations with all the other abilities tested. With a 90° display rotation, performance correlated only .25 with perceptual speed, but it correlated .69 with spatial orientation. With 180° rotation, the correlation with perceptual speed dropped to a negligible .04, but performance now correlated .40 with spatial

**Fig. 65**  Two combinations used in studying effects of display-control relations on task difficulty and on abilities required. (*From Fleishman, 17, p. 523.*)

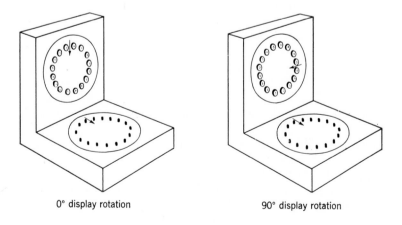

0° display rotation                    90° display rotation

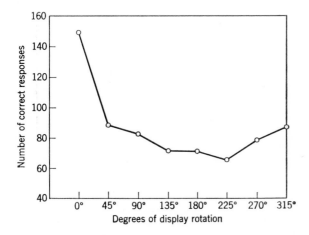

**Fig. 66**  Number of correct responses in relation to display-control compatibility. Display rotation of 0° represents complete compatibility. (*From Fleishman, 17, p. 527.*)

orientation and .40 with response orientation. Changing the relationship between display and control thus altered the nature of the task performed by the subject.

When movement of the control determines the direction of movement of the display, as in tracking, certain *population stereotypes* may affect performance. Several investigators have identified a number of prevalent associations between control movements and expected display movements (see 12; 43, ch. 14). Some of these associations are well known. For example, the large majority of persons brought up in our mechanized culture find it "natural" to turn the steering wheel in a clockwise direction in order to turn the car to the right. In other contexts, we expect a clockwise movement of a radio dial to increase the volume of sound, but we expect a clockwise movement of a water faucet to reduce the flow of water. The latter stereotype also applies to steam valves. Controls that violate such stereotypes cause annoyance, delay, and error.

A typical investigation designed to identify some of these population stereotypes was conducted by the Air Force (60). Using panels such as those illustrated in Figure 67, the subject was to "move" a light to the center position by rotating the knob. Actually rotation of the knob caused the lights in the row to turn on and off in sequence. Unknown to the subject, the equipment was so adjusted that the light moved toward the center regardless of the direction in which the knob was turned at the start of any one trial. Thus no direction was differentially rewarded. Any preferred directional association revealed by the data would therefore indicate the subject's own predisposition.

The three panels yielding the most clear-cut results are reproduced in Figure 67. Examination of panels A and B would suggest that clockwise movements are associated with "right" and "up," while counterclockwise movements are associated with "left" and "down." That the relation is not so simple as this, however, is indicated by the results obtained with panel C. Here most subjects

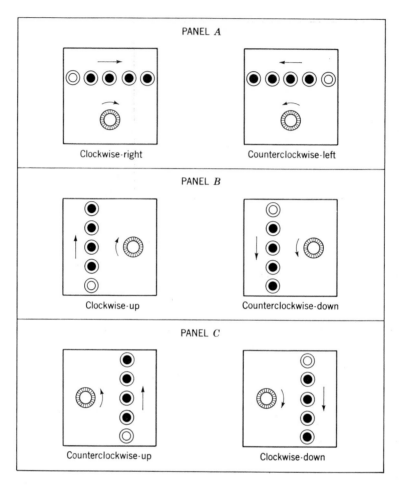

***Fig. 67*** Some examples of population stereotypes in display-control
relationships. (*Adapted from Warrick, 60.*)

chose counterclockwise for upward and clockwise for downward movements.
The answer seems to be that the preferred relation is one in which the display
moves in the same direction as the side of the control *nearer to it*. When the
position of the control is reversed, as in panels B and C, the "meaning" of
clockwise and counterclockwise rotation is correspondingly reversed.

  ***Coding of Controls.*** The rapid and correct identification of controls is important in many situations. Turning on the hot-water faucet when we want
cold water may be annoying or momentarily painful. Stepping on the accelerator instead of the brake pedal in a car or reaching for the wrong control
in an airplane can prove fatal. In an Air Force survey conducted during World
War II, for example, confusion between landing-gear and flap controls was reported to have caused 457 aircraft accidents within a 22-month period (44,
p. 607).

The identification of controls can be facilitated by coding each control in terms of some readily observable characteristic, such as its location, size, shape, or color. Thus if the cold-water faucet is always on the right and the hot-water faucet on the left, or if the cold-water faucet has a blue knob and the hot-water faucet a red knob, confusion will be greatly reduced. *Standardization* of such features is thus one way to facilitate the use of controls. The fact that controls are often in different positions in different models of cars, airplanes, or other equipment interferes with their effective operation (61). Under these conditions, uniform coding of controls with regard to shape, color, or some other characteristic will reduce the interference effects when the operator changes from one model to another.

Another factor determining the ease of identifying controls is their *discriminability*. Many experiments have been conducted to determine how far apart two controls must be, how much they must differ in size, or what shape they must have to be differentiated with a minimum of error (see 43, pp. 390–397). Special attention has been given to the shapes of handles for levers, switches, and adjustment controls of various sorts (30, 35, 36, 61). Shape of control handles is of particular interest because of its many usable variations, as contrasted, for instance, with the limited number of practicable sizes. Unlike colors, moreover, shapes can be identified tactually, when the operator's vision is otherwise occupied or when the control must be operated in dim light.

In one Air Force experiment on the tactual identification of knobs (36), 25 plastic shapes were mounted on rods that were bolted into a turntable, as shown in Figure 68. Each subject, wearing blindfold goggles, was given a test knob to explore for one second. The turntable was then rotated to a pre-designated point, and the subject felt each knob in turn until he found one that he thought was the test knob. The same procedure was repeated with each shape as a test knob. The order of test and comparison knobs was varied systematically to balance out intraserial effects. Forty Air Force pilots served as subjects.

An analysis of the frequency with which each shape was confused with every other shape revealed certain sets of shapes that were most clearly distinguishable. Figure 68 shows one set of eight shapes that were never confused with each other by any of the subjects. Comparison of results obtained with gloves and with bare hands showed no essential differences in the relative discriminability of shapes, although more errors were made in general when gloves were worn. Similarly, the investigation of horizontally mounted controls yielded about the same results as those obtained with vertically mounted controls, suggesting that mode of mounting or position in which the knob is grasped is not a critical factor in its identification.

A third way to facilitate identification of controls is to utilize *meaningful associations*. This technique is somewhat similar to the use of population stereotypes in establishing display-control directional relations. Certain well-known color symbols can be relied upon in coding controls. The association of red and green lights with "stop" and "go" and the identification of red with fire or danger of any sort are familiar examples. Meaningful symbols can also be incorporated in shape coding of controls. The Air Force now uses several control knobs whose shapes suggest their functions (see 43, p. 392). The landing-gear knob, for example, is shaped like a landing wheel and the flap-control knob is shaped like a wing.

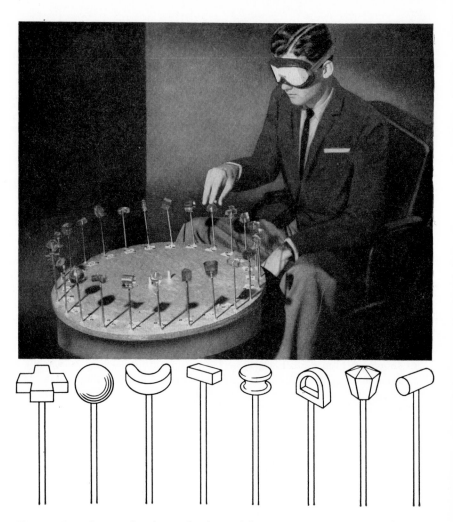

***Fig. 68*** Procedure employed in study of tactual discrimination of shapes
for use in coding aircraft control knobs. The eight shapes shown below
the photograph were never confused with each other. (*From Jenkins,
36, figs. 14.1, 14.6.*)


# MAN-MACHINE SYSTEMS

***Basic Concepts.*** If we were to name the one most distinctive contribution
of modern engineering psychology, it would probably be the concept of man-
machine systems. A schematic diagram of such a system is given in Figure
69. Essentially, this approach requires that we consider the man and the
machine he operates as interacting parts of a single system. Psychologists
began to use such an approach in their efforts to communicate with engineers.
It is characteristic of man-machine systems that the functions of the human
operator are described in engineering terminology. These functions include

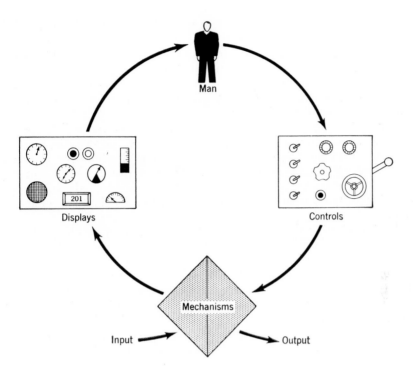

**Fig. 69** Schematic diagram of a man-machine system. (*Adapted from Taylor, 55, p. 250.*)

information receiving, data processing, and operation of controls. Inputs, such as temperature, amount of gasoline, direction and speed of motion, and the like, are translated by the mechanisms into signals, which are transmitted to the human operator by the displays. In many situations, of course, the operator receives at least some information directly, as from looking at the road when driving a car. The operator combines the new information with his stored knowledge and thereby decides upon a course of action, such as the operation of a particular control. The mechanism activated by the control in turn leads to a corresponding output, such as turning the car to the right or increasing the altitude of the plane.

In a *closed-loop system*, the results of the operator's actions are fed back into the displays, and such feedback produces constant readjustments in the operator's responses. The previously discussed tracking tasks are examples of closed-loop man-machine systems. A familiar closed-loop system not involving a human operator is a heating system controlled by a thermostat. When the room temperature drops below the setting, the thermostat turns on the burner. When this action causes the room temperature to rise to the designated level, the thermostat turns off the burner. In engineering parlance, such a closed-loop system is known as a "servomechanism."

Apart from facilitating interdisciplinary communication, the concept of man-machine systems has served to advance our understanding of human performance. This approach makes it evident that what has often been regarded as the performance of the man is actually total system performance. Changing the conditions in a tracking experiment, for example, may greatly improve the output of the man-machine system. But it cannot be assumed that the performance of the human operator has improved under these circumstances (55, 58). Improvement in system output resulting from changes in task variables should be distinguished from improvement in operator performance, such as that resulting from selection or training. The effects of stress on performance need to be similarly analyzed. In one experiment, the deterioration of performance with stress was found to be much more closely related to task variables than to operator variables (23). Thus performance of the intrinsically more difficult tasks deteriorated more under stress than did performance of the simpler tasks, regardless of the proficiency or training level of the operator.

By investigating the performance of the whole man-machine system, it is possible to specify the proportion of total system error attributable to each of its parts. As a result, effort can then be focused on improving those parts of the total operation that account for a major proportion of performance errors. Such an analysis may indicate that changes could most profitably be introduced in display characteristics, in control characteristics, or in the intervening data processing that the operator must perform. By altering the system dynamics, some of the data-processing load may be removed from the operator and built into the machine. The operator's task is thereby simplified, and the speed and accuracy of over-all system performance may be increased to unprecedented levels.

Another way in which system performance can be improved is by the introduction of a "quickening" device (56). Because of the speed at which jet planes travel, for instance, the pilot must make his next control movement long before the plane has finished responding to the preceding adjustment. With a quickening device in the system, the pilot will be able to read off from a predictor instrument where the plane *will be* in a few seconds if the controls remain steady. This makes the pilot's task less taxing and more manageable.

Some investigators have approached the problem from the opposite angle, inquiring into the effects of delayed sensory feedback (51, 52). For example, subjects carrying out such visual-motor tasks as writing, drawing, or maze tracing were not allowed to observe their performance directly but could follow it on a closed-circuit television screen. Introducing a delay of about half a second in such visual feedback caused a marked deterioration in both quality and speed of performance. This problem is of some relevance to space science, since earth-based guidance of lunar and planetary vehicles may depend upon the delayed feedback provided by televised images. Ongoing research is concerned with the effect of longer feedback delays and other conditions upon the operation of simulated remote-control systems (51).

The interchange of functions between man and machine is facilitated by the use of engineering models to describe human behavior. If the machine is to take over some of the functions of the human, these functions must first be specified in the terminology of physics and mathematics. Analyzing human behavior in terms of a new set of constructs and models should in turn provide psychologists with fresh insights, sharpen their concepts, and open up new fields of research (5, 55). The rapidly growing body of psychological research on information theory and on decision making illustrates some of the effects of engineering psychology upon basic psychological research (see 43, ch. 16).

*Link Analysis.* A technique that has proved useful in systems development is that of link analysis. By this method, data are gathered regarding operational connections between different units within a system. The units thus investigated may be individual dials or other signals on a display panel, individual controls on a control panel, different machines operated in succession by the same man or by different men, and individual operators working together within a system. A strong link between two controls, for example, would mean that they are often used in sequence and should therefore be placed close together. A strong link between two operators would mean that they must frequently communicate, hand each other materials, or interact in other ways.

The purpose of link analysis is to utilize the empirically observed connections among units in order to improve the arrangement of displays, controls, machines, and men. In this respect, it may be regarded as an extension of the problem of work layout considered in an earlier section of this chapter. Insofar as link analysis is concerned with connections among several workers, it also bears some relation to communication nets and to organization theory, discussed in Chapter 6.

There are basically two methods for obtaining link data: through observation of the system in operation and through the judgments of operators. Observational techniques are more suitable for determining frequency of link usage, while judgment techniques must usually be employed to estimate the relative importance of links. When the use of observational methods is not practicable, judgments must be relied upon for frequency data as well.

Direct or unaided observation may be adequate for a simple system consisting of few units. Motion pictures help in recording the manipulation of controls or the movement of men from one work station to another. For link analysis of visual displays, an eye camera may be employed. The eye camera photographs reflections of light from the eye. These reflections show the sequence of fixation points and the duration of each fixation. This method was used in an intensive link analysis of aircraft display instruments (37, 46). The percentage of times eye movements occurred from each display to every other was determined during different flight maneuvers, such as climbing, banking, and landing. In the same way, information was obtained regarding length of fixation, number of fixations per minute, and proportion of time spent fixating on each instrument. On the basis of all this information, the best arrangement of the six key indicators was identified, and this arrangement has now become standard in all military and commercial planes in the United States (see 43, p. 373).

When information is obtained on both frequency and importance of different links, it is customary to combine the two sets of link values into a composite index. For this purpose, frequency and importance must first be expressed in the same units. A three-point scale is commonly used, in which 1 represents the least and 3 the most frequency or importance. The composite link value can then be found by multiplying frequency and importance values for each link. These composite values can be presented in a schematic diagram, as illustrated in Figure 70.

The hypothetical system portrayed in Figure 70 includes three men and five machines. Three types of link are shown, namely, control links, visual communication links, and auditory communication links. Composite link values, which may range from 1 to 9, are given for each link. The upper part of Figure 70 contains the original arrangement of men and machines; the lower part contains the revised arrangement. The major objective of such rearrangement is to minimize the distance between units that have high link values. In general, the distance between units should be inversely related to their link values. A second objective is to minimize the number of crossovers of link connections.

**Fig. 70** Hypothetical example of rearrangement of men and machines as a result of link analysis. Link values are given in small circles on link connections. (*From McCormick, 43, p. 411.*)

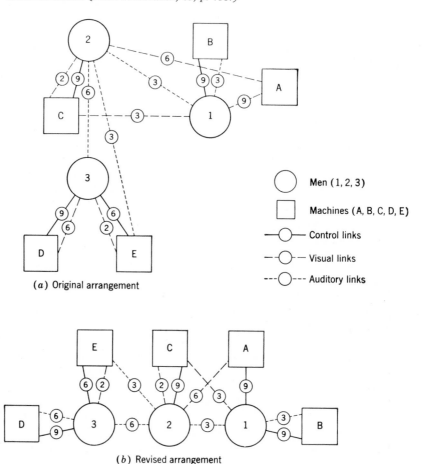

(*a*) Original arrangement

Men (1, 2, 3)

Machines (A, B, C, D, E)

Control links

Visual links

Auditory links

(*b*) Revised arrangement

These objectives can be approximated by inspection of the diagrams and by trial-and-error procedures. Mathematical techniques are also available to determine the arrangement that minimizes the link-by-distance relationships among units, although their application to large systems is very laborious. Any given layout, moreover, must usually be evaluated in terms of several criteria, such as visibility of visual displays, intelligibility of spoken communications (as a function of distance, cross talking, and other noise), amount of walking required, crowding and extent to which adjacent workers may interfere with each other's work, and other considerations relevant to the specific layout.

*System Simulation.* Another technique utilized by engineering psychologists is system simulation, which permits the investigation of man-machine systems under laboratory conditions (see 19, ch. 13). An example is provided by a long-range project conducted at the Laboratory of Aviation Psychology of Ohio State University (14). This investigation was concerned with air-traffic control systems, whose function is the safe and efficient control of aircraft within a terminal area of about 50 miles around the airport. By means of a specially designed electronic analog simulator, it was possible to present 30 independently controlled "aircraft," or target blips, on simulated radar scopes. A "pilot room" and a "radar control room" were set up in the laboratory (Figure 71). Both provided realistic representations of actual field situations. The subjects consisted of trained air-traffic controllers and pilots.

Several criteria of system performance were employed to study the effects of different task and procedural variables. Among these criteria were average fuel consumption, average amount of time required to bring an aircraft in or to take it out to a point 50 miles from takeoff, amount of deviation of incoming aircraft from the heading of the runway, and number of conflicts (defined as failure to maintain minimum separation between aircraft).

Among the many conditions investigated were various display characteristics; load variables, as illustrated by the rate at which aircraft enter the terminal area; and procedural variables, including communication procedures and types of instructions that controllers may issue to pilots. Organizational variables were also investigated. For example, how does the performance of two controllers working in a face-to-face situation compare with that of two controllers assigned to separate work stations? When two controllers work together, what are the effects of dividing responsibility between them on the basis of distance (farther aircraft controlled by one, nearer aircraft by the other) or on the basis of sectors (aircraft entering northern sector controlled by one, those entering southern sector by the other)?

It is anticipated that subsequent research conducted in this project will be concerned increasingly with problems of small-group organization and proficiency. By investigating small-group behavior under such carefully controlled laboratory conditions, this type of research cuts across the traditional areas of social and experimental psychology. Its findings are likely to extend far beyond the immediate practical problems under investigation and may ultimately contribute to basic psychological research.

Simulators have been used widely in the development of man-machine systems for space flight. Psychological research has been conducted with subjects confined for extended periods in sealed cabins that reproduce most of the living conditions of space cabins and require the performance of realistic control tasks (see 32). Another promising application of system simulation is

*Fig. 71* Simulated pilot room and radar control room used in research on air-traffic control systems. (*Courtesy of G. E. Briggs, Aviation Psychology Laboratory, Ohio State University.*)

to be found in the development of remote-control systems for earth-orbital satellites and for lunar or planetary vehicles (10, 51, 52). By means of simulators, it is possible to compare the efficiency of alternative control procedures and to investigate the effect of various conditions upon the performance of the total man-machine system.[1]

## SUMMARY

Although dating largely from World War II, modern research on human factors in equipment design was foreshadowed by the time-and-motion study of Taylor and Gilbreth, by certain investigations of the Great Britain In-

[1] Besides its use in the development and improvement of man-machine systems, simulation has been widely employed for training purposes, as illustrated in Chapter 5.

dustrial Fatigue Research Board, and by other early research. The immediate stimulus for the more recent involvement of psychologists in equipment design came from the realization that the complexity of machines was beginning to exceed man's capacity to operate them. Hence it became necessary to redesign the equipment so as to make the operator's job less demanding. In contrast to earlier psychological contributions to equipment design, modern engineering psychology is more extensive, systematic, research-oriented, and comprehensive in its approach.

One of the problems of equipment design is that of the spatial layout of work. This is illustrated by research on the pre-positioning of tools, the semicircular work space, and the proposed redesign of the typewriter keyboard. Another problem pertains to the improvement of displays through which information is transmitted to the operator. Although visual displays are the most common, auditory displays are particularly useful in certain situations. Some research has also been done on the potentialities of tactual displays. With regard to visual displays, extensive research has been conducted on the factors influencing speed and accuracy of dial reading, such as dial size and shape, length of scale units, number and spacing of scale markers, direction of pointer movements, size and style of letters and numerals, and the like. There is evidence of interaction between such display variables and procedural variables, such as type of reading required.

Research on control problems can be illustrated by the hundreds of experiments on tracking, most of which have investigated the effects of task variables upon tracking performance. Studies of display-control compatibility have been concerned with isomorphism of display and control patterns as well as with population stereotypes. A final example is provided by research on the coding of controls in terms of position, size, shape, or color. Confusion among controls can be reduced by standardizing similar controls, increasing the discriminability of different controls, and utilizing meaningful associations for the identification of controls.

The broadening scope of engineering psychology is best typified by its growing concern with man-machine systems. By describing the functions of the human operator in engineering terminology, such an approach makes it possible to transfer some of these functions from the man to the machine. The systems approach also permits the efficient arrangement of men and machines within a complex system. Two techniques that illustrate the procedures employed in system development are link analysis and system simulation. It is through the study of man-machine systems that the greatest improvements in speed and accuracy of operation have been achieved. It is through this approach, too, that engineering psychology is most likely to contribute to the advancement of basic psychological knowledge.

# REFERENCES

1. Adams, J. A. Human tracking behavior. *Psychol. Bull.*, 1961, **58**, 55–79.
2. Barnes, R. M. *Motion and time study.* (4th ed.) New York: Wiley, 1958.
3. Browne, R. C. Figure and ground in a two dimensional display. *J. appl. Psychol.*, 1954, **38**, 462–467.
4. Chapanis, A. *Research techniques in human engineering.* Baltimore: Johns Hopkins Press, 1959.
5. Chapanis, A. Men, machines, and models. *Amer. Psychologist*, 1961, **16**, 113–131.

6. Chapanis, A. Engineering psychology. *Ann. Rev. Psychol.*, 1963, **14**, 285–318.
7. Copley, F. B. *Frederick W. Taylor, father of scientific management.* New York: Harper, 1923. 2 vols.
8. Davis, D. D. W. An evaluation of the simplified typewriter keyboard, Part IV. *J. Bus. Educ.*, 1935, **11** (2), 19–21.
9. Dvorak, A., *et al. Typewriting behavior.* New York: Amer. Book Co., 1936.
10. Eddows, E. E. A new use for simulators: In the remote control of an earth-orbital satellite. *Amer. Psychologist*, 1961, **16**, 418.
11. Elkin, E. H. Effects of scale shape, exposure time, and display-response complexity on scale reading efficiency. *USAF WADC tech. Rep.*, 1959, No. 58–472.
12. Fitts, P. M. Engineering psychology and equipment design. In S. S. Stevens (Ed.), *Handbook of experimental psychology.* New York: Wiley, 1951. Pp. 1287–1340.
13. Fitts, P. M. Engineering psychology. *Ann. Rev. Psychol.*, 1958, **9**, 267–294.
14. Fitts, P. M., *et al.* Some concepts and methods for the conduct of man-machine system research in a laboratory setting. In G. Finch and F. Cameron (Eds.), *Air Force human engineering, personnel, and training research.* Washington: Nat. Acad. Sci.-Nat. Res. Coun., 1958. (Publ. No. 516.)
15. Fitts, P. M., and Deininger, R. L. S-R compatibility: Correspondence among paired elements within stimulus and response codes. *J. exp. Psychol.*, 1954, **48**, 483–492.
16. Fitts, P. M., and Seeger, C. M. S-R compatibility: Spatial characteristics of stimulus and response codes. *J. exp. Psychol.*, 1953, **46**, 199–210.
17. Fleishman, E. A. Factor structure in relation to task difficulty in psychomotor performance. *Educ. psychol. Measmt*, 1957, **17**, 522–533.
18. Forbes, T. W. Auditory signals for instrument flying. *J. aeronaut. Sci.*, 1946, **13**, 255–258.
19. Gagné, R. M. (Ed.) *Psychological principles in system development.* New York: Holt, Rinehart and Winston, 1962.
20. Gardner, J. F. Speed and accuracy of response to five different attitude indicators. *USAF WADC tech. Rep.*, 1954, No. 54–236.
21. Gardner, J. F., and Lacey, R. J. An experimental comparison of five different attitude indicators. *USAF WADC tech. Rep.*, 1954, No. 54–32.
22. Garvey, W. D., and Knowles, W. B. Response time patterns associated with various display-control relationships. *J. exp. Psychol.*, 1954, **47**, 315–322.
23. Garvey, W. D., and Taylor, F. V. Interactions among operator variables, system dynamics, and task-induced stress. *J. appl. Psychol.*, 1959, **43**, 79–85.
24. Geldard, F. A. Adventures in tactile literacy. *Amer. Psychologist*, 1957, **12**, 115–124.
25. Geldard, F. A. Some neglected possibilities of communication. *Science*, 1960, **131**, 1583–1588.
26. Gilbreth, F. B. *Motion study.* New York: Van Nostrand, 1911.
27. Gilbreth, F. B., and Gilbreth, Lillian M. *Fatigue study.* New York: Sturgis and Walton, 1916.
28. Gilmer, B. vonH. Toward cutaneous electro-pulse communication. *J. Psychol.*, 1961, **52**, 211–222.
29. Graham, Norah E. The speed and accuracy of reading horizontal, vertical, and circular scales. *J. appl. Psychol.*, 1956, **40**, 228–232.
30. Green, B. F., and Anderson, Lois K. The tactual identification of shapes for coding switch handles. *J. appl. Psychol.*, 1955, **39**, 219–226.
31. Griew, S., and Tucker, W. A. The identification of job activities associated with age differences in the engineering industry. *J. appl. Psychol.*, 1958, **42**, 278–282.
32. Hartman, B. O. Experimental approaches to the psychophysiological problems of manned space flight. *Lectures in Aerospace Med., USAF Aerospace Med. Center (ATC), Brooks AFB, Tex.*, 1961, No. 14.
33. Hawkes, G. R. Cutaneous communication: Absolute identification of electrical intensity level. *J. Psychol.*, 1960, **49**, 203–212.
34. Hoke, R. E. Improvement of speed and accuracy in typing. *Johns Hopkins Univer. Stud. Educ.*, 1922, No. 7.
35. Hunt, D. P. The coding of aircraft controls. *USAF WADC tech. Rep.*, 1953, No. 53–221.
36. Jenkins, W. O. The tactual discrimination of shapes for coding aircraft-type controls. In P. M. Fitts (Ed.), *Psychological research in equipment design.* (AAF Aviation

Psychology Program, Research Reports, Rep. No. 19). Washington: Govt. Printing Office, 1947. Pp. 199–205.

37. Jones, R. E., Milton, J. L., and Fitts, P. M. Eye fixations of aircraft pilots: IV. Frequency, duration, and sequence of fixations during routine instrument flight. *USAF, AF tech. Rep.,* 1949, No. 5975. (Wright-Patterson AFB, Dayton, Ohio.)

38. Klemm, O., and Sander, F. Experimentelle Untersuchungen über die Form des Handgriffes an Drehkurbeln. *Praktische Psychol.,* 1923, **4,** 300–302.

39. Legros, L. A., and Weston, H. C. On the design of machinery in relation to the operator. *Industr. Fat. Res. Bd, Rep. No.* 36, 1926.

40. Lincoln, R. S., and Smith, K. U. Systematic analysis of factors determining accuracy in visual tracking. *Science,* 1952, **116,** 183–187.

41. Loucks, R. B. An experimental evaluation of the interpretability of various types of aircraft attitude indicators. In P. M. Fitts (Ed.), *Psychological research on equipment design.* (AAF Aviation Psychology Program, Research Reports, Rep. No. 19.) Washington: Govt. Printing Office, 1947. Pp. 111–135.

42. McCollom, I. N., and Chapanis, A. *A human engineering bibliography.* San Diego, Calif.: San Diego State Coll. Found., 1956.

43. McCormick, E. J. *Human engineering.* New York: McGraw-Hill, 1957.

44. McFarland, R. A. *Human factors in air transport design.* New York: McGraw-Hill, 1946.

45. Melton, A. W., and Briggs, G. E. Engineering psychology. *Ann. Rev. Psychol.,* 1960, **11,** 71–98.

46. Milton, J. L., Jones, R. E., and Fitts, P. M. Eye fixations of aircraft pilots: V. Frequency, duration, and sequence of fixations when flying selected maneuvers during instrument and visual flight conditions. *USAF, tech. Rep.,* 1950, No. 6018. (Wright-Patterson AFB, Dayton, Ohio.)

47. Morgan, C. T., Cook, J., III, Chapanis, A., and Lund, M. W. (Eds.) *Human engineering guide to equipment design.* New York: McGraw-Hill, 1963.

48. Rubarth, B. Untersuchung zur Bestgestaltung von Handheften für Schraubenzieher und ännliche Werkzeuge. *Industr. Psychotech.,* 1928, **5,** 129–142.

49. Senders, Virginia, L. The effects of number of dials on qualitative reading of a multiple dial panel. *USAF WADC tech. Rep.,* 1952, No. 52–182.

50. Sleight, R. B. The effect of instrument dial shape on legibility. *J. appl. Psychol.,* 1948, **32,** 170–188.

51. Smith, K. U. *Delayed sensory feedback and behavior.* Philadelphia: Saunders, 1962.

52. Smith, W. M., McCrary, J. W., and Smith, K. U. Delayed visual feedback and behavior. *Science,* 1960, **132,** 1013–1014.

53. Squires, P. C. The shape of the normal work area. *USN med. Res. Lab. Rep.,* 1956, No. 275.

54. Stevens, S. S. Human engineering. *Amer. Psychologist,* 1957, **12,** 222.

55. Taylor, F. V. Psychology and the design of machines. *Amer. Psychologist,* 1957, **12,** 249–258.

56. Taylor, F. V. Simplifying the controller's task through display quickening. *Occup. Psychol.,* 1957, **31,** 120–125.

57. Taylor, F. V. Four basic ideas in engineering psychology. *Amer. Psychologist,* 1960, **15,** 643–649.

58. Taylor, F. V., and Birmingham, H. P. That confounded system performance measure—a demonstration. *Psychol. Rev.,* 1959, **66,** 178–182.

59. Tufts College Institute of Applied Experimental Psychology. *Handbook of human engineering data, second edition.* NAVEXOS P–643, 1952.

60. Warrick, M. J. Direction of movement in the use of control knobs to position visual indicators. In P. M. Fitts (Ed.), *Psychological research in equipment design.* (AAF Aviation Psychology Program, Research Reports, Rep. No. 19.) Washington: Govt. Printing Office, 1947. Pp. 137–146.

61. Weitz, J. The coding of airplane control knobs. In P. M. Fitts (Ed.), *Psychological research in equipment design.* (AAF Aviation Psychology Program, Research Reports, Rep. No. 19.) Washington: Govt. Printing Office, 1947. Pp. 187–198.

62. Woodson, W. E. *Human engineering guide for equipment designers.* Berkeley, Calif.: Univer. Calif. Press, 1954.

63. Wyatt, S., and Weston, H. C. Some observations on bobbin-winding. *Industr. Fat. Res. Bd, Rep. No.* 8, 1920.

# IV

*Consumer Psychology*

# 10

## *Scope and Methods of Consumer Psychology*

While personnel and engineering psychology are concerned primarily with the behavior of the individual as a producer, consumer psychology deals with his behavior as a consumer. This field of psychology began with the psychology of advertising and selling, whose object was effective communication from the manufacturer or distributor to the consumer. Through advertising, the consumer is informed about available products or services and about the particular ways in which they may meet his needs. Advertising itself dates from the earliest recorded periods of human history (see 26, ch. 1; 84; 90). The excavations of Pompeii, for example, disclosed advertisements for a variety of products or services, painted on the walls of public buildings. Newspaper advertising appeared shortly after the establishment of the first newspapers in the seventeenth century. Advertising psychology (31, 108) was launched during the first two decades of the present century with scattered laboratory studies and with the publication of books by such pioneers as Walter Dill Scott (93) and H. L. Hollingworth (40).

More recently, consumer psychology has been broadened to cover two-way communication, from consumer to producer as well as from producer to consumer. Communications from the consumer were first sought in the 1920s as a means of preparing more effective advertisements (58). Systematic inquiry into consumer needs and wants enabled the advertiser to identify those features of his product that would be of greatest interest to the consumer. Such consumer surveys led directly to the next step, which involved the consideration of consumer wants and preferences in the actual designing of products. The psychology of advertising has now been incorporated into the broader field of consumer psychology. One indication of the increasing vigor of this field of research is the formation in 1960 of a division of consumer psychology in the American Psychological Association and the establishment, that same year, of the *Journal of Advertising Research*.

The methods of consumer psychology are applicable to a number of fields besides that of developing and marketing industrial goods and services. One such application is to be found in public opinion polls, whose procedures are essentially the same as those of consumer surveys. Another example is provided by the well-designed research on food preferences conducted by the armed services as an aid in the planning of meals for military personnel. As a final illustration may be mentioned the use of advertising campaigns in connection with problems of general public interest. These campaigns have become a familiar part of the American scene. Their objectives range from the prevention of forest fires to the promotion of mental health. A specific example is provided by the advertising campaigns and the attitude surveys conducted by the U.S. Public Health Service in the effort to encourage widespread use of polio vaccine (45, 89). Whether such campaigns are undertaken by a government agency, a voluntary organization, an industrial corporation, or The Advertising Council, their success depends upon the same principles as all forms of advertising. In all of them, the communication must catch and hold the attention; it must be easily understood; and it must induce the appropriate action.

Modern consumer psychology covers a wide variety of problems, and its methods are correspondingly diverse.[1] In the present chapter we shall examine some of the typical research procedures followed in five major areas: testing the effectiveness of advertisements, radio and television research, personal salesmanship, consumer preferences and product design, and economic psychology.

## TESTING THE EFFECTIVENESS OF PRINTED ADVERTISEMENTS

Psychological studies of advertising vary in scope from the evaluation of a whole sales campaign, through a comparison of the relative merits of two alternative ads for the same product, to studies of specific features of ads, such as the legibility of printed type or the feelings aroused by different colors. Since the techniques employed in radio and television research will be discussed later in the chapter, this section will be concerned only with printed or visually presented advertisements, as illustrated by magazine, newspaper, direct-mail, car-card, and billboard advertising. For convenience, the procedures will be grouped under the following categories: consumer jury technique, readership surveys, controlled exposure studies, brand use surveys, analysis of coupon returns, and sales tests.[2]

*Consumer Jury Technique.* Although essentially an opinion test, the consumer jury technique is based on the opinions of a consumer sample, rather than on the opinions of advertisers. Because of the advertising specialist's continuing professional involvement with ads, his reactions to an ad are likely to be quite unlike those of the general public. Some large advertising agencies maintain a consumer panel so chosen as to be a representative sample of the consumer population. In terms of available data regarding age, sex, socioeconomic level, education, and other relevant variables, individuals may also be selected from such a panel so as to constitute appropriate samples for specific products, such as baby foods or Cadillacs.

Copies of ads may be submitted to consumer juries by mail or by personal interview, with such questions as the following: "Which of these two ads would interest you more?" "Which would be more likely to induce you to buy?" "Which of these two headlines would catch your attention more readily?" Despite their subjectivity, consumer jury tests often yield results that

[1] Much consumer research is published in sources not generally familiar to psychology students. A helpful guide to this literature, which lists bibliographies, abstracting journals, directories, and other relevant sources, can be obtained from the Advertising Research Foundation, New York (95).
[2] More detailed discussion of techniques for measuring advertising effectiveness can be found in Lucas and Britt (63).

claimed to have seen the ad was questioned about brand name and other aspects of the ad. The same procedure was followed with a representative group of the respondents who said they had *not* seen the ad before. In this way it was possible to determine how much the respondent could learn about each ad during the tachistoscopic exposure itself. Only those respondents who recalled more about an ad than this control amount were recorded under "proved recognition." The proved-recognized scores for the 30 ads ranged from 2 per cent to 32 per cent, suggesting that the technique is capable of discriminating widely among different ads. Its reliability was indicated by the very close agreement obtained in the two samples of 216 cases. The largest difference between the proved-recognized scores found in the two samples for any ad was less than 1 per cent.

**Controlled Exposure Studies.** Certain research procedures provide measures of the subject's responses to ads that are *initially* presented under controlled conditions. This approach differs from that of readership surveys, which measure the effects of uncontrolled everyday-life exposure to printed ads. For example, a specially prepared *dummy magazine* may be distributed to readers and then followed up with recall or recognition tests. The dummy magazine is so constructed as to hold constant all variables except those under investigation. Thus, if we wanted to test the effect of size of ads upon their attention and memory value, we would insert ads of different sizes in which such other characteristics as color, illustration, and position were equated. Dummy magazines may also be used in situations where the subject is observed—possibly through a one-way vision screen—while he thumbs through the magazine. The experimenter can thus determine directly which ads the subject looks at.

Similarly, ads may be exposed in a store window in accordance with some predetermined plan, while a concealed observer records the proportion of persons passing by who stop to look at each ad. Or subjects may be driven past a series of billboards and later tested for recall of their content. A number of laboratory studies have been concerned with subjects' reactions to specific features of ads, such as color, printing type, or illustration.

Observations of subjects' behavior toward ads can sometimes be made more objective and precise by the use of certain well-known laboratory instruments. *Eye cameras* have been employed to photograph the subjects' eye movements while he is looking at ads. This methods provides a continuous record of all eye fixations. With it we can determine the order in which different ads are examined, the amount of time spent looking at each, and the path followed by the eye as it explores the different parts of a single ad. Portable models of the eye camera have been developed for use in advertising field studies (35, pp. 282–285; 50; 68; 69). One such model is shown in Figure 72. It enables the subject to turn pages as he chooses and move his head freely. The magazine is read through what appears to the subject as a transparent glass but is in fact a partially silvered mirror that reflects an image of the face onto a motion-picture camera behind the subject.

Another useful instrument is the previously mentioned *tachistoscope,* which permits the rapid exposure of visual stimuli. Such an instrument could be used, for example, to determine the length of headline that can be correctly read at a glance. Adapted for field use, it can also be employed in testing ads prior to publication. Experimental ads can thus be compared as to the amount and

*Fig.* 72   Purdue Eye Camera in use. (*Courtesy of James S. Karslake.*)

clarity of information they convey during a quick, cursory inspection. Still another exposure device developed for use in advertising research is the Visual Testing Apparatus (VISTA) described and illustrated in Chapter 12. By means of this instrument, it is possible to control not only duration of exposure but also distance, illumination, and other stimulus variables.

Some use has also been made of the *galvanic skin reaction* to investigate the strength of emotional responses aroused by different ads. This familiar laboratory technique uses a galvanometer to detect the slight increases in secretion of the sweat glands that occur during emotional excitement (see 35, pp. 284–286).

*Brand Use Surveys.* The methods discussed so far have been concerned with reactions to the ads as such. Does the ad attract and hold attention? Does it make a lasting impression, so that it can be recalled or recognized later on? It is obvious that these are necessary but not sufficient conditions for effective advertising. The ultimate question is whether the ad succeeds in leading to appropriate action. Although more difficult to measure under controlled conditions than the attention or memory value of ads, buying behavior provides the most comprehensive index of advertising effectiveness.

Brand use surveys represent one technique for the investigation of buying responses. The survey may be conducted by mail, telephone, or house-to-house interviews. The respondent is merely asked what brand of a certain commodity, such as coffee or soap, is currently being used in the household. A single survey can conveniently cover a number of common household commodities. The frequency of brand use can be tied in with advertising by including questions about the magazines and newspapers that are read regularly in the home. Thus if brand A is advertised in magazine X, we can compare the frequency of use of brand A among readers and nonreaders of magazine X.

Several procedures may be followed to check on the accuracy of replies in brand use surveys. For example, the interviewer may arrange to return and collect empty containers, for which the respondent receives some premium. Or the interviewer may offer to buy old magazines for a nominal sum. A "pantry check" of the brands actually on the shelves at the time of the interview is sometimes feasible.

Starch (99) reports a 16-year study in which some 400,000 interviews were conducted to determine the relation between ad readership and reported product purchases. The study covered a total of about 45,000 ads appearing in the *Saturday Evening Post* or *Life*. Ad readership was measured by the seen-associated score obtained by the usual Starch procedure. In addition, respondents were questioned about purchases they had made during the first week after the publication of each ad. Results were analyzed so as to show net-ad-produced purchases (called "Netapps"). This index was derived from the proportion of ad readers who bought the product and the proportion of nonreaders of the ad who bought it. On this basis, Starch concluded that, on the average, the net effect of these magazine ads in increasing the number of buyers was 13.04 per cent. A limitation of this type of survey stems from the difficulty of analyzing cause-effect sequences. Did a respondent begin using the product because he saw the ad, or did he notice the ad because he was already using that brand?

Some attempt to disentangle these relations was made in special parts of the Starch study. For instance, 898 ad readers were paired with nonreaders of the same ads who had the same buying rate for the product before the ad appeared. Following the publication of the ads, those who had read the ads made 14.5 per cent more purchases than the nonreaders of the ads. Further supporting data were obtained by noting the increases in purchases by issue readers in the case of products that had stopped advertising in that magazine.

*Coupon Returns.* The analysis of coupon returns provides another opportunity to compare the effectiveness of ads appearing in magazines or newspapers. By keying the coupons in some convenient way, those belonging to each ad can be identified. Actual buying behavior can be studied if the coupon is used for mail-order purchases. When the coupon is inserted merely to test the attention value of different ads, it may offer a free sample, a recipe booklet, an informative brochure about the product, or some other inducement. Under these circumstances, however, we cannot assume that coupon returns indicate potential sales. Coupons are often filled out by children or by habitual clippers, who may clip the coupon just because they like to receive mail or because they cannot resist a free offer of any article. Thus, unless actual mail-order sales are involved, coupon returns indicate only the relative attention value of the ads themselves.

In any event, it is essential that both the nature of the offer and the physical characteristics of the coupon be held constant if the difference in returns is to reflect the relative effectiveness of the ads. The position of the coupon, for example, will greatly affect frequency of returns. Coupons in the outside bottom corner of the page are more conspicuous and easier to clip than coupons in the lower center of the page. And returns are nearly twice as frequent for the former than for the latter position (98).

The ads themselves should also be comparable in all characteristics except those under investigation. Ideally the ads should appear on the same page of the same issue of the same magazine. If less than full page in size, the ads should occupy the same position on the page. This apparently impossible feat can be accomplished through the *split-run technique.* By arrangement with the magazine or newspaper, one half of the copies of a given issue carry one ad, and the other half carry the other ad. Comparable distribution to all outlets is assured by having the two editions alternate as they come off the press.

Split-run tests may also be applied to ads that do not carry coupons, provided their distribution is controlled and the results can be tied in with the form of the ad employed. The two ads for Du Pont textile fibers reproduced in Figure 73 were among those investigated by a technique combining split run with a type of readership survey (71). Some time after the ads had been run in a technical magazine, a random sample of subscribers who had received each form were mailed a reprint of the appropriate ad from which all copy had been deleted. This was accompanied by a questionnaire asking the respondent to give the magazine in which the ad had appeared, the advertiser, the product, and the main idea of the advertising message. The replies to all four questions favored ad B, which featured present rather than future uses of the product. Such a copy-deleted test could not be used with ads whose illustrations provide cues to the product advertised. Moreover, when ads differ in several respects, as do those in Figure 73, it is impossible to identify the specific reason for the difference in their attention and memory value.

*Sales Tests.* The most obvious way to find out how well an ad works is to see what happens to sales after the ad is run. Although apparently simple,

Ad A

Ad B

**Fig. 73** Two ads used in a split-run test. (*See McNiven, 71;*
*reproduced by courtesy of E. I. duPont de Nemours & Company, Inc.*)

such sales tests are expensive and difficult to conduct. A major difficulty is that of ruling out the effect of other variables on sales. If there is a sudden spell of bad weather with a resulting increase in colds, the sale of cold remedies will rise regardless of advertising. In the effort to control these extraneous influences, sales tests are conducted simultaneously in several cities.

First, a number of typical and comparable cities are selected for study. Each new sales campaign to be tested is then introduced in a randomly chosen set of these cities. Other cities from the original group serve as controls in which no advertising is run or the current advertising is continued unchanged. Through special arrangement with retailers, a record of sales is kept for a designated number of weeks prior to the campaign, while it is in progress, and after its completion. Changes in sales in each of the experimental cities can then be evaluated in terms of concurrent changes in the control cities. Sales tests conducted in actual practice, however, often fall short of ideal requirements, especially with regard to comparability of experimental and control cities.

## RADIO AND TELEVISION RESEARCH

Much of the continuing research on radio and television deals with the size and composition of the audience reached by different programs. This research is similar to the readership surveys conducted with magazines and newspapers. The focus, however, is on the entire program rather than on the advertising or "commercials," on which relatively little direct research has been done. A second type of investigation is concerned with preferences and audience reaction in general. A third type, involving direct measurement of the sales effectiveness of radio and television advertising, is so far represented by few studies. The difficulty of obtaining sales data under adequately controlled conditions is undoubtedly a serious stumbling block in the way of this last type of research.

*Audience Size and Composition.*   Many techniques have been devised for finding out how many people listen to each program and who they are in terms of sex, age, education, socioeconomic level, geographical distribution, and other characteristics. The results of such surveys form the basis of the widely publicized ratings of programs and stations. No one survey method is completely satisfactory. Each has its own advantages and weaknesses, and each provides a somewhat different kind of audience information.[3]

One simple technique utilizes a *hidden offer*. At some inconspicuous point in the program, a free article is offered. The article chosen is one that is generally desirable and need not be related to the products advertised on the program. It is assumed that, owing to the "hidden" position of the offer, those who write in for the article have actually listened to all or most of the program, rather than having heard only the offer. This assumption is probably correct in general, although some respondents may have heard about the offer from a friend or neighbor. The latter objection, of course, also applies to

[3] A detailed evaluation of current broadcast rating procedures, with suggestions for needed research, is to be found in the Madow-Hyman-Jessen Report. Prepared by three eminent statisticians at the request of a congressional committee, this report has been summarized in one of the publications of the Advertising Research Foundation (73).

analyses of coupon returns. At best, the hidden-offer technique can provide only a rough comparison of the relative audience coverage of two or more programs in which similar offers are made.

*Telephone inquiries* are now a well-established method for evaluating the audience coverage of different programs. The survey may cover a designated period, such as the preceding day. In that case, the respondent is asked during what hours the radio or television was on and what programs were heard. He might also be asked who was listening to the program—how many men, women, and children. The replies to such a survey are obviously subject to errors of memory and other inaccuracies of report, despite the recency and brevity of the period covered.

To avoid these difficulties, the *coincidental technique* was evolved. In a telephone inquiry, the respondents are asked whether the radio (or television) is on at the time and if so what program is tuned in and what is the name of the sponsor or product advertised. The calls are made to a random sample of telephone owners, drawn from the telephone directory of each city. This type of survey provides the data for the well-known "Hooperating" of radio and television programs, prepared by the C. E. Hooper organization. With suitable sampling procedures, the coincidental telephone technique can also be used on a much smaller scale to investigate the coverage of local programs (75). For the latter purpose, as few as 20 or 30 calls may yield data at a satisfactory level of statistical significance.

A limitation of all telephone surveys arises from the fact that a sizable proportion of families own radios and television sets but have no telephone. In sample surveys conducted by the U.S. Census Bureau in 1960 and 1961, 22 per cent of all households had no telephone, and, of these, 70 per cent owned one or more television sets (103, 104). In a telephone sample, the lower-income families will be underrepresented. Hence, the sampling loss is likely to be selective with regard to programs, since the relative popularity of different programs varies with socioeconomic level. The total extent of radio listening or television viewing may also be related to telephone ownership. One survey found that nontelephone families listened to the radio on the average 44 per cent more hours per day than did telephone families (5). Estimates of total coverage, as well as of the relative audience size for different programs, may thus be distorted through the use of telephone samples.

Both *mailed questionnaires* and *personal interviews* have been employed in the effort to avoid the biases of telephone samples. Mail inquiries, however, are likely to yield a small proportion of returns, subject to a number of unknown selective factors. House-to-house interviews are regularly conducted in large metropolitan areas by a radio and television survey service known as *The Pulse*. Covering a 12-hour period, Pulse interviewers first ascertain during what times (if any) the respondent listened to the radio or watched television. They then show the respondent a roster of programs that were broadcast during each of these times, with the request that the respondent indicate those he heard or saw. Although obtaining a more representative sample than telephone surveys, this roster technique is subject to the limitations of all recognition tests.

A technique designed to avoid both the sampling limitations of telephone and mail surveys and the memory errors of mail and interview procedures utilizes a *mechanical recorder*. Originally developed by Stanton (96) for use with radios, this technique has undergone many mechanical improvements and now forms the basis of the *Nielsen Audimeter* (76). The Audimeter is a small electronic device that is installed in the home and keeps a record of all times when radio or television sets are in use, as well as the stations to which they are tuned. As many as four radio or television sets can be simultaneously covered by a single Audimeter. Once installed in a closet or other convenient place in the home, the device works silently and unobtrusively. New tape is inserted every two weeks, and the used tape is removed for analysis.

To be sure, the Audimeter does not show which members of the family listen to or watch each program, nor whether anyone at all is in the room at the time. Some people do turn on a radio and then forget about it, walking out of the room or even going out of the house without bothering to turn it off. That this does not occur as often as might be supposed, however, was indicated by an analysis of Audimeter results which showed that the average radio-listening period without change of station was only 28 minutes (5). Only 5 per cent of the listening periods were over 1 hour long, and 56 per cent were under 15 minutes.

***Audience Reaction.*** In the effort to obtain an objective record of audience preferences, Stanton and Lazarsfeld developed the *Program Analyzer* (see 41, 81). Representative samples of subjects, drawn from groups of volunteers, meet in a studio to listen to or view a program. Each subject is given a red and a green pushbutton and is instructed to press the green button during the parts of the program he likes and to press the red button during the parts he dislikes; when he is indifferent, he presses neither button (see Figure 74). Each red and green button is connected with pens that provide a continuous record on tape. Since time is simultaneously recorded on the tape, the parts of the program that each subject liked or disliked can be identified. After the observation period, subjects are usually questioned regarding the reasons for their likes and dislikes.

Figure 75 shows typical results obtained with the Program Analyzer. The height of the graph above and below zero indicates the number of subjects who liked or disliked each part, respectively. The trend line provides a single index that combines frequencies of liking, disliking, and indifference reactions for the group. This graph was taken from a comparative study of audience preferences in New York, Boston, and Hollywood (81). The results proved to be quite similar and suggest that tests conducted in the New York studio may provide a reliable index of national audience reactions, at least for certain types of programs.

Some research has also been done on radio and television *commercials*. The Schwerin Research Corporation, for example, has used rough, inexpensive film versions of television commercials in pretests of audience recall. Follow-up studies showed that the percentages of persons who remembered the brand name and at least one sales point were practically identical for the rough version and the finished version (92).

Preferences for different *types* of programs, such as classical music, news, and soap operas, have been investigated through personal interviews of representative national samples (57). These preferences have been analyzed with reference to age, sex, educational level, and other demographic variables. They have also been studied with reference to reading habits, attendance at motion

**Fig. 74**  Program Analyzer in operation. The lower photograph shows a close-up of the tapes on which each subject's responses are automatically recorded. (*Courtesy of Columbia Broadcasting Company.*)

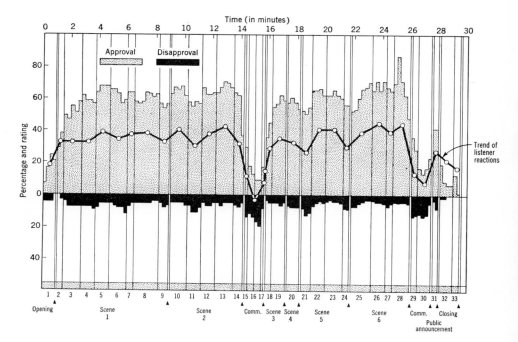

**Fig. 75** Profile of listener reactions to a radio program investigated with the Program Analyzer. (*From Peatman and Hollonquist, 81, p. 273.*)

pictures, participation in social activities, and personality traits (38, 57). Special studies of the content of soap operas and of the characteristics of their audiences suggest that many listeners regard the soap opera as a source of advice in solving their own problems, although the "advice" is usually superficial and unrealistic (3, 38). Mention should also be made of the use of depth interviewing and projective techniques in more intensive qualitative investigations of the emotional reactions of audiences to radio and television programs (28). These studies represent an application to radio and television of the techniques of motivation research to be discussed in Chapter 11.

    *Sales Effectiveness of Radio and Television Advertising.* Well-controlled studies of the effect of radio or television advertising are few. Generally these studies utilize some adaptation or combination of sales tests and brand use surveys. An outstanding example is a study reported by Stanton (97) on the effect of a radio program that had been broadcast for six months over a limited chain. By checking dealers' inventories and sales records, the investigators compared sales in two areas that were similar with regard to population, number of retail outlets, and previous sales of the product studied. In one area, however, the product was advertised by a radio program; in the other it was not. The survey showed 88 per cent more sales in the radio area than in the nonradio area. In the same study, households in the radio area were surveyed by the coincidental telephone technique to discover who was listening to the program. Brand use by these families was later ascertained through pantry inventories conducted in each home by field investigators. The results revealed that among the listeners the brand advertised on the program was used by 81 per cent more families than the next most popular brand; among the non-listeners, it was used by only 7 per cent more.

A study of the sales effectiveness of television advertising was conducted in Fort Wayne, Indiana, by the National Broadcasting Company (24). Field interviewers visited 7,500 households in the fall of 1953, before television was introduced to that city, and again in the spring of 1954, after one Fort Wayne station had been on the air for about five months. A total of 24 brands that were advertised on TV were analyzed with regard to purchases on the two occasions. In TV households, reported purchases of these brands rose by 6.0 per cent; in non-TV households, they rose by only 1.7 per cent (24, pp. A-15, A-16). The excess of purchases in TV households was larger for brands that devoted more time to TV advertising than for those devoting less time to it.

When brands advertised on TV were compared with those not advertised on TV, more striking differences were obtained. Among TV set owners, purchases of Scotties, a brand advertised on TV, rose from 15 to 40 per cent; in the same group, purchases of Kleenex, not advertised on TV, dropped from 35 to 32 per cent (24, p. 27). With the coming of television, those brands advertised on TV also showed marked improvements in measures of brand awareness, brand-product association, trademark recognition, slogan identification, brand reputation, and brand preference. Brands not advertised on TV, included in the questionnaire for control purposes, showed negligible or even negative changes in these measures over the same period (24, p. A-8).

## PERSONAL SALESMANSHIP

Salesmanship may be regarded as one form of advertising. Its purpose, like that of all advertising, is to show how a consumer want can be satisfied by a certain product or service. It is the most flexible form of advertising because it can be adapted fully to the needs, wants, and characteristics of each customer. The general approach, language, specific selling points, and all other aspects of the sales process can be chosen to suit the individual prospect. No other form of advertising permits this degree of individual adaptation. Moreover, the salesman can modify his approach as he observes the customer's reaction. The face-to-face sales situation provides immediate feedback to guide the course of the sales interview.

Books on salesmanship are plentiful. There is no shortage of opinions on how to be an effective salesman, but facts are scarce. Most books on salesmanship have been written by nonpsychologists. One of the few exceptions is a book by Husband (44). Although not based on research findings, this book provides a competent treatment of the subject that is in line with general psychological knowledge and contains many useful suggestions. More recently, Cash and Crissy (22) have tried to incorporate relevant facts and principles of psychology into a series of short, popularly written books for salesmen. Four volumes of this series have been published, and several more are in preparation.

Generalizations about salesmanship in the abstract are likely to be of little value because of the many varieties of selling. The wholesale salesman, the door-to-door salesman, and the salesclerk in a retail store are obviously performing different functions. Within any of these types of selling, moreover, problems and techniques vary widely with the nature of the product to be sold and the characteristics of the customers. The sex, age, education, and socioeconomic level of customers in a particular market will partly determine the sort of sales methods—and salesman—that will succeed. Similarly, an excellent shoe salesman may be a failure in selling electronic computers or life insurance. The fact that several different sales keys have been developed for scoring the Strong Vocational Interest Blank illustrates the specificity of salesman qualifications (see Chapter 3). Even for what appear to be closely related sales jobs, the interest patterns reflected in these scoring keys may be quite dissimilar (see 43).

Rather than trying to evolve generalized principles or "formulas" of effective salesmanship, psychologists have concentrated on the selection and training of salesmen for specific jobs. These were among the first problems that occupied such pioneers in applied psychology as Walter Dill Scott and Walter V. Bingham at the Carnegie Institute of Technology. Within Carnegie Institute's Division of Applied Psychology, which was organized in 1915, the Bureau of Salesmanship Research was established in 1916 and the Research Bureau for Retail Training in 1918 (see 31). The most promising technique for *salesman selection* has proved to be the empirically developed, weighted application blank (see Chapter 4). For high-level sales personnel, the selection procedures should include an intensive guided interview and a battery of tests chosen to fit the specific job. Attempts to devise general tests of "sales aptitude" have met with little success. This finding is not surprising in view of the specificity of qualifications for different sales jobs.

*Sales training* is receiving increasing attention. The initial on-the-job training period may vary from a few days of orientation to over a year of technical preparation. Refresher courses and periodic sales conferences are also a common practice in many companies. One objective of sales training is to acquaint the salesman with his product. The salesman needs up-to-date knowledge regarding the special characteristics of his product, its possible uses, and the comparative features of competing brands. This information provides him with concrete facts that he may use in his sales talk and in his answers to customer questions. With regard to the human-relations aspects of sales training, the objectives and procedures are quite similar to those of supervisory training (see Chapter 6). The various forms of role playing developed for use in supervisory training are especially suitable for salesmanship training (33).

Research on the *sales process* itself is very meager. A few laboratory studies have utilized ratings and other qualitative judgments of selected features of simulated sales interviews (e.g., 30, 67, 74). Although suggesting leads for further investigation, such studies are limited by their artificial conditions and subjective evaluations. Field studies of salesmen yield more realistic data, although conditions are difficult to control in such studies.

One study was concerned with the contribution of communication skills in sales effectiveness (79). From a group of women engaged in part-time door-to-door selling for a nationwide sales organization, 20 "more effective" and 17 "less effective" saleswomen were chosen on the basis of their sales records. An interviewer who had no knowledge of the subject's sales record evaluated each in selected aspects of oral communication, such as use of voice and language, listening behavior, utilization of emotional appeals, and dramatization. Several significant differences were found between the two groups, suggesting the desirability of considering communcation skills in selection and training programs for this type of selling.

Some provocative results were obtained in a field survey of driver-salesmen for a large company operating on a national scale (107). When such extraneous factors as geographic location and store differences were ruled out, sales records proved to be more closely associated with "sales methods" than with "sales personality." The men described by the field observers as "negative, colorless, weak, and drab," for example, were getting the same average size of order per stop as those described as "genial, cordial, familiar, easygoing, backslapping." On the other hand, those who began each call by making a count of the dealer's stock of the company's products received orders that averaged 2½ times as large as the orders obtained by salesmen who did not make this their first step. Similarly, those who told the dealer about the week's special offer before taking the regular order averaged 27 per cent more sales per call than did those who wrote up the regular order first.

The critical-incident technique (see Chapter 2) offers a promising approach to the analysis of selling behavior. This technique was used in a study conducted in the Minnesota Mining and Manufacturing Company, which employs over 1,000 salesmen (54). Each of 85 sales managers was asked to submit as many critical incidents as he could to illustrate both effective and ineffective behavior observed among his group of salesmen. A total of 96 usable incidents was reported, including 61 examples of effective behavior and 35 examples of ineffective behavior. The incidents fell into the following 15 categories (54, p. 56):

1. Following up: (*a*) complaints; (*b*) requests; (*c*) orders; (*d*) leads
2. Planning ahead
3. Communicating all necessary information to sales managers
4. Communicating truthful information to managers and customers
5. Carrying out promises
6. Persisting on "tough" accounts
7. Pointing out uses for other company products besides the salesman's own line
8. Using new sales techniques and methods
9. Preventing price cutting by dealers and customers
10. Initiating new sales ideas
11. Knowing customer requirements
12. Defending company policies
13. Calling on all accounts
14. Helping customers with equipment and displays
15. Showing nonpassive attitude

The largest number of incidents involved some form of follow-up. Persisting with tough customers and planning were also mentioned frequently. Although the factors cited differ in weight, failure with respect to any one of them could lead to failure on the entire job. The factors mentioned and their relative importance would of course vary somewhat with the type of selling, the product sold, and the company. Follow-up, for example, would undoubtedly be a less prominent factor for a retail salesclerk in a store than it was in this group of salesmen.

Studies such as these lend support to a concept of salesmanship that is rapidly gaining ground today. This is a concept based on customer-oriented selling, two-way communication, and service. An important aspect of the salesman's task is to learn all he can about the needs and wants of the individual customer. In wholesale and technical selling, this may entail extensive preparation and thorough study of individual companies. For the retail salesclerk, it means asking relevant questions and listening to the customer. It means, too, that the salesman should avoid such practices as jumping to conclusions, "sizing up" the customer prematurely, trying to fit every customer into a stereotype, or high-pressuring the customer into buying something he does not want. The last-named practice represents shortsighted selling, which leads more often to the return of merchandise than to the return of customers.

The current emphasis on product information in salesmen training programs provides the salesman with a store of knowledge from which he can choose relevant and useful facts to communicate to each individual customer. These concrete facts are of more interest to the customer than is the routine repetition of such empty phrases as "wonderful quality," "colossal bargain," and "a great buy." Finally, it is more important for the salesman to ask himself in what ways he can be of service to each customer than to try to change his own personality. With regard to "sales personality," there seems to be room for wide individual differences in successful selling. Each individual should try to utilize his unique pattern of traits to best advantage, rather than trying to follow someone else's rules for getting along with people.

## CONSUMER OPINION SURVEYS

*Purposes of Opinion Surveys.* It is now generally recognized that the development and marketing of consumer goods and services requires two-way communication. It is wasteful for the manufacturer to devise a product that *he* thinks consumers want and then use advertising and selling techniques to try to convince consumers that they do want it. A more effective procedure is to investigate consumer wants first and then develop products and services to meet those wants. It is better to avoid sales resistance than to overcome it.

Consumer surveys may be used as a guide in designing new products, in modifying existing products, or in preparing advertisements for products already on the market. The utilization of consumer research in product design may be regarded as an extension of engineering psychology (see Chapter 9). Consumer survey data may help not only in developing the product itself but also in designing the package or in choosing a trade name (see, e.g., 15). For the advertiser, consumer research provides information on those features of the product that are most important to the consumer. Do people who own electric clocks like them chiefly because of their high level of accuracy, because of their dependability, or because they do not require daily winding and setting? Consumer surveys may also reveal new uses for a product. When Kleenex was first developed, it was marketed as a facial tissue to remove cold cream. Its makers later learned, however, that many purchasers used it as a handkerchief. Accordingly, subsequent advertising focused on the merits of Kleenex for this purpose, stressing the fact that as a handkerchief it is cheap and sanitary and requires no laundering. The result was a sharp and continuing rise in sales, which made possible repeated reductions in price (36, p. 187; 77).

The procedures followed in conducting consumer surveys are essentially the same as those employed in *public opinion polls.* Although the preelection polls are undoubtedly the best-known examples, public opinion polls are regularly conducted to ascertain prevailing opinions on many political, economic, and social questions. The information gathered in such surveys over the years provides a valuable pool of raw data for social science research (see 19, 21, 88). Public opinion polls and consumer surveys are often handled by the same organizations. Many are conducted by commercial survey organizations, such as those established by George Gallup or by Elmo Roper. Certain universities have research bureaus that specialize in this type of survey, such as the Survey Research Center at the University of Michigan and the Bureau of Applied Social Research at Columbia University. Public opinion polls are regularly conducted by certain government agencies, notably the Department of Agriculture. Consumer surveys are also carried out by some advertising agencies and by large manufacturing companies.

**Sampling Problems.** Even when based on impressively large samples, opinion surveys may yield totally misleading results because of either poor methodology or a deliberate attempt to support a foregone conclusion. It is not difficult to find examples of surveys rendered worthless by inadequately trained or unscrupulous investigators. The best protection against such misrepresentations is a knowledge of how to evaluate an opinion survey. The basic problems, pitfalls, and procedures of opinion surveys have been fully discussed in several publications that should be consulted for further details (e.g., 12–14, 20, 70, 80, 86, 101).

Once we have decided what we want to ask in a survey, we need to determine *whom* to ask and *how* to ask it. The first question concerns sampling. Although there are several kinds of sampling procedure, a basic distinction is that between random and stratified sampling. A *random sample* is one in which each individual in the given population has an equal chance of being chosen and each choice is independent of every other choice. It could be illustrated by taking every tenth name in an alphabetical list of all names in the population. The traditional practice of "pulling a name out of a hat" accomplishes the same purpose.

A *stratified sample* is a miniature replica of the total population with respect to chosen variables. For example, if a sample is to be stratified with regard to education, the proportion of persons in each educational level, or "stratum," must be the same as that in the total population. If 8 per cent of the given population are college graduates, then 8 per cent of the persons included in the sample must be college graduates, and so on. The sample may be stratified separately with regard to several variables, such as age, sex, education, income level, and geographical location. In this case, the distribution of each of these variables in the sample would match its distribution in the population. A more precise procedure is to stratify the sample for all chosen variables simultaneously so that each cell in the cross-classification contains the correct proportion of persons. One cell of such a sample, for instance, might call for five female high school graduates between the ages of thirty and thirty-five. Because this procedure is very time-consuming, most surveys rely on the simpler type of stratification with no cross-classifications.

A number of surveys employ *area sampling,* in which small geographic units are sampled, rather than persons. In national surveys, this procedure requires the sampling of towns and rural areas. When applied within a city, it involves the sampling of blocks or other small units. Each interviewer is then given specific addresses at which he must call. Area sampling may itself be random, stratified, or a combination of both types.

*Sample size* is not as important as representativeness. Through the use of stratified samples it is possible to obtain precise estimates of population data with fewer cases than are needed with random sampling. Most national surveys now use between 3,000 and 5,000 cases. The percentages of each response obtained in such samples have sufficiently small sampling errors for most purposes.

By computing sampling errors, the investigator can determine the range within which the corresponding population percentages are likely to fall, as well as the significance of the differences between obtained percentages. For instance, he might find that 35 per cent of the respondents in the sample are dissatisfied with the refrigerator service provided by Company A. By computing the standard error of this percentage, he finds that the percentage of such dissatisfied customers in the population from which the sample was drawn may range from 33 to 37. By the same statistical procedures, he may establish that the percentage of complaints is significantly smaller for the refrigerator manufactured and serviced by Company B than it is for Company A's refrigerator.

Although a certain minimum sample size is required for reliable results, further increases in number of cases are generally wasteful. Moreover, large samples provide no guarantee that the results are accurate. One of the most famous examples of this point is the *Literary Digest* poll, based on the replies of 2½ million cases (see 2). This poll, which in 1936 predicted the election of a presidential candidate who was actually defeated by an overwhelming majority, highlights two faulty sampling procedures. First, the sampling was biased, since the mailing lists were obtained from telephone directories and automobile registrations. These sources yielded a sample that overrepresented higher-income groups and underrepresented lower-income groups. Second, the proportion of nonrespondents was high. Although there were approximately 2½ million respondents, the number of ballots sent out was 10 million.

Considerable research is now available on the effects of *nonresponse bias,* or *volunteer error,* upon the representativeness of samples (6, 18, 27, 42). This research demonstrates that survey respondents differ from nonrespondents in a number of characteristics that may be correlated with the answers they give. Similarly, persons who volunteer for any sort of investigation, whether in the laboratory or in the field, differ from those who do not volunteer. Differences have been found both in demographic variables, such as age, sex, occupation, and income level, and in personality characteristics, such as self-esteem, conventionality, and emotional adjustment (see 6). The specific differences undoubtedly vary with situational factors, such as the nature of the experiment, the topics covered in the survey, the sponsoring organization, and the data-gathering procedures.

In house-to-house interviews, some of the nonrespondents are persons who were not at home when the interviewer called. Unless proper precautions are taken, a daytime survey will underrepresent employed persons and will overrepresent elderly, retired persons and mothers of young children. Other nonrespondents are those who refuse to cooperate when contacted. Still a different situation is involved when a general call is issued for volunteers to participate in a laboratory study. With regard to mailed questionnaires, it has been found that those who respond are more likely to be favorably disposed toward the company or product than those who fail to respond.

Several procedures have been proposed for handling nonresponse bias. Repeated follow-ups may be employed to increase the proportion of respondents. A random sample of the nonrespondents in a mail survey may be personally interviewed. The demographic characteristics of the respondents may be compared with those of the total population or with the specifications originally laid down for the stratified sample. Or the nature and extent of nonresponse bias in the results may be estimated by comparing the replies obtained from early and late respondents or from those who responded to the initial request and those who responded to the follow-up. These findings may then be extrapolated to those who failed to respond at all.

*Questionnaire Construction.* A second major aspect of opinion-survey methodology is questionnaire construction. Poorly formulated questions can play as much havoc with survey results as can improper sampling procedures. The wording of questions and the general appearance and layout of the questionnaire are of primary importance in surveys conducted by mail. Questions used in telephone or house-to-house surveys, however, also need to be carefully formulated in advance.

The question writer can profitably examine the extensive research literature on the effects of different question forms upon replies (see, e.g., 11, ch. 7; 14; 20; 46; 56; 85). Acquaintance with the findings of this research will alert the investigator to certain common pitfalls he should avoid. The trend of opinion revealed in survey replies can be significantly altered and even reversed by changing the grammatical form of the question, the number of response options provided, or the order in which questions are presented (20, ch. 2). In a questionnaire on cooking ranges, significantly different percentages of preferences were obtained when alternatives were presented verbally or pictorially (105). The inclusion of emotionally toned terms such as "liberal" or "democratic" or the insertion of the name of a prominent person in an opinion questionnaire can substantially affect results.

Leading questions should of course be avoided. But some leading questions may appear innocuous to the investigator. Ambiguities are also difficult to detect, however well informed and experienced the writer may be. Since the writer knows what he wanted to say, he can rarely perceive other possible meanings in his question. Although much can be done in advance to improve the formulation of questions, *pretesting* provides the only sure way to iron out all difficulties. The questions should be pretested on persons typical of the respondent populations for which the survey is designed. Several revisions may be required to develop a satisfactory questionnaire.

The social desirability variable discovered in personality test responses (see Chapter 3) also affects the answers given in consumer surveys. The tendency to give what the respondent perceives as the socially more desirable answer is particularly strong in face-to-face interviews (20, ch. 5). If people are asked directly what magazines they read, for example, the replies will grossly overestimate the readership of such prestige magazines as the *Atlantic Monthly* and will show negligible readership for the pulp magazines, which actually sell by the millions (23, 60). For this reason, magazine and newspaper readership surveys employ indirect and check questions to ascertain whether or not the respondent has read the latest issue of a particular medium.

The growing body of research on individual response styles in questionnaire replies is highly relevant to consumer surveys. Such studies have revealed consistent individual differences in response styles, which may be correlated with other behavioral characteristics of the respondents. For instance, individuals differ in their tendency to answer "Yes" or "No" when asked whether they use a certain product, read a particular magazine, or look at a TV program (106). The "yea-sayers" are also more likely to express a clear-cut preference between two articles than are the "nay-sayers" and to give more favorable ratings to products, programs, and other items on which opinions are solicited. Insofar as these response styles reflect basic personality differences, they may serve as useful predictors of other behavior, such as impulse buying, susceptibility to persuasion, or preference for certain media. From another angle, however, a disproportionate number of yea-sayers or nay-sayers in a group could distort results in a variety of ways (see 106). Either an independent measure of this response tendency should be obtained for each subject, or questionnaires should be formulated so as to minimize its operation.

**Interviewer Variables.**  In telephone and face-to-face surveys, the selection, training, and supervision of field interviewers represent an important phase of the project. Survey results may be influenced in many ways by the interviewer's appearance and behavior. The interviewer's race, sex, and socioeconomic level have been found to affect responses to questions pertaining to race relations, sexual behavior, and labor or economic issues, respectively (see 4; 20, ch. 8; 48, ch. 7).

The interviewer's own opinion on the question under investigation likewise affects results (20, pp. 107–112). It is interesting to note that when results have been analyzed with regard to community size, interviewers' opinions have been found to affect the distribution of responses in small towns and rural areas, but not in large cities (20, p. 112). Among the possible reasons for this difference, the investigators pointed out that in smaller communities interviewers are more likely to be acquainted with their respondents. This fact may operate in two ways. First, interviewers consciously or unconsciously tend to choose respondents who share their views. Second, the respondents are more likely to know the interviewer's views and hence express an opinion that agrees with his.

Anything in the interviewer's appearance, dress, manner, or comments that tends to associate him with a certain point of view may bias interview results. This is true even when the cue may be false, as in the case of popular stereotypes. In a survey on the use of hard liquor, two interviewers happened to look like the popular stereotype of a "prohibitionist." The samples interviewed by these two investigators reported much less use of liquor than did those questioned by the other interviewers (94).

Respondents are also influenced by the interviewer's behavior during the interview. Any indication of agreement or disagreement by gesture, facial expression, or comment may affect subsequent responses. An experiment on verbal reinforcement was conducted in the form of a telephone survey of public opinion (39). Interviewers in one group were instructed to say "Good" when the respondent expressed agreement with the question, those in another group to say "Good" when he expressed disagreement. In two other groups, "Mm-hmm" was used as a reinforcement in the same ways. The response "Good" proved to bias the results significantly, while "Mm-hmm" did not.

When interviewer bias affects the respondent's answer—through appearance, behavior, or known opinion of the interviewer—the effect may be regarded as a special instance of the social desirability variable that operates in self-report techniques generally. Social desirability may be defined in terms of different groups with which the respondent identifies. There are very broad norms with regard to the moral and lawful behavior of civilized society; there are narrower national, regional, or class norms with reference to many questions of group relations, economic policy, patriotism, and the like; and there are still narrower norms established by the characteristics and behavior of the individual interviewer. "Interviewer bias" in the replies of respondents may thus be regarded in part as the subject's effort to give the "right answer" as defined by the immediate situation. Even with an interviewer who is a total stranger and whom they never expect to see again, most people are reluctant to "make a bad impression."

# PRODUCT TESTING

*Brand Identification and Brand Preference Studies.* It has often been asserted that different brands of many consumer goods are indistinguishable, once the brand labels and other artificial cues are removed. So-called "blind-fold" tests require careful methodological controls. Otherwise, either positive or negative results may be spurious. It is essential, of course, that all extraneous cues be effectively ruled out. For instance, touch cues might facilitate the identification of some brands of cigarettes. On the other hand, negative results need not indicate lack of discrimination (see 59, 102). Subjects may be unable to name brands correctly—especially in the case of obscure brands whose names are unfamiliar—even though they can discriminate the taste in a paired comparison test and may consistently prefer one of the brands. Another methodological problem arises from the presentation of several brands during the same experimental session. The procedures followed to eliminate sensory adaptation, prevent mixture of sensations, and otherwise ensure independence of observations may be inadequate or may themselves introduce cumulative effects.

Product testing provides an opportunity to apply the psychophysical methods of the psychology laboratory to consumer research. Both laboratory and field studies have been conducted on brand identification and brand preference with such commodities as cigarettes, cola beverages, shaving creams, bread, and beer (see 32, 59, 102). Two investigations are of particular interest because of their contributions to methodology.

One study was concerned with the ability to discriminate among three popular brands of cigarettes (59). The subjects were 246 college students, all chosen because they were habitual smokers, reported that they smoked one of the three brands under investigation, and actually had a package of that brand with them at the time of the test. The subjects, of course, did not know what brands were being used in the experiment. Tactual and visual cues were eliminated by covering the upper half of each cigarette with a gummed paper band. Each subject was asked to smoke only one cigarette, the three brands being used with different subjects in random order. The experimenter was in ignorance of the brand smoked by any one subject until that subject had left the room. Half of the subjects were asked to state whether they liked or disliked the cigarette; the other half were asked whether they thought it was or was not the brand they habitually smoked.

Both types of judgments were made with better than chance accuracy. In other words, subjects demonstrated significant ability to identify or differentiate their own brand. They also preferred their own brand significantly more often than the other two. To be sure, the differences were not large, and many "errors" occurred. But the fact that the discriminations were significantly better than chance suggests that the procedures followed in this experiment may be more sensitive than the brand-naming techniques, which have usually yielded negative results.

The other study chosen for illustration was a field investigation of beer consumption by a representative sample of families in one city (32). The consumer panel consisted of 20 families that were regular beer consumers, were willing to cooperate in the study, and constituted a stratified sample of the general beer-drinking population of that city with regard to social level. In contrast to most laboratory and field studies, which call for momentary expressions of preference, this study allowed a seven-day period for the development of preferences. Each day, 48 identical-looking bottles of free beer were delivered to each family. Included were 8 bottles of each of six brands, identified by the colors of the bottle caps. On any one day, subjects could thus continue to use the first brand tried or could keep trying new brands until they found one they liked. From one day to another, however, the color code was changed. Thus the subjects had to make a new set of choices each day. The subjects recorded the brands they drank each day (by color of caps), as well as their preferences. Empty bottles, bottle caps, and unused bottles were collected daily.

Significant brand differences were found both in number of bottles consumed and in recorded preferences. Expressed brand preferences agreed with data on consumption. Apparently beer drinkers *can* differentiate among certain brands even in the absence of brand names.

***Product Development Studies.***   A major use of product testing is to aid in the development of new products or the improvement of existing products. The experimental techniques employed for this purpose are quite varied, as are the problems investigated. A few examples will illustrate this diversity. When rayon was first put on the market, it encountered a certain amount of consumer resistance because of its unfamiliar "feel." Accordingly a study was conducted on the tactile sensations reported by subjects when feeling different, experimentally produced weaves of rayon fiber, as well as the pleasantness or unpleasantness of the sensations (87). Other studies have dealt with such questions as the perceived crispness of cereals stored in different kinds of packages, consumer preferences for oval or rectangular sponges, and the best color combination for a cake box (25). One experiment demonstrated that bread is perceived to be fresher when wrapped in cellophane than when wrapped in wax paper (17). The subjects judged the "freshness" of equally fresh loaves by the familiar practice of squeezing the loaf. The resulting tactual sensations were evidently influenced by the nature of the wrapper.

In designing new telephone equipment, the Bell Laboratories regularly conduct laboratory tests with small local samples, followed by field tests with larger and more representative consumer samples. An example is provided by a series of four laboratory studies conducted with all-numeral dialing (AND), in which numbers replace the letters of the traditional letter-numeral dialing (LND) system (49). Among the advantages of AND are that it requires less dial space and avoids the common confusions between the letter O and the number zero and between the letter I and the number one. It remains to be seen, however, how AND and LND compare in accuracy and convenience in actual use. Experiments were accordingly designed in which subjects were required to look up, dial, or recall the two kinds of telephone numbers under controlled but realistic conditions. Some experiments were conducted in a special test room, some in the subjects' own offices, and some in their homes. Each experiment extended over several weeks.

The two systems were compared with reference to speed and accuracy of performance as well as expressed preferences. Although it required slightly longer to memorize AND telephone numbers, the results generally favored the new system and did not reveal any serious difficulties in the changeover process. Field trials were initiated following the laboratory tests. The final decision will take into account the results of many such studies.

Mention should also be made of the use of *anthropometric data* in designing such consumer products as clothing; seats for railway cars, airplanes, automobiles, and auditoriums; household furniture; and telephone booths, to name only a few examples (see 65, ch. 13; 66, ch. 11). Although the collection and analysis of anthropometric measures are not strictly speaking product testing, they are consumer research in a broad sense. In the design of certain products, anthropometric measures are utilized together with behavioral data and consumer preferences.

Unlike opinion surveys and other verbal techniques, product testing can be applied to any kind of subject. An example of product testing with a rather special kind of consumer population is shown in Figure 76.

**Food Acceptance Studies.** The Quartermaster Food and Container Institute for the Armed Forces conducts extensive laboratory and field studies on food preferences (see 34, 82, 83). Although the immediate object of this research is to improve meal planning in the armed services, it has made significant methodological contributions to consumer psychology as a whole. Many of the techniques developed at the Quartermaster Institute are applicable to a variety of problems pertaining to the manufacturing and distribution of consumer goods. And some of the findings throw light on basic characteristics of the rating process.

Much of the research of the Quartermaster Institute is carried out in a specially built food acceptance laboratory, with individual booths for each subject. One investigation (82) was designed to see how closely results obtained with a civilian sample in this laboratory approximated those obtained with a soldier-consumer sample tested at an army camp by the same procedure. In both groups, each subject was served samples of 3 foods in a single test session. Four sessions were employed to test a total of 12 foods; the entire series was replicated in different combinations to provide estimates of reliability. The subject recorded his reaction to each food on a nine-interval graphic rating scale ranging from "like extremely" to "dislike extremely." This rating

*Fig. 76*   Some consumers are not human. A boxer participates in a
dog-food taste test. The different varieties of the product presented in the
three pans are weighed before they are given to the animal and again
after removal. (*Courtesy of The Quaker Oats Company.*)

scale, known as the "hedonic scale," is used regularly in the Quartermaster
Institute studies.

Both laboratory and field studies yielded satisfactory reliabilities, the coefficients ranging from .80 to .96. The correlations between laboratory and
field ratings assigned to the different foods proved to be equally high. It could
thus be concluded that pretesting of rations on civilian samples in the Quartermaster Institute laboratory represents a satisfactorily close approximation of
pretesting with soldier-consumer panels. Further research is in progress on
the correspondence between such laboratory-type tests and observations under
more natural conditions, including regular mess-hall feeding and the use of
rations in field maneuvers.

Another investigation was concerned with an analysis of preferences for
lists of named foods (91). This technique, which is a type of consumer opinion
survey, had generally yielded higher mean preference ratings for each food
than those obtained with laboratory taste tests. One reason for this discrepancy
may be found in the frame of reference used by respondents in rating named
foods. The individual's actual liking for any given food, such as beef stew,
will vary from one occasion to another partly as a function of variability in
ingredients, manner of preparation, and other characteristics of the particular

serving. In a laboratory taste test, the individual responds to the food as presented. In a purely verbal opinion survey, however, he is asked to judge the generalized food rather than a particular version of it. Are these generalized judgments based upon the respondent's average experiences with this food, upon the best examples he has encountered, or upon the poorest? It was to answer this question that the present investigation was undertaken.

Three groups of naval enlisted personnel were asked to rate, on the nine-interval hedonic scale, 54 individual foods falling into the eight classes listed in Table 14. The first group was given the standard normal instructions, which

**TABLE 14**   *Mean Preference Ratings of Foods as a Function of Instructions*
*(From Schutz and Kamenetzky, 91, p. 176)*

| Food Group | No. of Foods in Group | Instructions | | |
| --- | --- | --- | --- | --- |
| | | *Normal* | *"Best Servings"* | *"Poorest Servings"* |
| Main dishes | 12 | 6.78 | 6.76 | 6.05 |
| Vegetables | 10 | 5.50 | 5.39 | 4.90 |
| Desserts | 9 | 7.31 | 7.42 | 6.71 |
| Potatoes and starches | 6 | 6.94 | 6.97 | 6.11 |
| Soups | 5 | 5.85 | 5.74 | 5.43 |
| Breads | 5 | 7.40 | 7.43 | 6.84 |
| Breakfast foods | 4 | 6.75 | 6.78 | 6.03 |
| Beverages | 3 | 7.24 | 7.13 | 6.80 |
| All foods | 54 | 6.58 | 6.57 | 5.93 |

simply call for a rating of how much the respondent likes or dislikes the item. Subjects in the second group were asked to rate the "Best Serving" of each food they had ever eaten, and those in the third group were asked to rate the "Poorest Serving." For foods they had never eaten, all respondents were told to mark "Not Tried." As can be seen in Table 14, the mean ratings obtained in the three groups clearly demonstrate that, under normal survey conditions, subjects tend to rate the best example of each food they have encountered. For each class of foods, as well as for all classes combined, mean ratings with normal instructions are practically identical with those obtained for "Best Servings." The ratings for "Poorest Servings," on the other hand, are appreciably lower.

# ECONOMIC PSYCHOLOGY

A branch of consumer psychology that has been taking shape since World War II is economic psychology. Cutting across the fields of economics and psychology, this area of research employs some of the data-gathering procedures developed in consumer opinion surveys and in the previously discussed food acceptance methodology. In its analysis of consumer data, economic psychology combines concepts taken from psychology, mathematics, and economics. Two types of studies will be described to illustrate developments in this area.

*Operations Research.*   An important problem in economic psychology pertains to the way in which the results of consumer surveys can be used in
reaching decisions about the manufacturing and distribution of a product. In
solving this problem, psychologists have applied techniques drawn from the
broader field of operations research. Several attempts have been made to
develop mathematical solutions for utilizing consumer research data in product
planning and marketing. The manufacturer wants to know, for example, the
optimum quality level required to maximize consumer preference. Beyond a
certain point further increments in quality would be wasted. Consumers are
not interested in a desk that can withstand a weight of 1 ton, a watch that is
accurate to $1/1,000$ second, or a pair of shoes that will last 50 years. They
would be unwilling to pay for the additional cost required to achieve these
quality levels. The question then is to determine the last, or "marginal," quality
increment that does affect consumer preference.

To establish optimum quality levels empirically would be impracticable,
since it would require too many forms of each product. The usual consumer
testing of a few forms can show that some forms are preferred over others, but
it cannot establish a true optimum with regard to any product characteristic.
Benson (7–10) has proposed a systematic procedure based on the *marginal
preference model*. Essentially, this procedure requires the measurement of
consumer preferences for a limited number of product forms. From these data,
a mathematical function relating degree of preference to qualitative product
variables is established. The point of maximum preference can then be determined mathematically.

Another question is concerned with the particular combination of qualities
that will maximize consumer satisfaction (7, 8). For example, given a fixed
amount of money for manufacturing a toothpaste to sell at a particular price,
how should this money be apportioned to the various product qualities, such
as taste, cleansing efficiency, and foaminess? Still another question pertains
to the allocation of funds to packaging, advertising, and selling. Out of a 10-
cent cost per item, what proportion should be spent on manufacturing and
what proportion on marketing? This type of question can be answered by
measuring the increases in product preference that result when different
amounts are spent on each. From these data, the appropriate mathematical functions can be derived (8).

A study by Jones (47) illustrates the use of a mathematical model in predicting consumer purchases from preference data. The items investigated were
15 entrées served over a five-day period at a university faculty club. The list
of items, together with a seven-category rating scale, was mailed to 430 club
members, of whom 297 returned completed forms. The rated preferences, as
well as data on the relative popularity of different price levels, were used in
mathematically derived equations to predict the percentage of persons who
would actually purchase each of the three entrées appearing on the menu on
any given day. These predictions proved to be quite accurate. The mean difference between predicted and actual percentages was only 3 percentage
points.

With regard to the cost data, the maximum preference was for the inter-
mediately priced rather than for the cheapest items. Consumer reaction to
prices is itself an important problem in economic psychology. It is likely that
for many types of items price is perceived as a cue to quality. In the particular

situation investigated in this study, the prestige factor may also have affected choices (see 47). Faculty members lunching with colleagues may be reluctant to order the cheapest item on the menu—at least in some universities!

A brief overview of some of the ways in which operations research is being utilized in advertising is provided by a report of an operations research discussion group, prepared by the Advertising Research Foundation (78). One of the chief difficulties in the application of operations research techniques to advertising decisions is the lack of adequate data on some of the factors to be considered. When pertinent data are available, they often represent crude approximations unsuitable for complex mathematical analyses. Certain marketing questions of a relatively limited nature can, however, be satisfactorily answered by these techniques.

**Economic Attitudes and Buying Behavior.** Another aspect of economic psychology is illustrated by the research of Katona and his associates at the Survey Research Center of the University of Michigan (51–53). This approach utilizes interviews with representative samples of consumers and businessmen to investigate motives, attitudes, and expectations regarding broad economic questions. For instance, consumers are asked "Do you think that a year from now you people will be better off financially, or worse off, or just about the same?" and "Do you think that in the country as a whole during the next twelve months we will have good times financially, or bad times, or what?" (52, p. 16).

**Fig. 77**  Sales of durable goods in relation to index of consumer attitudes and disposable personal income. (*Adapted from Katona, 53, p. 52.*)

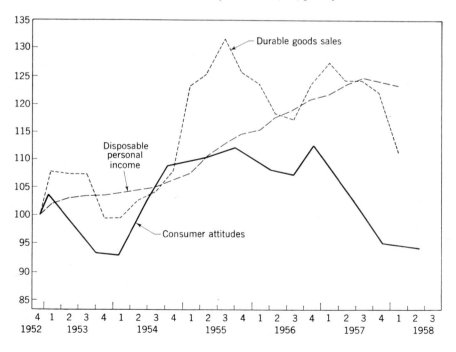

From the replies to a series of such questions, Katona computes an "index of consumer attitudes," which represents the over-all degree of optimism or pessimism expressed by the respondent. This index can be compared with various indices of economic behavior. Figure 77, for example, shows changes in consumer attitudes between 1952 and 1958 in relation to changes in sales of durable goods, such as automobiles and household appliances. It can be seen that major rises or declines in consumer "optimism" are followed by rises or declines in purchases, even though income continues to rise throughout this period. These findings support the view that demand is a function of both ability to buy and willingness to buy—the latter stemming from feelings of security or insecurity, confidence or uncertainty, optimism or pessimism, and other measurable attitudes.

Katona and his associates have used interview surveys to investigate a variety of economic problems. Repeated interviews of the same individuals permit a study of changes in attitudes, the factors leading to such changes, and the effect of the changes on individual buying behavior (52). Table 15 illustrates

**T A B L E  1 5**  *Purchase Rates of Families*
*with Different Attitudinal Classifications*
(*From Katona, 53, p. 85*)

| *Grouping of families by initial or final attitudes* | *Index value of number of durable goods purchases[a] by* | | |
| --- | --- | --- | --- |
| | *Optimists* | *Medium* | *Pessimists* |
| Initial attitudes, purchases in first 6 months | 1.15 | 0.95 | 0.88 |
| Initial attitudes, purchases in 12 months | 1.07 | 1.02 | 0.86 |
| Final attitudes, purchases in 12 months | 1.06 | 0.99 | 0.78 |
| *Grouping of families by change in attitudes* | *Improved attitudes* | *Unchanged attitudes* | *Deteriorated attitudes* |
| Purchases in first 6 months | 1.04 | 0.99 | 0.95 |
| Purchases in last 6 months | 1.11 | 0.95 | 0.87 |

[a] Income held constant.

one such analysis, in which initial attitudes and later changes in attitudes are both shown to be related to subsequent purchases of durable goods. For this purpose, respondents were classified into three groups, "Optimists," "Medium," and "Pessimists." Changes in attitudes were determined by interviewing the same respondents on two occasions over a one-year interval. Purchase of any durable goods within the year was ascertained during the second interview. These purchases have been recorded in Table 15 in terms of an index that adjusts for income differences among the different attitude groups. It can be seen that both initial and final attitudes are related to frequency of purchase during the year. It is also noteworthy that improvement in attitude is associated with higher frequency of purchase during the latter half of the period but shows a negligible relation to purchases during the first half. This is to be expected, since attitude changes were measured at the end of the period.

Among the other problems investigated by these procedures may be mentioned the relation of money saving to such factors as income, demographic variables, and attitudes. Several studies have been concerned with consumer motives in buying, for example, life insurance, one-family houses, and household appliances. Particular attention in this connection was given to the question of "saturation." What happens to purchases after consumer needs have been satisfied through the extensive availability of consumer goods? The results support the view that, when existing needs are gratified, other needs take their place. When a family buys their longed-for home, they need new appliances and furnishings. When they have acquired all the appliances they can use, they want new models with improvements, and so on.

## SUMMARY

Beginning with the psychology of advertising and selling, consumer psychology has gradually broadened to include research on consumer wants, preferences, attitudes, and buying behavior. The techniques of consumer psychology are also applicable to problems outside of business and industry, as illustrated by public opinion polls, public health campaigns, and meal planning in the armed services.

Procedures for testing the effectiveness of advertisements include the consumer jury technique, readership surveys, controlled exposure studies, brand use surveys, analysis of coupon returns, and sales tests. Radio and television research has been concerned with audience size and composition, audience reaction to specific programs or types of programs, and sales effectiveness of advertising. Among the techniques employed in such research are the hidden offer, telephone inquiries (including coincidental calls), mailed questionnaire, personal interviews, mechanical recorders such as the Nielsen Audimeter, and the CBS Program Analyzer. Some use has also been made of depth interviewing and projective techniques to investigate the emotional reactions of audiences.

Salesmanship may be regarded as the most flexible form of advertising. Because of the many varieties of selling, generalizations about effective salesmanship are likely to be of little value. Psychologists have concentrated on procedures for the selection and training of salesmen for specific jobs. Available research on the sales process, though meager, suggests the importance of a customer-oriented point of view, two-way communication, and service.

In any consumer opinion survey, the basic methodological problems concern sampling procedures and questionnaire construction. Sampling may be random or stratified, the latter requiring fewer cases. In area sampling, households in small geographical units are sampled, rather than persons. Sample size should be evaluated in terms of the resulting standard errors of percentages. Survey results must be checked for nonresponse bias and volunteer error. The questions employed in a consumer survey need to be formulated with care and pretested on a representative sample. In telephone and face-to-face surveys, interviewer variables must be taken into account.

Product testing may take many forms, as illustrated by brand identification and brand preference studies, product development studies, and food acceptance research. Economic psychology is a recent development within consumer psychology, which combines procedures from psychology, economics, and mathematics. Two rather different applications of it are to be found in operations research and in the study of economic attitudes in relation to buying behavior.

# REFERENCES

1. Advertising Research Foundation, Committee on Printed Advertising Rating Methods. *A study of printed advertising rating methods.* New York: Advert. Res. Found., 1956. 5 vols.
2. Albig, W. *Modern public opinion.* New York: McGraw-Hill, 1956.
3. Arnheim, R. The world of the daytime serial. In P. F. Lazarsfeld and F. N. Stanton (Eds.), *Radio research.* New York: Duell, Sloan & Pearce, 1944. Pp. 34–85.
4. Athey, K. R., Coleman, Joan E., Reitman, Audrey P., and Tang, Jenny. Two experiments showing the effect of the interviewer's racial background on responses to questionnaires concerning racial issues. *J. appl. Psychol.,* 1960, **44,** 244–246.
5. Audimeter. *Bus. Week,* 1939 (Oct. 21), No. 529, 34.
6. Bell, C. R. Psychological versus sociological variables in studies of volunteer bias in surveys. *J. appl. Psychol.,* 1961, **45,** 80–85.
7. Benson, P. H. A model for the analysis of consumer preference and an exploratory test. *J. appl. Psychol.,* 1955, **39,** 375–381.
8. Benson, P. H. Optimizing product acceptability through marginal preference analysis. In *Quality control and the consumer conference.* New Brunswick, N.J.: Rutgers, 1957. Pp. 3–30.
9. Benson, P. H., and Peryam, D. R. Preference for foods in relation to cost. *J. appl. Psychol.,* 1958, **42,** 171–174.
10. Benson, P. H., and Platten, J. H., Jr. Preference measurement by the methods of successive intervals and monetary estimates. *J. appl. Psychol.,* 1956, **40,** 412–416.
11. Bingham, W. V., Moore, B. V., and Gustad, J. W. *How to interview.* (4th ed.) New York: Harper & Row, 1959.
12. Blankenship, A. B. *Consumer and opinion research.* New York: Harper & Row, 1943.
13. Blankenship, A. B. (Ed.) *How to conduct consumer and opinion research.* New York: Harper & Row, 1946.
14. Blankenship, A.B., et al. Questionnaire preparation and interviewer technique. *J. Market.,* 1949, **14,** 399–433.
15. Blum, M. L., and Appel, V. Consumer versus management reaction in new package development. *J. appl. Psychol.,* 1961, **45,** 222–224.
16. Borden, N. H., and Lovekin, O. S. A test of the consumer jury method of ranking advertisements. *Publ., Grad. Sch. Bus. Admin., Harvard Univer.,* 1935, **22,** No. 2.
17. Brown, R. L. Wrapper influence on the perception of freshness in bread. *J. appl. Psychol.,* 1958, **42,** 257–260.
18. Burchinal, L. G. Personality characteristics and sample bias. *J. appl. Psychol.,* 1960, **44,** 172–174.
19. Campbell, A., Gurin, G., and Miller, W. E. *The voter decides.* New York: Harper & Row, 1954.
20. Cantril, H. *Gauging public opinion.* Princeton, N.J.: Princeton Univer. Press, 1944.
21. Cantril, H., and Strunk, Mildred. (Eds.) *Public opinion: 1935–1946.* Princeton, N.J.: Princeton Univer. Press, 1951.
22. Cash, H. C., and Crissy, W. J. E. *The psychology of selling.* Vols. 1–4. New York: Personnel Develpm. Associates, 1957–1958.
23. Cheskin, L., and Ward, L. B. Indirect approach to market reactions. *Harvard Bus. Rev.,* 1948, **26,** 572–580.
24. Coffin, T. E., Landis, J. B., and Baiman, M. W. *Strangers into customers.* New York: Nat. Broadcast. Co., 1955.
25. Corby, P. G. Product testing. In D. H. Fryer and E. R. Henry (Eds.), *Handbook of applied psychology.* New York: Holt, Rinehart and Winston, 1950. Pp. 351–355.

26. Crawford, J. W. *Advertising: Communications from management.* Boston: Allyn and Bacon, 1960.
27. Dalemius, T. Treatment of the non-response problem. *J. advert. Res.,* 1961, **1** (5), 1–7.
28. Dichter, E. Radio and television audience research. In D. H. Fryer and E. R. Henry (Eds.), *Handbook of applied psychology.* New York: Holt, Rinehart and Winston, 1950. Pp. 375–380.
29. Dodge, S. *A promising new approach to rating printed advertising.* New York: Advert. Res. Found., 1956.
30. Fay, E. J., and Middleton, W. C. Relationship between sales ability and rating of transcribed voices of salesmen. *J. appl. Psychol.,* 1942, **26**, 499–509.
31. Ferguson, L. W. The development of industrial psychology. In B. VonH. Gilmer (Ed.), *Industrial psychology.* New York: McGraw-Hill, 1961. Pp. 18–37.
32. Fleishman, E. A. An experimental consumer panel technique. *J. appl. psychol.,* 1951, **35**, 133–135.
33. Frey, J. M. Missing ingredient in sales training. *Harvard Bus. Rev.,* 1955, **33**, 126–132.
34. Gottlieb, D., and Rossi, P. H. A bibliography and bibliographic review of food and food habit research. *Quartermaster Food and Container Inst. for the Armed Forces, Library Bull.* No. 4, 1961.
35. Hattwick, M. S. *How to use psychology for better advertising.* Englewood Cliffs, N.J.: Prentice-Hall, 1950.
36. Hepner, H. W. *Modern marketing: Dynamics and management.* New York: McGraw-Hill, 1955.
37. Hepner, H. W. *Modern advertising: Practices and principles.* (3rd ed.) New York: McGraw-Hill, 1956.
38. Herzog, Herta. What do we really know about daytime serial listeners? In P. F. Lazarsfeld and F. N. Stanton (Eds.), *Radio research.* New York: Duell, Sloan & Pearce, 1944. Pp. 3–33.
39. Hildum, D. C., and Brown, R. W. Verbal reinforcement and interviewer bias. *J. abnorm. soc. Psychol.,* 1956, **53**, 108–111.
40. Hollingworth, H. L. *Advertising and selling.* New York: Appleton, 1913.
41. Hollonquist, T., and Suchman, E. A. Listening to the listener: Experiences with the Lazarsfeld-Stanton Program Analyzer. In P. F. Lazarsfeld and F. N. Stanton (Eds.), *Radio research.* New York: Duell, Sloan & Pearce, 1944. Pp. 265–334.
42. Howe, E. S. Quantitative motivational differences between volunteers and non-volunteers for a psychological experiment. *J. appl. Psychol.,* 1960, **44**, 115–120.
43. Hughes, J. L., and McNamara, W. J. Limitations on the use of Strong sales keys for selection and counseling. *J. appl. Psychol.,* 1958, **42**, 93–96.
44. Husband, R. W. *The psychology of successful selling.* New York: Harper & Row, 1953.
45. Ianni, F. A. J., Albrecht, R. M., and Polan, Adele K. Group attitudes and information sources in a poliovaccine program. *Publ. Hlth Rep.,* 1960, **75**, 665–671.
46. Jenkins, J. G. Characteristics of the question as determinants of dependability. *J. consult. Psychol.,* 1941, **5**, 164–169.
47. Jones, L. V. Prediction of consumer purchase and the utility of money. *J. appl. Psychol.,* 1959, **43**, 334–337.
48. Kahn, R. L., and Cannell, C. F. *The dynamics of interviewing; theory, techniques, and cases.* New York: Wiley, 1957.
49. Karlin, J. E. Human factors evaluation of a new telephone numerical dialing system. In E. A. Fleishman (Ed.), *Studies in personnel and industrial psychology.* Homewood, Ill.: Dorsey, 1961. Pp. 617–624.
50. Karslake, J. S. The Purdue Eye Camera: A practical apparatus for studying the attention value of advertisements. *J. appl. Psychol.,* 1940, **24**, 417–440.
51. Katona, G. *Psychological analysis of economic behavior.* New York: McGraw-Hill, 1951.
52. Katona, G. Attitude change: Instability of response and acquisition of experience. *Psychol. Monogr.,* 1958, **72**, No. 10.
53. Katona, G. *The powerful consumer: Psychological studies of the American economy.* New York: McGraw-Hill, 1960.

54. Kirchner, W. K., and Dunnette, M. D. Identifying the critical factors in successful salesmanship. *Personnel*, 1957, **34** (2), 54–59.
55. Koponen, A. *Mock readership survey*. New York: J. Walter Thompson, 1956.
56. Lazarsfeld, P. F. The art of asking why in marketing research. *Nat. market. Rev.*, 1935, **1**, 26–38.
57. Lazarsfeld, P. F., and Kendall, Patricia L. *Radio listening in America*. Englewood Cliffs, N.J.: Prentice-Hall, 1948.
58. Link, H. C. *The new psychology of selling and advertising*. New York: Macmillan, 1932.
59. Littman, R. A., and Manning, H. M. A methodological study of cigarette brand discrimination. *J. appl. Psychol.*, 1954, **38**, 185–190.
60. Longstaff, H. P., and Laybourn, G. P. What do readership studies really prove? *J. appl. Psychol.*, 1949, **33**, 585–593.
61. Lucas, D. B. A rigid technique for measuring the impression values of specific magazine advertisements. *J. appl. Psychol.*, 1940, **24**, 778–790.
62. Lucas, D. B. The ABC's of ARF's PARM. *J. Market.*, 1960, **25** (1), 9–20.
63. Lucas, D. B., and Britt, S. H. *Measuring advertising effectiveness*. New York: McGraw-Hill, 1963.
64. Lucas, D. B., and Murphy, M. J. False identification of advertisements in recognition tests. *J. appl. Psychol.*, 1939, **23**, 264–269.
65. McCormick, E. J. *Human engineering*. New York: McGraw-Hill, 1957.
66. McFarland, R. A. *Human factors in air transport design*. New York: McGraw-Hill, 1946.
67. McKinney, F. An empirical method of analyzing a sales interview. *J. appl. Psychol.*, 1937, **21**, 280–299.
68. McNamara, J. J. A new method for testing advertising effectiveness through eye movement photography. *Psychol. Rec.*, 1941, **4**, 399–460.
69. McNamara, J. J., and Tiffin, J. The distracting effect of nearby cartoons on the attention holding power of advertisements. *J. appl. Psychol.*, 1941, **25**, 524–527.
70. McNemar, Q. Opinion-attitude methodology. *Psychol. Bull.*, 1946, **43**, 289–374.
71. McNiven, M. A. Mail questionnaires for measuring industrial advertisements. *Proc. 5th ann. Conf., Advert. Res. Found.*, 1959, 67–74.
72. Marzoni, P., Jr. Some new light on advertising recognition measurement through a field test of the communiscope. *Assoc. nat. Advert., File Code No.* 16 b, 1958.
73. Mayer, M. The intelligent man's guide to broadcast ratings. *Advert. Res. Found. Rep.*, 1962.
74. Mitchell, G. E., and Burtt, H. E. Psychological factors in sales interviews. *J. appl. Psychol.*, 1938, **22**, 17–31.
75. Myers, L., Jr., and Gardner, E. F. An inexpensive method to determine the efficiency of a television program. *J. appl. Psychol.*, 1960, **44**, 39–43.
76. Nielsen, A. C. Two years of commercial operation of the Audimeter and the Nielsen Radio Index. *J. Market.*, 1945, **9**, 239–255.
77. Notes on the progress of Brand Names Research Foundation. *Sales Mgmt*, 1945, **54** (5), 68–74.
78. *Operations research in advertising: A summary of papers presented in ARF's Operations Research Discussion Group*. New York: Advert. Res. Found., 1961.
79. Pace, R. W. Oral communication and sales effectiveness. *J. appl. Psychol.*, 1962, **46**, 321–324.
80. Parten, Mildred B. *Surveys, polls, and samples: Practical procedures*. New York: Harper & Row, 1950.
81. Peatman, J. G., and Hollonquist, T. Geographical sampling in testing the appeal of radio broadcasts. *J. appl. Psychol.*, 1950, **34**, 270–279.
82. Peryam, D. R., and Haynes, J. G. Prediction of soldiers' food preferences by laboratory methods. *J. appl. Psychol.*, 1957, **41**, 2–6.
83. Peryam, D. R., Pilgrim, F. J., and Peterson, M. S. (Eds.) *Food acceptance testing methodology, a symposium*. Washington: Nat. Res. Coun., Adv. Bd, Quartermaster Res. Dev., 1954.
84. Presbrey, F. S. *The history and development of advertising*. Garden City, N.Y.: Doubleday Doran, 1929.
85. Ramond, C. K. *Questionnaires: A comprehensive bibliography*. New York: Advert. Res. Found., 1957.

86. Remmers, H. H. *Introduction to opinion and attitude measurement.* New York: Harper & Row, 1954.
87. Ripin, Rowena, and Lazarsfeld, P. F. The tactile-kinaesthetic perception of fabrics with emphasis on their relative pleasantness. *J. appl. Psychol.,* 1937, **21,** 198–234.
88. *The Roper Public Opinion Research Center at Williams College.* Williamstown, Mass.: Williams College, 1957.
89. Rosenstock, I. M., Derryberry, M., and Carriger, B. Why people fail to seek poliomyelitis vaccination. *Publ. Hlth Rep.,* 1959, **74,** 98–103.
90. Sampson, H. *A history of advertising from the earliest times.* London: Chatto & Windus, 1875.
91. Schutz, H. G., and Kamenetzky, J. Response set in measurement of food preference. *J. appl. Psychol.,* 1958, **42,** 175–177.
92. Schwerin, H. S. How pretests help to create better TV commercials. *Printers' Ink,* 1953, **243** (10), 60–63.
93. Scott, W. D. *The psychology of advertising.* Boston: Small, Maynard, 1908.
94. Skelly, Florence R. Interviewer-appearance stereotypes as a possible source of bias. *J. Market.,* 1954, **19,** 74–75.
95. *Sources of published advertising research.* New York: Advert. Res. Found., 1960.
96. Stanton, F. N. A new method for studying radio listening behavior. *Psychol. Bull.,* 1935, **32,** 703.
97. Stanton, F. N. A two-way check on the sales influence of a specific radio program. *J. appl. Psychol.,* 1940, **24,** 665–672.
98. Starch, D. *An analysis of 5,000,000 inquiries.* New York: Daniel Starch and Staff, 1930.
99. Starch, D. *Measuring product sales made by advertising.* Mamaroneck, N.Y.: Daniel Starch and Staff, 1961.
100. Starch, D., and Staff. How to use Starch readership studies: Part III. Readership and the advertisement's ability to communicate. *Starch Tested Copy,* 1959, No. 88.
101. Stephan, F. F., and McCarthy, P. J. *Sampling opinions: An analysis of survey procedures.* New York: Wiley, 1958.
102. Thumin, F. J. Identification of cola beverages. *J. appl. Psychol.,* 1962, **46,** 358–360.
103. U.S. Department of Commerce, Bureau of the Census. Characteristics of households with telephones, March 1960. *Curr. Popul. Rep.,* ser. P-20, No. 111, Aug. 2, 1961.
104. U.S. Department of Commerce, Bureau of the Census. Households with television sets in the United States, May 1961. *Curr. Housing Rep.,* ser. H-121, No. 8, Aug. 4, 1961.
105. Weitz, J. Verbal and pictorial questionnaires in market research. *J. appl. Psychol.,* 1950, **34,** 363–366.
106. Wells, W. D. The influence of yeasaying response style. *J. advert. Res.,* 1961, **1** (4), 1–12.
107. White, C. The mathematics of salesmanship. *Printers' Ink,* 1940, **41** (2), 34, 53–54.
108. Wulfeck, W. H. Role of the psychologist in market and advertising research. *J. appl. Psychol.,* 1945, **29,** 95–102.

# 11

## *Emotional and Motivational Factors in Buying Behavior*

Why do consumers use certain commodities or services? What do they like or dislike about a product? Why do they buy one brand rather than another? How can advertising arouse a desire for a product and lead to actual purchase? Although modern techniques of consumer research have focused attention upon questions such as these, the importance of emotional and motivational factors was recognized in the earliest writing on advertising psychology.

### APPEAL

The appeal is the message of an advertisement. It links the product or service advertised with consumer wants and needs. Whether the appeal is presented through written copy, illustration, spoken word, or television commercial, its object is to show how the commodity may satisfy consumer wants. Early textbooks on the psychology of advertising presented lists of "instincts," basic organic needs, or primary drives from which the advertiser might choose. Among these drives were hunger, thirst, sex, and the avoidance of pain or danger. These were followed by longer lists of secondary, or learned, drives, such as the needs for status or prestige, social approval, achievement, and cleanliness.

By looking through any current magazine or newspaper, one can easily find examples of advertising appeals based on each of these drives. One can also find evidence of the operation of one or more of these drives in most human activities. But merely labeling an activity as a manifestation of the hunger drive or the achievement drive tells us little about it. Nor are traditional lists of drives of much help to the ad writer. For one thing, the lists drawn up by different authors vary widely, especially with regard to the secondary drives. Classifications of drives are largely arbitrary and subjective. Psychologists are still a long way from a satisfactory understanding of motivation; no general agreement has been reached about the nature or operation of motives (see 34, pp. 253–272). Since basic experimental data in this field are still meager, consumer psychologists must rely upon their own applied research designed to answer specific questions.

The traditional concepts of drives, whether primary or secondary, are also too general to serve in the choice of advertising appeals. The hunger drive could be employed to advertise any food, from soup to candy. Yet there are vast differences between the appeal of a steaming bowl of soup on a cold day and that of a gift box of candy on one's birthday. Safety or the avoidance of danger is undoubtedly an important consideration in buying a car, but the actual choice between makes is often based on the automobile's role as a status symbol. Furthermore, buying decisions are often based on multiple and interlocking motives. In choosing a particular cake mix, the housewife may be influenced by her own craving for sweets, by pride in her achievement as a cook, by her need for social approval from family and guests, and by a desire to prove she can bake a better cake than her mother-in-law.

It might seem that a knowledge of the relative strength of different drives should help advertisers in their choice of appeal. But the strength of any drive is not a fixed quantity. Strength of primary drives depends upon degree of deprivation. When thwarted, some primary drives become overpowering. If breathing is hampered, the individual will fight violently for air. To a starving man, food becomes extremely important. But the advertiser is not addressing his message to starving consumers. When these primary drives are satisfied, other drives become prepotent.

The relative strength of secondary drives depends upon learning. Hence their strength will vary from one culture or subculture to another. Anthropology and differential psychology provide many examples of such group differences in the relative strength of drives (see 1, ch. 18). New drives develop as the individual's experiences change. For every drive, moreover, learning determines in large part what the individual does to satisfy it and what incentives he seeks. Cultural differences in eating customs and in food preferences provide a dramatic illustration of this fact.

Finally, in his choice of appeals the advertiser should take into account the specificity of buying motives. It is not so much a question of whether economy or prestige represents the stronger drive for a consumer. Rather it is a question of which is uppermost in his choice of a specific commodity. For the same consumer, economy may be foremost in the purchase of a washing machine, while prestige predominates in the choice of a car. The absurdity of trying to use the same "tried and true" appeal for very dissimilar products inspired the cartoon reproduced in Figure 78. The distinguished-looking man with the eye patch, featured repeatedly in Hathaway shirt ads (Figure 91), may sell shirts; but an eye patch on a dog would probably have little appeal for purchasers of dog food.

In selecting an effective appeal for a specific commodity, the advertiser can turn to the findings of opinion surveys and other types of consumer research. These techniques provide information on what consumers like or dislike about a product; what specific features led them to change brands; under what circumstances they made their most recent purchase of some durable commodity; how they use a particular product; and many other concrete questions about the role a particular product plays in the consumer's daily life. Analysis of subgroup results with regard to sex, age, socioeconomic level, or other variables may be helpful in the choice of suitable appeals for different consumer publics.

Many examples could be cited to illustrate the way in which consumer studies have affected the advertising of particular products. A manufacturer of a household product had been featuring the fact that his product "works faster." A consumer survey revealed that 58 per cent of the housewives who used the product said they did so because "it's easy on the hands," while only 2 per cent mentioned that "it's quicker" (20, p. 337). The most promising appeal had obviously been ignored in the previous advertising of this product.

A consumer study conducted for M & M candy found that for many persons

"*I know it's worked before, but will it sell dog food?*"

**Fig. 78**  Appeals are specific to the commodity. (*From The New Yorker, Dec. 30, 1961, p. 32. Drawing by O'Brian;* © *1961 The New Yorker Magazine, Inc.*)

candy eating is "associated with accomplishment of a job that the person who ate the candy considered disagreeable. The candy was a sort of reward or compensation for doing a tough job." Accordingly, M & M switched its advertising theme in two test markets from "Smooth, rich, creamy coated chocolate—everybody likes 'em" to "Make that tough job easier—you deserve M & M candy" (58, p. 87). Following this change in advertising appeals, sales in the two test areas rose from 17 per cent to 35 per cent of the national M & M total.

A third example is provided by advertisements for men's shoes, which traditionally stressed style, price, and details about the construction of the shoe. A survey of 5,000 men conducted for the Bostonian shoe company found that, when asked what they liked about the shoes they were wearing, 42 per cent of the men referred to "fit and feel," 32 per cent to "wear and tear," 16 per cent to "style and looks," and 9 per cent to "price and value" (16). On the basis of these results, the advertising appeal was changed, the shoes now being described in such terms as "walk-fitted." Again the change was followed by an improvement in sales.

Considerable attention has been given to the relative merits of *positive* and *negative appeals* in advertising. Essentially, a positive appeal portrays a pleasant situation that will follow the use of the product, while a negative appeal portrays an unpleasant situation that may occur if the product is not used. Negative appeals should not be confused with negative suggestion. The latter involves telling customers what *not* to do or calling attention to possible faults of competing products. Except under very special circumstances, negative suggestion should be avoided, since it may have the opposite effect from that intended. A familiar example of negative suggestion is that of telling a child not to play with matches. Such an admonition may suggest to him that matches are a potential plaything to be explored on the first opportunity, an idea that might never have occurred to him otherwise. Similarly, if women are told that the new, improved "Magicreme Supreme" will *not* enlarge pores, they may become alarmed about the possible ill effects of using *any* facial cream. Hence they may stop using facial creams altogether, instead of rushing to their nearest drug or department store to buy a jar of Magicreme.

Negative appeals, on the other hand, may be quite effective. For certain commodities, negative appeals can be made more dramatic and arresting than the corresponding positive appeals. An example of the continued and successful use of a negative appeal is shown in Figure 79. In all its advertising, this company has focused on the appeal that the Sanforized label on a garment is an assurance that the cloth will not shrink. Other examples of negative appeals can be found in the ads for products designed to protect against "halitosis," "B.O.," "coffee nerves," "tired blood," and the many other familiar advertiser diseases.

That negative appeals can be quite successful has been repeatedly demonstrated by survey data. In one extensive analysis of readership data, ads showing the unfavorable results of not using the product received much more attention than did ads showing the favorable results of using the product (47, p. 69). The former were also read by a larger proportion of persons than were the latter. Other studies have demonstrated the effectiveness of negative appeals for some commodities in terms of coupon returns and direct-mail sales (30, 31). On the other hand, there are many types of products for which negative appeals are inappropriate. The age and other characteristics of the consumers may also influence the relative effectiveness of positive and negative appeals. The results may likewise be affected by the specific way in which the negative appeal is presented. Thus, if the situation portrayed is too unpleasant, as in a detailed picture of a serious accident, people will simply turn away from the ad. Moreover, the emphasis should be placed on the action the individual may take to avoid the unpleasant situation. It is escape from fear that reinforces learning, rather than fear itself (34, p. 268).

Although the large majority of advertisements contain appeals, there are two well-known exceptions. One is the *reminder ad*, whose object is simply to keep the brand name before the public. Such ads serve to reinforce the associations with brand names that were established by other, conventional ads. They are effective with brands that are already familiar and widely ad-

## Why Betty bewares of some wash-and-wears

*Another Ballad by SANFORIZED-PLUS*

1. Fashion-conscious Betty Murray
Shopped at lunch-time in a hurry.
Bound for a week end, free from care,
Searched for a skirt tagged "wash-and-wear."

2. She slipped one on, it fit just fine
And Betty rejoiced—"This one is mine!"
Its pleats had a certain flirty flair
And the tag maintained "just wash and wear."

3. But, along came time to wash the garment
And Betts berated the unknown varmint
Who had put that label on her skirt!
Betty was angry and deeply hurt.

4. In place of pleats—a muss of wrinkles
And shrunk to boot! (Betts called it "shrinkles.")
The moral, friend, is save your trust
For items labeled "Sanforized-*Plus.*"

5. This reassuring label or tag
Will never make you weep or gag.
Attached to wash-and-wearable duds
Means style that lasts through tubs of suds.

## ·SANFORIZED·
TRADE ® MARK
—for protection against shrinkage

## ·SANFORIZED plus·
TRADEMARK
—for excellence in wash-and-wear performance

Cluett, Peabody & Co. permits use of its trademark "Sanforized-Plus", only on fabrics which meet its established test requirements for shrinkage, smoothness after washing, crease recovery, tensile strength, and tear strength. Fabrics bearing the trademarks "Sanforized" or "Sanforized-Plus" will not shrink more than 1% by the Government's standard test.

**Fig. 79** A negative appeal used repeatedly and successfully by the same company. In the issue of *Life* in which it appeared, this ad ranked first on the basis of "read most" women readers per advertising dollar. (*Courtesy of Cluett, Peabody, & Co.*)

vertised. Unless supported by other ads that do contain appeals, reminder ads would probably have little effect on sales.

Another type of ad that contains no appeal is the *institutional ad*. Although showing the name of the company, such ads make no mention of the merits of any products. Their object is to advertise the company as a whole, rather than any specific product. The ad may publicize some worthy cause, or it may feature the company's own beneficent activities. Insofar as the name of the company is included, such ads serve a reminder function. Their principal effects on product sales, however, presumably stem from the association of desirable feeling tones with the company and its products. If the company is perceived as public-spirited, farsighted, and generally on the side of Truth-Goodness-and-Beauty, people are likely to feel favorably disposed toward its products. The implications of this type of advertising will be seen more clearly in the light of the discussion of feeling tone in the next section, as well as the discussion of corporate image in the last section of this chapter.

## FEELING TONE

*Nature of Feeling Tone.* While the appeal in a printed ad or sales talk tells the consumer explicitly why he should purchase a commodity, other aspects of advertising may influence his reaction to the product in more subtle ways. Such effects have been variously described as "feeling tone," "atmosphere," "mood," and "indirect suggestion." Their operation can be illustrated by an early experiment (28). Interviewers made a house-to-house survey of hosiery preferences in one city. Four identical samples of hosiery were employed, three of which were packed in boxes containing a card of perfumer's blotting paper with faint perfumes. The four boxes were displayed in different parts of the room so that odors would not conflict. Each housewife was asked to examine the hosiery and indicate which was the best quality. Respondents apparently considered such characteristics as texture, weave, wearing quality, weight, and sheen, although all four pairs of stockings were identical in these respects and in every other way.

Tabulation of the expressed preferences showed that 50 per cent chose the stockings with a narcissus odor as being the best quality, while only 8 per cent chose those with no perfume. By chance, 25 per cent should have chosen each pair. Only 6 of the 250 respondents commented on the scent. Thus it appears that the perfume could engender a pleasant feeling tone toward the product even when subjects did not specifically notice it. This experiment also illustrates the spread of feeling tone beyond its immediate source. The fact that the housewives liked the perfume made them judge stockings more favorably.

A pleasant or unpleasant feeling tone aroused by any element of an advertisement may influence the consumer's reaction to the product. For this reason, the advertiser must inquire into the feeling tones associated with all aspects of the ad. It is relatively easy to recognize the role of illustrations in associating appropriate feeling tones with the product. In advertising soup, for instance, pictures can vividly suggest the glowing health of happy children, or the warmth and comfort of piping-hot soup on a blustery day, or the graciousness of an elegant dinner party. Other less obvious features of the ad may also arouse strong feelings that will spread to the product. An effective appeal in the ad's primary message may be worthless if an undesirable or inappropriate feeling tone is evoked by the colors, the printing type, or even a border design surrounding the ad. If the appeal is directed to elegance and daintiness while the printing type suggests cheapness and strength, the effects will clash and tend to cancel out rather than reinforcing each other.

*Color.* The association of colors with different feeling tones is widely recognized. Studies on the suitability of different colors for advertising various commodities were among the earliest conducted in the psychology of advertising (12; 43, pp. 452–462). Apart from its possible attention value (see Chapter 12) and its realism in portraying the commodity, color may arouse strong affective associations. Through common experiences, most people have learned to associate red with fire, blood, and danger; blue with cool rivers and lakes; orange and yellow with sunlight and comfortable warmth, and so on.

In one investigation (56), 94 college students were shown eight colors and were given a list of 11 "moods" described in such terms as: exciting, stimulating; distressed, disturbed, upset; calm, peaceful, serene; powerful, strong, masterful. The instructions were to name the one color that best represented the feelings described by each group of words. For each of the 11 moods, the choices showed a significant predominance of certain colors. For instance, for exciting and stimulating, 61 subjects chose red. For tender and soothing, 41 chose blue and 24 green; none chose red. Repetition of this experiment with different groups indicated that certain color associations, including those cited above, are quite consistent (36). Others vary with the demographic characteristics of the population, particularly its socioeconomic level. It should be added that changing the saturation or brightness of colors will considerably modify their associated feeling tones. Deep red and pink or navy and sky blue would hardly be expected to arouse the same feelings.

In a special experiment designed to test the common association of temperature with color, it was found that subjects' thresholds of "uncomfortable warmth" were unaffected by color of illumination (4). Nevertheless, when later questioned about the "amount of heat transmitted" by the different lights under which they had worked, the subjects judged the green and blue lights to be cooler than the white, yellow, or amber lights.

*Printing Types and Other Graphic Elements.* The printing type used in brand name, headline, or advertising copy should be legible, attractive, and appropriate. In a book, poor legibility of type may decrease speed and accuracy of reading and increase visual fatigue. But in an ad poor legibility reduces the motivation to read further. Even more important is the fact that the frustration experienced in trying to read such material will cause annoyance that may spread to the product.

Psychologists have done considerable research on the legibility of type (see 7, 40, 51, 52). Among the criteria employed to measure legibility are accuracy of perceiving letters or words in brief tachistoscopic exposures; reading speed and comprehension for long passages; distance at which letters, words, or sentences can be correctly read; indices of eye fatigue after continuous reading; and number and nature of eye movements made during reading. With more difficult reading, there is an increase in the number and duration of eye fixations and in the number of retracing movements. Eye movements are usually recorded with an eye camera, although increasing use is being made of electro-oculograms and other types of electrical recording.

Through all these techniques, it has been demonstrated that printing types vary significantly in legibility. Simple types are generally read faster than Old English or other types with elaborations and curlicues. The use of a type that can be read quickly and with little strain is particularly desirable in the copy of an ad, although some minimum standards of legibility should also be met in headlines and brand names. The relative legibility of different types varies somewhat with other factors, such as size, boldness (thickness of lines), width of margins, and interlinear spacing (7, 40).

The use of colored inks and colored backgrounds also affects legibility, chiefly by altering the degree of brightness contrast. Fastest reading and fewest eye fixations have been found with black print on a white background. About equally good are such combinations as green on white, blue on white, and black on yellow. At the other extreme are such combinations as red on green and black on purple. In one study, the latter combination slowed down reading rate by more than 50 per cent (40, p. 120).

Another factor that influences legibility is familiarity of both type and arrangement. Any unfamiliar feature tends to slow down reading. It is partly for this reason that a passage or headline printed in lower case is read at a faster rate than one set entirely in capitals (40, 41). The only advantage of a headline set in capitals is that it can be read at a greater distance than one set in lower case. This advantage is pertinent to the designing of billboards and road signs.

Familiarity of layout also facilitates reading. Bizarre arrangements of printed matter, sometimes used by advertisers as a means of gaining attention, may be self-defeating because of the frustration and annoyance they engender. Even certain layouts that have been found to be superior in tachistoscopic experiments yielded poorer results in the reading of long passages than did the less efficient but familiar arrangement of words along horizontal lines (8). With adult readers who have established certain reading habits, any change in layout of printed matter will increase reading difficulty, even when the new layout is better adapted than the old to the characteristics of human vision.

Besides legibility, the advertiser should consider the emotional reactions and associations aroused by different printing types. Decided preferences for different types have been found, and these preferences change with time (7). The types popular a generation ago appear quaint and old-fashioned today. That printing types arouse distinctive feelings has been repeatedly demonstrated. When subjects are asked to explain their likes or dislikes for different types, they volunteer such descriptive terms as "whimsical," "genteel," "aristocratic," "restful and soothing," or "intellectual" (7, p. 40). Advertisers have long tried to utilize these reactions by choosing types that express feeling tones appropriate to their products and to the appeals they wish to convey. Figure 80 illustrates a variety of types used in brand names to express such diverse qualities as elegance, dependability, dignity, informality, sturdiness, and so on.

In several early investigations, groups of subjects were given the names of abstract qualities and of commodities and were asked to rank printing types for their degree of appropriateness for each (10, 45, 48). The results show considerable agreement among individuals and give evidence of good internal

**Fig. 80**   Printing types that arouse widely different feeling tones.

consistency. For instance, when types were independently judged for their suitability in expressing cheapness and in expressing luxury, the two rank orders correlated — .94. The corresponding correlation for luxury and dignity was +.96, for cheapness and strength +.82, and for dignity and cheapness — .84. Rank orders assigned to the types with regard to their appropriateness in advertising various commodities also revealed considerable correlation. Thus the rank orders for jewelry and perfume correlated +.94, while those for jewelry and building materials correlated −.95. These correspondences are especially noteworthy in view of the fact that in this study a different group of subjects ranked the printing types for each quality and each commodity (45).

That feeling tones may be associated with such simple stimuli as *lines* was demonstrated in another early study (44). A total of 500 subjects were given a printed sheet containing 18 short lines, as well as a list of adjectives describing 13 classes of feelings, such as sad, merry, agitating, and powerful. The subjects were instructed to choose the one line that best expressed each of the 13 classes of feelings. The lines were drawn so as to represent different combinations of three variables: (1) direction (horizontal, upward, downward); (2) form (curved or angular); and (3) "rhythm," or number of waves per inch (slow, medium, fast). The results again showed considerable agreement among subjects. Thus for "sad," 86.3 per cent chose a curved rather than an angular line, 84.3 per cent chose a downward-sloping line, and 86.8 per cent chose a slow rather than a medium or fast rhythm. For "powerful," 85.1 per cent chose an angular line, 55.5 per cent chose an upward-sloping line, and 52.7 per cent chose a medium rhythm.

*Language.*    That distinct feeling tones can be aroused by sounds as well as by shapes is illustrated in Figure 81. Given the two meaningless forms and the two meaningless "words" shown in this figure, the vast majority of persons will associate the word containing the l and m sounds with the gently curving

*Fig. 81*  Feeling tones associated with forms and sounds.

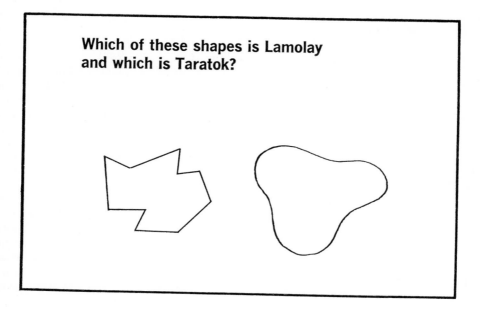

shape, and the word containing the t, r, and k sounds with the sharply angular shape. The feeling tones aroused by different sounds should be considered in devising brand names, as well as in selecting appropriate words for advertising copy (see, e.g., 23). In the choice of a brand name, meaningful associations should also be investigated, preferably in a consumer survey. Phonetically, one of the most beautiful combinations of sounds in the English language is "cellar door," but this name would hardly be suitable for a new perfume.

Another important factor in the success of a brand name is ease of pronunciation. Just like type that is difficult to read, a brand name that is difficult to pronounce tends to arouse annoyance and hostility. Because of the possible embarrassment resulting from mispronouncing the name, moreover, many customers will hesitate to ask for the product and will buy a more pronounceable competing brand instead. For mass-market items, such brand names as Baume Bengué, Djer-Kiss, Pro-phy-lac-tic, Nescafé, and Cinzano put an unnecessary burden on the consumer.

There are a number of instances in which a manufacturer became aware of the sales handicap resulting from a hard-to-pronounce brand name and did something about it. The makers of Baume Bengué, for example, began to insert "pronounced Ben Gay" under the name. Later, the name was changed to Ben Gay altogether. Another classic example is that of Suchard chocolate (17). Recognizing the difficulties that American consumers were having in pronouncing this name, the company began to print the slogan "Say Soo Shard" on the wrapper of each chocolate bar. This in turn led to the decision to adopt a live trademark in the form of an attractive little girl who was to be known as "Sue Shard." Eventually this little girl was featured in all advertisements for the company, through photographs, comic strips, radio commercials, and personal appearances.

Apart from word choice, many other aspects of language serve to arouse feeling tones that may be pleasant or unpleasant, appropriate or inappropriate. A passage consisting of short sentences, with a choppy, jerky rhythm, for example, is likely to suggest pep, sparkle, and liveliness; one written in longer sentences, with strings of modifiers and a slow, languorous rhythm, is more likely to suggest relaxation and reverie. The imagery evoked by language also needs to be considered. To say that "evaporated milk makes a fine curd in the stomach and is therefore more digestible than regular milk" could be factually correct, but it arouses imagery that is unappetizing. The whole question of ease of understanding and "readability" is also of some relevance to feeling tone but can be more appropriately discussed in Chapter 12.

## MOTIVATION RESEARCH

Finding out *why* people buy a certain product—or why they do anything, for that matter—is difficult. In answer to a direct question about the reasons for their choices or actions, people are likely to give rationalizations or "socially desirable" answers which may differ from their real motives. It was to meet these difficulties that the various techniques loosely grouped under "motivation research" were introduced into consumer psychology. The potentialities of motivation research fired the imagination of advertising men and of the general public alike. Articles and books soon appeared in the popular press, extolling its virtues (e.g., 32) or lambasting it as a dire threat to our privacy of thought and our freedom of action (e.g., 39). Fortunately, sober and well-balanced surveys of these techniques are also available (15, 19, 50).

The data-gathering procedures included under motivation research are many and varied. Some writers use the term so broadly as to cover any application of the methods of psychology, sociology, or anthropology to consumer problems. In its more usual, restricted sense, motivation research refers to the use of intensive, disguised, qualitative, clinical procedures in the study of buying motives. One of these techniques is *depth interviewing,* which may itself vary widely in the hands of different investigators (11; 50, chs. 3–5). At one extreme we find a fairly structured approach, with predetermined opening questions followed by nondirective probes. At the other extreme is psychoanalytic interviewing designed to explore emotional contexts, symbolic meanings, and fantasies that may be associated with a product; the origins of these associations are typically tracked down to early childhood experiences. Another variant is the *group interview,* which may be conducted either with a natural group such as a family or club or with a specially assembled consumer panel (50, ch. 6). This situation gives the respondents an opportunity to interact with each other, as well as to react directly to questions, sample products, demonstrations, films, or other stimuli presented by the interviewer.

Motivation research has also made extensive use of almost every available kind of *projective technique* (50, chs. 7–14). Among those most commonly employed may be mentioned both free and controlled word-association tests, sentence completion, and picture interpretation tests patterned after the Thematic Apperception Test. A number of studies have used cartoons in which the subject must supply the speech of one of the characters, as in the Rosenzweig Picture-Frustration Study. One such cartoon, used in a cigar survey, portrayed a man coming home from work and announcing to his wife, "I've decided to take up smoking cigars, dear." The wife's reply was to be filled in by the respondent (50, pp. 120–121). Such tests try to capitalize on the fact that a respondent is often willing to put in the mouth of a third person an opinion that he himself holds but is unwilling to express. The same idea can be utilized by merely wording an ordinary question in the third person. Instead of asking, "What do you think are the objectionable features of this cleanser?" we can say, "Some women who use this cleanser find a lot of faults with it. I wonder if you can guess what they are objecting to" (50, p. 104).

Another common technique is role playing, or visualization (19, pp. 74–79; 50, ch. 10). This technique was employed in a widely quoted study of the attitudes of housewives toward instant coffee (18). Although some form of powdered instant coffee had been on the market for many years, it had not been widely adopted at the time of this study. When directly questioned about their reasons for not using instant coffee, most housewives said that they did not like the flavor. Suspecting that this might be a rationalization, the investigator showed other samples of housewives a shopping list, with the request that they try to project themselves into the situation and describe the personality of the woman who bought the groceries. One group of 50 housewives was given list A; another group of 50 was given list B. As shown below, the two lists were identical except for the fifth item:

List A

1½ lb hamburger
2 loaves Wonder bread
bunch of carrots
1 can Rumford's Baking Powder
Nescafé instant coffee
2 cans Del Monte peaches
5 lb potatoes

List B

1½ lb hamburger
2 loaves Wonder bread
bunch of carrots
1 can Rumford's Baking Powder
Maxwell House coffee, drip grind
2 cans Del Monte peaches
5 lb potatoes

The descriptions obtained with the two lists were distinctly different. Among the women shown list A, which contained instant coffee, 48 per cent characterized the shopper as lazy, and an equal percentage said she did not plan her purchases well; 12 per cent called her a spendthrift; and 16 per cent said she was not a good wife. In the group shown list B, which contained a well-known brand of ground coffee, laziness was mentioned by only 4 per cent and bad planning by 12 per cent; no one in this group described the shopper as a spendthrift or said she was not a good wife. Adding a pie mix to *both* shopping lists, which were used with two new samples of housewives, brought the personality descriptions of the regular-coffee buyer closer to those of the instant-coffee buyer. Evidently it was the inclusion of a prepared food item that evoked the stereotype.

In still another part of the same study, responses to the original instant-coffee list were obtained from users and nonusers of instant coffee, as determined by a pantry check. The personality descriptions revealed several significant differences between the two groups of housewives. For example, 70 per cent of users and 18 per cent of nonusers characterized the shopper as economical; 29 per cent of users and no nonusers described her as a good housewife who planned well and cared about her family; 16 per cent of users and 55 per cent of nonusers said she could not cook or did not like to; and 19 per cent of users and 39 per cent of nonusers called her lazy.

Similar results were obtained by a simpler method in a Belgian survey regarding the use of soup mixes (19, p. 99). Three groups of housewives, classified as regular users, infrequent users, and nonusers, were asked, "For which among these six listed reasons do you think a woman might use soup mixes?" Only two of the answers were chosen with significantly different frequencies by the three groups. "She thinks soup mixes are as good as home-made soups" was checked by 73 per cent of regular users, 48 per cent of infrequent users, and 21 per cent of nonusers. On the other hand, "She is lazy" was the reason given by 35 per cent of regular users, 47 per cent of infrequent users, and 60 per cent of nonusers. It seems that fear of being considered lazy may be a common deterrent among nonusers of instant foods.

The reverse approach was followed in a British study of gasoline (or petrol, as it is called in Britain). Motorists were shown photographs of six men, of whom two were chosen as young and sporty types, two as solid and respectable citizens, and two as depressed and downtrodden types (19, pp. 78–79). Each respondent was told, "Here are some photographs of typical motorists. Would you look at them and tell me what sort of petrol you would guess that each of them habitually uses?" Only 3 per cent of those questioned said they could not tell from the photographs. The replies given by the other respondents revealed strong associations between certain brands and one or another of the given types, as can be seen in Table 16. Brand A seems to be more closely associated with the young and sporty type, Brand B with solid citizens.

**T A B L E   1 6**   *Stereotypes Associated with Different Brands of Gasoline* (*From Henry, 19, p. 79*)

| Gasoline Brand | Percentage ascribed to | | | |
| --- | --- | --- | --- | --- |
| | Young and sporty | Solid citizens | Depressed, downtrodden | Total |
| A | 61 | 29 | 10 | 100 |
| B | 26 | 51 | 23 | 100 |
| C | 34 | 35 | 31 | 100 |

Motivation research can serve as a source of hypotheses, which can subsequently be tested by objective, quantitative, large-scale procedures. It is thus most useful in the preliminary, exploratory stages of a consumer study. As a by-product, it can also suggest new advertising appeals to the copywriter. The effectiveness of ads prepared on this basis, however, needs to be determined empirically, as for any other ads. Even when several techniques are combined in the same study—as is often done—motivation research cannot provide conclusive answers about consumer behavior. Because of the many limitations of this research, its findings need to be verified by more objective procedures.

Most motivation research is conducted on small and unrepresentative samples. Depth interviewing, as well as certain projective techniques, require excessive expenditure of time on the part of trained investigators. The cost per case thus makes these procedures unsuitable for large-scale surveys. At the same time, the type of information gathered in motivation research is subject to wide individual differences. The emotional associations and motives investigated by motivation research are often of a highly personal nature and cannot be readily generalized. Once certain behavior patterns or feelings have been identified, it is necessary to determine what proportion of consumers in large, representative samples react in a similar way toward a given product.

Projective techniques of the sort used in motivation research have generally yielded little or no evidence of validity in personality studies. We certainly cannot assume that they provide valid indices of buying motives. In this area, as in personality testing, their validity remains to be demonstrated. The fact that in depth interviewing or projective testing the respondent may talk at great length does not necessarily mean that what he says is deep, nor that it is relevant to the behavior we are trying to predict.

In visualization, or role-playing, studies, such as those dealing with instant coffee and gasoline, we cannot be sure that the associations between product use and personality stereotypes are as strong or prevalent as the results suggest, nor that they actually affect buying behavior (see 22). When the interviewer asks subjects to give a personality description from a shopping list, for instance, he is forcing them to hunt around for any stereotype they can think of in the effort to comply with his request. Sad as it may be, few respondents have the self-confidence and courage to tell the interviewer that it can't be done. It is thus possible that many of the housewives who described the instant-coffee buyer as lazy did so only because they thought that was what the interviewer wanted them to say. The results merely show an awareness of the stereotype. They do not indicate its prevalence or strength. The fact that the undesirable stereotype was mentioned by more nonusers than users could mean simply that respondents are less likely to express disapproval of something that they themselves do. But this does not tell us what is cause and what is effect.

A common danger in motivation research is that the results may reflect the investigator's preconceived notions. Because of the uncontrolled and subjective nature of some of the techniques, it is virtually impossible to rule out the investigator's bias. The farfetched psychoanalytic interpretations offered by some practitioners of motivation research have little basis in verifiable facts. Under these conditions, too, it sometimes happens that different motivation researchers make inconsistent or opposite recommendations regarding the same product (see, e.g., 6, pp. 228–229).

It should also be recognized that motivation research is not new. It represents the application to consumer research of techniques that had long been in use in clinical psychology. Nor is motivation research the only way to study buying motives. If used with appropriate experimental designs, *direct questioning* can often yield the required information. Instead of asking a subject why he does something—which is a pretty big order anyway—we can ask him direct questions about what he does, how he does it, and when. Thus we could ask how long the respondent has been using his current brand of dentifrice, what other members of the family use it, what he disliked about his former brand, and so on. Or we can ask at what times a subject smokes more than usual and at what times less than usual, when he enjoys it most and when least, etc. (see 50, pp. 213–220).

To be most fruitful, questions should be formulated so as to test specific hypotheses. Sometimes the cross tabulation of replies to different questions can yield information that could not be obtained from an analysis of single questions. A good example can be found in an automobile survey conducted by Politz (46). The investigator hypothesized that the average motorist's judgment of the "pickup," or acceleration, of his car may be quite inaccurate and may be influenced by an irrelevant cue, namely, the amount of resistance encountered when pressing down the gas pedal. To test this hypothesis, he asked motorists two questions. In one part of the interview, the respondent was asked whether his car had good pickup. In another, he was asked about the ease of handling the car, the gas pedal being mentioned along with steering wheel, brake, and other controls. Engineering data about the cars indicated that stiff and soft accelerator springs occurred in about the same proportion in car models with high acceleration as in those with low acceleration. The survey replies showed, however, that, among motorists who reported difficulty in pressing and keeping down the accelerator, only 26 per cent said their car had good pickup; among those who reported that it was easy to press and keep down the accelerator, 61 per cent described their car as having good pickup. Softness of accelerator spring was thus perceived as additional horsepower.

In commenting upon this procedure, Politz wrote, ". . . the illusion that the interview has to obtain a 'true' answer from a given respondent is dispensed with; the answers are reactions and all we need to do is to observe and measure them as reactions" (46, p. 122). It is interesting to note that this is the approach followed in the development and use of most personality inventories (see 2, pp. 520–521). The questions in such inventories are not designed to elicit factual information but are treated as verbal stimuli to which subjects respond. The extent to which each response correlates with other behavioral indices is then empirically investigated. In discussing the construction of the Minnesota Multiphasic Personality Inventory, for example, Meehl wrote (33, p. 9):

. . . the verbal type of personality inventory is *not* most fruitfully seen as a "self-rating" or self-description whose value requires the assumption of accuracy on the part of the testee in his observations of self. Rather is the response to a test item taken as an intrinsically interesting segment of verbal behavior, knowledge regarding which may be of more value than any knowledge of the "factual" material about which the item superficially purports to inquire. Thus if a hypochondriac says that he has "many headaches" the fact of interest is that he *says* this.

This objective, empirical approach is well worth trying in consumer research as well.

## PERSONALITY STUDIES OF CONSUMERS

Knowledge about the characteristics of various consumer publics has been one of the objectives of consumer research from its earliest beginnings. Media research provides information on demographic characteristics of the audience reached by specific newspapers, magazines, and radio or television programs. Armed with this information, the advertiser can choose the medium most suitable for his product and can adapt the appeal, wording, and other features of his ad to the particular audience. Thus food ads will be more successful if placed in a magazine read by housewives. Ads for a single product, such as cigarettes, may be very differently expressed for a college paper, a trade journal, or a general family magazine. Within one medium, placing book ads on the book review page not only selects the persons interested in books but reaches them at a time when they are specifically oriented toward books.

To choose his medium effectively, as well as to prepare a successful ad, the advertiser needs to know as much as possible about the consumers who use his product. Beginning with such simple demographic variables as sex, age, and socioeconomic level, consumer studies have been extended to include personality characteristics. Motivation researchers have used depth interviewing and projective tests to find out how users of a product or brand differ from nonusers (11; 50, pp. 156–158). Other investigators have employed personality inventories for the same purpose. Personality factors have been studied in relation to such consumer variables as motion-picture preferences (49), amount of cigarette smoking (14), being overweight and hence a potential buyer of reducing products (27), and listening to soap operas (21).

An exploratory study of magazine readership used a special adaptation of the Allport-Vernon-Lindzey (A-V-L) Study of Values designed to fit the vocabulary and general information level of readers of mass-circulation magazines (13). The test was administered to 300 men and women in six cities. When subjects were classified according to their expressed interests in different types of fiction and nonfiction articles, many significant differences in A-V-L score patterns were found. In another study (53), 133 male business college students were given the Gordon Personal Profile and a disguised questionnaire containing questions on the use of various products, such as headache remedies, cigarettes, chewing gum, and deodorants. A number of low but significant relations were found between product use and personality test scores. For example, the use of headache remedies correlated negatively with ascendancy and emotional stability; the acceptance of new fashions correlated positively with ascendancy and sociability.

An unusually extensive and well-controlled study of consumer personality was conducted with the nationwide, representative consumer panel of the J. Walter Thompson Company (25, 26). The Edwards Personal Preference Schedule (EPPS) was administered to 8,963 adult men and women who were classified as heads of households. The EPPS, which was described in Chapter 3, is designed to measure the relative strength of 15 needs, such as achievement, affiliation, dominance, or change. In this study, significant mean differences in several needs were found among subgroups classified according to such demographic variables as age, sex, annual income, city size, and United States region. Such findings provide the advertiser with useful information about consumers in different markets.

A major part of the analysis consisted in the comparison of EPPS scores of consumer subgroups classified according to reported purchase of various commodities, such as cars, cigarettes, cosmetics, and paper towels. Subscribers to different magazines were similarly compared. Illustrative results obtained with male cigarette smokers and nonsmokers are given in Figure 82. The EPPS

*Fig. 82*   Mean scores on Edwards Personal Preference Schedule obtained by male cigarette smokers and nonsmokers. (*Adapted from Koponen, 26, p. 9.*)

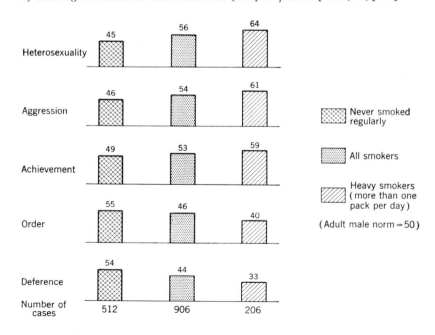

scores are expressed as percentiles based on adult male norms. The five scales listed on the graph yielded mean differences between nonsmokers and heavy smokers that were significant at the .01 level. The heavy smokers scored higher in expressed needs for sex, aggression, and achievement, while the non-smokers scored higher in the needs for order and deference, or compliance. Further breakdown of results showed that smokers of filter cigarettes scored significantly higher than nonfilter smokers on dominance, change, and achievement; the nonfilter smokers scored significantly higher on aggression and autonomy, or the need for independence.

In still another part of the same project, mail order purchases made in response to different appeals were checked against EPPS scores. In each case, two groups were chosen from persons who scored at opposite ends of the distribution in the need under investigation but who were matched in such variables as age, income, and city size. A sales promotion piece was deliberately written to appeal to individuals high in that particular need. These advertisements were mailed to the members of both groups, and the resulting sales in the two groups were compared. A mail order ad written around the appeal for change, for example, brought in over twice as many returns from the group scoring high on the need for change as from the group scoring low in this need. In general, these validation studies revealed significant but low relationships between EPPS scores and buying behavior. Other factors, such as price, product characteristics, and nature of the offer proved to be more important in determining frequency of returns. To be sure, the influence of personality factors on buying behavior may vary with the product. But the data so far available suggest that this influence is generally small.

## PRODUCT IMAGE

The terms "product image" and "product personality" refer to the composite of feeling tones and ideas associated with a product. Tea, for instance, was traditionally associated with old ladies, invalids, delicate china, and the affectations of the "tea shoppe." In the effort to change this image and to appeal to a wider public, advertisers began to feature pictures of young people and of rugged-looking men drinking tea for relaxation after work or sports (see Figure 83). For the same reason, such terms as "brisk," "robust," and "hearty" have been used more and more to describe tea in advertising copy.

Product image may also refer to a specific brand. Marlboro cigarettes were originally considered elegant and somewhat feminine. In the effort to alter this brand image, the company undertook an advertising campaign in which ranchers, hunters, and other sturdy outdoor types were shown smoking Marlboros and invariably displaying a tattoo mark. The previously cited British study indicated that different brands of gasoline have characteristic brand personalities. One was associated predominantly with young and sporty types, another with solid, respectable citizens.

Brand names and trademarks are often chosen so as to strengthen the desired brand image. The Campbell soup kids, Aunt Jemima, and Elsie the Borden cow are familiar examples. Of particular interest is the story of Green Giant peas (see 9, pp. 86–89). A small company in Minnesota—The Minnesota Valley Canning Company—began to market canned peas grown from a seed

***Fig. 83*** Use of advertising to modify a product image. (*Courtesy of Tea Council of the U.S.A., Inc.*)

Two of the winningest cowboys in rodeo today—both "tea men." Benny Reynolds, right, is World Champion All Around Cowboy. With him is Harley May, two-time Steer Wrestling Champion and President of the Rodeo Cowboys Association.

# Why these rodeo champs drink tea, the hot refresher

"I'd sure hate to crawl onto one of these broncs unless I felt like a million bucks," says Benny Reynolds. "It takes the best you've got. And that's exactly the reason most of us drink one or two cups of hot tea before the rodeoing starts. Between events, too. It helps quiet down the tension and gives you a good refreshing boost. Really

gets you feeling on top of things."

Why don't you get the good of tea, too? Make it your hot refresher for a week or so and see how good you feel about it. Lively satisfying taste,...clean, fresh feeling in your mouth . . . and the "just great" glow you have when you're relaxed but on your toes and ready for action. *Take Tea—You'll See!*

Winston Bruce on Stingaree. New World Champion Saddle Bronc Rider, Bruce started riding the bucking horses at 13. "And I've been a tea drinker about that long, too," he says. "I think it's the greatest refresher going."

TEA COUNCIL OF THE U.S.A., INC., A NONPROFIT ORGANIZATION

TEA
THE HOT
REFRESHER

that produced extra large peas. The company chose the brand name Green Giant and displayed a picture of a smiling green giant on the cans and in all advertisements of this product. Soon the green giant began to appear also on other canned goods prepared by this company, such as corn, and some of the other brand names were changed accordingly. Recognizing the popularity and effectiveness of this symbol, the company itself eventually changed its name to the Green Giant Company.

The Green Giant story illustrates a deliberate effort to transform a successful brand image into a corporate image. The reverse process is more common. In a well-established company, the strength of the corporate image increases public acceptance of each of its products. In some situations, however, it is better not to identify all products with a single corporate image. If a company makes both breakfast food and fertilizer, it would undoubtedly be desirable to have different brand names for the two lines and to keep the brand images distinct.

Even when two very similar products are involved, the use of a single brand name may be undesirable when the products are designed for different consumer publics or when some of their characteristics might conflict. This is illustrated by what may be regarded as a postscript to the Green Giant story recounted above. The same company is now marketing a type of canned peas whose principal feature is that they are *small*. Typical advertising copy for these peas asserts that "Their small size tells you, the minute you open the can, that these are not ordinary peas. . . . They have a subtle sweetness . . . that rivals the famed petits pois of France" (29). Under these conditions, it is understandable that the Green Giant company chose a *different* trade name for these peas.

Much of what was formerly described under the headings of "public relations" and "good will" has now been brought together under the concept of "corporate image" or "corporate personality" (see 5). Institutional advertising, mentioned in the first section of this chapter, is one of the recognized methods of building good will and developing a favorable corporate image. But to be effective, a corporate image needs to be much more than merely favorable—it must be specifically related to company objectives. A corporate image might, for example, suggest scientific advancement, old-fashioned goodness and dependability, elegance and distinction, or sturdiness and vigor. To combine or exchange these images might prove disastrous. A corporation cannot be all things to all people. It needs to formulate its objectives clearly and then set about developing a corporate image that fits these objectives. Conflicting and contradictory impressions tend only to confuse and weaken the corporate image.

To be sure, a corporation will be somewhat differently perceived by its different publics, including stockholders, employees, suppliers, distributors, customers, government officials, the press, and the communities in which it operates. Although recognizably different, these various corporate images will have a common core and will tend to influence each other. If a company's plants spread soot over the townspeople's homes or pollute their streams, these actions become a part of its corporate image. Advertising cannot do the whole job. The corporate image is affected by every aspect of a company's operation, from the quality of its products and the nature of its employee relations to the appearance of its buildings and grounds and the printing type used on its letterheads.

Nearly all techniques of consumer research have been used to investigate the public images of products, brands, or corporations (57). Not only direct questioning, but also depth interviewing, projective techniques, and other procedures of motivation research have been employed for this purpose. Motivation researchers have, in fact, done much to popularize the terms "product personality" and "corporate personality." Two relatively objective techniques that are well suited for image research are the Semantic Differential and the adjective checklist.

Originally developed for basic research on the psychology of meaning, the *Semantic Differential* has proved to be a useful tool in a wide variety of fields, from clinical psychology to advertising (38). Since the Semantic Differential provides a standardized and quantifiable procedure for measuring the connotations of any concept for the individual, it is particularly applicable to the study of product images and related problems (3, 24, 35, 57). Specifically, the respondent rates the product (or brand or company) on a seven-point graphic scale for each of a series of bipolar attributes, such as strong-weak, warm-cold, active-passive, friendly-unfriendly. Factorial analyses of the ratings for many different qualities have led to the identification of three principal factors: evaluative (e.g., good-bad, valuable-worthless), potency (e.g., strong-weak, large-small), and activity (e.g., active-passive, fast-slow). The evaluative factor generally accounts for the largest percentage of the total variance (38).

For each product investigated by means of the Semantic Differential, we can plot a "product profile" giving its mean ratings on the qualities rated. We can also find the total product score on each of the three factors or on all factors combined. The over-all difference between the profiles of two products can be expressed in terms of a composite index (37). In the study of corporate images, respondents are often asked to rate the ideal company on the same qualities on which they rate specific companies. The actual and ideal images can thus be compared by examining the profiles or by computing a total difference index.

The *adjective checklist* provides a simple basic procedure that has been used with a number of variations. Respondents are given a list of adjectives or descriptive phrases and asked to check those that apply to the particular product or company. Some of the variants of this technique are designed chiefly to dramatize the procedure and make it more interesting for the respondents (see 57). One modification is the chessboard technique, in which each adjective is printed on an individual square of the "chessboard." The respondent checks all the squares that apply to the object he is rating. Another variant uses pictures to represent the extremes of each quality to be rated.

A forced-choice variant of the adjective checklist was employed in an investigation of the product personality of different cars (54, 55). The first part of the study was conducted in 1956, before the introduction of the 1957 models. A list of 108 adjectives was presented to 100 undergraduate men, with the instructions that for each adjective they indicate which of three types of car owners it described best. The subjects recorded their responses by placing a check mark in one of three columns headed "Cadillac," "Buick," and "Chevrolet." The order of both the adjectives and the cars was rotated to avoid positional effects. The stereotypes associated with these three cars were clearly revealed in the responses. Among the traits most frequently attributed to

Cadillac owners were famous, important, and successful. Buick owners were described in such terms as middle-class, brave, and masculine. Chevrolet owners were characterized by such adjectives as poor, plain, and simple.

The respondents were also asked to compare Ford, Plymouth, and Chevrolet owners by means of the same checklist. Six months later, this procedure was repeated with a similar group of 100 respondents, about 70 per cent of whom had participated in the first test session. In the interval, the 1957 models of these cars had been introduced and vigorously promoted in advertising campaigns. Table 17 shows the results obtained on the two occasions.

**TABLE 17**  *Change in Product Personality*
*as Measured by an Adjective Checklist*
(*Data from Wells, Goi, and Seader, 55, p. 121*)

*Traits chosen as most typical of each car owner with frequencies exceeding chance expectations at .01 level, arranged in order of decreasing frequency*

| FORD | | PLYMOUTH | | CHEVROLET |
|---|---|---|---|---|
| | | *1956 Results* | | |
| masculine | merry | quiet | calm | ordinary |
| young | loud | careful | sad | fair |
| powerful | active | slow | thinking | common |
| good-looking | cool | silent | patient | |
| rough | tall | moral | honest | |
| dangerous | interesting | fat | understanding | |
| strong | sharp | gentle | content | |
| single | popular | | | |
| | | *1957 Results* | | |
| dangerous | active | high-class | | small |
| loud | proud | feminine | | low-class |
| rough | brave | important | | little |
| powerful | | rich | | simple |
| cross | | different | | ordinary |
| thin | | particular | | practical |

The youthful and dashing image of the 1956 Ford owner had become rougher, tougher, and less debonair in 1957. The Chevrolet owner appeared rather nondescript on both occasions. The most conspicuous change occurred in the image of the Plymouth owners. Of the 14 adjectives chosen with greater than chance frequency to characterize Plymouth owners in 1956, none remained in 1957. The pleasant, nice, and stodgy character associated with the 1956 models had now been replaced by a more glamorous and discriminating type of person.

These changes in product personality were in line with the changes that had occurred both in the cars and in the advertising. Thus a typical ad for the 1957 Plymouth asserted, "In one flaming moment, Plymouth leaps three full years ahead—the *only* car that dares to break the time barrier! Plymouth's traditionally great engineering brings you the fabulous new Fury '301' V-8 engine . . . revolutionary new Torsion-Aire ride . . . exhilarating sports car handling . . . new supersafe Total Contact brakes . . . dramatic Flight-Sweep Styling. The car you might have expected in 1960 is at your dealer's *now!"* (42). As the investigators aptly comment, "It is hard to believe that the quiet, careful, slow owner of an old Plymouth would dare go near a car with a Fury engine" (55, p. 121).

## SUMMARY

The appeal is the primary message of an advertisement, whose purpose is to show how a commodity can satisfy some consumer want. Lists of human drives can serve only as a very general guide to the advertiser. New drives develop as a result of experience. The relative strength of appeals varies for different products and for different consumer populations. By providing information on how consumers use products and on what they particularly like or dislike about different products, consumer surveys help in the selection of effective appeals. For a number of commodities, negative appeals may be more effective than positive appeals. Negative appeals, however, should be distinguished from negative suggestion, which is usually undesirable. Although most ads contain an appeal, two well-known exceptions are reminder ads and institutional ads.

Besides presenting explicit appeals, an advertisement can arouse the desired feeling tone and associate it with the product in more indirect ways. Since feeling tones tend to spread beyond their source, any aspect of the ad could lead to unfavorable, unsuitable, or conflicting associations with the product. Among the factors to be examined for appropriateness of feeling tone are illustration, color, printing type and other graphic elements, and language. In addition, type that is difficult to read or brand names that are hard to pronounce tend to produce frustration, annoyance, and embarrassment.

Motivation research utilizes depth interviewing and projective techniques in the study of buying motives. Among its many procedures are several varieties of intensive individual interviewing, group interviewing, word association, sentence completion, picture interpretation, cartoon tests modeled after the Rosenzweig P-F Study, and role playing, or visualization. The principal contribution of motivation research is to provide hypotheses for subsequent testing by more objective and quantitative methods applicable to large samples. Contrary to the claims of some motivation researchers, direct questioning can also yield information on consumer motivation, provided it is incorporated in suitable experimental designs.

Closely related to motivation research are personality studies of consumers. Users and nonusers of a product or brand have been compared in personality characteristics as well as in demographic variables. Interviewing, projective techniques, and personality inventories have been employed for this purpose. Some exploratory research has also been conducted on the relation between personality characteristics and actual buying response to specific appeals.

The concepts of product image, product personality, and corporate image have been popularized by motivation research. Nearly all techniques of consumer research have been utilized to investigate the public images associated with products, brands, or corporations. Two techniques that are often applied in this type of study are the Semantic Differential and the adjective checklist.

# REFERENCES

1. Anastasi, Anne. *Differential psychology.* (3rd ed.) New York: Macmillan, 1958.
2. Anastasi, Anne. *Psychological testing.* (2nd ed.) New York: Macmillan, 1961.
3. Anon. Mogul "Semantic Differential" aims to provide qualitative research data. *Advert. Age,* 1958, **29** (36), 3.
4. Berry, P. C. Effect of colored illumination upon perceived temperature. *J. appl. Psychol.,* 1961, **45**, 248–250.
5. Bristol, L. (Ed.) *Developing the corporate image; a management guide to public relations.* New York: Scribner, 1960.
6. Britt, S. H. *The spenders.* New York: McGraw-Hill, 1960.
7. Burt, C., Cooper, W. F., and Martin, J. L. A psychological study of typography. *Brit. J. statist. Psychol.,* 1955, **8** (pt. 1), 29–58.
8. Coleman, E. B., and Kim, I. Comparison of several styles of typography in English. *J. appl. Psychol.,* 1961, **45**, 262–267.
9. Crawford, J. W. *Advertising: Communications from management.* Boston: Allyn and Bacon, 1960.
10. Davis, R. C., and Smith, H. J. Determinants of feeling tone and type faces. *J. appl. Psychol.,* 1933, **17**, 742–754.
11. Dichter, E. Psychology in market research. *Harvard Bus. Rev.,* 1947, **25**, 432–443.
12. Dorcus, R. M. Habitual word associations to colors as a possible factor in advertising. *J. appl. Psychol.,* 1932, **16**, 277–287.
13. Engstrom, W. C., and Powers, Mary E. A revision of the study of values for use in magazine readership research. *J. appl. Psychol.,* 1959, **43**, 74–78.
14. Eysenck, H. J., Tarrant, Mollie, Woolf, Myra, and England, L. Smoking and personality. *Brit. med. J.,* 1960, 1 (5184), 1456–1460.
15. Ferber, R., and Wales, H. G. (Eds.) *Motivation and market behavior.* Homewood, Ill.: Irwin, 1958.
16. Giles, R. Bostonian shoe advertising is revolutionized after survey among 5,000 men. *Printers' Ink,* 1939, **188** (12), 25–32.
17. Grube, C. S. How the public learned to pronounce "Suchard." *Advert. Sell.,* 1947 (October), p. 68.
18. Haire, M. Projective techniques in market research. *J. Market.,* 1950, **14**, 649–656.
19. Henry, H. *Motivation research.* New York: Ungar, 1958.
20. Hepner, H. W. *Modern advertising: Practices and principles.* (3rd ed.) New York: McGraw-Hill, 1956.
21. Herzog, Herta. What do we really know about daytime serial listeners? In P. F. Lazarsfeld and F. N. Stanton (Eds.), *Radio research.* New York: Duell, Sloan & Pearce, 1944. Pp. 3–33.
22. Hill, C. R. Another look at two instant coffee studies. *J. advert. Res.,* 1960, 1 (2), 18–21.
23. Jones, E. S. Effect of letters and syllables in publicity. *J. appl. Psychol.,* 1922, **6**, 198–204.
24. Kjeldergaard, P. M. Attitude toward newscasters as measured by the semantic differential: A descriptive case. *J. appl. Psychol.,* 1961, **45**, 35–40.
25. Koponen, A. *Personality profile projects.* New York: J. Walter Thompson Co., 1958.
26. Koponen, A. Personality characteristics of purchasers. *J. advert. Res.,* 1960, 1 (1), 6–11.
27. Kotkov, B., and Murawski, B. A Rorschach study of the personality structure of obese women. *J. clin. Psychol.,* 1952, **8**, 391–396.
28. Laird, D. A. How the consumer estimates quality by subconscious sensory impression. *J. appl. Psychol.,* 1932, **16**, 241–246.
29. Le Sueur advertisement. *The New Yorker,* Feb. 10, 1962, p. 88.
30. Lucas, D. B., and Benson, C. E. The relative values of positive and negative advertising appeals as measured by coupons returned. *J. appl. Psychol.,* 1929, **13**, 274–300.
31. Lucas, D. B., and Benson, C. E. Some sales results for positive and negative advertisements. *J. appl. Psychol.,* 1930, **14**, 363–370.
32. Martineau, P. *Motivation in advertising.* New York: McGraw-Hill, 1957.
33. Meehl, P. E. An investigation of a general normality or control factor in personality testing. *Psychol. Monogr.,* 1945, **59**, No. 4.

34. Miller, N. E. Liberalization of basic S-R concepts: Extensions to conflict behavior, motivation and social learning. In S. Koch (Ed.), *Psychology: A study of a science.* New York: McGraw-Hill, 1959. (Study I, vol. 2.) Pp. 196–292.

35. Mindak, W. A. A new technique for measuring advertising effectiveness. *J. Market.,* 1956, **20**, 367–378.

36. Murray, D. C., and Deabler, H. L. Colors and mood-tones. *J. appl. Psychol.,* 1957, **41**, 279–283.

37. Osgood, C. E., and Suci, G. J. A measure of relation determined by both mean difference and profile information. *Psychol. Bull.,* 1952, **49**, 251–262.

38. Osgood, C. E., Suci, G. J., and Tannenbaum, P. H. *The measurement of meaning.* Urbana, Ill.: Univer. Ill. Press, 1957.

39. Packard, V. *The hidden persuaders.* New York: McKay, 1957.

40. Paterson, D. G., and Tinker, M. A. *How to make type readable.* New York: Harper & Row, 1940.

41. Paterson, D. G., and Tinker, M. A. Readability of newspaper headlines printed in capitals and lower case. *J. appl. Psychol.,* 1946, **30**, 161–168.

42. Plymouth advertisement. *Life,* 1956, **41** (19), 18–19.

43. Poffenberger, A. T. *Psychology in advertising.* Chicago: Shaw, 1928.

44. Poffenberger, A. T., and Barrows, Bernice E. The feeling value of lines. *J. appl. Psychol.,* 1924, **8**, 187–205.

45. Poffenberger, A. T., and Franken, R. B. Type face appropriateness. *J. appl. Psychol.,* 1923, **7**, 312–329.

46. Politz, A. Science and truth in marketing research. *Harvard Bus. Rev.,* 1957, **35** (1), 117–126.

47. Rudolph, H. J. *Attention and interest factors in advertising.* New York: Funk & Wagnalls (in assoc. with Printers' Ink Publ. Co.), 1947.

48. Schiller, G. An experimental study of the appropriateness of color and type in advertising. *J. appl. Psychol.,* 1935, **19**, 652–664.

49. Scott, E. M. Personality and movie preference. *Psychol. Rep.,* 1957, **3**, 17–18.

50. Smith, G. H. *Motivation research in advertising and marketing.* New York: McGraw-Hill, 1954.

51. Tinker, M. A. Recent studies of eye movements in reading. *Psychol. Bull.,* 1958, **55**, 215–231.

52. Tinker, M. A. *Legibility of print.* Ames, Iowa: Iowa State Univer. Press, 1963.

53. Tucker, W. T., and Painter, J. J. Personality and product use. *J. appl. Psychol.,* 1961, **45**, 325–329.

54. Wells, W. D., Andriuli, F. J., Goi, F. J., and Seader, S. An adjective check list for the study of "product personality." *J. appl. Psychol.,* 1957, **41**, 317–319.

55. Wells, W. D., Goi, F. J., and Seader, S. A change in product image. *J. appl. Psychol.,* 1958, **42**, 120–121.

56. Wexner, Lois B. The degree to which colors (hues) are associated with mood-tones. *J. appl. Psychol.,* 1954, **38**, 432–435.

57. Winick, C. How to find out what kind of image you have. In L. Bristol (Ed.), *Developing the corporate image; a management guide to public relations.* New York: Scribner, 1960. Ch. 3.

58. Yoell, W. A. Make your advertising themes match consumer behavior. *Printers' Ink,* 1952, **238** (12), 82–87.

# 12

## Perceptual and Cognitive
## Factors in Advertising

Advertising is a form of communication. In Chapter 11, we considered the message that the advertiser wishes to communicate, as illustrated by explicit appeals, feeling tones and atmosphere conducive to product acceptance, brand images, and corporate images. Whatever their objectives, advertising communications must be presented in such a way that they will be noticed, understood, retained, and accepted. To be sure, these are necessary but not sufficient conditions for advertising effectiveness. An ad may catch the eye, arouse interest, present its arguments clearly and convincingly, and still not sell the product. On the other hand, if no one notices an ad, it cannot affect sales no matter how meritorious it is in all other respects.

## MECHANICAL ASPECTS OF PRINTED ADS

Some of the earliest studies in the psychology of advertising were concerned with the effect of such ad characteristics as size, repetition, position, color, and illustration upon attention and retention. Continued research on these factors by a variety of methods has led to the accumulation of a considerable body of data that can serve as a general guide in the preparation of ads and in the planning of advertising campaigns. Detailed surveys of such data can be found in several sources (23, chs. 20–31; 29). Recent results have been derived largely from readership surveys of magazines or newspapers and from analyses of written inquiries, although eye cameras, tachistoscopes, and other laboratory techniques have also been employed.

*Readership Surveys.* A particularly well-controlled study of readership data was published by Rudolph (40) in 1947. Using Starch readership figures for 2,500 half-page and full-page *Saturday Evening Post* ads, Rudolph analyzed the effect of each ad characteristic while holding other features constant. Ads were regularly matched for product, company, size, and use of color, unless one of the latter variables was itself under investigation. For example, when studying the readership of right- and left-hand pages, Rudolph compared Texaco black-and-white full-page ads appearing on right and left pages. Readership ratios found in such subgroup comparisons were then averaged for all ads. Rudolph's findings have been corroborated by later Starch studies of more limited scope (see 44–46, 48, 51, 52) as well as by readership studies conducted by others. Some of the major results from these studies will be cited for illustrative purposes.

Increasing the *size* of an ad will generally increase its readership, but not in direct proportion to size. An ad that is doubled in size will have somewhat less than double the original readership. Moreover, the rate of increase in readership will itself depend upon the attention value of the original ad. A small ad that is noted by a large proportion of readers has less to gain by an increase in size than one noted by few readers.

Starch (46) has pointed out that, by chance alone, if 10 out of 100 readers notice a half-page ad, then doubling the size of the ad should attract 10 per cent of the remaining 90 readers, or 9 additional readers. Hence the full-page ad should attract 19, not 20, readers. On this basis, Starch proposes the following formula for predicting the effect of doubling ad size upon readership:

$$x = N + (100 - N) .01N$$

in which $N$ is the percentage of readers who noted an ad of given size and $x$ is the predicted percentage of those who will note an ad of twice the size. In simplified form, the formula reduces to:

$$x = 2N - .01N^2$$

Table 18 shows that the percentages predicted with this formula agreed quite closely with those obtained empirically. The data are based on 6,150 half-page

**TABLE 18**  *Relation between Ad Size and Readership*
(*From Starch, 46*)

| | Percentage "Noted" | | |
|---|---|---|---|
| Category | Obtained with half page | Obtained with full page | Predicted with full page |
| Black-and-white ads | | | |
| Men | 9.6 | 18.5 | 18.3 |
| Women | 10.1 | 20.6 | 19.2 |
| Two-color ads | | | |
| Men | 13.0 | 23.9 | 24.3 |
| Women | 6.3 | 11.6 | 12.2 |
| Four-color ads | | | |
| Men | 13.7 | 26.9 | 25.5 |
| Women | 25.4 | 44.9 | 44.3 |
| Total | 13.3 | 25.2 | 24.8 |

and 6,604 full-page ads surveyed by Starch over a four-year period. Readership scores were compared for half-page and full-page black-and-white ads in the same product category and appearing in the same magazine. The same analysis was repeated with two-color and with four-color ads.

Size of ads has been analyzed from several other points of view. One analysis of newspaper ad readership, for example, indicated that larger ads attract a greater proportion of nonusers than do smaller ads (21). This relationship is illustrated in Figure 84. Present users are likely to notice an ad for the product they use, regardless of ad size, because of their interest in the product itself. The nonuser, on the other hand, is more likely to respond to the mechanical factor of size. Small ads may thus be relatively effective in retaining present

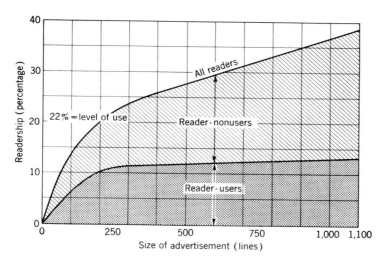

**Fig. 84** Relation of size of advertisement to readership by users and nonusers of product. (*From Hadley, 21, p. 55.*)

users and possibly inducing them to buy more of the product, while large ads may be more effective in attracting new users.

The additional space available in a large ad may be used in various ways. It is possible, of course, merely to magnify a small ad so as to fill up the space; but this is rarely done. In a larger ad, there is an opportunity to include more illustration and more text. Sometimes, the additional space is utilized simply as "white space," or unfilled background. Ads with a large proportion of white space tend to attract attention because of their novelty, stark simplicity, and startling appearance. White space may also be used to create a desired atmosphere. The ad reproduced in Figure 85 illustrates a liberal use of blank space in combination with an arresting headline to arouse interest and curiosity.

A second major factor that increases the number of readers reached by an ad is *repetition*. Each time an ad is repeated in a different issue of a magazine, it will be seen by a certain number of new readers, as well as by some who had seen it in the earlier issue. As a result, the total number of readers who notice the ad as well as the number who read it tends to remain approximately the same on successive repetitions. Moreover, the repeated exposure of those readers who notice the ad on more than one occasion serves to strengthen whatever impact the ad makes on them.

Starch (48) analyzed the readership data for 80 ads that had been inserted from two to eight times unchanged in different issues of the same magazine. The intervals between insertions ranged from two weeks to several months, the most common interval being one month. The results showed that each ad tended to retain the same readership level through all repetitions. Those ads with low initial readership were noted by a small proportion of readers on successive repetitions; those with high initial readership were noted by a large

**Fig. 85** Use of white space as an attention-getting device.
(*Courtesy of Rogers Corporation.*)

proportion of readers on each repetition. Such findings suggest the desirability of using successful ads repeatedly. Similar results have been obtained in other studies with business magazines (32) and with outdoor poster advertising (49).

A somewhat different procedure was followed in a well-designed experiment conducted with 150 *Saturday Evening Post* subscribers in a single city (37). By means of specially prepared copies of one issue, some readers were exposed to certain ads twice, some once, and some not at all. Each reader underwent all three conditions, but with different ads. As a check on actual exposure to the ad, a tiny glue seal held the test pages together in each copy. Only when this seal was broken was the exposure counted for that reader.

A few days after the last exposure, all subjects were asked to name the first brand that came to mind for various products. It was thus possible to determine how far exposure to an ad had raised the percentage of respondents who named a given brand above the percentage who named it in the unexposed control group. Reference to Figure 86 shows that, in terms of this index of brand familiarity, two exposures were about twice as effective as a single exposure. The advantage of two exposures proved to be equally large when subjects were questioned about their knowledge of and belief in the claims made by the different brands and when they were asked what brand they thought they would buy if they were to purchase the product on that day. Results pertaining to the respondent's willingness to buy the advertised product are also illustrated in Figure 86.

Considerable attention has been given to the *position* of an ad within magazines or newspapers. This question actually covers several independent questions. One has to do with choice of page within the medium. Extensive data have been gathered on the proportion of readers who look at each page in a newspaper or magazine. The results indicate that the content of different pages has more effect on reader traffic than does the physical position of the page. Placing an ad near a popular editorial feature gives it an advantage.

In magazines, ads on the cover pages (inside front cover, page 1, inside and outside back cover) do have a significant readership advantage of 30 to 64 per

**Fig. 86** Effect of repetition of magazine advertisements upon readers' reactions to advertised brands. (*From Politz, 37, pp. 14, 20; reproduced by permission of Curtis Publishing Company.*)

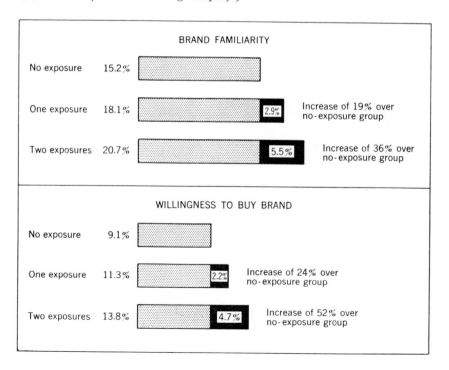

cent over inside pages (52). Among the inside pages, however, physical location seems to make little difference (51, 52). This uniformity of attention
value probably results from the increasing efforts of magazine publishers to
distribute the editorial content evenly throughout the medium. Whenever possible, of course, ads should be placed near relevant editorial features. Thus
food ads should be on or near the woman's page, book ads on or near the book
review pages, and so on. Such placement helps to select an interested audience
and also reaches the reader when he is particularly receptive to the product.

Advertisers have also been much concerned about right- and left-hand pages,
as well as right and left halves of single pages. Readership data, however, have
shown negligible differences between these positions when comparisons are
made under adequately controlled conditions (40). What differences are
found probably result from a variety of factors, including reading habits (from
left to right in our culture), habits of holding and turning pages, and customary placement of ads and features. For instance, in going through a magazine from front to back, the left-hand page is in motion when first seen and
hence will not be perceived as clearly as the right. A number of readers, however, have the habit of "thumbing through" a magazine from back to front, a
practice that reverses the advantage of right and left pages.

*Color* is now employed in the majority of magazine ads, and it is rapidly
being introduced in newspaper ads as well. How effective is such a use of color
in attracting reader attention? In Rudolph's analysis of readership data for
*Saturday Evening Post* ads, two-color ads, which use only one color besides
black, had only about 1 per cent higher readership than comparable black-and-
white ads (40, pp. 35–37). Since the additional cost of the two-color ads
averaged about 17 per cent, this use of color did not seem justified. However,
four-color ads, in which all colors can be realistically reproduced, averaged 54
per cent higher than black-and-white ads in readership figures and only 44 per
cent higher in cost. Today this cost differential has been reduced in some
media, a condition that increases the net advantage of colored ads.

In a later Starch analysis of 3,819 ads in two magazines, two-color ads again
showed no advantage over black-and-white ads in readership; but four-color
ads surpassed the black-and-white ads by 85 per cent for half-page ads and by
about 50 per cent for one-page and two-page ads (45). The latter difference
probably reflects the ceiling effect discussed earlier in connection with size
increments. An ad that is already attracting a large proportion of readers is
not likely to show marked gains in readership as further improvements are
introduced. In an analysis of reader-impression data for the same ads, however,
Starch found that color greatly augments the prestige value of the one- and
two-page ads. The four-color ads were mentioned over 2½ times as often as the
black-and-white as having outstandingly impressed the reader.

It might be noted that in two-color ads color is generally used not for
realistic portrayal but as an attention-getting device. When the printed matter
in a medium is largely black and white, the introduction of even a modicum
of color will catch the eye. This advantage is lost, however, in a medium which
uses color as lavishly as is done in most present-day American magazines.
Where color is still a novelty, as in newspapers, the addition of even a single
color to an ad will greatly enhance its attention value. In one newspaper survey, split-run tests of identical ads in black-and-white and with small quan-

tities of one color added showed substantial readership differences in favor of the colored ads (4).

Much depends, too, upon the way color is used in an ad. Some ads can be effectively presented without color and might gain little from the arbitrary addition of one or more colors. Others depend upon color to achieve realism, to display the attractive features of the product, or to create a suitable atmosphere. Average readership figures may be misleading when applied indiscriminately to individual ads. The introduction of color may produce spectacular gains in the effectiveness of some ads and negligible gains in others. If used injudiciously, moreover, color may render an ad worse than useless.

Like color, *illustrations* have been used with increasing frequency in advertising (26). Like color, too, illustrations serve many functions. They may be used to facilitate comprehension of ideas, to aid in the later identification of the product at the point of sale, or to arouse appropriate feeling tones. For certain classes of products, the illustration lets the product "speak for itself," as in the photograph of a delicious cake, a luxurious fur coat, or a decorative floor covering.

With regard to attention value, pictures of people generally rate high. An analysis conducted by Starch (43) indicated that ads portraying people were more often read than those showing only the product. Using the read-most index, which is based on the proportion of respondents who have read half or more of the text of an ad, Starch selected the 50 most widely read and the 50 least widely read ads from his records. The illustrations centered about people in 29 of the former and only 10 of the latter. Pictures of the product alone were found in none of the former and in 32 of the latter.

On the other hand, it should be noted that some of the most successful ads portray appetizing foods that can be prepared with the given product. This type of ad would feature, for example, not a package of flour, but a cake baked with that flour, along with a recipe for the cake. The Carnation Evaporated Milk ad reproduced in Figure 87 is an example of such an ad. When published in *Life* magazine, this full-page four-color ad received the following Starch ratings for women: noted 66 per cent, seen-associated 63 per cent, and read-most 29 per cent. In all three scores, it ranked first among women readers of that issue of *Life*. The ad also obtained an unusually high score when evaluated in terms of the Gallup-Robinson aided-recall technique (see Chapter 10).

Studies of the relative attention value of photographs and drawings (or "artwork") generally reveal a slight advantage of photographs (50). This difference, however, is not so large today as it once was, since current artwork is often so realistic as to be virtually indistinguishable from photographs. The findings of readership surveys were corroborated in a well-designed experimental study in which photographs and hand-drawn versions of the same ads were compared (61). A representative sample of 962 adults in New York City were asked to rank the ads for liking and believability. A recall test was also administered immediately after presentation of the ads. All three measures tended to favor the photographic versions. The one clear-cut exception was an ad containing a semihumorous illustration that could be better expressed in cartoon form.

An important consideration in the choice of illustration is its relevance to the product, the text, and the appeal. In the use of illustrations to attract attention,

**Fig. 87**  Effective use of illustration in a high-readership food ad. (*Courtesy of Carnation Company.*)

# NEW! THE PIE YOU CAN "BAKE ON ICE"

The secret is today's Carnation . . .

## The milk you can whip like cream— with ½ the fat calories

*Ordinary milk won't do!* Not even costly cream can make this pie so high, light, delicious. For this is the milk that *looks* like cream, *pours* like cream, *whips* even higher than cream – with ½ the fat calories, and at ½ the cost. Use Carnation like cream for delicious whipped desserts, rich-tasting coffee, smoother sauces, moister meat loaves, creamier-tasting mashed potatoes. (Even mixed with an equal amount of water, it's rich whole milk – for smoother cooking results at far less cost.) Change today to Carnation, the milk you can use like cream with ½ the fat calories, *and at ½ the cost of cream!*

**RECIPE:**

## NO COOKING! NO HOT OVEN! LEMONY-LUSCIOUS!

**NEW NO-BAKE WHIPPED ANGEL FOOD PIE**
(*Makes 9-inch single crust pie*)

| | |
|---|---|
| 1 3-ounce package lemon gelatin | ½ cup hot lemon juice |
| ⅓ cup sugar | 1 cup *undiluted* CARNATION EVAPORATED MILK |
| ⅔ cup hot water | |
| 1 teaspoon grated lemon rind | 2 tablespoons lemon juice 9-inch crumb crust* |

Dissolve gelatin and sugar in hot water and ½ cup *hot* lemon juice. Chill until consistency of unbeaten egg white. Add lemon rind. Chill Carnation in refrigerator tray until soft ice crystals form around edges of tray (15-20 minutes). Whip until stiff (1 minute). Add 2 tablespoons lemon juice; whip *very* stiff (2 minutes longer). Fold whipped Carnation into chilled gelatin mixture. Spoon into pie shell. Chill until firm (1 to 2 hours).

*For 9-inch crumb crust, mix 1½ cups graham cracker crumbs, 2 tablespoons sugar and ¼ cup melted butter. Line sides and bottom of 9-inch pie plate with crumb mixture.

there is the danger that the ad comes to be regarded as an end in itself. The advertiser should always remember that he is trying to sell the product, not the ad. Irrelevant, bizarre, or "arty" illustrations may attract attention to themselves but usually fail to associate the ad with the product or brand name (28, 44, 50).

A related question pertains to the specific audience that the advertiser wants to reach. The content and form of the illustration tend to select those who will read the ad. Advertisements containing pictures of women, for example, are more often read by women; those with pictures of men are more often read by men (40, p. 73). Although most men enjoy looking at a picture of a pretty girl, when they see such a picture in an ad they evidently assume that the ad is directed to women. Hence they are unlikely to read further. Women react in a similar fashion to ads featuring men.

*Factor Analysis of Ad Variables.* The potential usefulness of factor analysis in investigating the effectiveness of different features of advertisements was demonstrated in a study conducted with ads from a single issue of the *American Builder,* a monthly trade magazine (58). As in the studies discussed in the preceding section, the criterion of ad effectiveness was readership. The same technique could, however, be utilized with inquiries, sales records, or any other available criterion. The readership index employed in this study was the percentage of readers who recalled seeing any part of the ad. This is similar to the Starch "noted" score. The analysis was based on 137 ads, ranging in size from one-eighth of a page to four pages. Correlations were computed between the readership criterion and 34 mechanical and content variables of the ads. Of these variables, 19 were chosen for factor analysis because of significant criterion correlations, satisfactory rater reliability, and experimental independence.

The factor analysis yielded six factors, the first two of which accounted for more than half of the variance of readership scores. The first factor, accounting for 41 per cent of the readership variance of the ads, was described as a pictorial-color factor. Its three highest loadings on ad characteristics were found on "square inches of illustration," "number of pictures showing the product in use," and "number of colors." The second factor, accounting for an additional 12 per cent of readership variance, was identified as a size factor.

On the basis of these factorial results, the investigator worked out a regression equation for predicting ad readership from size of ad, number of colors, and square inches of illustration. For purposes of cross validation, this regression equation was applied to the readership scores of ads in six other trade and business magazines obtained by the same method with other readers. Correlations between the obtained and predicted readership scores ranged from .58 to .80 for different magazines, with a mean of .71. Although these findings are limited to the type of magazines and readers included in the study, they indicate considerable validity for the three rather simple predictors employed.

*Analysis of Written Inquiries.* The criterion of written inquiries has been employed to investigate the effectiveness of the major mechanical characteristics of ads, with results very similar to those obtained in readership studies. Several large-scale analyses of written inquiries have been published (39, 42, 47). In the most recent and most extensive of these studies, Starch (47) obtained from 75 companies confidential records covering 8,200 advertisements. The total number of inquiries analyzed was approximately 12 million, distributed over a 10-year period. As in the previously described analyses of readership records, the ads compared in studying any one variable, such as color, were matched as closely as possible in other variables, such as size, kind of product, company, kind of offer, and presence or absence of coupon. Differences in size of circulation among magazines were controlled by expressing number of inquiries in terms of per million circulation.

The results with regard to size of ad, color, and position are essentially the same as those obtained in readership studies. The role of illustration was not analyzed. The only significant differences between the two types of criteria were found in the case of repetition. Although readership scores remain virtually the same when an ad is reinserted in different issues, inquiries do decline. The drop for the second insertion is about 25 per cent. There are smaller declines for successive insertions, the returns leveling off at about 60 per cent of the original number. Such a decline is understandable, since readers who send a written request in response to an ad are unlikely to write again when they see the ad a second time. Thus the later returns come largely from new readers.

A comparison of the results of this investigation with those obtained through a similar analysis of written inquiries conducted by Starch some 30 years earlier is also of interest. With only one major exception, the conclusions drawn from the earlier study were corroborated by the later study. The exception pertains to the effect of position of the ad on number of inquiries. The earlier study, completed in 1930, found substantial differences in relation to position. Ads within the first 5 per cent of pages at the front and within the last 5 per cent of pages at the back elicited about 40 per cent more inquiries than did ads located in the middle of the issue. This advantage had disappeared at the time of the second survey. Starch observes that in the intervening 30 years magazines have deliberately sought to change their makeup so as to distribute reader interest evenly throughout their issues. The inquiry results suggest that they have largely succeeded in these efforts.

*Laboratory Techniques.* The direct observation of eye movements while subjects look at ads was one of the earliest techniques employed in psychological studies of advertising. Later investigations used eye cameras to obtain the same kind of data more precisely. Tachistoscopes have also been employed to determine what the subject sees on the page during his first very rapid glance. Immediately after each exposure, subjects are asked what they saw. Since the exposure is usually too brief to permit eye movements, the subjects will see only that which first catches the eye. By this method one can determine whether the objects seen first tend to occupy certain positions on the page, or to be colored, or to have definite shapes, and so forth.

Tachistoscopic presentation can be adapted for group testing by means of motion pictures or slide projectors. One study demonstrated a close correspondence between results obtained through a group tachistoscopic procedure and those obtained through the more laborious and time-consuming individual use of the eye camera (56). Every possible pair of 10 ads was exposed for a half second to a total of 154 subjects. Immediately after the presentation of each pair, the subjects were asked to indicate on a record sheet which of the two ads they would look at if they were given a second look. The Purdue Eye Camera was employed in a second test of the same 10 ads with 36 of the original subjects. Mean number of preferences for each ad, as determined in the group tachistoscopic test, correlated .79 with number of "first looks" recorded for each ad by the eye camera; the correlation of mean preference with number of seconds spent looking at the ad was .83. When corrected for unreliability of the eye camera measures, these correlations rose to .86 and .99.

Of particular interest is the methodology developed in a recent study of the "visual efficiency" of printed ads, conducted under the joint sponsorship of the Advertising Research Foundation and the Du Pont Company (3, 41). Visual efficiency of ads was investigated by means of an instrument developed for the purpose by HRB-Singer, Inc. A portable version of this device, now available for general use, is illustrated in Figure 88. Known as VISTA (Visual Testing Apparatus), the instrument provides four measures of the visual efficiency of ads. Three of these measures are concerned with the distance, illumination level, and duration of exposure at which an ad can be correctly recognized. The fourth is based on a test of binocular rivalry, in which two ads are presented simultaneously, one to each eye, to determine which one the subject perceives.

Against the four criterion measures of visual efficiency, the investigators checked 47 physical or mechanical ad variables. Among them were such traditional variables as area, color, and percentage of white space. Also included were two new sets of variables: one was concerned with the division

**Fig. 88** Visual Testing Apparatus (VISTA) for investigating visual efficiency of advertisements in terms of exposure time, distance, illumination, and binocular rivalry. (*Courtesy of HRB-Singer, Inc.*)

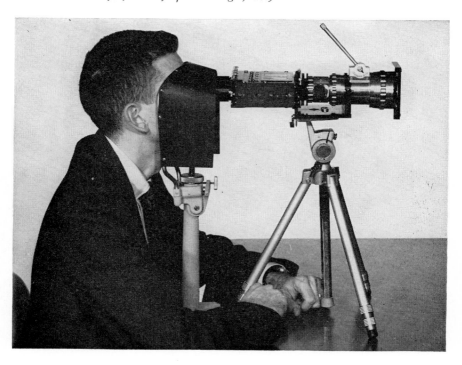

of an ad into its component parts, or visual units; the other, with the amounts of light reflected from the ad and its parts, from which ratios of brightness contrast could be computed.

Criterion measures of the visual efficiency of ads were obtained from 30 subjects. Of the 47 ad variables studied, 22 yielded significant correlations with one or more of the visual criteria. Multiple correlations of the six most predictive variables with each of the criterion measures ranged from .73 to .81. A type of cross validation was next carried out with specially constructed ads. On the basis of the previously identified ad variables, two high-scoring and two low-scoring ads were prepared for each of the four visual criteria.

Figure 89 shows an ad designed to score high and one designed to score low in the binocular-rivalry criterion. To obtain a high score in terms of this criterion, an ad should contain few perceptual units, should have an illustration low in reflectance, and should be in color. Its message should be stated directly in the headline, and the ad area should comprise approximately 10 per cent copy, 20 per cent illustration, and 70 per cent white space. When the specially constructed ads were tried out on 11 subjects, significant correspondences between predicted and actual visual effectiveness were found for most ads, although not all four criteria could be satisfactorily predicted.

This study was unusually well designed and offers several promising methodological leads. Much more information is needed, however, before its contribution can be assessed. The predictive value of the ad variables investigated needs to be checked with other types of subjects, other types of advertisements, and especially with other criteria of advertising effectiveness. To be recognized

*Fig. 89*   Two ads designed to score high and low in visual effectiveness as measured by binocular rivalry. (*From Snyder and Stover, 41, p. 16.*)

(Original in 4 colors)
High scoring

(Original in black and white)
Low scoring

quickly, at a distance, and under weak illumination is undoubtedly an asset for ads appearing on billboards or car cards. It remains to be determined, however, whether this kind of recognizability is a major factor in magazine and newspaper advertising. A unified illustration, an informative headline, and an abundance of white space are probably desirable in most display ads that receive only cursory inspection. Yet the highly cluttered full-page ads run in newspapers by some drugstores and supermarkets are undoubtedly successful. These ads are carefully perused by readers, who use them like a catalogue in their search for items on sale at bargain prices. These two contrasting types of ads illustrate the fact that the effectiveness of different ad variables must be evaluated in the light of the objectives of the particular ad.

## TRADEMARKS AND OTHER REDUCED CUES

*Reduced Cues in Advertising.* From a psychological standpoint, every trademark is a reduced cue. Its function is to serve as a stimulus for the recall of the product and company name. The trademark also tends to evoke the feelings and ideas that have become associated with the product through previous advertising and through the consumer's own contacts with the product. When the trademark is a direct representation of the brand name, as with Camel, Raleigh, Aunt Jemima, and Smith Brothers, the association is particularly easy to establish and the chances of confusion with other products or brands are minimized. Frequently, the trademark is chosen so as to symbolize a characteristic advantage of the product or service, which the advertiser wants to highlight. Examples are Bon Ami's newly hatched chick ("hasn't scratched yet") and the Prudential Life Insurance Company's Rock of Gibraltar ("the strength of Gibraltar").

It is not only the registered trademark that serves as a reduced cue. Any distinctive recurring feature of a company's advertising comes to stand for the product. An example of such a recurring element is the slogan. Some slogans, however, may not be closely associated with the brand name, even though they have strong attention value and are easily remembered in themselves. When subjects are given a list of slogans and asked to write the name of the company or brand that uses each, a sizable percentage give the wrong brand names for certain slogans. The surest way to avoid this confusion is to incorporate the brand name in the slogan, for example, "If it's Borden's, it's got to be good" or "I'd walk a mile for a Camel." When the brand name is *not* in the slogan, the advertiser must make certain that it is repeatedly and conspicuously linked with the slogan in his advertising.

Any other recurrent feature of a company's advertising can likewise function as a reduced cue. Characteristic color combinations, printing type, layout, writing style, decorative design, or nature of illustration can all become associated with a specific product. When a certain style of advertising has become strongly identified with one company, any attempt by a competitor to imitate it generally benefits the original company more than it benefits the imitator. Most observers attribute the ad to the original company, not even noticing the competitor's name. The effect will be a greater rise in sales for the original company than for the competitor (see 23, p. 440).

*Repetition with Variation.* To achieve continuity while avoiding monotony, advertisers often combine repetition of a major feature with variation of details. This type of advertising frequently takes the form of variations on a basic theme. Thus individual ads in a series may illustrate the same appeal by means of different incidents. Each ad would thus present the same message but express it differently. Or the same character may be portrayed in different settings. The use of familiar "trade characters" who recur in a company's advertisements not only facilitates product recognition but also helps to provide human interest and encourages the consumer to identify with the product. Successful examples of such trade characters include the Campbell kids (Figure 90), Elsie the Borden cow, Betty Crocker, and the man with the eye patch in the Hathaway shirt ads (Figure 91).

**Testing the Effectiveness of Trademarks and Trade Names.** Psychological research on the effectiveness of trademarks and trade names, or brand names, has been concerned with several different questions. One investigation undertook to measure the salience, meaning, and memory value of trademarks (5). Using a total of 166 subjects, the investigators compared the trademarks employed for the same product category by seven competing companies. By "salience," they meant the readiness with which the trademark could be seen and recognized. This characteristic was studied through successive tachistoscopic exposures of each trademark, which increased progressively from 1/50th of a second to 1 second.

Meaning was evaluated through the Semantic Differential (see Chapter 11, p. 306). A meaning index for each trademark was derived from the ratings it received on the good-bad, strong-weak, and active-passive scales. Memory was tested by exposing a single slide containing the seven trademarks for 15 seconds and, immediately upon its removal, asking subjects to write down all trademarks they recalled seeing. The order of the trademarks was rotated for different subjects to avoid positional effects. A memory score was computed for each trademark on the basis of the number of subjects who named it first, the number who named it second, and so on. When not named at all by a subject, it was scored zero for that subject. Apart from the methodological contributions of this study, a noteworthy finding concerns the high intercorrelations among the three indices of trademark effectiveness. These correlations ranged from .75 to .82 for the seven trademarks. In other words, trademarks that were readily perceived and that created a favorable feeling tone tended also to be recalled first.

The free association technique was used in a study of the stimulus value of trade names (18). Three equated groups of 100 students each were given the stimulus words Coca-Cola, Pepsi-Cola, and Dixie-Cola, respectively, with the instructions to write down the first word that came to mind. The associations showed considerable clustering, the large majority of subjects responding with one of a small number of words. The most frequent *total* association (regardless of stimulus) was "drink," given by 40 subjects for Pepsi-Cola, 32 for Coca-Cola, and 11 for Dixie-Cola. The predominance of this response to Pepsi-Cola probably resulted from the use of the word "drink" in a Pepsi-Cola advertising jingle current at the time. On the other hand, it is noteworthy that despite the Coca-Cola slogan, "Thirst knows no season," only two subjects gave the response "thirst" to the stimulus "Coca-Cola."

The second most frequent response was "Coca-Cola," given by 29 subjects to the stimulus "Dixie-Cola" and by 22 subjects to the stimulus "Pepsi-Cola."

**Fig. 90** A trade character in use for half a century. (*Courtesy of Campbell Soup Company.*)

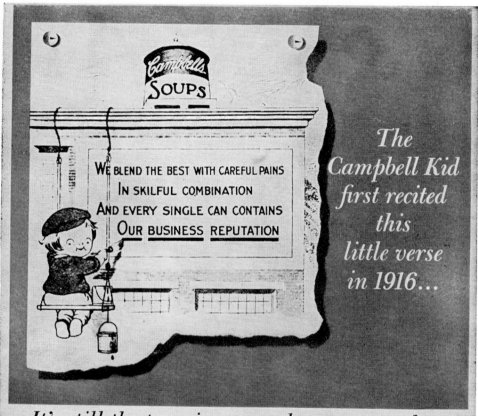

***Fig. 91*** Repetition with variation in a series of ads using the same trade character. (*Courtesy of C. F. Hathaway Co.*)

The third most frequent response was "Pepsi-Cola," given by 29 subjects to "Dixie-Cola" and by 10 subjects to "Coca-Cola." The frequency with which a less familiar brand name elicited a more familiar brand name in the same product category is of particular interest.

Another approach is illustrated by a "mock readership survey" designed to test the effect of brand names upon consumers' reactions to advertisements

(27). A total of 207 men and 212 women were interviewed by the usual procedures followed in readership surveys. The only difference was that none of the six advertisements shown to the respondents had appeared in print anywhere prior to the survey. One half of the subjects were shown a television ad with a well-known brand name (A), together with five ads of other products; the other half were shown the identical ads for the five other products and the same television ad, but with a much less popular brand name (B). The difference in popularity between the two brands is indicated by the fact that within the total sample about one-third of the respondents owned Brand A television sets, while less than 1 per cent owned sets of Brand B.

In the readership part of the study, 61.8 per cent of the men and 63.7 per cent of the women said they had seen one or more of the ads. The controlled comparison of the two television ads yielded 23.2 per cent recognition for the A ad and 12.7 per cent recognition for the B ad among the men; the corresponding percentages among the women were 22.4 and 11.8. Since the two groups of subjects who had seen the different versions of the television ad yielded no significant differences in their reported recognition of the remaining five ads, the differences between the results for Brand A and Brand B must be attributed to the effect of the brand names.

After looking at all six ads, the respondents were questioned about their recall of the ads. The main point of the TV advertisement (i.e., "clearer channels") was recalled three times as often for Brand A as for Brand B among the men and twice as often among the women. Such findings suggest that ads for well-known and widely used brands are read more closely and recalled better than are ads for less familiar brands. Finally, when asked to rate a number of characteristics of the TV sets pictured in the ads, such as the design of the set, respondents rated the A set higher than the B set.

**Generic Trade Names.** Sometimes a brand name becomes so strongly identified with a product that it comes to be used as a product name. Thus people may say Kleenex to mean any cleansing tissue or Jell-o to mean any gelatin dessert. Such a generic use of trade names has both legal and psychological implications. Legally, a company may lose its exclusive right to the name if it can be demonstrated that the name is commonly employed to designate a product category. This was the fate of such brand names as aspirin, cellophane, nylon, and linoleum. Psychologically, the generic use of trade names may lead to the indiscriminate purchasing of competing brands. It may also cause increasing dissatisfaction with the original brand as a result of the unrecognized use of inferior brands by the consumer.

An experiment conducted some twenty years ago with groups of college students demonstrated a simple technique for measuring the extent of generic use of trade names (25). After explaining the difference between generic product names and registered trade names, the experimenter presented the subjects with a list of names to be marked "trade name," "generic name," or "don't know." Over two-thirds of the subjects incorrectly marked such trade names as Dictaphone, Mimeograph, and Thermos Bottle as generic product names.

Today, many companies make special efforts in their advertising to protect their brand names against generic use. Some follow the precaution of employing a product name along with the brand name, as in Band-Aid adhesive bandage, Prestone antifreeze, and Scotch brand filament tape. Capitalizing the name, enclosing it in quotation marks, and always printing it in the same type are other common safeguards. The idea may also be embodied in a slogan, as, for example, "If it isn't an Eastman, it isn't a Kodak." An unusually thorough approach to the problem is illustrated by the continuing campaign conducted by Cluett, Peabody & Co. to educate consumers, retailers, and manufacturers regarding the meaning and proper use of their registered trademarks, Sanforized and Sanforized-Plus (see Figure 79, Chapter 11).

*Trade-name Confusion.* The legal problem of trade-name infringement arises from the psychological facts of verbal perception and discrimination. When reading a word, we do not normally perceive every letter in it. A few letters provide enough cues for the recognition of the whole word. Consequently, if certain letters are omitted, added, or substituted, the word may still be perceived in its original form.

In an early experiment on trade-name confusion, subjects were shown sets of 20 typewritten trade names at the rate of 1 per second (36). Immediately after exposure of one of these sets, 40 trade names were presented, including 20 new names, 10 from the original list, and 10 imitations of the remaining original names. The percentage of subjects who "recognized" an imitation as though it had appeared in the original list provided a direct measure of the extent of confusion between the two names. The 20 new names in the list yielded control data on the extent of "normal" confusion to be expected in such a recognition test.

Since the trade names investigated in this study had been involved in infringement proceedings, the results of the recognition test could be compared with the court decisions. Of 16 imitations that had been declared to be infringements because of name similarity, only 7 were confused by 50 per cent or more of the subjects, some being confused by as few as 20 per cent. On the other hand, among the trade names declared to be noninfringements, some were confused by as many as 50 per cent of the cases. It thus appears that the legal decisions were often inconsistent with the experimental findings. Since the latter represent a direct measure of empirically obtained confusion, the validity of the legal decisions appears questionable in such cases. It might be added that this type of study illustrates one way in which psychological research may be utilized in the legal profession, an application to be discussed further in Chapter 20.

A recent adaptation of the recognition method for measuring trade-name confusion is described by Weitz (60). In this method, four groups of respondents are examined by means of four different experimental procedures. In the first group, the original names appear on the initial list, while the imitations appear on the test list; in the second, the procedure is reversed. In the third, the originals appear on both lists; and in the fourth, the imitations appear on both. Several control measures can thus be obtained.

## SUBLIMINAL PERCEPTION

In the fall of 1957 widespread public alarm was aroused by the announcement of an "experiment" conducted by a commercial firm in a New Jersey motion-picture theater (see 2, 24, 31, 35). During the showing of the regular film, the words "Eat Popcorn" and "Drink Coca-Cola" were flashed alternately on the screen every 5 seconds for 1/3,000th of a second. Because of the extremely brief exposure, these stimuli were described as "subliminal," that is, below the limen, or threshold, of perception. Nevertheless, the firm claimed that over the six weeks when this procedure was followed the sale of popcorn from the lobby refreshment stand rose 57.5 per cent and that of Coca-Cola rose 18.1 per cent. The report of these results aroused widespread comment in the popular press. This type of advertising was variously described as "the super-soft sell," "the invisible sell," and "the little ad that wasn't there." Dismal pictures were painted of a nation of robots whose behavior could be controlled by suggestions of which they were not even aware. The protests and charges soon reached such proportions as to come before the United States Congress and the Federal Communication Commission.

The specific claims made regarding the New Jersey motion-picture demonstration could not be evaluated because of the refusal of the commercial organizaton to reveal the necessary details of procedure and results. Without such knowledge it is impossible to determine whether the reported increase in sales resulted from the subliminal advertising or from other uncontrolled factors. We would need to know, for instance, whether the size and nature of the audience were in any way unusual during the experimental period. Because of weather conditions, time of year, or the particular films shown, the audience might be larger than usual or might include a larger proportion of teen-agers, who are more likely to buy popcorn and Coca-Cola. Similarly, any changes made in the display of merchandise or in the operation of the sales booth itself would need to be investigated. It would also help to have more direct information on the buying behavior of the audience. Was there an increase in purchases made on the way in, before exposure to the subliminal advertising? How many customers made their purchases during the film showing and how many on the way out?

In the absence of adequate information on the above demonstration, we may turn to some recent well-controlled investigations. Designed to test specific claims about the subliminal control of behavior, these experiments have yielded largely negative results. In one study (9), two groups of students watched the same 30-minute instructional film. During the showing of this film, a slide was projected on the screen for .01 second at 10-second intervals. The slide used in the experimental group showed a spoon of rice with the words "Wonder Rice" printed below it; the slide used in the control group contained only four lines arranged in a meaningless way.

At the conclusion of the film, all subjects were shown a picture of the spoon of rice without the name and were asked whether they had ever seen it in a rice advertisement. A few individuals in both groups said they had seen it, but the proportion did not differ significantly in the two groups—in fact, it was slightly *higher* in the control group. Regardless of their answer to the first question, all subjects were asked which of two brands (Monarch or Wonder) they believed was more likely to be associated with the picture. Both groups chose Monarch much oftener than Wonder, but the difference between the groups was insignificant. Thus the experimental subjects' subliminal exposure to the words "Wonder Rice" failed to increase the probability of their associating this brand name with the picture.

In another experiment (6), the word "beef" was superimposed on a classroom film in flashes of 1/200th of a second every 7 seconds. The control group was shown only the film, with no additional stimuli. After viewing the film, the experimental and control groups showed no significant differences in their references to beef in sentence completion and word-association tests. Nor was there a significant difference in reported preferences for roast beef sandwiches, out of a given list of five common types of sandwiches. The experimental subjects, however, rated themselves as significantly more hungry than did the control group, even when time of day and interval since last meal were equated. Three of the original 108 subjects were eliminated from the analysis of results because when questioned they said they had seen a word on the screen. But it is interesting to note that only one saw "beef"; the other two perceived the word as "beer."

In still another experiment, subliminal perception was found to have no significant effect upon the subject's choice of "right" or "left" circles when required to guess which was correct in each trial (7). Unknown to the subjects, the words "Choose right" and "Choose left" were exposed tachistoscopically for durations of .01, .02, and .03 seconds in different parts of the experiment. The only subjects whose individual performance was better than chance later reported that they had seen the words and had followed the suggestion deliberately. In a learning experiment (59), performance in two different learning tasks was not significantly affected by the subliminal exposure of either correct or incorrect suggestions. In this experiment, the duration of subliminal exposure was based on an individually determined threshold for each subject.

Quite apart from its use in advertising and its potential dangers as a devious means of "behavior control," subliminal perception has been extensively studied in the psychological laboratory (see 1, 20, 31, 35). Research on subliminal perception dates back fully 100 years. Many experiments have demonstrated that subjects do respond in various ways to stimuli of which they report no awareness. Stimuli may fall below the "awareness" threshold because of low intensity, brief duration, or other characteristics. To understand the subject's reaction to such stimuli, it is essential to consider the nature of a sensory threshold. There is no single intensity such that stimuli above it are always perceptible and those below it always imperceptible. Sensitivity varies along a continuum; the transition from perceptible to imperceptible is gradual.

The specific threshold established for a given subject depends in part upon the *standard of accuracy*. If the subject must give a correct response 75 per cent of the time, he needs a more intense stimulus than he would need to give 50 per cent correct responses. The threshold also depends upon the nature of the *response indicator*. For instance, a stimulus may be too weak for the subject to report awareness of it. Nevertheless, if he is told to guess its location, he may be right significantly more often than by chance. Even weaker stimuli may lead to autonomic responses, such as a galvanic skin reaction to a word previously conditioned to an electric shock. Flashing such a word on a screen may evoke the conditioned galvanic response even when the word is too faint to be perceived in terms of other response indicators.

The problem of so-called subliminal perception thus reduces to that of threshold differences found with different response indicators. Reported awareness is a relatively crude and unreliable indicator. Such an awareness threshold will vary with the kind of directions given to subjects, the number and nature of available response categories, the serial position of stimuli, and other extraneous factors (20). This irrelevant variance tends to raise the threshold. An analogy may help to clarify the relationship among thresholds. Suppose you weigh yourself on an ordinary scale and find your weight to be 118 pounds. If you weigh yourself ten times during the day on such a scale, your weight will probably remain at 118 pounds. But repeated weighings on a highly sensitive laboratory scale will reveal systematic weight changes in the course of a 12-hour period. The latter could be described as "subliminal weight changes," which can be detected only with a delicate indicator.

By modifying the relative sensitivity of the two response indicators employed in a perception experiment, an investigator may artifically vary the extent of "subliminal perception" he finds from zero to any desired amount (20, p. 381). It can thus be seen that subliminal perception is not a special phenomenon but a methodological artifact. It is not a mysterious technique for "beaming ideas directly into the mind" while bypassing the individual's conscious defenses. Research on so-called subliminal perception can be more accurately described as the study of diverse responses to *weak stimuli*. So far there is no evidence to suggest that weak stimuli exert more influence on behavior than do strong stimuli. In fact, the reverse is generally found to be true.

With regard to the use of subliminal stimulation in advertising, it should also be noted that individuals vary in their sensory thresholds. Hence a word flashed on a motion-picture screen may fall well above the awareness threshold of some persons and may be clearly read by them; for others, it may be totally imperceptible in terms of all response indicators; and for still others it may fall in the desired intermediate, or subliminal, zone. These thresholds also vary within the same person from time to time. When weak stimuli are employed, moreover, the probability of *misperception* increases. Remember the students who saw "beer" instead of "beef." The advertiser who hopefully flashes the words "Buy Tasty Tea" on a motion-picture screen may find that many subjects actually perceive "Burn Trashy Ties"—a suggestion they may feel strongly tempted to accept when opening Christmas packages.

If at some future time it should be adequately demonstrated that subliminal stimulation can seriously influence a person's actions, then psychologists should look to their code of professional ethics to make sure that they will use these techniques for the benefit of the individual and not for ulterior gains. Under such circumstances, too, legal controls should be instituted against misuse of the techniques by unscrupulous persons. But, in our present state of knowledge, subliminal perception does not constitute a social threat.

# READABILITY

The term "readability" is most commonly used to mean the *difficulty level* of reading matter. In this sense, the easier a passage, the more readable it is. Reading ease is also affected by legibility of type, layout, and other mechanical features of the printed page. Similarly, one's interest in the topic influences the ease of reading. The measurement of readability, however, has centered on reading ease as determined by linguistic form. The principal question has been, "How can the writer express what he is trying to say so as to simplify the reader's task?"

*Vocabulary.* One factor that affects reading ease is the difficulty level of individual words. Frequency of use can serve as an index of word comprehension. Common words are more likely to be understood than rare words. A standard source of information on frequency of word usage is *The Teacher's Word Book of 30,000 Words,* compiled by Thorndike and Lorge (55). This book gives an alphabetical list of the more common English words, together with their frequency per million. The frequency data are based on several word counts utilizing a wide variety of sources, such as newspapers, magazines, children's books, textbooks for many subjects and at various academic levels, literary classics in prose and poetry, elementary school readers, business and private correspondence, mail-order catalogues, cookbooks, and United States postal regulations.

Words occurring 100 or more times per million and those occurring between 50 and 100 times per million are so designated. For words occurring between 1 and 49 times per million, specific frequencies are recorded. Supplementary lists of rare words, occurring less often than once per million, are also included. In addition, there is a list of the 500 and of the 1,000 most common words. The advertising copywriter can profitably check his word choice against these frequency lists. The use of rare words in an ad addressed to the general public will not only reduce comprehension and decrease readership but may also antagonize the reader.

**Readability Formulas.**   For more than forty years, psychologists and educators have been studying the effect of different linguistic factors upon reading ease. Those characteristics of reading matter found to correlate most highly with criteria of reading ease (such as comprehension, reading speed, or grade level of content) have been combined into readability formulas (see 8, ch. 3). These formulas are designed to estimate the difficulty level of a passage on the basis of such factors as word frequency, word length, number of abstract words, sentence length, sentence structure, and number of personal references. Since most of these factors are highly intercorrelated, the various formulas derived from them yield fairly similar results.

One investigator who has done much to publicize readability research is Rudolf Flesch. In 1946, three years after the completion of a doctoral dissertation on readability, Flesch published a popular book entitled *The Art of Plain Talk* (13). This book was followed by a series of other writing guides which also provided revisions and simplifications of the Flesch readability formula (15, 17). In developing his original formula, Flesch used as his criterion a series of graded passages from the McCall-Crabbs *Standard Test Lessons in Reading.* These passages had been standardized on the basis of number of questions correctly answered by children of known reading ability. The criterion of reading ease was thus based on empirically determined comprehension.

The most widely used form of the Flesch formula (14; 15, pp. 213–216) yields two measures, a "reading ease" score ($RE$) and a "human interest" score ($HI$). Reading ease is based on average word length in syllables ($wl$) and average sentence length in words ($sl$). These figures are inserted in the following formula:

$$RE = 206.835 - .846wl - 1.015sl$$

The human interest score is derived from the percentage of "personal words" ($pw$), such as proper names and personal pronouns, and the percentage of "personal sentences" (*ps*), such as spoken sentences, questions and other remarks directed to the reader, and exclamations. The formula used for this score is as follows:

$$HI = 3.635pw + .314ps$$

The unit to which all these measures are applied is a continuous 100-word passage. For reliable results, several random 100-word samples from the given selection are analyzed, and the counts are averaged.

**T A B L E  19**   *Interpretation of Flesch Reading Ease Score*
(*Data from Flesch, 15, pp. 149–150*)

| Description of Style | RE Score | Estimated Reading Grade | Typical Magazine |
|---|---|---|---|
| Very easy | 90–100 | 5th | Comics |
| Easy | 80– 90 | 6th | Pulp fiction |
| Fairly easy | 70– 80 | 7th | Slick fiction |
| Standard | 60– 70 | 8th–9th | Digests |
| Fairly difficult | 50– 60 | High school (10th–12th) | Quality |
| Difficult | 30– 50 | College (13th–16th) | Academic |
| Very difficult | 0– 30 | College graduate | Scientific |

In both of these formulas, the weights and constants were so chosen as to yield scores ranging from 0 to 100. The relative weights of the two factors in each formula were derived from correlations with the criteria of reading ease and human interest. Tables 19 and 20 provide an interpretation of these two scores in terms of academic levels and types of magazines.

To facilitate the computation of the Flesch *RE* and *HI* scores, tables have been prepared in which the scores can be found by merely entering the obtained word and sentence figures (11). Further simplifications of the Flesch formulas have subsequently been proposed by Flesch himself (17, ch. 6 and pp. 163–174) and by others (10, 12). Separate formulas have also been developed for measuring the level of abstraction of writing (16, 19). Although useful for special purposes, all such indices are highly intercorrelated (8, ch. 3;

**T A B L E  20**   *Interpretation of Flesch Human Interest Score*
(*Data from Flesch, 15, p. 151*)

| Description of Style | HI Score | Typical Magazine |
|---|---|---|
| Dramatic | 60–100 | Fiction |
| Highly interesting | 40– 60 | *New Yorker* |
| Interesting | 20– 40 | Digests |
| Mildly interesting | 10– 20 | Trade |
| Dull | 0– 10 | Scientific |

38). Abstract words, for example, tend to be longer than concrete words and to have lower frequency of usage.

**Readability and Readership.** Of all the readability formulas, those developed and popularized by Flesch have had the greatest impact upon journalists, advertising copywriters, and others interested in reaching mass audiences. Concern with the "Flesch index" of one's writing soon spread through these fields, with a resulting simplification of style (see 8, pp. 146–148). Empirical tests of the effects of such simplifications, however, have been few.

Split-run readership tests with easy and hard versions of the same articles have been conducted in such varied media as a Middle Western farm paper (30, 33, 34), a campus newspaper (53), and a company paper sent to employees (54). The readership gains reported for the simpler version range from zero (or a slight loss) to as high as 66 per cent. Among the factors determining these results are the absolute difficulty level of the versions as well as the amount of difference between them. Intrinsic interest of the content for the readers may also partly erase differences in reading ease. Another difficulty in interpreting results is that some of the versions differ in ways not measured by the Flesch scores. For example, the pair of articles yielding the largest readership difference (66 per cent) also differed in organization, the easier version being more systematically and clearly organized (see 8, pp. 104–105). In another case (53), the more difficult version sounded stilted and unnatural. It contained inappropriate words and circumlocutions that seemed to have been deliberately inserted to increase reading difficulty.

Another type of study has been concerned with the reading ease of existing material, rather than employing specially prepared versions. In an analysis of all major articles appearing in a single issue of the *Saturday Evening Post,* readership and degree of satisfaction were surveyed in a nationwide sample of 340 readers (22). An abstraction index computed for each article correlated −.79 with "finishing index," or proportion of readers starting the article who finished it. On the other hand, among those who finished an article, the proportion who rated it "excellent" correlated +.80 with the abstraction index.

In another study (57), the readability of editorial and advertising copy was compared in two magazines. The Flesch formulas for reading ease and human interest were applied to a random selection of issues of *Time* and *Newsweek* for two five-year periods: 1936–1940 and 1945–1949. In both periods and both magazines, advertising copy was easier to read on the average than editorial copy. The difference seemed to be shrinking, however. Advertising copy had become more difficult from the prewar to the postwar period, while editorial copy had become easier. The human interest scores showed negligible differences in the various comparisons. The type of comparisons made in this study are of particular interest, since the editorial content of a medium tends to "select" the audience. Hence an analysis of editorial content provides the advertiser with a useful guide to the difficulty level and style appropriate for such an audience.

**General Evaluation.** Readability formulas have met with a varied reception. They have been hailed enthusiastically as guides to good writing and attacked vigorously as mechanistic devices to stifle creativity and debase literature. After looking with horror at figures such as those reported in Tables 19 and 20, the critics have asked, "Should writers of science and literature try to raise their 'Flesch index' by imitating the style of pulp magazines and comic strips?"

The truth lies somewhere between these extreme views. Readability research *can* improve writing, but its findings must be used with discretion. Good writing depends on other factors besides those included in readability formulas. Then, too, there is undoubtedly an optimum difficulty level for different kinds of materials, as there is for different audiences. Intrinsically simple material becomes stilted, pretentious, and obscure when expressed in long words and intricate sentences. On the other hand, literary or scientific writings may lose in aesthetic value or in intellectual precision when oversimplified. Unusual words and subtle figures of speech may be a source of artistic delight in poetry. And the technical terms of science, mathematics, and logic represent a way of simplifying and clarifying complex masses of information that might otherwise prove unmanageable.

Simplicity and clarity of expression cannot be achieved by routine procedures. They are general goals of good writing that need to be pursued by whatever means are appropriate to the subject matter. Readership formulas *are* appropriate when the object is to maximize the communication of simple messages. This is the purpose of advertising copy, cookbooks, instruction sheets, training manuals, government bulletins, and similar forms of writing designed for mass audiences. It is to these forms of writing that readability formulas are most directly applicable.

## SUMMARY

For effective communication, the advertising message should be so presented as to be noticed, understood, retained, and accepted. The success of an ad in attracting and holding attention depends in part upon such mechanical factors as size, position, color, and illustration. Among the major techniques now used to study the effects of these factors are readership surveys, analysis of written inquiries, and laboratory techniques. Dummy magazines have been used in controlled experiments on readership. Factor analysis of ad variables has also been carried out with a readership criterion. Laboratory procedures adapted for the measurement of attention factors in advertising include eye cameras, tachistoscopes, and a specially developed instrument that permits control of distance, illumination, and exposure time as well as the binocular presentation of different ads.

Any feature that is repeated in a series of advertisements comes to serve as a reduced cue for the product and the company. Such reduced cues include, not only registered trademarks and brand names, but also slogans, trade characters, and other recurring aspects of ads such as color combination, printing type, layout, writing style, and nature of illustration. In an advertising campaign, repetition with variation provides continuity and familiarity without monotony. Psychological research on trademarks and trade names has been concerned with such questions as recognizability, retention, and associative value; effect of brand names upon consumers' reactions to ads; generic trade names; and trade-name confusion.

Subliminal perception is the process of responding to stimuli that fall below the threshold of verbally reported awareness. Essentially it refers to threshold differences associated with different response indicators, a problem on which extensive psychological research is available. Popular claims regarding the effectiveness of subliminal advertising in influencing buying behavior are as yet unverified. The findings of laboratory experiments suggest that subliminal stimulation cannot appreciably affect the behavior of mass audiences.

Readability research is concerned with the difficulty level of reading matter, as determined by its linguistic form. Among the factors affecting reading ease is vocabulary level, which can be checked against available word frequency counts. Readability formulas try to predict reading ease by an analysis of such variables as word frequency, word length, number of abstract words, sentence length, sentence structure, and number of personal references. Special formulas have been developed to gauge "human interest," "abstraction," and other aspects of reading matter. The formulas developed by Rudolf Flesch have been the most influential in journalism, advertising, and other mass media.

# REFERENCES

1. Adams, J. K. Laboratory studies of behavior without awareness. *Psychol. Bull.,* 1957, **54**, 383–405.
2. Advertising Research Foundation. *The application of subliminal perception in advertising.* New York: Advert. Res. Found., 1958.
3. Advertising Research Foundation. *The measurement and control of the visual efficiency of advertisements.* New York: Advert. Res. Found., 1962.
4. Are newspaper ads in color better read? *Printers' Ink,* 1955, **252** (9), 38–39.
5. Burdick, H. A., Green, E. J., and Lovelace, J. W. Predicting trademark effectiveness. *J. appl. Psychol.,* 1959, **43**, 285–286.
6. Byrne, D. The effect of a subliminal food stimulus on verbal responses. *J. appl. Psychol.,* 1959, **43**, 249–252.
7. Calvin, A. D., and Dollemayer, Karen S. Subliminal perception: Some negative findings. *J. appl. Psychol.,* 1959, **43**, 187–188.
8. Chall, Jeanne S. *Readability: An appraisal of research and applications.* Columbus, Ohio: Ohio State Univer. Press, 1958.
9. Champion, J. M., and Turner, W. W. An experimental investigation of subliminal perception. *J. appl. Psychol.,* 1959, **43**, 382–384.
10. England, G. W., Thomas, Margaret, and Paterson, D. G. Reliability of the original and simplified Flesch reading ease formulas. *J. appl. Psychol.,* 1953, **37**, 111–113.
11. Farr, J. N., and Jenkins, J. J. Tables for use with the Flesch readability formulas. *J. appl. Psychol.,* 1949, **33**, 275–278.
12. Farr, J. N., Jenkins, J. J., and Paterson, D. G. Simplification of Flesch reading ease formula. *J. appl. Psychol.,* 1951, **35**, 333–337.
13. Flesch, R. *The art of plain talk.* New York: Harper & Row, 1946.
14. Flesch, R. A new readability yardstick. *J. appl. Psychol.,* 1948, **32**, 221–233.
15. Flesch, R. *The art of readable writing.* New York: Harper & Row, 1949.
16. Flesch, R. Measuring the level of abstraction. *J. appl. Psychol.,* 1950, **34**, 384–390.
17. Flesch, R. *A new way to better English.* New York: Harper & Row, 1958.
18. Foley, J. P., Jr. The use of the free association technique in the investigation of the stimulus value of trade names. *J. appl. Psychol.,* 1944, **28**, 431–435.
19. Gillie, P. A simplified formula for measuring abstraction in writing. *J. appl. Psychol.,* 1957, **41**, 214–217.
20. Goldiamond, I. Indicators of perception: I. Subliminal perception, subception, unconscious perception: An analysis in terms of psychophysical indicator methodology. *Psychol. Bull.,* 1958, **55**, 373–411.
21. Hadley, H. D. How readership is affected by size of an advertisement. *Advert. Agency,* 1950, **43** (7), 50–51, 122, 128; (8), 54–55, 112.
22. Haskins, J. B. Validation of the abstraction index as a tool for content-effects analysis and content analysis. *J. appl. Psychol.,* 1960, **44**, 102–106.

23. Hepner, H. W. *Modern advertising: Practices and principles.* (3rd ed.) New York: McGraw-Hill, 1956.
24. Institute of Practitioners in Advertising. *Subliminal communication.* London: Inst. Practition. Advert., 1958.
25. Jenkins, J. G. The generic use of trade names. *J. appl. Psychol.,* 1941, **25**, 697–702.
26. Klapp, O. E. Imitation value in advertising. *J. appl. Psychol.,* 1941, **25**, 243–250.
27. Koponen, A. *Mock readership survey.* New York: J. Walter Thompson Co., 1956.
28. Laslett, H. R. The value of relevancy in advertisement illustrations. *J. appl. Psychol.,* 1918, **2**, 270–279.
29. Lucas, D. B., and Britt, S. H. *Advertising psychology and research.* New York: McGraw-Hill, 1950.
30. Lyman, H. B. Flesch count and readership in a midwestern farm paper. *J. appl. Psychol.,* 1949, **33**, 78–80.
31. McConnell, J. V., Cutler, R. L., and McNeil, E. B. Subliminal stimulation: An overview. *Amer. Psychologist,* 1958, **13**, 229–242.
32. McGraw-Hill Research, Laboratory of Advertising Performance. How repeat advertisements affect readership. *Data Sheet* 3040, 1962.
33. Murphy, D. R. Test proves short words and sentences get best readership. *Printers' Ink,* 1947, **218**, (2), 61–62.
34. Murphy, D. R. How plain talk increases readership 45% to 66%. *Printers' Ink,* 1947, **220**, (12), 35–37.
35. Naylor, J. C., and Lawshe, C. H. An analytical review of the experimental basis of subception. *J. Psychol.,* 1958, **46**, 75–96.
36. Paynter, R. H., Jr. A psychological study of trade-mark infringement. *Arch. Psychol.,* 1920, No. 42.
37. Politz, Alfred, Media Studies. *The Rochester study.* Philadelphia: Curtis, 1960.
38. Rubenstein, H., and Aborn, M. Learning, prediction, and readability. *J. appl. Psychol.,* 1958, **42**, 28–32.
39. Rudolph, H. J. *Four million inquiries from magazine advertising.* New York: Columbia Univer. Press, 1936.
40. Rudolph, H. J. *Attention and interest factors in advertising.* New York: Funk & Wagnalls (in assoc. with Printers' Ink Publ. Co.), 1947.
41. Snyder, M., and Stover, R. Can visual effectiveness of advertisements be controlled? *Proc. 7th ann. Conf., Advert. Res. Found.,* 1961, 11–18.
42. Starch, D. *An analysis of 5,000,000 inquiries.* New York: Daniel Starch & Staff, 1930.
43. Starch, D. Why readership of ads has increased 24%. *Advert. Sell.,* 1946, **39** (8), 47, 154.
44. Starch, D. Just how important is readership? *Tested Copy,* 1954, No. 64.
45. Starch, D. How do size and color of advertisements affect readership? *Tested Copy,* 1956, No. 74.
46. Starch, D. Readership and size of advertisement. *Starch Tested Copy,* 1957, No. 82.
47. Starch, D. *An analysis of 12 million inquiries.* Evanston, Ill.: Media/Scope, 1959.
48. Starch, D. How does repetition of advertisements affect readership? *Starch Tested Copy,* 1960, No. 89.
49. Starch, D. Should outdoor posters be repeated? *Starch Tested Copy,* 1960, No. 89.
50. Starch, D. Readership of drawings and photographs. *Starch Tested Copy,* 1961, No. 91.
51. Starch, D. Do inside positions differ in readership? *Starch Tested Copy,* 1961, No. 95.
52. Starch, D., and Staff. Is preferred position worth it? *Starch Tested Copy,* 1961, No. 94.
53. Swanson, C. E. Readability and readership. *Journalism Quart.,* 1948, **25**, 339–343.
54. Swanson, C. E., and Fox, H. G. Validity of readability formulas. *J. appl. Psychol.,* 1953, **37**, 114–118.
55. Thorndike, E. L., and Lorge, I. *The teacher's word book of 30,000 words.* New York: Teach. Coll., Columbia Univer., Bur. Publ., 1944.
56. Tiffin, J., and Winick, D. M. A comparison of two methods of measuring the

attention-drawing power of magazine advertisements. *J. appl. Psychol.*, 1954, **38**, 272–275.

57. Trenchard, K. I., and Crissy, W. J. E. Readability of advertising and editorial copy in *Time* and *Newsweek*. *J. appl. Psychol.*, 1952, **36**, 161–163.

58. Twedt, D. W. A multiple factor analysis of advertising readership. *J. appl. Psychol.*, 1952, **36**, 207–215.

59. Vernon, J. A., and Badger, D. H. Subliminal stimulation in human learning. *Amer. J. Psychol.*, 1959, **72**, 265–266.

60. Weitz, J. A study of trade name confusion. *J. Market.*, 1960, **25** (2), 54–56.

61. Winick, C. Art work versus photography: An experimental study. *J. appl. Psychol.*, 1959, **43**, 180–182.

# V
## *Clinical Psychology*

# 13

# *Diagnosis*

The focus of clinical psychology is on the individual. Clinical psychologists work with persons who have intellectual or personality disorders. Today clinical psychologists are functioning in a variety of settings, including not only hospitals and outpatient clinics, but also industry, schools, prisons, courts, government agencies, and the armed services. In industry, for example, the number of employees with personality disorders is large enough to constitute a serious problem (24, chs. 20 and 21; 49). Such emotional difficulties occur at all levels, from unskilled labor to top management, and range from the mild problems of essentially normal persons to full-blown psychoses. The effects of these conditions upon job performance may take many forms, including excessive absenteeism, increased accident rate, deterioration of output, and disruption of co-worker morale.

The practice of clinical psychology utilizes findings and techniques from many branches of psychology, such as abnormal psychology, personality theory, and psychological testing. The specific activities of clinical psychologists consist chiefly of diagnosis, therapy, and research, although the emphasis placed upon each varies widely with the work setting and with the individual psychologist. Moreover, these three functions are frequently intertwined. Research may be specifically concerned with the validity of diagnostic tools or with the effectiveness of different types of therapy. Similarly, diagnostic and therapeutic procedures are indistinguishable in certain types of clinical practice, such as psychoanalysis. It is only for convenience that in this book diagnosis, therapy, and research are discussed in separate chapters.

Both clinical psychology (Chapters 13–15) and the closely related field of counseling psychology (Chapters 16–17) are marked by an abundance of unresolved issues and active controversies. In part, this situation stems from complexity of subject matter and from the comparative youth of these fields. Another factor making for diversity of opinion, however, is that both theory and practice in these fields tend to be highly colored by human values. Discussions of the objectives of counseling and psychotherapy, or definitions of "mental health," for example, often touch closely upon one's concept of a "good life." Thoughtful clinical and counseling psychologists have faced these issues, as will be noted in several connections in these chapters. But unanimity has by no means been attained. While complacency certainly does not characterize any field of applied psychology, turbulence and struggle are especially typical of the clinical and counseling areas. Although this introductory book focuses primarily upon what is presently known, many problems remain to be solved. The fact that much can be found in the common ground, about which considerable agreement exists, should not lull the reader into assuming an absence of controversy.

## OBJECTIVES OF CLINICAL DIAGNOSIS

In the present context, the term "diagnosis" is used in its broadest sense, to cover all aspects of clinical evaluation or assessment. Essentially diagnosis is a fact-finding process. Among the various objectives of the diagnostic process in clinical psychology, four can be clearly identified: (1) screening and classification, (2) personality description, (3) prediction of outcome, and (4) attainment of insight by the client.

**Screening and Classification.**   To the layman, diagnosis generally means attaching labels to people. This is the traditional approach to diagnosis, which clinical psychology has inherited from nineteenth-century psychiatry. In psychiatric hospitals, a good deal of attention is still given to the categorizing of patients by various diagnostic labels. It is generally recognized, however, that such labels can serve only for purposes of preliminary screening and rough classification.

A major diagnostic distinction is that between mental deficiency and personality disorders. In terms of intelligence test performance, *mental deficiency* usually corresponds to an IQ of 70 or less. Within this category, further subdivisions are traditionally made into three levels: mild (IQ 50 to 70), moderate (IQ 20 to 50), and severe (IQ below 20). A more functional classification that is rapidly gaining acceptance recognizes those cases requiring custodial or nursing care, those that are trainable by specialized individual procedures, and those that are teachable in special classes. Decisions regarding the disposition of individual cases, moreover, should be based on a comprehensive study of the individual's present functioning level, his developmental history, his family background, his physical condition, and other pertinent data.

Although psychological research on mental deficiency has lagged behind the investigation of other disorders, it now constitutes a very active area of research. Some progress has already been made toward an understanding of the nature and causes of mental deficiency. Organic defects underlying certain forms of mental deficiency, such as phenylketonuria and mongolism, have been identified. Some suggestive research has been done on the role of cultural deprivation in the production of intellectual retardation. There has also been an upsurge of interest in the training and rehabilitation of mental defectives. Further information regarding psychological work with mental defectives can be found in several recent books covering different aspects of the problem (37, 42, 62, 66).

Among personality disorders, psychoses are commonly distinguished from neuroses. *Psychoses* represent the more severe disorders, which usually require institutionalization. The largest single group of psychotics, accounting for about half of the chronic patients in state hospitals, are diagnosed as *schizophrenic*. Although including several forms with distinct behavior patterns, schizophrenia as a whole is characterized by extreme withdrawal, loss of contact with other persons, and emotional dulling. Also typical of schizophrenia are such symptoms as hallucinations, disorganization of thought processes, and peculiar mannerisms of speech and gesture. In the catatonic form, the patient may remain motionless in bizarre postures for hours. In the paranoid form, he may have delusions in which he believes, for example, that he is being persecuted for some fanciful reason.

Although less common than schizophrenia, *manic-depressive psychoses* constitute another widely recognized category. These conditions are characterized by periods of extreme depression, hopelessness, and slowing down of thought and action and by periods of elation, overactivity, and flight of ideas, in which one thought leads to the next through superficial associations. The same patient may exhibit both types of behavior at different times; or either type alone may alternate with periods of normality. Hallucinations and delusions may occur during both depressed and manic phases.

Mention should also be made of *organic psychoses,* which have identifiable physical pathology resulting from such factors as drugs, alcohol, senile deterioration, or brain injuries. By contrast, such disorders as schizophrenia and manic-depressive psychoses are sometimes described as "functional" or "psychogenic," since no physiological basis has been conclusively demonstrated for them. Many psychologists object to these terms, however, because they imply more knowledge of etiology than is currently available. Although extensive research on the causes of these disorders is in progress, their etiology still remains largely unknown.

*Neuroses* (or psychoneuroses) are relatively mild personality disorders in which the individual remains in touch with reality and shows no gross disorders of thought or action. These conditions are generally considered to be psychogenic and amenable to treatment by psychological techniques. Unlike the psychotic, who may be blissfully unaware of reality, the neurotic typically feels miserable. Often his emotional problems interfere with interpersonal relations and lower his productive capacity in school or on the job. Because he is aware that something is wrong and is unhappy about his condition, the neurotic is more likely to seek and continue treatment than is the psychotic and he is more likely to cooperate actively in the treatment.

One of the most characteristic neurotic reactions is anxiety. The individual experiences feelings of dread and apprehension out of all proportion to the situations that arouse them. The anxiety may also be generalized, or "free-floating," rather than being associated with any specific stimulus. In some cases, traditionally classified as "anxiety hysteria," minor environmental stresses produce attacks of acute anxiety accompanied by palpitation of the heart, profuse sweating, difficulty in breathing, and tremors.

Another traditional neurotic category is "conversion hysteria," in which the individual develops some physical ailment, such as paralysis of his right arm, that enables him to escape from an unbearable emotional situation. Other types exhibit "phobias," or irrational fears of specific objects or situations, such as claustrophobia (fear of closed-in places) or acrophobia (fear of heights). Still another example is the "obsessive-compulsive" type, characterized by persistent thoughts of a useless or irrational nature or by a strong compulsion to perform certain meaningless acts, like repeated hand washing. A particularly dramatic form of neurotic behavior is that in which the individual dissociates himself from unpleasant life situations by forgetting who he is and other details of his life. In rare cases, such amnesia may last for several years, the individual assuming a new name, working at a different occupation, and living his life apart from his earlier contacts. Also rare is the condition of "multiple personality," in which the individual alternates between two or more distinct personalities (see, e.g., 72, 73).

These and other types of neurotic reactions have been traditionally classified into specific "syndromes," or associated groups of symptoms. Surveys of such diagnostic categories, as well as fuller descriptions of both psychotic and neurotic behavior, can be found in textbooks of psychiatry or abnormal psychology (see, e.g., 8, 32). Most clinical psychologists, however, avoid the use of specific diagnostic labels in evaluating individual cases. More and more it is being recognized that the syndromes of the classical diagnostic systems do not fit the cases encountered in practice. In fact, "textbook cases" that do fit the descriptions are hard to find.

Some attempts have been made to develop new systems of classification, especially for psychotic behavior, by investigating the empirical concomitance of symptoms within individual cases. Several studies have employed the techniques of correlation and factor analysis for this purpose and have proposed sets of categories corresponding to the factors thus identified (14; 18, ch. 1; 23; 27; 45; 82). Although these studies provide many suggestive findings, no single schema of classification has emerged that has met with general acceptance.

Part of the resistance to the adoption of a new system of classification undoubtedly stems from the inconvenience of effecting a change-over in institutional records. From a different angle, however, many clinical psychologists reject all attempts to place individuals into diagnostic categories. They point out that, even when derived from empirically established correlation of symptoms, these categories still represent only group trends. The combination of specific symptoms of maladjustment is unique to each individual. Then, too, behavior traits vary in degree from person to person. Any classification in terms of presence or absence of a given symptom is therefore unrealistic.

Still another argument against the use of diagnostic categories is that psychological disorders are not "disease entities," like pneumonia or scarlet fever. To classify an individual as a catatonic schizophrenic tends to create the misleading impression that he is suffering from a specific psychological "disease." In reality, however, he manifests a collection of loosely related disorders of behavior that may have complex causes and probably require different treatment in individual cases. Rather than being identified as symptoms of "mental illness," such behavior disorders are coming to be recognized more and more as direct manifestations of the conflicts and problems of daily living. This point of view has been most clearly expressed by Szasz in a book entitled *The Myth of Mental Illness* (69).

***Personality Description.*** A major objective of the clinical psychologist's diagnostic function is to provide a personality description of the individual case. Such a description is unique for each person, covering the specific behavioral difficulties the individual manifests as well as the antecedent circumstances that led to their development. In contrast to traditional diagnostic labels, such a personality description is a full and detailed report. Its object is to facilitate the understanding of what makes the individual behave as he does and to serve as a guide for planning specific therapeutic procedures. It also differs from the traditional diagnostic approach in its utilization of a normal rather than a pathological orientation. The patient's behavior is seen as an exaggeration or distortion of behavior mechanisms commonly used by normal persons in meeting the conflicts and frustrations of daily living.

The terms, concepts, or constructs employed in such personality descriptions vary somewhat with the personality theory favored by the particular clinician, although considerable progress has been made in integrating these different points of view. Typically, behavior is described in terms of the *adjustment mechanisms* that the individual utilizes to cope with his emotional problems, resolve conflicts, and reduce anxieties and tensions. Detailed discussions of these adjustment mechanisms can be found in books on the psychology of adjustment, mental hygiene, or personality (e.g., 48, 64).

A few examples will suffice to show what is meant by an adjustment mechanism. One way in which an individual may react to an unpleasant or conflictual situation is by *escape,* as in excessive daydreaming. Another escape mechanism is illustrated by the shy, seclusive person, who thereby avoids exposure to possible embarrassment, failure, or abuse in social contacts. The extreme withdrawal of the schizophrenic may be recalled in this connection. A familiar *defense* mechanism is rationalization, whereby the individual tries to "explain away" the source of conflict. Thus the failing student may assure himself that "enjoying life" and "being a regular fellow" are more important than "being a grind" and earning good grades. A related mechanism is projection, or the practice of attributing our shortcomings to someone else. The student who justifies his failure by proclaiming that the instructor did not teach the course properly typifies this kind of defensive behavior. In the psychotic, such rationalizations and projections may take the form of a highly organized delusion. The patient may thus become convinced that he is really a brilliant scientist who is being kept prisoner by his enemies—and possibly "brainwashed" in the process.

All typical psychotic and neurotic reactions, including phobias, compulsions, obsessions, amnesias, psychogenic ailments, and so forth, can be reformulated in terms of adjustment mechanisms. Since they are applied to specific types of behavior rather than to the individual as a whole, adjustment mechanisms permit more descriptive flexibility than is possible with traditional diagnostic categories. Moreover, these mechanisms provide hypotheses for exploring the sources of the individual's behavioral aberrations.

It should be noted that all these adjustment mechanisms may be effectively employed by normal persons in certain situations. As used by neurotics and psychotics, however, they represent ineffectual and superficial solutions for the individual's emotional problems. They fail to eliminate his tensions and anxieties, although they may temporarily reduce their intensity. Furthermore, the individual's irrational behavior is itself disabling and hence creates new difficulties of varying degrees of severity. The purpose of therapy is to replace these ineffective problem-solving devices with more effective solutions.

**Prediction of Outcome.** One of the objectives of clinical evaluation is prognosis, or prediction of outcome. Since outcome may be defined in many ways, the prediction problem covers several more or less related questions. One question pertains to the probability of improvement, recovery, or deterioration in the absence of therapy. Such information is useful, for example, in matching control and experimental samples in research on the effects of therapy. It also contributes to practical decisions regarding the disposition of individual cases.

Another question concerns the individual's response to therapy. Thus, if an outpatient clinic has a long waiting list, cases can be selected on the basis of their estimated chances of improving with therapy. If those who fail to return after one or two visits and those who continue in therapy but derive no benefit from it can be weeded out in advance, available therapeutic resources can be more effectively utilized. In accepting clients for psychotherapy, moreover, most clinical psychologists make an effort to screen out the type of cases that do not respond well to this form of therapy.

With institutionalized cases, a further question is that of posthospital adjustment. Decisions regarding discharge depend upon this type of prediction. The criteria against which such predictions can be tested include rehospitalization within specified periods of time, as well as various indices of the individual's level of functioning in the community. Among these indices may be mentioned objective records of educational or vocational achievement, ratings by family members and other associates, and the individual's own report of his feelings.

It can be readily seen that the criteria of outcome vary widely. This variation complicates research on the effectiveness of different forms of therapy, a difficulty that will be examined further in Chapter 15. For the present purpose, it is apparent that the validity of any given predictor may differ from one type of outcome to another. Considerable research has been done on the prognostic use of both tests and case history data in the effort to provide a systematic basis for clinical prediction (see 15, 19, 44, 56, 81, 83). An example of a relatively promising test developed to predict response to psychotherapy is Barron's Ego-Strength Scale (4). Consisting of those items from the Minnesota Multiphasic Personality Inventory that differentiated between improved and unimproved psychoneurotic groups, this scale proved successful when cross-validated against improvement criteria in several new samples (4, 19).

Analysis of case history material on schizophrenics has suggested a useful distinction between process and reactive schizophrenics (33, 39). One of the chief differentiating features of these two groups is found in the onset of the disorder, which is slow and gradual in the process group and sudden in the reactive group. In the latter cases, too, the psychotic condition is often precipitated by a highly stressful experience. There is fairly extensive evidence to show that prognosis is more favorable for the reactive than for the process group. Other systematic analyses of premorbid data have yielded promising indices for forecasting schizophrenic adjustment both in the hospital and upon restoration to the community (56).

A final example is provided by a survey of posthospital adjustment of discharged patients (15). In terms of both rehospitalization and community-adjustment criteria, this study showed that the environmental milieu to which the patient returns is a major factor in the success of his posthospital adjustment. For instance, married women with young children were more likely to make a good adjustment than were single women living with their parents or other relatives. Data regarding the condition of these cases at the time of admission and discharge indicated that this difference in adjustment could not be attributed to selective factors. The investigators suggest that a family milieu in which the patient is required to take responsibility, as in managing a home and caring for young children, is more conducive to recovery than one in which the "sick" role is accepted and even encouraged by solicitous relatives.

The same study found that educational and socioeconomic variables are significantly related to outcome. Women who were college graduates, for instance, made a much more successful posthospital adjustment and were less often rehospitalized than women with only a grade school education. A similar relation was found between outcome and socioeconomic status. It should be noted that educational and socioeconomic factors may enter the picture in at least two ways. They not only determine certain features of the posthospital milieu to which the individual returns but also reflect characteristics of the patient himself—such as intellectual level, persistence, and self-confidence—that may be directly related to outcome.

*Attainment of Insight.* An important goal of the fact-finding, or exploratory, aspect of the clinical process is the attainment of insight by the client. Although any discussion or sharing of diagnostic findings with the client may contribute to such insight, certain clinical approaches are primarily oriented toward this objective. In nondirective, or client-centered, therapy, the principal goal is to encourage the client to verbalize his anxieties and examine his problems. Through such self-exploration, the individual comes gradually to understand his motives and actions. The insight he thus gains, it is believed, will enable him to deal with his own conflicts and to manage his behavior more effectively.

Similarly, psychoanalysis is specifically designed to make the individual aware of the origins of his emotional difficulties, which are often traced back to early childhood experiences. Free association and dream analysis are among the psychoanalytic techniques used for this purpose. Other common clinical procedures, such as play techniques and psychodrama, are also employed, with the dual objective of furthering the clinician's understanding of the client and the client's understanding of himself.

The utilization of diagnostic techniques for the promotion of client insight illustrates the *interrelation of diagnosis and therapy* in clinical psychology. Insight plays an important part in the major forms of psychotherapy (see, e.g., 28, ch. 4). The methods cited above for the attainment of insight represent well-known therapeutic procedures. As such, they will be considered more fully in Chapter 14. They are mentioned here simply to highlight the fact that, in much current clinical practice, diagnosis and therapy cannot be differentiated with regard to temporal sequence, methods, or objectives. Even a brief contact during which the client has an opportunity to describe his problem to a clinician may have therapeutic value. For that matter, when the client decides to consult a clinician and puts that decision into practice by keeping his first appointment, that action itself may contribute to his recovery.

There is also a growing tendency among clinical psychologists to de-emphasize diagnosis, especially in the narrow sense of advance understanding by the clinician (see, e.g., 52). Many believe that such advance understanding of the client's problems does not speed up therapy. Some are even skeptical about the contribution of causal understanding in general to the treatment process. To be sure, diagnostic procedures of various sorts are still widely employed in clinical practice, and extensive research is being devoted to their evaluation (see Chapter 15). Nevertheless, the gradual recognition that at least some of these techniques are of doubtful validity has opened up the whole question of whether they serve any useful function.

## SOURCES OF INFORMATION IN CLINICAL DIAGNOSIS

In the effort to understand the client's problems, clinical psychologists may turn to three major sources of data, namely, case history, psychological tests, and diagnostic interview (see 22; 28, part III; 64, pp. 491–513). Depending upon their theoretical orientation, the setting in which they function, and the type of client with whom they are dealing, clinicians will vary in the extent to which they employ each of these sources.

*Case History.* Utilizing a reverse longitudinal approach, the case history, or anamnesis, provides data about the client's reactional biography. It covers family background and current familial situation, educational and vocational history, and other important facts regarding the individual's physical and psychological development from the prenatal stage to the present. Information may be gathered through interviews with the client himself, members of his family, teachers, employers, co-workers, friends, or anyone else who has had contact with the client. School and employment files, agency reports, court records, and other official sources may be consulted. Unless an adequate medical report is already available, a medical examination is usually requested to round out the picture and to identify any conditions that may require treatment by a physician. In certain settings, the services of a social worker are utilized in obtaining at least part of the case history material.

*Psychological Tests.* In clinical practice, psychological tests are commonly employed to determine general level of intellectual functioning and to check for evidence of intellectual impairment or deterioration. A wide variety of personality tests is also available for investigating emotional disorders, strength of various needs, interests, attitudes, adjustment mechanisms, self concepts, interpersonal relations, and many other facets of behavior. Major types of tests used in clinical practice will be examined in later sections of this chapter.

*Interviewing Techniques.* The diagnostic interview represents a particularly important part of the process of clinical assessment (6, ch. 13; 28, ch. 15). Although a single intensive interview may serve for this purpose, frequently a series of interviews is required. In a diagnostic interview, the client has the opportunity to describe his problem as he sees it and to talk freely and fully about himself. Interest generally centers on how the client perceives events in his life and how he reacts to them, rather than on the objective events as such. Clinicians differ, however, in the extent to which they ask questions designed to elicit information about specific behavior difficulties, sources of conflict, or symptoms. In the nondirective approach, for example, the client is simply encouraged to talk about anything he considers important.

Although the interview is largely a medium for verbal communication, it also provides many opportunities for direct behavioral observations. Facial expressions, laughter, crying, blushing, muscular tics and grimaces, gestures, posture, and other expressive reactions serve as additional cues to the client's feelings. In the more severely disturbed cases, such symptoms as hallucinations, delusions, and flight of ideas may become apparent in the course of the interview.

For maximal effectiveness, the interview requires good *rapport* between clinician and client. Essentially this means that the client must have confidence in the clinician, so that he feels free to communicate. Ordinarily an individual shows some resistance to discussing or even thinking about certain highly emotional matters. There are several ways in which the clinician may help to overcome such resistance. Privacy and confidentiality of communication are of course essential. Through his own comments and behavior, moreover, the clinician can indicate that he is interested, attentive, and seriously concerned about the client's problems. The clinician's manner should be warm, friendly, and relaxed, while at the same time remaining impersonal and professional.

Most clinical psychologists today put the greatest emphasis on the establishment of a *permissive atmosphere*. By this is meant that the clinician refrains from judging or evaluating anything the client communicates—he expresses neither approval nor disapproval but concentrates on understanding and clarifying the client's own feelings. Although "permissiveness" is most closely associated with the client-centered school of clinical practice, its advantages—at least at certain stages—are quite generally recognized. In actual practice, however, it is difficult for any clinician to withhold entirely all expressions of approval or disapproval. Differential reinforcement of topics for discussion or of different types of patient responses is likely to be provided even by the most nondirective of clinicians. Some research findings on the effects of subtle cues in the clinician's behavior upon the course of client responses will be considered in Chapter 15.

It should also be noted that in much current clinical practice the diagnostic interview merges imperceptibly with the therapeutic interview. This is particularly true of those approaches that stress the therapeutic value of the client-therapist relationship.

# NATURE OF CLINICAL JUDGMENT

Two more or less related questions can be asked about the clinician's diagnostic function: *"What* does he do?" and *"How well* does he do it?" A fair amount of research and considerable discussion have been devoted to both questions. Nevertheless, psychologists are still a long way from reaching satisfactory answers. The only matter on which complete agreement could be obtained today is that "the nature of clinical judgment" is a topic that will guarantee a lively symposium.

***Person Cognition.*** What the clinician does in assessing a client may be regarded as a special case of person cognition, or interpersonal perception (3, 9, 20, 21, 63, 70). Through what process does *anyone* come to know and understand another person? This is a broad question that has been approached from the standpoints of epistemology, the psychology of perception, and concept formation, among others. Investigations of the accuracy of interpersonal perception and of the factors that affect it are beset with methodological pitfalls that have only recently been recognized. Generalizations about one's ability to judge others are misleading unless they specify the type of judgment and the circumstances under which it is made. Moreover, spurious impressions of accuracy can arise from failure to control certain variables, such as degree of resemblance between judge and subject or degree of resemblance between subject and a group stereotype in terms of which the judge may be responding (20, 21).

In understanding another person, the individual often relies upon *assumed similarity* to himself. He can thus use his own experience in interpreting the behavior of another. Although he cannot directly observe another's aches and pains or feelings of joy and sadness, he can identify them through facial expressions, gestures, verbal reports, and other overt cues that he has learned to associate with his own feelings. Assumed similarity between a newcomer and familiar others, such as one's relatives, friends, or former clients, is an extension of this mechanism. When this approach is followed in trying to understand someone quite unlike oneself—or unlike one's earlier acquaintances—it is likely to be misleading. Errors may thus arise when clinicians make diagnostic or prognostic inferences about a client whose cultural background, education, or socioeconomic level differs markedly from their own (see, e.g., 75).

*The Clinician's Data-gathering Function.* The diagnostic role of the clinician can be described in terms of data gathering and data interpreting. We shall begin by considering what the clinician can contribute to the process of data gathering. First, by establishing and maintaining rapport, he may elicit from the client facts about his life history not readily accessible in other ways. Such life-history data provide a particularly sound basis for understanding an individual and predicting his future behavior (13, 43). The life history has been aptly described as "an unbiased population of events which is as convincing an operational definition of a person as one can hope for" (13, p. 21). It might be added that the more factual data one has from the life history, the less filling-in needs to be done in the interpretive process.

In his search for facts, the clinician can also be guided by the client's own responses. He may thus form tentative hypotheses that suggest the direction of further probing. Such interlocking of data gathering and interpretation represents both an advantage and a potential danger of clinical interviewing. On the one hand, it permits more flexibility of search and more effective utilization of cues than would be possible with a test, questionnaire, or other standardized procedure. On the other hand, if the clinician puts undue confidence in his early hypotheses, he may look only for data that support them. By the type of questions he asks and the way he formulates them or by subtle expressions of agreement or disagreement, he may influence what the client reports. Sarbin and his associates (63) call this process "soliciting" as contrasted to "probing." Such biased data-gathering techniques undoubtedly account for the remarkably uniform etiologies found among the clients of some psychoanalysts.

Another way in which the clinician contributes to the fact-finding process is by serving as a stimulus in an interpersonal situation (61, 63). In this regard, the clinical interview may be regarded as a situational test (see Chapter 3). It provides a sample of the client's interpersonal behavior, observed under more or less controlled conditions.

*The Clinician's Interpretive Function.* There has been much discussion of the interpretive, or data-processing, function of the clinician. Some have argued for a special process of "clinical intuition" that is qualitatively different from other forms of inference. Belief in such a process arises partly from the fact that clinicians are often unable to report the cues they employ in reaching a conclusion (7; 63, ch. 8). The mystery disappears, however, when we realize that many of our perceptions utilize cues that are inaccessible to self-examination. A classical example is visual depth perception. We regularly perceive the world in three dimensions, without being able to specify the cues we employ in this process. Similarly, after exposure to a test protocol, a set of test scores, a case history, or a face-to-face interaction with a client, the clinician may assert that the patient is creative, or a likely suicide, or a poor psychotherapy risk, even though he cannot verbalize the facts he used in reaching such a conclusion. Being unaware of the cues that mediated his inference, the clinician is also unaware of the probabilistic nature of the inference. As a result, he may falsely associate a feeling of complete certainty with his "intuition."

A number of investigations have been concerned with the comparative validity of clinical versus statistical predictions (see 25, ch. 10; 35; 47; 50; 51; 63, ch. 10; 68). Given the same set of facts, such as test scores or life-history data, will clinical judgment provide more accurate predictions of subsequent behavior than would be obtained by the routine application of a regression equation or other empirically derived prediction formula? The large majority of studies have found statistical prediction to be at least as good as clinical prediction, and sometimes better.

It is difficult to generalize from such studies, however, because the results are undoubtedly affected by the nature of the data to be interpreted, the type of criterion behavior to be predicted, and the characteristics of the clinician. Not only the amount of training and experience of the clinician, but also the soundness of the theoretical framework within which he operates, will influence the validity of his judgments. If a clinician is guided by a bizarre and unverified personality theory, his prediction success may be poorer than that of the crudest statistical procedures. The process of clinical judgment probably varies widely from one clinician to another. Insofar as the clinician functions as an instrument, he needs to be individually validated, just like a test. Moreover, since clinical judgment is probably not a single trait, the clinician's validity must be separately investigated for different types of prediction, which have been classified according to type of client, type of outcome, and other relevant variables.

Several attempts have been made to analyze what clinicians do to arrive at their inferences (2, 16, 34, 36, 38, 46, 50, 63, 74). It is frequently claimed that clinical judgment, as contrasted to statistical data-processing techniques, is peculiarly suited to understanding the uniqueness of individuals. In the course of his interactions with a client, the clinician is able to develop constructs, categories, or trait concepts that are specifically fitted to the individual case. He can also take into account patterns of traits or events. His interpretation of any single fact, such as a test score, can be made contingent upon other variables, such as another test score or some biographical facts.

Furthermore, in his interpretations the clinician is able to incorporate rare events, whose frequency is too low to permit their use in statistical prediction. Although any one such event occurs very infrequently, it may significantly affect outcome in an individual case. Moreover, *different* "rare events" will be encountered often enough to have a substantial effect upon the decisions reached in large numbers of cases. In this connection, Meehl quotes the old paradox that "an improbable event is one that hardly ever happens, but nevertheless something improbable happens almost every day" (50, p. 25).

In focusing upon the uniqueness of the individual case, we must not lose sight of the fact that people also exhibit a great deal of similarity. Without such similarity, the science of psychology could never have developed. In fact, society and civilization would be impossible, and human relations would be chaotic. In the clinical context, it is the pronounced similarity among individuals that enables the clinician to utilize the technique of assumed similarity, to refer to test norms, or to draw upon personality theories developed through research on other persons. With regard to the clinician's consideration of patterns and interrelations of facts, it should be noted that such analyses can also be incorporated in statistical prediction formulas (see, e.g., 34). Although for most purposes linear regression equations based on simple additive combination of terms have proved sufficiently accurate, more complex combinations of variables can be handled by appropriate mathematical techniques. Such mathematical models have in fact been used in an effort to discover the type of model actually followed by different clinicians (34).

With diagnostic procedures in their present stage of development, there is much that the clinician must do, because neither tests nor statistical prediction formulas are available to do the whole job. For many years to come, clinicians will probably continue to use a combination of clinical judgment and such statistical aids as norms, expectancy tables, and regression equations. Clinicians need to be constantly aware of the probabilistic nature of all their inferences, whether derived from clinical judgment or statistical procedures. And they should make continuing efforts to check the validity of their predictions in terms of empirical follow-ups. Whether it will ever be practicable —or even theoretically possible—to program all of the clinician's diagnostic functions on a computer is still a moot point.

## INTELLIGENCE TESTING

Almost every type of test may be used by a clinician in individual cases. Tests of academic achievement, for example, are often useful in clinical work with children. Vocational apitude and interest tests may be required to help solve a special problem with an adolescent or adult client. Certain types of tests, however, were designed chiefly as clinical instruments. It is with these tests that we shall be concerned in the remaining sections of this chapter. Only a few examples of tests in each category will be cited. For a fuller discussion the reader is referred to textbooks on psychological testing (e.g., 1, 10) and to books on the practice of clinical psychology (e.g., 22; 28, chs. 16–20; 57). Apart from providing an overview of the sort of tests used by clinicians, the present survey will familiarize the reader with certain concepts relevant to the discussion of therapy and of clinical research to be given in the next two chapters.

*Stanford-Binet Intelligence Scale.* Among the best-established clinical instruments are intelligence tests. Although the concept of intelligence still needs much theoretical clarification, traditional intelligence tests have proved their worth empirically for many practical purposes. Typically, such tests yield an objective index of the individual's general level of intellectual functioning. The test that has been used for this purpose longer than any other is the Stanford-Binet. Originally developed by Terman at Stanford University from an earlier test introduced by Binet in 1905, the Stanford-Binet was most recently revised in 1960 (71). This form of the test extends from the age of two years to the superior adult level, but it is used most commonly with children. Most of the items are oral, although some require the subject to read, write, draw, or carry out simple manipulative tasks.

Like most intelligence tests designed for clinical use, the Stanford-Binet is an individual test. It can be administered to only one subject at a time and requires a trained examiner. Although more time-consuming and much harder to give and score than group tests, individual tests provide additional information for the clinician. Thus in such a situation it is possible to observe the subject's work methods, attitudes, and problem-solving techniques, as well as the finished product. Interpersonal reactions, emotional responses, and other incidental behavior can likewise be noted. Individual tests also provide a better opportunity for establishing rapport with each subject than do group tests.

The Stanford-Binet yields a single score expressed as a deviation IQ with a mean of 100 and an SD of 16. A particular advantage of this test stems from the wealth of interpretive data that has accumulated through many years of clinical use. Clinicians have thus had a chance to learn inductively what to expect from individuals at different Stanford-Binet IQ levels.

***The Wechsler Scales.*** The Wechsler Adult Intelligence Scale (WAIS), like its earlier version, the Wechsler-Bellevue, was specially developed as a clinical instrument for adult testing (77, 78). Standardized in 1955 on a representative nationwide adult sample, the WAIS provides separate norms for successive age levels between sixteen and sixty-four years. Supplementary norms were also established on a special old-age sample extending to seventy-five years and over, tested in a Middle Western city.

The WAIS yields a total deviation IQ ($M = 100$, $SD = 15$), as well as separate Verbal and Performance IQs. The Verbal IQ is based on six orally administered tests utilizing verbal and numerical content; the Performance IQ is derived from five subtests using nonverbal symbols, pictures, geometric forms, and cutout parts of objects to be assembled by the subject. A simple item used for demonstration purposes in one of the picture tests is reproduced in Figure 92. The subject's task in this test is to rearrange a set of cards in the proper order so as to tell a story. Figure 93 shows a subject taking another of the performance tests, in which designs are copied by arranging blocks with painted sides.

The Wechsler Intelligence Scale for Children (WISC) was prepared as a downward extension of the original Wechsler-Bellevue (76). It, too, provides Verbal, Performance, and Full Scale IQs and is quite similar to the WAIS in form and content. Norms are available for every four-month interval between the ages of five and fifteen years.

***Fig. 92*** Demonstration item from the WAIS Picture Arrangement Test. (*Reproduced by permission. Copyright 1955, The Psychological Corporation.*)

*Fig. 93*  A subject taking the WAIS Block Design Test. (*Courtesy of The Psychological Corporation.*)

**Performance and Nonlanguage Scales.**  A number of less well-known tests have been developed for use with special groups, such as infants and preschool children (see 1, ch. 11). Others have been designed for testing persons unable to take the usual type of test, such as the deaf, the orthopedically handicapped, children with reading disabilities, illiterates, and foreigners with a language handicap. There are several nonlanguage group tests that require no reading; some can be administered without the use of language altogether, the instructions being presented by means of gestures, pantomime, and demonstrations. For individual testing, performance tests are generally employed for several of the special handicaps mentioned above. Since most nonlanguage and performance tests tap chiefly perceptual and spatial rather than verbal and numerical functions, they are also used in clinical practice to provide a better-rounded picture of the individual's intelligence. The Performance Scale of the previously mentioned WAIS and WISC was included chiefly for this purpose.

In a few tests, the attempt has been made to eliminate, not only language, but also knowledge and skills that are specific to a particular culture. An example of such an intelligence test designed for cross-cultural testing is the Progressive Matrices (58), previously described and illustrated in Chapter 3. This test, it will be recalled, consists of 60 matrices, or designs, from each of which a piece has been removed. The subject must choose the missing piece from six or eight given inserts. Because it is a nonverbal test requiring the eduction of relations among abstract items, this test is particularly useful in clinical practice as a supplement to the usual verbal type of intelligence test. Still another application is in the testing of persons with severe motor handicaps, as in cerebral palsy, with whom the Progressive Matrices have proved quite successful. When administering the test to such cases, the examiner points to each piece in turn, while the subject signifies assent or dissent through some convenient signal.

**Tests of Intellectual Impairment.** Several types of tests have been designed as clinical instruments for assessing intellectual impairment. Such tests are used to detect intellectual deterioration resulting from brain damage (or "organicity"), psychotic disorders, senility, or other pathological conditions. They are sometimes employed to help differentiate between mental deficiency and psychosis, as well as between mental defectives with or without brain damage. Many of these tests are only loosely standardized, being designed chiefly to give the clinician an opportunity to make qualitative observations. Others have relatively standardized procedure and empirical norms.

Available tests of intellectual impairment are based on the premise of a differential deficit in different functions. Among the functions found to be most sensitive to pathological processes are memory for newly learned material, perception of spatial relations, and abstraction, or concept formation. The individual's performance on these tests is usually compared with his performance in a function that is relatively resistant to deterioration. Vocabulary test scores or scores on predominantly verbal intelligence tests are often used for the latter purpose. An index of the individual's prior intellectual level, from which he subsequently deteriorated, can also be obtained from his educational or occupational status or from intelligence tests he may have taken in the past.

The Wechsler scales are sometimes used to find a deterioration index, as well as to identify diagnostic signs of various psychotic and neurotic disorders (78). All these measures are based on inequalities of performance from one subtest to another. Although employed by some clinicians and recommended by the test author, these applications of the Wechsler scales have many technical weaknesses that make them of doubtful value (see 1, pp. 320–325).

An example of a special test for measuring intellectual impairment is the Benton Visual Retention Test (5). This test combines perception and memory by having the subject reproduce designs from memory. In the procedure usually followed, each of 10 cards containing simple geometric figures is exposed briefly. Immediately upon its removal, the subject draws what he saw on the card.

Another well-known type of test utilizes the sorting of objects or forms to investigate the subject's concept formation (see 1, pp. 329–330; 26; 57, vol. I,

*Fig. 94*   Objects employed in a sorting test for evaluating concept formation. (*Courtesy of The Psychological Corporation.*)

ch. 3). Thus the subject may be given a set of circles, squares, and triangles in different colors, with the instructions to place together those that belong together. Whether he groups the pieces according to form or color, he is then asked to sort them in another way. In this test, interest is focused on the subject's ability to shift from one basis of classification to another. In the sorting test illustrated in Figure 94, common objects are employed in a variety of sorting situations. For example, the examiner selects an article and asks the subject to pick out the others that belong with it. The examiner also places objects in groups on some basis, such as color, shape, material, or use, and asks the subject to say why they belong together. The same object may be included in several different groupings, such as eating utensils, toys, and metal objects. Hence the subject is again required to shift from one attribute of an object to another in the reclassifications.

## PERSONALITY TESTING

The term "personality test" is conventionally used to designate techniques for assessing the emotional, social, and motivational aspects of behavior. It should be noted that neither personality nor intelligence represents an entity. Each refers merely to certain characteristics of the individual's behavior. Moreover, everything the individual does is influenced by both intellectual and personality factors. How well the individual performs an intellectual task depends in part upon his motivation, interests, and emotional adjustment. Conversely, the way in which he resolves an emotional difficulty and his reaction to psychotherapy are affected by his intellectual level. Application of the previously discussed tests of intellectual impairment demonstrates the effects of severe emotional difficulties upon intellectual functioning.

Although personality tests vary widely with respect to reliability, validity, and adequacy of norms, such tests as a whole are not so well constructed nor so successful as those in the intellectual area. For this reason, personality tests are employed chiefly as exploratory tools in clinical practice. In assessing personality traits, most clinicians rely heavily upon life-history and interview data. Of the many personality tests available to the clinician, we shall consider three major types: (1) self-report inventories, (2) projective techniques, and (3) measures of self concepts and personal constructs.

**Self-report Inventories.** In a self-report inventory, the individual answers a series of written questions about his typical feelings, attitudes, and actions. This technique has been used in measuring such varied characteristics as vocational interests, race prejudice, interpersonal relations, and neuroticism. Standardized inventories have been prepared for use with different age groups, from the elementary school to the adult level. Some are designed for essentially normal persons; others were developed within clinical settings to detect emotional maladjustments.

Among clinically oriented inventories, the most widely known is undoubtedly the Minnesota Multiphasic Personality Inventory, or MMPI (12, 17, 29, 30, 31, 80). Originally developed "to assay those traits that are commonly characteristic of disabling psychological abnormality," the MMPI consists of 550 statements which the subject is to classify as *True, False,* or *Cannot Say* with regard to himself. In the individual form of this test, which is the form more commonly used in clinical practice, each statement is printed on a card, and the subject places the card in the appropriate category in a box. The items range widely in content, covering such areas as: health, psychosomatic symptoms, neurological disorders, and motor disturbances; sexual, religious, political, and social attitudes; educational, occupational, family, and marital questions; and common neurotic or psychotic behavior disturbances, such as obsessive and compulsive states, delusions, hallucinations, ideas of reference, phobias, and the like. A few illustrative items are reproduced below:

I do not tire quickly.
I am worried about sex matters.
When I get bored I like to stir up some excitement.
I believe I am being plotted against.

In its regular administration, the MMPI provides scores on the following 10 scales:

| | |
|---|---|
| 1. Hs: Hypochondriasis | 6. Pa: Paranoia |
| 2. D: Depression | 7. Pt: Psychasthenia |
| 3. Hy: Hysteria | 8. Sc: Schizophrenia |
| 4. Pd: Psychopathic deviate | 9. Ma: Hypomania |
| 5. Mf: Masculinity-femininity | 0. Si: Social introversion |

Eight of these scales consist of items that differentiated between patients with specified clinical syndromes and a normal control group of approximately 700 persons. These scales were developed empirically by criterion keying of items, the criterion being traditional psychiatric diagnosis. Items for the Masculinity-femininity (Mf) scale were selected in terms of frequency of responses by men and women. The Social introversion (Si) scale was added later, on the basis of research on normal subjects. A special feature of the MMPI is its utilization of four so-called "validity" scales (?, L, F, K). These scales are not concerned with validity in the technical sense but provide checks on carelessness, misunderstanding, malingering, and the operation of special response sets and test-taking attitudes.

Scores on the MMPI scales are expressed as standard scores with a mean of 50 and an SD of 10. These standard scores are used in plotting profiles, as illustrated in Figure 95. A score of 70 or higher—falling 2 SD's or more above the mean—is generally taken as the cutoff point for identifying possible pathological deviations. The interpretation of MMPI profiles is much more complex than the labels originally assigned to the scales might suggest. The test manual and related publications now caution against literal interpretation of the clinical scales. For example, we cannot assume that a high score on the Schizophrenia scale indicates the presence of schizophrenia. Other psychotic groups show high elevation on this scale; and schizophrenics often score high on other scales. Moreover, such a score may occur with a normal person. It is partly to prevent possible misinterpretations of scores on single scales that the code numbers o to 9 have been substituted for the scale names in later publications on the MMPI.

The original clinical scales of the MMPI were based on a traditional psychiatric classification which, though popular, rests upon a questionable theo-

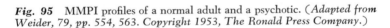

**Fig. 95**   MMPI profiles of a normal adult and a psychotic. (*Adapted from Weider, 79, pp. 554, 563. Copyright 1953, The Ronald Press Company.*)

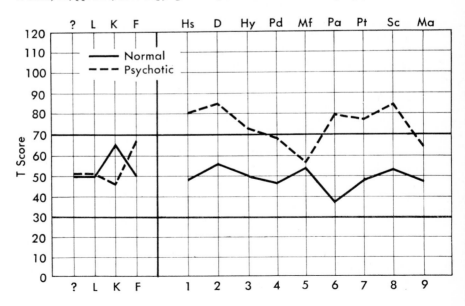

retical foundation. As we saw in the first section of this chapter, the artificiality of these categories has been a matter of concern in clinical psychology for a long time. The fact that such categories prove unsatisfactory in actual practice is now generally conceded. Another difficulty is that a high score on any one MMPI scale may have different implications depending upon the individual's scores on other scales. It is the score pattern, or profile, rather than the scores on individual scales that must be considered. To facilitate the interpretation of score patterns, a system of numerical profile coding has been developed. In such codes, the sequence and arrangement of scale numbers show at a glance which are the high and which the low points in the individual's profile. For instance, the code 49–2 signifies high scores in scale 4 (Pd) and scale 9 (Ma) in decreasing order of size and a low score in scale 2 (D). A mass of interpretive clinical material has been gathered and published, showing the characteristics of persons who obtain each coded profile on the MMPI (see 12, 17, 30, 31).

The MMPI has also served as an item pool for the construction of about 200 special scales, most of them developed by independent investigators to meet specific needs (see 12). Both normal and clinical populations have been employed in selecting items for these scales against a wide variety of criteria. Examples include scales assessing Ego Strength, Manifest Anxiety, Dependence, Dominance, Prejudice, and Social Status.

Insofar as items are selected and their scoring weights determined by empirical criterion keying, they may be regarded as verbal stimuli to which the subject responds when he takes the inventory. These responses are interpreted in terms of their empirically established correlations with criterion data. Thus, if a person reports that he has been generally unsuccessful in his undertakings, the point at issue is not his actual degree of success but the fact that he gives such a response. This approach to self-report inventories is effectively characterized by Meehl in a statement about the MMPI which was quoted in Chapter 11 (p. 301) in a different connection.[1]

***Projective Techniques.*** Although projective techniques have been employed for a variety of purposes—including personnel selection, executive evaluation, and motivation research—their principal application is in clinical psychology. Most of them require individual administration by a specially trained examiner. And they yield a mass of qualitative data along with (or in place of) quantitative scores. It will be recalled from Chapter 3 that projective techniques as a group are characterized by the use of a relatively *unstructured* task, which allows considerable freedom in the subject's response. The underlying hypothesis is that, when test stimuli and instructions are vague and equivocal, the individual's responses will reveal his own basic personality characteristics.

There is almost no limit to the kinds of tasks or situations that can serve as a basis for projective testing. Available techniques are many and varied. One of the earliest was the "free association test," in which the subject is given a list of disconnected words, to each of which he must respond with the first word that comes to mind. Another test employing verbal stimuli is the sentence completion test. Subjects are given the opening words of a series of sentences

---

[1] Other examples of personality inventories were described in Chapter 3. The use of self-report inventories in the measurement of interests is discussed in Chapters 3 and 16.

and are required to write suitable endings. Frequently the instructions stress the fact that the sentences should express the subject's own feelings. The sentence stems are chosen so as to permit wide latitude in the responses. Typical examples are: "I feel . . ."; "What annoys me . . ."; "My father. . . ." The responses are evaluated or coded in various ways. Thus they might be rated for degree of maladjustment indicated; or they might be checked for the number of references to a particular theme, such as insecurity, hostility, or parental conflict.

One of the best-known projective instruments, the Rorschach, utilizes ink-blots as stimuli (59). Developed in 1921 by the Swiss psychiatrist Herman Rorschach, this test utilizes 10 cards, each containing a bilaterally symmetrical but otherwise irregular blot, similar to that illustrated in Figure 96. Some of the cards are in black, white, and gray; others are in color. As the subject is shown each blot, he is asked to tell what he sees—what the blot could represent. Different systems of administration vary in the details of procedure and scoring, but all require a good deal of qualitative interpretation in translating the subject's responses into broad personality characteristics. Although content is considered to some extent, the most common scoring systems are based predominantly on formal characteristics of the responses. For example, scores are derived from such data as: number of associations elicited by the whole blot and number elicited by details of the blot; number of times the subject

*Fig. 96*   An inkblot of the type employed in the Rorschach technique.

responds to form and to color; frequency with which he perceives movement, as well as kind of movement perceived (human, animal, etc.); and the ways in which the subject perceives shading.

Several projective techniques employ pictures as stimuli. In the Thematic Apperception Test (TAT), which was cited in Chapter 3, black and white pictures are presented individually with the instructions to make up a story to fit each picture (53). The subject is told to describe what is happening in the picture, to indicate what the characters are feeling and thinking, and to give the outcome. The content of the pictures is sufficiently unstructured to permit wide freedom of interpretation. A typical TAT picture is reproduced in Figure 97. Evaluation of responses is largely qualitative, drawing heavily upon Murray's personality theory.

A different use of pictures is illustrated by the Rosenzweig Picture-Frustration Study (P-F), based on the author's theory of frustration and aggression (60). The test booklet contains a series of cartoon-like drawings, each depicting a frustrating situation commonly met in daily life. One of the characters in each cartoon is saying something that either causes the frustra-

**Fig. 97**   One of the pictures used in the Thematic Apperception Test. (*Reprinted by permission of the publishers from Henry Alexander Murray, Thematic Apperception Test, Cambridge, Mass.: Harvard University Press, Copyright, 1943, by The President and Fellows of Harvard College.*)

tion or calls attention to it. The reply of the frustrated character is to be filled in by the subject. One item from this test is shown in Figure 98. Responses are analyzed in various ways. For example, direction of aggression is classified as "extrapunitive," or turned outward upon the environment; "intropunitive," or turned inward upon the subject; and "impunitive," or turned off in an attempt at glossing over or evading the situation.

With regard to the contributions they can make to clinical assessment, projective techniques differ widely among themselves. Some appear more promising than others because of sounder theoretical orientation, more favorable empirical findings, or both. About some there is a voluminous research literature; about others little is known. Although each instrument obviously must be evaluated on its own merits, certain general statements can be made about the projective approach to personality assessment.

On the positive side, projective techniques are effective in "breaking the ice" and establishing rapport during initial contacts with a client. They are also applicable to a wide variety of subjects. Several available techniques involving nonverbal media can be used successfully with young children, illiterates, or persons with language handicaps. Projective tests, moreover, are

*Fig. 98*   Typical item from Rosenzweig Picture-Frustration Study. (*Reproduced by permission of Saul Rosenzweig.*)

less susceptible to faking than are self-report inventories, since their purpose is generally disguised. In addition, the subject soon becomes engrossed in the task and is hence less likely to resort to the habitual restraints and defenses of interpersonal communication. At the same time, because of its unstructured nature, the task is usually less threatening than those encountered in intelligence and aptitude tests.

When evaluated in terms of their technical qualities as tests, however, projective instruments generally fare rather poorly. Most are inadequately standardized with regard to both administration and scoring procedures. Consequently, results are likely to vary as a function of the examiner. With a few notable exceptions, norms are inadequate. Normative data either are lacking or are based on small and unrepresentative samples. Frequently, not enough information is given about normative samples to permit an evaluation of the norms. For many projective tests, reliability is difficult to determine because of the nature of the test and the absence of parallel forms. When obtained, reliability coefficients are often low. Empirical studies of validity have also yielded disappointing results for most projective tests. Positive findings have sometimes been obtained because of inadequate controls and other methodological deficiencies.

Some of the special problems encountered in the evaluation of projective techniques will be considered in Chapter 15, in connection with clinical research. In their present state of development, projective techniques should be regarded as interviewing aids rather than as psychometric tools. Their chief usefulness lies in providing leads to be followed up by the clinician.

**Self Concepts and Personal Constructs.** Although self-report inventories and projective techniques represent the most numerous and best-known devices for personality assessment, many other approaches are being actively pursued (see 1, ch. 21). Investigators have experimented with tests of perception, controlled association, aesthetic preference, and humor responses, among others. Of particular interest for clinical psychology are techniques for exploring self concepts and personal constructs. These techniques are closely allied with some of the personality theories and systems of psychotherapy to be discussed in the next chapter. A common feature of such techniques is their concern with the way in which the individual views himself and others. In this respect, they reflect the influence of phenomenological psychology, which focuses on how events are perceived by the individual (41, 65). The individual's self-description thus acquires primary importance in its own right, rather than being regarded as a poor substitute for other types of behavioral observations. Interest also centers on the extent of self-acceptance shown by the individual.

One of the special procedures for investigating self concepts is the Q *sort,* developed by Stephenson (67). In this technique, the subject is given a set of cards containing statements or trait names and is asked to sort them into piles according to their applicability to himself, from "most characteristic" to "least characteristic." The items may come from a standard list but more often are designed to fit the individual case. To ensure a uniform distribution of ratings, a forced-normal distribution may be used, the subject being instructed to place a specified number of cards in each pile (see Chapter 4).

Q sorts have been employed to study a variety of psychological problems. In the clinical investigation of individual personality, the subject is often asked to re-sort the same set of items according to different frames of reference. For example, he may sort the items as they apply to himself and to other persons, such as his father, mother, wife, or therapist. Q sorts can also be obtained for the individual as he actually thinks he is (real self) and as he would like to be (ideal self). A cumulative measure of the differences between real- and ideal-self sorts provides an index of self-acceptance. To observe change, Q sorts may be obtained repeatedly at different stages in the course of psychotherapy.

Q technique represents an attempt to systematize self-rating procedures. It can also be employed as a basis for rating others. For example, a clinician may record his evaluation of an individual by means of a Q sort. Although some of the statistical procedures that have been employed in analyzing Q-sort data are questionable (11), the Q sort provides a useful rating technique for both clinical practice and research.

Another relevant technique is the *Semantic Differential,* originally developed by Osgood and his associates (54) as a tool for research on the psychology of meaning. This technique has subsequently proved useful in a variety of fields, including that of personality assessment. The Semantic Differential represents a standardized and quantified procedure for measuring the connotations of any given concept for the individual. Each concept is rated on a seven-point bipolar graphic scale defined by a pair of opposites such as good-bad, strong-weak, or fast-slow. Every concept to be investigated is rated in turn on each scale, as illustrated below:

| CHILD | large | ___:___:___:___:___:___:___ | small |
| HATRED | tense | ___:___:___:___:___:___:___ | relaxed |
| SEX | strong | ___:___:___:___:___:___:___ | weak |
| CHILD | valuable | ___:___:___:___:___:___:___ | worthless |

Some of the scales can be applied literally to a particular concept, as in the rating of CHILD on the large-small scale. Many of the scales are obviously interpreted figuratively, as when a person is described as "cold." When a scale appears totally inapplicable to a concept, the subject would presumably check the middle position.

Intercorrelations and factorial analyses of different scales have revealed three major factors: *Evaluative,* with high loadings in such scales as good-bad, valuable-worthless, and clean-dirty; *Potency,* found in such scales as strong-weak, large-small, and heavy-light; and *Activity,* identified in such scales as active-passive, fast-slow, and sharp-dull. The evaluative factor is the most conspicuous, accounting for the largest percentage of total variance. Responses on the Semantic Differential can be analyzed in several ways. For example, the connotations of all concepts rated by an individual can be investigated by computing the "score" of each concept in the three principal factors described above. The factor loadings can be more easily visualized by means of three-dimensional models, as illustrated in Figure 99. These models are taken from an intensive study of a case of multiple personality, in which the patient shifted back and forth between sharply contrasted "selves" (72, 73). The one self, designated "Eve White," was meek, self-critical, frustrated, and unhappy. The other, "Eve Black," was irresponsible, self-centered, fun-loving, and mischievous. "Jane," a third, more highly integrated and better-adjusted personality, emerged in the course of therapy and seemed eventually to be replacing the other two.

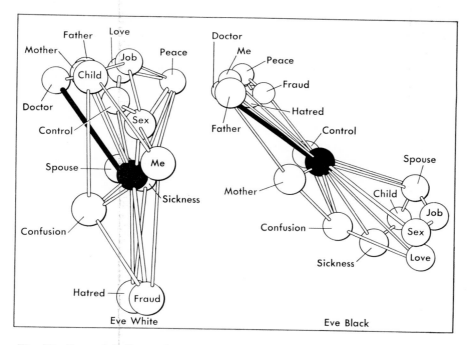

*Fig. 99*  Semantic Differential patterns found in a case of multiple personality. (*From Osgood and Luria, 55, pp. 584, 585.*)

An independent analysis of the Semantic Differential patterns of Eve White and Eve Black led to personality descriptions that agreed remarkably well with the case reports of the therapists (54, 55). Figure 99 shows these patterns as they appeared early in therapy. In these diagrams, "good" is at the top, "active" at the left, and "weak" toward the reader. The dark circle is the zero point for all three dimensions. The dark line connecting this circle to Doctor (who retained approximately the same position in all diagrams) serves to orient the patterns in "semantic space." A number of contrasts are apparent between the two patterns. Eve White places Me much lower in the evaluative dimension than does Eve Black. The latter also shows less differentiation of concepts along the evaluative (up-down) dimension. Eve Black's distorted values are further indicated by her placing Hate and Fraud along with Peace, Father, Doctor, and herself toward the good end of the scale, while Child, Spouse, Job, Sex, and Love are classified with Confusion and Sickness toward the bad end. In Eve White's pattern, the separation of Love and Sex and the neutral position of Spouse reflect some of her adjustment difficulties in marriage. Changes occurring in the course of therapy were accompanied by shifts in the position of concepts in later Semantic Differential patterns.

A technique devised specifically as an aid in clinical practice is the *Role Construct Repertory Test* (Rep test) developed by George A. Kelly (41). This test has certain features in common with several other personality tests, notably the Semantic Differential and the various sorting tests used to study concept formation. In the Rep test, however, the objects to be sorted are persons who are important in the subject's life. And, unlike the Semantic Differential, the Rep test requires the subject himself to designate the categories or constructs in terms of which he classifies these persons. The Rep test was developed within the context of Kelly's personality theory. A basic proposition of this theory is that the concepts or constructs an individual uses to perceive objects or events influence his behavior. In the course of psychotherapy, it is frequently necessary to build new constructs and to discard some old constructs before progress can be made.

The Rep test is designed to help the clinician identify some of the client's important constructs about people. Although the test can be administered in many ways, one of its simpler variants will serve to illustrate its essential characteristics. In this variant, the subject is first given a Role Title List and asked to name a person in his experience who fits each role title. A few examples are: a teacher you liked; your father; your wife or present girl friend; a person with whom you have been closely associated recently who appears to dislike you. The examiner next selects three of the persons named and asks, "In what *important way* are two of them alike but different from the third?" This procedure is repeated with many other sets of three names, in which some of the same names may occur in different combinations. The Rep test yields a wealth of qualitative data. A simplified factor-analytic procedure has also been developed for the quantitative identification of constructs that are important for each individual.

An example of the many variations that can be introduced into the Rep test is provided by a study of adolescent adjustment (40). In the adaptation developed in this study, the subject uses each of the constructs that emerge from the first part of the test to rate himself as he is at the time, as he was five years ago, and as he would like to be five years hence. He also estimates how each person named earlier in the test would rate him on the same constructs. Several of the measures obtained by this procedure differentiated significantly among a group of adolescents rated as well adjusted by their teachers, a group rated as poorly adjusted, and a group referred to a clinic for emotional problems.

## SUMMARY

While functioning in a variety of settings, clinical psychologists are typically concerned with individuals who are experiencing difficulties of an emotional or intellectual nature. The principal activities of clinical psychologists can be classified as diagnosis, therapy, and research. These activities are frequently intertwined, their relative importance varying widely with the clinician.

In its broadest sense, diagnosis corresponds to the fact-finding aspect of clinical practice. Its objectives include screening and classification, personality description, prediction of outcome, and attainment of client insight. In the classification of psychological disorders, a basic distinction is that between mental deficiency and emotional problems, the latter being further subdivided into psychoses and neuroses. More specific syndromes have been identified, but the application of these traditional psychiatric categories has many drawbacks. Characteristically, the clinical psychologist is interested in a detailed personality description of the individual case, with its unique combination of problems, adjustment mechanisms, and antecedent circumstances. The predictive validity of both tests and life-history data has been investigated against such criteria as reaction to therapy, postinstitutional adjustment, and improvement or deterioration in the absence of therapy. The interrelation of diagnosis and therapy is illustrated by those forms of psychotherapy that emphasize the therapeutic value of the client's insight into the nature and origin of his problems.

The major sources of data available to the clinician include case history, psychological tests, and diagnostic interview. Considerable discussion and some research have been devoted to the nature and effectiveness of clinical judgment. The clinician's diagnostic task can be regarded as a special case of the general process of person cognition. With regard to both data gathering and interpretation, there are a number of ways in which the services of a skilled clinician are needed. Whether objective diagnostic techniques and statistical prediction formulas can eventually assume the entire diagnostic function remains a debatable question.

Currently, clinicians utilize a number of psychological tests in conjunction with life-history and interview data. Among the tests most frequently used for clinical purposes are individual intelligence tests, special tests of intellectual impairment, personality inventories, projective tests, and various measures of self concepts and personal constructs.

# REFERENCES

1. Anastasi, Anne. *Psychological testing.* (2nd ed.) New York: Macmillan, 1961.
2. Arnhoff, F. N. Some aspects of clinical judgment. *J. clin. Psychol.,* 1960, **16**, 123–128.
3. Bakan, D. Clinical psychology and logic. *Amer. Psychologist,* 1956, **11**, 655–662.
4. Barron, F. An ego-strength scale which predicts response to psychotherapy. *J. consult. Psychol.,* 1953, **17**, 327–333.
5. Benton, A. L. *Benton Visual Retention Test, Revised Edition.* New York: Psychol. Corp., 1955.
6. Bingham, W. V., Moore, B. V., and Gustad, J. W. *How to interview.* (4th ed.) New York: Harper & Row, 1959.
7. Buck, R. C., and Seeman, W. Clinical judges and clinical insight in psychology. *Phil. Sci.,* 1955, **22**, 73–85.
8. Coville, W. J., Costello, T. W., and Rouke, F. L. *Abnormal psychology.* New York: Barnes & Noble, 1960.
9. Cronbach, L. J. Processes affecting scores on "understanding of others" and "assumed similarity." *Psychol. Bull.,* 1955, **52**, 177–193.
10. Cronbach, L. J. *Essentials of psychological testing.* (2nd ed.) New York: Harper & Row, 1960.
11. Cronbach, L. J., and Gleser, Goldine C. Review of Stephenson, W. The study of behavior: Q-technique and its methodology. *Psychometrika,* 1954, **19**, 327–330. (See also reply by Stephenson, pp. 331–333.)
12. Dahlstrom, W. G., and Welsh, G. S. *An MMPI handbook: A guide to use in clinical practice and research.* Minneapolis: Univer. Minn. Press, 1960.
13. Dailey, C. A. The life history as a criterion of assessment. *J. counsel. Psychol.,* 1960, 7, 20–23.
14. Degan, J. W. Dimensions of functional psychoses. *Psychometr. Monogr.,* 1952, No. 6.
15. Dinitz, S., Lefton, M., Angrist, Shirley, and Pasamanick, B. Psychiatric and social attributes as predictors of case outcome in mental hospitalization. *Soc. Probl.,* 1961, 8, 322–328.

16. Donahoe, J. W. A dimensional analysis of clinical judgment. *J. consult. Psychol.*, 1960, **24**, 96.
17. Drake, L. E., and Oetting, E. R. *An MMPI codebook for counselors.* Minneapolis: Univer. Minn. Press, 1959.
18. Eysenck, H. J. *Handbook of abnormal psychology.* New York: Basic Books, 1961.
19. Fulkerson, S. C., and Barry, J. R. Methodology and research on the prognostic use of psychological tests. *Psychol. Bull.*, 1961, **58**, 177–204.
20. Gage, N. L., and Cronbach, L. J. Conceptual and methodological problems in interpersonal perception. *Psychol. Rev.*, 1955, **62**, 411–422.
21. Gage, N. L., Leavitt, G. S., and Stone, G. C. The intermediary key in the analysis of interpersonal perception. *Psychol. Bull.*, 1956, **53**, 258–266.
22. Garfield, S. L. *Introductory clinical psychology: An overview of the functions, methods, and problems of contemporary clinical psychology.* New York: Macmillan, 1957.
23. Gerard, R. W., *et al.* The nosology of schizophrenia. *Amer. J. Psychiat.*, 1963, **120**, 16–29.
24. Gilmer, B. vonH., *et al. Industrial psychology.* New York: McGraw-Hill, 1961.
25. Goldman, L. *Using tests in counseling.* New York: Appleton-Century-Crofts, 1961.
26. Goldstein, K., and Scheerer, M. Abstract and concrete behavior; an experimental study with special tests. *Psychol. Monogr.*, 1941, **53**, No. 2.
27. Guertin, W. H. A factor analytic study of schizophrenic symptoms. *J. consult. Psychol.*, 1952, **16**, 308–312.
28. Hadley, J. M. *Clinical and counseling psychology.* New York: Knopf, 1958.
29. Hathaway, S. R., and McKinley, J. C. *Minnesota Multiphasic Personality Inventory.* Minneapolis: Univer. Minn. Press, 1951.
30. Hathaway, S. R., and Meehl, P. E. *An atlas for the clinical use of the MMPI.* New York: Psychol. Corp., 1951.
31. Hathaway, S. R., and Monachesi, E. D. *An atlas of juvenile MMPI profiles.* Minneapolis: Univer. Minn. Press, 1961.
32. Henderson, D. K., and Batchelor, B. C. *A textbook of psychiatry for students and practitioners.* (9th ed.) London: Oxford Univer. Press, 1962.
33. Herron, W. G. The process-reactive classification of schizophrenia. *Psychol. Bull.*, 1962, **59**, 329–343.
34. Hoffman, P. J. The paramorphic representation of clinical judgment. *Psychol. Bull.*, 1960, **57**, 116–131.
35. Holt, R. R. Clinical *and* statistical prediction: A reformulation and some new data. *J. abnorm. soc. Psychol.*, 1958, **56**, 1–12.
36. Holtzman, W. H. Can the computer supplant the clinician? *J. clin. Psychol.*, 1960, **16**, 119–122.
37. Hutt, M. L., and Gibby, R. G. *The mentally retarded child.* Boston: Allyn and Bacon, 1958.
38. Kahn, M. W. Clinical and statistical prediction revisited. *J. clin. Psychol.*, 1960, **16**, 115–118.
39. Kantor, R. E., Wallner, J. M., and Winder, C. L. Process and reactive schizophrenia. *J. consult. Psychol.*, 1953, **17**, 157–162.
40. Kasper, S. Measurement of adjustment in adolescents: An extension of personal construct theory and methodology. *Psychol. Monogr.*, 1962, **76**, No. 6.
41. Kelly, G. A. *The psychology of personal constructs. Vol. 1. A theory of personality.* New York: Norton, 1955.
42. Kirk, S. A., *et al. Early education of the mentally retarded.* Urbana, Ill.: Univer. Ill. Press, 1958.
43. Kostlan, A. A method for the empirical study of psychodiagnosis. *J. consult. Psychol.*, 1954, **18**, 83–88.
44. Lorr, M., Katz, M. M., and Rubinstein, E. A. The prediction of length of stay in psychotherapy. *J. consult. Psychol.*, 1958, **22**, 321–327.
45. Lorr, M., O'Connor, J. P., and Stafford, J. W. Confirmation on nine psychotic symptom patterns. *J. clin. Psychol.*, 1957, **13**, 252–257.
46. McArthur, C. Analyzing the clinical process. *J. counsel. Psychol.*, 1954, **1**, 203–207.
47. McHugh, R. B., and Apostolakos, P. C. Methodology for the comparison of clinical with actuarial predictions. *Psychol. Bull.*, 1959, **56**, 301–308.

48. McKinney, F. *Psychology of personal adjustment.* (3rd ed.) New York: Wiley, 1960.
49. McMurry, R. N. Mental illness: Industry's 3 million dollar burden. *Advanc. Mgmt,* 1960, **25** (9), 18–20.
50. Meehl, P. E. *Clinical vs. statistical prediction: A theoretical analysis and a review of the evidence.* Minneapolis: Univer. Minn. Press, 1954.
51. Meehl, P. E. A comparison of clinicians with five statistical methods of identifying psychotic MMPI profiles. *J. counsel. Psychol.,* 1959, **6**, 102–109.
52. Meehl, P. E. The cognitive activity of the clinician. *Amer. Psychologist,* 1960, **15**, 19–27.
53. Murray, H. A. *Thematic Apperception Test.* Cambridge, Mass.: Harvard Univer. Press, 1943.
54. Osgood, C. E., *et al. The measurement of meaning.* Urbana, Ill.: Univer. Ill. Press, 1957.
55. Osgood, C. E., and Luria, Zella. A blind analysis of a case of multiple personality using the semantic differential. *J. abnorm. soc. Psychol.,* 1954, **49**, 579–591.
56. Phillips, L. Case history data and prognosis in schizophrenia. *J. nerv. ment. Dis.,* 1953, **117**, 515–525.
57. Rapaport, D. *Diagnostic psychological testing: The theory, statistical evaluation, and diagnostic application of a battery of tests.* Chicago: Year Book Publ., 1945.
58. Raven, J. C. *Guide to using Progressive Matrices* (1938). London: Lewis, 1956. (U.S. distributor, Psychol. Corp.)
59. Rorschach, H. (Transl. by P. Lemkau and B. Kronenburg.) *Psychodiagnostics: A diagnostic test based on perception.* Berne: Huber, 1942. (1st German ed., 1921; U.S. distributor, Grune & Stratton.)
60. Rosenzweig, S. *Rosenzweig Picture-Frustration Study.* St. Louis, Mo.: Author, 1947–1949.
61. Sarason, S. B. *The clinical interaction, with special reference to the Rorschach.* New York: Harper & Row, 1954.
62. Sarason, S. B. *Psychological problems in mental deficiency.* (3rd ed.) New York: Harper & Row, 1959.
63. Sarbin, T. R., Taft, R., and Bailey, D. E. *Clinical inference and cognitive theory.* New York: Holt, Rinehart and Winston, 1960.
64. Shaffer, L. F., and Shoben, E. J., Jr. *The psychology of adjustment: A dynamic and experimental approach to personality and mental hygiene.* (2nd ed.) Boston: Houghton Mifflin, 1956.
65. Snygg, D., and Combs, A. W. *Individual behavior: A perceptual approach to behavior.* (Rev. ed.) New York: Harper & Row, 1959.
66. Stacey, C. L., and DeMartino, M. F. (Eds.) *Counseling and psychotherapy with the mentally retarded; a book of readings.* New York: Free Press, 1957.
67. Stephenson, W. *The study of behavior: Q-technique and its methodology.* Chicago: Univer. Chicago Press, 1953.
68. Sydiaha, D. On the equivalence of clinical and statistical methods. *J. appl. Psychol.,* 1959, **43**, 395–401.
69. Szasz, T. S. *The myth of mental illness.* New York: Hoeber-Harper, 1961.
70. Taft, R. The ability to judge people. *Psychol. Bull.,* 1955, **52**, 1–28.
71. Terman, L. M., and Merrill, Maud A. *Stanford-Binet Intelligence Scale: Manual for the third revision, Form L-M.* Boston: Houghton Mifflin, 1960.
72. Thigpen, C. H., and Cleckley, H. M. A case of multiple personality. *J. abnorm. soc. Psychol.,* 1954, **49**, 135–151.
73. Thigpen, C. H., and Cleckley, H. M. *The three faces of Eve.* New York: McGraw-Hill, 1957.
74. Thorne, F. C. Clinical judgment: A clinician's viewpoint. *J. clin. Psychol.,* 1960, **16**, 128–134.
75. Wainwright, W. H. Cultural attitudes and clinical judgment. *Int. J. soc. Psychiat.,* 1958, **4**, 105–107.
76. Wechsler, D. *Wechsler Intelligence Scale for Children.* New York: Psychol. Corp., 1949.
77. Wechsler, D. *Wechsler Adult Intelligence Scale.* New York: Psychol. Corp., 1955.
78. Wechsler, D. *The measurement and appraisal of adult intelligence.* (4th ed.) Baltimore: Williams & Wilkins, 1958.

79. Weider, A. (Ed.) *Contributions toward medical psychology.* Vol. 2. New York: Ronald, 1953.
80. Welsh, G. S., and Dahlstrom, W. G. (Eds.) *Basic readings on the MMPI in psychology and medicine.* Minneapolis: Univer. Minn. Press, 1956.
81. Windle, C. Psychological tests in psychopathological diagnosis. *Psychol. Bull.,* 1952, **49,** 451–482.
82. Wittenborn, J. R., Holzberg, J. D., and Simon, B. Symptom correlates for descriptive diagnosis. *Genet. Psychol. Monogr.,* 1953, **47,** 237–301.
83. Zubin, J., *et al.* A biometric approach to prognosis in schizophrenia. In P. H. Hoch and J. Zubin (Eds.), *Comparative epidemiology of the mental disorders.* New York: Grune & Stratton, 1961. Pp. 143–203.

# 14

## *Therapy*

Many kinds of therapy are used today in treating emotional disorders. The choice of therapy depends partly upon the nature and severity of the disorder and upon such client characteristics as age and intellectual level. To a considerable extent, however, the type of therapy employed reflects the training and theoretical persuasion of the therapist, the available facilities, and other extraneous factors. The same behavioral symptoms may be treated quite differently by different therapists; and several types of therapy may be combined in treating a single individual. There are very few forms of treatment that are wholly specific to a given emotional disorder. In psychology, as contrasted to medicine, one rarely if ever finds a disorder in which the diagnosis directly determines the treatment.

Evaluating the relative effectiveness of different forms of therapy for emotional disorders is very difficult. Some of the methodological problems presented by such evaluative studies will be illustrated in Chapter 15. For the present it should be noted that there is little conclusive evidence to demonstrate that one therapy is better than another for any given case, or even that any therapy is effective at all. Both clinical psychologists and psychiatrists are often in the position of applying a therapeutic procedure because they feel it will do no harm and may do some good. But there is no certainty about how well any given therapy will work or why. The rationale underlying different types of therapy varies from unknown to tentative. Since the practical demands of the situation call for some action, the therapist does the best he can within the available state of knowledge.

In the present chapter, the different approaches to therapy will be considered under four major headings: somatic therapies, environmental therapy, psychotherapy, and the preventive and positive measures represented by a comprehensive mental health point of view.

## SOMATIC THERAPIES

All somatic therapies are administered by a medical practitioner or under his immediate supervision. In the use of these therapies, psychologists may collaborate with physicians in several ways. The clinical psychologist may help in determining which patients are most likely to benefit from a particular therapy and in evaluating progress in the course of therapy. Sometimes psychotherapy, conducted by a psychologist, is combined with somatic therapy. In some cases, in fact, somatic therapy may be administered chiefly to make the patient more amenable to psychotherapy. Perhaps the most important contribution psychologists can make to the development of somatic therapies is in the area of research. The special methodological controls and experimental designs required in this type of research provide a fruitful field for the psychologically trained investigator. It is chiefly as background for some of the research problems to be considered in Chapter 15 that somatic therapies are introduced in this section.

Somatic therapies are themselves quite varied, being grouped together only because of their common medical nature (see 38). The introduction of a new somatic therapy usually arouses widespread optimism and exaggerated expectations, only to be followed by skepticism and a more sober evaluation. Some therapies that were popular one or two decades ago have been largely replaced by newer techniques. A few are currently in an exploratory stage. For example, some research has been conducted on the effects of nutritional therapy, involving the experimental administration of glutamic acid, selected vitamins, or other nutritive substances to both mentally retarded and emotionally disturbed subjects (3, 87). The results, although suggestive, are still inconclusive and controversial.

In the practical application of any somatic therapy, one must consider the likelihood of undesirable side effects, of either a physiological or psychological nature. Some side effects have been demonstrated with all the commonly used somatic therapies, although the incidence and severity of such effects vary with the individual patient, the dosage level, and other circumstances. Little is known, however, about the specific patient variables that determine the rather pronounced individual differences found both in side effects and in responsiveness to the various somatic therapies. Among the major somatic therapies are psychosurgery, shock therapy, and the many therapies covered by the broad area of psychopharmacology.

*Psychosurgery.* The results of animal experiments on the extirpation of brain tissue, as well as the observation that human personality changes sometimes followed brain injuries or the removal of frontal lobe tumors, led some neuropsychiatrists to try brain surgery in the treatment of emotional disorders (see 23, 38, 44, 90). Psychosurgery is a general name for the application of surgical techniques in treating functional, as contrasted to organic, disorders (see Chapter 13). Several specific procedures have been developed for this purpose. The original technique, commonly known as "lobotomy," involved the severing of the corticothalamic tracts that connect the thalamus with the frontal lobes of the cerebral cortex. Later variations limited the operation to more narrowly circumscribed areas and employed simpler surgical procedures.

Various combinations of neurological and psychological mechanisms have been proposed to account for the therapeutic effects of psychosurgery (see 90). Available evidence in support of any of these explanations is meager. The most clearly demonstrated effects are a reduction in anxiety and in emotional tension. Such improvement, however, may be accompanied by one or more undesirable effects, such as apathy, emotional flatness, decrease in drive and energy, irresponsibility, aggressiveness, poor judgment, impaired skill in problem solving, increase in perseverative responses, and loss in spontaneity. Such behavioral effects have been demonstrated through clinical observations of human patients, animal experiments, or both (90). Today psychosurgical techniques are considered only when other, less drastic forms of therapy have failed.

*Shock Therapy.* Under the general category of shock therapy are grouped a number of procedures for artificially inducing comatose or convulsive states. The specific techniques were usually suggested by accidental observations made either in the treatment of other disorders in human patients or in the course of animal experimentation. Although several hypotheses have been formulated to explain the rationale of such therapies, in either physiological or psychological terms, none has been conclusively established (14, 79). The principal agents currently employed in shock therapy are insulin and electricity.

*Insulin coma therapy* (38) is employed mainly with schizophrenics. In this treatment, insulin is administered in large enough doses to cause severe hypoglycemia, or sugar deficit in the blood. When the brain is thus deprived of its chief food, the individual sinks into a coma. He is allowed to remain in this condition for periods ranging up to about an hour, at which time the coma is terminated by the administration of sugar. The treatments are usually repeated daily over a few weeks. As the patient recovers from each comatose period, he exhibits confusion, amnesia, perceptual disorientation, and other disturbances, which gradually disappear.

In *electroconvulsive therapy* (ECT), convulsive seizures are induced by passing an electric current through the cerebral cortex (14, 38, 79). The patient feels no pain, since the electric shock produces unconsciousness immediately. The seizure lasts about a minute, but the patient usually remains stuporous for about an hour. Treatments are generally administered several times a week, the total duration of the series depending upon the patient's response to treatment and his rate of improvement. ECT is used chiefly with cases in which depression is either the principal feature or a major symptom. Severe impairment of memory is an immediate effect of the treatments but lessens gradually. Whether there is any permanent cognitive loss as a result of ECT or other types of shock therapy is difficult to ascertain because of inadequate controls in most investigations with human patients. Animal experiments, however, suggest that some permanent cognitive changes may occur (see 14, 79). In the decision to utilize any somatic therapy, the therapist must weigh the possibility of permanent deleterious side effects against the chances that the patient will remain in a seriously disturbed condition or even deteriorate if untreated.

**Psychopharmacology.** Drugs have been used in the treatment of mental disorders in many ways and for a long time (see 15, 38, 83, 84). Mention has already been made of insulin coma therapy. Prior to the introduction of electroshock, several drugs were also employed to induce convulsions. A different application of drugs is illustrated by *narcoanalysis*, in which psychotherapeutic techniques are introduced while the patient is in a narcotically induced trance. The relaxed state produced by the drug permits the patient to relive traumatic experiences that would otherwise have provoked too much anxiety.

Still another example is provided by the use of drugs in research on the nature of mental disorders, conducted with either animal subjects or normal volunteers (83; 84, ch. 1). Certain drugs, when administered to normal individuals, produce temporary symptoms similar to those found in psychotic patients. Because they "mimic" psychotic symptoms, these drugs have been named *psychotomimetic*. Since hallucinations are among their usual effects, they are also called "hallucinogens." Considerable research has centered around lysergic acid diethylamide (LSD), which induces schizophrenic-like symptoms, including disturbances of perception and thought, hallucinations, and mood changes.

Of all the psychoactive drugs, those that have aroused the strongest public interest are undoubtedly the so-called *tranquilizers*. In general, the effect of such drugs is to reduce anxiety and agitation. They are now widely used in mental hospitals to calm hyperactive and aggressive patients. As a result, there has been a sharp decline in the need for physical restraint, isolation, locked wards, and other traditional methods for controlling highly disturbed patients. It has also been reported that tranquilizers serve more specifically to counteract delusions, hallucinations, and other cognitive disorders (84, ch. 2).

Figure 100 shows the results of a five-year survey conducted in the state mental hospitals of New York (9, 10). The findings are typical of those obtained in other American state hospitals following the introduction of tranquilizers. It will be seen that, as the number of patients put on tranquilizing drugs rises, the number requiring restraint drops sharply. Beginning in the second year of drug therapy, the total state hospital population also declined. This decline resulted from an increase in the number of patients discharged as improved, rather than from changes in number of admissions. Representing the first reversal in the rising trend of American state mental hospital populations, this finding was particularly dramatic.

While indicating that the introduction of tranquilizers into overcrowded and understaffed mental hospitals was undoubtedly a wise move, this type of survey fails to identify the specific factors that brought about the improvement. The investigators themselves point out that during the last three years of the survey conspicuous administrative changes were made in the state hospitals. That these changes may themselves have been of primary therapeutic value will be seen

**Fig. 100**   Trends in adoption of tranquilizers, use of restraint, and total patient population in New York State mental hospitals, 1954–1959. (*From Brill and Patton, 10, p. 498.*)

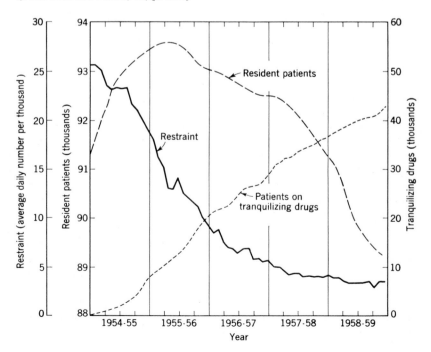

in the following section, dealing with environmental therapy. Even prior to the official innovations in hospital organization and procedures, the use of tranquilizers probably affected the attitudes of the hospital staff toward the patients. As patients become easier to manage, the behavior of the hospital personnel toward them takes on more constructive and therapeutic qualities. It has been observed, in fact, that the administration of tranquilizers to mental hospital patients may improve the behavior of the staff as much as that of the patients (35, p. 39).

Surveys such as the one cited illustrate forcefully the distinction between applied and basic research. Although the results are clear with regard to the introduction of tranquilizers within a specific context, with its peculiar complex of circumstances, they tell us little that can be generalized to other situations and other sets of circumstances. For the latter purpose, we need the highly controlled experimental designs to be considered in Chapter 15. In this connection it is relevant to note that tranquilizers have failed to produce such dramatic effects in other countries where the shift to therapeutic environments in mental hospitals had antedated the advent of tranquilizers (18, pp. 5–18; 35, p. 47; 83, pp. 681–682).

Any statistical survey of hospitalized populations, moreover, presents a number of methodological difficulties that preclude conclusive interpretation of results. It is possible, for example, that various social and economic developments may have reduced the total number of psychotics available for institutionalization. Such a decline may fail to show up in admission rates if more and more patients with milder disorders are admitted. Since milder disorders tend to have a higher recovery rate, however, such a trend *could* account at least in part for the increasing proportion of discharges and the resulting drop in mental hospital populations (56, 96).

Even the most enthusiastic exponents of tranquilizers recognize that not all types of cases are helped by these drugs. Among those who generally fail to improve or are adversely affected are depressed, apathetic, or withdrawn patients and deteriorated, passive schizophrenics (84). Another limitation in the application of tranquilizers arises from the occurrence of a number of adverse side effects, of both a medical and a behavioral nature. The latter range from sleepiness and drowsiness to severe motor symptoms including tremors and extreme stiffness. Little is as yet known about possible long-range or irreversible effects. All side effects, it should be noted, vary with the specific drug employed, the dosage, and the individual to whom it is administered. With small doses of the milder tranquilizers, side effects are negligible for most persons. From another angle, it has been cautioned that the indiscriminate use of tranquilizers may suppress anxiety below a desirable minimum and may thus reduce social sensitivity, ambition, and the restlessness that spurs one to constructive action.

There is some evidence to suggest that the difference in the effects of tranquilizers and of sedatives (such as the barbiturates) is one of degree (40). In larger doses, tranquilizers affect cognitive and psychomotor performance, alertness, and other psychological functions in much the same way as do sedatives. An important advantage of tranquilizers, however, is that they are not habit-forming to any significant degree. There are almost no reports of addiction to any of the tranquilizing drugs, although with very large doses of some tranquilizers withdrawal symptoms have been noted (84. ch. 7).

Mention should also be made of the more recently developed "psychic energizers," or antidepressants (84, ch. 3). These drugs are believed to be useful in the treatment of depressed patients. They should not be regarded as the opposites of tranquilizers, however, since the two types of drugs have several effects in common. Moreover, tranquilizers themselves do not represent a homogeneous class, since individual tranquilizers vary in many ways. The classification of such psychoactive drugs is not so simple as their popular names imply. Each drug needs to be examined individually with respect to therapeutic value, side effects, and other properties.

Despite the waves of enthusiasm that have greeted each new somatotherapy, there is no one "miracle cure" for mental disorders. The various somatic therapies described above continue to be used with different cases, the choice of specific therapy depending upon the nature of the disorder, individual patient characteristics, and other circumstances. Several therapies may be tried in turn with the same individual. Since so many mental disorders orginate in the individual's inability to cope with problems of daily life, somatic therapies are coming to be regarded more and more as adjuncts to psychotherapy. The psychoactive drugs, even more than earlier forms of somatic therapy, are used increasingly to render the withdrawn, uncommunicative, unresponsive, agitated, or aggressive patient accessible to psychotherapy. It should be borne in mind that to reduce the anxiety arising from unsolved problems is not in itself a solution.

## ENVIRONMENTAL THERAPY

Environmental therapy covers any manipulation of the client's environment outside of the formally scheduled therapeutic session. Its object is to improve the individual's behavioral adjustment by modifying physical or interpersonal aspects of his surroundings, or both. Environmental therapy may be applied within the ordinary contexts of daily life, such as home, school, and job, or within an institutional setting. Under the latter category are included some conspicuous innovations that are rapidly altering the psychological climate of mental hospitals.

*Environmental Therapy in Daily Life.*   Therapeutic environmental modifications are most commonly utilized with children, although in certain situations they are also useful as supplementary procedures with adult clients. Therapists differ in the extent of their active intervention in the client's outside activities. Nondirective therapists, for example, maintain that any efforts by the therapist to influence the client's outside environment would interfere with psychotherapy. Hence they limit their activities to the therapeutic hour itself. Some psychotherapists, on the other hand, make extensive use of environmental manipulation. Environmental therapy alone is rarely enough, however, since part of the difficulty usually lies within the individual. In some forms of psychotherapy, the client is given specific therapeutic tasks to perform or roles to assume outside of the therapeutic hour and is expected to report on the results during the subsequent session.

Environmental manipulations undertaken for therapeutic purposes may cover any phase of daily living. To reduce stress and provide a more wholesome milieu, the therapist may recommend a change of job or possibly a short vacation for an adult client. For a child, he may arrange a transfer to a different school or to another class within the same school. When the child's home is highly unfavorable and resistant to improvement, foster home placement may be indicated as a last resort. In other cases, the individual may be guided into recreational activities specially suited to his needs. Joining a club, going to camp, participating in sports, or cultivating a hobby might each have therapeutic value for a given individual.

An important aspect of environmental therapy involves counseling with significant persons in the client's life, such as parents, spouse, teachers, and employers. Modifying the attitudes of these associates toward the client and giving them a better understanding of his problems may go a long way toward reducing stress and interpersonal conflicts. In psychotherapy with children, it is customary to require one parent—and sometimes both—to meet regularly with a therapist. The latter may not be the same therapist who works with the child, but in that case both therapists work closely together. It sometimes happens that the parents are more in need of psychotherapy than the child and that the child's problems disappear when the parents resolve their own emotional difficulties.

Some environmental modifications may require the specialized resources of social service agencies. In environmental therapy, psychologists often collaborate closely with social workers. Furthermore, certain types of adjustment problems are commonly handled by social workers themselves, whose approach is characteristically that of environmental manipulation. Psychiatric caseworkers are social workers specially trained to work with maladjusted individuals.

**Institutional Environments.**   Institutionalization itself may be regarded as a form of environmental therapy. In an institution, it is possible to manipulate all aspects of the individual's environment for 24 hours a day. Until quite recently, however, institutions have been so organized as to serve principally a custodial rather than a therapeutic function. With their overcrowding and understaffing, their emphasis upon security and restraint, and their deadening inactivity, state mental hospitals have often contributed to the deterioration of chronic cases in the "back wards." Sitting idly on benches from morning till night is not therapeutic. The longer the individual lives in such a psychological vacuum, the farther he retreats from reality.

Today the atmosphere of mental hospitals is rapidly changing, as the concept of a *therapeutic community* replaces that of a custodial institution (18; 27; 29, pp. 218–222; 35, ch. 2; 57). This approach was first explored in institutions for children and adolescents, where the possibility of re-education and rehabilitation was more readily apparent (see, e.g., 7; 18, pp. 11–13). The decade of the 1950s saw its large-scale application in American state mental hospitals. Tranquilizers undoubtedly contributed much to the ensuing improvements in both staff attitudes and administrative practices. Locked wards were gradually abolished, and the "open hospital" became standard. Under these conditions, most patients became more tractable and less aggressive, and their general behavior improved rather than deteriorated. To what extent these changes resulted from the use of tranquilizing drugs and to what extent they resulted from institutional reorganization cannot be readily determined. It is certainly true that tranquilizers were introduced in American hospitals at a time when the mental health professions were ready for the many administrative innovations that were facilitated by these drugs.

The inactivity and custodial atmosphere typical of earlier institutions is giving way to *milieu therapy*. Essentially this therapy is an attempt to utilize all the patient's daily experiences for therapeutic purposes. Considerable emphasis is placed upon the cooperation of all hospital personnel who come in contact with patients, from the director of the hospital to ward attendants and janitors. The attitudes of staff members toward patients is a major aspect of milieu therapy. In this regard milieu therapy reflects the therapeutic utilization of interpersonal relations, which is characteristic of the chief forms of psychotherapy to be discussed in the next section.

Activity on the part of the patient is likewise stressed. In one form of milieu therapy, known as "total push" therapy, constant and varied activity is the predominant feature, even somatic therapies of various sorts being introduced largely for their psychological value (see 29, pp. 218–219; 65). Occupational, or work, therapy has long been recognized as an adjunct to other forms of treatment. In milieu therapy, it assumes more importance and becomes more highly diversified. Patients are given training and experience in vocational activities suited to their individual abilities. Working in sheltered workshops that are conducted along realistic lines affords direct preparation for returning to the outside community. Paying the patient for work he does while in the institution may have good motivational value and is a common practice in European hospitals. Recreational and social activities, like parties, outings, cookouts, motion pictures, art, music, and sports, are also part of the program. These activities provide practice in interpersonal contacts, as well as opportunities to be creative, to experience success, and to obtain other satisfactions. Trips and visits to theaters, museums, and other recreational resources help to reestablish contact with the outside community.

Treating each patient as an individual and boosting his morale by improving his own appearance and that of his surroundings are additional aspects of milieu therapy. Increasing emphasis is also being placed upon patient government, through regular group discussions, committees, and other techniques for patient participation in planning and decision making (18, pp. 129–146; 26).

Although all the above developments are examples of milieu therapy, the essential characteristic of this type of therapy is the utilization of all hospital resources in an integrated therapeutic program. What is included in the therapeutic program may vary widely from one institution or one ward to another. Somatic therapies and psychotherapy are often incorporated in the total program. Ideally the content of the program should be adapted to the needs of the individual patient. For some, a highly structured environment with rigid schedules may be desirable; for others, maximum freedom in the choice and scheduling of activities may be most effective. The nature of the specific activities would obviously vary as a function of individual patient characteristics. From another angle, size of institution and patient-staff ratio are limiting factors in milieu therapy.

In line with the current trend toward rehabilitation and resumption of normal community living, mention should also be made of the establishment of day hospitals, night hospitals, week-end hospitals, halfway houses, and other arrangements for partial institutional treatment (16; 18, pp. 163–176; 35, pp. 180–182; 42; 88; 93). In a *day hospital,* the patient reports for therapy from 9 to 5 on weekdays, while continuing to live in his own home. It is obvious that such an arrangement implies the application of milieu therapy. There would be no point in having patients come to the hospital to sit on benches from 9 to 5. Even less disruption of normal living is involved in the *night hospital,* which enables the patient to continue with his job or other regular daytime activities, while reporting to the hospital for treatment in the evenings. Depending upon his specific needs, the patient may remain overnight at the hospital or return home after the evening sessions. *Halfway houses* are designed to aid in the rehabilitation of former mental hospital patients and to facilitate their transition to community living. With developments such as these, the sharp distinction between inpatient and outpatient care is disappearing. Instead, there are now available a wide variety of therapeutic schedules, from a one-hour therapy session to complete hospitalization, which may be adapted to the needs of the individual patient.

## PSYCHOTHERAPY

**General Characteristics.** In the New York State certification law for psychologists, psychotherapy is defined as "the use of verbal methods in interpersonal relationships with the intent of assisting a person or persons to modify attitudes and behavior which are intellectually, socially, or emotionally maladaptive" (55, p. 50). Elsewhere psychotherapy has been described as "a series of very specialized conversations with a skilled clinician" (69, p. 514). To be sure, psychotherapy is not always strictly verbal, especially when applied to young children; but it always involves some means of communication between therapist and client.

Regardless of their theoretical persuasion, practically all clinical psychologists today agree that the *interpersonal relationship* between therapist and client is an important element in psychotherapy—if not the most important. The personality of the clinician and his behavior toward the client during the session are thus an integral part of the therapeutic process. It is also generally recognized that psychotherapy is a *learning process.* The individual acquired his maladaptive responses through past learning; psychotherapy offers him a method for unlearning these responses and replacing them with new responses of a more adaptive nature.

The general nature of the client-therapist relationship was described briefly in Chapter 13, in connection with the question of rapport in clinical interviewing. Essentially, this relationship can be characterized as warm, nonthreatening, accepting, and permissive. In his interactions with the therapist, the individual gradually discovers that, no matter what he says, he will not be criticized, blamed, or rejected. The strict confidentiality observed also reassures him that his behavior during the therapy hour will lead to no aversive consequences in his daily life. The therapeutic relationship thus provides a "safe" situation in which the individual can try out new interpersonal behavior. In this respect, the clinician serves the same function as the training devices and simulators used in flight training. The learner can make mistakes without danger to himself. The client's interaction with the therapist helps him to understand his reactions to people in general and enables him to develop new ways of feeling and thinking about himself and others.

Several psychologists have tried to explain the process of psychotherapy in terms of learning principles (5; 20; 29, ch. 7; 50; 69, ch. 16; 71; 72; 94; 95).

Since psychologists differ in their theoretical orientation with regard to both learning and psychotherapy, no one explanation would find general acceptance. It should also be borne in mind that therapeutic procedures developed largely on an empirical basis; it was only later that theoretical rationales were formulated to support them. A few examples will suffice to illustrate how learning theory has been applied to psychotherapy.

A major goal of all psychotherapy is the overcoming of anxieties and the elimination of defenses built up against these anxieties in the form of behavioral symptoms. Within the context of a secure and emotionally satisfying therapeutic relationship, the client is encouraged to verbalize his anxieties and the situations that led to them. Talking about an anxiety-provoking situation approximates the experience of reliving it. The symbolic, verbal reinstatement of the situation arouses much of the anxiety associated with the situation itself (see 51). Through the processes of extinction and counterconditioning, the original responses to these situations tend to disappear and are replaced by the more positive affective responses of security and confidence aroused by the therapeutic situation. Through stimulus generalization, these newly acquired responses tend to be evoked by similar situations subsequently encountered outside of therapy (69, ch. 16). The individual may also develop a generalized learning set that will make him better able to solve emotional and interpersonal problems in the future (47).

In psychotherapy, timing is important. If too much anxiety is aroused early in therapy, conditioning may occur in the wrong direction. The therapeutic situation itself might thus become anxiety-provoking and intolerable for the client. Anxiety must be aroused very gradually and only after a sufficiently secure therapeutic relationship has been established. As the client overcomes his initial anxiety and learns to cope with it, he can safely progress to a consideration of situations evoking more severe anxiety. As anxiety is reduced, the individual is able to examine his problems rationally and work out more effective ways of handling them (20, ch. 14).

In the course of therapy, the client's self concept also tends to change in a favorable direction. Under the influence of the therapist's accepting attitude, the client experiences a growing sense of his own personal worth. Insofar as this response generalizes to other persons he encounters outside of the therapeutic situation, the client will exhibit more confidence and security in interpersonal relations. There is evidence to suggest that feelings of personal worth tend to be accompanied by a more favorable evaluation of others (see, e.g., 70, 81). These newly aroused attitudes on the client's part will in turn elicit more favorable responses from his associates. Hence a cycle of positive behavior and reinforcement is started in the individual's real-life experiences whereby the effects of therapy are further generalized.

One might ask why verbalizations are used to mediate the conditioning that occurs during psychotherapy. Why not work directly with the maladaptive behavior we are trying to eliminate? The answer is that we can, if the behavior is of the sort that can be readily evoked in the therapeutic situation. Extinction and counterconditioning have been successfully applied to the elimination of phobias, compulsions, motor tics, and other specific symptoms (see 5, 94, 95). In a classical early experiment (36), a child's fear of furry objects was overcome by having a rabbit in the room while the child was eating. During the initial sessions, of course, anxiety had to be minimized by keeping the rabbit caged and at a distance and by leaving him in the room only a short time. After repeated sessions, fear responses were eliminated, not only to the rabbit, but also to other furry objects, through stimulus generalization.

The traditional objection to such an approach is that it treats the "symptoms" rather than the "cause." This objection, however, seems to be based on an inappropriate analogy with organic disease. A toothache is only an indicator of dental decay. But in behavior disorders the maladaptive responses themselves constitute the disorder. This distinction provides a further example of the inapplicability of the disease analogue to psychological disorders (see Chapter 13). It is the object of therapy to change the maladaptive responses (see 5, 22, 50). Whether such behavioral changes can be effected more successfully when the responses are regarded as "symptoms" of some underlying adjustment mechanism remains to be demonstrated. These "underlying mechanisms" are, after all, unverified hypotheses contributed by the therapist, rather than observable facts contributed by the client.

**Scope of Psychotherapy.** Many clinical psychologists set a number of limitations upon the type of client they will accept for psychotherapy (see 8, ch. 5; 20, ch. 15). The requirements vary considerably with the theoretical orientation of the therapist and the form of psychotherapy he practices. Because of the heavy reliance upon verbal communication in most types of psychotherapy, minimum educational and intellectual levels are often specified. Background factors that would affect the client's motivation for therapy are sometimes considered. The various indices for predicting response to therapy that were cited in Chapter 13 are also relevant in this connection. Psychotherapy has been traditionally employed with neurotics and with essentially normal persons who want help with some of their emotional problems. More recently, however, there has been a growing interest in the application of psychotherapy to schizophrenics and other severely disturbed cases (13, 17). It will be recalled that somatic therapies have been used increasingly for the purpose of making psychotics accessible to psychotherapy.

Surveys of the relationship between type of therapy employed and patient variables have consistently shown that socioeconomic level is an important factor (11; 32, ch. 9; 33; 64). The higher the individual's socioeconomic level, the greater are his chances of being accepted for psychotherapy in outpatient clinics, of being assigned to a relatively experienced therapist, and of continuing in therapy. Patients in lower socioeconomic levels are more likely to receive somatic or simply custodial treatment than psychotherapy. These differences remain even when cost, availability of therapists, and similar extraneous factors are ruled out.

Since socioeconomic level is itself related to educational and intellectual levels, the latter factors undoubtedly account in part for the more limited use of psychotherapy with lower-class patients. Another contributing factor is the discrepancy between the socioeconomic levels of therapist and client. The more similar the client's and therapist's cultural backgrounds are, the easier it will be for the therapist to understand and communicate with the client (11, 86, 92). The concept of assumed similarity discussed in Chapter 13 may be recalled in this connection. Still another reason is to be found in the motivations, attitudes, and expectations of persons in different socioeconomic levels. Motivation for therapy will tend to be higher when the patient has more to look forward to in terms of vocational achievement, social status, and other tangible rewards of improved emotional adjustment (20, ch. 15). Persons in higher socioeconomic levels tend to perceive therapy as a means of maintaining status in their immediate social environment (33). They also have a better understanding of psychotherapy and a more rationalistic approach to their emotional problems than do persons in lower socioeconomic levels. The latter are more likely to perceive their emotional disorders as a disease for which they expect a quick-acting, somatic remedy (11; 32, ch. 11; 92).

So far we have concentrated upon the common features of psychotherapy. Even these features, however, are more characteristic of some forms of psychotherapy than of other forms. In the field of psychotherapy, "schools" still thrive. There are currently many varieties of psychotherapy, each with its loyal adherents (8, 12, 30, 80). One recent survey listed 36 different systems (30). It is heartening to note, however, that the trend is toward eclecticism. Well-trained clinical psychologists recognize that different forms of psychotherapy may be required for different clients and that no one form is universally to be preferred. In a survey of the members of the APA Division of Clinical Psychology, conducted in 1960, 49 per cent of those engaged in psychotherapy described their orientation as "eclectic" (45). Like its clients, psychotherapy itself becomes better integrated as it grows toward maturity.

To illustrate more fully what psychotherapists do, we shall briefly examine in the next two sections two of its most widely practiced forms, namely, psychoanalysis and client-centered therapy. Although psychotherapy is predominantly individual and verbal in its techniques, two important procedural variants are group therapy and play therapy. Each may be employed by clinicians with widely varying theoretical orientations. These procedures will be considered in the last two sections.

**Psychoanalysis.** The theory and techniques of psychoanalysis originated during the last quarter of the nineteenth century in the work of Sigmund Freud, a Viennese physician who became interested in the treatment of emotional problems (see 52, chs. 22 and 23). Freud's approach to these problems still provides the general framework for psychoanalysis, although many changes in specific therapeutic procedures and in theoretical rationale have been introduced (see 20; 29, ch. 4; 69, ch. 14). The principal object of psychoanalysis is to uncover repressed impulses and forgotten experiences that are believed to underlie present behavioral symptoms. The client is thereby given an insight into possible causes of his maladaptive behavior. He is also enabled to relive emotionally the incidents in which the repression occurred. As he becomes aware of his repressed impulses in a context of reduced anxiety, he is able to bring them under rational control. In the classical psychoanalysis of Freud, the origins of emotional difficulties were traced to early childhood experiences. Among neoanalysts, the causes of symptoms are more often sought in the individual's present interpersonal relations. Partly for this reason, the newer psychoanalytic therapies generally require less time than classic psychoanalysis, a condition which makes them applicable to a wider range of clients.

Among the special techniques employed by psychoanalysts are free association and dream analysis. In the former, the client is asked to report everything that comes to mind; nothing is to be held back, however irrelevant, absurd, or embarrassing it may seem. To facilitate such free association, the client traditionally reclined on a couch, with the analyst seated outside his field of vision. Today the procedure is more flexible: the client may sit, lie down, or walk around as he wishes. Although the couch has remained the symbol of psycho-analysis in popular thinking, some contemporary analysts have discarded it altogether. Dream analysis is utilized by psychoanalysts as another source of cues to unconscious or repressed impulses, which, they maintain, appear in dreams in disguised and symbolic form. The dreams reported by the client may be interpreted directly by the analyst in terms of common psychoanalytic symbols, or they may serve as the starting point for further free association by the client.

With regard to the client-therapist relationship, psychoanalysts emphasize the process of transference. By "transference" is meant that in the course of therapy the patient identifies the therapist with a parent or some other important person in his life and projects upon him the emotions he feels toward that person. These feelings may be positive, such as dependence and love, or negative, such as hostility and antagonism. The therapist uses the transference relation-ship as a device to help the client relive his earlier emotional experiences. As the treatment progresses, the transference itself is gradually terminated by explaining its source to the client.

It is apparent that active interpretation by the therapist is a major feature of psychoanalysis. The analyst interprets the client's dreams, his casual re-marks and slips of the tongue, the apparently irrelevant content of his free associations, and the feelings the client expresses toward the analyst himself. When resistance is encountered in free association, he interprets it as evidence of repression and calls the client's attention to the defenses he is using against anxiety-provoking content. By bringing together disparate bits of information that the client provides, the analyst offers him an explanation of the source of his symptoms. In building up such an explanation, the psychoanalyst asks probing questions to elicit additional facts. All too often the inquiry may take the form of what Sarbin and his associates describe as "soliciting" rather than "probing" (see ch. 13). There is thus a danger that the resulting ex-planation will reflect the psychoanalyst's theoretical views more closely than it does the personality dynamics of the particular client.

In its early forms, psychoanalytic theory was expressed largely in terms of crude physical analogies and figures of speech. Most of its propositions were so formulated as to be untestable. For instance, if a client agreed with the analyst's interpretation of a symptom, that was regarded as supporting evidence of the correctness of the explanation; if he disagreed with it, his reaction was attributed to repression of anxiety-evoking material. With such a highly sub-jective approach, it is little wonder that different schools of psychoanalysis quickly developed, each with its highly partisan protagonists.

In its later evolution, psychoanalysis has moved closer to the science of psychology. Its language has become less fanciful, and its claims are more often verifiable—even though still largely unverified. A promising beginning has been made by some psychologists in their attempts to explain psycho-analytic concepts and procedures in terms of learning theory (see, e.g., 20). Such reformulations make it possible to design experiments to test psycho-analytic hypotheses. Examples of this type of research will be considered in Chapter 15.

**Client-centered Therapy.** Also known as "nondirective counseling," client-centered therapy was first described in 1942 by Carl R. Rogers, an American psychologist (58, 59, 60). In contrast to psychoanalysis, client-centered therapy reduces interpretation by the therapist to a minimum (82). The basic postulate of client-centered therapy is that the individual has the capacity to identify the sources of his emotional problems and to work out effective solutions, once he is freed from disabling anxieties and feelings of insecurity. To accomplish this goal, the client-centered therapist establishes a permissive, accepting, non-threatening therapeutic relationship. He refrains from probing, interpreting, advising, persuading, or suggesting. He serves the function of an active listener, trying to understand fully what the client says and feels, and making every effort to perceive situations from the client's point of view.

An important part of the therapist's task is to reflect and clarify the client's feelings by restating the client's remarks. This clarification of feeling is illustrated in the following excerpt from a recorded interview with a young woman of twenty. The excerpt begins near the end of the first interview (77, pp. 139–141).[1]

*Cl.* I realize, of course, that it all began a long time ago—because everything begins somewhere. I wasn't just—somehow or other something failed somewhere along the line. And I guess we sort of have to get at it, a sort of re-education. But I don't feel as though I can do it myself.

*Th.* You realize that the roots must go a long way back, and that at some point you will have to start in reworking it, but you're not sure whether you can do it.

*Cl.* That's right. (*Pause*) It's just the idea that I can see myself going through life this way, fifty, sixty, and seventy years old—still thinking these horrible thoughts. And it just doesn't seem worthwhile—I mean, it's so ridiculous. While everybody else is going their way and living life, I'm sort of at the edge, and looking on. It just isn't right.

*Th.* The future doesn't look very bright when you look at it that way.

*Cl.* No. (*Long pause*) I know I'm lacking in courage, that's the big thing I'm lacking. That must be it, 'cause other people aren't swayed so easily. It's a funny thing, though—when I think of those—those qualities, I always think of them, I don't know, not as realities, but as something that's far off somewhere. It's a hard thing to explain these things. It's just as though—it's—it's true but I laugh at it in a way. Sort of a feeling that I am sort of sneering at it—but I know it must be true 'cause other people go around expressing those things. It's a very confused feeling.

*Th.* Logically, you realize that courage is one of your deficiencies, but inside yourself you find yourself laughing at that notion and feeling that it doesn't really have anything to do with you. Is that it?

*Cl.* That's right. I always sort of make myself different. That's it.

*Th.* M-hm. You sort of say that might apply to other people but it's not for you because you're different.

*Cl.* I don't know whether that's exactly right or not. I can't put my finger on it. Sometimes I feel lonely and sometimes I feel another way. Do you have cases this bad?

*Th.* You really wonder whether anybody else could be—

*Cl.* I think I'm worse than anybody that I know. That's just it. I feel as though I am terribly, terribly low. It just does not seem worth—bothering with it, it doesn't seem worthwhile, that I can't get up there to first base.

*Th.* You think about making the struggle, but it doesn't seem possible.

*Cl.* That's right. I just wonder what other people do when they find problems and stuff. I just wonder whether they see it through or try to find out something else.

*Th.* You feel that you'd like to know how somebody else would handle it.

[1] Cl. stands for "client," Th. for "therapist."

Through systematic analyses of recorded interviews, client-centered therapists have conducted extensive research on the therapeutic process itself (61, 67, 70, 76, 81). These studies indicate that in the course of client-centered therapy there is an increase in the number of statements showing insight and self-understanding, as well as in statements regarding client plans and decisions. Similarly, a comparison of early and late therapeutic sessions shows an increase in number of statements expressing positive attitudes toward self and a decrease in statements expressing negative attitudes toward self. The individual's self concept comes to resemble his ideal concept more closely in the course of therapy. Acceptance of others and respect for others also increase with the growing acceptance of oneself. The methodology of these studies and their broader implications regarding the effectiveness of therapy will be considered in Chapter 15.

**Group Therapy.** Although group activities and group discussions were utilized therapeutically in different settings since the beginning of the century, the widespread adoption of current methods of group psychotherapy dates from World War II (29, ch. 10; 31; 39; 54; 74). First introduced as a means of coping with a shortage of therapists, group therapy was soon seen to have a number of intrinsic advantages. In its most usual form, it has much in common with individual psychotherapy. A group of 5 to 10 persons meet once or twice a week for several months to discuss their emotional problems. The therapist, who serves as discussion leader, tries to create a permissive atmosphere that reduces resistance and defensiveness. Each participant describes his own experiences and difficulties as he feels inclined and comments upon the experiences of other group members. An informal atmosphere is maintained, with group members sitting around a table or in some other casual grouping.

Most persons are eventually able to relive emotionally charged experiences as well in group therapy as they can in individual therapy—and sometimes better. Recognizing that others have similar problems enables them to consider their own problems more objectively. Participation in group therapy helps to break down feelings of isolation so common among emotionally disturbed persons. It also gives the individual a more extensive and realistic field in which to practice interpersonal behavior than is provided by individual psychotherapy.

To insure maximal effectiveness, participants in group therapy are usually screened for various characteristics, and groups are assembled with special reference to age and sex distribution, type of problems, and other relevant variables. Group therapy may be employed exclusively or in combination with individual psychotherapy. When the two approaches are combined, they may run parallel or individual psychotherapy may be used in advance to prepare the client for group therapy.

There are fully as many varieties of group as of individual psychotherapy. The therapist may play a very active role in steering discussion and interpreting member reactions; or he may be nondirective, limiting his remarks to acceptance, restatement of content, and clarification of feelings. Psychoanalytically oriented group therapists utilize transference reactions, which develop not only toward the therapist but also toward other group members.

Group therapy has been employed with special groups, such as members of a single family, mothers of emotionally disturbed children, or former patients who meet periodically for mutual support and continuing therapeutic experiences. Such well-known national groups as Alcoholics Anonymous (43) and Recovery, Inc. (89) employ some form of group therapy. The latter organization was founded in 1937 by recovered patients who had been treated at the Psychiatric Institute of the University of Illinois Medical School. Group therapy may also be combined with other group activities. In one Veterans Administration hospital, for example, a *group living program* was introduced, in which small, family-like groups of schizophrenics participated for several months in a joint program of social, educational, recreational, and work activities, as well as in group psychotherapy (91). Results were promising when compared with those of somatic therapies and of a traditional institutional activity program.

*Psychodrama* (48) is a variant of group therapy. In this technique, the client acts out unrehearsed parts on a stage, with other clients in the audience. The therapist usually assigns roles, directs the performance, and interprets the individual's behavior. Supporting parts are played by therapeutic assistants or by other clients. The individual may play himself in realistic situations from his daily life; he may play the roles of other persons in his life, such as his father; or he may improvise imagined roles. Psychodrama is designed to provide emotional release as well as self-insight. Role playing is a simplified version of psychodrama which does not require a theatrical setting or special props. It is used with clinical groups, as well as in certain types of training, some of which were illustrated in Chapter 5.

**Play Therapy.** Because children have difficulty in verbalizing their emotional problems, play therapy is often employed in either individual or group form (4, 21, 25, 49). In the play session, the child has an opportunity to act out his anxieties, hostilities, aggressions, and other disturbing feelings. Among the media utilized for this purpose are puppets, dolls, toy furniture, clay, sand, and finger paints.

Therapy sessions are usually conducted in a room that is as indestructibly furnished as possible, and the child is allowed to do what he wishes, within broad limits. Through his accepting and nonthreatening manner, the therapist establishes a warm, secure interpersonal relationship with the child, just as he does in the verbal interaction with adult clients. In this safe context, the child obtains emotional release from his manipulations of the play materials. With the aid of interpretations or clarification by the therapist, the child may also gain insight into his own motives and feelings.

Figure 101 shows a little girl caring for a baby doll in play therapy. Using dolls that represent mother, father, and siblings, the child can enact family themes revealing attitudes that she would have difficulty in communicating verbally.

# THE MENTAL HEALTH MOVEMENT

The mental health movement is a broad social movement that has been gaining momentum since World War II. Its recent upsurge is characterized by a growing public awareness of mental health problems, governmental support of mental health activities, and the cooperative efforts of several professional specialties, including medicine, psychology, and social work. A significant development within this movement was the enactment of the

*Fig. 101*  A child using dolls in play therapy. (*From Ginott, 25, p. 54.*)

Mental Health Study Act of 1955 by the Congress of the United States and its implementation by the Joint Commission on Mental Illness and Health (35). With the help of 36 participating organizations representing many disciplines, this Commission conducted extensive investigations of the country's mental health problems and available resources for meeting them and submitted a set of recommendations for action.

Although the term "mental health" has misleading connotations, it has become so strongly associated with the movement that it would be difficult to replace it with a more precise expression, such as "effective behavior" (2, 75). It seems more expedient to redefine the term within its present context. The current mental health movement is characterized not only by renewed efforts to treat and rehabilitate severely disturbed cases but also by an increased emphasis on prevention, on the development of positive mental health, and on a comprehensive approach that encompasses all aspects of daily life. Because of its special concern with preventive measures and its broad social orientation, the mental health movement is logically an aspect of the general public health movement.

**Prevention.**  One of the objectives of the mental health movement is to increase facilities for identifying and treating mild and incipient disorders. Known as "secondary prevention," this approach tries to reach the individual before he develops more serious difficulties. Community mental health clinics for outpatient treatment are an important resource for this purpose. The Joint Commission report (35, p. xii) calls attention to another potential source of help for referral and for direct handling of minor problems, namely, the persons to whom individuals in trouble generally turn and those in a position to spot trouble in its early stages. Examples include clergymen, family physicians, teachers, public welfare workers, scoutmasters, and many others. Short training courses and the availability of professionally trained mental health consultants would enable these persons to function more effectively in their role of "mental health counselors."

An exploratory survey conducted in a lower-class district in New York City was concerned with the ability to recognize mental illness and the recommendations and referral practices of community leaders in various fields (19). A number of significant differences were found among leaders in different fields, such as religion, education, business, and politics. Although necessarily limited in its findings, this study illustrates the kind of information that is needed in planning for the better utilization of community leaders in mental health activities.

Still another way to encourage secondary prevention is to modify public attitudes toward emotional disorders—an admittedly difficult task. Several well-conducted attitude surveys have demonstrated that emotionally disturbed persons still encounter widespread social rejection (35, ch. 3; 53). By the very nature of their difficulties, such persons lack social appeal. They are likely to be uncooperative or hostile even toward those who try to help them. Their behavior often estranges them from family and friends. Their social rejection engenders further withdrawal and hostility, which in turn lead to more rejection in a continuing cycle. Breaking this cycle, it will be recalled, is one of the objects of psychotherapy. Unfortunately, the social stigma that still attaches to "mental illness" makes the mildly troubled individual reluctant to seek professional help and makes his associates hesitate to recommend it. That attitudes toward the mentally disturbed *can* be altered, however, is illustrated by the excellent work done through the college student volunteer program with highly deteriorated state hospital patients (35, pp. 88–93; 85).

A more direct attack, of course, is through primary prevention, i.e., the prevention of even minor difficulties that need professional help. This objective requires that the experiences of persons in general—especially in childhood —be so structured as to strengthen their ability to withstand the strains and stresses of daily living. It has been repeatedly observed that mental health is a way of reacting to problems rather than an absence of problems (6; 28; 35, ch. 4; 75). Happy, well-adjusted persons may have many worries, but they know how to cope with them.

***Positive Mental Health.*** There is an increasing interest in the positive goal of attaining mental health as contrasted to the purely negative goal of avoiding mental illness (34, 37, 75). The range of persons that the mental health movement tries to reach is thus greatly extended. It is clear that many essentially normal persons have emotional problems with which they can be helped. Surveys of random samples of the general population have repeatedly revealed a high incidence of emotional problems (28, 78). In one of the studies sponsored by the Joint Commission, for example, a representative nationwide sample of American adults living at home was intensively interviewed (28). In this group of approximately twenty-five hundred persons, nearly one respondent in four said he had at some time had an emotional or interpersonal problem for which professional help would have been useful. Only one in seven, however, had actually sought help. And, of these, 42 per cent had consulted clergymen, 29 per cent general physicians, 18 per cent psychiatrists or psychologists, and 10 per cent social agencies or marriage clinics.

An even more important aspect of the present focus on positive mental health is the recognition that mental health means more than freedom from emotional difficulties. Several attempts have been made to define mental health in terms of active attainment of important goals rather than mere adjustment (see, e.g., 34, 37, 46, 68, 73, 75). In this connection, it should be noted that any definition of either mental illness or mental health implies value judgments (see 41, 66, 75). With regard to the negative end of the scale there is considerable agreement, at least within a given culture. Thus most persons in contemporary Western civilization would agree on the maladaptive and undesirable nature of such behavior deviations as violent acts of aggression, hallucinations and delusions, or the sort of intellectual disorganization that makes it impossible to attend school or hold a job. With regard to the positive end of the scale, however, values differ more widely among groups and among individuals.

Definitions of mental health inevitably reflect these differences in values, although some may evade the problem by their vagueness. Mental health has been variously described in such terms as creativity, spontaneity in interpersonal relations, integrated personality, correct perception of oneself and of one's environment, autonomy, self-actualization and continued growth, richness of experience, and active mastery of environment. These are undoubtedly worthy values, but others could easily be added to the list. In specific situations, moreover, some values may conflict with others, thus requiring judgments of relative strength. Nondirective, or client-centered, therapists have come closest to defining mental health without reference to a specific value system (62). Essentially, their object is to free the individual from debilitating tensions and anxieties so that he may more effectively pursue his own goals. One cannot escape the fact, however, that even this goal of individual freedom represents a prior value judgment on the part of the therapist. Moreover, the individual's own values reflect the earlier influences to which he was exposed in home, church, school, and community.

We need to recognize that mental health may be attained in very different ways by different persons. And we need to recognize that the value systems presupposed by these varying concepts of mental health lie outside the domain of science. To be sure, scientific research can help in clarifying and in implementing values. It can, for instance, reveal cultural differences in value systems and the variables associated with such differences. It can also help to make explicit the values underlying an individual's behavior. This knowledge should increase the individual's ability to make his choices deliberately rather than by default.

**Comprehensive Approach.**   It is apparent that both the prevention of emotional disorders and the fostering of positive mental health as now envisaged require a broad, comprehensive program. Among the fields encompassed by such a program are family life, education, and employee relations. Training programs for marriage and parenthood provide an opportunity for improving not only child-rearing practices but also all interpersonal relations within the family. The schools can contribute much to mental health through both curricular and extracurricular activities, interpersonal relations of the child with his peers, and teacher-pupil relations. Much of what was said in Chapter 6 regarding employee relations, supervisory practices, and organizational structure is obviously relevant to the promotion of mental health. Some exponents of the mental health movement think in even broader terms, to include community development and the application of mental health principles to large-scale social planning. Crime, delinquency, and even war, they argue, are in part problems of mental health. We can certainly grant that such conditions represent malfunctions in interpersonal systems, to borrow a concept from engineering psychology.

What roles can the psychologist play in this far-flung program? Thoughtful analyses of the psychologist's unique pattern of qualifications suggest that he can serve best through research and consultation (2, 24, 35, 63). Research, both basic and applied, is urgently needed in the area of mental health. Although much is being done in the effort to alleviate emotional disturbance and to promote positive mental health, there is little objective evidence regarding the effectiveness of any specific procedures.

With regard to service functions, the professionally trained psychological consultant, working through practitioners in other fields with a minimum of mental health training, can greatly extend his sphere of operations. There is a vast discrepancy between the need for mental health services and the trained manpower available to meet this need (1). Consequently, direct work with single clients, as in individual psychotherapy, can reach only a very small proportion of persons requiring psychological services. Even apart from this personnel shortage, however, it is likely that psychologists will function increasingly as mental health consultants in the future. The growing emphasis on prevention and on positive mental health would seem to point in this direction.

## SUMMARY

The many kinds of available therapies for treating emotional disorders may be grouped under somatic therapies, environmental therapies, psychotherapy, and preventive mental health procedures. Somatic therapies, requiring the services of a licensed physician, are illustrated by psychosurgery, shock therapies, and various applications of psychopharmacology. The introduction of tranquilizers has led to a spectacular rise in the recovery rate of American state mental hospital patients. A major factor in these results appears to be the role of tranquilizers in making patients more amenable to psychotherapy and indirectly improving staff morale. Other, more direct effects of such drugs have not yet been conclusively established in adequately controlled experiments. Environmental therapy includes the therapeutic manipulation of environmental factors, both in daily life (such as home, school, job, and recreational contexts) and in institutions. A growing emphasis on milieu therapy is rapidly transforming mental hospitals from custodial institutions to therapeutic communities.

Psychotherapy is practiced in many forms, reflecting the varied theoretical orientations of the therapists. In the most general terms, it can be described as the use of verbal or other means of communication in a nonthreatening interpersonal situation which facilitates the alleviation of anxiety and the elimination of maladaptive behavior through a learning process. Two widely used types of psychotherapy are psychoanalysis and client-centered therapy. Group therapy is being employed increasingly, either in place of individual psychotherapy or in conjunction with it. Psychodrama and role playing are special variants of group therapy. Play therapy is commonly utilized with children, in lieu of the predominantly verbal techniques employed with adults. The current mental health movement is concerned not only with the treatment and rehabilitation of institutionalized mental patients but also with preventive measures and with the fostering of positive mental health through comprehensive social and educational programs.

# REFERENCES

1. Albee, G. W. *Mental health manpower trends.* New York: Basic Books, 1959.
2. American Psychological Association, Ad Hoc Planning Group on the Role of the APA in Mental Health Programs and Research. Mental health and the American Psychological Association. *Amer. Psychologist,* 1959, **14**, 820–825.
3. Astin, A. W., and Ross, S. Glutamic acid and human intelligence. *Psychol. Bull.,* 1960, **57**, 429–434.
4. Axline, Virginia M. *Play therapy.* Boston: Houghton Mifflin, 1947.
5. Bandura, A. Psychotherapy as a learning process. *Psychol. Bull.,* 1961, **58**, 143–159.
6. Barron, F. *Personal soundness in university graduate students.* Berkeley, Calif.: Univer. Calif. Press, 1954.
7. Bettelheim, B., and Sylvester, Emmy. Milieu therapy: Indications and illustrations. *Psychoanal. Rev.,* 1949, **36**, 54–68.
8. Brammer, L. M., and Shostrom, E. L. *Therapeutic psychology: Fundamentals of counseling and psychotherapy.* Englewood Cliffs, N.J.: Prentice-Hall, 1960.
9. Brill, H., and Patton, R. E. Analysis of 1955–1956 population fall in New York State mental hospitals in first year of large-scale use of tranquilizing drugs. *Amer. J. Psychiat.,* 1957, **114**, 509–517.
10. Brill, H., and Patton, R. E. Analysis of population reduction in New York State mental hospitals during the first four years of large-scale therapy with psychotropic drugs. *Amer. J. Psychiat.,* 1959, **116**, 495–509.
11. Brill, N. Q., and Storrow, H. A. Social class and psychiatric treatment. *Arch. gen. Psychiat.,* 1960, **3**, 340–344.
12. Burton, A. (Ed.) *Case studies in counseling and psychotherapy.* Englewood Cliffs, N.J.: Prentice-Hall, 1959.
13. Burton, A. (Ed.) *Psychotherapy of the psychoses.* New York: Basic Books, 1961.
14. Campbell, D. The psychological effects of cerebral electroshock. In H. J. Eysenck (Ed.), *Handbook of abnormal psychology.* New York: Basic Books, 1961. Ch. 16.
15. Cole, J. O., and Gerard, R. W. (Eds.) *Psychopharmacology: Problems in evaluation.* (NAS-NRC Publ. No. 583) Washington: Nat. Acad. Sci.–Nat. Res. Coun., 1959.
16. Craft, M. Psychiatric day hospitals. *Amer. J. Psychiat.,* 1959, **116**, 251–254.
17. Dawson, J. G., Stone, H. K., and Dellis, N. P. (Eds.) *Psychotherapy with schizophrenics.* Baton Rouge, La.: La. State Univer., 1961.
18. Denber, H. C. B. *Research conference on therapeutic community held at Manhattan State Hospital, Ward's Island, New York.* Springfield, Ill., Thomas, 1960.
19. Dohrenwend, B. P. Some aspects of the appraisal of abnormal behavior by leaders in an urban area. *Amer. Psychologist,* 1962, **17**, 190–198.
20. Dollard, J., and Miller, N. E. *Personality and psychotherapy: An analysis in terms of learning, thinking, and culture.* New York: McGraw-Hill, 1950.
21. Dorfman, Elaine. Play therapy. In C. R. Rogers, *Client-centered therapy: Its current practice, implications, and theory.* Boston: Houghton Mifflin, 1951. Ch. 6.
22. Eysenck, H. J. *The dynamics of anxiety and hysteria.* New York: Praeger, 1957.

23. Freeman, W., and Watts, J. *Psychosurgery in the treatment of mental disorders and pain.* Springfield, Ill.: Thomas, 1950.
24. Gelfand, S., and Kelly, J. G. The psychologist in community mental health. *Amer. Psychologist,* 1960, **15**, 223–226.
25. Ginott, H. G. *Group psychotherapy with children: The theory and practice of play therapy.* New York: McGraw-Hill, 1961.
26. Gralnick, A., and D'Elia, F. Role of the patient in the therapeutic community: Patient-participation. *Amer. J. Psychother.,* 1961, **15**, 63–72.
27. Greenblatt, M., Levinson, D. J., and Williams, R. H. (Eds.) *The patient and the mental hospital: Contributions of research in the science of social behavior.* New York: Free Press, 1957.
28. Gurin, G., Veroff, J., and Feld, Sheila. *Americans view their mental health: A nationwide interview survey.* New York: Basic Books, 1960.
29. Hadley, J. M. *Clinical and counseling psychology.* New York: Knopf, 1958.
30. Harper, R. A. *Psychoanalysis and psychotherapy: 36 systems.* Englewood Cliffs, N.J.: Prentice-Hall, 1959.
31. Hobbs, N. Group-centered psychotherapy. In C. R. Rogers, *Client-centered therapy: Its current practice, implications, and theory.* Boston: Houghton Mifflin, 1951. Ch. 7.
32. Hollingshead, A. B., and Redlich, F. C. *Social class and mental illness: A community study.* New York: Wiley, 1958.
33. Imber, S. D., Nash, E. H., and Stone, A. R. Social class and duration of psychotherapy. *J. clin. Psychol.,* 1955, **11**, 281–284.
34. Jahoda, Marie. *Current concepts of positive mental health.* New York: Basic Books, 1958.
35. Joint Commission on Mental Illness and Health. *Action for mental health: Final report of the Joint Commission on Mental Illness and Health.* New York: Basic Books, 1961.
36. Jones, Mary C. A laboratory study of fear: The case of Peter. *J. genet. Psychol.,* 1924, **31**, 308–315.
37. Jourard, S. M. *Personal adjustment: An approach through the study of healthy personality.* (2nd ed.) New York: Macmillan, 1963.
38. Kalinowsky, L. B., and Hoch, P. H. *Somatic treatments in psychiatry: Pharmacotherapy; convulsive, insulin, surgical, other methods.* New York: Grune & Stratton, 1961.
39. Klapman, J. W. *Group psychotherapy: Theory and practice.* New York: Grune & Stratton, 1946.
40. Klerman, G. L., et al. Sedation and tranquilization. *Arch. gen. Psychiat.,* 1960, **3**, 4–13.
41. Korner, I. N. Of values, value lag, and mental health. *Amer. Psychologist,* 1956, **11**, 543–546.
42. Kramer, B. M. *Day hospital: A study of partial hospitalization in psychiatry.* New York: Grune & Stratton, 1962.
43. Lee, J. P. Alcoholics Anonymous as a community resource. *Soc. Wk,* 1960, **5**, 20–26.
44. Lewis, N. D., Landis, C., and King, H. E. *Studies in topectomy.* New York: Grune & Stratton, 1956.
45. Lubin, B. Survey of psychotherapy training and activities of psychologists. *J. clin. Psychol.,* 1962, **18**, 252–256.
46. Lynn, D. B. A model man for applied psychology. *Amer. Psychologist,* 1959, **14**, 630–632.
47. Magaret, Ann. Generalization in successful psychotherapy. *J. consult. Psychol.,* 1950, **14**, 64–70.
48. Moreno, J. L. *Psychodrama.* Beacon, N.Y.: Beacon House, 1946.
49. Moustakas, C. E. *Children in play therapy.* New York: McGraw-Hill, 1953.
50. Mowrer, O. H. *Learning theory and personality dynamics.* New York: Ronald, 1950.
51. Mowrer, O. H. The psychologist looks at language. *Amer. Psychologist,* 1954, **9**, 660–694.
52. Murphy, G. *An historical introduction to modern psychology.* (Rev. ed.) New York: Harcourt, Brace & World, 1949.
53. Nunnally, J. C., Jr. *Popular conceptions of mental health: Their development and change.* New York: Holt, Rinehart & Winston, 1961.
54. Powdermaker, Florence B., and Frank, J. D. *Group psychotherapy: Studies in*

*methodology of research and therapy*. Cambridge, Mass.: Harvard Univer. Press, 1953.

55. Psychology—Law, rules and information. *Handbook 51, Prof. Educ., Univer. State of N.Y., State Educ. Dept.* (Albany, N.Y.), 1962.

56. Pugh, T. F., and MacMahon, B. *Epidemiologic findings in U.S. mental hospital data.* Boston: Little, Brown, 1962.

57. Rapoport, R. N. *Community as doctor: New perspectives on a therapeutic community.* Springfield, Ill.: Thomas, 1961.

58. Rogers, C. R. *Counseling and psychotherapy: Newer concepts in practice.* Boston: Houghton Mifflin, 1942.

59. Rogers, C. R. *Client-centered therapy: Its current practice, implications, and theory.* Boston: Houghton Mifflin, 1951.

60. Rogers, C. R. *On becoming a person: A therapist's view of psychotherapy.* Boston: Houghton Mifflin, 1961.

61. Rogers, C. R., and Dymond, Rosalind F. (Eds.) *Psychotherapy and personality Change.* Chicago: Univer. Chicago Press, 1954.

62. Rogers, C. R., and Skinner, B. F. Some issues concerning the control of human behavior: A symposium. *Science,* 1956, **124,** 1057–1066.

63. Sanford, F. H. Psychology and the mental health movement. *Amer. Psychologist,* 1958, **13,** 80–85.

64. Schaffer, L., and Myers, J. K. Psychotherapy and social stratification: An empirical study of practice in a psychiatric outpatient clinic. *Psychiatry,* 1954, **17,** 83–93.

65. Schnore, M. M. Re-evaluation of "total push" therapy with regressed schizophrenic patients. *Amer. Psychologist,* 1961, **16,** 367.

66. Scott, W. A. Research definitions of mental health and mental illness. *Psychol. Bull.,* 1958, **55,** 29–45.

67. Seeman, J. A study of the process of nondirective therapy. *J. consult. Psychol.,* 1949, 13, 157–168.

68. Seeman, J. Toward a concept of personality integration. *Amer. Psychologist,* 1959, 14, 633–637.

69. Shaffer, L. F., and Shoben, E. J., Jr. *The psychology of adjustment: A dynamic and experimental approach to personality and mental hygiene.* (2nd ed.) Boston: Houghton Mifflin, 1956.

70. Sheerer, Elizabeth T. An analysis of the relationship between acceptance of and respect for self and acceptance of and respect for others in ten counseling cases. *J. consult. Psychol.,* 1949, **13,** 169–175.

71. Shoben, E. J., Jr. Psychotherapy as a problem in learning theory. *Psychol. Bull.,* 1949, **46,** 366–393.

72. Shoben, E. J., Jr. Some observations on psychotherapy and the learning process. In O. H. Mowrer (Ed.), *Psychotherapy: Theory and research.* New York: Ronald, 1953. Pp. 120–129.

73. Shoben, E. J., Jr. Toward a concept of the normal personality. *Amer. Psychologist,* 1957, **12,** 183–189.

74. Slavson, S. R. (Ed.) *The fields of group psychotherapy.* New York: Int. Univer. Press, 1956.

75. Smith, M. B. Research strategies toward a conception of positive mental health. *Amer. Psychologist,* 1959, **14,** 673–681.

76. Snyder, W. U. An investigation of the nature of nondirective psychotherapy. *J. gen. Psychol.,* 1945, **33,** 193–224.

77. Snyder, W. U. *Casebook of non-directive counseling.* Boston: Houghton Mifflin, 1947.

78. Srole, L., et al. *Mental health in the metropolis: The midtown Manhattan study,* vol. 1. New York: McGraw-Hill, 1962.

79. Stainbrook, E. Shock therapy: Psychologic theory and research. *Psychol. Bull.,* 1946, **43,** 21–60.

80. Stein, M. I. *Contemporary psychotherapies.* New York: N.Y. Univer. Press, 1961.

81. Stock, Dorothy. An investigation into the interrelations between the self concept and feelings directed toward other persons and groups. *J. consult. Psychol.,* 1949, **13,** 176–180.

82. Strupp, H. H. An objective comparison of Rogerian and psychoanalytic techniques. *J. consult. Psychol.,* 1955, **19,** 1–7.

83. Trouton, D., and Eysenck, H. J. The effects of drugs on behaviour. In H. J.

Eysenck (Ed.), *Handbook of abnormal psychology*. New York: Basic Books, 1961. Ch. 17.

84. Uhr, L., and Miller, J. G. (Eds.) *Drugs and behavior*. New York: Wiley, 1960.

85. Umbarger, C. C., et al. *College students in a mental hospital: An account of organized social contacts between college volunteers and mental patients in a hospital community*. New York: Grune & Stratton, 1962.

86. Wainwright, W. H. Cultural attitudes and clinical judgment. *Int. J. soc. Psychiat.*, 1958, **4**, 105–107.

87. Watson, G., and Currier, W. D. Intensive vitamin therapy in mental illness. *J. Psychol.*, 1960, **49**, 67–81.

88. Wechsler, H. Halfway houses for former mental patients: A survey. *J. soc. Issues*, 1960, **16** (2), 20–26.

89. Wechsler, H. The self-help organization in the mental health field: Recovery, Inc., a case study. *J. nerv. ment. Dis.*, 1960, **130**, 297–314.

90. Willett, R. A. The effects of psychosurgical procedures on behaviour. In H. J. Eysenck (Ed.), *Handbook of abnormal psychology*. New York: Basic Books, 1961. Ch. 15.

91. Williams, M., McGee, T. F., Kittleson, Shirley, and Halperin, L. An evaluation of an intensive group living program with schizophrenic patients. *Psychol. Monogr.*, 1962, **76**, No. 24.

92. Williams, W. S. Class differences in the attitudes of psychiatric patients. *Soc. Probl.*, 1957, **4**, 240–244.

93. Winick, C. Psychiatric day hospitals: A survey. *J. soc. Issues*, 1960, **16** (2), 8–13.

94. Wolpe, J. Reciprocal inhibition as the main basis of psychotherapeutic effects. *Arch. Neurol. Psychiat.*, 1954, **72**, 205–226.

95. Wolpe, J. *Psychotherapy by reciprocal inhibition*. Stanford, Calif.: Stanford Univer. Press, 1958.

96. Zubin, J. The revolution in psychopathology and its implications for epidemiology. Paper read at Amer. Psychol. Assoc., Chicago, September, 1960.

# 15

## Clinical Research

In the preceding chapter, attention was called to the pressing need for research in the field of mental health. This need stems partly from the fact that few techniques currently in use for diagnostic or therapeutic purposes have been adequately validated. In addition, it is hoped that basic research will open up new approaches to problems of mental health. The Joint Commission on Mental Illness and Health emphasized the importance of basic research in mental health programs (52, p. viii). The same emphasis is to be found in the reports of special conferences dealing with the role of psychologists in mental health (111) and the training and functions of psychologists in general (37). Moreover, it is in research that the clinical psychologist, as contrasted to other mental health professionals, can make his most distinctive contribution (37, 111). Even in his service functions, the clinical psychologist with a research orientation can operate more effectively than one who is trained only as a practitioner. With research training, he is better able to evaluate innovations and to incorporate new developments into his practice. In a field that is rapidly evolving, rigid commitment to existing techniques can only retard progress.

Before World War II, the gap between clinical and experimental psychology was very wide. The rapid growth of clinical psychology since that time has been accompanied by some *rapprochement* between the two fields. The gap is still evident, but it has narrowed. To be sure, psychologists differ in their reaction to this gap. Some deplore its existence and urge further narrowing. Others insist it is inevitable and argue for a realistic acceptance of two kinds of psychologists. Nevertheless there are promising signs that psychologists *can* function effectively in the dual role of scientist-practitioner. Clinicians, on the one hand, have become more critical about their techniques and more willing to test their hypotheses. Experimentalists, on the other, have been doing more and more research on problems arising out of clinical contexts.

A particularly clear sign of this *rapprochement* can be seen in the increasing interest in the development or identification of statistical techniques suitable for clinical data (13, chs. 7 and 8; 14; 46; 110; 121). Several of these techniques are designed for the intensive study of single cases. Others make it possible to handle several variables simultaneously, a situation likely to occur in naturalistic clinical settings. Procedures for investigating interaction effects among different variables, for measuring complex nonlinear relations, and for analyzing patterns of responses are further examples. The growth of nonparametric or distribution-free statistics is also a boon to the clinical researcher, whose data often fail to meet the assumptions underlying traditional statistical formulas. A related development is to be found in the increasing number of publications dealing with the experimental designs required in clinical studies (e.g., 21, 120).

In the preceding chapters, some research findings were cited in connection with diagnostic and therapeutic procedures. In the present chapter, however, the focus will be on methodological problems and experimental design in clinical research. Because of the wide scope of clinical research and the variety of problems it encompasses, this chapter can do no more than sample the types of problems investigated and present one or two illustrative studies of each type.

## VALIDATION OF DIAGNOSTIC TECHNIQUES

A major area of applied research in clinical psychology pertains to the validation of tests and other diagnostic techniques. Because of the extensive use of projective techniques in clinical practice and the many unverified claims made about them, these techniques offer many opportunities for research. Since the validation of these techniques also presents many methodological pitfalls, it provides good illustrative material for the purposes of the present chapter (see 4, ch. 20).

Inadequate experimental designs or inappropriate statistical analyses may have the effect of producing spurious evidence of validity where none exists. An example is the contamination of either criterion or test data. Thus the criterion judges may have access to the subjects' test protocols (see Chapter 2). Conversely, the examiner may have obtained cues about the subject's behavior from remarks made by the subject while taking the test, or from case-history material or other non-test sources. The best control for the latter type of contamination in validation studies is provided by *blind analysis,* in which the test record is interpreted by a scorer who has had no contact with the subject and who has no information about him other than that contained in the test protocol.

A more subtle source of error is illustrated by *stereotype accuracy.* Certain descriptive statements, such as might occur in a Rorschach protocol, may apply widely to persons in general, or to young men, or to hospitalized mental patients, or to whatever category of subjects is sampled by the particular investigation. Agreement between criterion and test data with regard to such statements would therefore yield a spurious impression of validity. Some control for this error is needed, such as a measure of congruence between the test evaluation of one subject and the criterion evaluation of another, control subject in the same category (see, e.g., 104, p. 9). The spurious validity arising from stereotype accuracy will be recognized as somewhat similar to the "Barnum effect" described in Chapter 2.

From a different angle, an individual's responses may depend more upon the specific testing technique employed than upon his general behavioral characteristics. Insofar as behavioral descriptions based upon a single testing technique have validity, they should exhibit stability across techniques. To check on this aspect of validity, Campbell and Fiske (11) proposed a *multitrait-multimethod validation process* whereby the correlations of the same traits measured by different methods are compared with the correlations of different traits measured by both the same and different methods. Common variance due to method might result from response sets and other test-taking attitudes that would increase the uniformity of the subject's performance on a particular test or type of test. Unless the trait correlations are appreciably higher than the method correlations, there is obviously no point in describing an individual in terms of the given trait categories. For example, if aggressiveness and obsessiveness as measured by Test A correlate higher than do measures of aggressiveness derived from Tests A and B, there is some question about the value of the construct "aggressiveness" as measured by these two tests.

Meehl (68) describes an adaptation of the Campbell-Fiske procedure involving essentially the correlation between Q sorts of two persons evaluated on the same test (e.g., the Rorschach) and the correlation between Q sorts of the same person evaluated on two different tests (e.g., Rorschach and TAT). The first correlation would show the degree of similarity between the trait patterns of two different persons and would reflect stereotypes and sorting bias arising from the test and the scorers. The second correlation would show the degree of similarity between the trait patterns of the same person as measured by two different tests. The latter could be scored by the same or different scorers.

A common source of spurious validity is failure to *cross-validate* (see Chapter 2). Because of the large number of possible diagnostic signs that can be derived from most projective techniques, it is likely that by chance alone some of them will discriminate significantly between criterion groups. It should be recalled that by chance approximately 5 per cent of the diagnostic signs investigated ought to discriminate at the 5 per cent level of significance, 1 per cent at the 1 per cent level, and so on. The validity of a scoring key based on such diagnostic signs, however, would collapse to zero when the test is cross-validated in a new sample.

The traditional interpretations of many projective test responses are expressed in the form of "dispositional constructs" (98, p. 229), such as "unconscious feelings of inferiority." Such interpretations cannot be fully validated unless reformulated in terms of *observable behavior* as, for example, "will buy a more expensive car than he can afford" or "will drop names of important persons" (98, p. 229). Without these behavioral predictions, we can determine only whether two independent observers or scorers arrive at the same dispositional construct by applying different diagnostic procedures to the same individual. Agreement under these conditions may be looked upon as a first step toward validation. But such validation must be regarded as tentative, because the agreement may simply reflect a common theoretical bias on the part of the two observers, a bias that is broad enough to encompass different diagnostic techniques.

Inadequacies of experimental design may also have the effect of underestimating the validity of a diagnostic instrument. One example is provided by the use of an *inadequate criterion*. In Chapter 13 we noted various objections to the application of such traditional psychiatric categories as schizophrenia and anxiety hysteria. If this type of diagnostic category is used as the sole criterion for checking the validity of a personality test, negative results are inconclusive. A lack of correspondence in this case might indicate the weakness of the criterion rather than the invalidity of the predictor. Another important question pertains to the skill, training, and experience of the *clinician* who interprets the test protocol. Because of the active part played by the clinician in this interpretation, test validity cannot be evaluated independently of certain clinician variables.

Insignificant validity coefficients may also result from a failure to take *interaction effects* into account. For example, the hypothesized relation between aggression in fantasy (as revealed, for instance, in TAT stories) and aggression in overt behavior may be too complex to be tested by a single validity coefficient. Depending upon other concomitant personality characteristics, high aggression in fantasy may be associated with either high or low overt aggression. There is some evidence to suggest that, if strong aggressive tendencies are accompanied by high anxiety or fear of punishment, expressions of aggressions will tend to be high in fantasy and low in overt behavior. When anxiety and fear of punishment are low, however, high fantasy aggression is associated with high overt aggression (83, 87).

A lack of significant correlation between expressions of aggression in TAT stories and in overt behavior in a random sample of cases would thus be consistent with the stated hypothesis, since the relation is positive in some individuals and negative in others. Obviously, however, such a lack of correlation is also consistent with the hypothesis that the TAT has no validity in detecting aggressive tendencies. A similar methodological problem is illustrated by hypotheses of defensiveness, which maintain that in the more highly defensive individuals overt behavior should be negatively correlated with strength of emotional needs, while in the less defensive individuals overt behavior and emotional needs should be positively correlated (116). What these problems require, of course, is more complex experimental designs that permit the measurement of interaction effects through an analysis of results in previously identified subgroups (83, 87, 116).

Still another condition that may lower the validity indices obtained with projective techniques pertains to the *unevenness of coverage* of such procedures. Because of their unstructured nature, projective techniques may provide different kinds of information regarding different individuals—or even regarding the same individual when evaluated by different scorers (16, p. 129; 44, p. 22; 68, p. 21). One person's TAT responses, for example, may reveal a good deal about his aggression and little or nothing about his achievement drive; another person's TAT record may permit a thorough assessment of the strength of his achievement drive, while indicating little about his aggression. This lack of uniformity in the kinds of information yielded in individual cases may help to explain the low validities found when projective test responses are analyzed for a single trait across a group of persons. Similarly, Q sorts force the scorer to evaluate each subject in all traits, a requirement that is clinically unrealistic (68, p. 21).

Much of the published literature on the evaluation of projective tests is inconclusive because of one or more of the methodological difficulties mentioned above or because of the use of inappropriate statistical techniques (4, ch. 20; 15; 25). On the other hand, a few recent studies reflect the *rapprochement* of clinical and experimental psychology in the sophistication of their experimental designs (see, e.g., 44, 62, 104, 116).

For purposes of illustration, we may consider an investigation of four personality tests conducted by Little and Shneidman (62). First, a single examiner administered the Rorschach, TAT, MAPS, and MMPI[1] to each of 12 adult male patients in a Veterans Administration hospital. The 12 subjects included three in each of the following diagnostic categories: neurotic, psychotic, psychosomatic, and normal (fracture and surgery cases with no record of emotional disorders). A detailed case history, or anamnesis, for each subject was also obtained independently through a series of intensive interviews.

Both test and anamnestic data were independently analyzed by two groups of judges, designated as test judges (TJ) and anamnesis judges (AJ). The former comprised 48 clinical psychologists, selected from lists of recognized experts on each of the four tests employed; the latter included 23 psychiatrists and one psychologist. Each TJ performed a blind analysis for four subjects on the test for which he was a skilled interpreter. Each AJ prepared a blind anamnestic evaluation for two subjects. The only additional information available to either test or anamnesis judges was that the subjects were all white, Protestant, male veterans between the ages of 22 and 33 years and with high school education. Specifically, both test and anamnesis judges performed the following five tasks: (1) diagnostic labeling of the subject; (2) rating subject's degree of maladjustment on a linear scale; (3) completing a 76-item Q sort on the subject; (4) answering 117 true-false items about the subject, typical of statements made in psychological test reports, and indicating degree of confidence in each answer; and (5) answering 100 true-false items of a relatively factual nature about the subject's past and present life and reporting degree of confidence in each answer. To provide a measure of scorer reliability, each TJ repeated the entire analysis of one case after a lapse of 10 days.

The results were analyzed statistically to measure congruencies among the personality evaluations of each subject as determined by the different techniques and different judges. With regard to diagnostic labels, there was little correspondence between the categories assigned by the test judges and the subject's previously established diagnosis. The test judges also disagreed widely among themselves. There was a strong tendency, moreover, to classify the normal subjects as neurotic or psychotic and to rate them as maladjusted. This tendency probably reflects in part the strongly pathological orientation in the experience of the clinicians and possibly in the context in which the tests were developed.

Of particular interest are the results of the more detailed analyses of Q sorts and other personality descriptions. Although somewhat higher than chance, the degree of agreement among the different evaluations was quite low. Not only were congruencies between anamnestic and test results low, but little agreement was also found from one test to another and even among different judges using the same test. The 10-day reliability check showed that individiual judges agreed closely with their former evaluations with regard to diagnostic label and degree of maladjustment, but not with regard to detailed personality descriptions. All in all, the findings of this study raise considerable doubt about the clinical value of the instruments investigated. On the other hand, it should be noted that this investigation does not meet all the method-

---

[1] The MMPI is a self-report personality inventory, described in Chapter 13; the Rorschach, TAT, and MAPS are projective techniques, the first two of which were also described in Chapter 13. In the MAPS (Make A Picture Story) technique, the subject selects cardboard figures and a backdrop, which he assembles on a miniature stage, and then tells a story about them.

ological objections raised against clinical validation studies. For example, the
Q sorts and true-false statements may have imposed unrealistic and unduly
demanding conditions upon the test interpreters, by requiring them to evaluate
all traits for all individuals.

## STUDIES OF THE PROCESS OF PSYCHOTHERAPY

Research on the process of psychotherapy has been concerned with such
questions as the effect of therapist variables upon the psychotherapeutic
process, the specific ways in which therapists function, and the changes in
client behavior that occur in the course of psychotherapy. In contrast to studies
of the outcome of psychotherapy, to be discussed in the next section, this
research is limited to what goes on during the psychotherapeutic sessions
themselves. Most of this "process" research has been conducted by client-
centered psychotherapists (see 90; 95, pp. 96-107), although the same procedures have been applied to a more limited extent to psychoanalytic and
other forms of psychotherapy (6, 18, 29, 31, 80, 101, 112, 113).

*Changes in the Course of Therapy.* Process research has been greatly
advanced by the application of two techniques, namely, the recording of
psychotherapeutic sessions and content analysis. With the client's permission,
therapeutic sessions have been recorded by phonographic, wire, or tape recorders and then transcribed. When these records are employed for either
research or teaching purposes, of course, all identifications of individual clients
are eliminated. Content analysis is a technique for classifying the meaningful
content (as opposed to grammatical and other formal properties) of the verbal
responses of client and therapist. Several schemas of classification have been
worked out for this purpose, the specific categories varying with the objectives
of the study and the theoretical framework of the investigator (6, 18, 20, 80,
106).

A typical study conducted with client-centered psychotherapy will serve to
illustrate the procedure. Seeman (100) analyzed over 6,500 client and therapist
statements taken from 60 therapeutic sessions with 10 clients. Using a previously developed schema (106), he classified client responses into four categories: (1) expressions of problems or symptoms, (2) simple acceptances of
therapist response, (3) indications of understanding or insight, and (4) discussions or explorations of plans for the future. The frequency of each of the
four types of response was determined separately for successive fifths of the
psychotherapeutic process in order to reveal any changes that occurred during
therapy. The results can be seen in Figure 102. In the course of psychotherapy,
the percentage of statements dealing with problems or symptoms declined
sharply, while the percentage of those showing understanding or insight rose.
Discussions of future plans also increased during the later sessions. Simple
acceptance of therapist response rose in the early part of therapy and then
declined slowly.

As a further index of the effectiveness of psychotherapy, Seeman computed
the ratio between number of statements showing understanding or insight
and the sum of these statements and those expressing problems or symptoms.
When the data from all clients were combined, this ratio rose from the first to
the last fifth of the psychotherapeutic process. Moreover, the rise tended to be
greater for those clients whom the therapists rated as most improved than for

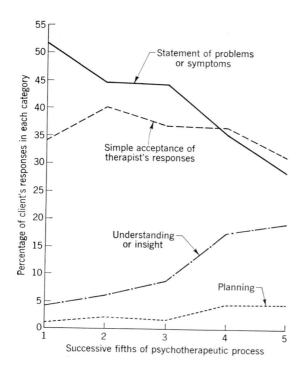

*Fig. 102* Changes in client responses during client-centered psychotherapy. (*Data from Seeman, 100, p. 161.*)

those rated as least improved. The latter finding, however, may be a methodological artifact, since the therapist's rating of client improvement was probably influenced by client statements in the course of therapy. Another finding of the same study was that attitudes expressed by clients in the present tense tended to become more positive and less negative in the course of therapy, while attitudes expressed in the past tense showed the reverse change. Apparently the past was viewed with less favor and the present with increasing optimism following therapy.

Several other progressive changes have been identified in the course of psychotherapy. Defensiveness tends to decrease as therapy proceeds (39, 79). Similarly, expressions of hostility increase as the anxiety associated with such feelings is reduced through therapy (79). Such findings suggest an increasing ability to recognize and express feelings freely in the course of therapy.

A number of studies by psychologists of the client-centered school have been concerned with changes in the client's self concept. With therapy, the self concept tends to become more favorable and comes to resemble more closely the individual's self-ideal concept, or the way he would like to be. These changes have been investigated by having the client perform a Q sort with reference to his real self as he perceives it and his ideal self, at different stages of therapy. In one study of 25 cases (10), the mean correlation between self and ideal sorts before therapy was −.01, as contrasted with a mean correlation of .58 found with normal control subjects. After therapy, the mean client correlation rose to .38. In a follow-up after an interval of six months to a year, this mean showed a negligible drop to .31. The mean control correlation remained virtually unchanged over the time intervals covered.

Although the observed changes in self-acceptance in the course of psychotherapy are consistent with the underlying rationale of client-centered therapy, their interpretation is not so simple as might seem at first sight (see 17). One difficulty arises from the fact that different indices of self-acceptance do not correlate very highly with each other and hence may be measuring different constructs. Much more information is needed on the generality of self-acceptance with reference to measuring techniques, traits or items, situations, and time. Another difficulty is that the meaning of high self-acceptance scores is ambiguous. In such scores, self-acceptance may be confounded with defensiveness, lack of insight into one's emotional difficulties, or the tendency to choose socially desirable answers on personality inventories.

**Therapist Variables.** In the effort to learn more about the therapeutic relationship, some investigators have studied the effects of therapist characteristics and therapist responses upon client behavior during therapy. For example, certain characteristics of the therapist's responses, such as the accuracy with which he reflects client feelings or the degree of his unconditional positive acceptance of the client, have proved to be significantly related to the extent of intrapersonal exploration that the client undertakes during group therapy (114). Some studies on individual psychotherapy have found that "insight" and "discussion of plans" by the client are more likely to follow nondirective than directive therapist responses and that resistance to the therapist and to the therapeutic process more often follow directive responses (95, pp. 247–259; 106).

Of particular interest is the evidence of *interaction* among client, therapist, and process variables (95, pp. 247–259; 107). These findings suggest that, because of their individual personality characteristics, some therapists may function more effectively with one type of therapy, while others may function more effectively with a different type. Similarly, pre-therapy personality characteristics of clients affect their responses to different therapists and to different therapeutic processes. The importance of compatibility between therapist and client is indicated by this research. There is also evidence of a close correspondence between client's feelings toward therapist and therapist's feelings toward client. In an intensive study of the psychotherapeutic relationship between one therapist and 20 clients (107), both therapist and clients filled out specially constructed "affect scales" pertaining to their feelings toward each other, following each therapeutic session. For all sessions combined, the correlation between client and therapist affect for the 20 cases proved to be .70.

Still another approach is illustrated by an investigation of the effect of therapist response upon the frequency of client responses in different content categories (80). This study is of particular interest because it demonstrates that even in nondirective therapy the subtle approval or disapproval implicit in the therapist's remarks influences the subsequent frequency of various kinds of client responses. Among the response categories that were consistently approved by the therapist were expressions of client independence; among those that were disapproved were intellectual defenses and feelings of anxiety about independence. A comparison of the pooled categories of approved responses with the pooled categories of disapproved responses over eight hours of psychotherapy yielded the results shown in Figure 103. It can be seen that the proportion of approved responses rose sharply, while the proportion of disapproved responses dropped sharply, in the course of therapy. That subtle verbal reinforcement by the therapist will significantly affect the subsequent course of the client's responses has been repeatedly confirmed by other investigators (e.g., 1; 88; 91; 96; 97; 113, pp. 61–94).

*Physiological Measures.* The research considered thus far has dealt exclusively with verbal responses. Considerable information is also available regarding changes in physiological indices of anxiety during psychotherapy. Both laboratory and clinical studies provide extensive evidence showing that such physiological measures as galvanic skin reaction, heart rate, blood pressure, muscle tension, and gastric motility can serve as indicators of emotional conflict areas during therapeutic sessions, can indicate quantitatively the extent of emotional involvement, and can reflect changes in client behavior as therapy progresses (78, chs. 18–19; 95, pp. 160–208). Such physiological changes can be detected in moment-by-moment comparisons within a single therapy session, as well as in the comparison of different sessions.

In view of the foregoing findings, it would seem that physical indices of anxiety should provide a good measure of the effectiveness of therapy. Several difficulties arise, however, when the indices are employed for this purpose (65; 95, pp. 160–208). First, the intercorrelations among different anxiety indicators are rather low. There is considerable specificity in the autonomic response pattern of different persons (57; 95, pp. 160–208). Thus one individual might consistently show his maximal response to stress in blood-pressure rise, another

**Fig. 103**   Effect of therapist approval or disapproval upon frequency of client statements in different categories. (*From Murray, 80, p. 11.*)

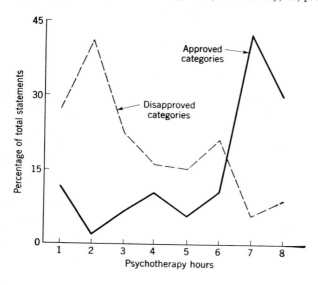

in heightened muscle tension, and a third in increased finger sweating. It would therefore be misleading to employ a single physiological variable for all cases.

A second difficulty stems from the fact that physiological indicators of anxiety cannot be taken directly as indices of therapeutic effectiveness but must be interpreted in the light of other behavioral data (95, pp. 160–208). For instance, physiological measures cannot differentiate between the reduction of stress resulting from neurotic defenses and that resulting from the resolution of conflicts. Many psychotherapists maintain that anxiety should rise and then decline in the course of therapy, as defensive symptom systems are broken down and new responses are developed. It is apparent that anxiety indicators need to be considered in combination with other information about the client and interpreted against previously formulated theoretical expectancies.

A final limitation is common to all measures taken during the therapeutic process, whether they be physiological or verbal. Any change observed in the course of psychotherapy may be restricted to the therapeutic situation. The therapist's nonthreatening and accepting attitude, for instance, may gradually lead to a reduction in the anxiety the client experiences *while talking to the therapist about emotional problems*. It is, of course, an underlying assumption of therapeutic practice that these response changes will generalize from talking to other behavior and from the therapeutic situation to other situations of daily living. On theoretical grounds, there is good reason to expect this generalization to occur. But it must be recognized that process studies as such can provide no evidence for such generalization.

## EVALUATING THE OUTCOME OF THERAPY

A particularly difficult field of clinical research is that concerned with the evaluation of therapy. Although hundreds of studies have been published in this area, few have yielded conclusive results. Serious methodological problems make it difficult to determine the effectiveness of somatic therapies as well as psychotherapy. A review of over 500 publications on a leading tranquilizer, for example, found only 37 studies that met even minimum standards of scientific acceptability (43). Surveys of published studies on psychotherapy with adult neurotics (24; 26, ch. 18) and with children (59) failed to find satisfactory evidence that psychotherapy facilitates recovery. To be sure, that which is unproved is not thereby disproved. When small samples are employed, for example, only very large effects can be significantly established. Much larger samples than are ordinarily available would be required to demonstrate slight treatment effects (32, p. 187). Similarly, unreliable measuring instruments, inadequate criteria of improvement, or the unskilled application of a therapeutic technique may artificially reduce the difference in outcome between treated and untreated samples.

*Criteria of Outcome.* One of the most persistent problems in outcome research centers around the criteria of outcome (113, pp. 320–324; 119). How can we judge whether or not the individual has improved? One way is to ask the client about his own feelings. Such information could be obtained either through an informal report or through a standardized self-evaluation, as in a personality inventory or Q sort. A difficulty with this approach arises from defense mechanisms, which may make the client's self-report totally misleading. Another source of error has been described as the "hello-goodbye" effect (42). When a client is seeking therapy, he is likely to exaggerate his difficulties because of a subtle social obligation to justify his appeal for help; when about to terminate therapy, on the other hand, he is likely to overestimate his improvement and satisfaction out of courtesy and gratitude toward the therapist. For many persons, it may be difficult to say they feel no better after a professionally trained therapist has devoted many hours to helping them. Suggestion would also operate, insofar as the individual expects to benefit from therapy.

If we rely upon the therapist's evaluation of the patient's improvement, we encounter similar difficulties. Being ego-involved in the therapeutic process, the therapist cannot be considered an unbiased observer. Having diligently applied a form of therapy in whose efficacy he believes, the therapist certainly expects to find improvement. Although not subject to this bias, objective measures of verbal and physiological changes during therapy, such as those employed in process research, have the limitation that they may be specific to the therapeutic situation. There is some evidence to suggest that client responses during therapeutic sessions may be unrelated to external indices of progress (50).

A fourth type of outcome criterion is based upon the ward behavior of institutionalized patients. Several objective rating scales have been developed to evaluate this behavior. One such scale consists of 150 items to be marked by nurses in reporting on the patient's ward behavior during the preceding week (9). To what extent improved adjustment to the sheltered institutional environment will generalize to behavior outside the institution must of course be checked for specific therapies and for different kinds of patients.

A fifth and final type of outcome index utilizes follow-up data regarding the individual's behavior in real-life situations. Such data may range from length of time the individual remains outside the hospital to evidence of job and family adjustment and associates' evaluations of interpersonal behavior. Although theoretically this type of criterion would seem to be the most satisfactory, it is difficult to apply because of inequalities in the environments to which different persons must adjust. The experimenter has no control over the circumstances of the individual's life and little knowledge about them. A patient may return to the hospital within six months or may fail to adjust to his job, not because of the inadequacy of the therapy, but because of the unusually stressful nature of his environment.

In view of the many special problems presented by each criterion of outcome, it is not surprising to find that the intercorrelations among different types of criteria are often low (32). A patient may be greatly improved according to one criterion and unimproved according to another. In a well-controlled study of the relative effectiveness of three forms of psychotherapy with patients in a Veterans Administration hospital, there was little relation between outcome criteria based on ward behavior and those based on a six-month follow-up after discharge; and there was little relation between these criteria of outcome and those based on self-report inventories or Q sorts (27).

Even among follow-up criteria, moreover, the relative effectiveness of different therapies differed depending upon whether a hospitalization or an employment criterion was chosen.

Duration of follow-up also makes a difference in the results. A survey (109) of many studies on shock therapies and psychosurgery showed a considerably higher recovery and improvement rate among treated than among untreated cases immediately following therapy. But the difference declined with time and had virtually disappeared within five years (see Figure 104). These somatic therapies may thus hasten improvement by patients who would eventually recover if untreated. Even this effect, of course, is a notable accomplishment if it can be conclusively established.

It should also be noted that the choice of a criterion of outcome involves some value judgment (22; 95, pp. 1–9). The question of what constitutes mental health, discussed in Chapter 14, is also relevant to the evaluation of therapy. Therapists differ, for example, in the relative value they place upon individual freedom and upon conformity and adjustment as goals of therapy. Clients also vary with regard to these values, partly as a function of socioeconomic background and other cultural factors. Such value differences represent one of the variables in the compatibility of client and therapist that may in turn affect the success of psychotherapy. All of the foregoing problems indicate the desirability of investigating the outcome of therapy in terms of multiple criteria and of specifying fully the criteria employed in each study.

*Selection of Subjects.* A second major methodological question pertains to the choice of both experimental and control subjects. Because of the likelihood of interaction between client variables and types of therapy, it is important to work with groups or subgroups that are homogeneous with regard to relevant variables. Which variables are relevant depends somewhat upon the type of therapy under investigation and the objectives of the study. Client characteristics that are likely to make a difference can be identified in part from earlier empirical findings and in part from the theoretical rationale underlying the therapy. Any study, however, should probably control, as a bare minimum, such variables as age, sex, socioeconomic level, duration of illness, type of onset (sudden or gradual), and diagnostic category (95, pp. 10–26; 120). The expected improvement and recovery rates among untreated cases vary as a function of these patient characteristics. For instance, the base rate of improvement is considerably higher for manic-depressives than for schizophrenics (32, 109). When feasible, of course, more precise specifications regarding symptoms, emotional problems, and adjustment mechanisms are desirable, in view of the inadequacies of traditional diagnostic categories.

In any evaluation of therapy, it is particularly important to use a control group matched with the experimental group in all of the previously mentioned variables. It is the function of the control group to indicate what improvement (or deterioration) would occur in the absence of the specific therapy under investigation. Changes occurring in the control group should reflect "spontaneous recovery" occurring as a result of nonspecific treatments (such as institutionalization) and of the many uncontrolled and unknown events in the individual's day-by-day experiences.

Unless special care is exercised in matching treated and control groups, selective bias is likely to influence group assignments. There is a strong tendency to place in the control groups cases with poorer prognosis (109). It has been demonstrated that the recovery rate of control groups used in studies of somatic therapies is significantly lower than that of the general untreated mental hospital population prior to the introduction of these specific therapies. Figure 104 provides a striking demonstration of this difference, based upon a careful analysis of published surveys of schizophrenics that were conducted prior and subsequent to the introduction of shock therapies and psychosurgery. It can be seen that, in the five-year follow-ups, there is virtually no difference between treated and general untreated samples, while the control groups employed in the various investigations of these therapies showed a much lower recovery rate.

In experiments with outpatients, control cases are sometimes drawn from waiting lists. This procedure presents several difficulties. It is likely that many such cases will obtain help elsewhere, especially if the waiting period is long. They may in any event lose contact with the clinic and be unavailable for follow-ups. The fact that they have not been accepted for therapy may heighten the feeling of rejection that so often characterizes their interpersonal attitudes.

The waiting period may also be utilized to provide an own-control for cases later accepted for therapy. In a relatively well-designed experiment using this procedure, 22 self-referred neurotic clients were compared during equal periods of waiting and of nondirective therapy (12). The waiting period

**Fig. 104** Outcome for institutionalized schizophrenics given custodial treatment during pre-therapy era and for those used as controls in somantic-therapy studies. (*Adapted from Staudt and Zubin, 109, p. 185.*)

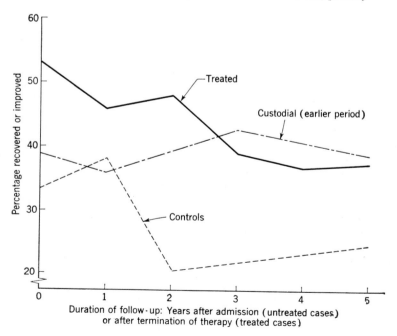

ranged from 3 to 24 weeks and averaged slightly under 9 weeks. The over-all results showed a significant advantage of therapy over waiting period as reflected by Q sorts but not by TAT performance. Improvement during therapy was greater with experienced than with inexperienced therapists. These findings need to be qualified by the limitations inherent in outcome indices obtained during therapy sessions, by any attitudinal effects of the waiting period, and by the possible influence of temporal and sequential factors.

***Experimental Design.*** There are many problems of experimental design that must be considered in planning or evaluating any study on the effects of therapy (see, e.g., 21; 115, chs. 5 and 6). Some of these problems are common to all outcome research in clinical psychology; others are specific to the evaluation of a particular form of treatment. As examples, we shall consider two problems, one pertaining chiefly to psychotherapy and the other to drug therapy.

With regard to *psychotherapy,* it is difficult to separate the influence of a specific therapy from the more general effect of any sort of therapeutic attention. The latter underlies "total push" and other milieu therapies. Control subjects who receive no discernible form of treatment may deteriorate or fail to improve because of feelings of hopelessness and neglect. It is largely for this reason that several investigators have advocated—and some used—one form of psychotherapy as a control for another. In some studies, different therapies are simply evaluated against each other; in others, a minimal "control" therapy is introduced, which is less time-consuming and more superficial than the other forms of psychotherapy (see, e.g., 27; 95, pp. 10–26).

In experimental designs calling for multiple therapies, the role of the therapist must be considered. If different therapists are employed with each type of therapy, differences among therapists will be confounded with differences among therapies. If the same therapists are assigned to all therapies in some balanced design, the interaction of therapist and type of therapy should be investigated. It is likely that each therapist will be most successful with the therapy he prefers and in which he is most experienced. In addition, it is highly desirable for outcome studies to be so designed as to permit the measurement of interactions between client characteristics and type of therapy (see 21). One form of psychotherapy may be more effective with certain types of disorders or certain kinds of persons; another form may be more effective with others.

In the evaluation of *drug therapies,* control procedures must be such as to rule out the placebo effect (63; 103; 115, ch. 6). The term "placebo," derived from a Latin verb meaning "to please" or "to placate," originally referred to a pharmaceutically inactive substance prescribed when no specific remedy was available for the patient's condition. More recently, placebos have come to be employed in drug experiments to control the effects of suggestion on both subjects and observers. The customary procedure is to administer a placebo to some subjects and the experimental drug to others in a form that makes the two indistinguishable. In the "double-blind" technique, the identity of drug and placebo (or control) cases is not revealed to either subjects or observers (e.g., therapists, nurses, attendants, examiners).

Some drugs present a more difficult control problem because they produce recognizable side effects, such as dizziness or motor incoordination. It would thus be an easy matter for subjects and observers to determine who had received the placebo and who had received the drug. Under these circumstances, it is desirable to use an "active placebo," which simulates the side effects of the drug but does not contain the specific pharmaceutical agent under investigation. This problem is not likely to arise in research on the common tranquilizers and energizers, unless very large doses are employed.

The need for stringent control procedures in drug research was vividly demonstrated in a simulated drug-therapy study conducted with 120 hospitalized psychiatric patients (63). With the exception of the investigators and the medical director of the hospital, all staff members and participating patients were under the impression that a new tranquilizer and a new energizer were being evaluated. Although the two kinds of tablets differed in size, color, and taste, both kinds actually contained the same inert placebo. On the basis of their specific psychiatric disorders, 60 patients were selected for the "tranquilizer" study and 60 for the "energizer" study. Each group was divided into matched experimental and control groups, the latter receiving no tablet. The "drugs" were administered for a 6-week period, preceded and followed by 2-week base-line periods with no drug. Weekly ratings on a behavioral rating scale were recorded for each patient by the nurses. Patients, psychiatrists, and nurses also made a subjective evaluation of the degree to which each patient had been helped by the therapy.

According to the subjective evaluations, from 53 to 80 per cent of the patients appeared to have benefited from these "drugs." Such findings are not unlike those reported in some equally subjective and uncontrolled studies in support of the psychiatric use of certain drugs. In terms of the better controlled comparison of behavior ratings of experimental and control groups, the alleged tranquilizer produced a statistically significant improvement. The alleged energizer failed to do so, probably because energizers were newer and less widely accepted than tranquilizers at the time of the study. All that the results demonstrate, of course, is the effect of suggestion upon patients, staff, or both.

# RESEARCH ON THE CAUSES OF
# MENTAL DISORDERS

Investigations of the nature and causes of intellectual and emotional disorders constitute a large portion of the basic research underlying clinical psychology. The phenomenal growth of clinical psychology since World War II has been accompanied by a vigorous and comprehensive attack on problems of etiology. This research has drawn upon a multitude of disciplines, from genetics and biochemistry to sociology and communication theory. Because the major emphasis in this book is on applied rather than on basic research, etiological studies will be sketched rather briefly, in order merely to suggest the varied approaches that are currently being explored.

Especially promising are certain large-scale interdisplinary projects, such as the Schizophrenia and Psychopharmacology Project conducted jointly at the University of Michigan and the Ypsilanti State Hospital (35). Believing that progress in the understanding and treatment of schizophrenia requires the identification of different syndromes that may be loosely grouped under this category, the investigators organized the project around the problem of classification. For the purposes of this study, a special research ward was established, in which diet and other details of patient care were carefully controlled. For each experimental patient, as well as for several control groups, data were gathered through psychiatric interviews, case histories, records and ratings of ward behavior, a specially developed battery of psychological tests, and an extensive series of physiological and biochemical measures. Preliminary analysis of the intercorrelations among several hundred variables thus measured revealed certain clusters that cut across biological, psychological, and clinical indices. These clusters differentiated significantly among such diagnostic groups as paranoid schizophrenics, other schizophrenics, patients with chronic brain syndrome, and other nonschizophrenic psychotics. Longitudinal studies also indicated that some of these clusters tended to shift under drug action, thus providing further corroboration of the concomitance of certain measures. This project also covered many studies of a more specific nature, dealing with biochemical, physiological, and psychological factors associated with schizophrenia. The findings of these studies have been separately reported in an extensive list of publications.

Still better control of conditions is provided by a long-range research project in progress at the National Institute of Mental Health (55). In this study, a small and carefully selected group of schizophrenic patients live in an experimental ward with controlled diet and other uniform living conditions, while a group of normal control subjects live under approximately comparable conditions in a similar ward. This procedure represents the most far-reaching attempt as yet undertaken to minimize the operation of extraneous variables in comparative studies of schizophrenics and normals.

**Heredity.**   The extent to which hereditary factors contribute to the etiology of mental disorders is still largely unknown.[2] Since the experimentally controlled, selective-breeding procedures of animal genetics cannot be applied to human subjects, knowledge about human heredity must be derived from relatively indirect and uncontrolled sources. Thus human geneticists have investigated the extent of consanguinity (marriage of close relatives) in the families of persons with a given disorder, the incidence of a disorder in relatively isolated inbred communities, and the occurrence of a disorder in different members of the same family (26, ch. 8; 51, ch. 1). Because of insufficient information about the operation of other factors, however, these approaches rarely provide conclusive evidence of hereditary influences.

Data on family resemblances in a given trait or condition are particularly difficult to interpret because families represent environmental as well as biological units. Even physical disorders may run in families without necessarily being hereditary. Beriberi shows high concentration in certain families, not because of a genetic basis, but because of a vitamin deficiency in the family diet. Members of the same family not only share many features of a common environment but also interact with each other. Hence there are many opportunities for mutual influence. Quite apart from heredity, an illiterate mother provides a less stimulating intellectual environment for her children than does a mother with a college degree. A more subtle but potentially effective factor is social expectancy. Since relatives are expected to resemble each other, any chance similarity between them is likely to be noticed and

[2] For an introduction to the heredity-environment problem in psychology, see 2 (chs. 3, 4, and 9) and 3.

magnified. The expected similarities may in turn influence the individual's self concept and his subsequent psychological development.

It is only when a defect is transmitted according to a simple and easily identified hereditary mechanism that data on familial incidence can demonstrate its genetic origin. For example, if a characteristic depends upon a single recessive gene, its observed familial incidence can be checked against the expected distribution derived from Mendelian ratios (see 2, pp. 270–274). Such simple hereditary mechanisms have been identified for only a few human conditions. Among them are certain rare and extreme forms of mental deficiency, such as phenylketonuria and the amaurotic idiocies. These types of mental deficiency have also been traced to metabolic disorders, which in turn stem from biochemically defective genes. Knowledge about the many intervening physiological steps, from defective gene to behavior disorder, helps to clarify the hereditary basis of the disorder. For most psychological disorders, however, this type of information is unavailable.

In the effort to rule out some of the uncontrolled factors of familial studies, several investigators have worked with identical (monozygous) and fraternal (dizygous) twins. Since they develop from a single fertilized ovum, identical twins have identical sets of genes. Fraternal twins, on the other hand, are no more alike in heredity than ordinary siblings, although they are born at the same time. The usual procedure in twin studies is to locate individual cases of twins who manifest a particular disorder. The incidence of the disorder among the co-twins and other relatives of these "index cases" is then investigated. When both members of a pair of related persons (twins, siblings, parent-child, etc.) exhibit the same disorder, they are described as "concordant"; when only one member shows the disorder, the pair is described as "discordant."

The twin-study method was employed in an extensive research project on schizophrenia conducted by Kallmann and his associates (53). Beginning with 953 twin index cases (268 identical and 685 fraternal), all of whom were institutionalized in New York State and diagnosed as schizophrenic, the investigators proceeded to determine which, if any, of the relatives had been similarly diagnosed. The principal results are summarized in Table 21. It will be seen that 86.2 per cent of the identical twin pairs, as contrasted to 14.5

**TABLE 21**   *Concordance Rates for Schizophrenia as Determined for 953 Twin Index Cases in New York State*
(*Data from Kallmann, 53, p. 146*)

| Type of Kinship | Concordance Rate[a] |
|---|---|
| Monozygous twins | 86.2 |
| Dizygous twins | 14.5 |
| Full siblings | 14.2 |
| Half siblings | 7.1 |
| Step siblings | 1.8 |
| Parents | 9.3 |
| Expectancy in general population: 0.7–0.9 | |

[a] Corrected for age to allow for the fact that the expectancy rate for schizophrenia varies with age.

per cent of the fraternal twin pairs, were concordant. It is particularly note-worthy that the concordance rate for fraternal twins is practically the same as that for siblings. The findings of this study have been roughly corroborated by less extensive surveys conducted in other countries (see 51, ch. 2; 53).

Although such data strongly suggest the operation of hereditary factors in schizophrenia, the conclusiveness of the evidence has been questioned on several grounds (51, ch. 2). A number of studies have shown, for example, that identical twins receive more similar parental treatment and have closer contact with each other than do fraternal twins (see 2, pp. 287–288). Thus environmental differences are not ruled out when the two types of twins are compared. In addition, certain procedural biases may have operated in the samples investigated (51, ch. 2; 92). Because of their striking physical re-semblance, for example, identical twins are more likely to be noticed than fraternal twins when both members of a twin pair are hospitalized in the same institution. A larger proportion of concordant identicals than concordant fraternals might thus come to the attention of investigators. Since the diagnosis of schizophrenia is so loosely applied, moreover, the fact that a patient's identical co-twin is known to be schizophrenic may increase the probability that he is also so classified.

***Organic Factors.*** Any organic defects identified as causal factors in mental disorders may themselves have either a hereditary or an environmental origin. On the one hand, defective genes may produce metabolic disorders that ultimately lead to mental deficiency or other behavioral disturbances. On the other hand, psychological disorders may result from a number of condi-tions in the prenatal environment, such as toxins, bacterial infections, nutri-tional inadequacies, and X-ray irradiation (see 7, 33). Brain injuries occurring during the birth process, as well as neonatal anoxia, may also cause intellectual defects and other psychological abnormalities. Severe diseases like meningitis or encephalitis in early childhood may have similar results.

The effects of many of these conditions have been investigated experi-mentally in animals as well as through follow-up studies of human infants. In a well-controlled animal experiment, for example, oxygen deprivation dur-ing gestation or immediately after birth significantly decreased the learning performance of rats and cats at maturity (69). In another study (38), 355 new-born infants were classified into those who had had normal birth, those who had experienced anoxia, and those who had undergone other birth complica-tions (prematurity, injuries, etc.). Three years later, the children were given neurological and psychological examinations. To control observer bias, the examiners had no knowledge of the subjects' original classification. The anoxia cases performed significantly more poorly on the Stanford-Binet and other psychological tests and showed signs of neurological impairment. Similar but more varied results were obtained with other birth complications. This study supported the view that "minimal brain damage," too slight to cause con-spicuous disorders like cerebral palsy, may nevertheless produce behavioral deficiencies.

Following an extensive survey of many different complications of gestation and birth, Pasamanick and his associates (56, 60) proposed a "continuum of reproductive casualty." By this they meant that varying degrees of prenatal or natal trauma will lead to a continuum of effects ranging from mild intellectual or emotional disorders to severe mental deficiency, cerebral palsy, and death. The data for this survey were obtained retrospectively, by examining the birth certificates and obstetrical records of children whose subsequent condition was known. In the same survey (86), an analysis of results by socioeconomic level showed a marked excess of prenatal and natal abnormalities in lower socioeconomic levels, probably resulting from dietary deficiencies and inferior maternal care during pregnancy. These findings suggest a possible basis for some of the socioeconomic differences that are consistently found both in intelligence test performance and in the incidence of emotional disorders.

Organic factors have also been extensively investigated in connection with the etiology of schizophrenia (8; 35; 51, parts II and III; 55; 89; 94). Significant differences between schizophrenics and normals have been found in electroencephalograms, incidence of structural defects of cortical neurones, metabolic processes, blood chemistry, and endocrine functions. Several investigators have measured the toxicity of the serum of schizophrenics, using various animal forms as test objects. Research with psychotomimetic drugs, which simulate psychotic symptoms in normal persons, suggests that schizophrenia may be characterized by a disordered metabolic response to stress, which in turn derives from a biochemical defect (94). This hypothesis could also account for the effect of certain tranquilizers in terms of their specific biochemical action.

All this research activity is opening up promising new approaches to the etiology of schizophrenia and other psychological disorders. At this stage, however, conclusions would be premature. In interpreting the findings of any study in this area, we must bear in mind, first, that schizophrenia is a broad and loosely applied diagnostic category, which actually covers a variety of behavioral difficulties. Different forms of schizophrenia may have different etiologies. Even the same symptoms may result from different factors in different persons. It is likely, too, that organic and experiential factors interact in the development of schizophrenic disorders. Thus either hereditary or environmentally produced organic deficiencies may make the individual more vulnerable to psychological stress. In the absence of severely stressful experiences, however, behavioral disturbances may fail to develop even in one who is organically predisposed to them.

When organic differences are found between schizophrenics and normals, we must also consider the possibility that the differences may be a result of emotional stress, degree of activity, nutritional state, and other variables associated with either the psychotic condition itself or with institutionalization (see 48; 55; 89, ch. 7). It was found, for example, that the serum of schizophrenics oxidized adrenaline more rapidly than did the serum of normal controls. Further investigation, however, demonstrated that this difference resulted from a vitamin C deficiency in the diet of the institutionalized schizophrenics (5). When this variable was controlled, the difference between schizophrenics and normals disappeared. Several other alleged biochemical differences between schizophrenics and normals likewise disappeared when checked in the well-controlled study at the National Institute of Mental Health (55), cited earlier in this chapter (p. 410).

***Experiential Factors.***  In line with the recognition that learning plays an important part in the development of adjustment mechanisms, problem-solving techniques, and other response variables, there has been an increasing amount of research on the relation between experiential factors and psychological disorders. Particular interest has centered on familial experiences during the formative years of childhood, although adult experiences in different cultures and subcultures have also received attention. Only a few examples will be cited to illustrate some of the approaches followed in this broad and active area of current research.

One group of studies has investigated the mothers (and occasionally the fathers) of schizophrenics—their personality characteristics, their attitudes toward children, and their child-rearing practices. Although the studies differ in many ways and have yielded some conflicting results, certain suggestive trends have emerged (see 47; 51, chs. 10–14; 54). The term *schizophrogenic mother* has been introduced to refer to the type of mother whose behavior tends to induce schizophrenia in her offspring. Such mothers have been described as emotionally immature, dominant, rigid, restrictive, and manifesting extremes of either rejection or overprotectiveness toward the child. They tend to be impervious to the child's feelings and to discourage the development of autonomy. Another characteristic attributed to them is "intrusiveness," or an unwillingness to give the child any privacy, even in his thoughts. According to one hypothesis, the schizophrogenic mother, because of her own emotional conflicts, habitually gives the child conflicting and mutually incompatible communications of feelings and ideas (40; 51, ch. 13).

The foregoing data have been gathered by a variety of techniques, including interview, questionnaire, and psychological test studies of the mothers, as well as retrospective reports by patients. The latter procedure, of course, is subject to perceptual distortions by the emotionally disturbed informant. Some investigators have utilized a short situational test to observe the interpersonal relations of parents and child (34). In a much more intensive investigation of the total family pattern, schizophrenic patients and their parents lived together on a psychiatric ward in a research center for as long as 2½ years (51, ch. 12). In a few families, normal siblings also lived on the ward for as much as a year. All family members participated in joint psychotherapy sessions as a family unit. Data were gathered through these therapeutic sessions as well as through daily observations by nurses and ward attendants. In all these studies, it is difficult to disentangle cause-and-effect relations. We do not know to what extent the abnormal behavior of the patient may have led to the disturbed family relations. Only a longitudinal study could answer this question conclusively.

*Cultural differences in family patterns* were highlighted in a study of the specific symptoms of schizophrenic patients differing in national origin (105). The subjects were two groups of male schizophrenics in a Veterans Administration hospital. While closely equated in age, education, socioeconomic level, religion, and number of American generations, one group was of Irish and the other of Italian extraction. Both personality test performance and ratings of ward behavior revealed significant group differences in the nature of the schizophrenic symptoms. The Irish-Americans showed a greater tendency toward imaginative and fantasy behavior and more inhibition of motor expression; the Italian-Americans were more overtly aggressive and impulsive. The investigators related these findings to subcultural differences in child-rearing practices and family constellation, as well as to other cultural factors. A later study, dealing with female schizophrenics from the same two national groups, revealed very similar differences in symptoms (28).

Another approach is concerned with *epidemiology,* or the distribution of mental disorders with reference to various population characteristics (45, 58, 84, 85, 99, 108). Of particular interest is the greater incidence of mental disorder among lower than among higher socioeconomic levels. This difference has been repeatedly demonstrated and persists when selective factors have been ruled out by a variety of procedures. Among the many possible conditions contributing to these differences are child-rearing practices, educational level, amount of psychological stress encountered in occupational and other adult activities, and class differences in attitudes toward mental health and therapy.

A comparison of the socioeconomic level of the patients themselves with that of their parents sheds some light upon the probable influence of specific etiological factors. Surveys conducted in America reveal that the fathers of schizophrenics tend to be in the same occupational level as the patients (45). Hence the conditions associated with low socioeconomic level have been operative since the patient's childhood. In British surveys, on the other hand, the occupational distribution of the fathers is fairly typical of that found in the general population, while the schizophrenic sons tend to cluster in the unskilled labor level (75). In neither country, however, can the low occupational status of the patients be attributed to a downward drift on the part of the patients themselves, since the patients tended to remain in the same occupational level throughout their own working life. These analyses illustrate the complexity of conditions to be considered in interpreting epidemiological findings. Nevertheless, the epidemiological approach holds much promise for both the understanding of mental disorders and the identification of preventive measures.

Finally, mention should also be made of the extensive anthropological literature pertaining to *mental abnormalities in different cultures* (see 2, pp. 617–619; 23; 30; 41; 51, ch. 10; 61; 117). Not only the total incidence of mental disorders, but also the relative frequency of such syndromes as schizophrenia and manic-depressive psychoses or of anxiety and conversion hysteria, vary widely among cultures. Moreover, some syndromes appear to be specific to certain cultures and absent in others. The social history of our own culture shows temporal changes and "fashions in abnormality," as illustrated by the dancing manias of the Middle Ages and by the conspicuous decrease in the frequency of hysterical anesthesias and motor disorders between the two world wars. The whole problem is further complicated by the fact that behavior that is deviant or disabling in one culture may be accepted and even favored in another (2, pp. 614–617).

# INTEGRATION OF CLINICAL AND EXPERIMENTAL APPROACHES

With the growing interest in basic research on mental disorders, more and more efforts are being made to integrate clinical and experimental approaches in this area. As a result, clinical observations, laboratory studies of human subjects, and animal experiments tend to be combined in the formulation and testing of hypotheses. On the one hand, controlled experiments provide objective tests of clinical "hunches" and working hypotheses; on the other, psychotherapy contributes to a fuller understanding of normal personality. Because the non-threatening psychotherapeutic situation induces the client to communicate more freely and fully than he does in most other interpersonal contexts, it can provide a unique data-gathering opportunity.

Although the research possibilities of the combined clinical and experimental approach are still largely unexplored, a number of psychologists representing different theoretical orientations have made notable contributions in this direction. Following an early observation by Pavlov in the course of his conditioning experiments, several investigators have established "experimental neuroses" in dogs, cats, rats, sheep, and other animals by exposing them to conflict situations (see 26, ch. 19; 102, pp. 112–118). The usual procedure is to condition approach and avoidance responses to the same or very similar stimuli. For example, cats conditioned to open a food box and eat when a buzzer or a light was turned on were later stimulated by an air blast as they approached the food box (66). The resulting indications of anxiety and disorganization of behavior were more intense and lasting than those following simple stimulation by an air blast. Through several subsequent studies, it was demonstrated that it was the conflictual nature of the situation that produced the behavioral symptoms observed in these experiments.

To facilitate the formulation of testable hypotheses, a number of psychologists have applied concepts derived from general psychology to the description of neurotic and psychotic behavior. Some have used concepts from information theory (70), others from sensory deprivation (51, pp. 269–272; 93), and still others from developmental psychology (36). Because of the key position it occupies in all psychology, learning theory has been employed most widely in proposed explanations of behavioral deviations. These formulations have been prepared within the framework of different learning theories (see, e.g., 19, 64, 76, 77, 118).

One of the most thoroughgoing formulations, which has stimulated extensive research, is that given by Dollard and Miller in their book on *Personality and Psychotherapy* (19) and extended in later publications by Miller and his co-workers (see 72). These investigators first reformulated common psychoanalytic concepts such as repression, displacement, and transference in terms of the conditioned-reaction learning theory developed by Hull (49). Together with a group of their associates and students at Yale University, they then designed and conducted controlled animal experiments to test the various hypotheses generated by these theoretical formulations. Finally, they checked clinical observations of the behavior of patients in psychotherapy against their experimental findings. Working within the same theoretical framework, Mednick (67) has more recently proposed an interpretation of both acute and chronic schizophrenia in terms of anxiety level and stimulus generalization.[3]

Of the many investigations conducted by Miller and his associates, one will be described to illustrate the general approach. This study deals with the mechanism of displacement, which has been used widely in clinical psychol-

[3] See also the critique of this formulation and the rejoinder in *Psychol. Bull.*, 1959, **56**, 313–316.

ogy to explain symptom formation. Briefly, displacement refers to the substitution of another stimulus or response for the one that arouses excessive anxiety. Like other symptom mechanisms, displacement has been interpreted as a defense against intolerable anxiety. Miller and his associates formulated an explanation of displacement in terms of stimulus generalization and conflict (71–74, 81, 82). Through a series of ingenious experiments with rats, they demonstrated that, as stimulus similarity decreases, avoidance responses decline more rapidly than approach responses. In technical conditioning terminology, the generalization gradient is steeper for avoidance than for approach. By similar procedures, it was shown that avoidance falls off more rapidly than approach along a distance gradient. Thus, in a conflict situation, in which food and an electric shock are associated with the same goal object, the rat will approach part way and then stop.

Combining these displacement and conflict hypotheses, Murray and Berkun (81) conducted an experiment with the apparatus illustrated in Figure 105. The rats were first given approach training in the wide white alley, in which they could obtain food by raising the lid of the food box. In the second series of trials, they received an electric shock upon contact with the food box but still found food within it. This represents a typical conflict situation. In the third part of the experiment, the walls with windows, shown in Figure 105, were inserted and the rats were again placed in the wide white alley. No shock was used, and food was available in the white alley only. It was anticipated that the conflict of approach and avoidance would lead to an initial approach response for a short way along the white alley. According to the displacement hypothesis, the animal should then move to the medium-width gray alley. After proceeding some distance along this alley, the increasing strength of the avoidance response should again halt progress, and the animal should displace to the still less similar narrow black alley. The more different the new alley, the closer the rat should approach the food end.[4] Following repeated training with food in the white alley and no shock, the substitute responses should gradually be eliminated, and the original direct response in the white alley should reappear.

The empirical findings of the rat experiments confirmed these hypotheses. This experiment in turn provided a theoretical model for explaining behavior during psychotherapy. It was applied, for example, in predicting the course of the client's verbal expressions of hostility toward various persons in his life as psychotherapy progressed. Neither the displacement model nor the conflict model alone fitted the observed results. It was only when the two were combined that the sequence of events in psychotherapy confirmed expectation.

It is beyond the scope of this book to consider the detailed formulations of these hypotheses and the nature of the evidence gathered to test them. The interested reader is urged to examine the original publications, especially the article by Murray and Berkun (81). For the present purpose this research was cited only to illustrate the possibility of combining theoretical formulations, clinical observations, and controlled laboratory experiments in an integrated research program.

[4] In the apparatus used, the most dissimilar alley is also farthest from the original alley. For the present purpose, however, it does not matter whether the gradient is one of dissimilarity, distance, or a combination of the two.

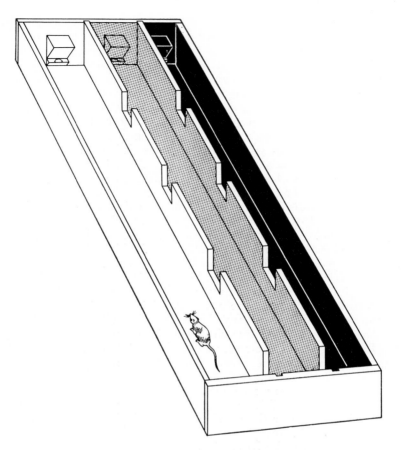

***Fig. 105*** Apparatus used in studying combined effects of stimulus generalization and avoidance-approach conflict in rats. (*From Murray and Berkun, 81, p. 50.*)

## SUMMARY

The gap between clinical practice and research has been narrowing since World War II. A major area of applied research in clinical psychology is concerned with the validity of diagnostic procedures, particularly projective techniques and other special clinical instruments. In the validation of such instruments, special attention must be given to questions of blind analysis, stereotype accuracy, multitrait-multimethod validation, cross validation, translation of test protocols into testable behavioral predictions, adequacy of criterion measures, interaction effects, and unevenness of coverage of the same test for different persons.

Investigations of the psychotherapeutic process deal with changes in client behavior in the course of therapy, the specific ways in which different therapists function, and the effect of therapist characteristics upon the progress of psychotherapy. Process research has been greatly furthered by the recording of psychotherapeutic sessions and by content analysis of the verbal responses of client and therapist. Q sorts have been used by the client-centered school to measure changes in self concepts in the course of psychotherapy. Appreciable interactions have been found among client, therapist, and process variables. The effects of subtle verbal reinforcement by the therapist upon client responses have been repeatedly demonstrated. Besides verbal responses, physiological indices of anxiety have also been investigated in the course of psychotherapy.

It is particularly difficult to obtain conclusive measures of the outcomes of therapy. Among the criteria of outcome employed for this purpose are client self-report, therapist's evaluation, objective measures of behavioral changes during therapy sessions, ward behavior, and follow-up data in real-life situations. Representativeness and comparability of experimental and control groups are essential but difficult to achieve. There is also need for control procedures to eliminate the influence of suggestion.

Research on the causes of mental disorders is an interdisciplinary venture spanning many fields, from biochemistry to anthropology. The sources of intellectual and emotional disorders have been sought in heredity, organic conditions, and experiential factors. Basic research that integrates clinical and experimental approaches is beginning to make vital contributions both to clinical practice and to the science of psychology. The reformulation of clinical concepts in terms of learning theory has been especially productive of research that cuts across clinic and laboratory.

# REFERENCES

1. Adams, J. S., and Hoffman, B. The frequency of self-reference statements as a function of generalized reinforcement. *J. abnorm. soc. Psychol.,* 1960, **60**, 384–389.
2. Anastasi, Anne. *Differential psychology.* (3rd ed.) New York: Macmillan, 1958.
3. Anastasi, Anne. Heredity, environment, and the question "How?" *Psychol. Rev.,* 1958, **65**, 197–208.
4. Anastasi, Anne. *Psychological testing.* (2nd ed.) New York: Macmillan, 1961.
5. Angel, C., *et al.* Serum oxidation tests in schizophrenic and normal subjects. *Arch. Neurol. Psychiat.,* 1957, **78**, 500–504.
6. Auld, F., Jr., and Murray, E. J. Content-analysis studies of psychotherapy. *Psychol. Bull.,* 1955, **52**, 377–395.
7. Benda, C. E., and Farrell, M. J. Psychopathology of mental deficiency in children. In P. H. Hoch and J. Zubin (Eds.), *Psychopathology of childhood.* New York: Grune & Stratton, 1955. Pp. 56–81.
8. Brackbill, G. A. Studies of brain dysfunction in schizophrenia. *Psychol. Bull.,* 1956, **53**, 210–226.
9. Burdock, E. I., Hardesty, Anne S., Hakerem, G., and Zubin, J. A ward behavior rating scale for mental hospital patients. *J. clin. Psychol.,* 1960, **16**, 246–247.
10. Butler, J. M., and Haigh, G. V. Changes in the relation between self-concepts and ideal concepts consequent upon client-centered counseling. In C. R. Rogers and Rosalind F. Dymond (Eds.), *Psychotherapy and personality change: Co-ordinated research studies in the client-centered approach.* Chicago: Univer. Chicago Press, 1954. Ch. 4.
11. Campbell, D. T., and Fiske, D. W. Convergent and discriminant validation by the multitrait-multimethod matrix. *Psychol. Bull.,* 1959, **56**, 81–105.
12. Cartwright, Rosalind D., and Vogel, J. L. A comparison of change in psycho-neurotic patients during matched periods of therapy and no therapy. *J. consult. Psychol.,* 1960, **24**, 121–127.

13. Cattell, R. B. *Factor analysis: An introduction and manual for the psychologist and social scientist.* New York: Harper & Row, 1952.
14. Chassan, J. B. Statistical inference and the single case in clinical design. *Psychiatry,* 1960, **23**, 173–184.
15. Cronbach, L. J. Statistical methods applied to Rorschach scores: A review. *Psychol. Bull.,* 1949, **46**, 393–429.
16. Cronbach, L. J., and Gleser, Goldine C. *Psychological tests and personnel decisions.* Urbana, Ill.: Univer. Ill. Press, 1957.
17. Crowne, D. P., and Stephens, M. W. Self-acceptance and self-evaluative methodology. *Psychol. Bull.,* 1961, **58**, 104–121.
18. Dollard, J., and Auld, F., Jr. *Scoring human motives: A manual.* New Haven, Conn.: Yale Univer. Press, 1959.
19. Dollard, J., and Miller, N. E. *Personality and psychotherapy: An analysis in terms of learning, thinking, and culture.* New York: McGraw-Hill, 1950.
20. Dollard, J., and Mowrer, O. H. A method of measuring tension in written documents. *J. abnorm. soc. Psychol.,* 1947, **42**, 3–32.
21. Edwards, A. L., and Cronbach, L. J. Experimental design for research in psychotherapy. *J. clin. Psychol.,* 1952, **8**, 51–59.
22. Ehrlich, R., and Wiener, D. N. The measurement of values in psychotherapeutic settings. *J. gen. Psychol.,* 1961, **64**, 359–372.
23. Ellenberger, H. Cultural aspects of mental illness. *Amer. J. Psychother.,* 1960, **14**, 158–173.
24. Eysenck, H. J. The effects of psychotherapy: An evaluation. *J. consult. Psychol.,* 1952, **16**, 319–324.
25. Eysenck, H. J. Personality tests: 1950–1955. In T. H. Fleming (Ed.), *Recent progress in psychology.* London: Churchill, 1959. Pp. 118–159.
26. Eysenck, H. J. (Ed.) *Handbook of abnormal psychology: An experimental approach.* New York: Basic Books, 1961.
27. Fairweather, G. W., *et al.* Relative effectiveness of psychotherapeutic programs: A multicriteria comparison of four programs for different patient groups. *Psychol. Monogr.,* 1960, **74**, No. 5.
28. Fantl, B., and Schiro, J. Cultural variables in the behavior patterns and symptom formation of 15 Irish and 15 Italian female schizophrenics. *Int. J. soc. Psychiat.,* 1959, **4**, 245–253.
29. Fiedler, F. E. A method for objective quantification of certain countertransference attitudes. *J. clin. Psychol.,* 1951, **7**, 101–107.
30. Field, M. J. *Search for security: An ethno-psychiatric study of rural Ghana.* Evanston, Ill.: Northwestern Univer. Press, 1960.
31. Frank, G. H. On the history of the objective investigation of the process of psychotherapy. *J. Psychol.,* 1961, **51**, 89–95.
32. Fulkerson, S. C., and Barry, J. R. Methodology and research on the prognostic use of psychological tests. *Psychol. Bull.,* 1961, **58**, 177–204.
33. Furchtgott, E. Behavioral effects of ionizing radiations. *Psychol. Bull.,* 1956, **53**, 320–334.
34. Garmezy, N., Farina, A., and Rodnick, E. H. Direct study of child-parent interactions: I. The structured situational test. A method for studying family interaction in schizophrenia. *Amer. J. Orthopsychiat.,* 1960, **30**, 445–452.
35. Gerard, R. W., *et al.* The nosology of schizophrenia. *Amer. J. Psychiat.,* 1963, **120**, 16–29.
36. Goldman, A. E. A comparative-developmental approach to schizophrenia. *Psychol. Bull.,* 1962, **59**, 57–69.
37. *Graduate education in psychology.* Washington: Amer. Psychol. Assoc., 1959.
38. Graham, Frances K., Ernhart, Claire B., Thurston, D., and Craft, Marguerite. Development three years after perinatal anoxia and other potentially damaging newborn experiences. *Psychol. Monogr.,* 1962, **76**, No. 3.
39. Haigh, G. Defensive behavior in client-centered therapy. *J. consult. Psychol.,* 1949, **13**, 181–189.
40. Haley, J. Direct study of child-parent interactions: III. Observation of the family of the schizophrenic. *Amer. J. Orthopsychiat.,* 1960, **30**, 460–467.
41. Harvey, W. A. Changing syndrome and culture: Recent studies in comparative psychiatry. *Int. J. soc. Psychiat.,* 1956, **2**, 165–171.

42. Hathaway, S. Some considerations relative to nondirective counseling as therapy. *J. clin. Psychol.*, 1948, **4**, 226–231.
43. Heilizer, F. Critical review of some published experiments with chlorpromazine in schizophrenic, neurotic, and normal humans. *J. chron. Dis.*, 1960, **11**, 102–148.
44. Henry, W. E., and Farley, Jane. The validity of the Thematic Apperception Test in the study of adolescent personality. *Psychol. Monogr.*, 1959, **73**, No. 17.
45. Hollingshead, A. B., and Redlich, F. C. *Social class and mental illness: A community study.* New York: Wiley, 1958.
46. Holt, R. R. Some statistical problems in clinical research. *Educ. psychol. Measmt*, 1950, **10**, 609–627.
47. Horowitz, Frances D., and Lovell, L. L. Attitudes of mothers of female schizophrenics. *Child Develpm.*, 1960, **31**, 229–305.
48. Horwitt, M. K. Fact and artifact in the biology of schizophrenia. *Science*, 1956, **124**, 429–430.
49. Hull, C. L. *Principles of behavior.* New York: Appleton-Century-Crofts, 1943.
50. Hunt, J. McV. A social agency as the setting for research. *J. consult. Psychol.*, 1949, **13**, 69–81.
51. Jackson, D. D. (Ed.) *The etiology of schizophrenia.* New York: Basic Books, 1960.
52. Joint Commission on Mental Illness and Health. *Action for mental health: Final report of the Joint Commission on Mental Illness and Health.* New York: Basic Books, 1961.
53. Kallmann, F. J. *Heredity in health and mental disorder: Principles of psychiatric genetics in the light of comparative twin studies.* New York: Norton, 1953.
54. Kaufman, I., *et al.* Treatment implications of a new classification of parents of schizophrenic children. *Amer. J. Psychiat.*, 1960, **116**, 920–924.
55. Kety, S. S. Biochemical theories of schizophrenia. Parts I and II. *Science,* 1959, **129**, 1528–1532; 1590–1596.
56. Knobloch, Hilda, and Pasamanick, B. Syndrome of minimal cerebral damage in infancy. *J. Amer. med. Assoc.*, 1959, **170**, 1384–1387.
57. Lacey, J. I., and Lacey, Beatrice C. Verification and extension of the principle of autonomic response stereotypy. *Amer. J. Psychol.*, 1958, **71**, 50–73.
58. Leighton, Dorothea C. Community study of mental health: Preliminary findings of the distribution of persons with symptoms of psychiatric significance in relation to social environment. In *Milbank Memorial Fund, 1956 Annual Conference.* New York: Milbank Memorial Fund, 1957. Pp. 68–77.
59. Levitt, E. E. The results of psychotherapy with children: An evaluation. *J. consult. Psychol.*, 1957, **21**, 189–196.
60. Lilienfeld, A. M., Pasamanick, B., and Rogers, M. Relationship between pregnancy experience and the development of certain neuropsychiatric disorders in childhood. *Amer. J. publ. Hlth,* 1955, **45**, 637–643.
61. Linton, R. *Culture and mental disorders.* Springfield, Ill.: Thomas, 1956.
62. Little, K. B., and Shneidman, E. S. Congruencies among interpretations of psychological test and anamnestic data. *Psychol. Monogr.*, 1959, **73**, No. 6.
63. Loranger, A. W., Prout, C. T., and White, Mary A. The placebo effect in psychiatric drug research. *J. Amer. med. Assoc.*, 1961, **176**, 920–925.
64. Lundin, R. W. *Personality: An experimental approach.* New York: Macmillan, 1961.
65. Martin, B. The assessment of anxiety by physiological behavioral measures. *Psychol. Bull.*, 1961, **58**, 234–255.
66. Masserman, J. H. *Behavior and neurosis.* Chicago: Univer. Chicago Press, 1943.
67. Mednick, S. A. A learning theory approach to research on schizophrenia. *Psychol. Bull.*, 1958, **55**, 316–327.
68. Meehl, P. E. The cognitive activity of the clinician. *Amer. Psychologist*, 1960, **15**, 19–27.
69. Meier, G. W., Bunch, M. E., Nolan, C. Y., and Scheidler, C. H. Anoxia, behavioral development, and learning ability: A comparative-experimental approach. *Psychol. Monogr.*, 1960, **74**, No. 1.
70. Miller, J. G. Information input overload and psychopathology. *Amer. J. Psychiat.*, 1960, **116**, 695–704.
71. Miller, N. E. Theory and experiment relating psychoanalytic displacement to stimulus-response generalization. *J. abnorm. soc. Psychol.*, 1948, **43**, 155–178.

72. Miller, N. E. Liberalization of basic S-R concepts: Extensions to conflict behavior, motivation, and social learning. In S. Koch (Ed.), *Psychology: A study of a science*. New York: McGraw-Hill, 1958. Vol. 2, pp. 198–292.

73. Miller, N. E., and Kraeling, D. Displacement: Greater generalization of approach than avoidance in a generalized approach-avoidance conflict. *J. exp. Psychol.*, 1952, **43**, 217–221.

74. Miller, N. E., and Murray, E. J. Displacement and conflict: Learnable drive as a basis for the steeper gradient of avoidance than of approach. *J. exp. Psychol.*, 1952, **43**, 227–231.

75. Morrison, S. L. Principles and methods of epidemiological research and their application to psychiatric illness. *J. ment. Sci.*, 1959, **105**, 999–1011.

76. Mowrer, O. H. *Learning theory and personality dynamics*. New York: Ronald, 1950.

77. Mowrer, O. H. *Learning theory and behavior*. New York: Wiley, 1960.

78. Mowrer, O. H., *et al. Psychotherapy: Theory and research*. New York: Ronald, 1953.

79. Murray, E. J. A case study in a behavioral analysis of psychotherapy. *J. abnorm. soc. Psychol.*, 1954, **49**, 305–310.

80. Murray, E. J. A content-analysis method for studying psychotherapy. *Psychol. Monogr.*, 1956, **70**, No. 13.

81. Murray, E. J., and Berkun, M. M. Displacement as a function of conflict. *J. abnorm. soc. Psychol.*, 1955, **51**, 47–56.

82. Murray, E. J., and Miller, N. E. Displacement: Steeper gradient of generalization of avoidance than of approach with age of habit controlled. *J. exp. Psychol.*, 1952, **43**, 222–226.

83. Mussen, P. H., and Naylor, H. K. The relationships between overt and fantasy aggression. *J. abnorm. soc. Psychol.*, 1954, **49**, 235–240.

84. Myers, J. K., and Roberts, B. H. *Family and class dynamics in mental illness*. New York: Wiley, 1959.

85. Pasamanick, B., *et al.* A survey of mental disease in an urban population: II. Prevalence by race and income. In B. Pasamanick (Ed.), *The epidemiology of mental disorder*. Washington: Amer. Assoc. Adv. Sci., 1959. Pp. 183–201.

86. Pasamanick, B., Knobloch, Hilda, and Lilienfeld, A. M. Socioeconomic status and some precursors of neuropsychiatric disorder. *Amer. J. Orthopsychiat.*, 1956, **26**, 594–601.

87. Pittluck, Patricia. The relation between aggressive fantasy and overt behavior. Unpublished doctoral dissertation, Yale Univer., 1950.

88. Quay, H. The effect of verbal reinforcement on the recall of early memories. *J. abnorm. soc. Psychol.*, 1959, **59**, 254–257.

89. Roessler, R., and Greenfield, N. S. (Eds.) *Physiological correlates of psychological disorder*. Madison, Wis.: Univer. Wis. Press, 1962.

90. Rogers, C. R., and Dymond, Rosalind F. (Eds.) *Psychotherapy and personality change: Coordinated research studies in the client-centered approach*. Chicago: Univer. Chicago Press, 1954.

91. Rogers, J. M. Operant conditioning in a quasi-therapy setting. *J. abnorm. soc. Psychol.*, 1960, **60**, 247–252.

92. Rosenthal, D. Problems of sampling and diagnosis in the major twin studies of schizophrenia. *J. psychiat. Res.*, 1961, **1**, 116–134.

93. Rosenzweig, N. Sensory deprivation and schizophrenia: Some clinical and theoretical similarities. *Amer. J. Psychiat.*, 1959, **116**, 326–329.

94. Rubin, L. S. Recent advances in the chemistry of psychotic disorders. *Psychol. Bull.*, 1959, **56**, 375–383.

95. Rubinstein, E. A., and Parloff, M. B. (Eds.) *Research in psychotherapy*. Washington: Amer. Psychol. Assoc., 1959.

96. Salzinger, K., and Pisoni, Stephanie. Reinforcement of verbal affect response of normal subjects during the interview. *J. abnorm. soc. Psychol.*, 1960, **60**, 127–130.

97. Sapolsky, A. Effect of interpersonal relationships upon verbal conditioning. *J. abnorm. soc. Psychol.*, 1960, **60**, 241–246.

98. Sarbin, T. R., Taft, R., and Bailey, D. E. *Clinical inference and cognitive theory*. New York: Holt, Rinehart and Winston, 1960.

99. Scott, W. A. Social psychological correlates of mental illness and mental health. *Psychol. Bull.,* 1958, **55**, 65–87.
100. Seeman, J. A study of the process of non-directive therapy. *J. consult. Psychol.,* 1949, **13**, 157–168.
101. Seeman, J. Psychotherapy. *Ann. Rev. Psychol.,* 1961, **12**, 157–194.
102. Shaffer, L. F., and Shoben, E. J., Jr. *The psychology of adjustment: A dynamic and experimental approach to personality and mental hygiene.* (2nd ed.) Boston: Houghton Mifflin, 1956.
103. Shapiro, A. K. A contribution to the history of the placebo effect. *Behav. Sci.,* 1960, **5**, 109–135.
104. Silverman, L. H. A Q-sort study of the validity of evaluations made from projective techniques. *Psychol. Monogr.,* 1959, **73**, No. 7.
105. Singer, J. L., and Opler, M. K. Contrasting patterns of fantasy and motility in Irish and Italian schizophrenics. *J. abnorm. soc. Psychol.,* 1956, **53**, 42–47.
106. Snyder, W. U. An investigation of the nature of nondirective psychotherapy. *J. gen. Psychol.,* 1945, **33**, 193–224.
107. Snyder, W. U. *The psychotherapy relationship.* New York: Macmillan, 1961.
108. Srole, L., et al. *Mental health in the metropolis: The midtown Manhattan study,* vol. 1. New York: McGraw-Hill, 1962.
109. Staudt, Virginia M., and Zubin, J. A biometric evaluation of the somatotherapies in schizophrenia. *Psychol. Bull.,* 1957, **54**, 171–196.
110. Stephenson, W. *The study of behavior: Q-technique and its methodology.* Chicago: Univer. Chicago Press, 1953.
111. Strother, C. R. (Ed.) *Psychology and mental health.* Washington: Amer. Psychol. Assoc., 1956.
112. Strupp, H. H. Psychotherapy. *Ann. Rev. Psychol.,* 1962, **13**, 445–478.
113. Strupp, H. H., and Luborsky, L. (Eds.) *Research in psychotherapy,* vol. 2. Washington: Amer. Psychol. Assoc., 1962.
114. Truax, C. B. The process of group psychotherapy: Relationships between therapeutic conditions and intrapersonal exploration. *Psychol. Monogr.,* 1961, **75**, No. 7.
115. Uhr, L., and Miller, J. G. (Eds.) *Drugs and behavior.* New York: Wiley, 1960.
116. Wallach, M. A., Green, L. R., Lipsitt, P. D., and Mineheart, Jean B. Contradiction between overt and projective personality indicators as a function of defensiveness. *Psychol. Monogr.,* 1962, **76**, No. 1.
117. Weinstein, E. A. *Cultural aspects of delusion: A psychiatric study of the Virgin Islands.* New York: Free Press, 1962.
118. Wolpe, J. *Psychotherapy by reciprocal inhibition.* Stanford, Calif.: Stanford Univer. Press, 1958.
119. Zax, M., and Klein, A. Measurement of personality and behavior changes following psychotherapy. *Psychol. Bull.,* 1960, **57**, 435–448.
120. Zubin, J. Design for the evaluation of therapy. *Proc. Assoc. Res. nerv. ment. Dis.,* 1953, **21**, 10–15.
121. Zubin, J., et al. Symposium: Statistics for the clinician. *J. clin. Psychol.,* 1950, **6**, 1–76.

# VI

*Counseling Psychology*

# 16

# The Work of the
# Counseling Psychologist

"Counseling" is a broad term that covers many different functions. A professional counselor, moreover, may have been trained in psychology, social work, education, the ministry, or a number of other fields. It is only since the 1950s that the title of "counseling psychologist" was adopted to designate a fully trained psychologist, typically at the Ph.D. level, who specializes in counseling functions. The term "counselor" is commonly employed to refer to persons operating at a lower professional level and with less training.

Historically, counseling psychology originated in the vocational-guidance movement (51). The early vocational counselors concentrated on the dissemination of information about jobs. Following the rapid growth of psychological testing after World War I, tests were widely employed to investigate the individual's qualifications for different kinds of work. Still later came the recognition that vocational choices and vocational adjustment are intimately related to personality development and to total life adjustment. As a result, the functions of the vocational counselor were broadened to include a study of the whole individual. Concurrently, the rise of the mental health movement, the introduction of employee counselors in industry, and other developments highlighted the need for counselors to deal with a number of personal problems other than those associated with vocational choice. At this stage, counseling merged with clinical psychology.

Some psychologists today use the terms "clinical psychology" and "counseling psychology" interchangeably and recognize no difference between the two fields (see, e.g., 38, 66, 67). To be sure, there is much overlapping in the activities of most clinical and counseling psychologists. Among individual practitioners, moreover, some counseling psychologists can readily be found who in their functions resemble a particular clinical psychologist more closely than two clinical psychologists resemble each other. Nevertheless, the two fields as a whole can be differentiated, as will be shown in a later section of this chapter. This differentiation has received formal recognition by the psychological profession (1). Thus the American Board of Examiners in Professional Psychology issues separate diplomas in clinical and in counseling psychology. Similarly, the Education and Training Board of the American Psychological Association accredits university training programs independently in these two specialties. The American Psychological Association has also had separate divisions in the clinical and counseling fields since 1945, when a divisional structure was first introduced into the association. On the other hand, the overlap between clinical and counseling psychology is suggested by the close similarity in actual course requirements in university training programs in these two fields (64).

## VARIETIES OF COUNSELING

Counseling psychologists work in many contexts. Schools and colleges represent one of the principal settings for their activities. An increasing number are being employed in industrial and business organizations, government agencies, and the armed services. Others work in hospitals, rehabilitation centers, vocational-guidance bureaus, marital clinics, and other community agencies. To a large extent, the setting in which a counseling psychologist operates determines the type of problems with which he must deal.

*Vocational counseling* still represents a major part of the work of most counseling psychologists, particularly those employed in student counseling bureaus of high schools and colleges (15). Because of its central position in the entire counseling field, vocational counseling will be discussed more fully in later sections of this chapter as well as in the next chapter. A closely related area is that of *educational counseling*. Frequently the selection of a program of studies is implied in a vocational decision. In its own right, however, educational counseling is concerned with such decisions as whether or not to attend college, the choice of a particular college, what curriculum to pursue, or what specific courses to elect. Educational counselors may also deal with problems of study skills, reading disabilities, and other academic difficulties.

Educational counseling is often conducted on a part-time basis by classroom teachers. To a more limited extent, such part-time counselors may also provide vocational counseling within academic settings, from the elementary school through the college level. In such situations, a counseling psychologist or other guidance specialist may direct the counseling program or serve as a consultant in its administration. Counseling psychologists also conduct in-service training and special training institutes for educational and vocational counselors and participate in the general training programs conducted in schools of education. More will be said about these functions in connection with the relations of psychology to education, to be considered in Chapter 18.

Guidance functions are now regarded as an integral part of the daily classroom activity of elementary and high school teachers. Accordingly, guidance techniques are regularly included in teacher training programs, and several books on guidance have been directed specifically to the needs of teachers (see e.g., 46, 59). Group counseling techniques suitable for use in a school situation have also been developed (44, 47, 91). There is evidence that such group procedures may be as effective as individual counseling under certain circumstances (83, ch. 13). At the college level, counseling functions are generally integrated in the student personnel program, which covers also housing, student activities, student government, health services, and other extracurricular matters (60). To aid in the vocational counseling of college students, a number of books have been written for use by the students themselves (e.g., 37, 58).

*Employee counseling* in industry was ushered in by the Hawthorne Studies, discussed in Chapter 6. The growing recognition of the importance of employee morale has led to the appointment of employee counselors in many industrial, business, and governmental organizations. The activities of such counselors are usually quite varied, ranging all the way from assistance in locating suitable housing to counseling on emotional problems. The problem need not be directly related to the job. For some maladjusted employees, the source of the difficulty may be at home or in some other problem arising off the job.

Depending upon the employee counselor's professional qualifications and the time available per client, he may handle problems himself or make appropriate referrals. In any event, an employee counselor would not himself undertake long-term psychotherapy with seriously disturbed individuals. In order to establish an effective counseling relationship, the employee counselor should have no administrative duties or authority. Only under these conditions would the employee feel completely free to discuss his problems with the counselor. In some companies, employee counseling is carried on by independent consulting psychologists on a part-time basis. This practice is followed especially in the counseling of executive personnel.

*Rehabilitation counseling* is a relatively recent but rapidly expanding field of activity for the counseling psychologist (38, ch. 12; 40; 55; 88). The rehabilitation counselor works with the orthopedically handicapped, the tubercular, the cardiac, the blind, the deaf, and other types of disabled persons. One of the recently formed divisions of the American Psychological Association is concerned with psychological aspects of disability (see Appendix A), and in 1958 the association sponsored a special institute on psychology and rehabilitation (94). There is also a growing body of psychological research dealing with the characteristics and problems of the physically disabled (6, 22, 95).

Counseling of the physically handicapped must be closely coordinated with remedial and training programs. Such counseling may have several objectives. In the case of children, the physical disability is likely to have delayed psychological development through the curtailment of normal experiences. Such children may require not only special educational programs but also interpersonal experiences for normal personality growth. Handicapped persons of any age tend to have special emotional problems, such as feelings of insecurity or hostility and various types of defensive reactions. These reactions often stem from a feeling of being different from one's associates. An important goal of rehabilitation counseling is the development of a realistic and constructive attitude toward one's handicap. Emotional acceptance of prosthetic and other adaptive devices is a closely related problem.

The successful adjustment of the disabled person often requires counseling with family, teachers, employers, and other associates who interact with the individual in significant ways. Vocational counseling is also an important aspect of the rehabilitation program. The physical disability limits the vocational opportunities available to a young person entering the world of work and often makes a return to the former job impossible for a previously employed worker. Satisfactory work adjustment can be achieved by a combination of intensive testing with realistic work samples, special training, experience in sheltered workshops, and eventual job placement. Such a program needs to be closely integrated with a medical evaluation of the limits set by the physical disability (see, e.g., 34).

Patients who have been institutionalized for serious emotional disturbances may also require rehabilitation before resuming their normal activities. Today the scope of rehabilitation counseling has been broadened to cover mental as well as physical disabilities (94). A noteworthy development in this connection is the gradual inclusion of psychiatric patients in rehabilitation centers originally established to care for the physically disabled. The Institute for the Crippled and Disabled in New York City has successfully initiated such an extension of its services. Similar institutes throughout the country have begun to accept a few psychiatric patients, although no formal recognition of this function is included in their objectives. Since the physically disabled often have psychiatric problems, institutes designed to serve such patients may already have the facilities and experience for handling psychiatric disabilities.

*Old-age counseling* is concerned with the vocational and personal guidance of older persons, with retirement problems, and with the special intellectual and emotional disorders associated with old age. Practical concern with the problems of advanced age has been stimulated by the relatively large number of older persons in our society. As medical progress and better living conditions lengthen the life span, the proportion of older persons in the population continues to increase. Gerontology, or the study of old age, and geriatrics, dealing with diseases of old age, are now thriving fields of research and professional specialization.

The active interest of psychologists in these fields is evidenced by the establishment of a Division on Maturity and Old Age in the American Psychological Association and by an increasing amount of research on the changes occurring beyond maturity in intelligence, special aptitudes, emotional reactions, interests, and attitudes (see 2, pp. 238-258; 10; 11; 71). The use of longitudinal approaches, large representative samples, and improved experimental designs is beginning to clarify the nature and causes of these changes. Special attention has also been given to the industrial skills of older workers and to ways of maximizing their effective utilization (e.g., 92).

The adjustment problems of older persons provide a fertile field for the application of psychotherapy, but one that has not yet been adequately explored (65). Among very old persons, intellectual and emotional deterioration is likely to have some organic basis. But, even in these cases, experiential factors play a significant part, and psychotherapeutic techniques are likely to bring about some improvement. As in the case of rehabilitation counseling with the handicapped, the psychological counseling of the aged often needs to be coordinated with medical care and with social work.

Another area in which psychologists can make a contribution is that of *marriage counseling* (49, 50). Beginning with the pioneer work of Terman (79), a limited amount of research has been conducted on psychological factors making for marital adjustment and compatibility (see, e.g., 17; 48; 54; 69, pp. 578-581; 80). To date, sociologists have been somewhat more active than psychologists in this area. Marital counseling itself spans many fields, including medicine, genetics, psychology, religion, social work, law, and home economics. The specific functions of marital counselors might range from planning a family budget to analyzing the hereditary transmission of a rare defect. Within this context, the psychologist is typically concerned with questions of compatibility in choice of marital partner and with the solution of interpersonal conflicts in family living. The latter may call for psychotherapy with one or both partners. Problems of child-rearing and parent-child relations are also of obvious relevance. Although psychology has much to contribute to marriage counseling, this is so far one of the least-developed fields of counseling psychology (49, 72).

It is apparent that counseling with regard to emotional problems, attitudes, and interpersonal relations runs through all forms of counseling. In addition, some individuals seek the help of a counselor explicitly because of an emotional problem. A recent college survey indicated the prevalence of emotional problems among college students and the need for college counselors equipped to handle them (12). But even when the referral problem pertains to a vocational decision, an educational question, or some other specific and relatively "impersonal" matter, the root of the difficulty often lies in a personality problem. Moreover, personality difficulties frequently complicate and aggravate other problems.

Counseling with regard to emotional problems is usually designated as *personal counseling*, although it is also known as adjustment counseling, psychological counseling, or short-term psychotherapy. It is in this area that the psychologist can make his most distinctive contribution. Furthermore, the counseling psychologist recognizes the close interrelation of all adjustment problems and therefore functions at a broad level regardless of the type of counseling involved. His orientation tends always to be toward counseling the whole individual. It is in connection with personal counseling, too, that the work of the counseling psychologist comes closest to that of the clinical psychologist. Hence at this point it is appropriate to examine more fully the relation between these two fields.

## RELATION BETWEEN CLINICAL AND COUNSELING PSYCHOLOGY

There are unquestionably many similarities between the functions of a clinical and a counseling psychologist. For both, the interpersonal relation between psychologist and client is of prime importance. As in clinical practice, the counseling relationship is nonthreatening, confidential, permissive, and accepting (83, pp. 14-17). Similarly, counseling depends upon verbal communication. Most counseling psychologists employ some variant of the client-centered, or nondirective, approach discussed in Chapter 14, although many combine this approach with considerable information giving of a fairly directive type. Classical psychoanalysis is least likely to be used in a counseling situation.

What of the differences? Perhaps the primary difference is that the aim of clinical psychology is to *change* the individual's basic personality structure and personal constructs, while the aim of counseling psychology is to enable the individual to *utilize* his present resources most effectively in solving problems. Tyler (82; 83, ch. 11) has introduced the concept of "minimum-change therapy" to characterize the counseling process. Its object is to bring about readjustment with a minimum of personality change rather than to delve into the sources of anxieties and conflicts.

While psychotherapy tries to alter a client's anxiety level, defensiveness, and other generalized response habits, counseling concentrates on the solution of specific problems, such as poor study habits or lack of social poise, that may be interfering with effective functioning (8). It is also concerned with the making of decisions and plans regarding educational, vocational, and other courses of action. The counseling psychologist, however, does not as a rule give advice or tell the client what he should do. It is now generally felt that to do so would reinforce habits of dependency rather than facilitate personal growth.

Because it does not undertake to restructure a client's personality or to provide insight into all his emotional conflicts, counseling characteristically requires less time than does psychotherapy. It will be recalled that duration of treatment also differentiates nondirective therapy from psychoanalysis (Chapter 14). In many ways, the differences between counseling and clinical psychology are similar to those between the nondirective and the psycho-analytic approaches. Among client-centered, or nondirective, practitioners, the distinction between counseling and psychotherapy is most likely to be blurred.

Another difference between clinical and counseling psychology is that the former focuses on weaknesses to be overcome, while the latter focuses on positive strengths to be developed (82; 83, ch. 11). Typically the counselor is not concerned with ferreting out personality deficiencies that are adequately controlled. Rather he concentrates on the utilization of any available assets that he can identify in the particular client. Slight shifts in the direction in which an individual is moving may enable him to capitalize on these assets and to bypass obstacles. The counseling psychologist looks for the normalities found even in abnormal persons, whereas the clinical psychologist and, to a greater extent, the psychiatrist look for the abnormalities found even in normal persons. In its emphasis upon positive development and the prevention of maladjustment, counseling is consistent with the aims of the mental health movement (Chapter 14). Perhaps, as we learn more about the causes and prevention of mental disorders, there will be an increasing demand for counseling psychologists and a decreasing need for clinical psychologists.

Unlike psychotherapy, counseling frequently requires the giving of factual information (39; 83, ch. 9). Thus, in educational and vocational counseling, the individual needs information about job requirements and opportunities, suitable schools and courses of study, effective study skills, or test norms in terms of which he may evaluate his own performance. Such information should be provided when it will help the client to think realistically and constructively about his problems. The counselor may impart the information himself during an interview, or he may refer the client to appropriate persons or to readily available published sources. In any event, the information should be presented in such a way as to be understood and accepted. Effective communication, including sufficient feedback from the client, is essential to this aspect of counseling.

The counselor himself also needs to be familiar with up-to-date and dependable sources of information in his particular area of operation. Since vocational counseling plays such an important part in the activities of most counselors, a knowledge of the world of work is a common requirement in the training of counseling psychologists. In fact, the inclusion or noninclusion of courses on occupational information often represents the principal difference between the basic training of counselors and clinical psychologists (64).

The type of client with whom clinical and counseling psychologists work has often been cited as another difference between the two fields. It is certainly true that in general the counseling psychologist works with more nearly normal persons who may want help in making a specific decision or who may have minor personality difficulties. Hahn (39) sums it up by saying that the counseling psychologist is most often concerned with persons whose anxiety level is interfering and disruptive rather than disabling or disintegrative. To be sure, this distinction is only relative. On the one hand, some clinical psychologists will accept no severely disturbed cases for psychotherapy; they exclude all psychotics, as well as neurotics with symptoms of long standing. On the other hand, some counseling psychologists work with hospitalized psychotic patients. In the latter cases, however, the counseling psychologist is concerned with the rehabilitation and vocational adjustment of the patient rather than with treatment of his psychotic condition. Frequently such counseling is introduced shortly before discharge, to enable the individual to make a more effective job and community adjustment. An example is the extensive program in counseling psychology conducted in Veterans Administration hospitals.

The difference between clinical and counseling psychology has also been described in terms of the characteristic orientations and attitudes of the psychologists who specialize in the two areas. It has been suggested, for example, that counseling psychologists resemble industrial psychologists more closely than they do clinical psychologists (39). In contrast to the clinical psychologist, the counseling psychologist is more likely to rely upon objectively constructed tests and empirical norms than upon subjective qualitative approaches. He relies less on clinical judgment or projective tests and more on structured ability and interest tests. Counseling psychologists often have to work closely with members of other professions, as was apparent in the preceding section. They must therefore be able to function effectively in various settings and to cooperate with persons whose training and background are very unlike their own. In several of these contexts, counseling psychologists also tend to have administrative and managerial responsibilities.

Still another point of view about the relation of clinical and counseling psychology has been expressed by Vance and Volsky (89). While maintaining that clinical and counseling *processes* can be differentiated, they argue that these two kinds of treatment are often required by the same client and hence should not be artificially separated in practice. On these grounds they advocate combined training in clinical and counseling processes for each practitioner.

## USE OF TESTS IN COUNSELING

*Types of Tests Used in Counseling.* Tests may be helpful in any kind of counseling but are most often employed to facilitate educational and vocational decisions. All types of tests may be used in counseling and probably are, but certain types clearly predominate. For a detailed treatment of tests that are of special interest to vocational counselors, the reader is referred to Super and Crites (78). General surveys of available tests can be found in current texts, such as Anastasi (3) and Cronbach (21). The preliminary discussion of the use of tests in personnel selection given in Chapter 3 is also relevant.

In counseling, *intelligence tests* are commonly employed to determine the

individual's general ability level, with special reference to his scholastic aptitude. Persons engaged in different occupations differ significantly in mean
intelligence test scores. The clearest demonstration of these differences was
provided by the analyses of intelligence test scores of large samples of men
in the United States Army during both world wars (32, 74). Figure 106
illustrates the results with a few occupations selected from different portions
of the total range. There are probably many reasons for these occupational
differences, but a major factor is undoubtedly the educational level required
for different types of work. The professions and other occupations calling

*Fig. 106*   Scores on the Army General Classification Test in relation to
civilian occupation. (*Data from Stewart, 74, pp. 5–13.*)

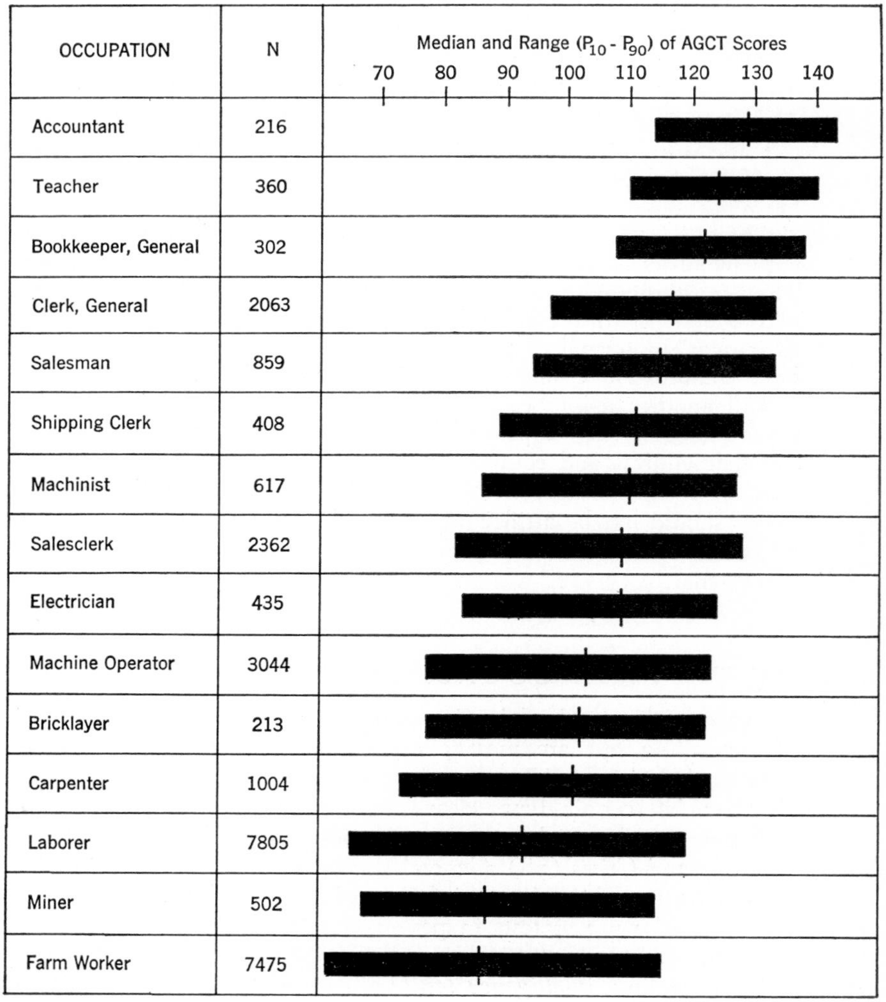

| OCCUPATION | N | Median and Range ($P_{10}$ - $P_{90}$) of AGCT Scores |
|---|---|---|
| Accountant | 216 | |
| Teacher | 360 | |
| Bookkeeper, General | 302 | |
| Clerk, General | 2063 | |
| Salesman | 859 | |
| Shipping Clerk | 408 | |
| Machinist | 617 | |
| Salesclerk | 2362 | |
| Electrician | 435 | |
| Machine Operator | 3044 | |
| Bricklayer | 213 | |
| Carpenter | 1004 | |
| Laborer | 7805 | |
| Miner | 502 | |
| Farm Worker | 7475 | |

for a high level of education typically show a higher average and a narrower range of intelligence test scores than do routine clerical and manual occupations.

Since most intelligence tests are primarily measures of scholastic aptitude, one of their applications to counseling is in predicting educational achievement and in estimating the highest educational level the individual is likely to reach. Intelligence tests are especially useful at the elementary school ages, when differentiation into separate abilities has not yet advanced very far (see 2, pp. 357–361). Typically, counselors rely on group tests of intelligence, which may of course be administered either individually or in groups, and which are available for different levels ranging from the primary grades to the graduate school.

For educational counseling, intelligence tests are often supplemented with *achievement tests* in different areas. Of particular interest are tests of reading and arithmetic skills. Special disabilities in these skills—particularly in reading—may seriously interfere with over-all educational achievement. *Special aptitude tests* are frequently administered in individual cases as demanded by the particular circumstances. When considering a special educational program or making vocational plans, the individual may need information regarding his manual dexterity or other motor skills or about his mechanical, clerical, artistic, or musical aptitudes. Tests are available to aid evaluation in all these areas.

*Multiple aptitude batteries* are of particular relevance to counseling problems because they provide a profile of scores in relatively independent abilities. Combining the principal abilities covered by intelligence tests with other broad aptitude areas, they enable the individual to explore his major strengths and weaknesses. While a global intelligence test score may indicate general level of expected educational or vocational attainment, a profile of scores on a multiple aptitude battery is more helpful in the choice of a field of specialization.

A multiple aptitude battery that has been in use long enough to permit the accumulation of extensive validity data is the Differential Aptitude Tests (7). Sample items from each of the eight tests comprising this battery can be found in Figure 107. A score profile on the Differential Aptitude Tests was reproduced in Figure 15 (Chapter 3). Designed for grades 8 through 12 and for unselected adults, this battery was prepared principally for use in educational and vocational counseling. The General Aptitude Test Battery developed by the United States Employment Service (25) is employed widely in vocational counseling. Other generally available aptitude batteries have not yet been sufficiently validated to be considered ready for use in individual counseling (see 3, ch. 13; 77).

*Interest tests* are undoubtedly one of the most popular counseling instruments. Essentially these tests are self-report inventories in which the individual records his likes and dislikes or his relative preferences for many kinds of familiar activities, people, or objects. In the Kuder Preference Record (52), the individual always compares three items, among which he marks the one he likes best and the one he likes least. For example, would he rather visit an art gallery, browse in a library, or visit a museum; would he rather collect autographs, coins, or butterflies? The responses are scored with reference to 10 broad interest areas: Outdoor (agricultural, naturalistic), Mechanical, Com-

## VERBAL REASONING.

Choose the correct pair of words to fill the blanks. The first word of the pair goes in the blank space at the beginning of the sentence; the second word of the pair goes in the blank at the end of the sentence.

...... is to water as eat is to ......

    A.   continue —— drive
    B.   foot —— enemy
    C.   drink —— food
    D.   girl —— industry
    E.   drink —— enemy

**The correct answer is C.**

## NUMERICAL ABILITY.

Choose the correct answer for each problem.

| Add | 13 | A | 14 |  | Subtract | 30 | A | 15 |
|-----|----|---|----|--|----------|----|---|----|
|  | 12 | B | 25 |  |  | 20 | B | 26 |
|  | —  | C | 16 |  |  | —  | C | 16 |
|  |    | D | 59 |  |  |    | D | 8 |
|  |    | E | none of these |  |  |    | E | none of these |

**The correct answer for the first problem is B; for the second, E.**

## ABSTRACT REASONING.

The four "problem figures" in each row make a series. Find the one among the "answer figures" which would be the next in the series.

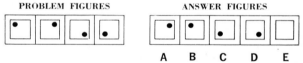

**The correct answer is B.**

## SPACE RELATIONS.

Which one of the following figures could be made by folding the given pattern? The pattern always shows the outside of the figure. Note the three grey surfaces.

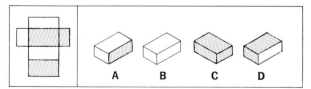

**The correct answer is D.**

*Fig. 107a*   Sample items from the Differential Aptitude Tests. (*Reproduced by permission. Copyright 1963, The Psychological Corporation.*)

## MECHANICAL REASONING.

Which man in this picture has the heavier load?

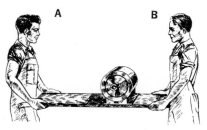

The correct answer is B.

## CLERICAL SPEED AND ACCURACY.

In each test item, one of the five combinations is underlined. Find the same combination on the answer sheet and mark it.

TEST ITEMS

SAMPLE OF ANSWER SHEET

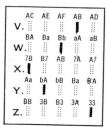

## LANGUAGE USAGE: I. SPELLING.

Indicate whether each word is spelled right or wrong.

W.   man

X.   gurl

## LANGUAGE USAGE: II. GRAMMAR.

Decide which of the lettered parts of the sentence has an error and mark the corresponding letter on the answer sheet. If there is no error, mark E.

Ain't we / going to / the office / next week?
    **A**       **B**       **C**       **D**

**Fig. 107b**   Sample items from the Differential Aptitude Tests. (*Reproduced by permission. Copyright 1963, The Psychological Corporation.*)

putational, Scientific, Persuasive, Artistic, Literary, Musical, Social Service, and Clerical. In addition, there is a verification scale for detecting carelessness or failure to follow directions.

It should be noted that Kuder scores indicate relative interest in these 10 areas, rather than absolute amount of interest. A flat profile might thus indicate that the individual is equally interested or equally uninterested in all of them. The test is constructed on the same principle as a Q sort, in which comparisons are made within the individual. A sample profile of scores on the Kuder is reproduced in Figure 108. This subject has his strongest interests in the literary field, with social service and outdoor interests following very closely. Other interest areas are low, the mechanical being unusually weak.

The Vocational Interest Blank developed by Strong (75) yields separate scores in each of about fifty occupations in the men's form and about thirty in the women's form. The construction of these keys was described in Chapter 3. Essentially, a high score in any given occupational key means that the individual's interests resemble those of persons engaged in that occupation. It suggests that he would find that occupation and his colleagues in it congenial and that he would fit in well with their way of life. For guidance purposes, the total pattern of occupational scores is customarily taken into account. It may be just as important to know which occupational groups the individual is most unlike as it is to know which groups he resembles most closely.

Figure 109 shows the standard profile chart on which Vocational Interest Blank scores are reported. The shaded areas represent the expected range of "chance scores," indicating neither agreement nor disagreement with the interests of that group. For illustrative purposes, the mean score of a group of 47 medical students on each key available at the time of testing has been marked with an x. As might be anticipated, this group obtained its highest mean score on the physician key. Other high scores were found on the dentist and chemist keys.

With regard to the use of the Vocational Interest Blank in counseling, it should be noted that most of its keys pertain to occupations at the professional or higher business levels. Few are available for skilled trades and none below that level. Clark (19) has developed another interest inventory with occupational scoring keys for several skilled trades. Attempts to develop interest keys for lower-level jobs have generally failed (see 23). This lack of differentiation in the interest patterns of workers at the lower occupational levels may be related to the finding that at these levels job satisfaction is more often associated with factors extrinsic to the work itself, while at higher job levels it is more often associated with the nature of the work (see Chapter 6).

Other types of *personality tests* are used to a much more limited extent in counseling. The lack of adequate validity data about most of these instruments requires that they be interpreted with considerable caution and checked against other sources of information about the individual. Personality inventories may be employed as a preliminary screening device to identify persons who should be referred for psychotherapy. Or they may be used by the counselor to focus discussion upon personal problems and to help the counselee to understand his own behavior.

Despite its original pathological orientation, the Minnesota Multiphasic

**Fig. 108**  Profile on Kuder Preference Record—Vocational. (*Record form reproduced by permission of Science Research Associates.*)

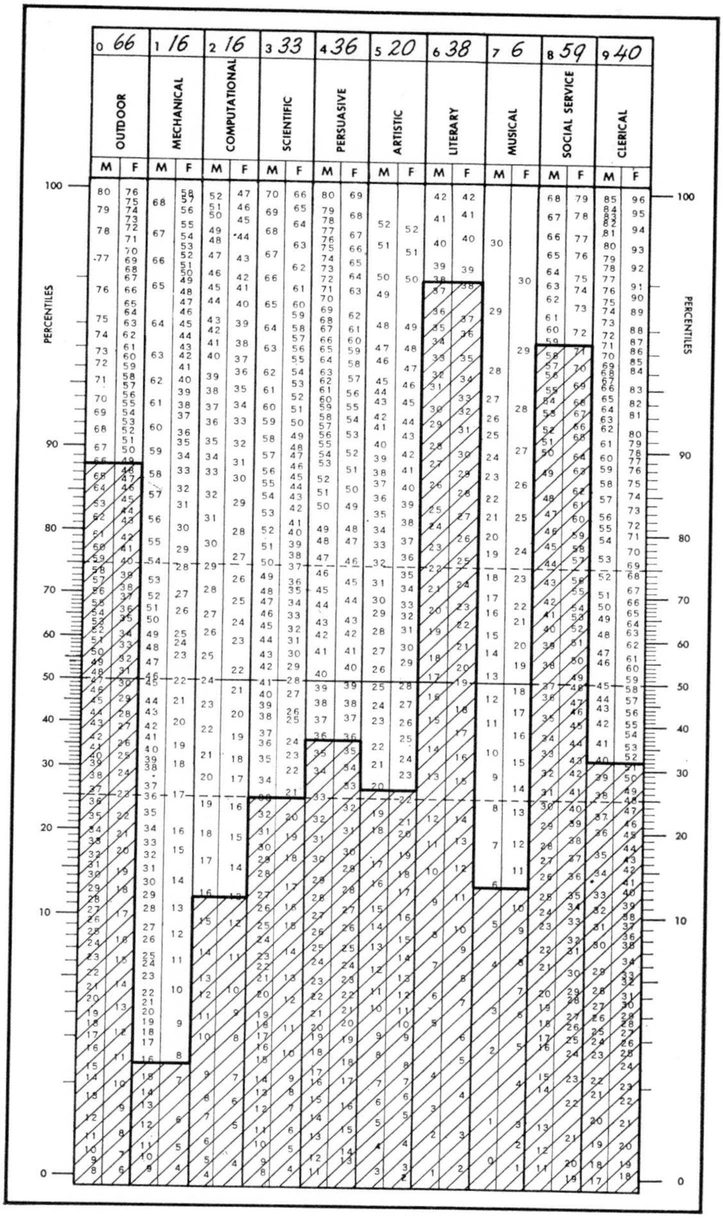

## Report on Vocational Interest Test for Men
(See other side for explanation)

Name .................................................... Age......... Date............. Agency or school ................................................. Case no..........

| Group | Occupation | Raw Score | Standard Score | Score (0–65) |
|-------|-----------|-----------|----------------|---------------|
| I | Artist | | 32 | X (≈33) |
| | Psychologist (rev.) | | 29 | X (≈31) |
| | Architect | | 33 | X (≈36) |
| | Physician (rev.) | | 46 | X (≈44) |
| | Psychiatrist | | — | |
| | Osteopath | | — | |
| | Dentist | | 41 | X (≈40) |
| | Veterinarian | | — | |
| II | Physicist | | — | |
| | Chemist | | 38 | X (≈38) |
| | Mathematician | | 28 | X (≈27) |
| | Engineer | | 35 | X (≈31) |
| III | Production Manager | | 31 | X (≈29) |
| IV | Farmer | | 37 | X (≈35) |
| | Carpenter | | 19 | X (≈19) |
| | Printer | | 33 | X (≈31) |
| | Math. Sci. Teacher | | 34 | X (≈30) |
| | Policeman | | 29 | X (≈24) |
| | Forest Service | | 24 | |
| | Army Officer | | — | |
| | Aviator | | — | |
| V | Y.M.C.A. Phys. Dir. | | 29 | X (≈28) |
| | Personnel Manager | | 24 | X (≈24) |
| | Public Administrator | | — | |
| | Vocational Counselor | | — | |
| | Y.M.C.A. Secretary | | 18 | X (≈18) |
| | Soc. Sci. Teacher | | 24 | X (≈24) |
| | City School Supt. | | 21 | X (≈21) |
| | Minister | | 21 | X (≈21) |
| VI | Musician | | 34 | X (≈33) |
| VII | C.P.A. Partner | | — | |
| VIII | Senior C.P.A. | | 26 | X (≈26) |
| | Junior Accountant | | 22 | X (≈22) |
| | Office Worker | | 28 | X (≈28) |
| | Purchasing Agent | | 26 | X (≈26) |
| | Banker | | 23 | X (≈23) |
| | Mortician | | — | |
| | Pharmacist | | — | |
| IX | Sales Manager | | 25 | X (≈25) |
| | Real Estate Slsmn. | | 33 | X (≈33) |
| | Life Insurance Slsmn. | | 28 | X (≈28) |
| X | Advertising Man | | 32 | X (≈32) |
| | Lawyer | | 36 | X (≈36) |
| | Author-Journalist | | 36 | X (≈36) |
| XI | President | | 30 | X (≈30) |
| | Occupational Level | | | |
| | Masculinity-Femininity | | | |
| | Specialization Level | | | |
| | Interest Maturity | | | |

Column headers (Standard Score scale): C (0–30), B− (30–35), B (35–40), B+ (40–45), A (45–65)

**Fig. 109** Report form of Strong Vocational Interest Blank, showing mean scores of a group of medical students. (*Reproduced by permission of Stanford University Press; data from Strong, 76, p. 421.*)

Personality Inventory (41) has been used extensively in counseling normal persons and a considerable amount of relevant research has accumulated. On the basis of data obtained with this test from more than four thousand college students examined in a college counseling center, Drake and Oetting prepared a codebook for interpreting MMPI profiles in this context (24). A few self-report inventories have been specially developed for normal persons, and their scores are expressed in terms of needs, motives, and interpersonal response modes rather than in terms of pathological deviations. Examples of such inventories include the Edwards Personal Preference Schedule (26), the California Psychological Inventory (35), and the Minnesota Counseling Inventory (9).

**Integrating Tests into the Counseling Process.** Under the influence of the nondirective, client-centered approach, counseling psychologists have put increasing emphasis upon the counseling process itself as a means of contributing to the client's development. In keeping with this viewpoint, several psychologists have given considerable attention to the way in which tests are introduced into the counseling process—how the tests are selected, when and how they are administered, and how the results are communicated to the counselees (13, 33, 83). Some feel that what tests are chosen and how the individual scores on them are less important questions than how the tests are incorporated into the counseling process.

Taking tests is itself regarded as a significant experience for the counselee. It is not to be thought of as an independent activity, but as a part of the total counseling experience. As such, it is a kind of "reality testing," providing the counselee with an opportunity to check his aspirations, plans, and self concept against objective standards. The individual's attitude toward taking tests may also be quite revealing and may in turn affect his test performance. One student may feel threatened if he believes that the decision to enter the college of his choice hinges on his test score. Another may hope that a low test score will help to dissuade an overambitious father from pushing him into a vocation for which he has neither interest nor aptitude.

Unlike test scores obtained in other situations, the information obtained from counseling tests is primarily for the use of the client himself. One exception is the occasional administration of preliminary tests to decide whether the client should be retained in counseling or referred elsewhere. In general, counseling tests should serve to stimulate client interest in areas or courses of action he has not previously considered and should provide him with the information he needs to make decisions. Tests are not a substitute for decision making by the client but should help to clarify the alternatives among which he must choose. Tests should therefore be introduced to answer specific questions or solve problems presented by the client.

It should also be noted that test results are more helpful in making negative than in making positive decisions. It is easier to determine on the basis of test scores which occupations or courses of study to rule out than which to elect. This follows from the fact that a certain minimum aptitude, interest pattern, or whatever the test measures is a necessary but not a sufficient condition for success in a given area. Individuals lacking such a qualification are likely to fail. But those who meet the requirement are not assured of success, since the latter depends on many additional personal and circumstantial factors.

In nondirective counseling, the client frequently participates in the selection of tests (13, 14, 33, 66, 83). Some counselors introduce no tests at all until and unless the client requests them. Others regularly employ tests but ask the client to choose those he would like to take from a given list. This technique is said to work better than one might anticipate, especially if certain cautions are observed. Most counselees lack the technical competence to evaluate tests. Hence the list from which a choice is made should contain only tests that are appropriate for the client and that have satisfactory reliability, validity, and norms. A simple explanation of the type of information each test provides may be given orally by the counselor or included in the list. Another approach is to have the client specify the kind of question he would like answered about himself, whereupon the counselor chooses the specific test for that purpose.

A possible difficulty may arise from misconceptions about the purpose of tests and incorrect notions about their nature, which many counselees have acquired from popular sources. The counselee may say he wants to take a test "to find out what kind of work I should do" or "to find out if I'm normal." Again, he may want to take tests as a means of evading a discussion of his real problem or for some other defensive reason. In all these cases, the counselor needs to pursue the matter sufficiently and possibly to provide appropriate information to cut through the superficial responses and enable the counselee to make a more intelligent decision about test taking.

On the positive side, it has been argued that client participation in test selection has many advantages over a completely counselor-directed program (13, 33). If the client cannot see the relevance of the tests to his immediate problem, he may simply drop out of counseling. The same result may follow if the client is not emotionally ready to submit to a realistic appraisal of himself. When the client is convinced of the need for testing and understands its purpose, on the other hand, he will be better motivated to do his best on ability tests and to answer truthfully on self-report inventories. He will also be more likely to accept test findings, rather than reacting defensively toward them.

The client's own reaction to information about a list of tests from which he must choose may also shed light on attitudes and other relevant facts. For example, the counselor might learn that a student is overanxious about school examinations or that he has a hobby indicating considerable mechanical aptitude. Finally, participation in test selection gives the client an opportunity to practice decision making.

As in many other interpersonal relations, the most effective degree of client participation in test selection depends upon the interaction of client, counselor, and situational variables. The first includes such client characteristics as age, intelligence, sophistication about tests, and emotional maturity; the second includes the counselor's personality characteristics, theoretical orientation, and attitudes toward directive and nondirective techniques; the third includes the context (school, community agency, hospital, etc.), the nature of the problem (educational, vocational, personality, etc.), the time available, and similar questions. The importance of these interactions is one of the few clearly established findings of research on different methods of selecting tests for counseling (33, 83). There is apparently no one best way for all circumstances.

The way in which test findings are communicated to the client is another important consideration in the counseling process. The counselor must take into account what the test score will mean to the client in the light of the latter's individual attitudes, goals, anxieties, and conflicts. He must be ready to detect expressions of rejection, hostility, and rationalization toward the test scores on the client's part. When such reactions occur, they must be accepted as one more fact regarding the client's behavior.

Test findings need not be reported in the form of scores, since these may be misunderstood by a psychometrically unsophisticated client. Rather they should be stated as expectancies or probabilities of concrete events, such as graduation from a given college, and should be directly related to the questions the client set out to answer. Test results should not be introduced until the client is ready to discuss them. Even then, the discussion should remain sufficiently flexible so that tangential topics brought up by the client may be followed up. The client should also be encouraged to integrate test findings with other self-knowledge, such as his achievement in different academic courses, his job experiences, his interests in various activities, and the like. Such integration tends to dispel any "mystery" that attaches to psychological tests. When related to similar observations from everyday life, tests are more likely to be correctly perceived as behavior samples obtained under standardized conditions.

The counselor in a school or college has the opportunity to accumulate longitudinal data about each counselee over a period of several years. It is customary in such situations to keep a *cumulative record* for each individual, including test data, biographical information, and continuing observations of his reactions toward different teachers, courses, extracurricular activities, and other school experiences. Under these circumstances, the counselor himself has usually had repeated contacts with the individual over a long time span. When properly employed, the cumulative record should prove extremely helpful. It can provide a wealth of information and a picture of developmental trends that no cross-sectional counseling contacts could equal. In practice, however, there is a danger that the keeping of cumulative records may become just one more mechanical chore in a busy schedule. The use of complicated and rigid forms may detract from the spontaneous recording of significant observations and the meaningful interpretation of developmental trends.

Another potential advantage available to counselors in school systems lies in their opportunity to do certain kinds of research. Because they have access to large numbers of students who go through similar criterion situations, such counselors are often in a better position than clinicians to conduct applied research with data already in their files. For example, entering students can be followed up through four years in the same college. The validity of tests and other predictors can thus be investigated, and empirical norms and cutoff scores can be established. Similar studies can be conducted with graduates of a single school who have entered a particular college in large numbers over a period of years, or possibly with groups who have been employed in a single community industry.

Finally, the counselor should accumulate information regarding the criterion situations about which his clients must make predictions. In educational counseling, for example, he must keep up with current data regarding schools and colleges in which his clients may be interested. Routine information regarding formal requirements, curriculum, financial aid, and the like, can be found in school and college catalogues and in a number of standard handbooks (e.g., 20, 56, 57).

There are many other characteristics of schools and colleges, however, that should be considered by a client. For example, it is well established that the average level and range of scholastic aptitude test scores vary widely among colleges. The differences are so large that there is little overlap between the top and bottom colleges in these scores. Colleges also differ in their psychological climate and in the kinds of environmental pressures they put upon the student. Research has revealed differences among colleges in such characteristics as relative strength of theoretical and practical values, emphasis placed upon social conformity and acceptance by others, extent of extracurricular participation, degree of student concern with social action and international problems, and pressure to achieve as contrasted to an easygoing atmosphere (62, 63, 73). Quite apart from his intellectual qualifications, a student might be a misfit in one of these college environments and an outstanding leader in another.

In vocational counseling, knowledge about jobs is of such basic importance that it has received special attention from the earliest beginnings of the vocational-guidance movement. This type of information will be considered in the next section.

## OCCUPATIONAL INFORMATION

Because vocational decisions play a prominent part in the counseling process in schools, colleges, community agencies, Veterans Administration hospitals, and other contexts, the counseling psychologist must have ready access to dependable sources of occupational information. The scope and complexity of the modern world of work necessitate special efforts to organize and systematize such information.

Vocational information includes knowledge about available fields of work and types of jobs, nature of the work, worker qualifications, training requirements, pay rates, working schedules and hours, vacation provisions, retirement plans and other fringe benefits, characteristics of the working environment, and many other specific facts of interest to the potential worker. It involves knowledge about national trends as well as local conditions. Obviously, no one person could acquire all this information. Even if he could do so, moreover, his store of knowledge would begin to go out of date at once. What the vocational counselor tries to do instead is to become familiar with *sources* of occupational information and with methods for evaluating it, keeping it up to date, and making it available to clients. Available sources of occupational information have been surveyed in a number of books (e.g., 5, 36, 43, 70). Such books are frequently used as texts in occupational information courses for counseling psychologists.

Counseling centers in schools, colleges, community agencies, and other settings generally maintain a library and file of vocational information materials for use by counselors and clients. Such collections include reference books and journals, as well as monographs, pamphlets, and leaflets dealing with specific fields, industries, or companies. Some texts on vocational information devote a whole chapter just to the question of how to classify and file these vocational materials so that they can be most readily located when needed (e.g., 43, ch. 6). To keep their information up to date, counseling centers also subscribe to publication services which provide fresh material periodically.

Because of the tremendous quantity and uneven quality of occupational literature, the counselor needs to be selective. Some years ago, the National Vocational Guidance Association (61) prepared a set of standards for evaluating an occupational monograph or pamphlet. The principal requirements are recency, objectivity, and readability. Owing to the rapid obsolescence of vocational information, the date when the information was obtained is a major consideration. Objectivity can often be evaluated by examining the source of the publication. Government agencies, such as the Department of Labor, as well as private publishing firms that prepare occupational materials, are usually motivated only to provide information. A specific industry or company, on the other hand, is likely to present a more biased picture because of its interest in recruitment. Popular sources are frequently concerned with the entertainment value of their material and may therefore give dramatized or glamorized versions. This does not imply, of course, that vocational material prepared by a popular magazine or by a company or industry is necessarily biased.

In publications to be used by clients, it is desirable that the information be interestingly presented and readily understood by the type of person for whom it is intended. By and large, occupational information materials tend to be too difficult for their readers. In one investigation, the Flesch formulas described in Chapter 12 were used to measure the reading ease and human interest of 78 occupational information booklets from a wide variety of government and private sources (16). Nearly two-thirds were rated as "very difficult," or at the level of a typical scientific magazine; another 32 per cent were rated as "difficult." With regard to human interest, about two-thirds fell into the "dull" category and about a third into the "mildly interesting."

Among the general sources of occupational information available to the counselor, an outstanding publication is the *Occupational Outlook Handbook*, prepared by the United States Bureau of Labor Statistics (85). This book summarizes trends in the number of persons employed in different fields. For example, in recent decades the proportion of persons in the professions has been steadily increasing, as have the proportions in clerical and sales jobs. At the same time, the proportion in unskilled labor jobs has been decreasing, as machine production and automation have taken over more and more of their functions. The *Handbook* also contains detailed information regarding several hundred major occupations, chosen with special reference to the interests of students and other young people seeking guidance. The data given for each occupation include nature of the work, number and nature of workers employed, where employed, training and qualifications, lines of advancement, employment trends and outlook, earnings and working conditions, and where to go for further information. The presentation is sufficiently simple for a junior high school student. To keep the material up to date, the *Handbook* is revised biennially. In addition, supplementary information is provided in a periodical, the *Occupational Outlook Quarterly*.

One of the major contributions to the organization and systematization of occupational information was the preparation of the *Dictionary of Occupa-*

*tional Titles* (DOT) by the United States Employment Service (87). The DOT provided for the first time a comprehensive classification of jobs, with definitions of each job title and a uniform numerical coding system. Volume I defines each of about twenty-two thousand job titles in terms of the duties performed. To obtain this information, job analysts observed samples of workers in many different jobs in a nationwide survey. Supplementary information was gathered from such sources as libraries, employers, trade and labor organizations, and public employment offices. Some eighteen thousand alternate titles for the jobs are also listed and cross-indexed. All titles in volume I are arranged alphabetically. In volume II, on the other hand, the same titles are arranged according to an occupational classification, with similar jobs grouped together.

In both volumes, all job titles are accompanied by their code numbers. Hence a counselor or client can look under the appropriate codes in volume II for jobs in which he might be interested and can then turn to volume I for the corresponding job descriptions. The code numbers include five or six digits. Of these the first digit denotes the major field, or level, such as professional and managerial, clerical and sales, skilled labor, and unskilled labor. Successive digits refer to increasingly finer subdivisions. For example, the digit 1 in the first place designates the broad category of clerical and sales occupations; 1–01 represents "bookkeepers and cashiers, except bank cashiers"; and 1–01–05 corresponds to "budget clerk." Similarly, 4–78–021 is the code number for a skilled turret lathe operator. Another volume of the DOT is concerned with the classification of entry occupations. These are jobs that require no experience and through which an individual may enter a field of work (86).

Although the publication of the DOT did much to introduce order and uniformity in occupational information, its classification system is crude and deficient in a number of ways. Some alternative classifications will be considered in Chapter 17. With regard to the DOT itself, the development of a new schema of classification has been in progress for several years and is expected to replace the original coding system in 1964 (27–29). By means of a nine-digit code, this system will classify occupations on the basis of worker functions (reflecting trait requirements), work field, and product or service. To date, the system has been applied to a list of 4,000 jobs (84). The information given for each job includes general educational requirements, specific vocational preparation, aptitudes, interests, temperamental characteristics, physical capacities, and special working conditions (e.g., cold, heat, noise). The estimated trait requirements are based on ratings by job analysts. Aptitude patterns on the General Aptitude Test Battery are also included when available.

As in the case of psychological tests, we may inquire into the ways in which occupational information can be incorporated into the counseling process (see 43, chs. 10–12; 83, ch. 8). Like tests, occupational materials can be most effectively introduced when a specific need for them arises, to answer questions raised by the client. Generally, however, it is better to postpone the consideration of occupational data until after some preliminary interviewing and possibly testing. Otherwise, a detailed examination of a specific field of occupation may lead to a premature structuring of the client's problem around vocational questions or to a premature vocational choice.

Vocational information may serve several purposes in the process of vocational planning. One is the exploration of the world of work. The client may be looking for ideas about fields in which he would be interested and may want a general picture of the work performed in various jobs. It is in such cases that counselors often turn to comprehensive sources like the DOT and the *Occupational Outlook Handbook* to help the client investigate likely fields and identify jobs not previously familiar to him. A second use of vocational information is to aid the client in choosing among specific occupations. For this purpose, the client needs fuller information regarding the alternatives he is considering. Such information should not only cover obvious job characteristics but should also give some notion of the total way of life that a particular vocational choice implies. Finally, occupational information may be required to implement a vocational decision. For example, the client may need information about apprenticeships and union regulations in a skilled trade, about the educational requirements for law or medicine, about the offerings of different graduate schools in his chosen field, or about the availability of scholarship aid in various colleges. A single client may require occupational information at any one or more of these stages in his vocational planning.

As for the method of presenting the information, the counselor may transmit the required data orally, refer the client to published sources, or combine the two procedures. Noting the client's reaction to the information and reflecting the client's feelings are important aspects of the counselor's contribution in this connection. Many supplementary methods can be employed to facilitate and augment the information-gathering process (see, e.g., 43). Schools frequently conduct regular courses on occupations, which may utilize several techniques of group guidance. This approach is helpful in providing a preliminary over-all view of the world of work and in encouraging the student to think about relevant questions. Other procedures include group conferences with representatives of different fields, plant tours, and part-time or summer jobs. Ideally, techniques such as these should supplement individual counseling. If used alone, they may yield an inadequate or distorted picture of the occupations surveyed.

# EVALUATING THE EFFECTIVENESS OF COUNSELING

***Test Validation Studies.*** Research on the effectiveness of counseling has been concerned with several different aspects of the counseling process. Any data on the predictive validity of the tests employed in counseling are of course relevant. Several longitudinal investigations have analyzed the relation between test scores and later vocational choices or indices of vocational adjustment, when the tests were not administered in connection with counseling. An unusually extensive study of this type was conducted by Thorndike and Hagen (81). In 1955 and 1956, these investigators sent a questionnaire to about seventeen thousand men who in 1943 had taken a comprehensive test battery when applying for cadet training in the United States Air Force. Approximately ten thousand responded. For purposes of analysis, the tests were grouped into five categories: general intelligence or scholastic aptitude, numerical fluency, visual perception, mechanical ability, and psychomotor skills. Responses to a large number of items in a specially devised biographical inventory were also available. Initial test scores and biographical inventory responses were first analyzed in terms of the individual's present job. Within each job group, the predictors were then correlated with each of seven criteria of job adjustment, such as earned income and self-ratings for job success and for job satisfaction.

Among the 124 occupational categories analyzed, several could be clearly differentiated in terms of level and pattern of test scores, as well as in responses to biographical inventory items. For example, accountants and auditors averaged very high in numerical fluency and high in general intelligence; they were about average in visual perception, below average in psychomotor skills, and very low in mechanical ability (Figure 110). Architects were distinctly high in visual perception; carpenters scored higher in mechanical ability than in general intellectual tests. To be sure, individual differences in scores within each occupational group were large, and overlapping among groups was considerable. Moreover, there were a number of occupations that yielded flat profiles with no outstandingly high or low scores. Nevertheless, the results show considerable correspondence between the type of work in which these men were employed and their test performance some thirteen years earlier.

Neither test scores nor biographical inventory items, on the other hand, proved to have any validity in predicting degree of job success within any one occupation. The correlations with the various criteria of job adjustment were no different from what would be found by chance.

Despite its ambitious scope, this study has many limitations, which its authors describe fully. As a result of self-selection as well as preliminary screening by the Air Force, the available sample was clearly unrepresentative

*Fig. 110* Means and standard deviations of 235 accountants and auditors on a multiple aptitude battery. Vertical bar shows mean; distance between arrowheads corresponds to ± 1 SD.(*From Thorndike and Hagen, 81, p. 25.*)

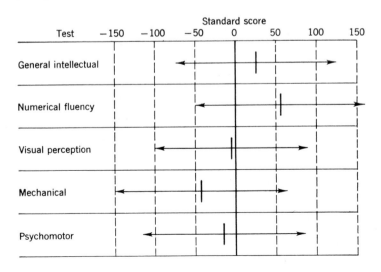

of its age group. The proportion of nonrespondents leaves the way open for further bias in the final sample. The number of persons in single occupational groups was often quite small. Even when similar occupations were combined and the smallest groups eliminated, nearly half of the remaining categories contained fewer than fifty cases. At the same time, the men classified within each group were generally heterogeneous with regard to nature of work performed, even when their occupation was nominally the same. Finally, it is obvious that the criteria of job adjustment were very crude. Most of these limitations are such as to reduce the likelihood of finding significant correlations between predictors and criterion measures. The differentiation of vocational groups in terms of initial aptitude patterns, on the other hand, was sufficiently pronounced to emerge despite these methodological handicaps.

It should be noted, furthermore, that other longitudinal studies of narrower scope have obtained very similar results (see 83, pp. 118–120). Both vocational and educational groups can be differentiated in terms of their initial score patterns on aptitude and interest tests. But, within such groups, the tests generally show little relation to degree of success. Even when scores from different tests are weighted and combined in such a way as to simulate the sort of judgments a counselor might make in predicting a client's suitability for a particular vocation, no significant correlation is found between these predictions and indices of job success (53).

The fact that tests can differentiate among occupational and educational groups probably reflects the selective processes that normally accompany admission and survival in these groups. Through self-sorting, screening, and subsequent dropping out, persons who are unsuited for a particular course of study or job are unlikely to remain in it long. It is the purpose of tests, of course, to reduce the waste in this natural selection by steering persons away from unsuitable choices in advance. Among those who meet the minimum prerequisites for survival in an educational or vocational category, however, the degree of success or satisfaction attained depends upon such a complex interplay of personal and situational variables that test scores alone are of little help in predicting it. This conclusion is supported by the common finding that negative prediction from test scores can be made with more accuracy than can positive prediction (30).

An ongoing nationwide survey of high school students may eventually provide more definitive answers to the sort of questions investigated by the above studies. Known as Project TALENT, this research began in 1960 with the administration of a comprehensive battery of aptitude and achievement tests, as well as interest and personality inventories, to approximately 440,000 high school students (31). Information about each school and its guidance program was also obtained. In comparison with earlier studies, this project provides a wider coverage of tests and a larger and more representative sampling of subjects. The group was carefully chosen so as to yield a stratified sample of students enrolled in public, parochial, and private high schools throughout the country. In addition, in order to secure national norms for one complete age group, fifteen-year-olds not in high school were also tested. Present plans call for questionnaire follow-ups to be conducted 1, 5, 10, and 20 years after high school graduation.

**Use of Tests in Counseling.** Some investigations have been concerned more directly with the effect of using tests in the counseling process. In these studies the results are generally more promising than when tests were administered without counseling. Indices of job success and job satisfaction do show significant relations with predictions made from test scores under these conditions (see 83, pp. 116–117, 273–277).

Typical of these studies is a British investigation conducted in the 1940s (45). A total of 1,639 young people who were leaving school at the age of fourteen to go to work were followed up after a two-year interval, and an additional 603 were followed up after four years. At the time of school leaving, half of the entire group was counseled on the basis of test information. The other half had only a vocational planning interview, which was standard procedure for school leavers. The jobs subsequently held by all counselees were classified into "accordance" and "non-accordance" posts depending upon whether they were or were not consistent with the counselor's recommendations. A two-way comparison could thus be made, between tested and nontested counselees and between those who had and those who had not followed counselor's advice. The criteria of occupational adjustment employed in this analysis were based on estimates of suitability for the job, secured from the subjects and from their employers.

Consistent results were obtained with all criteria and in both two-year and four-year follow-ups. The counselees who had been tested made better job adjustments than those who had not. Within the tested group, those who were in accordance jobs were more successful than those in non-accordance jobs, but this was not true in the group counseled without tests. Furthermore, tested counselees who began in non-accordance jobs tended to shift in the direction of accordance jobs, whereas in the nontested group shifts tended to be away from counselor recommendations.

This study and others following the same general procedures clearly indicate the value of tests in vocational counseling. That these results are more favorable than those of follow-ups based on test scores alone may reflect the influence of the counseling process itself. In the interaction between counselor and client, other relevant factors can be integrated with test scores in choosing a suitable course of action. Moreover, the individual's participation in the counseling process itself may have facilitated self-insight and personal development in ways that were beneficial to subsequent vocational adjustment. Tests provide opportunities for reality testing that may contribute to the effectiveness of this experience.

***Attainment of Self-knowledge.***   The emphasis placed by the above studies on whether or not the counselee followed the counselor's recommendations is characteristic of the earlier, more "directive" approach to counseling. The recent swing toward nondirective and client-centered techniques is reflected in a corresponding shift in research. Studies conducted since the 1950s have concentrated more heavily on the effect of different aspects of the counseling process upon self-knowledge (33, ch. 14; 83, ch. 7). A common procedure is to compare test scores in abilities or interests with self-ratings obtained before and after counseling or in a counseled and a control group. A smaller discrepancy between test scores and self-ratings or between counselor's and client's ratings is regarded as evidence of better self-insight.

There are a number of methodological weaknesses in this approach. The adequacy of counselor evaluation or test scores as a criterion for measuring accuracy of self-knowledge is certainly questionable. Furthermore, self-ratings obtained after the counselee has been told his test scores or his counselor's evaluations may be contaminated by this knowledge. The individual may be simply parroting what he has heard without necessarily revising his self concept. On the other hand, if counseling fails to bring about the expected evidence of improved self-knowledge, it is impossible to determine why. It may mean that the tests or the counselor's evaluations were in error, that the counselee was poorly motivated to profit from counseling, that he rejected the knowledge because of defensiveness, or that the counselor did not communicate the information effectively. In view of these various methodological difficulties, it is not surprising that this type of research has so far yielded inconsistent and inconclusive results.

**Global Studies of Counseling Effectiveness.** Other studies have been designed to check the over-all effectiveness of educational or vocational counseling in terms of follow-up criteria (see 83, ch. 13). Although the findings of different studies are not entirely consistent, they generally show that the counseling of high school and college students has a favorable effect upon their subsequent academic and vocational adjustment. Such generalizations, of course, need to be qualified in terms of counselor characteristics, type of counseling, and nature of client problems. Several studies suggest, for example, that college students with marginal scholastic aptitude are unlikely to improve in academic achievement as a result of the usual counseling procedures (see 83, pp. 271–272).

One of the most extensive and carefully controlled investigations of counseling effectiveness was the Wisconsin Counseling Study (68). This study was concerned with the effects of a long-range guidance program rather than with those of a single counseling experience. In a research project extending over 8 years, a guidance program was established in four representative Wisconsin high schools. Participating students were followed up 6 months, 2½ years, and 5 years after graduation.

Studies that compare self-selected counselees with non-counseled control cases are subject to the unknown influence of motivational differences between the two groups. Even when the counseled and control subjects actually compared are matched a posteriori for a number of variables, there is no control over motivation to improve and tendency to use effective methods in solving life problems. It is likely that the group that seeks counseling spontaneously excels initially in these respects. This common methodological difficulty was avoided in the Wisconsin study by assigning students at random to the experimental and control groups. A total of 870 sophomores in the four high schools were placed in the two groups. Those in the experimental group were counseled during the remaining three years of high school by members of the university staff, who used generally accepted techniques of testing and interviewing. The control subjects received no counseling.

The results were consistently favorable to counseling, although the differences between counseled and control groups were not large. In comparison with the control subjects, the counselees achieved slightly better academic records both in high school and in subsequent education, were more realistic about their weaknesses, were less dissatisfied with their high school experiences, were more consistent about their vocational choices, made better progress in their chosen employment after graduation, and were more likely to continue their education to high school graduation and beyond.

A somewhat different application of counseling is illustrated by the Demonstration Guidance Project conducted in New York City (96, 97). The object of this project was to identify promising pupils from a culturally deprived neighborhood and to stimulate them to reach higher educational and vocational goals. Surveys have repeatedly shown that, even when adequate financial assistance is available, qualified high school students from lower socioeconomic levels are much less likely to go to college than are students from higher socioeconomic levels with the same intellectual qualifications (see 4, 42, 90). Moreover, achievement at the elementary and high school levels, as well as intelligence test performance, tends to be adversely affected by the attitudinal and intellectual climate typically found in underprivileged homes. Children from such homes not only have a dearth of intellectual stimulation but also have little incentive for educational advancement.

The Demonstration Guidance Project was a pilot program aimed to counteract these environmental deficiencies. The project was begun with about seven hundred pupils in the seventh, eighth, and ninth grades of a junior high school and was continued for six years, thus giving the youngest of the three groups time to complete high school. The procedure included an intensive counseling program with both individual and group guidance; counseling and social work with parents; remedial instructional programs; and cultural enrichment both in school and through field trips and visits to museums, art exhibitions, theaters, concerts, and the like. Clinical services were also provided in many individual cases, and financial assistance was made available when needed.

Although final results have not yet been fully analyzed, the data gathered so far appear promising. Questionnaire surveys of pupils, parents, and teachers indicate that for most students the program provided substantial help in their choice of career, encouraged them to continue in high school until graduation and to consider the possibility of college, broadened their interests and their participation in cultural activities, improved their social adjustment and their attitude toward school, and raised their self-esteem. The dropout rate of this group in high school was approximately 20 per cent, as compared with about 40 per cent for other classes. Of particular interest are the marked improvements in educational achievement and the mean rise of about 9 IQ points on a verbal intelligence test, which is significant at the .01 level. The latter increase is all the more notable when contrasted with the decline in IQ with age usually found in culturally deprived groups. With regard to the various influences operating during the program, the investigators comment that the students' intimate relation with their guidance counselor seemed to be a major factor in their improvement (96, p. 250). Because of the large number of independent variables and the absence of a comparable control group, however, it is impossible to draw causal conclusions from this study.

Mention should also be made of investigations of the effectiveness of *personal counseling* in both academic settings and elsewhere. Insofar as this type of counseling is a form of psychotherapy, the research on the outcomes of psychotherapy discussed in Chapter 15 is also relevant here. Within the framework of counseling, we can repeat the conclusion reached from clinical research: so far, the effectiveness of counseling for personal adjustment has not been satisfactorily demonstrated (8; 83, chs. 11 and 13). The difficult methodological problems presented by both process and outcome research, which were considered in Chapter 15, make the designing of definitive studies on personal counseling extremely difficult.

*Theoretical Analyses of Counseling.* At a different level of evaluation, psychologists, educators, and members of related disciplines have examined the goals, underlying assumptions, and philosophy of counseling. The rapid expansion of counseling activities and the increasing professionalization of counseling services since the mid-fifties have led to some searching analyses of the responsibilities of the counselor. Typical of such examinations of the counselor's role is Wrenn's *The Counselor in a Changing World* (93). Representing the report of a commission appointed to consider guidance in American schools, this book describes needed developments in school counseling in the light of projected changes in our culture. The author explores the implications of societal changes for the functions and training of counselors. Of particular interest is the analysis of the "culturally encapsulated counselor," who is unresponsive to both temporal changes and subcultural differences in the value systems he employs in his counseling practice. Furthermore, because counseling is typically concerned with the client's plans for the future, it is not enough for the counselor to evaluate his information in terms of its present accuracy; he must also check it against rate and direction of change.

Since discussions of the objectives of counseling reflect both the value systems and the theoretical orientations of the discussants, it is not surprising that the conclusions reached are quite divergent. This is one of the areas of current controversy and ferment alluded to in the opening of Chapter 13. The diversity of opinions held regarding the goals of counseling is richly illustrated in a series of articles published in 1962 in an issue of the *Harvard Educational Review* devoted to an examination of guidance (18). Dealing principally with the functions of the counselor within a school setting, these articles cover such questions as: the role of counseling in shaping and modifying behavior, rather than merely predicting behavior; the influence of both the immediate school context and the broader societal setting upon counseling goals and practices; the unwitting "smuggling" into the counseling process of values that may not be explicitly recognized by the counselor; the impact of counseling upon education and its place in the total educational process; and the issue of social conformity versus spontaneity and individuality as counseling goals. For an adequate appreciation of the wealth of provocative ideas provided in this symposium, the reader is urged to consult the original articles.

# SUMMARY

Counseling psychologists work in many settings and perform a variety of functions. Although they may specialize in one type of counseling, such as vocational, educational, employee, rehabilitation, old-age, marriage, or personal counseling, fully trained counseling psychologists recognize the interrelation of all adjustment problems and focus on the counseling of the whole person. While there are many similarities between clinical and counseling psychology, the fields as a whole can be differentiated in terms of objectives, type of client, duration of professional relationship with client, extent of information giving, and orientation of practitioners. In none of these variables, however, is the distinction so sharp as to preclude overlapping of the two fields.

Among the types of tests most commonly used in counseling are general intelligence tests, educational achievement tests, special aptitude tests, multiple aptitude batteries, interest inventories, and personality inventories. Under the influence of the client-centered approach, counseling psychologists have placed increasing importance upon the ways in which tests are integrated into the counseling process. In counseling, psychological tests are used chiefly for the information of the client himself, to increase his self-knowledge and help him in making decisions. Some nondirective counselors leave the choice of tests up to the client. If applied within certain limits, this practice may make for a better counseling relationship and a more effective utilization of test results by the client. Counselors working in school systems generally have access to longitudinal data about their counselees in the form of cumulative records.

Because of the importance of vocational decisions in most counseling activities, counseling psychologists need to be familiar with sources of occupational information. An up-to-date and systematically organized library or file of occupational materials should be available for the use of clients as well as counselors. The development of the *Dictionary of Occupational Titles* by the United States Employment Service introduced a comprehensive, uniform classification and coding system for occupations, a classification which is now in process of revision. Like psychological tests, occupational information needs to be integrated into the total counseling process.

Research on the effectiveness of counseling has been concerned with the long-range predictive validity of counseling tests, the effect of using tests in the counseling process, the influence of different aspects of the counseling process upon self-knowledge, and the over-all success of counseling programs in terms of follow-up criteria. All of these questions present serious methodological problems, only a few of which have been satisfactorily solved in available research. Thoughtful analyses of the underlying philosophy of counseling reveal wide diversity in value systems and theoretical orientation.

# REFERENCES

1. American Psychological Association, Division of Counseling Psychology, Committee on Definition. Counseling psychology as a specialty. *Amer. Psychologist*, 1956, **11**, 282–285.
2. Anastasi, Anne. *Differential psychology.* (3rd ed.) New York: Macmillan, 1958.
3. Anastasi, Anne. *Psychological testing.* (2nd ed.) New York: Macmillan, 1961.
4. Andrew, D. C., and Stroup, F. College attendance of high ability high school seniors. *Educ. Rec.*, 1960, **41**, 258–265.
5. Baer, M. F., and Roeber, E. C. *Occupational information.* (2nd ed.) Chicago: Sci. Res. Assoc., 1958.
6. Barker, R. G., et al. *Adjustment to physical handicap and illness: A survey of the social psychology of physique and disability.* (Rev. ed.) New York: Soc. Sci. Res. Coun., 1953.
7. Bennett, G. K., Seashore, H. G., and Wesman, A. G. *Differential Aptitude Tests (1963 Edition), Forms L and M.* New York: Psychol. Corp., 1963.
8. Berdie, R. F. A program of counseling interview research. *Educ. psychol. Measmt*, 1958, **18**, 255–274.
9. Berdie, R. F., and Layton, W. L. *Minnesota Counseling Inventory.* New York: Psychol. Corp., 1953–1957.
10. Birren, J. E. Psychological aspects of aging. *Ann. Rev. Psychol.*, 1960, **11**, 161–198.
11. Birren, J. E. (Ed.) *Handbook of aging and the individual.* Chicago: Univer. Chicago Press, 1959.

12. Blaine, G. B., Jr., and McArthur, C. C. *Emotional problems of the student*. New York: Appleton-Century-Crofts, 1961.
13. Bordin, E. S. *Psychological counseling*. New York: Appleton-Century-Crofts, 1955.
14. Bordin, E. S., and Bixler, R. H. Test selection: A process of counseling. *Educ. psychol. Measmt*, 1946, **6**, 361–373.
15. Brayfield, A. H. Counseling. *Ann. Rev. Psychol.*, 1963, **14**, 319–350.
16. Brayfield, A. H., and Reed, Patricia A. How readable are occupational information booklets? *J. appl. Psychol.*, 1950, **34**, 325–328.
17. Burgess, E. W., and Cottrell, L. S. *Predicting success or failure in marriage*. Engle-wood Cliffs, N. J.: Prentice-Hall, 1939.
18. Carle, R. F., Kehas, C. D., and Mosher, R. L. (Eds.) Guidance—An examination. *Harvard educ. Rev.*, 1962, **32**, No. 4.
19. Clark, K. E. *The vocational interests of nonprofessional men*. Minneapolis, Minn.: Univer. Minn. Press, 1961.
20. *The College Handbook*. New York: Coll. Entr. Exam. Bd (various editions).
21. Cronbach, L. J. *Essentials of psychological testing*. (2nd ed.) New York: Harper & Row, 1960.
22. Cruickshank, W. M. (Ed.) *Psychology of exceptional children and youth*. Englewood Cliffs, N.J.: Prentice-Hall, 1955.
23. Darley, J. G., and Hagenah, Theda. *Vocational interest measurement: Theory and practice*. Minneapolis, Minn.: Univer. Minn. Press, 1955.
24. Drake, L. E., and Oetting, E. R. *An MMPI codebook for counselors*. Minneapolis, Minn.: Univer. Minn. Press, 1959.
25. Dvorak, Beatrice J. The General Aptitude Test Battery. *Personnel. Guid. J.*, 1956, **35**, 145–154.
26. Edwards, A. L. *Edwards Personal Preference Schedule*. New York: Psychol. Corp., 1953–1959.
27. Fine, S. A. The structure of worker functions. *Personnel Guid. J.*, 1955, **34**, 66–73.
28. Fine, S. A., and Heinz, C. A. The estimates of worker trait requirements for 4000 jobs. *Personnel Guid. J.*, 1957, **36**, 168–174.
29. Fine, S. A., and Heinz, C. A. The functional occupational classification structure. *Personnel. Guid. J.*, 1958, **37**, 180–192.
30. Fisher, J. The twisted pear and prediction of behavior. *J. consult. Psychol.*, 1959, **23**, 400–405.
31. Flanagan, J. C., et al. *The talents of American youth, I. Design for a study of American youth*. Boston: Houghton Mifflin, 1962.
32. Fryer, D. Occupational intelligence standards. *Sch. Soc.*, 1922, **16**, 273–277.
33. Goldman, L. *Using tests in counseling*. New York: Appleton-Century-Crofts, 1961.
34. Gorthy, W. C., et al. Vocational evaluation by work sample technic and its de-pendence upon medical contributions. *Arch. phys. Med. Rehab.*, 1959, **40**, 238–242.
35. Gough, H. G. *California Psychological Inventory*. Palo Alto, Calif.: Consult. Psy-chologists Press, 1956–1957.
36. Greenleaf, W. J. *Occupations, a basic course for counselors*. Washington: Govt. Printing Office, 1951.
37. Greenleaf, W. J. *Occupations and careers*. New York: McGraw-Hill, 1955.
38. Hadley, J. M. *Clinical and counseling psychology*. New York: Knopf, 1958.
39. Hahn, M. E. Counseling psychology. *Amer. Psychologist*, 1955, **10**, 279–282.
40. Hamilton, K.W. *Counseling the handicapped in the rehabilitation process*. New York: Ronald, 1950.
41. Hathaway, S. R., and McKinley, J. C. *Minnesota Multiphasic Personality Inventory*. New York: Psychol. Corp., 1951.
42. Hollinshead, B. S. *Who should go to college?* New York: Columbia Univer. Press, 1952.
43. Hoppock, R. *Occupational information: Where to get it and how to use it in coun-seling and teaching*. New York: McGraw-Hill, 1957.
44. Hoyt, K. B., and Moore, G. D. Group procedures in guidance and personnel work. *Rev. educ. Res.*, 1960, **30**, 158–167.
45. Hunt, E. Patricia, and Smith, P. Vocational psychology and choice of employment. *Occup. Psychol.*, 1945, **19**, 109–116.
46. Hutson, P. W. *The guidance function in education*. New York: Appleton-Century-Crofts, 1958.

47. Katz, M. R. *You: Today and tomorrow.* (3rd ed.) Princeton, N.J.: Educ. Test. Serv., 1959.
48. Kelly, E. L. Marital compatibility as related to personality traits of husbands and wives as rated by self and spouse. *J. soc. Psychol.*, 1941, **13**, 193–198.
49. Kimber, J. A. M. The science and the profession of psychology in the area of family relations and marriage counseling. *Amer. Psychologist*, 1959, **14**, 699–700.
50. Kimber, J. A. M. An introduction to the marriage counselor and his work. *Psychol. Rep.*, 1961, **8**, 71–75.
51. Kitson, H. D. Psychology in vocational adjustment. *Personnel Guid. J.*, 1958, **36**, 314–319.
52. Kuder, G. F. *Kuder Preference Record—Vocational.* Chicago: Sci. Res. Assoc., 1934–1956.
53. Latham, A. J. Job appropriateness: A one-year follow-up of high school graduates. *J. soc. Psychol.*, 1951, **34**, 55–68.
54. Locke, H. J. *Predicting adjustment in marriage.* New York: Holt, Rinehart and Winston, 1951.
55. Lofquist, L. H. *Vocational counseling with the physically handicapped.* New York: Appleton-Century-Crofts, 1957.
56. Lovejoy, C. E. *Lovejoy's college guide.* New York: Simon and Schuster. (Various editions.)
57. Lovejoy, C. E. *Lovejoy's vocational school guide.* New York: Simon and Schuster. (Various editions.)
58. Martinson, W. D. *Educational and vocational planning.* Chicago: Scott, Foresman, 1959.
59. Miller, F. W. *Introduction to guidance.* Columbus, Ohio: Merrill, 1961.
60. Mueller, Kate H. *Student personnel work in higher education.* Boston: Houghton Mifflin, 1961.
61. National Vocational Guidance Association. Distinguishing marks of a good occupational monograph. *Occupations*, 1939, **18**, 129–130.
62. Pace, C. R. Five college environments. *Coll. Bd Rev.*, 1960, **41**, 24–28.
63. Pace, C. R., and Stern, G. G. An approach to the measurement of psychological characteristics of college environments. *J. educ. Psychol.*, 1958, **49**, 269–277.
64. Paterson, D. G., and Lofquist, L. H. A note on the training of clinical and counseling psychologists. *Amer. Psychologist*, 1960, **15**, 365–366.
65. Rechtschaffen, A. Psychotherapy with geriatric patients: A review of the literature. *J. Geront.*, 1959, **14**, 73–84.
66. Rogers, C. R. *Counseling and psychotherapy: Newer concepts in practice.* Boston: Houghton Mifflin, 1942.
67. Rogers, C. R. *Client-centered therapy: Its current practice, implications, and theory.* Boston: Houghton Mifflin, 1951.
68. Rothney, J. W. M. *Guidance practice and results.* New York: Harper & Row, 1958.
69. Shaffer, L. F., and Shoben, E. J., Jr. *The psychology of adjustment: A dynamic and experimental approach to personality and mental hygiene.* Boston: Houghton Mifflin, 1956.
70. Shartle, C. L. *Occupational information: Its development and application.* (3rd ed.) Englewood Cliffs, N. J.: Prentice-Hall, 1959.
71. Shock, N. W. The role of research in solving the problems of the aged. *Gerontologist*, 1961, **1**, 14–16.
72. Steiner, Lee R. Re: Marriage counselors. *Amer. Psychologist*, 1960, **15**, 363–364.
73. Stern, G. G., Stein, M. I., and Bloom, B. S. *Methods in personality assessment.* New York: Free Press, 1956.
74. Stewart, Naomi. A.G.C.T. scores of army personnel grouped by occupation. *Occupations*, 1947, **26**, 5–41.
75. Strong, E. K., Jr. *Strong Vocational Interest Blank for Men, Revised; Strong Vocational Interest Blank for Women, Revised.* Palo Alto, Calif.: Consult. Psychologists Press, 1938–1959.
76. Strong, E. K., Jr. *Vocational interests of men and women.* Stanford, Calif.: Stanford Univer. Press, 1943.
77. Super, D. E. (Ed.) *The use of multifactor tests in guidance.* Washington: Amer. Personnel Guid. Assoc., 1958. (Repr. from *Personnel Guid. J.*, 1956–1957.)

78. Super, D. E., and Crites, J. O. *Appraising vocational fitness by means of psychological tests* (Rev. ed.) New York: Harper & Row, 1962.
79. Terman, L. M. *Psychological factors in marital happiness.* New York: McGraw-Hill, 1938.
80. Tharp, R. G. Psychological patterning in marriage. *Psychol. Bull.,* 1963, **60,** 97–117.
81. Thorndike, R. L., and Hagen, Elizabeth. *Ten thousand careers.* New York: Wiley, 1959.
82. Tyler, Leona E. Minimum change therapy. *Personnel Guid. J.,* 1960, **38,** 475–479.
83. Tyler, Leona E. *The work of the counselor.* (2nd ed.) New York: Appleton-Century-Crofts, 1961.
84. United States Bureau of Employment Security. *Estimates of worker trait requirements for 4000 jobs as defined in the Dictionary of Occupational Titles.* Washington: Govt. Printing Office, 1956.
85. United States Bureau of Labor Statistics. *Occupational outlook handbook.* Washington: Govt. Printing Office, 1963.
86. United States Employment Service. *Dictionary of occupational titles, entry occupational classification.* Vol. 4. (Rev. ed.) Washington: Govt. Printing Office, 1944.
87. United States Employment Service. *Dictionary of occupational titles.* (2nd ed.) Vols. 1 and 2. Washington: Govt. Printing Office, 1949. (Suppl. 1955.)
88. United States Office of Vocational Rehabilitation. *Counseling for psychological acceptance of disability.* Washington: OVR, Dept. Hlth Educ. Welf., 1954.
89. Vance, F. L., and Volsky, T. C., Jr. Counseling and psychotherapy: Split personality or siamese twins? *Amer. Psychologist,* 1962, **17,** 565–570.
90. Warner, W. L., Havighurst, R. J., and Loeb, M. B. *Who shall be educated?* New York: Harper & Row, 1944.
91. Warters, Jane. *Group guidance: Principles and practices.* New York: McGraw-Hill, 1960.
92. Welford, A. T., *et al. Skill and age; an experimental approach.* London: Oxford Univer. Press, 1951.
93. Wrenn, C. G. *The counselor in a changing world.* Washington: Amer. Personnel Guid. Assoc., 1962.
94. Wright, Beatrice A. *Psychology and rehabilitation.* Washington: Amer. Psychol. Assoc., 1959.
95. Wright, Beatrice A. *Physical disability: A psychological approach.* New York: Harper & Row, 1960.
96. Wrightstone, J. W. Demonstration guidance project in New York City. *Harvard educ. Rev.,* 1960, **30,** 237–251.
97. Wrightstone, J. W., *et al.* Demonstration guidance project. *Res. Rep. No.* 43, *Bur. Educ. Res., N.Y.C. Bd Educ.,* 1961. (Mimeographed.)

# 17

# *Psychology of*
# *Vocational Choice*

The most distinctive area of research in counseling psychology is that dealing with occupational choices. What are the determinants of such choices? When and under what conditions are vocational decisions made? What kinds of satisfactions do individuals seek in their work? How do these satisfactions differ among persons who choose different occupations? That counseling psychologists should focus upon occupations in their research programs is understandable for a number of reasons. First, there is the historical association of counseling with vocational problems. It will be recalled that the vocational-guidance movement was the principal factor contributing to the rise of counseling psychology. Even today, when the scope of counseling has broadened considerably, many counseling psychologists still function predominantly in the vocational field.

To be sure, the counseling psychologist typically considers vocational problems within the context of the client's over-all emotional adjustment. It is recognized that the vocational problem presented by the client may itself arise from emotional immaturity, insecurity, inability to face reality or make decisions, a difficult familial situation, or other problems of personal adjustment. Conversely, there is increasing realization that occupation itself plays a central role in one's total life adjustment. Emotional problems frequently stem from job tensions and frustrations, while absorbing and rewarding work can be highly therapeutic. Similarly, maladjustments can often be prevented through satisfying work activities. Not only the work itself, but also its many associated experiences, can contribute to the individual's total adjustment. Of considerable importance to mental health, for instance, are acceptance by fellow workers and the feelings of security and belongingness that come from identification with an occupational group.

## OCCUPATION AS A WAY OF LIFE

*Rationale.* Choosing an occupation is equivalent to choosing a way of life (5; 49, ch. 23; 58; 59, ch. 2). For one thing, the individual spends a large proportion of his waking time on the job. But the influence of one's occupation extends well beyond working hours. For the vast majority of people in our culture, the nature of their work is the single most important determiner of social status. When trying to "place" a new acquaintance, people ask, "What *is* Wilson?" and are told that he is a lawyer, or a carpenter, or a hairdresser. The income derived from work helps to shape one's general style of living—the neighborhood in which he lives, the sort of house or apartment he occupies, the car he drives, the kind of vacation he can afford. One's job determines the distribution of work and leisure in both daily and seasonal schedules—as illustrated by the jobs of physician, long-distance truck driver, free-lance writer, schoolteacher, and bank clerk. Some jobs limit the places where one may live —as illustrated by the jobs of forest ranger, mining engineer, music critic, and investment broker. In many other kinds of work, some geographical mobility is required for maximal vocational advancement. A research chemist or a professor of philology must be free to go where the best opportunities are available in his field of specialization. He may be a native Californian with all his family ties in the San Fernando valley, but his best job offer may come from Harvard.

Occupations differ in many other ways that may be significant to an individual worker. They may influence one's habitual dress, as witnessed by our stereotypes of white-collar and blue-collar jobs and of the businessman in the gray flannel suit. They differ widely in the physical and psychological surroundings in which the work is done. Contrast, for example, the neatness and order of the normal working environment of a surgeon with that of a construction foreman or the interpersonal contacts of a bill collector with those of a commercial artist. Friendships are often work-determined. People tend to spend their leisure hours with co-workers, business associates, or professional colleagues. Nor is it at all unusual for an individual to marry someone he or she has met through job contacts.

Many kinds of work are associated with characteristic sets of values that frequently extend into one's personal life. If some of these values are not consonant with the individual's own values, the resulting conflict may be quite disruptive. In view of the degree to which vocational decisions imply the choice of a whole way of life, it becomes easier to understand the success of interest tests such as the Strong Vocational Interest Blank (5, 15). Persons in different occupations are in fact characterized by distinctive interest patterns and sets of values that reach beyond the work itself into nearly every aspect of daily living.

It might be added that among women it is not only the so-called "career" women who need to be concerned about occupational differences. The job of housewife is by no means uniform. Much has been written about the peculiar problems and way of life of the wives of medical doctors, career officers in the armed services, and business executives. Although these examples have been widely publicized and dramatized, the same principle holds in all walks of life. The husband's occupation permeates and colors every facet of the wife's world in much the same way that it affects his own.

From a different angle, the choice of an occupation can be seen as a way of establishing one's identity. Super (58–60) has repeatedly pointed out that vocational choice is the implementation of a self concept. He argues that "satisfaction in one's work and on one's job depends on the extent to which the work, the job, and the way of life that goes with them, enable one to play the kind of role that one wants to play" (58, p. 189).

More specifically, occupations are chosen to meet needs (see 33, chs. 7 and 8). The economic need to earn one's livelihood is only one of many such needs. It can ordinarily be met by any one of many jobs, among which the individual chooses on the basis of other needs. For some persons, rate of pay may be so closely linked with one or more of their major goals that it will be the determining factor in a job decision. But, for most persons, other needs either determine or significantly affect vocational choices. Thus one person may put such a high value on personal freedom and independence that he can only be happy as a free-lance or self-employed worker. Another functions best when he is the center of attention—a need that could be satisfied by many occupations, ranging from actor to information clerk. Still another requires the security that comes from working in a highly structured situation in which he is relieved of all responsibility for decision making.

These needs are not necessarily verbalized (19). The individual may simply feel that he *must* paint or that an office job is not for him, without being able to explain why. It is one of the objectives of counseling to make the individual aware of the motives underlying such convictions. When needs are recognized as such, they are more readily brought under rational control and less likely to lead to unrealistic decisions. Throughout such a process, however, the counselor must operate within the framework of the client's needs, which may differ from those of the counselor. This is one of the reasons why the counselor cannot choose a "suitable" occupation for the client without at least some interaction with the client. Parenthetically, the consideration of needs in vocational decisions highlights one difference between the characteristic approaches of clinical and counseling psychologists. If, for example, a client has a deep-rooted feeling of insecurity, the clinician typically attempts to change the client's personality so that he may overcome the insecurity, whereas the counselor helps the client choose a vocation in which emotional insecurity is not a serious drawback.

**Occupational Personality Patterns.**    There is a mounting accumulation of research literature dealing with personality differences among occupational groups. The most comprehensive survey of studies published prior to 1956 is provided by Roe (49, chs. 13–20). Summaries of portions of this literature prepared from different points of view can be found in several other sources (1, ch. 13; 15, ch. 4; 30; 59, ch. 16; 62; 69, pp. 172–176). A number of studies have appeared more recently and others are in progress (4, 12, 29, 31, 32, 36–39, 53, 55, 73). Some of this research has been conducted by psychologists, although sociologists and members of other disciplines have contributed extensively to this topic. The methodology ranges from rather subjective biographical approaches to moderately well-controlled applications of questionnaires, interviewing techniques, personality inventories, and projective tests. A wide variety of occupations has been investigated, including those of scientists in a number of fields, mathematicians, engineers, medical students, psychiatric residents, schoolteachers, architects, and many others. Some investigators have compared student groups specializing in different fields, such as accounting and creative writing (52). Others have worked with persons employed in the various occupations; a few have concentrated on scientists who have attained a high degree of eminence in their fields.

Data on developmental history and childhood experiences of persons in different occupations were generally obtained retrospectively during interviews with the adult subjects. A notable exception is the longitudinal study of a group of California children with initial Stanford-Binet IQs of 140 or higher, conducted by Terman and his associates. Among the many analyses of the voluminous follow-up data obtained in this project is a comparison of the men who eventually became physical scientists with those specializing in social science, law, or the humanities (64). Out of a total of about 500 items, including test scores, ratings, and biographical data, 108 differentiated between the two groups at the .05 level of significance or better. Most of these discriminating items dealt with interests, including evidence of early scientific interest in childhood and scores on the Strong Vocational Interest Blank.

The close association between vocational interests and other personality characteristics has been suggested by a number of studies with the Strong VIB (see 2, pp. 556–559; 15, ch. 4). An example is an investigation of 100 Air Force officers conducted at the University of California (see 15, pp. 128–129). Each subject took a battery of tests, including the Strong VIB, and also underwent an intensive assessment program through interviews and other observational techniques. On the basis of all available information, subjects were described by eight clinical psychologists in terms of 76 given personality variables. Correlations of these trait ratings with each of the VIB occupational keys revealed a number of statistically significant correlations. The personality descriptions associated with high scores on two of these keys are summarized below:

*High scorers on Mathematician Key:* Self-abasing, concerned with philosophical problems, introspective, lacking in social poise, lacking confidence in own ability, sympathetic, reacts poorly to stress, not persuasive in personal contacts, not an effective leader, not ostentatious, not aggressive or socially ascendant

*High scorers on Real Estate Salesman Key:* Self-indulgent, guileful, cynical, opportunistic, aggressive, persuasive, ostentatious, may arouse hostility in others, not sympathetic, not concerned with philosophical problems, not lacking confidence in own ability, not self-abasing

Available published research on occupational personality patterns provides many promising hypotheses, but as yet few differences have been conclusively established. The number of cases investigated is often small. Few studies have included control groups. It is therefore impossible to determine whether the personality characteristics found in a given occupational group differentiate that occupation from others or whether they are common to men at a particular age level, who have attained a certain degree of vocational success, or who resemble the experimental subjects in other ways. For instance, in Roe's studies of eminent scientists, the results pointed strongly to the importance of prestige motivation, strong inner drive, sustained effort, and absorption in work to the exclusion of other interests (47, 48). There is no way of knowing to what extent these qualities are also typical of men who have achieved distinction as artists, writers, business executives, statesmen, or workers in any other field.

In studies that compared two or more occupational groups, the findings were rarely cross-validated on new samples to determine which of the observed differences might have resulted from chance. Even when significant personality differences are conclusively established between occupational groups, it is often impossible to analyze cause-effect relations. To what extent do salesmen become dominant and extroverted because of the demands of their jobs, and to what extent were they that way to begin with? Only longitudinal studies can adequately answer this kind of question.

At best, what occupational differences have been found in personality patterns represent group trends. For many kinds of work, one could probably write personality sketches that would roughly fit a majority of persons in that occupation. This sort of information is useful in counseling insofar as it gives the counselee some idea of the kind of person with whom he is most likely to associate if he chooses a given type of work. But, within any occupational group, the range of individual differences is fully as wide in personality variables as it is in aptitudes. Nor are these differences necessarily associated with different degrees of success. The breadth and flexibility of most occupations are such that different persons may succeed in them for different reasons. Individuals may choose specialties (as in law or medicine) that are consonant with their own needs, interests, and values. Even a single job can often be structured by the individual to fit his own aptitude and personality pattern. Moreover, the same job in different companies or under different supervisors may call for very different personality traits. Specific jobs as well as occupational fields undoubtedly vary in the degree of specialization and restructuring that they permit. This is one of the variables that should be considered in making vocational decisions.

*Job Satisfaction and Individual Needs.* The studies cited in the preceding section were concerned chiefly with comparisons *among* occupational groups. Another approach is to investigate the correlates of job satisfaction *within* an occupation. For example, 72 men employed predominantly in professional and semiprofessional jobs filled out a questionnaire designed to assess the strength of 12 needs, such as those for recognition, achievement, self-expression, economic security, and independence (51). The subjects also rated their general job satisfaction and the degree to which their job permitted the satisfaction of each of the 12 needs. A multiple correlation of .58 was found between job satisfaction and the extent to which the individual's two strongest needs were satisfied by his job.

In another study (8), 81 nurses were given several self-report inventories designed to assess, among other things, the individual's concept of her actual and ideal occupational roles, her self concept, and her vocational satisfaction. The results supported the hypothesis that, the larger the discrepancy between self concept and perceived occupational role, the lower the vocational satisfaction. Discrepancy between ideal and actual occupational roles was also negatively correlated with vocational satisfaction.

There is some evidence that persons with a high achievement drive tend to prefer occupations with higher status or prestige. In a group of 53 young veterans, a correlation of .74 was found between the individual's achievement drive as assessed by a projective test and the prestige level of the occupation he chose (41).

A series of studies conducted in Columbus, Ohio, investigated more directly the relation between job satisfaction and perceived job status (34, 45, 46). The research was prompted by the difficulty of recruiting professional mental health personnel for state institutions, as well as by the high turnover rate among persons in these jobs. The principal sample consisted of 400 persons, including 80 in each of the following occupations: psychiatrists, psychologists, social workers, teachers, and nurses. In each occupational group, 40 persons were employed in state institutions and 40 in other settings (clinics, agencies, public schools, general hospitals, or private practice). There was also a control group selected by area sampling of Columbus, Ohio.

By means of a series of rating scales filled out by the subjects, it was demonstrated that the needs for recognition, status, and prestige are closely related to job satisfaction among these professional workers. Discrepancies between expected and perceived job status were associated with low job satisfaction. Another common source of dissatisfaction was a discrepancy between wanted and available intellectual stimulation on the job. For all the professional groups studied, both perceived status and job satisfaction were found to be lower for institutional than for noninstitutional samples. These findings highlight the fact that need satisfaction may differ, not only among occupations, but also among work settings within the same occupation.

The increasing emphasis upon the contribution of motivational factors to occupational choice and job satisfaction has led to the development of several instruments for measuring vocational needs. In an attempt to identify common factors or dimensions in the variables measured by these scales, Crites (14) administered three available inventories yielding 11 scores to 300 college students. In these inventories, the subject rates types of work, ranks job incentives, or records degree of liking for various items. A factor analysis of the 11 scores yielded five independent factors: material security versus job freedom, personal status versus social service, social approval, system (self-created order and planfulness), and structure (externally imposed orderliness, working on schedule, clearly defined duties).

Although motivational factors undoubtedly play an important part in vocational adjustment, there is a danger that they may be overemphasized at the expense of performance factors. As vocational counselors have moved in the direction of personal counseling, with its more nearly clinical orientation, they have tended to lose sight of the realistic goal of job performance. Brayfield (72) has cautioned against this de-emphasis of performance and has advocated a closer integration of industrial and counseling psychology. He writes, "We need the healthy antidote of a performance-oriented industrial psychology to balance the uncritical acceptance of the self-realization goal of vocational counseling" (72, p. 42).

***Childhood Experiences and Occupational Choice.*** Early family experiences have been cited as a principal source of the emotional needs and value systems that underlie vocational choices (20, 49, 50). Case histories provide many examples of such childhood influences. The individual's reaction to authority on the job may reflect his early relation with one or both parents. A worker may seek security on the job as a result of uncertainty and insecurity in his early family environment. A more specific hypothesis in terms of parent-child relations has been proposed by Roe (50). Protecting or demanding parental attitudes, according to this hypothesis, predispose the individual to seek occupations dealing with persons; rejecting, neglecting, and casual parental attitudes predispose him to seek occupations dealing with things, or "nonpersons." Despite the readiness with which case-history material can be found to illustrate these childhood influences, systematic tests of this hypothesis have failed to support it (23, 25, 71). The general procedure has been to compare recalled parent-child relations of persons engaged in different occupations. No significant relations were found between childhood familial relations and such occupational choices.

The limited number of occupations investigated in some of these studies may have been poorly chosen to represent contrasting need patterns. A more serious methodological weakness is the reliance on subjects' recollections of childhood conditions. A longitudinal approach would provide more dependable data. It is quite likely, however, that the etiology of vocational choices is more complex than this hypothesis presupposes. While childhood familial relationships may be of primary significance for some persons, other factors may affect the development of emotional needs in other instances. Experiences in school, contacts with adults and age mates outside the family, and innumerable other circumstances of daily life may play a part. Moreover, the characterization of familial environment in terms of a single variable such as warmth—or in terms of a few categories such as protecting, demanding, and rejecting—may be an oversimplification. The interaction among members of a family is highly intricate and may affect individual members differently.

## THE CLASSIFICATION OF OCCUPATIONS

*Dimensional Classifications.* Psychological research on occupations has quite naturally led to attempts to classify occupations in terms of psychologically meaningful dimensions. The original DOT classification, while representing a significant achievement in its comprehensiveness and general applicability, had many drawbacks. One of its principal weaknesses stems from the mixture of different dimensions, or principles of classification. This confusion can be readily seen by examining its major categories, which correspond to the first digit of the occupational code, as shown in Table 22. The professional

**T A B L E   2 2**   *Major Occupational Categories in Original Dictionary of Occupational Titles* (*Data from 70, p. ix*)

| Category | Code Number |
|---|---|
| Professional and managerial | 0 |
| Clerical and sales | 1 |
| Service | 2 |
| Agricultural, fishery, forestry, and kindred occupations | 3 |
| Skilled | 4, 5 |
| Semiskilled | 6, 7 |
| Unskilled | 8, 9 |

and managerial category is a combination of level and field of work; clerical and sales, as well as service occupations, refer predominantly to fields; agriculture and related occupations are classified together because of the setting in which the work is performed; and the last three categories are obviously based on level of skill required. The finer subdivisions within each major category show the same mixture of classification principles. For example, the service occupations are further broken down into domestic, personal, protective, and building services. These groups combine work setting with nature of work done.

Several substitute classifications have been proposed for use in counseling and research, in which at least two of the dimensions of the DOT classification are separated (see, e.g., 26, 49, 59). The most obvious distinction is that between level and field. *Level* is identified with such occupational variables as income, social status and prestige, intelligence, general educational requirements, degree of authority, freedom and independence of action, and amount of responsibility for decision making (49, ch. 11; 59, ch. 3). Because these social and psychological variables are highly intercorrelated, it is feasible to classify occupations unidimensionally with regard to this composite definition of level. Although individual jobs might be differently ranked in terms of one or another of these variables, there is little difficulty in placing them in broad categories on this basis. With regard to worker requirements, occupational levels are differentiated principally in terms of educational level and performance on scholastic aptitude or general intelligence tests.

*Field* of work refers to the type of activity performed. Although operating at the same level, for example, a bricklayer and an electrician are in different fields, as are a physiologist and a professor of English literature. Psychologically, field corresponds closest to differences in aptitude patterns and in interests. Certain other personality differences may also characterize special fields, but the evidence for such differences is still meager, as indicated in the preceding section.

Super (59, ch. 3) has added a third dimension to this occupational classification, which he calls *enterprise*. This dimension refers to the setting or industry in which the work is performed, such as agriculture, transportation, or government. Although not so basic psychologically as the classifications into level and field, choice of enterprise may be quite important in individual cases. A person who finds it oppressive to work indoors could profitably explore opportunities in agriculture and kindred occupations; one who has a deep-rooted aversion to bureaucratic procedures might be well advised to eschew employment in a government agency. Jobs in the same field and at the same level may appeal to very different kinds of persons when performed in different settings. Compare, for example, the jobs of three chemists, one employed in a university, another in a government laboratory, and the third in a manufacturing plant. The previously cited studies of mental health professionals working in institutional and noninstitutional settings may also be recalled in this connection.

The three-dimensional schema of classification proposed by Super is illustrated in Figure 111. In this classification, Super combined the Standard Industrial Classification prepared by the United States Bureau of the Budget with a modified version of the level-and-field classification suggested by Roe (49, chs. 11–12). Within each field, typical occupations have been listed at different levels. Thus, for the Outdoor-physical field, examples range from athletic coach (level 2) to deckhand (level 6); for the Social-personal field, they range from social scientist (level 1) to attendant (level 6). Enterprise, corresponding to the third dimension, cannot be plotted directly on paper but has been indicated in perspective. The broken line illustrates the three-dimensional classification of one job, that of "civil engineer employed in conservation work with the National Park Service." This job is classified in level 2, field V (Mathematics-physical sciences), and enterprise A (Agriculture, forestry, fisheries).

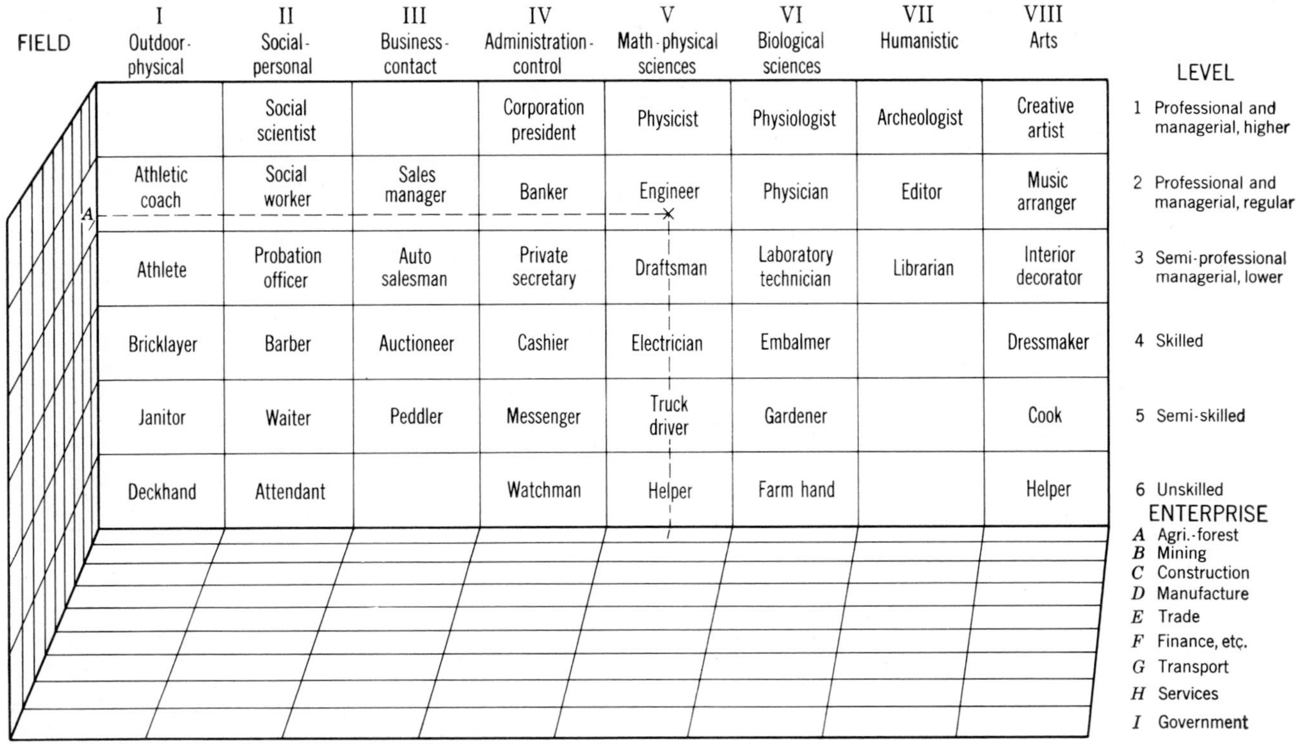

| FIELD | I Outdoor-physical | II Social-personal | III Business-contact | IV Administration-control | V Math-physical sciences | VI Biological sciences | VII Humanistic | VIII Arts |
|---|---|---|---|---|---|---|---|---|
| 1 Professional and managerial, higher | Athletic coach | Social scientist | | Corporation president | Physicist | Physiologist | Archeologist | Creative artist |
| 2 Professional and managerial, regular | | Social worker | Sales manager | Banker | Engineer | Physician | Editor | Music arranger |
| 3 Semi-professional managerial, lower | Athlete | Probation officer | Auto salesman | Private secretary | Draftsman | Laboratory technician | Librarian | Interior decorator |
| 4 Skilled | Bricklayer | Barber | Auctioneer | Cashier | Electrician | Embalmer | | Dressmaker |
| 5 Semi-skilled | Janitor | Waiter | Peddler | Messenger | Truck driver | Gardener | | Cook |
| 6 Unskilled | Deckhand | Attendant | | Watchman | Helper | Farm hand | | Helper |

LEVEL
1 Professional and managerial, higher
2 Professional and managerial, regular
3 Semi-professional managerial, lower
4 Skilled
5 Semi-skilled
6 Unskilled

ENTERPRISE
A Agri.-forest
B Mining
C Construction
D Manufacture
E Trade
F Finance, etc.
G Transport
H Services
I Government

*Fig. 111*   A scheme for classifying occupations by level, field, and enterprise. (*Adapted from Super, 59, fig. 1, p. 48. Harper & Row, Publishers, Inc., 1957.*)

*Classifications According to Trait Patterns.* In the attempt to integrate job classifications more closely with worker requirements, psychologists have for some time been exploring the trait patterns demanded by different jobs. Among the early efforts in this direction is a set of ratings of 123 occupations according to their minimum requirements in 24 traits, prepared for use in the vocational-guidance program of the British National Institute of Industrial Psychology (42).

The Minnesota Occupational Rating Scales (MORS) represent a more extensive and systematic application of the same type of rating procedure (44). In these scales, each of 432 occupations has been rated for the amount of each of seven abilities which it requires. The traits include academic ability, mechanical ability, social intelligence, clerical ability, musical talent, artistic ability, and physical agility. For every occupation, each of these seven traits is rated on a four-point scale (A to D). These ratings were based on the pooled judgments of vocational psychologists.

The 432 occupations are first arranged alphabetically, each with its corresponding ability pattern. To facilitate the use of the scales in counseling, the same occupations are reclassified in several other ways on the basis of their ability patterns. For example, one classification groups together all occupations requiring the A level and those requiring the B level of each ability in turn. It should be noted that, in the MORS, level is rated for *each* of the seven traits, rather than for the job as a whole as was done in the previously described dimensional classifications. With regard to mechanical ability, for example, an electrical engineer and a toolmaker fall into the A level, while a street sweeper and a lawyer fall equally into the D level (44, p. 20).

Mention should also be made of the empirically established Occupational Ability Patterns based on General Aptitude Test Battery scores (24). Each of these Occupational Ability Patterns shows the minimum cutoff score in critical aptitudes for a given job. These score patterns were found by administering the complete battery to samples of workers in many different occupations. Critical aptitudes were those in which workers in a given job excelled the general norms, as well as those yielding significant correlations with criteria of job success. Occupational Ability Patterns have so far been developed for over five hundred occupations.

Both the MORS ratings and the GATB score patterns are limited to aptitudes. More recently, counseling psychologists have been exploring the possibility of incorporating interests, needs, and other personality factors into the descriptions and classifications of occupations (e.g., 7, 30, 31). The functional classification of occupations, to be employed in the forthcoming revision of DOT, includes some interest and personality variables (18). This classification, which was briefly described in Chapter 16, represents an extension of the approach followed in the MORS. Ratings by job analysts were again utilized to establish worker requirements in general educational development, specific vocational preparation, 11 aptitudes, 10 interest areas, 12 "temperament" qualities (such as need for variety and change or ability to perform under stress), and 6 physical traits. Occupational Ability Patterns on the GATB will also be included for all jobs for which they are available. The application of this functional classification to all DOT jobs will undoubtedly be the most ambitious vocational classification project yet undertaken.

## VOCATIONAL DECISIONS

One of the most important objectives of all counseling is to facilitate the making of effective decisions. In contrast to the charlatan, who is likely to hand his client a ready-made solution for his problems or to choose a specific occupation for him, the counseling psychologist concentrates on improving the individual's own decision making. Effective vocational decisions require accurate knowledge regarding both abilities and wants or needs. Tests help in this connection, as does much of the verbal interaction between counselor and counselee. In addition, effective decisions require knowledge about occupations, which counseling likewise tries to provide. Finally, they require the ability to think clearly—to combine available information in predicting outcomes, to weigh alternative courses of action, and to make choices that adequately reflect all relevant factors.

Vocational planning normally involves, not one decision, but a multitude of decisions, which typically extend over a period of several years. Many preliminary decisions may have to be made and implemented before the individual finally enters his chosen field of work. Moreover, people's wants and their suitability for different kinds of careers may change with time. Jobs also change. In our rapidly evolving society, new fields of work constantly emerge, and even familiar jobs may become drastically altered. All these circumstances call for flexibility in the vocational decisions made at any one stage. Also relevant is the multipotentiality of both persons and jobs, to which we have repeatedly alluded. Any one person is qualified for many different jobs, not just for a single job. Conversely, a given occupation may be successfully pursued in many different ways by different persons.

The goal of vocational counseling is *not* early commitment to an ultimate vocational choice. Rather, counseling contributes to vocational decisions in at least three ways. First, it helps the individual in making immediate decisions as demanded by his present environment. For instance, a junior high school student may have to choose among different types of schools, curricula, or courses; or he may have to decide whether to continue his education or take a job. Such decisions require that the individual consider the general direction in which he wants to go and the major future implications of his decision. But there will be many opportunities for modifying the direction later and for making more specific choices in the light of subsequent experience.

In the second place, counseling may provide knowledge about oneself and about the world of work that will be used later—perhaps several years later —when the occasion demands it. At the time of counseling, the individual may have reached no decision at all. But as a result of the information he acquired, he may accept or reject a specific job when it is offered to him. If it contributed to the wisdom of that decision, counseling was effective. Finally, the counseling process offers an opportunity to learn more effective procedures for decision making itself. This experience is designed to help the individual make wiser and more satisfying decisions in solving future problems of daily life.

Occupational choice represents a *synthesis* between wishes and reality, between what one wants and what one learns he can attain (59, ch. 21). Through continuing interaction with his environment, the individual tests his personal needs, aptitudes, and other attributes against the demands and resources of society. In the process of growing up, he has an opportunity to explore different roles through fantasy, play activities, schoolwork, extracurricular functions, household tasks, and part-time or temporary jobs. Specific interests probably develop in much the same way. As Strong put it, "An interest is an expression of one's reaction to his environment. The reaction of liking-disliking is a resultant of satisfactory or unsatisfactory dealing with an object" (57, p. 682). This resultant obviously depends upon the characteristics of the individual as well as upon the characteristics of the particular objects he encounters and the circumstances under which he does so.

The extent to which one's vocational choices are reality-oriented may be related to his general personality adjustment. A study designed to test this hypothesis was conducted with 100 boys between the ages of fifteen and nineteen who had been referred to a community counseling center for vocational counseling (54). The group included 50 "definitely maladjusted" referrals from psychiatric hospitals and clinics and 50 "better adjusted" referrals from schools and similar sources. In the course of counseling, each boy was asked to state two vocational choices in order of preference. On the basis of the counselor's information about the boy and the jobs, each choice was given a "reality-deviation score."

Analysis of these scores revealed that both first and second choices were significantly more realistic among the well-adjusted than among the maladjusted boys. This difference was larger for the first than for the second choices. Moreover, among the well-adjusted the first choices tended to be more realistic than the second, while the reverse was true among the maladjusted. Although such findings do not permit an analysis of cause-effect relations, the more realistic reaction of the well-adjusted subjects is of interest in its own right. Insofar as counseling can lead the individual to make more realistic choices, it may contribute to his over-all adjustment. On the other hand, the counselor must guard against any tendency to brand as unrealistic vocational aspirations that fail to conform to his own set of values or vocational plans that reveal the courage and breadth of vision to pursue a novel or difficult path.

Tyler (68; 69, ch. 14) has focused attention upon the important role of decisions in the individual's general development. Within any lifetime, only a small fraction of one's "potentialities" can be realized. A person may have the qualifications to become a distinguished surgeon, writer, *and* statesman, but there is not enough time to be all three. Choices must be made throughout life and each in turn limits and determines the direction of subsequent development.

At the outset, these limits are set largely by external circumstances. For instance, a newborn infant *could* learn any existing language—or even a nonexisting language that someone might devise. But what he actually learns to speak is quickly narrowed down to the language of his parents. As the child becomes older, however, the limits of his development are established more and more by his own choices—whether he spends more time on schoolwork or play, whether he plays baseball or collects stamps, the companions he chooses, the books he reads, and so forth. Although available opportunities, decisions by other persons, and his own physical and psychological attributes continue to set many limits upon his behavior, the individual himself participates increasingly in the process. At every choice point he encounters, he helps to set his own limits and to shape his future experiences.

In this concept of choice, Tyler sees a rationale for the successful predictions of occupational choice made with such instruments as the Strong Vocational Interest Blank. A high score on this inventory signifies that the individual's pattern of choices resembles that of persons in a given occupation. This in turn should help us to predict how he will choose in similar circumstances in the future.

Much research on the nature of choices remains to be done. Tyler (67) describes an ongoing longitudinal study of children's expressed likes and dislikes from the first grade through high school. The interest or choice patterns of these subjects during their high school years are being analyzed with reference to many concurrent and earlier variables. The influence of positive and negative factors in the choice process is another question investigated in the same project. To what extent are choices based on the rejection of what one dislikes and to what extent on the acceptance of what one likes? Some data on this question have also been obtained by comparing like and dislike responses on the Strong VIB (3, 67).

Vocational choice can be analyzed in the light of *decision theory*. There is a growing number of psychological experiments conducted within the framework of decision theory, which should provide some of the basic research for counseling. Decision theory began as an attempt to put the decision-making process into mathematical form so that available information may be used to arrive at the most effective decision under given circumstances. The mathematical procedures employed in decision theory are often quite complex, and few are in a form permitting their immediate application to psychological problems. Nevertheless, the basic concepts of decision theory help in formulating and clarifying the decision process. A simple and readable introduction to these concepts can be found in a book by Bross (9). A more detailed treatment oriented toward applications to psychological research is given by Edwards (16).

Essentially, decisions are based upon: (1) predicted probability of different outcomes; (2) estimates of risks involved or seriousness of failure; and (3) consideration of the relative value or importance of different goals. In vocational decisions, information about the individual's capabilities, obtained from tests or other sources, together with job information, provides the data for predicting outcomes. Thus the individual, with the help of the counselor, might estimate his chances of completing an apprenticeship as machinist or of graduating from medical school. The consequences of making a bad decision help to establish the certainty level we require to take action. If the consequences of failure are slight, we may be willing to try a course of action even though there is a high probability of failure.

Both decision theory and counseling psychology recognize the fundamental importance of values in the decision process. The fact that to be workable the individual's decisions must be consonant with his own value system provides one more reason why counselors cannot make decisions for clients. In decision theory, the mathematical expression of the relative values of different outcomes constitutes a particularly thorny problem. Values, however, inevitably enter into decision making; decision theory merely requires that they be made explicit.

Most available psychological research on the decision process is exploratory and deals with questions that are far removed from the counseling situation.

A few studies concerned more specifically with vocational decisions provide suggestive findings. There is some evidence, for example, that college students who are undecided about their career plans and are unable to specify a vocational choice tend to be more reluctant to take risks and place a higher value on security than do those reporting definite career plans (see 69, p. 209). It is likely that an unrealistic demand for certainty makes for indecisiveness in vocational planning. A potential source of raw data for applied research on decision making is to be found in counseling interviews that deal with decision problems. So far virtually no use has been made of such data.

An excellent example of the practical application of vocational counseling principles is provided by a workbook entitled *You: Today and Tomorrow* (35). Designed for a group guidance unit at the eighth- and ninth-grade level, this workbook introduces the student to vocational problems and provides exercises in self-appraisal, in the utilization of educational and vocational information, and in decision making. Data regarding abilities can be obtained from intelligence, multiple aptitude, or achievement tests administered in the regular school-testing program, as well as from the student's grade record. In addition, there is provision for the student to consider his schoolwork, extracurricular activities, hobbies, and other experiences in the appraisal of his abilities, interests, and values. The handbook presents problems and information in an interesting and highly readable style. An excerpt is reproduced in Figure 112.

With its accompanying teacher's guide, *You: Today and Tomorrow* is suitable for use by a classroom teacher in a program extending over about thirty class sessions. Its focus is on the student's immediate task of choosing a high school curriculum, both for its direct effect on later vocational choices and for its value as a paradigm in decision making. Preliminary evaluation studies indicated that the program was well received by students, teachers, and school counselors. Pretests and posttests demonstrated significant learning of key concepts. In one study, pupils were intensively interviewed before and after their participation in the program (22). Indices of maturity in educational and vocational planning, derived from the interview records, showed highly significant improvement. Because of the lack of a control group, however, it is impossible to determine how much of this gain may have resulted from the repetition of the interview or from other intervening experiences.

# VOCATIONAL DEVELOPMENT

**Rationale.** The recognition that vocational decisions are made over a period of many years has led to the concept of vocational development, which has found its fullest expression in the work of Super and his associates (59, 61). Drawing upon both developmental psychology (10) and sociological analyses of occupational behavior (21, 40), Super discusses the process of vocational adjustment in terms of five stages. The first is the *growth* stage, extending from birth to about the age of fourteen. During this period, the child begins to develop a self concept. Through observation of parents and other adults in the family circle, he first becomes acquainted with different roles that an individual may play in our culture. As he grows older, his available role models are augmented through his contacts in school and in other situations outside the home. Still other roles may be encountered vicariously in books, movies, or television.

So we can see that the information we get from a forecast or prediction is only one fact that goes into making a wise decision. A lot does depend on the *chances* in our favor or against us. But a lot also depends on the *value* or importance of our goals; and a lot depends on the seriousness or danger of our *risks*.

A trackman who has jumped 21 feet in 8 out of 10 tries would be foolish to try to jump across a 20-foot chasm just to pick a few blueberries on the other side. But what if he were being chased by an angry grizzly bear?

So in deciding which high school course to take, or in setting goals for your future education and occupation, you will want to consider not only your chances of success or failure. You will want to consider also *how serious it would be to fail* and *how important it would be to succeed*.

*Fig. 112*   Excerpt from *You: Today and Tomorrow*—a group guidance program for junior high school students. (*From Katz, 35, p. 34.*)

From an early age, the child begins to "try on" different roles in play or in fantasy. He may become in turn a cowboy, policeman, fireman, or astronaut. At this level, needs are uppermost in his selection of roles. It is only later that he begins to consider interests, then abilities, and still later job requirements and opportunities. The apparently irrational occupational roles assumed in childhood make good sense when examined within their own context. Typically, the young child is dominated by adults who restrict his freedom of action and protect him from danger. Against such a background, his needs for independence, for power over others, and for adventure find outlets in play. If asked what he wants to be when he grows up, the child is also likely to name an occupation within his limited repertory of knowledge that seems to fulfill these needs.

In recognizing that an occupational role *can* help to meet his needs, the child has taken the first step in his vocational development. With time, he finds increasing opportunities for realistic tryout of vocational roles. As he (or she) carries out household chores, works in the neighbor's yard, baby-sits, tinkers with mechanical gadgets, plays baseball, takes violin lessons, or studies different subjects in school, the process of reality testing begins.

The second stage proposed by Super is that of *exploration*, covering adolescence and early adulthood. This is a period of extensive reality testing, with consequent modification of the self concept. It is at this stage that important educational decisions are first faced and vocational goals are first seriously examined. For these reasons, vocational counseling has traditionally focused on this period. At this stage the individual also undertakes more formal work-role tryouts through part-time, temporary, and trial jobs.

The third stage is that of *establishment*. After some preliminary trial-and-error and floundering, most persons show a tendency to "settle down" in a particular line of work. Stabilization and advancement are typical of this stage. The individual comes to identify with his chosen field of work; he accumulates experience that ties him more closely to that field; and he assimilates the general way of life associated with his job. The fourth stage is one of *maintenance*. Continuing in the same field of work, the individual at middle age typically concentrates on retaining the position he has attained on the job, at home, and in the community. He either enjoys the fruits of his labor or accepts his frustrations. This stage leads finally to occupational *decline*, as indicated by reduction in vocational activity and eventual retirement.

Like any system of stages employed to describe human development, this schema is admittedly an oversimplification. While helping to focus attention upon developmental sequences and upon tendencies characterizing different life periods, it is limited in a number of ways. First, the developmental process is continuous, and any description of it in terms of discrete stages is only an approximation. Second, there are wide individual differences in the time of onset and duration of each stage. In some persons, one or more stages may be skipped altogether. Individual career patterns, for example, vary in the number and nature of job shifts (40; 59, ch. 5). These differences in mobility are also associated with the nature of the work. Thus for semiskilled or clerical work, changing jobs usually entails no loss and may represent a gain. For work requiring a long period of professional preparation or for jobs in which considerable premium is put on experience, on the other hand, earlier decisions are more nearly irrevocable, and the typical career pattern is very stable. Similar differences may be found at later stages. Some persons continue to advance in their work throughout life. For them, there never comes a time for mere maintenance of the *status quo* or for decline in productivity.

When these limitations are borne in mind, the above stages can provide a convenient framework for organizing a mass of discrete facts. They can serve to establish norms against which individual development can be evaluated. And they help to generate testable hypotheses for research.

A related concept is that of *developmental tasks* (17, 27, 61). In vocational development as in other forms of human development, the individual encounters typical behavioral demands and problems at different life stages from the preschool period to the age of retirement. Although both the problems and the appropriate reactions vary somewhat among cultures and subcultures, modal requirements can be specified within a given cultural setting. Each of the vocational life stages described above makes characteristic demands upon the individual. Mastery of the developmental tasks of earlier stages influences the individual's handling of the behavioral demands of the next.

Super (61) has used this concept of developmental tasks in his treatment of *vocational maturity*. The individual's vocational maturity is measured in terms of his mastery of the vocational tasks of his age level or his effectiveness in coping with the characteristic problems of his life stage. For example, among the vocational developmental tasks of an elementary schoolchild are the choice of daily activities suited to one's capacities, the assumption of responsibility for one's acts, and the undertaking of cooperative enterprises. Vocational developmental tasks of a man in his sixties might include, among others, planning for any necessary curtailment of work load or change of functions, as well as realistic consideration of retirement prospects. *Vocational adjustment* at any stage is the resultant of interaction between the individual's vocational maturity and the reality demands of the situations he encounters. Thus, while vocational maturity is defined in terms of the individual's behavior, his vocational adjustment is defined in terms of the outcomes of his behavior (59, p. 187). At any stage of vocational development, moreover, vocational maturity implies sufficient flexibility to permit the individual to modify his occupational activities and life style to meet the demands of changing personal and societal situations.

**Career Development Studies.**   The concepts of developmental tasks and vocational maturity provided the theoretical framework for a 20-year longitudinal investigation of approximately one hundred ninth-grade boys, initiated by Super and his associates (61, 63). The subjects were all attending a public high school in an urban community in New York State, chosen as typical of American cities in many socioeconomic indices. A mass of data were gathered through tests, questionnaires, and a series of four semistructured interviews with each subject. Further data were obtained from records of school achievement, reports of extracurricular and community activities, peer ratings, interviews with parents, and other miscellaneous sources. Several indices of vocational development were formulated and applied to the group. The resulting measures were intercorrelated and factor analyzed. On the basis of these analyses, the following indices were identified as the best measures of the construct "vocational maturity" at this age level: concern with choice (awareness of need for choice and knowledge of factors affecting choice), acceptance of responsibility for choice and planning, specificity of planning for the preferred occupation, and use of resources in obtaining occupational information.

The findings suggested that the major vocational developmental task at the junior high school level is that of preparing to make vocational choices. For the ninth-grade boy, vocational maturity is shown, not by the wisdom or consistency of the ultimate vocational goal he chooses, but rather by the way he handles the preliminary planning and exploration required at this stage. Correlations with many personal and background variables were also found in the effort to investigate factors associated with vocational maturity. As defined in this study, vocational maturity tended to be positively correlated with intelligence, parental occupational level, extent of cultural stimulation provided in the home, level of boy's own occupational choice, and enrollment in a college preparatory curriculum. It is thus possible that the indices chosen in this study may be more appropriate for assessing the vocational maturity of boys planning to enter higher-level occupations than for those planning to enter lower-level occupations.

Despite the impressive accumulation of data, the results of this initial, cross-sectional analysis of data must be regarded as tentative and exploratory. The anticipated follow-ups of the same group of boys will undoubtedly permit a more definitive evaluation of initial findings. By its very nature, vocational maturity cannot be adequately defined without longitudinal data. Specifically we must know how each of the proposed indices of vocational development changes with age and how it correlates with measures of subsequent vocational adjustment in the individual. Otherwise we are unable to evaluate deviations above or below the group norm in any of the variables.

Equally significant data should be provided by several other longitudinal studies of career development that are now in progress both in this country and elsewhere (see 6, 65). Cross-sectional studies of more limited scope are also helping to round out the picture. In one study of high school boys, for example, self-estimates of aptitudes and interests were correlated with test scores obtained on the same variables (43). These correlations were higher for twelfth-graders than for ninth-graders, suggesting an improvement in self-knowledge and an increasingly realistic orientation as the boys progressed through high school. It might be added parenthetically that the previously cited group guidance unit for the junior high school, entitled *You: Today and Tomorrow* (35), represents a direct application of the vocational development rationale and of the specific developmental tasks proposed by Super and his associates.

*Life-span Counseling.* The increasing emphasis placed upon vocational development, as contrasted to single vocational choices, has been paralleled by a conception of vocational counseling as a continuing process. Life-span counseling is now widely advocated. Such counseling is needed to help the child keep up with the developmental tasks of his age level in preparation for later vocational choices and to guide the adolescent and young adult through his vocational explorations and successive approximations. Following entry into the world of work, other decisions must be made about specific jobs within one's chosen field and about job changes to improve job satisfaction, to facilitate vocational advancement, or for any number of individual reasons.

In special cases, a drastic reassessment of occupational choice may be required at any age level. This is true of an individual who discovers he made an unsuitable choice at an earlier stage, or one whose needs and values have altered radically with time, or one who has suffered a physical disability through injury or disease. The tubercular, the heart patient, and the disabled war veteran are common examples of the need for vocational counseling during early or late maturity. Still other examples are provided by a married woman who is suddenly widowed or by an older woman whose children have grown up and who would like to enter or reenter the world of work.

Vocational counseling of older workers is now receiving more and more attention. The special vocational problems encountered at this stage may revolve around changes in the nature or amount of work done on the present job, transfer to a more suitable type of job, or complete retirement from work. Research on problems of retirement has so far concentrated on exploratory surveys of attitudes, plans, problems, and effects on both the individual and his family. The tools have been largely questionnaires and interviews (e.g., 11, 13, 28, 66). A project conducted at Cornell introduced an important methodological improvement by gathering longitudinal data at four points in time: before retirement and after intervals of two, four, and five years (56). Comparisons were also made between retired workers and those still gainfully employed. The study included 4,032 workers in 259 industrial, governmental, and other organizations distributed over the entire country. Mention should also be made of the growing body of research on the vocational skills of older workers (e.g., 74).

Finally, it is being recognized increasingly that vocational counseling should not be limited to cross-sectional "crisis counseling," i.e., counseling given when the individual faces a serious problem. With its positive and preventive orientation, counseling should help to forestall crises. Moreover, a counselor can function most effectively if he maintains continuing, long-term contact with the same client. Super (59, ch. 23) proposes that such a relationship might be comparable to the typical relationship one has with a family physician, dentist, minister, or lawyer. The individual seeks help when he feels the need for it and possibly for an occasional checkup. But on these occasions he continues to consult the same counselor, who thus accumulates enough background information to be of maximum service to the client. The continuing contacts that a school counselor maintains with his counselees, as supplemented by cumulative records, approximate such a relationship. But in the counseling of adults, this pattern is so far largely untried, except possibly in the case of employee counseling in certain industrial corporations.

## SUMMARY

A major area of research in counseling psychology concerns the process of occupational choice and the nature of vocational development. In selecting an occupation, the individual chooses a way of life. One's occupation is likely to affect not only his income level and general social status but also many specific aspects of daily life. Job satisfaction and general emotional well-being are contingent upon the extent to which a person's work satisfies needs and values that are significant to him. There is a considerable accumulation of data on personality patterns characteristic of persons in different occupations, but the findings are often difficult to interpret because of procedural inadequacies. Some research has also been done on the relation between job satisfaction and need satisfaction and on the role of childhood experiences in vocational choice.

Both occupational research and vocational counseling call for occupational classifications based upon psychologically meaningful categories. Dimensional classifications have utilized the concepts of level, field, and enterprise. Trait patterns have been employed in other classifications, such as those followed in the *Minnesota Occupational Rating Scales* and in the forthcoming revision of the *Dictionary of Occupational Titles*.

Vocational choice involves, not one, but a series of decisions made over a period of years. It is one of the objectives of counseling to facilitate decision making by providing self-knowledge, occupational information, and training in the decision process. Occupational choice represents a synthesis between individual wants or needs and the demands and limitations of reality. An effective decision takes into account the probabilities of different outcomes, the risks involved, and the individual's value system. Throughout life, decisions made by the individual set limits upon his subsequent experiences and help to determine the direction of his development. Psychological research on the decision process, which has barely begun, should eventually make significant contributions to counseling psychology.

Counseling psychologists now emphasize the continuity of vocational development throughout life. In describing this developmental process, Super identifies five stages: growth, exploration, establishment, maintenance, and decline. Each stage presents its characteristic developmental tasks. An individual's vocational maturity is defined in terms of his mastery of the vocational tasks appropriate to his age. Longitudinal studies of vocational development have been initiated both in America and in other countries. A practical application of psychological knowledge regarding developmental tasks as well as decision making can be found in a group guidance program entitled *You: Today and Tomorrow*. There is increasing recognition of the need for life-span vocational counseling, since each life stage presents characteristic problems of its own. Counseling can be made more effective by the establishment of a continuing relationship between counselor and client. Vocational adjustment requires flexibility to reorient oneself to changing societal demands and individual capabilities throughout life.

# REFERENCES

1. Anastasi, Anne. *Differential psychology.* (3rd ed.) New York: Macmillan, 1958.
2. Anastasi, Anne. *Psychological testing.* (2nd ed.) New York: Macmillan, 1961.
3. Berdie, R. F. Likes, dislikes, and vocational interests. *J. appl. Psychol.*, 1943, **27**, 180–189.
4. Bogard, H. M. Union and management trainees: A comparative study of personality and occupational choice. *J. appl. Psychol.*, 1960, **44**, 56–63.
5. Bordin, E. S. A theory of vocational interests as dynamic phenomena. *Educ. psychol. Measmt*, 1943, **3**, 49–65.
6. Borow, H. Research programs in career development. *J. counsel. Psychol.*, 1960, **7**, 62–70.
7. Brender, M. Toward a psychodynamic system of occupational classification. *J. counsel. Psychol.*, 1960, **7**, 96–100.
8. Brophy, A. L. Self, role, and satisfaction. *Genet. Psychol. Monogr.*, 1959, **59**, 263–308.
9. Bross, I. D. J. *Design for decision.* New York: Macmillan, 1953.
10. Bühler, Charlotte. *Der menschliche Lebenslauf als psychologische Problem.* Stuttgart: Hirzel, 1933.
11. Burgess, E. W., *et al.* Occupational differences in attitudes toward aging and retirement. *J. Geront.*, 1958, **13**, 203–206.
12. Cleveland, S. Personality patterns associated with the professions of dietitian and nurse. *J. Hlth hum. Behav.*, 1961, **2**, 113–124.
13. Corey, L. G. Psychological adjustment and the worker role: An analysis of occupational differences. *J. appl. Psychol.*, 1959, **43**, 253–255.
14. Crites, J. O. Factor analytic definitions of vocational motivation. *J. appl. Psychol.*, 1961, **45**, 330–337.

15. Darley, J. G., and Hagenah, Theda. *Vocational interest measurement: Theory and practice.* Minneapolis: Univer. Minn. Press, 1955.
16. Edwards, W. The theory of decision making. *Psychol. Bull.,* 1954, **51**, 380–417.
17. Erikson, E. H. *Childhood and society.* New York: Norton, 1950.
18. Fine, S. A., and Heinz, C. A. The estimates of worker trait requirements for 4000 jobs. *Personnel Guid. J.,* 1957, **36**, 168–174.
19. Forer, B. R. Personality factors in occupational choice. *Educ. psychol. Measmt,* 1953, **13**, 361–366.
20. Friend, Jeannette G., and Haggard, E. A. Work adjustment in relation to family background. *Appl. Psychol. Monogr.,* 1948, No. 16.
21. Ginzberg, E., *et al. Occupational choice: An approach to a general theory.* New York: Columbia Univer. Press, 1951.
22. Gribbons, W. D. Evaluation of an eighth grade group guidance program. *Personnel Guid. J.,* 1960, **38**, 740–745.
23. Grigg, A. E. Childhood experience with parental attitudes: A test of Roe's hypothesis. *J. counsel. Psychol.,* 1959, **6**, 153–155.
24. *Guide to the use of the General Aptitude Test Battery. Section III: Development.* Washington: Govt. Printing Office, 1962.
25. Hagen, D. Careers and family atmospheres: An empirical test of Roe's theory. *J. counsel. Psychol.,* 1960, **7**, 251–256.
26. Hahn, M. E., and MacLean, M. S. *Counseling psychology.* (2nd ed.) New York: McGraw-Hill, 1955.
27. Havighurst, R. J. *Human development and education.* New York: Longmans, Green, 1953.
28. Havighurst, R. J. The social competence of middle-aged people. *Genet. Psychol. Monogr.,* 1957, **56**, 297–375.
29. Heist, P. Personality characteristics of dental students. *Educ. Rec.,* 1960, **41**, 240–252.
30. Holland, J. L. A theory of vocational choice. *J. counsel. Psychol.,* 1959, **6**, 35–45.
31. Holland, J. L. Some explorations of a theory of vocational choice: I. One- and two-year longitudinal studies. *Psychol. Monogr.,* 1962, **76**, No. 26.
32. Holt, R. R., and Luborsky, L. *Personality patterns of psychiatrists: A study of methods for selecting residents.* Vols. 1 and 2. New York: Basic Books, 1958.
33. Hoppock, R. *Occupational information: Where to get it and how to use it in counseling and teaching.* New York: McGraw-Hill, 1957.
34. Jacobson, F. N., Rettig, S., and Pasamanick, B. Status, job satisfaction, and factors of job satisfaction of state institution and clinic psychologists. *Amer. Psychologist,* 1959, **14**, 144–150.
35. Katz, M. R. *You: Today and tomorrow.* Princeton, N.J.: Educ. Test. Serv., 1959.
36. Kirchner, W. K., Dunnette, M. S., and Mousley, N. Use of the Edwards Personal Preference Schedule in the selection of salesmen. *Personnel Psychol.,* 1960, **13**, 421–424.
37. MacKinnon, D. W. Satisfaction with self as person and in professional role. *Amer. Psychologist,* 1961, **16**, 365.
38. Merton, R. K., Reader, G. G., and Kendall, Patricia L. (Eds.) *The student physician: Introductory studies in the sociology of medical education.* Cambridge, Mass.: Harvard Univer. Press, 1957.
39. Merwin, J. C., and DiVesta, F. J. A study of need theory and career choice. *J. counsel. Psychol.,* 1959, **6**, 302–308.
40. Miller, D. C., and Form, W. H. *Industrial sociology.* New York: Harper & Row, 1951.
41. Minor, C. A., and Neel, R. G. The relationship between achievement motive and occupational preference. *J. counsel. Psychol.,* 1958, **5**, 39–43.
42. Oakley, C. A., Macrae, A., and Mercer, E. O. *Handbook of vocational guidance.* London: Univer. London Press, 1937.
43. O'Hara, R. P., and Tiedeman, D. V. Vocational self concept in adolescence. *J. counsel. Psychol.,* 1959, **6**, 292–301.
44. Paterson, D. G., Gerken, C. d'A., and Hahn, M. E. *Revised Minnesota Occupational Rating Scales.* Minneapolis: Univer. Minn. Press, 1953.
45. Rettig, S. Status and job satisfaction of the professional: A factor analysis. *Psychol. Rep.,* 1960, **6**, 411–413.

46. Rettig, S., Jacobson, F. N., and Pasamanick, B. The motivational pattern of the mental health professional. *Psychiat. Res. Rep.* (*Amer. Psychiat. Assoc.*), 1958, No. 10.
47. Roe, Anne. A psychological study of eminent biologists. *Psychol. Monogr.,* 1951, **65**, No. 14.
48. Roe, Anne. A psychological study of physical scientists. *Genet. Psychol. Monogr.,* 1951, **43**, 121–235.
49. Roe, Anne. *The psychology of occupations.* New York: Wiley, 1956.
50. Roe, Anne. Early determinants of vocational choice. *J. counsel. Psychol.,* 1957, **4**, 212–217.
51. Schaffer, R. H. Job satisfaction as related to need satisfaction in work. *Psychol. Monogr.,* 1953, **67**, No. 14.
52. Segal, S. J. A psychoanalytic analysis of personality factors in vocational choice. *J. counsel. Psychol.,* 1961, **8**, 202–210.
53. Siegelman, M., and Peck, R. F. Personality patterns related to occupational roles. *Genet. Psychol. Monogr.,* 1960, **61**, 291–349.
54. Small, L. Personality determinants of vocational choice. *Psychol. Monogr.,* 1953, **67**, No. 1.
55. Stern, G. G., *et al.* Two scales for the assessment of unconscious motivations for teaching. *Educ. psychol. Measmt,* 1960, **20**, 9–29.
56. Streib, G. F., Thompson, W. E., and Suchman, E. A. The Cornell study of occupational retirement. *J. soc. Issues,* 1958, **14** (2), 3–17.
57. Strong, E. K., Jr. *Vocational interests of men and women.* Stanford, Calif.: Stanford Univer. Press, 1943.
58. Super, D. E. A theory of vocational development. *Amer. Psychologist,* 1953, **8**, 185–190.
59. Super, D. E. *The psychology of careers; an introduction to vocational development.* New York: Harper & Row, 1957.
60. Super, D. E. Vocational adjustment in terms of role theory. *Voc. Guid. Quart.,* 1957, **5**, 139–141.
61. Super, D. E., *et al. Vocational development: A framework for research.* New York: Teach. Coll., Columbia Univer., Bur. Publ., 1957.
62. Super, D. E., and Bachrach, P. B. *Scientific careers and vocational development theory: A review, a critique, and some recommendations.* New York: Teach. Coll., Columbia Univer., Bur. Publ., 1957.
63. Super, D. E., and Overstreet, Phoebe L. *The vocational maturity of ninth grade boys.* New York: Teach. Coll., Columbia Univer., Bur. Publ., 1960.
64. Terman, L. M. Scientists and non-scientists in a group of 800 gifted men. *Psychol. Monogr.,* 1954, **68**, No. 7.
65. Tiedeman, D. V., and O'Hara, R. P. The Harvard studies in career development: In retrospect and in prospect. *Harvard Stud. Career Develpm.,* 1960, No. 15a. (Grad Sch. Educ., Harvard Univer.—Mimeographed)
66. Tuckman, J., and Lorge, I. *Retirement and the industrial worker: Prospect and reality.* New York: Teach. Coll., Columbia Univer., Bur. Publ., 1953.
67. Tyler, Leona E. Distinctive patterns of likes and dislikes over a twenty-two year period. *J. counsel. Psychol.,* 1959, **6**, 234–237.
68. Tyler, Leona E. Toward a workable psychology of individuality. *Amer. Psychologist,* 1959, **14**, 75–81.
69. Tyler, Leona E. *The work of the counselor.* (2nd ed.) New York: Appleton-Century-Crofts, 1961.
70. United States Employment Service. *Dictionary of occupational titles.* (2nd ed.) Vol. 1. Washington: Govt. Printing Office, 1949. (Suppl. 1955.)
71. Utton, A. C. Recalled parent-child relations as determinants of vocational choice. Unpublished doctoral dissertation, Teach. Coll., Columbia Univer., 1960.
72. Viteles, M. S., Brayfield, A. H., and Tyler, Leona E. *Vocational counseling: A reappraisal in honor of Donald G. Paterson.* Minneapolis: Univer. Minn. Press, 1961.
73. Walther, R. H. Self-description and occupational choice. *Amer. Psychologist,* 1961, **16**, 429.
74. Welford, A. T., *et al. Skill and age; an experimental approach.* London: Oxford Univer. Press, 1951.

# VII
## *Psychology and Other Professions*

# 18

# Psychology and Education

In the next three chapters we shall consider certain applications of psychology to other professional fields. In these roles, the psychologist works predominantly (though not exclusively) through other professional personnel rather than directly with clients, applicants, employees, students, or other recipients of his services. He may function as a consultant, making recommendations that are implemented by others. He may be engaged in the training of professional personnel in schools of education, medicine, business, home economics, social work, nursing, theology, and other specialties. Finally, he may conduct joint research with members of another profession. The interprofessional contacts of any one psychologist may of course cover one or more of these three types of relationships.

To be sure, some psychologists employed in schools, courts, hospitals, and other institutions do work directly with clients and may even devote most of their time to such immediate personal services. When they do so, however, their functions are so similar to those of clinical or counseling psychologists as to be virtually indistinguishable from them. In the present section, therefore, the focus will be on the interprofessional activities of psychologists working in these settings.

Mention should also be made of the extensive contributions of psychologists to testing programs for the selection of professional school students, the specialty certification of professional personnel, and the evaluation of applicants for professional posts. Examples of large-scale programs developed and administered by psychologically trained test specialists are provided by the Medical College Admission Test, the Law School Admission Test, and the National Teacher Examinations, among others (see 3, pp. 472–485). In these programs, the psychologist functions in the same way as he does in any personnel selection situation. Since the problems and techniques of personnel selection were discussed in Chapters 2, 3, and 4, nothing further need be said about this role of psychologists in relation to other professions.

Although psychologists have established professional relationships with many fields (see 146, chs. 8 and 11), three have been singled out for special discussion because of their present or potential scope. These are the fields of education, medicine, and law, each of which will be examined in a separate chapter. Even in these fields, however, the contributions of psychology are not so fully developed or so highly structured as they are in the other psychological specialties discussed earlier in the book. The roles of psychologists in these fields are in a state of flux and will undoubtedly undergo considerable reorganization and clarification in the years ahead.

Psychologists who work in the field of *education* can be differentiated into school psychologists and educational psychologists. Although the two groups have much in common in training and functions, their distinctness was recognized by the establishment of two separate divisions in the American Psychological Association, devoted to these two specialties (see Appendix A). Similarly, some universities now offer separate training programs leading to graduate degrees in the two fields. The University of Chicago, for example, initiated these differentiated programs in 1962.

The functions of the school psychologist have much in common with those of counseling and clinical psychologists but are performed exclusively in a school setting. The educational psychologist, on the other hand, is most likely to be found on the faculty of a school of education or in an educational research bureau. As in the distinction between clinical and counseling psychology, that between school psychology and educational psychology is one of degree. The focus of activity in the two specialties can be clearly differentiated, but there is much overlapping of functions and individual variation. The first section of this chapter is concerned with the work of the school psychologist. The remaining three sections, dealing with teacher training, educational research, and the educational applications of teaching machines and other technological developments, fall within the area of educational psychology.

## THE SCHOOL PSYCHOLOGIST

*Functions.* The functions and responsibilities of a school psychologist vary widely with the school and the community in which he is employed. Nevertheless, questionnaire surveys, national conferences, and published descriptions of these functions reveal certain areas of general agreement (see 29; 48, ch. 1; 68; 98; 146, ch. 8; 147). The most common function is one of diagnosis, broadly defined. This involves individual intelligence and personality testing; fact-finding interviews with the pupil, as well as with teachers, parents, and others who have significant contacts with him; observation of the pupil in the classroom, on the playground, and in other school contexts; and study of the pupil's cumulative school record.

These diagnostic procedures are followed by recommendations for remedial action, which are usually carried out by other professional personnel, such as the child's classroom teacher or the school social worker. In some cases, the psychologist may recommend remedial instruction to make up for special educational deficiencies, as in reading or arithmetic. In still other cases, he may recommend placement in a special class or special school. Conferences with parents may also be utilized in the effort to improve the child's home situation and parental relations. In all these procedures, it is apparent that the school psychologist relies heavily upon environmental therapy (see Chapter 14).

A major source of current controversy regarding the functions of the school psychologist pertains to psychotherapy. Some school psychologists maintain that they should also conduct psychotherapy with individual children, especially when community and other clinical resources are inadequate. On the other hand, a majority of spokesmen for school psychology deemphasize this role. All agree, of course, that any contact between the psychologist and the child may and should serve a therapeutic function. The disagreement centers around more intensive, long-term psychotherapy.

Apart from the various arguments that have been mustered for and against psychotherapy by school psychologists, there is the inescapable fact that the school psychologist rarely has the time required to carry out this function unless he concentrates on a few seriously disturbed cases and neglects all other obligations. It has been estimated that to provide one school psychologist for every three thousand schoolchildren in the nation would require some fifteen thousand school psychologists (146, p. 167). The number currently available is close to one-tenth of that figure. To be sure, school psychologists are quite unevenly distributed among school systems. But even in those systems that are most liberally provided with such services, the available number of psychologists is not such as to permit extensive individual psychotherapy. When school psychologists work in this capacity, they do so chiefly as an auxiliary or emergency measure. The bulk of their contribution is made through other professional personnel.

Even if the available supply of school psychologists were to be greatly augmented, it would still be desirable for them to work principally through teachers and others who have daily contact with the children. Such an approach is in keeping with the objectives of the mental health movement in its emphasis upon prevention and upon the fostering of effective psychological development through good teaching practices (1). In school as elsewhere, mental health is not something to be acquired in a special department or at certain hours, but is a by-product of one's experiences in daily living. Successful school achievement, for example, is as important to the mental health of the schoolchild or college student as is successful job performance to the mental health of an adult worker.

Depending upon the needs of a particular school system and the availability of other personnel, school psychologists may and frequently do perform a number of other functions. They may assist in organizing and administering the school's group testing program. Because of their special training, they can also be of help in the interpretation of test results and in the evaluation and selection of new tests. Frequently they conduct in-service training of teachers in such areas as test interpretation, detection of emotional problems in children, giving of "psychological first aid" in the classroom, and application of the mental health point of view to teaching. They can also make a contribution to curriculum development, to the improvement of cumulative records, and to various administrative procedures. Often they are called upon to participate in PTA meetings, address various civic groups, and perform other public-information functions. In some schools, psychologists conduct remedial training programs in basic educational skills, although the desirability of their doing so has been questioned on the grounds that they can use their time more effectively. Special teachers trained in remedial work should carry on this instruction. Opinion is also divided as to whether school psychologists should engage in research as a part of their regular duties. For many school psychologists this may be an academic question because of time pressures.

**Referral Problems and Sources.**  The kinds of problems for which children are referred to a school psychologist are quite varied. The most visible type is the behavior problem of an aggressive or disruptive nature that interferes with the normal operation of the school. Other kinds of emotional adjustment problems are also a common cause of referral. Learning difficulties of a general or specific nature, as in reading or arithmetic, are another frequent complaint. Some cases are referred because of physical handicaps that require special placement or adjustment in instructional techniques. The psychologist may be consulted, too, with regard to gifted children whose educational programs should be enriched or accelerated to suit their abilities.

Although the classroom teacher is the most common referral source, other school personnel may have opportunities to detect problems and to make referrals or seek the advice of the school psychologist. Among them are the school nurse and physician, the social worker, and special teachers. At the high school level, self-referrals by students are not unusual. Other ways of identifying individuals in need of help include group screening procedures utilizing teachers' ratings or screening guides, as well as checklists or inventories filled out by pupils. When such group procedures are followed by screening interviews, they will usually help to detect problem cases not otherwise identified. Visits by the school psychologist to classes and to other school activities may also bring to his attention pupils who are not adjusting satisfactorily. Cumulative records and group testing programs can help to identify pupils with learning problems and with special talents or defects.

*Training.*    With regard to training, the school psychologist must cut across the fields of psychology and education. Although there are a few dissenting voices, it is the general consensus that he is not merely a clinical psychologist who works in a school building. He works not only *in* a school but *through* it. He serves as a consultant to educational personnel, and he utilizes the school environment as a therapeutic medium. For these reasons, he needs an understanding of the educational process and some knowledge about the organization and administration of school systems, their available resources, and the roles of their specialized personnel.

Within psychology, he should have a firm foundation in the general science of behavior, with special training in such areas as child or developmental psychology, personality adjustment, psychological testing, and clinical and counseling methods. Whether conducted in a department of psychology, a department of education, or jointly in both departments, university training programs for school psychology require the cooperative services of psychology and education faculty. It is particularly important that in his practicum training the school psychologist have adequate opportunity to work with children. Training in clinical psychology is often limited to adult cases, unless special efforts are made to include experience with children (see 97; 147, ch. 2). Teaching experience has also been recommended, although other types of practicum experience in the schools may provide a realistic orientation to the sort of environment in which the school psychologist will work.

*Growth and Legal Status.*    As a professional specialty, school psychology has been making rapid strides since midcentury. In 1948, the APA Division of School Psychologists had 88 members; in 1963, this number had grown to 856, representing nearly a tenfold increase over a 15-year period. Since a sizable proportion of APA members are not affiliated with any division and a number of school psychologists may not even be members of the APA, it has been estimated that the total number of psychologists functioning in this capacity may be of the order of 1,500 (146, p. 167). This number, of course, is still far below even the most conservative estimates of current need (29).

Approximately half of the states now have certification laws for school psychologists (63). The educational requirements for certification vary from the M.A. to the Ph.D. level. Among psychologists themselves, it is recognized that school psychologists should have doctoral level training, although the M.A.

level is sufficient for the more routine testing functions performed by school psychologists in some school systems (29). It is recommended, however, that the latter job level be designated by a more restricted job title, such as psychometrist, psychometric technician, or psychological examiner.

**Relation to Guidance Counselors.** In one respect, the functions of a school psychologist are more similar to those of clinical psychologists than to those of counseling psychologists: the school psychologist does not normally provide vocational orientation or educational and vocational counseling. In most school systems, these functions are handled by guidance counselors. Parenthetically, one wonders why such a redundant term was chosen to describe this function. Since "guidance" and "counseling" are often used synonymously, calling someone a "guidance counselor" has been likened to naming a girl "Mary Marie" (146, p. 168). Having become deeply entrenched in educational nomenclature, however, this term will undoubtedly persist.

Guidance counselors are rarely trained as counseling psychologists. Training requirements for this position vary widely from state to state and are often quite limited. In some states, in fact, guidance counselors may be classroom teachers with no formal preparation or special experience in counseling functions. To help remedy some of these limitations in training, the National Defense Education Act of 1958 appropriated funds for short intensive training institutes for school guidance counselors (140). Many such institutes have now been conducted throughout the country. Whatever his level of training and sophistication, the guidance counselor represents one more type of specialized educational personnel with whom the school psychologist needs to maintain effective working relations (see 147, pp. 257–260).

# PSYCHOLOGY IN TEACHER TRAINING

**Objectives.** Courses in educational psychology are designed to augment the teacher's understanding of human behavior, rather than to provide specific "rules" for effective teaching. Psychological training should make available to prospective teachers knowledge about child behavior, learning processes, adjustment mechanisms, and other relevant areas. Such information should help the teacher to make a wiser choice of teaching procedures when confronted with specific situations. As in other fields of application, psychological training should provide the teacher with a point of view toward human behavior and a method for solving interpersonal problems as they arise. It should help him to decide what to look for and what questions to ask in trying to understand situations encountered in the classroom.

Such an approach is in sharp contrast to the learning of prescribed teaching techniques. There are many reasons why a set of rules or techniques cannot serve as a satisfactory guide to effective teaching. Teaching situations are complex, and each is unique in its totality. Moreover, teaching procedures very probably interact with teacher variables, as well as with learner and task variables. A procedure effective in the hands of one teacher may fail dismally when attempted by another. Since teaching is basically an interpersonal relationship, there is good reason to expect the same sort of interaction between teaching method and teacher characteristics that is found between therapeutic techniques and therapist variables in clinical psychology (see Chapter 15).

Classroom atmosphere depends largely upon the teacher. If the teacher feels insincere, hypocritical, or uncomfortable with the procedures he employs, the classroom atmosphere suffers as a consequence. Recognizing the importance of these conditions for teacher effectiveness, Rogers writes:

To know when he has reached the limit of his own internal comfort, and to feel easy in refusing to function in ways that are not comfortable for him, is another aspect of the genuineness of his attitudes. If he behaves in some way that is not natural for him, simply because he feels that he should do so, this is quickly sensed by the group and damages the group atmosphere (115, p. 401).

Still another type of interpersonal relation that may be recalled in this connection is that between supervisor and employees, discussed in Chapter 6. There, too, no set of rules could be universally applied, because of the interactions between supervisor, worker, and situational variables. Also relevant are the findings on leadership climate, considered in Chapters 5 and 6. As in the case of industrial supervision, the leadership climate in which teachers themselves must function is likely to influence their classroom behavior. If permissive and pupil-centered teaching procedures have been authoritatively even though subtly imposed upon a teacher by his own supervisor, their application can hardly be genuine and whole-hearted.

**The Psychology of Learning.**    Although emphasis on different topics has shifted from time to time, most educational psychology texts today focus on learning processes (see, e.g., 26, 37, 74, 78, 84, 107). It is obvious that the effective management of learning is the central problem of education. To be sure, information from several other areas of psychology is relevant; but the value of such information to the educator stems chiefly from its application to the facilitation and guidance of learning. It should be noted, too, that learning covers much more than what is formally taught in school. The pupil, whether he be academically successful or unsuccessful, is constantly learning many things, such as attitudes toward peers and authority figures, habits of fair play and sportsmanship, neurotic symptoms, decision-making techniques, prejudices and superstitions, and a host of other reactions that may be desirable or undesirable. The teacher needs to be alerted to the vast multiplicity of learning that goes on in the school situation. An understanding of learning processes is thus relevant to every aspect of education, from the fostering of mental health to the choice of specific methods for teaching reading or arithmetic.

The potential contribution that psychology can make to education is still largely unrealized. Oddly enough, the gap between the two fields is widest in the area of learning, where the greatest contribution would be expected (see 32, 46, 55, 91, 126). From time to time, psychologists have attempted to survey what psychology has to offer to education (e.g., 11, 130). To a large extent, every educational psychology text tries also to do this. Insofar as these books undertake to give a coordinated picture of recommended teaching practices, however, they fill in extensively from personal opinions of educational leaders, educational folklore, and other experimentally unverified sources.

Another regrettable tendency in educational psychology is that of drawing unwarranted conclusions and overgeneralizing from isolated laboratory experiments. Most laboratory investigations of both animal and human learning, for example, were designed to contribute toward the development of learning theory. When examined in isolation and outside of this context, they often appear trivial. It is only when they are considered in relation to other experiments and within their appropriate theoretical framework that their significance can be recognized. Certainly such experiments were not designed to test (or support!) the effectiveness of specific teaching procedures. What is needed for the latter purpose is applied research on school learning, similar to the research on military training problems initiated during World War II (see Chapter 5).

There is relatively little well-designed learning research that is explicitly oriented toward education. The reasons for this deficit can be found partly in psychology and partly in education (see 91, 138). The confusion between basic and applied research in this field has also served to delay progress. Melton (91) has pointed out that education bears the same relation to psychology that engineering bears to the physical sciences. Bridging the gap between education and psychology, the educational psychologist must design the curricula and teaching procedures that utilize the science of learning and must then carry out the necessary applied research to test the effectiveness of these procedures in school situations.

To be sure, there is a mass of published educational research on such topics as reading and arithmetic and on comparative evaluations of different methods of teaching these subjects (see 18, 49). The results are often inconclusive, however, owing to inadequacies in experimental design, control of conditions, or statistical analysis of data. Because of the many variables that operate in a classroom situation and because the relative effectiveness of teaching methods may vary with learner characteristics and with the objectives of instruction, complex experimental designs are needed for a conclusive evaluation of teaching methods.

A knowledge of learning theory and of laboratory experiments on learning can contribute in at least two ways to the development of an empirically based educational technology. First, it can provide methodological guidance in the planning and execution of applied research in educational contexts. Second, the learning principles identified in the laboratory can lead to a deeper understanding of school learning. Out of such understanding may come suggestions for specific educational procedures to be evaluated through applied classroom research. The learning principles cited in Chapter 5 in connection with industrial and military training are also relevant to school learning. They pertain to such questions as motivation, stress and anxiety, active learner participation, feedback and immediacy of reinforcement, and the distribution of learning, among others.

Since education is expected to equip the individual to meet effectively situations encountered in later life, *transfer of training* is of primary concern to the educator. Of particular interest are the conditions that facilitate transfer, such as the presentation of the learning task in a variety of contexts and the explicit formulation of concepts and principles. There is some evidence suggesting that principles worked out by the learner himself transfer more readily to other situations than do principles that are given to him (58, 73, 127). The optimal combination of guidance and empirical discovery, however, undoubtedly varies with task variables, learner variables, and learning objectives (41, 73, 77, 109).

Education deals largely with the learning of *meaningful verbal materials*, as contrasted with motor learning or rote verbal learning. There has recently been an upsurge of research, both basic and applied, on the nature of meaningfulness, its effect on learning and transfer, and ways of increasing its utilization in the learning process (5, 6, 22, 43, 100, 142, 143). Also relevant are studies on concept formation in children as a function of task and learner variables (e.g., 101, 102).

The importance of *motivation* in the learning process is generally recognized. The need for complex experimental designs that permit the assessment of interaction effects is well illustrated by a recent Swedish investigation of the effects of praise and blame on schoolchildren's achievement in arithmetic (69). In this experiment, the relative influence of praise and blame was found to vary with the child's initial performance level, his anxiety level, his attitudes toward the teacher, and the type of task (whether mechanical computation or problem solving).

Still another major concern of educational psychologists is represented by the concept of *learning readiness*. Essentially, "readiness" refers to the presence of prerequisite skills and knowledge that enable the learner to profit maximally from a certain kind of instruction. Individual differences in the reading readiness of first-grade schoolchildren provide a familiar example. At one time, readiness was considered largely in terms of maturation. To be sure, the attainment of certain minimum physical prerequisites facilitates some kinds of learning. Unless he can make the necessary auditory discriminations, the child cannot learn to speak by the usual procedures; without the ability for fine motor coordination, he cannot manipulate a pencil in writing. Most school learning, however, is not so closely bound up with sensorimotor development. In the mastery of educational tasks, the importance of prior learning has come to be increasingly recognized (12). More and more emphasis is being placed upon the hierarchical development of knowledges and skills, whereby the acquisition of simpler concepts equips the individual for the learning of more complex concepts at any age.

Of particular interest in connection with readiness is a series of experiments by Harlow (57) on learning sets. These experiments, conducted on both monkeys and children, demonstrated that, when learning a series of similar problems, the individual gradually establishes certain learning sets that facilitate the learning of the required discriminations. Through such an experience, the individual is thus "learning how to learn." This concept is especially relevant to education, so much of which is designed to equip the individual for later learning. Through this approach, readiness can be seen as a special application of transfer of training, since it reflects the facilitating effect of prior learning upon present learning. In human learning, the acquisition of effective learning procedures can be accelerated by guidance from the teacher. "How to study" programs are aimed at the same objective.

Since midcentury, there is evidence that the gap between laboratory research on learning and educational technology is narrowing. Psychologists and educators, acting both as individuals and through their professional associations, have been making special efforts to bring about closer contacts between the two fields. Books are beginning to appear that interpret learning theory for educators and concentrate on the implications of learning principles for school instruction (e.g., 50). The rising interest in education as a factor in national defense and the growing demand for scientists and other highly trained personnel has led to increased government support of educational research. All this activity is beginning to bear fruit in some comprehensive and well-designed research projects on school learning. Eventually, the results of these studies should provide a more solid foundation for the teaching of educational psychology.

**Other Areas of Psychology.** Prospective teachers generally receive preparation in certain other areas of psychology, either in separate courses or as part of a comprehensive course in educational psychology. *Developmental, child,* or *adolescent* psychology is designed to orient teachers toward developmental changes in behavior and to familiarize them with the particular age groups they expect to teach. A closely related area is that of *individual and group differences.* Knowledge regarding the nature, origins, and extent of individual differences helps in understanding the behavior of individual children in the classroom. Educators also need to consider the implications of physical and psychological sex differences and of the sex roles institutionalized by a particular culture (2, ch. 14; 79; 96). In recent years, too, there has been a growing concern with the educational problems of children from culturally deprived backgrounds. In many parts of the country, a number of special remedial and developmental programs have been instituted for such children, ranging from the preschool to the high school level.

The teacher also needs to be acquainted with the special problems and educational needs of several types of "exceptional children," including the intellectually gifted (38, 61, 145), the creative (45, 131), the mentally retarded, the physically handicapped, and the emotionally disturbed (56, 72, 75, 76, 117). Many school systems have special classes for children in these various categories, taught by specially qualified teachers. Such teachers are usually required to have more training in psychology than are regular classroom teachers.

To function effectively in the modern school, the teacher must have considerable familiarity with *psychological testing,* with special reference to group intelligence tests and achievement tests. An elementary knowledge of the nature and interpretation of test scores and simple statistical procedures for handling such scores is also helpful. Techniques for developing and evaluating classroom examinations are generally taught in this connection too. Several current texts on measurement and evaluation have been specially written for use in teacher training (e.g., 44, 134).

Modern education has for some time included among its major goals the development of a healthy personality and the prevention of emotional maladjustment. The current mental health movement has stimulated interest in a reexamination of these goals (1; 33; 65; 66, part 6; 82; 121, pp. 552-566). In its report, the Joint Commission on Mental Illness and Health (see Chapter 14) devoted a separate volume to the role of the schools in mental health (1). It is generally recognized that teachers need an elementary introduction to the psychology of adjustment, including common adjustment mechanisms and the nature and sources of mild behavioral abnormalities. This background will help them in identifying children for referral to special services as well as in administering "psychological first aid" in the classroom. It should also assist them in establishing effective teacher-pupil relations and in maintaining a classroom atmosphere conducive to mental health.

A specific example of psychological research that is pertinent to teacher training in mental health is the comprehensive investigation of the causes, nature, and effects of anxiety among schoolchildren, conducted by Sarason and his associates (119). Of all the emotional problems of the schoolchild, anxiety is one of the least likely to be recognized by teachers, because of its minimal observable manifestations. This is particularly true of the bright anxious child who does acceptable or even superior school work, although he could do still better if he were free from his disruptive anxieties.

Finally, there is a growing tendency to include some *social psychology* in teacher training (21, 139). Examples of research areas in social psychology that are relevant to education include leadership, attitudes and prejudice, intergroup relations, competition and cooperation, interaction of individuals in face-to-face groups, conformity, internalization of social norms, and sociometry.

## RESEARCH AND DEVELOPMENT

The term "educational research" has many meanings (7, 8, 137). Since the educational profession has its roots in such diverse fields as philosophy, history, economics, government, and psychology, its concept of research reflects the variety of practices traditionally designated as research in these fields. Thus what the educator calls research includes many activities that fall outside the realm of research as defined in psychology and other natural sciences.

Another source of confusion stems from the early identification of educational research in America with the compilation of educational statistics. Under this heading, masses of data are regularly gathered on such topics as the supply and demand of teachers, salaries of teachers in different parts of the country, distribution of pupils in schools and classes, attendance, and other administrative details (39, 138). It was for such record-keeping purposes that the Office of Education was originally established by the Federal government. The same objectives led to the organization of research bureaus and the appointment of research directors in individual school systems. Another area that has often been loosely included under educational research is curriculum development. Even when empirical outcome studies were conducted in school settings, they were often undertaken to justify a particular educational program to the public rather than to test hypotheses. Such studies usually lacked adequate control data and their experimental designs did not permit the isolation of the many variables involved.

Against this background, psychological research made little headway. After its promising beginnings early in the century through the efforts of such pioneers as E. L. Thorndike at Columbia and C. H. Judd at Chicago, educational psychology made slow progress for nearly half a century. It was not until the late 1950s that research in this field began to show new vigor, as noted in the preceding section. Even now, much of the research in educational psychology is carried on by investigators who are not themselves connected with schools. Although some of the larger school systems are becoming more receptive to such outside investigators, there are still many barriers to the effective utilization of schools for research purposes (34, 97).

Within school systems themselves, there are as yet few research bureaus conducting well-designed psychological research. In some of the largest city school systems, however, administrative research and curricular research have become differentiated from educational research. These three types of research may be conducted by different bureaus, as in the New York City system. Under these conditions, the educational research bureau can concentrate its activities on test construction and evaluation, learning and teaching research, and broader educational experiments.

In this section we shall look at some examples of educational research in which psychologists are making significant contributions. In order to give some notion of the range of potential contribution, specific examples have been chosen from widely diverse areas. Some represent highly developed fields of research; others concern problems on which research has barely begun. In their approach, the investigations fall at various points along the continuum of basic and applied research. Only a few examples are reported for purposes of illustration. Many more types of studies could be cited, including some of those mentioned in the preceding section.

**Evaluation and Measurement.** Traditionally, educational psychologists have made their greatest contribution in test construction and in the development of statistical methods for analyzing test results. In this area, educational psychologists have also attained a relatively high level of technical sophistication. The content of such publications as the *Journal of Educational Psychology* and *Educational and Psychological Measurement,* for instance, reveals both the predominant concern of educational psychologists with testing problems and the soundness of their procedures in this area. Besides contributing to the development and validation of tests, psychologists have conducted considerable applied and basic research on a number of factors that affect test performance. For instance, several studies have been concerned with the influence of practice and coaching on test scores (see 3, pp. 54–57). Another problem, with broad implications for educational practice, is that of "test anxiety." In a series of studies on both school children and college students, extensive data were gathered on the origins of this anxiety, its effects on test performance and on school achievement, and its relation to anxiety in other situations (119).

Not only do schools employ nearly every available kind of psychological test in their operational programs, but they are also the principal consumers of certain types of tests specially devised for educational purposes. In the construction of the latter tests, psychologists and educators work in close collaboration. The effective interprofessional relations that have been established in test construction are in sharp contrast to those characteristic of learning research.

One category of tests developed to meet a specific educational need is that of *readiness tests* (3, ch. 17; 44). These tests are designed to implement the previously discussed concept of educational readiness in various areas. One of their chief uses is in assessing the child's qualifications for schoolwork upon school entrance. Readiness tests for this level have much in common with intelligence tests for children in the primary grades. In the readiness tests, however, special emphasis is placed upon those abilities found to be most important in learning to read; some attention is also given to the prerequisites of numerical thinking and to the sensorimotor control required in learning to write. Among the specific functions covered are visual and auditory discrimination, motor control, verbal comprehension, vocabulary, quantitative concepts, and general information. Figure 113 shows sample items from two of the tests included in the Metropolitan Readiness Tests (62). Consisting of six tests, this battery yields separate scores in reading readiness, number readiness, and total readiness for first-grade schoolwork.[1]

At higher educational levels, readiness tests are commonly known as "prognostic tests," but their objectives are essentially the same. By measuring prerequisite skills and knowledge, these tests attempt to predict how well the individual will perform in a particular course of study. Frequently they include the learning of sample tasks similar to those that will be encountered in the course. Among the most widely used prognostic tests are those de-

[1] A revision of these tests is in progress.

**Fig. 113** Sample items from Metropolitan Readiness Tests. (*Reproduced by permission of Harcourt, Brace & World.*)

Test 1. *Word Meaning.* In the first row, the subject marks the baby; in the second row, the house.

Test 4. *Matching.* In each row, the subject marks the picture which is identical to the one in the circular frame.

subsequently adapted some of the Guilford tests for use with younger subjects and have employed them, along with new tests, in educational research projects extending from the preschool to the high school level (42, 45, 103, 133, 135, 136). An example of a test that is effective with young children is the "Improvements" test, in which the child is given toys — such as nurse kit, fire truck, and dog — and is asked to think of ways for changing each toy so it would be "more fun to play with" (135, 136). Thinking up unusual uses for common objects, such as a toy, a tin can, or a brick, illustrates another technique that has proved applicable over a wide age range (45, 53, 135, 136).

A common finding in these investigations is that creativity involves many intellectual factors *not* covered by traditional intelligence tests. In unselected populations, the correlations between creativity tests and intelligence tests fall largely between .20 and .40; in relatively homogeneous samples of individuals at high intellectual levels, the correlations may be zero or even negative (133). These relationships were illustrated in a study of high school students conducted by Getzels and Jackson (45). From a population of 449 high school students attending the University of Chicago laboratory school, two groups were selected for intensive study: one high in intelligence but not in creativity, the other high in creativity but not in intelligence. The High Intelligence group consisted of 28 students who were in the top 20 per cent in IQ[2] when compared with students of the same age and sex, but were below the top 20 per cent on a battery of five creativity tests; the High Creativity group consisted of 26 students falling in the top 20 per cent on the creativity battery but below the top 20 per cent in IQ.

In school achievement, both the High Creativity and the High Intelligence groups excelled the total school population by the same amount. Since the High Creativity group did not differ significantly in IQ from the total school population, such students would traditionally be regarded as "overachievers." These findings highlight the artificiality of the overachievement concept, as well as its dependence upon the particular measure of scholastic aptitude used to predict achievement level. Getzels and Jackson employed several other rating and testing techniques in their comparison of the two groups. In general, the High Creativity students tended to express unconventional values and aspirations, to place a high value on humor, and to utilize unusual associations in their fantasy productions.

All these findings were closely corroborated in an extensive investigation of elementary schoolchildren conducted by Torrance (135, 136). Achievement tests again revealed no differences between the High Intelligence and High Creativity groups. Nevertheless teachers rated the High Creativity cases as less desirable pupils, less ambitious, and less hardworking than the High Intelligence cases. Humor and playfulness were again conspicuous in the creative child's behavior. Other parts of Torrance's continuing project are concerned with such problems as the creative pupil's estrangement from his peers, influences in and out of school that tend to interfere with the development of creative behavior, and the application of certain techniques of creativity training to schoolchildren (132, 135, 136).

With regard to the relation between intelligence test performance and

[2] As determined from Stanford-Binet, WISC, or Henmon-Nelson group tests of intelligence.

creativity, Torrance reports that if only the top 20 per cent in IQ had been considered, approximately 70 per cent of his High Creativity group would have been excluded. Surveys in several schools and with a variety of intelligence tests yielded remarkably similar results in this respect. On the other hand, in Torrance's study, as well as in that of Getzels and Jackson, there were sizable groups of children who fell above the cutoffs in *both* intelligence test scores and creativity measures. More data on such cases would have helped to round out the picture.

In an investigation conducted by Gallagher and his associates (42) with intellectually gifted junior high school students, the focus was on the verbal interaction that occurs in the classroom between teachers and pupils. Tape recordings of such interactions were obtained for a total of 60 sessions of 12 different classes in science, mathematics, social studies, and English. The tape scripts, with supplementary observations by two classroom observers, were analyzed in terms of a specially developed system of classification derived from Guilford's creativity research. The major categories in this classification system included: cognitive memory, convergent thinking, divergent thinking, evaluation, and routine incidental remarks.

The results of these analyses of verbal interaction for each pupil were studied in relation to such other data as written class assignments of a creative nature, performance on creativity tests of the Guilford type, attitudinal and self-concept measures, and home and familial characteristics. The study also provides suggestive data on the types of teacher behavior that lead to creative pupil responses in classroom situations. In its general approach, this project represents a "process study" of teaching, which is analogous to the process studies of psychotherapy described in Chapter 15.

**Teacher Characteristics.** Investigation of the characteristics of effective and ineffective teachers is crucial to both selection and training of teachers. It also represents one approach to the study of the teaching process itself. Educators have been trying to assess and predict teacher effectiveness for a long time, but the large majority of the studies have contributed little because of methodological deficiencies (see 93, 95). A major difficulty is that of finding adequate *criteria* of good teaching. This difficulty stems largely from the multiplicity of educational objectives and the lack of agreement regarding their relative importance. It is quite likely that teaching effectiveness is not a unitary characteristic. A teacher who is highly effective in promoting one educational goal, such as mastery of knowledge and skills, may be relatively ineffective in furthering other goals, such as emotional adjustment, creativity, or the development of desirable interpersonal attitudes. In research on teacher effectiveness, there is need for complex experimental designs that permit a measurement of possible interactions between teacher characteristics, on the one hand, and educational objectives, teaching methods (lecture, discussion, projects, etc.), subject matter, and pupil characteristics on the other.

Specific criteria of teacher effectiveness may utilize either product or process measures. Product criteria are based upon changes in pupil behavior after exposure to a given teacher. Comparison of achievement test scores before and after a term's work illustrates the application of such a criterion. Although logically the most satisfactory, this type of criterion measure is often impracticable because of the difficulty of controlling the influence of other factors on pupil change.

Process criteria involve systematic classroom observation of teacher behavior, teacher-pupil interactions, and "classroom climate." The use of such criteria is based on the assumption that certain teaching practices are intrinsically more desirable and are generally accepted as such. Agreement could undoubtedly be reached regarding some practices, especially in their more extreme forms. But on the whole, concepts of effective teaching still leave much room for controversy. Insofar as teacher behavior cannot be readily separated from pupil behavior, both are generally included in process criteria. In this case, the pupil behavior observed is an immediate response in the classroom situation. Product criteria, on the other hand, are concerned with long-range and more lasting changes in pupil behavior.

In an attempt to systematize the observation of teaching behavior, the American Council on Education initiated a six-year, nationwide investigation of this problem (118). Known as the Teacher Characteristics Study, this investigation comprised approximately 100 separate research projects requiring the participation of more than 6,000 elementary and high school teachers in about 1,700 public, private, and parochial schools. In the basic study, teachers were independently observed in the classroom by two to four trained observers. The rating scales developed for this purpose covered 22 traits, identified through the critical-incident technique as well as through an examination of published studies of teacher and pupil behavior. Intercorrelation and factorial analysis of the ratings yielded three major factors, or dimensions, common to both elementary and high school groups. These dimensions were described as: (1) warm, understanding, friendly vs. aloof, egocentric, restricted teacher behavior; (2) responsible, businesslike, systematic vs. evading, unplanned, slipshod teacher behavior; (3) stimulating, imaginative vs. dull, routine teacher behavior. Other major parts of the study were concerned with the development of paper-and-pencil instruments for predicting these and other dimensions of teacher behavior and with the comparison of various subgroups in these instruments.

A different approach was followed by Heil and his associates in an intensive study of 55 teachers from nine public elementary schools in Brooklyn, New York (59, 60). In this study, the criterion measures were *pupil gains* over a school year in (1) achievement test scores and (2) friendliness as determined by a sociometric instrument. It is noteworthy that, within the restricted population of professionally trained teachers investigated, little or no relation was found between these criteria of pupil gains and classroom observations of teacher behavior. This is a common finding in studies that compared the two kinds of criteria.

Among the most significant findings of the study are those obtained with specially developed indices of pupil and teacher personality. The results showed several interactions between the two sets of variables. For example, pupils characterized as "conformers" made greater gains with one type of teacher, while those characterized as "opposers" improved more with another type of teacher. There were also interactions between teacher personality and subject matter, some types of teachers obtaining the greatest gains in arithmetic and science, others in reading. This research is now being replicated in other parts of the country. Studies on college teaching suggest similar interactions at that level, although relevant data are as yet very meager (88).

The type of teacher who obtained the best over-all results in the Heil study was described as emphasizing structure, order, and planning, while exhibiting warm interpersonal relations and sensitivity to children's feelings. The authors point out that the high work-orientation and planfulness of this type of teacher is in sharp contrast to some interpretations of "permissiveness." The description of these effective teachers recalls at least two dimensions identified in the Teacher Characteristics Study, namely, "warm, understanding, friendly" and "responsible, businesslike, systematic." There are also some interesting parallels with the dimensions of supervisory behavior discussed in Chapter 6. It will be recalled that the most effective supervisors were those who rated high in both the "Consideration" and "Structure" dimensions. Since a major part of the teacher's role consists in serving as a group leader or supervisor, it is reasonable to expect such similarities.

**Teaching Media.** An increasing number of experimental psychologists who had been engaged in military research on training media have been turning their attention to educational problems. Evidence of such interest may be found in the reports of several conferences organized to survey the educational implications of available training research (36, 47, 99). Much of this research centers around training media (see also Chapter 5). In the broadest sense, such media include any method for communicating information or providing an opportunity to learn. Among such media should be listed textbooks, instructors, classmates, and even solitary intellectual activity (36, pp. 196–206).

Particular attention has been given to so-called *audio-visual media,* involving the use of motion-picture films, tape recordings, sound filmstrips, and television. Such media have been used in at least three ways. First, they may serve as teaching aids (along with charts, mock-ups, demonstrations, and similar materials) to supplement conventional teaching methods. Second, they may carry the major instructional load in special educational programs for such groups as the physically handicapped, hospitalized patients, prisoners, or adults who find it impracticable to attend classes because of distance, lack of time, domestic responsibilities, or other reasons. Finally, they may constitute the primary instructional media in regular school classes. Obviously it is this third application that has the broadest implications for the future of education.

Research on audio-visual media may be subdivided into evaluative studies of specific instruments and experimental investigations of variables that influence learning. The first type is concerned with effectiveness of a single film, television course, or other instrument within a particular context. Typical of the earlier research in this field, these evaluative studies sought to answer such questions as "Can students learn through television?" or "How does the amount learned from this film compare with the amount learned from conventional instruction?" Because the many variables involved in the methods under investigation are not isolated, it is impossible to generalize the findings of such evaluative studies beyond the situations investigated. For example, the results would be restricted to a particular film as compared to a particular instructor using face-to-face communication.

A more recent development, dating largely from World War II, is the systematic and controlled investigation of individual variables in relation to the effectiveness of audio-visual training media. Although the bulk of this research was conducted in military contexts, studies of school learning are gradually appearing. Most available investigations deal with films, but their findings usually apply equally well to television. Among the many variables investigated are different ways of providing active student responses in the course of learning and the relative effectiveness of these procedures (85, 86). Overt responses have also been compared with covert, or mental, responses. Different types of feedback, reinforcement, and knowledge of results have likewise been investigated. Other factors include such stimulus characteristics as color, animation (e.g., moving arrows, pop-on labels), and difficulty level of accompanying oral commentary as measured by Flesch formulas or other readability indices. Still other studies have been concerned with repetition, review, rest pauses, organization of learning units within a film, and techniques for calling attention to certain aspects of the film, as through advance instructions and preliminary or interpolated tests.

Some attention has also been given to the *instructor as a training medium* (36, pp. 22–33). When regarded simply as an instrument for conveying information, the instructor has both advantages and disadvantages in comparison with mechanized media. In the film, all students can be exposed to carefully planned teaching by the best available instructors. Along with oral communication, the film can employ visual demonstrations that might otherwise be impracticable or even impossible in a classroom situation. Chief among the special advantages of a live instructor, on the other hand, is his opportunity to adjust his presentation to the characteristics of different audiences and to respond to continuous feedback from his listeners. If a film fails to put a point across, it keeps right on going. But if a lecturer is faced by puzzled frowns, blank stares, or signs of restlessness, he can try again or change his approach.

Suggestive findings on the influence of audience feedback upon the effectiveness of communication were provided by an experiment in which students drew complex geometric patterns that were described orally by the experimenter but were not seen by the class (83). Several feedback conditions were investigated, ranging from zero feedback, with the experimenter behind a screen and no questions or noise permitted, to free feedback, with the audience in view and questions permitted. Results showed that, with more feedback, accuracy of communication increased, confidence was higher on the part of both experimenter and students, and less hostility was manifested by the students.

The instructor may also function as a discussion leader (36, pp. 28–31). In this connection, some of the exponents of client-centered counseling and psychotherapy have been exploring the possibilities of *student-centered teaching* (see 36, pp. 28–31; 88; 115, ch. 9; 116, chs. 13–15). In applying these techniques to teaching, one should note certain essential differences between teaching and psychotherapy. Rogers (115) points out, for example, that, while the therapist responds only by clarifying feelings and attitudes, the teacher must respond to both intellectual content and emotional attitudes expressed by the group. The teacher should acquaint his students with sources of information, opportunities for practicing skills, and other relevant resources with which they can implement their objectives. He himself also serves "as a flexible resource to be utilized by the group in the ways which seem most meaningful to them" (115, p. 402).

Student-centered teaching may be quite effective for attaining certain educational objectives and for teaching certain types of subject matter. For other purposes, however, different procedures are likely to be more satisfactory. The relative success of student-centered teaching probably varies, too, with the educational level and other qualifications of the students and with the personality characteristics of the instructor. An interesting illustration of such interaction effects was provided by an experiment in which students were randomly assigned to four instructional procedures varying in degree of student contacts with other students and with an instructor (10). A significant interaction was found between instructional procedure and sociability (or social introversion-extroversion) as measured by a standardized personality inventory. Thus, in the group taught by the lecture method, the *less* sociable students made significantly greater achievement gains than did the more sociable; among those assigned to small autonomous discussion groups with no instructor, on the other hand, the *more* sociable students made significantly greater achievement gains than did the less sociable.

In this discussion of instructional media, no mention has been made of recent applications of teaching machines and programmed instruction to education. These developments are of such magnitude and potential significance as to justify their separate treatment in the following section.

## TEACHING MACHINES AND OTHER TECHNOLOGICAL DEVELOPMENTS

***Teaching Machines.*** In Chapter 5, teaching machines were briefly discussed, along with training devices and simulators, with special reference to their uses in industrial and military training. It will be recalled that teaching machines are essentially instructional devices that afford an opportunity for active learner participation, provide immediate feedback or knowledge of results, and permit each individual to progress at his own pace. As early as 1924, Pressey developed a teaching machine that was an adaptation of a self-scoring test (87, pp. 35–41; 94; 104). The student answered multiple-choice questions by pressing a key on the machine. If his answer was correct, the machine automatically exposed the next item; if it was incorrect, the machine did not advance to the next item until the correct key was pressed.

Over the next thirty years, Pressey and his students developed other forms of this device and gathered data indicating its effectiveness in accelerating classroom learning (36, 87, 105). This type of teaching machine, which Pressey still advocates, differs from the more common current types in that it represents an *adjunct* to traditional instruction, or a training aid, rather than a method for accomplishing the complete instructional task (106). Such a teaching machine presupposes that some initial learning has already occurred through textbook reading, lectures, laboratory work, field trips, or other instructional procedures.

Pressey's original teaching machines had little effect upon educational practices, probably because they were introduced at a time when neither education nor society at large was ready for such innovations. It was not until about 1958 that the current teaching machine movement got under way; but since that time it has proceeded at a frenetic pace. Several factors contributed to this development. Learning theory had made many advances over the preceding quarter century and at least some learning theorists were beginning to turn their attention to the educational implications of their research. An important milestone in this connection was Skinner's 1954 article on "The Science of Learning and the Art of Teaching" (123). Another influence stemmed from the training technology of World War II, with its automatic training devices developed in the urgency of military needs. Still another contributing factor was the shortage of qualified teachers, combined with various pressures upon educational systems to augment their instructional facilities.

The development of teaching machines and their educational implications have been surveyed in a number of books (e.g., 31, 40, 67, 125) and many articles (e.g., 35, 94, 128). A good introduction to the learning theory underlying these technological developments is given by Green (50). The most comprehensive source is the volume assembled by Lumsdaine and Glaser (87) for the Department of Audio-Visual Instruction of the National Educational Association. While most educational psychologists feel that teaching machines will probably make a valuable and lasting contribution to education, they have become concerned about the overemphasis on "hardware" and gadgetry that characterizes the present movement. Some commercial distributors, moreover, have been promoting the sale of teaching machines too vigorously and too soon.

In the effort to help potential users to evaluate the bewildering array of available self-instructional materials, psychologists and educators have tried to provide some guidelines. An example is an interim statement about teaching machines issued jointly in 1961 by the American Psychological Association, the American Educational Research Association, and the Department of Audio-Visual Instruction of the National Educational Association (120). As observed in this statement, it is not the "machine" that teaches, but rather the instructional content or program of materials presented through the machine. Such a program needs to be evaluated from the standpoint of both curriculum development and learning technology. Of interest in this connection is a project under way at Educational Testing Service to develop practical, quality control standards for programmed learning (129). Also noteworthy are the organized efforts to induce a wider participation by teachers in the construction and testing of teaching machine programs (80).[3]

***Programmed Learning.*** "Programming" of auto-instructional materials refers to the preparation of the content of a teaching program. Particular attention is given to the formulation of specific steps into which the subject matter is analyzed and the sequence in which these steps are presented. There are two major programming techniques, identified with Skinner (87, part III; 124) and Crowder (27, 28), respectively. Both types are designed to provide self-sufficient instructional programs, in contrast to the approach represented by Pressey.

Skinner's programming technique is a direct outgrowth of his learning theory and his basic laboratory research with animals. Known as *linear programming*, this technique employs the same sequence of steps for all individuals. The material to be learned is presented in small, easy steps, formulated so as to reduce the possibility of response errors to a minimum. For each item, the learner "constructs" his response either by writing or by moving sliders that cause the desired letters or numbers to appear. Knowledge of results follows immediately upon completion of each response. Figures 116 and 117

[3] See also publications of The Center for Programed Instruction, Inc., New York.

*Fig. 116* College student using a Skinner-type teaching machine. (*Courtesy of B. F. Skinner.*)

show a college student and a schoolchild using machines which require these two response modes.

The object of the Skinnerian technique is to elicit or "shape" the correct response by prompting or response cueing. The needed information is conveyed by the items themselves through a wide variety of ingenious prompts, a few of which are illustrated in Table 23. By easy steps that virtually assure success and hence positive reinforcement of responses, the individual progresses from items providing maximal prompting to items providing minimal prompting. This process of progressive cue reduction is called "vanishing" and is basic to Skinner's method of shaping responses.

In contrast to Skinner's linear programming, Crowder employs a *branching* technique. This type of program characteristically utilizes multiple-choice

**Fig. 117** Schoolchild using Skinner-type arithmetic teaching machine. (*Courtesy of B. F. Skinner.*)

**TABLE 23** *A Set of Frames Employed in Skinner Programming to Teach a Third- or Fourth-grade Pupil to Spell a Word* (*From Skinner, 124, p. 972*)

1. **Manufacture** means to make or build. Chair factories manufacture chairs. Copy the word here:

☐ ☐ ☐ ☐ ☐ ☐ ☐ ☐ ☐ ☐

2. Part of the word is like part of the word **factory**. Both parts come from an old word meaning *make* or *build*.

m a n u ☐ ☐ ☐ ☐ u r e

3. Part of the word is like part of the word **manual**. Both parts come from an old word for *hand*. Many things used to be made by hand.

☐ ☐ ☐ ☐ f a c t u r e

4. The same letter goes in both spaces:

m ☐ n u f ☐ c t u r e

5. The same letter goes in both spaces:

m a n ☐ f a c t ☐ r e

6. **Chair factories** ☐ ☐ ☐ ☐ ☐ ☐ ☐ ☐ ☐ ☐ chairs.

rather than constructed responses. Depending upon the response option chosen
by the individual, he is channeled through a different route. If he chooses the
correct response, the machine moves on to the next item. A wrong response,
however, is followed by explanations and review designed to correct the error
specific to that response. Wrong responses thus route the individual through
remedial branches or detours. Since all these alternative routes are built into
the program, the Crowder technique is also described as "intrinsic programming." Another feature of the Crowder technique is that new information is
presented by conventional methods of communication. Each item exposed on
the viewing screen of the machine typically contains an informational passage
followed by multiple-choice questions on that unit. The steps in this type of
program are also larger than in the Skinner type. Rather than trying to
eliminate errors, Crowder programming utilizes errors to clarify communication
through remedial loops. An example of a teaching machine designed for use
with Crowder programming is reproduced in Figure 118.

Although most teaching machine programs follow either the Skinner or the
Crowder approach, individual features of the two methods may be recombined

**Fig. 118**   A teaching machine designed for use with Crowder programming.
(*AutoTutor Mark II, reproduced by courtesy of U.S. Industries, Educational
Science Division.*)

in different ways and a number of minor variations have been worked out.[4] Each method has certain advantages and disadvantages, and their relative merits have been widely debated. Because of the multiplicity of educational objectives and the diversity of subject matter to be taught, it appears likely that different methods will be suitable for different purposes (15). This is true of Pressey's adjunct programming, as well as of the linear and branching types of programming described above. Moreover, auto-instructional techniques should be considered together with other, more conventional instructional procedures in designing effective educational systems.

Teaching machines undoubtedly have much to contribute. They save teacher time that would be spent on such routine tasks as drill, grading papers, and record keeping. But even more important is the fact that teaching machines can accomplish certain teaching functions more efficiently than conventional teaching procedures. They can, for example, provide individualized tutorial instruction to a whole class simultaneously. The results that can be achieved with such improved procedures have barely been glimpsed. For instance, logic and other "advanced" subjects have been successfully taught to elementary schoolchildren; and three-year-olds have been taught to read and write (see 50, p. 197). These findings challenge the traditional educational concept of readiness.

Teaching machines also lend themselves to the teaching of new developments in science and other rapidly expanding fields, for which it would be difficult to find enough adequately trained teachers (80). From a different angle, teaching machines permit a more complete control of conditions for applied research on school learning. With such automated devices, one factor at a time can be isolated and varied systematically. The effect of individual differences among teachers, which complicates the interpretation of most classroom experiments, can thus be ruled out.

Of particular interest, too, is the possibility of utilizing teaching machines with delinquent, mentally retarded, behavior-problem, and other types of children who may have developed negative attitudes toward teachers and other authority figures. The impersonal nature of the teaching machine and the high proportion of successful responses serve to counteract these earlier attitudes (15, 89, 90). Because of the saving in teaching personnel and hence in total instructional cost, teaching machines are also useful in prisons and other institutional settings. An exploratory study of the application of teaching machines is under way at the Draper Correctional Center in Elmore, Alabama (89, 90). Still another application of teaching machines is to be found in the educational programs of underdeveloped countries, particularly for literacy training and for elementary courses in science and mathematics. Teaching machines have already been introduced on an experimental basis in several African nations.[5]

The art of programming itself, ushered in by teaching machines, is beginning to influence other teaching media. Programmed textbooks on many subjects have been prepared in accordance with both Skinnerian and Crowder principles (e.g., 28, 64). Conventional classroom lectures have been made more

[4] A comprehensive survey of auto-instructional devices and the types of programming for which they are suitable is given by Kopstein and Shillestad (81). The United States Office of Education publishes a guide to available instructional programs for use in schools.

[5] See, e.g., the October, 1962, issue of *Auto-Instructional Devices*.

effective by giving some attention to the programming of their content. In fact, one investigation found no significant differences in student achievement as a result of using teaching machines, programmed texts, or programmed lectures, although all three of these methods proved superior to ordinary lectures (114). Programming may also be useful as a teacher training experience, in introducing the teacher to concrete applications of learning principles to the sort of material she plans to teach (80). Teaching machines may succeed in breaking down the wall that has for so long separated the learning laboratory from the classroom. If they accomplish no more than this, the effort that has gone into their development will have been well spent.

**Systems Development.** The concepts of man-machine systems utilized in engineering psychology (see Chapter 9) are also finding applications in education. In the terminology of engineering psychology, teaching machines are "closed-loop" systems, since they provide continuous feedback. By contrast, films, television, and formal lectures are "open-loop" systems, in which information flows in only one direction. By means of computers, many aspects of educational systems can be simulated and hence investigated under controlled conditions. Computers, along with computer-based teaching machines, can be utilized in every major activity of educational systems, including instruction, student guidance, and administration.

In several centers, exploratory research is in progress on the use of computers in automated instructional systems (24; 81, pp. 81–90). An example is the ongoing IBM project on computer-controlled teaching machines (24, pp. 171–190; 108; 144). A digital computer can simulate any type of teaching machine. Owing to its flexibility, extensive storage capacity or "memory," and rapid decision-making power, it can also come close to simulating the "conversational interaction" between a human tutor and an individual student. In the IBM project, programs have been prepared and tried out for teaching such varied subjects as stenotypy, psychological statistics, and German reading. Information is initially presented by means of a textbook, although individual reading assignments are given out by the computer. Using an electric typewriter, the student constructs his responses (as in Skinner programming), but the instructional sequence follows a branching pattern (as in Crowder programming). However, the branching is not predetermined or intrinsic to the program but is tailored to the individual student. On the basis of each student's stored response history, the computer chooses individual items and assembles exercises appropriate to the student's own past performance.

In a more comprehensive approach, psychologists at System Development Corporation (17; 20; 24, pp. 191–204; 122) have been experimenting with a simulated school conducted in a specially built Computer-based Laboratory for Automated School Systems (CLASS). This laboratory contains classroom facilities for 20 students, a guidance center, and a principal's office. Three aspects of the educational process are being investigated in an integrated system: (1) individual teaching machines with highly flexible, computer-controlled programming; (2) group instruction by means of films, television, and conventional teaching procedures; (3) centralized data processing for administrative, student-guidance, and planning functions.

Some attention is also being given to other potential uses of computers in educational systems (24, pp. 3–12; 25; 30; 141). One example is the development of information-retrieval systems utilizing computer-based libraries at regional or national centers. Through such a system, students, instructors, and research workers could obtain information on the current state of knowledge in any area of the sciences or arts, without an individual searching process. Information now scattered in several geographically remote libraries could thus be made available simultaneously to an individual in any given location.

Another illustration is provided by the utilization of computers in making administrative decisions regarding students, staff personnel, equipment, and other educational matters. Computers are already in use in many school districts to process administrative data such as attendance records, registration statistics, payroll, budgetary appropriations, and the like. Their application can be further extended to provide the required information for allocating and scheduling rooms, equipment, and other educational resources for more effective use; for helping students as well as colleges to make decisions regarding college admissions; for placement of students in courses suited to their qualifications; and for diagnosing learning difficulties requiring remedial instruction. A related application is in training teachers and educational administrators in decision-making functions. For this purpose, operational gaming procedures could be devised similar to the management games discussed in Chapter 5. Within a period of months, such computer-controlled games could provide the trainee with the equivalent of several years of experience in decision making within the appropriate context.

# SUMMARY

Chief among the fields in which psychologists work in a consulting or collaborative relation with other professional personnel are education, medicine, and law. Within the field of education, the roles of psychologists may be differentiated into those of school psychologist and educational psychologist. Although the functions of school psychologists vary widely from school to school, they consist largely in the diagnostic testing and interviewing of individual pupils, followed by recommendations for remedial action. Working through teachers and other educational personnel, the school psychologist utilizes the school environment as a therapeutic medium.

Educational psychologists are concerned principally with teacher training and educational research. Texts and courses on educational psychology focus upon the learning process, although there is still a wide gap between the psychology of learning and the technology of teaching. It is recognized that the preparation of teachers should also include some familiarity with other areas of psychology, notably developmental psychology, differential psychology, psychological testing, the psychology of adjustment, and social psychology.

The term educational research has traditionally included many activities that fall outside the domain of research as defined in science. With a few notable exceptions, research in educational psychology made little progress until midcentury. At that time, several developments in education, in psychology, and in society at large contributed to an upsurge of psychological research in educational contexts. Even before that time, psychologists had been working effectively with educators in test construction and in the analysis of test results. Currently, educational psychologists are also conducting research in such areas as those of ideational problem solving, creativity, teacher characteristics, and teaching media.

Teaching machines and programmed instruction represent one application of the psychology of learning to teaching methods. Teaching machines are automatic devices that provide for active learner participation, immediate feedback, and individual pacing. The instructional content presented by the teaching machine is known as a program. There are two major programming techniques, namely, linear and branching programming. Exploratory research is under way on the use of computers in the operation of teaching machines, as well as on broader applications of computers to educational systems.

# REFERENCES

1. Allinsmith, W., and Goethals, G. W. *The role of schools in mental health.* New York: Basic Books, 1962.
2. Anastasi, Anne. *Differential psychology.* (3rd ed.) New York: Macmillan, 1958.
3. Anastasi, Anne. *Psychological testing.* (2nd ed.) New York: Macmillan, 1961.
4. Anderson, H. H. (Ed.) *Creativity and its cultivation.* New York: Harper & Row, 1959.
5. Ausubel, D. P. The use of advance organizers in the learning and retention of meaningful verbal material. *J. educ. Psychol.,* 1960, **51**, 267–272.
6. Ausubel, D. P., and Fitzgerald, D. Organizer, general background, and antecedent learning variables in sequential verbal learning. *J. educ. Psychol.,* 1962, **53**, 243–249.
7. Banghart, F. W. (Ed.) *First annual symposium on educational research.* Bloomington, Ind.: Phi Delta Kappa, 1960.
8. Barr, A. S. Research methods. *Encycl. educ. Res.* (3rd ed.), 1960, pp. 1160–1166.
9. Bartlett, F. C. *Thinking.* London: Allen and Unwin, 1958.
10. Beach, L. R. Sociability and academic achievement in various types of learning situations. *J. educ. Psychol.,* 1960, **51**, 208–212.
11. Bell, J. E., *et al. New directions in learning: Contributions of philosophy, psychology, and education.* Riverside, Calif.: Calif. Assoc. Sch. Psychologists and Psychometrists, 1960.
12. Blair, G. M., and Jones, R. S. Readiness. *Encycl. educ. Res.* (3rd ed.), 1960, pp. 1081–1086.
13. Bloom, B. S., *et al. Taxonomy of educational objectives, handbook I: Cognitive domain.* New York: Longmans, Green, 1956.
14. Bloom, B. S., and Broder, L. G. *Problem solving processes of college students.* Chicago: Univer. Chicago Press, 1950. (*Suppl. educ. Monogr.,* No. 73.)
15. Briggs, L. J. The probable role of teaching machines in classroom practice. *Theory into Practice,* 1962, **1**, 47–56.
16. Bruner, J. S., *et al. A study of thinking.* New York: Wiley, 1956.
17. Bushnell, D. D., and Cogswell, J. F. A computer based laboratory for the study of automation in education systems. *Amer. Psychologist,* 1961, **16**, 379.
18. Buswell, G. T. Arithmetic. *Encycl. educ. Res.* (3rd ed.), 1960, pp. 63–77.
19. Carroll, J. B., and Sapon, S. M. *Modern Language Aptitude Test.* New York: Psychol. Corp., 1959.
20. Carter, L. F. Automated instruction. *Amer. Psychologist,* 1961, **16**, 705–710.
21. Charters, W. W., Jr., and Gage, N. L. *Readings in the social psychology of education.* Boston: Allyn and Bacon, 1963.
22. Cieutat, V. J. Group paired-associate learning: Stimulus vs. response meaningfulness. *Percept. mot. Skills,* 1961, **12**, 327–330.
23. Cooperative Test Division, Educational Testing Service. *Sequential Tests of Educational Progress.* Princeton, N.J.: Educ. Test. Serv., 1956–1962.
24. Coulson, J. E. (Ed.) *Programmed learning and computer-based instruction.* New York: Wiley, 1962.

25. Coulson, J. E., *et al.* Symposium: Possible applications of recent technological developments to educational systems. *Amer. Psychologist,* 1962, **17**, 324.
26. Cronbach, L. J. *Educational psychology.* (2nd ed.) New York: Harcourt, Brace & World, 1963.
27. Crowder, N. A. Automatic tutoring by means of intrinsic programming. In E. Galanter (Ed.), *Automatic teaching: The state of the art.* New York: Wiley, 1959. Pp. 109–116.
28. Crowder, N. A. Automatic tutoring by intrinsic programming. In A. A. Lumsdaine and R. Glaser (Eds.), *Teaching machines and programmed learning: A source book.* Washington: Nat. Educ. Assoc., 1960. Pp. 286–298.
29. Cutts, Norma E. (Ed.) *School psychologists at midcentury: A report of the Thayer Conference on the functions, qualifications, and training of school psychologists.* Washington: Amer. Psychol. Assoc., 1955.
30. DeCarlo, C. R. Information systems in the educational environment. *Proc. 1962 invit. Conf. test. Probl., Educ. Test. Serv.,* 1963, 91–101.
31. Deterline, W. A. *An introduction to programmed instruction.* Englewood Cliffs, N.J.: Prentice-Hall, 1962.
32. Estes, W. K. Learning. *Encycl. educ. Res.* (3rd ed.), 1960, pp. 752–770.
33. Farnsworth, D. M., Glidewell, J. C., Pratt, D., and White, R. W. Mental health in education. *Teach. Coll. Rec.,* 1961, **62**, 263–297.
34. Fattu, N. A. The role of research in education: Present and future. *Rev. educ. Res.,* 1960, **30**, 409–421.
35. Fattu, N. A. Training devices. *Encycl. educ. Res.* (3rd ed.), 1960, pp. 1529–1535.
36. Finch, G. (Ed.) *Educational and training media: A symposium.* (NAS–NRC Publ. No. 789.) Washington: Nat. Acad. Sci.–Nat. Res. Coun., 1960.
37. Frandsen, A. N. *Educational psychology: The principles of learning in teaching.* New York: McGraw-Hill, 1961.
38. French, J. L. (Ed.) *Educating the gifted.* New York: Holt, Rinehart and Winston, 1959.
39. Froelich, G. J. Research bureaus. *Encycl. educ. Res.* (3rd ed.), 1960, pp. 1155–1160.
40. Fry, E. *Teaching machines and programmed learning.* New York: McGraw-Hill, 1962.
41. Gagné, R. M., and Brown, L. T. Some factors in the programing of conceptual learning. *J. exp. Psychol.,* 1961, **62**, 313–321.
42. Gallagher, J. J., and Aschner, Mary J. A preliminary report on analyses of classroom interaction. *Merrill-Palmer Quart.,* 1963, **9**, 183–194.
43. Gannon, D. R., and Noble, C. E. Familiarization (n) as a stimulus factor in paired-associate verbal learning. *J. exp. Psychol.,* 1961, **62**, 14–23.
44. Gerberich, J. R., Greene, H. A., and Jorgensen, A. N. *Measurement and evaluation in the modern school.* New York: McKay, 1962.
45. Getzels, J. W., and Jackson, P. W. *Creativity and intelligence: Explorations with gifted students.* New York: Wiley, 1962.
46. Glaser, R. Psychology and instructional technology. In R. Glaser (Ed.), *Training research and education.* Pittsburgh: Univer. Pittsburgh Press, 1962. Ch. 1.
47. Glaser, R. (Ed.) *Training research and education.* Pittsburgh: Univer. Pittsburgh Press, 1962.
48. Gottsegen, M. G., and Gottsegen, Gloria B. (Eds.) *Professional school psychology.* New York: Grune & Stratton, vol. 1, 1960; vol. 2, 1963.
49. Gray, W. S. Reading. *Encycl. educ. Res.* (3rd ed.), 1960, pp. 1086–1135.
50. Green, E. J. *The learning process and programmed instruction.* New York: Holt, Rinehart and Winston, 1962.
51. Guilford, J. P. Three faces of intellect. *Amer. Psychologist,* 1959, **14**, 469–479.
52. Guilford, J. P. Factors that aid and hinder creativity. *Teach. Coll. Rec.,* 1962, **63**, 380–392.
53. Guilford, J. P., *et al.* A factor-analytic study of creative thinking: I. Hypotheses and description of tests. *Rep. Psychol. Lab., Univer. So. Calif.,* No. 4, 1951.
54. Guilford, J. P., Wilson, R. C., and Christensen, P. R. A factor-analytic study of creative thinking: II. Administration of tests and analysis of results. *Rep. Psychol. Lab., Univer. So. Calif.,* No. 8, 1952.
55. Haggard, E. A. The proper concern of educational psychologists. *Amer. Psychologist,* 1954, **9**, 539–543.

56. Haring, N. G., and Phillips, E. L. *Educating emotionally disturbed children.* New York: McGraw-Hill, 1962.

57. Harlow, H. F. The formation of learning sets. *Psychol. Rev.,* 1949, **56**, 51–65.

58. Haslerud, G. M., and Myers, Shirley. The transfer value of given and individually derived principles. *J. educ. Psychol.,* 1958, **49**, 293–298.

59. Heil, L. M., Powell, Marion, and Feifer, I. *Characteristics of teacher behavior related to the achievement of children in several elementary grades.* Brooklyn, N.Y.: Brooklyn Coll. Bookstore, 1960.

60. Heil, L. M., and Washburne, C. Characteristics of teachers related to children's progress. *J. Teacher Educ.,* 1961, **12**, 401–406.

61. Henry, N. B. (Ed.) *Education for the gifted.* Chicago: Univer. Chicago Press, 1958.

62. Hildreth, Gertrude H., and Griffiths, Nellie L. *Metropolitan Readiness Tests.* New York: Harcourt, Brace & World, 1949–1950.

63. Hodges, W. L. State certification of school psychologists. *Amer. Psychologist,* 1960, **15**, 346–349.

64. Holland, J. G., and Skinner, B. F. *The analysis of behavior: A program for self-instruction.* New York: McGraw-Hill, 1961.

65. Hollister, W. G. Current trends in mental health programming in the classroom. *J. soc. Issues,* 1958, **15** (1), 50–58.

66. Hountras, P. T. (Ed.) *Mental hygiene: A text of readings.* Columbus, Ohio: Merrill, 1961.

67. Hughes, J. L. *Programed instruction for schools and industry.* Chicago: Sci. Res. Assoc., 1962.

68. Inglis, S. A., Jr. Perceptions of the role of the school psychologist. *Calif. J. educ. Res.,* 1959, **10**, 36–41.

69. Johannesson, I. Effects of praise and blame upon achievement and attitudes of schoolchildren. In Å. G. Skard and T. Husén (Eds.), *Child and education.* Copenhagen: Munksgaard, 1962. Pp. 184–197. (Proc. 14th int. Congr. appl. Psychol.)

70. John, E. R. Contributions to the study of the problem-solving process. *Psychol. Monogr.,* 1957, **71**, No. 18.

71. Johnson, D. M. Formulation and reformulation of figure concepts. *Amer. J. Psychol.,* 1961, **74**, 418–424.

72. Kephart, N. C. *The slow learner in the classroom.* Columbus, Ohio: Merrill, 1960.

73. Kersh, B. Y. The adequacy of "meaning" as an explanation for the superiority of learning by independent discovery. *J. educ. Psychol.,* 1958, **49**, 282–292.

74. Kingsley, H. L., and Garry, R. *The nature and conditions of learning.* (2nd ed.) Englewood Cliffs, N.J.: Prentice-Hall, 1957.

75. Kirk, S. A. *Educating exceptional children.* Boston: Houghton Mifflin, 1962.

76. Kirk, S. A., et al. *Early education of the mentally retarded.* Urbana, Ill.: Univer. Ill. Press, 1958.

77. Kittell, J. E. An experimental study of the effects of external direction during learning on transfer and retention of principles. *J. educ. Psychol.,* 1957, **48**, 391–405.

78. Klausmeier, H. J. *Learning and human abilities: Educational psychology.* New York: Harper & Row, 1961.

79. Komarovsky, Mirra. *Women in the modern world: Their education and their dilemmas.* Boston: Little, Brown, 1953.

80. Komoski, P. K. Programing by teachers for the school curriculum. *Center for Programed Instruction, Publ. No. 109,* 1962.

81. Kopstein, F. F., and Shillestad, Isabel J. A survey of auto-instructional devices. *U.S. Air Force, Aeronaut. Syst. Div., ASD Tech. Rep. 61–414,* 1961.

82. Krugman, M. (Ed.) *Orthopsychiatry and the school.* New York: Amer. Orthopsychiat. Assoc., 1958.

83. Leavitt, H. J., and Mueller, R. A. H. Some effects of feedback on communication. *Hum. Relat.,* 1951, **4**, 401–410.

84. Lindgren, H. C. *Educational psychology in the classroom.* (2nd ed.) New York: Wiley, 1962.

85. Lumsdaine, A. A. Experimental research on instructional devices and materials.

In R. Glaser (Ed.), *Training research and education.* Pittsburgh: Univer. Pittsburgh Press, 1962. Ch. 9.

86. Lumsdaine, A. A. (Ed.) *Student response in programmed instruction: A symposium.* Washington: Nat. Acad. Sci.–Nat. Res. Coun., 1961.
87. Lumsdaine, A. A., and Glaser, R. *Teaching machines and programmed learning.* Washington: Nat. Educ. Assoc., 1960.
88. McKeachie, W. J. Procedures and techniques of teaching: A survey of experimental studies. In N. Sanford (Ed.), *The American college: A psychological and social interpretation of the higher learning.* New York: Wiley, 1962. Ch. 8.
89. McKee, J. M., and Slack, C. W. Preliminary findings of the Draper Correctional Center project in education and rehabilitation by self-instruction. Unpubl. Rep., Draper Correctional Center, Elmore, Ala., June, 1961.
90. McKee, J. M., and Watkins, J. C. A self-instructional program for youthful offenders. Unpubl. Rep. Draper Correctional Center, Elmore, Ala., May, 1962.
91. Melton, A. W. The science of learning and the technology of educational methods. *Harvard educ. Rev.,* 1959, **29**, 96–106.
92. Merrifield, P. R., Guilford, J. P., Christensen, P. R., and Frick, J. W. The role of intellectual factors in problem solving. *Psychol. Monogr.,* 1962, **76**, No. 10.
93. Mitzel, H. E., and Ryans, D. G. Teacher effectiveness. *Encycl. educ. Res.* (3rd ed.), 1960, pp. 1481–1491.
94. Morrill, C. S. Teaching machines: A review. *Psychol. Bull.,* 1961, **58**, 363–375.
95. Morsh, J. E., and Wilder, Eleanor W. Identifying the effective instructor: A review of the quantitative studies 1900–1952. *USAF Pers. Train. Res. Cent. Res. Bull.,* 1954, No. AFPT RC-TR-54-44.
96. Mueller, Kate H. *Educating women for a changing world.* Minneapolis: Univer. Minn. Press, 1954.
97. Mullen, Frances A. The school as a psychological laboratory. *Amer. Psychologist,* 1959, **14**, 53–56.
98. Mullen, Frances A. (Ed.) *The psychologist on the school staff.* Washington: Amer. Psychol. Assoc., 1958.
99. National Research Council, Advisory Board on Education. *Psychological research in education.* (NAS-NRC Publ. No. 643.) Washington: Nat. Acad. Sci.–Nat. Res. Coun., 1958.
100. Noble, C. E. Meaningfulness (m) and transfer phenomena in serial verbal learning. *J. Psychol.,* 1961, **52**, 201–210.
101. Osler, Sonia F., and Fivel, Myrna W. Concept attainment: I. The role of age and intelligence in concept attainment by induction. *J. exp. Psychol.,* 1961, **62**, 1–8.
102. Osler, Sonia F., and Trautman, Grace E. Concept attainment: II. Effect of stimulus complexity upon concept attainment at two levels of intelligence. *J. exp. Psychol.,* 1961, **62**, 9–13.
103. Piers, E. V., Daniels, J. M., and Quackenbush, J. F. The identification of creativity in adolescents. *J. educ. Psychol.,* 1960, **51**, 346–351.
104. Pressey, S. L. A simple apparatus which gives tests and scores—and teaches. *Sch. Soc.,* 1926, **23**, 373–376.
105. Pressey, S. L. Development and appraisal of devices producing immediate automatic scoring of objective tests and concomitant self-instruction. *J. Psychol.,* 1950, **29**, 417–477.
106. Pressey, S. L. Teaching machine (and learning theory) crisis. *J. appl. Psychol.,* 1963, **47**, 1–6.
107. Pressey, S. L., Robinson, F. P., and Horrocks, J. E. (3rd ed.) *Psychology in education.* New York: Harper & Row, 1959.
108. Rath, G. J., Anderson, Nancy S., and Brainerd, R. C. The IBM Research Center teaching machine project. In E. Galanter (Ed.), *Automatic teaching: The state of the art.* New York: Wiley, 1959. Pp. 117–130.
109. Ray, W. I. Pupil instruction vs. direct instruction. *J. exp. Educ.,* 1961, **29**, 271–280.
110. Rimoldi, H. J. A. A technique for the study of problem solving. *Educ. psychol. Measmt,* 1955, **15**, 450–461.
111. Rimoldi, H. J. A. Problem solving as a process. *Educ. psychol. Measmt,* 1960, **20**, 449–460.

112. Rimoldi, H. J. A., *et al.* Training in problem solving. *Loyola Univer. Psychometr. Lab., Publ. No. 27*, 1962.
113. Rimoldi, H. J. A., Haley, J. V., and Majewska, Sister M. Canisia. Decision processes in mathematical thinking. *Loyola Univer. Psychometr. Lab.* (In press, 1963.)
114. Roe, A. Automated teaching methods using linear programs. *J. appl. Psychol.*, 1962, **46**, 198–201.
115. Rogers, C. R. *Client-centered therapy: Its current practice, implications, and theory.* Boston: Houghton Mifflin, 1951.
116. Rogers, C. R. *On becoming a person: A therapist's view of psychotherapy.* Boston: Houghton Mifflin, 1961.
117. Rothstein, J. H. (Ed.) *Mental retardation: Readings and resources.* New York: Holt, Rinehart and Winston, 1961.
118. Ryans, D. G. *Characteristics of teachers: Their description, comparison, and appraisal.* Washington: Amer. Coun. Educ., 1960.
119. Sarason, S. B., *et al. Anxiety in elementary school children.* New York: Wiley, 1960.
120. Self-instructional materials and devices. *Amer. Psychologist*, 1961, **16**, 512.
121. Shaffer, L. F., and Shoben, E. J., Jr. *The psychology of adjustment: A dynamic and experimental approach to personality and mental hygiene.* (2nd ed.) Boston: Houghton Mifflin, 1956.
122. Silberman, H. F. A computer as an experimental laboratory machine for research on automated teaching procedures. *Behav. Sci.*, 1960, **5**, 175–176.
123. Skinner, B. F. The science of learning and the art of teaching. *Harvard educ. Rev.*, 1954, **24**, 86–97.
124. Skinner, B. F. Teaching machines. *Science*, 1958, **128**, 969–977.
125. Smith, W. I., and Moore, J. W. *Programmed learning: Theory and research.* Princeton, N. J.: Van Nostrand, 1962.
126. Spence, K. W. The relation of learning theory to the technology of education. *Harvard educ. Rev.*, 1959, **29**, 84–95.
127. Stephans, J. M. Transfer of learning. *Encycl. educ. Res.* (3rd ed.), 1960, pp. 1535–1543.
128. Stolurow, L. M. Teaching machines and special education. *Educ. psychol. Measmt*, 1960, **20**, 429–448.
129. Stolurow, L. M., Kulkarni, S. S., Jacobs, P. I., and Maier, M. *Programed instruction: Some problems and technical recommendations.* Princeton, N. J.: Educ. Test. Serv., 1963.
130. Symonds, P. M. *What education has to learn from psychology.* (3rd ed.) New York: Teach. Coll., Columbia Univer., Bur. Publ., 1960.
131. Taylor, C. W. The creative individual: A new portrait in giftedness. *Educ. Leadership*, 1960, **18** (1), 7–12.
132. Taylor, C. W., and Barron, F. *Scientific creativity: Its recognition and development.* New York: Wiley, 1963.
133. Taylor, C. W., and Holland, J. L. Development and application of tests of creativity. *Rev. educ. Res.*, 1962, **32**, 91–102.
134. Thorndike, R. L., and Hagen, Elizabeth. *Measurement and evaluation in psychology and education.* (2nd ed.) New York: Wiley, 1961.
135. Torrance, E. P. Current research on the nature of creative talent. *J. counsel. Psychol.*, 1959, **6**, 209–216.
136. Torrance, E. P. *Guiding creative talent.* Englewood Cliffs, N.J.: Prentice-Hall, 1962.
137. Travers, R. M. W. *An introduction to educational research.* New York: Macmillan, 1958.
138. Travers, R. M. W. A study of the relationship of psychological research to educational practice. In R. Glaser (Ed.), *Training research and education.* Pittsburgh: Univer. Pittsburgh Press, 1962. Ch. 17.
139. Trow, W. C., *et al.* Psychology of group behavior: The class as a group. *J. educ. Psychol.*, 1950, **41**, 322–338.
140. Tyler, Leona E. *The national defense counseling and guidance training institutes program. A report of the first fifty institutes.* Washington: Govt. Printing Office, 1960.
141. Tyler, R. W. The role of machines in educational decision-making. *Proc. 1962 invit. Conf. test. Probl., Educ. test. Serv.*, 1963, 102–113.

142. Underwood, B. J. Verbal learning in the educative processes. *Harvard educ. Rev.*, 1959, **29**, 107–117.
143. Underwood, B. J., and Schulz, R. W. *Meaningfulness and verbal learning.* Philadelphia: Lippincott, 1960.
144. Uttal, W. R. On conversational interaction. *IBM Res. Rep.*, RC–532, Sept. 14, 1961.
145. Ward, V. S. *Educating the gifted: An axiomatic approach.* Columbus, Ohio: Merrill, 1961.
146. Webb, W. B. (Ed.) *The profession of psychology.* New York: Holt, Rinehart and Winston, 1962.
147. White, Mary A., and Harris, M. W. *The school psychologist.* New York: Harper & Row, 1961.

# 19

## Psychology and Medicine

The role of emotional, motivational, and interpersonal factors in medical practice has long been recognized. In fact, such recognition antedates modern scientific medicine, being of primary significance in the ministrations of the medicine men of early preliterate cultures. In more recent times, physicians have generally been aware of the importance of many "psychological" factors in the daily practice of medicine. Examples include the contribution of doctor-patient relations and of the doctor's "bedside manner" to the patient's recovery; the need for considering personality, familial, and cultural factors in diagnosing a patient's condition; and the dependence of physical improvement upon the individual patient's cooperation and his motivation to recover.

Despite the many potential applications of psychological knowledge to medicine, however, contacts between the two fields were negligible until quite recently. Even books on the psychology of medical practice or the psychology of physical illness were often written, not by psychologists, but by psychiatrists (see, e.g., 9, 44). This was also true of courses or units on psychology taught in medical schools. With their strongly pathological orientation, psychiatrists are likely to provide a distorted picture of the psychologically normal patients encountered in other branches of medicine. Moreover, the training and experience of psychiatrists emphasize clinical practice rather than basic behavioral science. Consequently, their notions of human behavior tend to derive from uncontrolled personal observation and selected cases rather than from systematic and controlled experimentation.

It was not until after World War II that professional contacts between psychology and medicine attained significant proportions, and even now the potential contributions of psychology in this field are largely undeveloped. Originally, the contacts occurred almost entirely between clinical psychologists and psychiatrists and were limited to psychodiagnostic functions. Later, an increasing number of referrals for psychodiagnosis started to come from other medical specialists, such as pediatricians, internists, neurosurgeons, plastic surgeons, obstetricians, and endocrinologists (63). This trend reflected a growing realization among medical practitioners that a standardized assessment of the patient's emotional responses, intellectual functioning, and other psychological characteristics would in many cases facilitate the diagnosis of physical difficulties. After midcentury, the role of psychologists in medical practice expanded to include consulting relations in other than diagnostic functions. The growth of collaborative psychological research in medical settings and of medical school teaching by psychologists was also characteristic of this period. Finally, contacts with medicine were no longer limited to clinical psychologists but came to include counseling, experimental, physiological, developmental, social, and practically all other kinds of psychologists.

## PSYCHOLOGY IN MEDICAL PRACTICE

In every major phase of medical practice, psychology can contribute in two principal ways: (1) by providing knowledge and orientations that improve the physician's performance of his own functions; (2) by providing the services of psychologists as consultants or as participating members of interprofessional teams. These two avenues of contact between psychology and medicine are not entirely distinct. Psychological orientations, for example, may be acquired by the physician, not only during medical school training, but also in the course of consulting and collaborative relationships with psychologists. In the present section, we shall illustrate the types of contributions psychology can make to diagnosis, treatment, rehabilitation, and preventive medicine.

*Diagnosis.* Mention has already been made of the increasing use of psycho-diagnostic referrals in nearly every branch of medicine. In such cases, the physician integrates the psychodiagnostic data with medical data in arriving at his diagnosis. In his own diagnostic functions, moreover, every physician relies at least in part upon information elicited from the patient through interviewing techniques. Training in effective interviewing procedures is thus as relevant to this field as it is to personnel selection (Chapter 4) or to the practice of clinical psychology (Chapter 13). Much can be accomplished by simply recording and playing back typical diagnostic interviews, thereby alerting the physician to common errors (see 49, chs. 1 and 10). Some familiarity with the findings of psychological research on interviewing procedures is also helpful (see Chapter 4).

For a variety of reasons, the medical interview presents special difficulties for effective communication and hence requires a particularly skillful interviewer. For the patient, the situation is emotionally loaded and is likely to arouse ambivalent attitudes. On the one hand, the patient wants to communicate fully in order to obtain maximum help from the physician. On the other hand, he is reluctant to face the possibility that he may require long or unpleasant therapy or that he may be suffering from a serious disease. The combination of these conflicting tendencies may distort the patient's report in a number of ways. The patient's emotional involvement also heightens his suggestibility. He will thus be quick to respond to slight cues in the physician's queries that may suggest symptoms he had not really observed. He is also likely to read unintended meanings into the physician's remarks, tone of voice, and other expressive reactions. Communication is further obscured by differences in language between physician and patient. Such differences may arise, not only from medical terminology and from the different connotations of common words to layman and physician, but also from possible differences in socio-economic level, general education, and cultural background.

Mention should also be made of the extent to which medical diagnosis utilizes introspective report regarding the intensity, qualitative characteristics, and localization of pain, as well as other bodily sensations. The extensive psychological research on sensory and perceptual responses and on the factors influencing their accuracy is pertinent to an evaluation of such reports. A more specific example is provided by the detailed visual examinations conducted in ophthalmology. The standard psychophysical procedures of the psychological laboratory have much to contribute to these examinations.

*Treatment.* There has been a growing interest in the nature of the interpersonal relation between physician and patient and in the part which this relation plays in the recovery process (see, e.g., 44, 54, 67). Theoretical analyses of this relation have been proposed in terms of the attitudes of both patient and physician toward each other. The patient's attitudes, for example, may vary from passive dependence or awed admiration to skepticism or active resistance. The physician, on his part, may exhibit varying degrees of empathy and warmth or impersonal objectivity and aloofness. The physician-patient relationship may also be characterized in terms of a continuum ranging from authoritarian control, through guidance, to mutual participation. In all its aspects, the relationship varies as a function of the nature and severity of the patient's illness, the personality and intellectual characteristics of both patient and physician, the physician's reputation, the patient's earlier contacts with physicians, and many other circumstances.

Although empirical data on the effects of the physician-patient relationship are meager, it seems evident that the nature of this relationship will be reflected in the patient's cooperation in carrying out medical orders. That the relationship itself may have therapeutic value is also widely recognized. Contact with a physician in whom the patient has confidence frequently provides an emotional "lift" accompanied by a noticeable amelioration of symptoms. In many cases, this effect may contribute to the patient's ultimate recovery.

From another angle, familiarity with a patient's cultural background may prove very helpful to the physician (3, 77). Behavior that might appear bizarre and irrational becomes intelligible when viewed against the frame of reference of the patient's own culture. Deep-rooted cultural beliefs and traditions may profoundly affect attitudes toward illness, doctors, hospitals, and other medical matters. A doctor who understands the patient's culture enjoys an advantage, not only in arriving at a correct diagnosis, but also in presenting required therapeutic procedures in ways that are acceptable to the patient.

The application of psychology to medical practice has been furthered by the recent movement toward *comprehensive medicine* (35, 39, 64). Arising as a reaction against the increasing specialization of medical practice during the first half of the twentieth century, comprehensive medicine focuses on the treatment of the whole person. With the gradual disappearance of the family doctor, medicine was losing sight of the patient. Comprehensive medicine is an effort to reverse this trend. Illness is viewed, not as a specific disorder of an isolated organ, but as a complex relation between the organism and his environment (39). The environmental stresses to which the organism is subjected may range from bacterial infection to interpersonal relations and cultural pressures. The resulting physiological and behavioral changes depend partly upon the nature of these environmental stresses and partly upon the state of the individual at the time. This state in turn reflects the individual's heredity and the residual effects of his previous life experiences.

In the effort to train medical students in the practice of comprehensive medicine, medical schools have been experimenting with a number of specially designed instructional procedures, such as joint teaching by different departments on hospital wards, continuing case studies of individual patients, and family care programs (42, 62). In the family care programs, each medical student is assigned a particular family whose members he treats in their natural environment during his medical training. This procedure permits a continuing relationship between the medical student and individual patients, as well as providing him with relevant information about the family setting and home background of the patients.

The participation of psychologists themselves in medical treatment is exemplified by the appointment of psychologists in hospitals for orthopedic disabilities, tuberculosis, and other physical disorders. There is a growing recognition that in these settings the psychologist can function most effectively as a consultant to ward physicians, nurses, and other staff members (14; 40, ch. 24). Rather than spending a few hours a week with a handful of patients, the psychologist can thus help the hospital staff to deal more effectively with the daily problems arising in patient care. This staff-oriented approach is in line with the milieu therapy of psychiatric patients described in Chapter 14. It is also similar to the role of the school psychologist insofar as the latter works through teachers and other school personnel who are in daily contact with the child (Chapter 18).

**Rehabilitation.**  The rehabilitation movement originated after World War I in an effort to facilitate the vocational readjustment of disabled war veterans. It was not until after World War II, however, that the movement underwent a significant expansion in scope and functions (30, 31, 104). At that time, its objectives were broadened to include not only vocational training and placement but also personal, familial, and community adjustment. The categories of patients reached by rehabilitation services were also increased to cover all types of injuries and illnesses, including psychiatric disorders. For any patient, it was recognized that convalescent care should serve to prepare the individual for a return to community living. Depending upon the nature of the disorder, the duration of the illness, and the severity of residual handicap, the rehabilitation program may vary from a brief counseling session to a long period of extensive retraining.

Today rehabilitation is typically carried on by teams of professional workers drawn from many fields, including physicians, nurses, physical therapists, occupational therapists, speech therapists, psychologists, social workers, vocational counselors, prosthetic specialists, and others. The focus is on the total adjustment of the individual to his environment, rather than on the disability as such. Moreover, it is generally recognized that the individual's reaction to his disability is often more important than the disability itself in determining his work capacity and general adjustment. The attitudes of family, employers, teachers, and other significant associates are also major factors in the patient's progress.

The psychologist's role on the rehabilitation team includes not only assessment and counseling of the patient himself but also consultation with other team members. Accurate assessment of motor and intellectual skills, emotional traits, motivation, and attitudes is of fundamental importance in planning the rehabilitation program, in determining the effectiveness of remedial procedures, and in detecting progressive changes in the patient. In severely disabled persons, even slight increments or decrements in function may drastically alter capacity for self-care, for job performance, and for other practical activities. Consequently, precise and repeated assessments of abilities are needed. On the basis of his continuing evaluation of the patient through testing and interviewing, the psychologist can help in the planning and revision of the rehabilitation program at all stages. In his consultative functions, he can also enhance the psychological orientation of the other team members, alerting them to the psychological aspects of the patient's adjustment to disability.

**Preventive Medicine.** In both individual medical practice and public health programs, preventive medicine needs the cooperation of the lay public. The availability of preventive medical techniques such as the use of polio-vaccine can be of no help if the public does not take advantage of them. Early detection and treatment of such conditions as cancer and tuberculosis likewise depend upon the knowledge and attitudes of the individual patients. To be effective, preventive medicine requires a well-informed public with appropriate attitudes toward disease prevention.

Public information campaigns in the field of preventive medicine can utilize the methodology and research findings of consumer psychology (see Chapter 10). In the first place, data are needed about existing public attitudes or misinformation that may interfere with the adoption of any given preventive measure. Superstitions, cultural traditions, and deep-rooted emotional reactions that would cause resistance must be identified. For example, efforts have been made to investigate such questions as why people fail to seek poliomyelitis vaccination, why they oppose community water fluoridation, and why they do not report for treatment following a cancer diagnosis (46, 50, 71, 76).

In one survey, the investigator contacted the families of 227 patients who had received a diagnosis of cancer and who later died of cancer without having reported for treatment (see 46, p. 430). In one-third of these cases, the reasons given for failure to return for treatment were fear and unwillingness to admit the diagnosis. Such findings illustrate an all too frequent reaction to certain illnesses that have acquired an aura of mystery and dread. "Fear of knowing" undoubtedly keeps many persons from even seeking a diagnosis. In a more recent survey (55), 808 New York City residents were interviewed regarding their medical histories, past health behavior, and current health attitudes. Results showed that delays in seeking medical care occurred significantly more often for cancer symptoms than for other medical symptoms. Delay in seeking care for cancer was also found to be associated with low educational and socioeconomic levels.

Knowledge about prevailing public attitudes is a necessary first step in planning a public information campaign. The next step is to choose effective means of communication (47, 81). "Media research" is as relevant here as in the advertising of consumer goods. One survey, for example, was concerned with the sources of public information about poliovaccine (47). Both socioeconomic and urban-rural differences were found in the extent to which individuals received their information from physicians, newspapers, radio, and other media. Another investigator compared the effectiveness of different types of illustrated lectures on dental hygiene (28). He found that a straight factual presentation was more successful in improving the oral-hygiene practices of high school students than were the more emotional, fear-arousing lectures. Although a few psychologists are currently working on problems such as these, pertinent research is still very meager. We certainly know much more about people's attitudes toward political issues and canned soups than about their attitudes toward preventive medicine.

# PSYCHOLOGY IN MEDICAL EDUCATION

Current interest in the role of psychologists in medical schools is evidenced by the number of conferences, symposia, professional committees, and articles that have been concerned with it (17, 34, 35, 45, 51, 52, 58, 59, 63–65, 82, 90, 98). All this activity has been concentrated into little more than a decade. Prior to World War II, psychologists were rarely employed by medical schools. What little psychology was included in medical school curricula was taught by psychiatrists. With the growth of clinical psychology following World War II, psychologists began to appear on medical school faculties on a part-time basis, to give one or two lectures in psychiatry courses and to demonstrate psychological tests during the students' clinical years. Later, training in psychology came to be regarded as the "basic science training" for psychiatry. Still later—and more slowly—it is being recognized as one of the basic sciences for the training of all medical students, along with physiology, anatomy, biochemistry, and other biological sciences (59). Concurrently, there has been a marked upsurge of research activities by psychologists in medical schools.

As the area of participation broadened, the number of psychologists in medical schools rose sharply. A 1952 survey (65) revealed that 73 per cent of the country's medical schools employed one or more psychologists on their staff. The total number of psychologists so employed was 255, over half being on full-time appointments. Within the next 10 years, this number rose to approximately 600, and nearly every 4-year medical school in the country was represented (66, p. 234).

The amount of formal instruction currently provided by psychologists in medical schools ranges from a few lectures in a course given jointly by several departments to full responsibility for one or more courses. There is a growing trend toward establishing separate divisions or departments of "medical psychology" or "behavioral science" (45, 58, 59, 90, 98). The latter may also include some work in medical sociology and cultural anthropology (90). Among the specific courses most often taught by psychologists, as reported in a 1955 survey (64), were psychometric or psychodiagnostic techniques, general introductory psychology, abnormal psychology, the psychology of personality, and the professional role of the psychologist in a medical setting. Among the other courses offered in at least a few medical schools were developmental psychology, electroencephalography, psychotherapy, and research methods in clinical psychology. Since the time of this survey, there has been an increase in "basic science" courses, such as physiological and experimental psychology (59).

The students taught by psychologists in medical schools include general medical students in both their basic science and clinical years, as well as psychiatric residents. Increasingly, psychologists are participating in the training of residents in other specialties, such as pediatrics, neurology, and ophthalmology. Psychologists also contribute to the training of students in certain allied professional fields, including nursing, occupational therapy, physical therapy, and social work (64).

Much of the time of psychologists employed in medical schools is spent, not in formal course instruction, but in other functions that may indirectly serve an instructional purpose (64, 66). Thus psychologists participate in case conferences, in collaborative diagnostic studies, in pyschotherapy, and in joint research projects with members of other departments. Under certain circumstances, counseling and even short-term psychotherapy with students may have a training function, especially when directed toward the improvement of interpersonal relations with patients.

In dental schools, for example, there is little or no course work in psychology, although about half of these schools do employ psychologists, usually on a part-time basis (66). In these schools, psychologists perform chiefly testing and counseling functions. They may also conduct intensive workshops for practicing dentists (e.g., 37, 38). Insofar as these procedures provide increased self-knowledge and a better understanding of interpersonal relations with patients, they are similar to some of the techniques employed in management development programs (see Chapter 5). They should thus be regarded as an integral part of professional training.

In both formal and informal contacts with students and professional colleagues, the psychologist can also make a distinctive contribution through his research orientation. He can transmit relevant research findings, not only to students in basic science courses, but also to clinical instructors. Drawing upon his knowledge of research methodology in behavioral science, he can instill a more critical and inquisitive attitude toward the results of research. The prospective medical practitioner needs to develop some skill in the evaluation of research findings. If he is to keep abreast of current developments in his medical practice, he must be able to assess published reports of new research, to detect possible sources of error in the data, and to determine what conclusions can properly be drawn from the results. Still another way in which a research orientation can help the medical practitioner is in patient diagnosis. Insofar as the diagnostic process requires the formulation and testing of a series of interlocking hypotheses, research training should improve its effectiveness. Medical diagnosis thus represents one more example of the potential contribution of research training to professional practice, as discussed in several earlier contexts in this book (see Chapters 1, 4, 13).

## PSYCHOLOGY IN MEDICAL RESEARCH

*Overview.* One of the chief contributions that psychologists can make to medicine is in the area of research. Both in medical schools and in other medical settings, the number of psychologists engaged in interdisciplinary research projects is growing rapidly. In this research, psychologists collaborate not only with medical practitioners but also with specialists in other basic sciences, such as physiology, neurology, biochemistry, and pharmacology. Among the well-established areas of such collaborative research are electroencephalography (23), motion sickness, and the environmental stresses of space travel (Chapter 8). The latter two areas illustrate the effective collaboration of psychologists with medical personnel and other biological scientists in the military services. It is also interesting to note that one of the events leading to research on sensory deprivation (Chapter 8) was the observation that polio patients confined in respirators for long periods of time experienced feelings of strangeness, hallucinations, and other cognitive disturbances (88).

A relatively new but rapidly growing area of collaboration between psychology and medicine is to be found in psychopharmacology (33, 68, 92). Much of the psychological research on drugs pertains to their use in the understanding and treatment of psychiatric disorders (Chapter 15). The total contribution of psychology to pharmacology, however, covers other medical uses of drugs, including relief of pain and specific therapies for physical disorders. It is being increasingly recognized, for example, that any drug designed for medical use should be tested for "behavioral toxicity," that is, for any adverse side effects it may have upon psychological functioning (92, ch. 7). For this purpose, almost every available kind of psychological test has been used, from measures of simple sensory and motor functions to tests of complex intellectual and personality traits (92).

In the testing of drugs prior to their release for medical use, psychological research techniques are being employed at every stage, from preliminary animal research, through experimental studies with human subjects, to clinical tests. In animal research, behavioral measures are proving more sensitive than physiological measures in detecting drug effects, and psychologists are now trying to develop a standardized battery for testing the effects of any new drug on animals. Skinner boxes and other refined instruments for measuring animal behavior are beginning to appear in the pharmacology departments of medical schools. Drug companies are also beginning to employ psychologists to conduct drug research with animals (see, e.g., 80).

In both experimental studies on normal human volunteers and clinical field tests on patients, psychology has much to offer to methodology. Examples of these contributions include the use of psychological tests or rating scales for objective and quantitative assessment of behavioral changes, the application of appropriate sampling and matching procedures in assigning subjects to experimental groups, the utilization of the double-blind technique (Chapter 15) to control the influence of suggestion on subjects and observers, and the designing of experiments that permit effective statistical analyses of results.

Research on psychopharmacology, as well as in other areas of medical and psychological collaboration, is also contributing to basic knowledge about behavioral science. From the standpoint of the research psychologist, collaboration with medicine opens up new research settings in hospitals, clinics, and other agencies and provides access to many types of subjects not heretofore available. It also permits the use of techniques such as drug administration that require medical collaboration. Apart from their therapeutic values, drugs are being used experimentally to produce temporary and limited "biochemical lesions" in the nervous system. By interfering with selected biochemical events these techniques can shed light on the operation of different parts of the nervous system in normal behavior. For this purpose, drugs have several advantages over earlier methods of extirpation and other types of surgical intervention. Not only is drug administration a simpler and better controlled procedure than surgical techniques, but the effects of drugs are also reversible. Because of this reversibility and the reduction of risk, some drug research can be safely conducted with human subjects. The precision with which drug administration can be controlled and manipulated, moreover, makes possible a clearer delineation of the physiological mechanisms underlying behavioral changes. Psychopharmacology illustrates the reciprocal contribution of collaborative research to both medical practice and the advancement of psychological knowledge.

Understandably, it is in physiological psychology that the bulk of collaborative research with medicine is to be found. Currently, the greatest activity is occurring in the newly emerging field of psychopharmacology, as the above discussion suggests. Nevertheless, research contacts between psychology and medicine are not limited to physiological problems. Other areas of psychology have developed specialized research methodologies that are applicable to medicine. Of the many potential applications, three will be described below to illustrate the variety of possible contributions from both physiological psychology and other areas.

**Nature and Alleviation of Pain.**   The subject of pain is obviously of concern to medical practitioners, while falling clearly in the domain of psychological research. Pain and its relief have been investigated by psychologists, physiologists, neurologists, and pharmacologists, among others (10). Collaborative projects cutting across these fields, however, are of relatively recent origin. Specific studies have ranged from introspective analyses to the identification of sensory receptors and neurological correlates of pain. Their objectives have also varied widely, extending from the formulation of a basic theory of pain to the evaluation of individual techniques for its elimination or diminution. Among the techniques that have been explored for the relief of chronic pain, as in cancer patients, are prefrontal lobotomy (see Chapter 14), drugs, hypnosis, and placebos (4).

A noteworthy finding of much of the psychological research on pain is that pain-relieving agents may eliminate the discomfort and anxiety associated with pain without raising the pain threshold or altering pain sensations themselves. Thus the individual can still identify the pain, localize it, and discriminate it from other sensations such as touch or temperature, but he no longer finds it intolerable or unpleasant (4, 8). Physiological alterations, such as blood pressure changes, ordinarily associated with the discomfort of pain may also disappear under these conditions.

Laboratory studies of experimentally produced pain have yielded inconsistent results (4, 43). This is not surprising in view of the many methodological problems presented by pain research. The more carefully controlled investigations, however, have failed to find any significant change in pain threshold following administration of such analgesics as aspirin, codeine, and morphine (see, e.g., 25, 27, 91). What differences were obtained could be attributed to placebo effects and other extraneous variables. For example, one investigator found that phenobarbital produced threshold changes similar to those produced by morphine (25). Since the side effects of phenobarbital and morphine in the dosages employed were indistinguishable to most of the subjects, phenobarbital served as an "active placebo" in this experiment (see Chapter 15).

Of particular methodological interest was the finding that repeated stimulation of the same spot on the skin produces a consistent rise in pain threshold (25, 91), as illustrated in Figure 119. Such a finding calls into question the positive conclusions of earlier drug studies employing repeated stimulation of a single spot. It also points up the multiplicity of variables that must be controlled in this type of research and the complex experimental designs required to achieve adequate control. Another relevant consideration is that there may be different varieties of pain, which are mediated by different neurological mechanisms. Drugs that relieve one type of pain may thus yield negative results with another type.

**Process of Medical Diagnosis.**   A very different kind of research is illustrated by exploratory studies of the process of medical diagnosis and by the

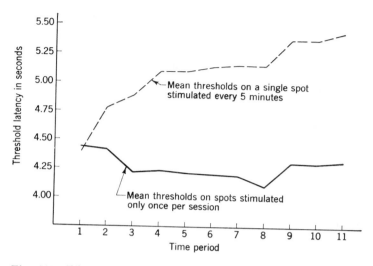

**Fig. 119** Effect of repeated stimulation of same spot on pain threshold for radiant heat. (*From Sweeney, 91, p. 46.*)

development of techniques for evaluating and training such diagnostic skills. Rimoldi and his associates (74, 75) have developed the Test for Diagnostic Skills, which focuses on the diagnostic process rather than on the final diagnosis. After being given preliminary information about a case, including admission data and chief complaints, the examinee proceeds by requesting additional information as needed. Such information, which he obtains by choosing the appropriate cards, covers questions he might ask the patient, manipulative techniques he might wish to use in his examination of the patient, diagnostic tests he might order, and so forth. The particular items requested, as well as the order in which they were requested, provide the basis for evaluating the individual's diagnostic performance.

Several types of scores can be found with the Test of Diagnostic Skills. Some of these scores are based on the number of questions asked and the utility of these questions in terms of the final diagnosis; others pertain to the order in which the questions are asked. The utility of a question is determined by the frequency with which it was asked by a criterion group, such as practicing physicians or medical school faculty. The sequence of questions is analyzed by newly developed techniques of pattern analysis, some of which are being adapted for machine scoring.

In an exploratory study, the Test of Diagnostic Skills was administered to 100 junior medical students, 230 senior medical students, and 50 physicians, drawn from five medical schools (74, 75). The responses of these three groups differed in a number of ways. With regard to number of questions asked, the junior students asked the most and the physicians the least. These differences, furthermore, were largely restricted to items dealing with history and interview data. The junior students asked questions that were often irrelevant or redundant, or they tended to follow wrong clues. With the physician group

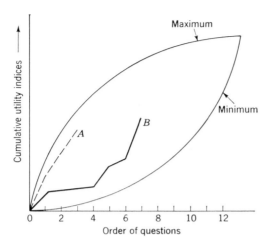

**Fig. 120**  Utility of acquired information as a function of order of questions for skilled and unskilled diagnosticians. (*From Rimoldi, 74, p. 77.*)

as a criterion, utility scores computed for the students were higher for seniors than for juniors. Thus, in the specific questions asked, the seniors agreed more closely with physicians than did the juniors. These group differences, too, were found largely with questions pertaining to history and interview information.

Of special interest is the analysis of these utility values in relation to sequence of questions. As the individual approaches the final diagnosis, the cumulative utility value of the information he has gathered rises. The more skillful diagnostician reaches a high utility value more quickly than does the poorer diagnostician, as illustrated in Figure 120. The cumulative index for student A rises almost as rapidly as is theoretically possible. That of student B, on the other hand, shows a plateau between questions 1 and 4. Student B accumulated practically no relevant information between these questions.

Mention should also be made of current research on the possible uses of computers and other types of automated information-processing systems as aids in medical diagnosis (29, 70, 87, 93, 95). At the start, these techniques are being explored with reference to relatively specific diagnostic problems, such as the interpretation of records from electroencephalographs, electrocardiographs, radiographs, and polygraphs (29). Another preliminary approach involves statistical analyses of variables for the diagnosis of a single disease, such as coronary artery disease (95). Multiple regression equations can be utilized for this purpose, just as in the development of personnel selection batteries (see Chapter 3). Eventually, computer techniques will be applied to the processing of more complex and varied combinations of diagnostic data.

**Norms and Related Measurement Problems.**   Insofar as medical diagnosis utilizes measurement, it requires norms for the interpretation of results. In evaluating data on body weight, heart rate, blood pressure, biochemical analyses, or any other objective measure, the physician either explicitly or implicitly compares the results with those expected under normal conditions. This process requires a knowledge of typical results, as well as of the range of "permissible variation." Available norms, however, are often crudely expressed and based on inadequate samples and unsystematic surveys (60, 69, 87, 99, 103).

In a 1951 article in the *British Medical Bulletin*, Wootton, King, and Smith (103) wrote: "Probably the most common use of blood analysis is in diagnosis. This involves comparing the results obtained from the patient being examined with those found in similar persons in normal health. It is therefore surprising how inadequate is the detailed information on the results obtained from normal subjects" (103, p. 307). In an effort to improve this situation, these investigators analyzed blood samples from 100 normal volunteers of both sexes between the ages of eighteen and fifty. A few of the blood constituents measured in this sample yielded distributions closely approximating the normal curve, as illustrated in Figure 121; but the majority yielded highly skewed distributions, as illustrated in Figure 122. Consequently, the use of means and standard deviations would have been inappropriate. Instead, the authors reported norms in terms of percentile measures, that is, the ranges covered by the middle 80 per cent and by the middle 98 per cent of the cases.

Published tables of biological norms frequently give means and variability estimates that may be misleading because of the form of the distribution. With skewed distributions, the median or mode would be more appropriate than the mean as a measure of central tendency. Normal range is often estimated by taking a distance of approximately two standard deviations on either side of

**Fig. 121**   Distribution of a blood constituent in a normal sample: plasma albumin. (*From Wootton, King, and Smith, 103, p. 307.*)

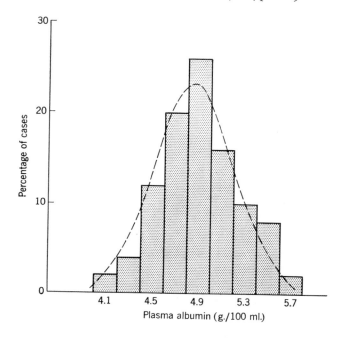

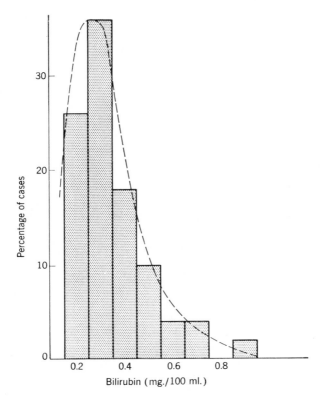

**Fig. 122**  Distribution of a blood constituent in a normal sample: bilirubin.
(*From Wootton, King, and Smith, 103, p. 308.*)

the mean, with no knowledge of normality of distribution. For some physiological variables, moreover, the published estimates of range are based, not on
data analysis, but on the subjective judgment of an investigator "experienced
in measuring the quantity in question" (89).

Apart from the possible use of inappropriate statistical measures, available
biometric norms have other deficiences. The samples from which they are
derived are often small and unrepresentative. When compared with the
normative samples employed in standardizing psychological tests, most of the
samples utilized in biometric surveys appear quite inadequate. Published ranges
of the concentration of different blood constituents, for example, are often
based on samples of fifty cases or less, and sometimes on as few as five cases
(99, p. 57).

The need for systematic medical norms stems from the wide variability found
among normal persons. In a book entitled *Biochemical Individuality,* Williams
(99) reports data gathered in his own laboratories, as well as published findings of other investigators, showing wide individual differences in metabolic
patterns, as indicated by the chemical composition of saliva and urine. In the

same book, he cites the extensive individual differences observed in virtually all anatomical and physiological variables, from stomach shape and size to heart rate. In his writings, Williams has repeatedly urged that medical prac-tice pay more heed to individual differences in bodily functions and that adequate data regarding such differences be collected.

Among the most extensive collections of biometric data are those pertaining to height and weight (69). Many thousands of cases have been included in the routine measurement of infants, schoolchildren, military recruits, inmates of prisons and other institutions, and applicants for life insurance policies. Special groups such as industrial workers and students have also been surveyed. Despite the impressive size of these samples, however, representative data are not available for certain segments of the population, such as adult women. For medical use, moreover, weight norms need to be specified with reference to age, sex, height, and possibly other anthropometric indices, such as chest cir-cumference. For such detailed breakdowns, representativeness of sampling is even more important than for general group comparisons. The variability of norms in different regions and at different times must also be taken into ac-count. Temporal changes in physical characteristics of populations call for periodic revisions of norms (69).

In the diagnostic use of quantitative data, some attention should also be given to errors of measurement. These errors result in part from temporal fluctuations in the individual's own condition. For many functions, systematic data on normal intraindividual fluctuations are lacking (87). Variations also occur in the results obtained by different examiners or by different laboratories that perform diagnostic tests (87, 103). All these types of measurement error are analogous to those assessed by the reliability coefficients of psychological tests, and similar procedures could be used to estimate their magnitudes. A knowledge of the measurement error inherent in diagnostic measurements is essential for their proper interpretation. In addition, the extent of such measure-ment error can often be reduced by controlling sources of variation through further standardization of procedures. An obvious example is that of controlling the previous exertion and present emotional state of the patient in measuring heart rate.

In many diagnostic measures the distributions of healthy and pathological cases overlap. Empirical determination of the extent of such overlap would obviously be helpful. Since diagnosis is usually based on a combination of measures, statistical studies of combinations and patterns of variables would likewise be fruitful (103). Finally, there is need for more longitudinal studies to determine the predictive validity of diagnostic measures. In the previously mentioned article, Wootton, King, and Smith (103) cite a longitudinal study conducted with infants suffering from haemolytic disease of the newborn, a condition resulting from blood-group incompatibility of mother and offspring. Several indices of the severity of the disease were checked against subsequent mortality. The most valid proved to be the haemoglobin concentration in the blood of the umbilical cord. With this index, an expectancy graph was pre-pared with which an infant's chances of survival could be estimated. These estimates are useful, not only in individual prognosis, but also in evaluating the effectiveness of different therapies.

It is apparent that the collection and analysis of quantitative data for use in medical diagnosis involve many concepts and techniques familiar in psychometrics. It would thus seem that the collaboration of psychometrically trained psychologists with medical statisticians, pathologists, and other medical specialists should prove fruitful. So far, however, the contributions of psychologists to this area of medicine have been minimal.

## PSYCHOSOMATIC MEDICINE

Since midcentury, the term "psychosomatic" has become familiar, not only in medical and psychological literature, but also in popular speech. Much publicity has been given to such "psychosomatic illnesses" as peptic ulcer, high blood pressure (essential hypertension), rheumatoid arthritis, and bronchial asthma. Conceptually, psychosomatic disorders can be differentiated from malingering, in which the individual deliberately fakes or falsely reports a symptom to gain some ulterior end. They can also be differentiated from such neurotic symptoms as hysterical paralyses and loss of sensitivity, for which no organic basis can be found (see Chapter 13). The term psychosomatic is typically applied to those physical disorders in which emotional stresses have led to identifiable organic pathology. We must hasten to add, however, that some writers use the term more broadly and with varied emphases. Moreover, the above threefold distinction is not always easy to apply in practice. And any individual patient may exhibit symptoms classifiable under two or even all three types.

***Historical Development.*** The concept of psychosomatic illness is an old one, dating from some of the earliest recorded writings (see 100, ch. 3). Even the term psychosomatic is not very new, having been proposed at least as early as 1818 (100, p. 41). Nevertheless, the current psychosomatic movement in medicine and the widespread recognition of psychogenic factors in physical disorders is of recent origin. The publication in 1935 of Dunbar's book on *Emotions and Bodily Changes* (21), which surveyed relevant world literature of both experimental and clinical nature, did much to launch the movement. *The Journal of Psychosomatic Medicine* began publication in 1939, and the Psychosomatic Society[1] was organized in 1942. The high incidence of psychosomatic disorders among military personnel and among civilians exposed to wartime stresses during World War II also contributed to the growing concern with these problems.

Several antecedent developments in psychology, physiology, and psychiatry contributed to the rise of the modern psychosomatic movement. A major contribution stems from research on the *effects of psychological factors upon physiological functions*, as studied in both man and animals. The pioneer animal experiments of Pavlov (72) on the conditioned salivary reflex and of Cannon (13) on physiological effects of intense emotional stimuli are outstanding examples of this research. The more recent investigations of Selye (83, 84) on the "general adaptation syndrome" following prolonged exposure to any kind of stress have thrown further light upon the role of certain hormones in mediating physiological responses to stress. More limited experimental studies on human subjects as well as clinical observations on patients

1 When first established, this society was known as the Society for Research in Psychosomatic Problems. In 1950, the name was changed to Psychosomatic Society (21, p. 73).

provided additional data on changes in blood pressure, respiration, gastric motility, glandular secretions, and other physiological reactions resulting from emotional stress. Such research has established that temporary and reversible physiological changes accompany anxiety and other emotional states. In addition, there is evidence that excessive and continued emotional stress may lead to chronic disturbances of physiological functions and to permanent tissue damage.

Among the other developments that contributed to the emergence of psychosomatic medicine may be mentioned *constitutional type theories* (see 2, ch. 6). These typologies have a long history but are best known to psychologists through the work of Kretschmer (53) and Sheldon (85). The earliest expositions of constitutional type theories were concerned with the relation between body build and susceptibility to different diseases. In later formulations, body build came to be associated with characteristic personality patterns as well as with proneness to specific diseases. Such theories thus helped to stimulate investigations into the personality characteristics of persons suffering from given diseases.

Still another major influence, especially evident in psychiatric writings on psychosomatic medicine, is *psychoanalysis* (see 21, 36). Beginning with Freud, many psychoanalysts have proposed theories regarding the role of conflicts, repressions, and other psychoanalytic mechanisms in the development of physical diseases. These theoretical speculations, bolstered by selected examples from clinical practice, have often led to descriptions of the typical personality of patients suffering from different psychosomatic disorders. Such popular phrases as "ulcer type" and "coronary personality" have their origins in these theories. Some psychoanalysts have approached the problem through the symbolic psychoanalytic significance of different organ systems, which allegedly determines the specific psychosomatic disorders each person is likely to develop.

**Research Methodology.** Current research on psychosomatic problems reflects the influence of these varied approaches. Following the earlier exploratory work, *animal experiments* have been more directly concerned with the production and alleviation of specific psychosomatic symptoms (1; 7; 11; 12; 48, pp. 49–51; 63–69; 78; 79; 96). By exposing rats, dogs, cats, monkeys, and other animals to conflictual and stressful situations, experimenters have been able to induce peptic ulcers, asthmalike symptoms, and other familiar psychosomatic disorders.

In one such experiment (11, 12), pairs of monkeys were placed in restraining chairs where they could be given brief electric shocks on the feet every 20 seconds. By pressing a lever at least once during each 20-second interval, the experimental member of the pair (facetiously designated as the "executive" monkey) could avoid the shock for both. Figure 123 shows the experimental and control monkeys in their restraining chairs. Both have levers within easy reach, but the lever on the side of the control animal is inactivated. Although both animals were subjected to the same physical stress, consisting of equally frequent shocks of the same intensity, only one was under the additional psychological stress of having to press the lever. Physical observations both during the experiment and after death revealed marked gastrointestinal ulceration in the experimental monkeys, while the control animals showed no gastrointestinal complications.

It is thus apparent that neither the restraint nor the shocks employed in

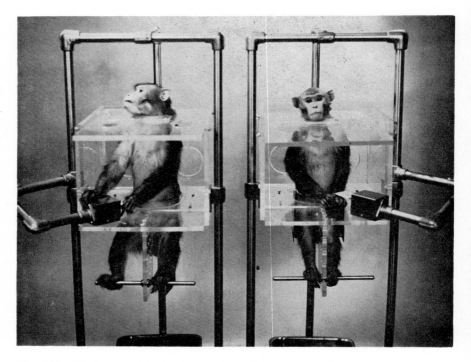

*Fig. 123* Monkeys participating in experimental investigation of peptic ulcers. Animal on the left can avoid shock for both by pressing lever; control animal's lever is inactivated. (*See Brady, 11, 12; United States Army photograph.*)

this experiment could account for the ulceration. The essential factor centered in the responses required of the experimental member of the pair. Physiological records indicated an excess secretion of gastric acid in the experimental monkeys, which was the immediate physiological cause of ulcer development. The "rest" and "work" schedules followed in the experiment also appeared to be an important factor in the situation. When six-hour rest periods with the shock turned off were alternated with six-hour work periods during which the animal must press the lever to avoid shock, most experimental monkeys developed ulcers. With other schedules, requiring either longer or shorter work periods, ulcers failed to develop. It is possible that the relation of the stress periods to some physiological cycle is a relevant factor, but more research is needed to identify the exact etiological mechanism.

Short-term experiments of a milder nature have been performed with *human volunteers* (48, pp. 48–49; 100–102). The subject is exposed to a stressful stimulus while various physiological measures are recorded and compared with those obtained under emotionally neutral circumstances. In clinical situations, the discussion of an emotionally charged topic may serve as the stressful situation. In such experiments, it is essential that the situation be one that has genuine emotional significance for the particular subject. This requires considerable knowledge about the individual's attitudes, values, and prior experiences. With suitable emotional stimuli, physiological changes have been demonstrated in a variety of bodily functions, including respiration, blood pressure, heart rate, sweat secretion, muscle potentials in different parts of the body, and acid secretion in the stomach.

Of particular interest are the studies of a few patients who as a result of injury or for therapeutic reasons have a gastric fistula that permits direct observation of the gastric mucosa, or inner lining of the stomach (24, 101). Figure 124 illustrates results obtained with one of these patients during a conversation that aroused anger and hostility. It can be seen that stomach contractions were intensified, hydrochloric acid production was more then doubled, and the gastric mucosa reddened as it became engorged with blood.

A third and related approach consists in the *longitudinal observation of patients with psychosomatic disorders.* Through such continuing observations, periods of remission or exacerbation of the physical symptoms can be correlated with life experiences. Published reports of such studies indicate a tendency for the patient's physical condition to worsen during periods of emotional stress. Because of the difficulty of maintaining contact with patients for long periods, an adaptation of this method utilizes case-history data (19). Some practitioners employ a "life chart" in which each row corresponds to a year in the patient's life. In appropriate columns on this chart, they record the patient's medical condition and any significant life events occurring during the year. Again published records indicate fairly close correspondence between experiential factors and the course of such disorders as peptic ulcer and rheumatoid arthritis (19).

**Fig. 124**   Changes in gastric mucosa observed in a subject with a gastric fistula during an emotionally stressful situation. (*Wolf and Wolff, 101,* p. 298. *From Contributions toward medical psychology, edited by Arthur Weider. Copyright 1953, The Ronald Press Company.*)

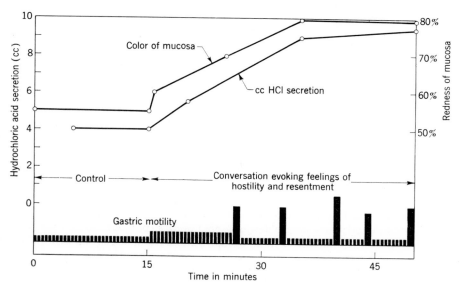

The analysis of life charts is less satisfactory than direct longitudinal observation, since it must rely upon the patient's report, and it leaves room for selective bias on the part of both patient and investigator. Both methods, moreover, are limited in that contact with the subject occurs after he is in an advanced stage of some somatic disorder. Physiological studies of individuals in the process of responding to life stresses, prior to the onset of pathology or during an early stage in the development of the disorder, are more illuminating, though more difficult to conduct. One such longitudinal study of Army inductees during World War II demonstrated that both physiological and personality variables contribute to the development of ulcers under stressful conditions (97).

From a different angle, psychiatrists and psychologists have investigated the *personality characteristics of patients suffering from a specific physical disorder.* Much of the literature on psychosomatic medicine is concerned with the results of this type of study (see 21, 36, 41, 57, 61). Many of these published personality descriptions are derived from selected cases observed under uncontrolled clinical conditions. Data were usually gathered by interviewing. When tests were employed, they were often of questionable validity. More objective studies with random samples and moderately well-matched control groups have usually failed to confirm the hypothesized relations between personality variables and type of disorder.

A further difficulty in the application of this method is the impossibility of inferring causal relations. If, for example, coronary patients manifest excessive anxiety, we do not know whether this condition existed prior to the onset of the physical disability or whether it is the patient's reaction to his physical handicap and to the frustrations it imposes. Only a longitudinal study begun prior to the onset of the physical disorder could answer this question. A further complication arises from the possible behavioral effects of reduced blood supply to the brain, changes in blood content, and other physiological aspects of the disease itself (31, pp. 101–102). Drugs administered to treat the physical disorder may also influence emotional and intellectual responses.

A fifth approach, which is receiving increasing attention, is that of *epidemiology.* By comparing the relative frequency of a disorder in different segments of the population, the epidemiologist can test hypotheses about causal influences (15). Analyses of the prevalence of certain diseases in different occupational groups provide one example of such an approach. It is noteworthy in this connection that surveys conducted in several countries have found peptic ulcer to be significantly more common among foremen than among craftsmen or higher-level executives (22). Contrary to popular belief, it is not the top-level executive who is most likely to develop ulcers. Although much more information is needed to arrive at a causal interpretation of such findings, one of the proposed explanations is that role conflicts may increase the emotional stress of the foreman's job.

Another application of the epidemiological approach is illustrated by a series of studies in progress in a recently industrialized area of North Carolina (15, 16). In these studies, the investigators set out to test the hypothesis that the incongruities and conflicts presented by cultural change, as in migration or in the industrialization of a farming community, produce stresses likely to result in increased rates of psychological, somatic, and social ill health. Over the preceding half century, the community under investigation had changed from a mountain village of approximately one hundred population to a small industrial city of about five thousand population. Since the population had remained racially quite homogeneous and was drawn almost wholly from the nearby farming area, this community provided a relatively controlled situation for study. As hypothesized, the "second-generation" factory workers, whose fathers were also employed in industry, had fewer health problems than the "first-generation" employees, whose fathers were farmers. The emotional stresses accompanying the readjustments and culture conflicts of these first-generation factory workers were thus reflected in poorer health conditions (16).

*Current Trends.* Today it is being increasingly recognized that the relation between emotional stress and somatic disorders is more complex than that implied in the personality-type theories. Because of methodological weaknesses, studies purporting to show the association of characteristic personality profiles with specific psychosomatic syndromes are of questionable value. An examination of the proposed personality descriptions, moreover, reveals considerable similarity among the traits attributed to persons with different diseases, such as peptic ulcer, hypertension, and rheumatoid arthritis (see, e.g., 41, pp. 205–208). Empirical observations, in fact, suggest that any given psychosomatic symptom could be the expression of several different emotions and that a given emotion could lead to a variety of psychosomatic symptoms (36, ch. 5). Such a finding is also consistent with present knowledge about the transient physiological expressions of emotional states (56). It is likewise relevant to note that shifts from one type of symptom to another, as from asthma to eczema, are not unusual (36, p. 66; 41, p. 203).

A parallel trend in psychosomatic medicine is to regard *all* diseases as having both psychogenic and somatogenic components, rather than labeling a few as psychosomatic. This trend is illustrated by the extension of psychosomatic medicine to include more and more specialties, such as surgery, gynecology, ophthalmology, and dentistry (21, chs. 1 and 17; 36). But, at a more basic level, the concept of psychosomatic medicine is being broadened to mean a consideration of the total reacting organism in his environment. Psychosomatic medicine thus stands for a point of view applicable to the practice of all medicine, rather than representing a branch of medicine. This approach will be recognized as virtually identical with that of comprehensive medicine, described earlier in this chapter.

# SOMATOPSYCHOLOGY

*General Nature.* Psychosomatic medicine began with investigations of the somatic effects of such psychological factors as emotional stress. Beginning at the opposite angle, some psychologists have been studying the individual's psychological reactions to physical illness or disability. Barker and his associates (5, 6, 105) have coined the term "somatopsychology" for this field. Although this is a new and relatively unexplored research area, it has attracted widespread interest through its practical implications for rehabilitation programs.

In somatopsychology, the individual's body is regarded "as a tool for behavior, and as an object with social significance to himself and others" (6, p. 419). For example, an orthopedic disability that seriously affects locomotion and other motor responses will interfere with social interaction, with schooling, and with other normal childhood activities. Such experiential limitations, unless remedied by other means, will retard intellectual growth and alter personality development in various ways. Another way in which conspicuous physical anomalies may affect psychological development is through the reactions of associates. Pity, avoidance, oversolicitousness, rejection, repulsion, and many other emotionally charged attitudes tend to make the disabled individual's social environment different from that of physically normal persons. The individual's self concept and his own attitude toward his disability are likely to be profoundly affected by his atypical experiences.

**Long-term Psychological Effects.** Exploratory studies have been conducted on the psychological effects of many types of physical disability, including deafness, blindness, amputation, facial disfigurement, tuberculosis, poliomyelitis, cerebral palsy, multiple sclerosis, and paraplegia, among others (5, 30, 31, 86, 105). Patients in these different categories have been investigated through intensive case studies, interviews, questionnaires, and psychological tests. An example of a projective technique developed especially for studying the attitudes of amputees toward their disability and toward the wearing of artificial limbs is given in Figure 125. Patterned after the Rosenzweig Picture-Frustration Study, this test consists of nine cartoons portraying potentially awkward or embarrassing social situations that may be encountered in daily life by an arm amputee (73, 86). The subject's responses are scored with regard to self-acceptance, reality facing, and desire for independent function.

The results of such studies show that there is no consistent association between specific forms of disability and particular personality characteristics. There are no psychological traits that uniformly differentiate, let us say, the blind, the deaf, or the orthopedically handicapped from persons with other disabilities or from physically normal persons. As a group, the severely disabled tend to show some maladjustment, in the form of anxiety, depression, and social isolation. Even these group differences, however, are slight, and the overlapping with physically normal persons is extensive.

Studies of physically disabled individuals, on the other hand, reveal that the physical disability often has a profound effect upon behavior. The discrepancy between individual and group results arises from the fact that the psychological effect of disability takes many different forms in different persons. The end result in the individual's behavior depends upon a three-way interaction among: (1) nature and severity of handicap; (2) individual personality and ability variables; and (3) situational variables in home, school, job, and social contexts (5; 6; 105, ch. 15). Heterogeneity in the effects of specific physical disabilities upon individual behavior is one of the best-established findings of somatopsychology. The individual's attitude toward his disability is an important link in the chain of circumstances leading to particular behavioral effects.

**Immediate Reactions to Illness.** While the above research pertains to long-range and relatively permanent effects of physical disability upon intellectual and personality development, several investigators have been concerned with the individual's immediate response to illness, hospitalization, and treatment. This approach is illustrated by an extensive series of studies undertaken cooperatively by psychologists in a number of Veterans Administration hospitals. In the first of these studies, data were obtained from nearly eight hundred male patients hospitalized for pulmonary tuberculosis (94). This disease was

Hostess (who knows nothing about the guest):

*Check One*

1. Thank you. I shall help myself to coffee and cake.                    ___
2. Thank you. I shall try to manage both, but if not would you
   mind if I find a small table?                                         ___
3. Thank you. I'll have some coffee. (Cake seems too hard to
   handle, John thinks to himself.)                                      ___
4. Thank you. Would you mind helping me with the cake? I'll
   take the coffee.                                                      ___
5. Thank you. I'll appreciate it if you would set the coffee and
   cake down for me.                                                     ___
6. No thank you. (I'd like some, but what's the use, John
   thinks to himself.)                                                   ___
7. Thank you. Would you mind helping me? It would be
   somewhat easier                                                      ___
8. Thank you. I'll try and manage. (John thinks to himself,
   I'll bet she feels sorry for me.)                                     ___

*Fig. 125*  Typical item from projective test designed to assess attitudes of
amputees toward their disability and toward the use of prosthetic devices.
(*From Peizer, 73, p. 52.*)

chosen because it presents a particularly difficult adjustment problem during
treatment. Because the disease is contagious, the patient must be isolated.
Treatment is slow and frustrating, the patient being hospitalized for long
periods during which he may feel perfectly fit. In addition, the threats of
possible lung surgery and permanent disability evoke anxiety and depression.
   In the study, rating scales, interviews, and questionnaires were used to
arrive at criterion indices of hospital adjustment and of subsequent community

adjustment. These indices were correlated with biographical data and with scores on a battery of psychological tests. One of the suggestive findings of the study was that the type of person who adjusts well to the hospital tends to make a poorer community adjustment after discharge. Conversely, those making a good community adjustment tended to be more resistant to the regimentation and inactivity typical of the tuberculosis ward. The passivity, acquiescence, and dependence conducive to good hospital adjustment contrast sharply with the personal qualities demanded by the posthospital environment. Only one psychological variable, anxiety, was found to be detrimental to both hospital and community adjustment.

A more intensive investigation of 32 patients in the tuberculosis division of a county hospital was conducted by Derner (20). Information was obtained through a series of guided interviews, self-report inventories, and projective techniques. The results gave no evidence of a characteristic personality pattern associated with tuberculosis, although feelings of apprehension, fearfulness, and depression were common. The patients' responses also indicated a pervasive concern with their illness and with bodily condition in general. An attempt to check on the alleged euphoria and undue optimism of tubercular patients yielded inconclusive results. Several findings pointed to an underlying conflict between dependency needs and independency needs in the course of hospitalization and rehabilitation. Patients differed widely in their response to this conflict, as was also suggested by the findings of the more recent and more extensive Veterans Administration study cited above.

Patients' reactions to a diagnosis of cancer and to their subsequent hospitalization and treatment also provide a fruitful field for psychological research (18). Because of the high death rate from some forms of this disease, insufficient knowledge about its nature, the possibility of disfiguring surgery, and the many superstitious beliefs associated with it, cancer engenders unusually high anxiety in most patients. Attitudes of relatives also play an important part in the patient's reaction to this disease. The psychologist in a cancer hospital can do much to reduce misunderstandings and allay anxieties.

Even with terminal cancer patients, psychological counseling for the acceptance of death has much to contribute to the patient's emotional well-being (18). To perform effectively in this role, the psychologist needs much more information than is now available about individuals' attitudes toward their own death. This is an area of psychological research that has been largely neglected, but its importance is gradually coming to be recognized by psychological investigators. A beginning has been made in exploring attitudes toward death held by individuals at different age levels, from early childhood to old age (26, chs. 6–8). Surveys of terminally ill patients suggest, among other findings, that feelings of being abandoned and rejected often augment the patient's dread (18; 26, ch. 8). As might be anticipated, a given patient's reaction to imminent death depends upon many individual and situational variables. But most patients want to discuss their impending death and resent evasiveness and withdrawal by their associates.

**Relation between Patient Attitudes and Recovery.**   Still another type of investigation is concerned with the effect of patient attitudes upon recovery from illness. In the previously mentioned study of patients with pulmonary tuberculosis in Veterans Administration hospitals, biographical and test data were also correlated with indices of recovery as determined from X-ray films and bacteriological tests (94). Favorable response to treatment was found to be significantly correlated with freedom from anxiety and with personal confidence. Rapid recovery also tended to be associated with an "experimenting," intellectual orientation as contrasted with a cautious and conservative attitude. Although these specific findings should be regarded as tentative and preliminary, the fact that patients in identical physical condition may respond very differently to treatment has long been recognized in clinical practice.

Similar observations have been reported by physicians treating cancer patients, and some exploratory research has been undertaken to identify psychological characteristics associated with differential recovery rate. Independent research projects conducted at different hospitals have provided suggestive evidence that patients' attitudes toward their illness and other personality characteristics are related to the likelihood of recovery from certain forms of cancer (18, 32). Findings from joint psychological and biochemical research suggest the role of hormones as a possible mediating factor in this relationship. Although available information is far too meager to permit any conclusions at this time, preliminary results are sufficiently promising to justify further research along these lines.

With these studies on the effect of attitudes upon recovery from physical illness we have come full circle and are back to a psychosomatic relationship. By now it should be apparent that the separation of different types of relation between psychological factors and physical illness, while desirable for purposes of analysis, cannot be sharply maintained in practice. The way in which an individual adjusts to the complex changes in his life pattern brought about by illness or physical disability depends to a large extent upon his pre-disability personality. If his reaction includes anxiety and depression, these attitudes will in turn exert a psychosomatic effect upon the subsequent course of the illness, as well as upon his ability to cope with the social, economic, and other problems that it engenders. Both psychosomatic medicine and somatopsychology can thus be recognized as two aspects of the general approach designated as comprehensive medicine.

## SUMMARY

Although the role of psychological factors in medical practice has been recognized for centuries, it was not until after World War II that contacts between psychology and medicine attained significant proportions. Even now, the potential contributions of psychology to medicine are largely undeveloped. In medical practice, psychology can aid in diagnosis, treatment, rehabilitation, and prevention. Apart from his utilization of psychodiagnostic data, the physician can profit from psychological knowledge in conducting medical interviews and in evaluating introspective reports by patients. In treatment, the role of interpersonal relations between physician and patient is widely recognized. The trend toward comprehensive medicine, with its emphasis upon the whole patient in his environment, has advanced the application of psychology to medicine. In rehabilitation, the psychologist typically functions as a member of a team composed of physicians and other professional workers. Preventive medicine requires effective two-way communication between lay public and public health personnel. Its problems thus have much in common with those of consumer psychology.

Since midcentury, the participation of psychologists in medical school teaching has grown rapidly, as manifested both by the increasing number of psychoogists so employed and by the broadening scope of their functions. A major contribution that psychology can make to medicine is in research. Examples of collaborative psychological research conducted in medical settings include electroencephalography, studies of environmental stresses of flight and space travel, psychopharmacology, investigations of the nature and relief of pain, analyses of the process of medical diagnosis, and the improvement of physiological norms and of diagnostic measurement.

Modern psychosomatic medicine dates from the mid-thirties. Its antecedents stem from such varied sources as physiological psychology, constitutional type theories, and psychoanalysis. Current research techniques include the artificial production of psychosomatic disorders in animals, experimental investigation of the effects of stress upon human physiological functions, longitudinal observations and case studies of patients with psychosomatic disorders, and personality studies of patients with different physical syndromes.

Somatopsychology begins from the opposite angle, focusing upon the psychological effects of physical illness and disability. It is concerned with both long-range effects upon intellectual and personality development and immediate responses to illness, hospitalization, treatment, and impending death. Some suggestive data have been reported on the effect of patients' attitudes and other personality characteristics upon recovery from such illnesses as tuberculosis and cancer. Both somatopsychology and psychosomatic medicine may be regarded as particular aspects of comprehensive medicine.

# REFERENCES

1. Ader, R., Tatum, R., and Beels, C. C. Social factors affecting emotionality and resistance to disease in animals. *J. comp. physiol. Psychol.*, 1960, **53**, 446–458.
2. Anastasi, Anne. *Differential psychology.* (3rd ed.) New York: Macmillan, 1958.
3. Apple, D. (Ed.) *Sociological studies of health and sickness: A source book for the health professions.* New York: McGraw-Hill, 1960.
4. Barber, T. X. Toward a theory of pain: Relief of chronic pain by prefrontal leucotomy, opiates, placebos, and hypnosis. *Psychol. Bull.*, 1959, **56**, 430–460.
5. Barker, R. G., *et al. Adjustment to physical handicap and illness: A survey of the social psychology of physique and disability.* Rev. ed. New York: Soc. Sci. Res. Coun., 1953.
6. Barker, R. G., and Wright, Beatrice A. Disablement: The somatopsychological problem. In E. Wittkower and R. Cleghorn (Eds.), *Recent developments in psychosomatic medicine.* Philadelphia: Lippincott, 1954. Pp. 419–435.
7. Beach, F. A. "Psychosomatic" phenomena in animals. *Psychosom. Med.*, 1952, **14**, 261–276.
8. Beecher, H. K. *Measurement of subjective responses.* New York: Oxford Univer. Press, 1959.
9. Bellak, L. (Ed.) *Psychology of physical illness; psychiatry applied to medicine, surgery, and the specialties.* New York: Grune & Stratton, 1952.
10. Berger, F. M. (Ed.) Non-narcotic drugs for the relief of pain and their mechanism of action. *Ann. N.Y. Acad. Sci.*, 1960, **86**, 1–310.
11. Brady, J. V. Ulcers in "executive" monkeys. *Scient. Amer.*, 1958, **199** (4), 95–104.
12. Brady, J. V., *et al.* Avoidance behavior and the development of gastroduodenal ulcers. *J. exp. Anal. Behav.*, 1958, **1**, 69–73.

13. Cannon, W. B. *The wisdom of the body.* New York: Norton, 1932.
14. Casner, D. Staff-centered clinical psychology in a tuberculosis hospital. *J. clin. Psychol.,* 1953, **9**, 151–155.
15. Cassel, J., Patrick, R., and Jenkins, D. Epidemiological analysis of the health implications of culture change: A conceptual model. *Ann. N.Y. Acad. Sci.,* 1960, **84**, 938–949.
16. Cassel, J., and Tyroler, H. A. Epidemiological studies of culture change. *Arch. environ. Hlth,* 1961, **3**, 25–33.
17. Chesler, Julia. Teaching medical students the principles of mental health. *J. med. Educ.,* 1959, **34**, 674–679.
18. Cobb, Beatrix. Cancer. In J. F. Garrett and Edna S. Levine (Eds.), *Psychological practices with the physically disabled.* New York: Columbia Univer. Press, 1962. Pp. 231–260.
19. Cobb, S. Technique of interviewing a patient with psychosomatic disorder. In A. Weider (Ed.), *Contributions toward medical psychology.* New York: Ronald, 1953. Ch. 10.
20. Derner, G. F. *Aspects of the psychology of the tuberculous.* New York: Hoeber-Harper, 1953.
21. Dunbar, Flanders. *Emotions and bodily changes.* New York: Columbia Univer. Press, 1954. (1st ed. 1935.)
22. Dunn, J. P., and Cobb, S. Frequency of peptic ulcer among executives, craftsmen, and foremen. *J. occup. Med.,* 1962, **4**, 343–348.
23. Ellingson, R. J. Brain waves and problems of psychology. *Psychol. Bull.,* 1956, **53**, 1–34.
24. Engel, G. L., and Reichsman, F. A study of an infant with a gastric fistula: I. Behavior and the rate of total hydrochloric acid secretion. *Psychosom. Med.,* 1956, **18**, 374–398.
25. Fangman, J. J. The effects of morphine on two forms of experimental pain. Unpublished doctoral dissertation, Fordham Univer., 1963.
26. Feifel, H. (Ed.) *The meaning of death.* New York: McGraw-Hill, 1959.
27. Feleppa, Evelyn M. The effect of acetylsalicylic acid on the pricking pain threshold as determined by radiant heat. Unpublished master's dissertation, Fordham Univer., 1961.
28. Feshbach, S. The consequences of fear-arousal in public health education. In Lise Ostergaard (Ed.), *Clinical psychology.* Copenhagen: Munksgaard, 1962. (Proc. 14th int. Congr. appl. Psychol., vol. 4.)
29. Flood, W. H. Computer-aided medical diagnosis. *Ment. Hlth Res. Inst. (Ann Arbor, Mich.),* 5th ann. Rep., 1961, p. 28.
30. Garrett, J. F. (Ed.) *Psychological aspects of physical disability.* Washington: Govt. Printing Office, 1952. (OVR, Rehab. Serv. Ser. No. 210.)
31. Garrett, J. F., and Levine, Edna S. (Eds.) *Psychological practices with the physically disabled.* New York: Columbia Univer. Press, 1962.
32. Gengerelli, J. A., and Kirkner, F. J. (Eds.) *The psychological variables in human cancer.* Berkeley, Calif.: Univer. Calif. Press, 1962.
33. Gerard, R. W. *et al.* The nosology of schizophrenia. *Amer. J. Psychiat.,* 1963, **120**, 16–29.
34. Gilmer, B. von H., and Mensh, I. N. Psychology in other professional schools. *Amer. Psychologist,* 1956, **11**, 676–679.
35. Greenfield, N. S. A brief appraisal of the role of clinical psychology in medical education. *Amer. Psychologist,* 1960, **15**, 624–625.
36. Grinker, R. R. *Psychosomatic research.* (Rev. ed.) New York: Grove Press, 1951.
37. Gustav, Alice. Evaluation of dentist-patient relationship by means of a psychological test. In J. L. Blass (Ed.), *Motivating patients for more effective dental service.* Philadelphia: Lippincott, 1958. Pp. 5–11.
38. Gustav, Alice. Use of two tests in brief counseling. *J. counsel. Psychol.,* 1960, **7**, 228–229.
39. Guze, S. B., Matarazzo, J. D., and Saslow, G. A formulation of principles of comprehensive medicine with special reference to learning theory. *J. clin. Psychol.* 1953, **9**, 127–136.
40. Hadley, J. M. *Clinical and counseling psychology.* New York: Knopf, 1958.
41. Hamilton, M. *Psychosomatics.* New York: Wiley, 1955.

42. Hammond, K. R., et al. *Teaching comprehensive medical care: A psychological study of a change in medical education.* Cambridge, Mass.: Harvard Univer. Press, 1959.

43. Hardy, J. D., Wolff, H. G., and Goodell, Helen. *Pain sensations and reactions.* Baltimore: Williams & Wilkins, 1952.

44. Hollender, M. H. *The psychology of medical practice.* Philadelphia: Saunders, 1958.

45. Horowitz, M. J., et al. Psychology as a basic science in medical education. *Neuropsychiatry,* 1959, **5**, 43–74.

46. Hunt, Thelma. Psychology in medicine. In J. S. Gray (Ed.), *Psychology in use.* (2nd ed.) New York: Amer. Book, 1951. Ch. 10.

47. Ianni, F. A. J., Albrecht, R. M., and Polan, Adele K. Group attitudes and information sources in a poliovaccine program. *Publ. Hlth Rep.,* 1960, **75**, 665–671.

48. Jores, A., and Freyberger, H. (Eds.) *Advances in psychosomatic medicine.* New York: Brunner, 1961.

49. Kahn, R. L., and Cannell, C. F. *The dynamics of interviewing: Theory, technique, and cases.* New York: Wiley, 1957.

50. Kegeles, S. S., et al. Symposium: Social and psychological phenomena related to the acceptance of water fluoridation. *Amer. Psychologist,* 1960, **15**, 439–440.

51. Knopf, I. J. Summary report on the conference on psychology in medical education. *Amer. Psychologist,* 1956, **11**, 684–685.

52. Knopf, I. J., et al. Conference on psychology in medical education. *Neuropsychiatry,* 1957, **4**, 93–107.

53. Kretschmer, E. *Physique and character.* (Transl. from 2nd ed. by W. J. H. Sprott.) New York: Harcourt, Brace, 1925.

54. Kutner, B. Physician-patient relationships: A theoretical framework. In J. G. Peatman and E. L. Hartley (Eds.), *Festschrift for Gardner Murphy.* New York: Harper & Row, 1960. Pp. 258–273.

55. Kutner, B., and Gordan, G. Seeking care for cancer. *J. Hlth hum. Behav.,* 1961, **2**, 171–178.

56. Lacey, J. I., and Lacey, Beatrice C. Verification and extension of the principle of autonomic response stereotypy. *Amer. J. Psychol.,* 1958, **71**, 50–73.

57. LeShan, L., and Reznikoff, M. A psychological factor apparently associated with neoplastic disease. *J. abnorm. soc. Psychol.,* 1960, **60**, 439–440.

58. Lubin, B., et al. Symposium: The psychologist in undergraduate medical education. *J. nerv. ment. Dis.,* 1961, **133**, 108–129.

59. McGuire, F. L., et al. Symposium: Psychology in medical education—trends and developments. *Amer. Psychologist,* 1962, **17**, 341.

60. McKinlay, P. L. The measurement of normality. *Brit. med. Bull.,* 1951, 7, 275–277.

61. Marshall, S. Personality correlates of peptic ulcer patients. *J. consult. Psychol.,* 1960, **24**, 218–223.

62. Matarazzo, J. D. Comprehensive medicine: A new era in medical education. *Hum. Organiz.,* 1955, **14** (1), 4–9.

63. Matarazzo, J. D. The role of the psychologist in medical education and practice: A challenge posed by comprehensive medicine. *Hum. Organiz.,* 1955, **14** (2), 9–14.

64. Matarazzo, J. D., and Daniel, R. S. The teaching of psychology by psychologists in medical schools. *J. med. Educ.,* 1957, **32**, 410–415.

65. Mensh, I. N. Psychology in medical education. *Amer. Psychologist,* 1953, **8**, 83–85.

66. Mensh, I. N. Psychology and other professions. In W. B. Webb (Ed.), *The profession of psychology.* New York: Holt, Rinehart and Winston, 1962. Ch. 11.

67. Meyer, B. C. Some psychiatric aspects of surgical practice. *Psychosom. Med.,* 1958, **20**, 203–214.

68. Miller, N. E. Some recent studies of conflict behavior and drugs. *Amer. Psychologist,* 1961, **16**, 12–24.

69. Morant, G. M. Measurements of the growth and form of British people. *Brit. med. Bull.,* 1951, 7, 316–319.

70. Overall, J. E., and Williams, C. M. Models for medical diagnosis. *Behav. Sci.,* 1961 **6**, 134–141.

71. Paul, B. D., Gawson, W. A., and Kegeles, S. S. (Eds.) Trigger for community conflict: The case of fluoridation. *J. soc. Issues,* 1961, **17**, No. 4.
72. Pavlov, I. P. *Lectures on conditioned reflexes.* (Transl. by W. H. Gantt.) New York: Int. Publ. Co., 1928.
73. Peizer, E. Studies of the upper extremity amputee. I. Design and scope. *Artif. Limbs,* 1958, **5** (1), 4–56.
74. Rimoldi, H. J. A. The test of diagnostic skills. *J. med. Educ.,* 1961, **36**, 73–79.
75. Rimoldi, H. J. A., Haley, J. V., and Fogliatto, Hermelinda. The test of diagnostic skills. *Psychometr. Lab., Loyola Univer., Publ. No. 25,* 1962.
76. Rosenstock, I. M., Derryberry, M., and Carriger, B. Why people fail to seek poliomyelitis vaccination. *Publ. Hlth Rep.,* 1959, **74**, 98–103.
77. Savitz, H. A. The cultural background of the patient as part of the physician's armamentarium: Four case studies. *J. abnorm. soc. Psychol.,* 1952, **47**, 245–254.
78. Sawrey, W. L. Conditioned responses of fear in relation to ulceration. *J. comp physiol. Psychol.,* 1961, **54**, 347–348.
79. Sawrey, W. L., Conger, J. J., and Turrell, E. S. An experimental investigation of the role of psychological factors in the production of gastric ulcers in rats. *J. comp. physiol. Psychol.,* 1956, **49**, 457–461.
80. Scheckel, C. L. The effect of chlorpromazine (Thorazine) and Chlordiazepoxide (Librium) on delayed matching responses in the *Macaca Mulatta.* Unpublished doctoral dissertation, Fordham Univer., 1963.
81. Seidenfeld, M. A. Mass media and health communication. *Amer. J. occup. Ther.,* 1959, **13**, 185–188.
82. Sells, S. B. The purposes of psychology curricula in medical education. *Amer. Psychologist,* 1956, **11**, 679–683.
83. Selye, H. The general adaptation syndrome and the diseases of adaptation. *J. clin. Endocrinol.,* 1946, **6**, 117–230.
84. Selye, H. The general-adaptation-syndrome in its relationships to neurology, psychology, and psychopathology. In A. Weider (Ed.), *Contributions toward medical psychology: Theory and psychodiagnostic methods.* New York: Ronald, 1953. Ch. 11.
85. Sheldon, W. H., and Stevens, S. S. *The varieties of temperament.* New York: Harper & Row, 1942.
86. Siller, J., and Silverman, Sydelle. Studies of the upper-extremity amputee. VII: Psychological factors. *Artif. Limbs,* 1958, **5** (2), 88–116.
87. Smith, P. A. Some problems and approaches to automation of medical diagnosis. *Behav. Sci.,* 1961, **6**, 88–91.
88. Solomon, P., Leiderman, P. H., Mendelson, J., and Wexler, D. Sensory deprivation: A review. *Amer. J. Psychiat.,* 1957, **114**, 357–363.
89. Spector, W. S. (Ed.) *Handbook of biological data.* Philadelphia: Saunders, 1956.
90. Straus, R. A department of behavioral science. *J. med. Educ.,* 1959, **34**, 662–666.
91. Sweeney, D. R. Dolorimetry and its value as a method of evaluating analgesic agents. Unpublished doctoral dissertation, Fordham Univer. 1962.
92. Uhr, L., and Miller, J. G. (Eds.) *Drugs and behavior.* New York: Wiley, 1960.
93. Vandenberg, S. G. Medical diagnosis by computer: Recent attempts and outlook for the future. *Behav. Sci.,* 1960, **5**, 170–182.
94. Vernier, Claire M., et al. Psychosocial study of the patient with pulmonary tuberculosis: A cooperative research approach. *Psychol. Monogr.,* 1961, **75**, No. 6.
95. Ward, J. H., Jr., and Hook, Marion E. Use of regression analysis and electronic computers in the prediction of coronary artery disease. *Behav. Sci.,* 1962, **7**, 120–126.
96. Warren, I. A., and Kobernick, S. D. Studies with experimental neurosis and drug-induced ulceration of the colon in dogs. *Psychosom. Med.,* 1960, **22**, 443–447.
97. Weiner, H., et al. Etiology of duodenal ulcer. I. Relation of specific psychological characteristics to rate of gastric secretion (serum pepsinogen). *Psychosom. Med.,* 1957, **19**, 1–10.
98. West, L. J. Behavioral sciences in the medical school curriculum. *J. med. Educ.,* 1959, **34**, 1070–1076.
99. Williams, R. J. *Biochemical individuality: The basis for the genetotrophic concept.* New York: Wiley, 1956.

100. Wittkower, E., and Cleghorn, R. (Eds.) *Recent developments in psychosomatic medicine.* Philadelphia: Lippincott, 1954.
101. Wolf, S., and Wolff, H. G. Life situations, emotions, and gastric function: A summary. In A. Weider (Ed.), *Contributions toward medical psychology.* New York: Ronald, 1953. Ch. 13.
102. Wolff, H. G. Life stress and bodily disease. In A. Weider (Ed.), *Contributions toward medical psychology.* New York: Ronald, 1953. Ch. 14.
103. Wootton, I. D. P., King, E. J., and Smith, J. M. The quantitative approach to hospital biochemistry. *Brit. med. Bull.,* 1951, 7, 307–311.
104. Wright, Beatrice A. *Psychology and rehabilitation.* Washington: Amer. Psychol. Assoc., 1959.
105. Wright, Beatrice A. *Physical disability: A psychological approach.* New York: Harper & Row, 1960.

# 20

# *Psychology and Law*

With its heavy reliance upon precedent, the practice of law is characteristically resistant to change. Current laws as well as judicial procedures are often based upon outdated theories of human behavior and are at variance with experimentally established facts. This cultural inertia is generally defended on the grounds that law, dealing as it does with matters of life and death and other momentous decisions, must move cautiously. Thus it is argued that "new" findings, concepts, and techniques provided by a rapidly developing science such as psychology cannot be accepted as guides in legal practice until they have become so firmly established as to meet with virtual unanimity among psychologists themselves.

The effect of this policy, however, is that the psychological principles actually followed in legal practice are sometimes so manifestly obsolete as to be almost unanimously rejected by psychologists.[1] In all practical action, decisions must be made in the absence of complete certainty. Under such circumstances, wisdom requires that all the information available at the time be utilized in choosing the best course of action. Modern medicine provides a good example of this approach. For most diseases, there is no therapy that guarantees 100 per cent success. Nor would there be complete agreement about the best therapy to follow in any particular case. Yet this state of affairs is not used to justify a continuation of the medical practices of the Middle Ages.

Today there are several indications within the field of law that efforts are being made to bring legal practice into closer touch with modern society and with developments in both natural and social sciences. Among law professors, jurists, and law enforcement officers, a few outstanding individuals have encouraged research into social problems and have introduced techniques and findings of modern science into their own work. Within psychology, there has been sporadic interest in legal problems during the past fifty years. Such early books as Burtt's *Legal Psychology* (16) and Robinson's *Law and the Lawyers* (116) illustrate a variety of ways in which psychologists may contribute to law. Still other facets of the field are covered in more recent books on *Psychology for Law Enforcement Officers* (32) and *Legal and Criminal Psychology* (138). Applied psychological research specifically concerned with legal problems is still meager. Teaching by psychologists in law schools is likewise limited to an occasional course here and there. In many different ways, however, psychologists are beginning to establish contacts with the legal profession. In the following sections, the types of contributions that psychology can make to law will be illustrated in a variety of contexts, ranging from courtroom procedures and the treatment of individual delinquents and criminals to the formulation of laws and the development of national and international policies.

[1] This dilemma is reminiscent of what in statistics are known as Type I and Type II errors.

## TESTIMONY AND COURT PROCEDURE

Oddly enough, the psychology of testimony represents one of the earliest areas of applied psychology. Among the pioneers in this research was William Stern, who not only conducted studies of his own but also edited a journal on this topic, *Beiträge zur Psychologie der Aussage,* published at Leipzig during the first decade of this century.[2] During the same period, Alfred Binet, of intelligence test fame, was also conducting research and publishing on the psychology of testimony (12). In America, Harvard professor Hugo Münsterberg wrote *On the Witness Stand* (99) in 1908, a book summarizing relevant psychological studies. Between 1909 and 1917, the *Psychological Bulletin* published annual reviews on the psychology of testimony, prepared by G. M. Whipple. Research on problems of testimony continued until the early 1930s, after which activity lapsed for some twenty years. Since about 1955, however, interest in the topic has revived (35). The current approach is characterized by a broadened scope and by the collaboration of psychologists with members of other professions, notably sociology and law.

**Contributions of General Experimental Psychology.** Much of what psychology can contribute to the evaluation of courtroom testimony is derived from established facts of sensation, perception, memory, and other familiar areas of experimental psychology (10; 16, chs. 2–4; 113). Among the most relevant findings are those pertaining to: localization of sounds; visual illusions, such as the overestimation of vertical as contrasted to horizontal distances, the overestimation of filled as contrasted to unfilled spaces, and the influence of contextual factors upon length estimation as illustrated by the Müller-Lyer illusion; estimation of short time intervals and of the speed of moving vehicles; and adaptation phenomena, such as shifts between light-adapted and dark-adapted vision and adaptation effects in the perception of odors, temperature, and other continuing stimuli. In another area, studies of incidental memory suggest that more reliance can be placed upon the testimony of a witness who realized he might later have to report on the events he observed than on one who observed them casually and with no effort to memorize facts. Contrary to legal folklore, strong emotion at the time of observation or subsequent report tends to increase the probability of error.

A recent example of the bearing that psychological research on perception may have upon the evaluation of legal testimony is provided by the case of a Canadian hunter who, mistaken for a deer, was shot and killed by his companions (130). The victim was wearing faded red coveralls and was seen just before sunset on a very overcast day. The first pertinent psychological observation derives from the Purkinje phenomenon. As illumination diminishes, colors at the red end of the spectrum decrease in brightness faster than do those at the blue end. Consequently, red objects are among the first to lose their color as light fades. A second relevant psychological fact concerns the effect of set, or expectation, upon the perception of an ambiguous stimulus. The hunters, who were eagerly scanning the landscape for deer, perceived the moving object as a deer. When a policeman later observed a man under the same conditions, knowing it was a man, he perceived the object as a man.

[2] This journal was superseded in 1908 by the much broader *Zeitschrift für angewande Psychologie,* also edited by Stern. It is interesting to note that the first journal of applied psychology evolved from a publication initially devoted to the psychology of testimony.

*Aussage Tests.* First employed by William Stern, the Aussage test is now commonly known in the psychological literature by its original German name, meaning "testimony" or "report." In this test, a group of subjects are shown a picture or a short motion-picture film; or a brief and startling episode is enacted before them (13, ch. 10; 131; 142). In the latter case, the subjects are not usually told in advance that they will be questioned about their observations. For example, a stranger may burst into the classroom and engage in an altercation with the instructor; or an assistant may come rushing in and announce that some white rats have escaped from the laboratory. Later, the subjects are asked to report on what they witnessed, giving details of appearance, dress, speech, and actions of the participants.

By this procedure, accuracy of report may be investigated in relation to a number of variables, such as length of delay, prior instructions, suggestion, degree of emotional involvement, observer characteristics, and so on. One of the principal findings of this research is that errorless reports are rare. The usual reaction is to fill in the gaps in one's observation or recall of the scene with plausible details that are consistent with the individual's general perception of the event. The subject is often certain that he actually observed such a detail, although it was only suggested by the context. Under these conditions, moreover, agreement among several witnesses is no guarantee of factual correctness, nor is it evidence of collusion. Such spurious consistency may result simply from constant errors that affect the responses of different persons. Thus another deep-rooted legal tradition regarding the validity of testimony is called into question.

It is interesting to note that Stern (131) recommended the use of Aussage tests in the training of law students. By observing their own performance in the role of witness, prospective lawyers could thus gain a realistic understanding of the limitations of courtroom testimony.

*Method of Interrogation.* Among the conditions commonly investigated by means of Aussage tests is the method of eliciting information from the witness (10; 13, ch. 10; 16, chs. 5 and 6). Several early experiments consistently demonstrated that with free narration, in which the witness reports the incident in his own words, accuracy is higher than with direct questioning. When asked specific questions, most persons give more details than in a free recital, but a larger percentage of their report is wrong. Under the more hostile or confusing type of questioning involved in cross-examination, accuracy tends to drop still further.

Some data are also available regarding the form of the question (16, pp. 119–123; 103). Leading questions that suggest a particular answer obviously tend to encourage false recall. Questions containing a hidden assumption likewise have a strong suggestive effect. If asked whether the defendant held the gun in his right or left hand, a witness may honestly come to believe he saw a gun that was not actually there. Even the grammatical form of a question may exert an influence upon the response (16, ch. 5; 103). "Wasn't there a car parked in front of the bank?" is a more suggestive question than "Was there a car parked in front of the bank?" Directing attention to the witness himself as observer tends to increase response accuracy and caution. "Did you see a car?" is more likely to elicit a correct response than "Was there a car?"

It is also noteworthy that, when subjects are asked to indicate which facts they would be willing to report under oath, error is reduced but not eliminated

(16, pp. 153–155). For most persons, an appreciable proportion of error remains even among those facts they feel sufficiently sure about to affirm under oath.

**Other Aspects of Courtroom Procedure.** Psychological research on other aspects of courtroom procedure is so far quite limited (138, chs. 5 and 6). Some suggestive data have been gathered on variability in the sentences passed by different judges for similar crimes (10, pp. 203–204; 38; 39). In one study of six New Jersey judges, the median sentences for the same type of offenses varied from 6 to 12 months (39). The percentage of cases sentenced to the penitentiary by the same judges ranged from 34 to 57. Individual judges also differ in the relative severity of sentences they impose for specific crimes, such as sex crimes as compared with other types of crimes.

Although theoretically a judge's decision should be "impersonal," it is inevitable that the decisions actually reached are influenced by the individual judge's personality, point of view, and experiential background. That such individual variables may affect judicial decisions even at the highest level was demonstrated in a factorial analysis of decisions by justices of the United States Supreme Court (137). Based on the voting records of the nine judges over a two-year period, the study covered 115 cases in which there were at least two dissenting votes. The factor pattern showed that the nine judges fell into subgroups exhibiting significant and consistent differences in voting behavior.

Somewhat more information is available on factors affecting the behavior of a jury (10; 16, ch. 7; 96; 138, ch. 5; 142). Jury members' perception of the reported facts, as well as their ultimate decision in the case, may be influenced by any prejudices they may have toward racial, national, religious, economic, occupational, or other groups. Social stereotypes and snap judgments based on appearance or mannerisms may likewise affect the jury's evaluation of defendant, witnesses, and other participants in the trial.

Apart from such general considerations, applicable to all human interactions, some research has been specifically concerned with the American jury system (8; 60; 61; 96; 133; 134; 138, ch. 5). In much of this research, which was conducted jointly by psychologists, sociologists, and members of the legal profession, the subjects were jurors drawn by lot from regular jury pools. Either mock trials or recorded proceedings of actual trials were employed. The jury deliberations were in turn recorded and subsequently analyzed with regard to a number of factors, such as the effect of foreman personality upon jury decisions; sex, socioeconomic, and educational differences in relation to participation and influence; and the proportion of time devoted to different topics during jury deliberations.

Other experiments have been conducted with groups of law school or college students and have dealt with more limited questions. Several studies have investigated the effect of order of presentation upon persuasiveness of evidence (56, 57, 98, 142, 143). In one of these experiments (143), a detailed report of a criminal case was divided into 13 sections and read to groups of pre-law students acting as jurors. At the end of each section, the subjects rated their belief in the defendant's innocence or guilt on a nine-point scale. Figure 126 shows the median rating assigned by the group after each installment of evidence was heard. Installment 13 has been omitted from the graph, since it was merely the verdict of the actual trial jury. It can be seen that the judg-

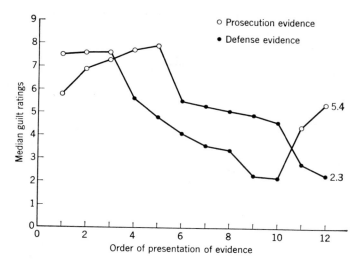

**Fig. 126** Effect of order of presentation upon persuasiveness of evidence. (*Data from Weld and Roff, 143, pp. 619, 622.*)

ment of guilt rose with successive presentation of prosecution evidence and dropped with successive presentation of defense evidence.

To test the effect of order of presentation, the same evidence was presented in a different order to each of two groups. When all the prosecution evidence was given first and the defense evidence second, the final median guilt rating was 2.3. When the series began and ended with prosecution items, with the defense items sandwiched in between, the final median guilt rating was 5.4. In the latter arrangement, the prosecution evidence had more influence because of a recency effect. Other studies have demonstrated both primacy and recency effects (57, 98). Under ordinary courtroom conditions, primacy and recency effects tend to be equally strong (98). With different modes of presentation and different time schedules, either one or the other effect may predominate (98).

# LIE DETECTION AND STRESSFUL INTERROGATION

The preceding section was concerned with testimony given by a witness who is motivated to be accurate and truthful. In many types of interrogation, however, the respondent tries to conceal or disguise facts or to mislead the investigator in other ways. The procedures discussed in this section share the common objective of obtaining correct information under the latter conditions.

*Development of Lie Detection.* Like the psychology of testimony, psychological research on lie detection dates from the beginning of this century. Among its pioneers were Benussi (7), Marston (93, 94), Larson (75, 76), Keeler (see 78, 79), and Summers (135, 136). Current procedures of lie detection represent a special application of two techniques long familiar in the psychological laboratory, namely, free association and the measurement of physiological indices of emotion.

Basically, all lie detectors compare the subject's responses to critical and neutral stimuli. The critical stimuli are associated with the specific crime under investigation. Suppose the crime was the theft of a green purse containing, among other things, $34 in cash, a visiting card with the name Henry Donohue, and a book of matches from the Morningside Coffee Shop. In that case, the words "green," "34," "Henry Donohue," and "Morningside" could be used as critical stimuli in a free association test. Neutral stimuli could be chosen so as to match the critical stimuli as closely as possible. Thus among the neutral words could be those for other colors, numbers, and proper names, such as "blue," "yellow," "28," "47," "John Edwards," "Herbert Reilly," "Everglade," and so forth. The critical words would of course be scattered at random among the neutral words.

If the subject's responses to the critical words are significantly different from his responses to the neutral words, in terms of speed, failure to respond, repetition of stimulus word, repetition of an earlier response, or other features, guilty knowledge is indicated. To the innocent subject, critical and neutral words are indistinguishable. This procedure is not applicable when all details of the crime have been widely publicized. It is based on the assumption that at least some details can be found that are known only to the guilty party. Many variants of the technique have been developed. Instead of stimulus words for free association, the investigator may use a series of questions, to be answered "Yes" or "No," or a set of multiple-choice questions. For instance, a list of addresses may be given at only one of which a burglary was committed.

Physiological measures of emotional excitement may be employed along with any of the verbal techniques described above. Any indices of emotion could be used, but the most common are changes in respiration, blood pressure, and galvanic skin responses (see 24, 78, 79). In the galvanic skin response (GSR), increased secretion of the sweat glands is detected by a rise in the electrical conductivity of the skin. When physiological measures are employed, the criterion of lying or guilt is again a consistent difference in response to critical and neutral items. Several physiological measures are often combined into a single recording instrument, known as a "polygraph." This term, which literally means "multiple graphic record," is commonly used as a generic name for lie detectors.

**Practical Applications of Lie Detectors.** Today lie detectors are used widely for a number of purposes (78, 79, 144). As early as 1953, it was estimated that approximately one hundred police departments were using such tests (144). In police work, lie detectors are employed chiefly in the preliminary examination and screening of suspects. Outstanding examples of their long-continued and effective application are provided by the Police Department of Berkeley, California, where the technique was introduced by Larson, and by the Chicago Police Scientific Crime Detection Laboratory, where it was introduced by Keeler. In addition, lie detectors are used regularly by several government agencies, such as the Atomic Energy Commission, and by all branches of the military services. They are also finding extensive application in banks, hotels, retail stores, and industrial plants, both in personnel selection and in periodic examination of employees.

Surveys of the correctness of the conclusions reached by polygraphic techniques have generally yielded encouraging results (144). Estimates of the performance of well-trained and experienced examiners usually run to about 75 to 80 per cent correct decisions, 15 to 20 per cent uncertain, and 2 to 5 per cent incorrect decisions. Some highly experienced practitioners claim close to 100 per cent accuracy for the records that they can interpret with confidence, after excluding doubtful or ambiguous cases. Because of the nature of the technique, moreover, the errors are usually failures to detect guilt; rarely is an innocent person shown to be guilty by the lie detector. The high optimism engendered by these surveys must be tempered by a consideration of the unsystematic and uncontrolled nature of the data on which they are based. Field studies of lie detection techniques in practical use need to be checked by controlled experimentation, of which there is still a dearth.

So far lie detection data have only rarely been admitted as evidence in court trials (144). Occasionally such data are admitted with the prior consent of both parties in the litigation. In such cases, both parties agree to submit to a lie detection test administered by an examiner who is acceptable to both and whose remuneration is shared equally by them. The findings of the test are then presented by the examiner as expert testimony and are considered along with other evidence by the judge or jury.

Whether in a legal setting or elsewhere, a lie detector should be employed only with the examinee's consent and with his knowledge of what the procedure is designed to accomplish. The ethical question of invasion of privacy is relevant in this connection. With the increasing professionalization of polygraph examiners, more attention is being given to the rights of the subject, necessary precautions in the use of lie detectors, and other matters of professional ethics (78). There is also growing concern with questions of training, standards, and certification. Training programs in lie detection techniques are conducted by universities, police departments, the military services, and private organizations. An important step in the improvement of lie detection practices was the establishment in 1949 of the Academy for Scientific Interrogation, a professional organization of leading practitioners from police departments, the Armed Forces, and other settings (78, vol. 2).

It should be noted that, while some psychologists are engaged in lie detection work, the majority of practitioners in this field are nonpsychologists. The amount of psychological training that these practitioners have received varies widely. There is an obvious need for the closer involvement of psychologists in consultation, training, and research on lie detection.

**Research on Lie Detection.**   The recent renewal of interest in all aspects of interrogation has been accompanied by a resurgence of research on lie detection (see, e.g., 24, 33, 70, 84, 85). To obtain better control of conditions, experiments are typically conducted with "simulated crimes," although every effort is made to achieve realism. For example, in a recent study by Kubis (70), conducted under Air Force sponsorship, volunteer college students participated in a simulated theft experiment. The experimental crime consisted in taking money from a coinbox attached to a pamphlet rack. The money was eventually returned, but the subjects did not learn about this condition until the end of the experiment.

In this experiment, subjects were grouped into sets of three, one of whom served as "thief," one as "lookout," and the third as "innocent suspect." The importance of avoiding detection at all stages was impressed upon the participants. Each subject was examined by several standardized verbal procedures, while his physiological responses were recorded. Figure 127 shows a subject with attached apparatus, including chest pneumograph for obtaining breathing records, plethysmograph cuff inserted over middle finger of right hand for blood pressure measurement, and palmar electrodes strapped to each hand for recording galvanic skin response. All examiners who conducted the lie detection tests and analyzed records were in ignorance of the roles assigned to individual subjects.

One of the objects of this study was to try to objectify the evaluation of records with a view to their ultimate handling by a computer. In this connection, a promising finding was that analysts who worked only from the records did as well as the examiners who had contact with the subjects during the test. For all experimenters, the percentage of correct identifications ranged from 73 to 92, with no uncertain category permitted. All these percentages exceeded the chance expectancy of 33 per cent correct by large and highly significant

*Fig. 127*   Lie detection apparatus for measuring changes in breathing, blood pressure, and galvanic skin response. (*Courtesy of Joseph F. Kubis; see 70.*)

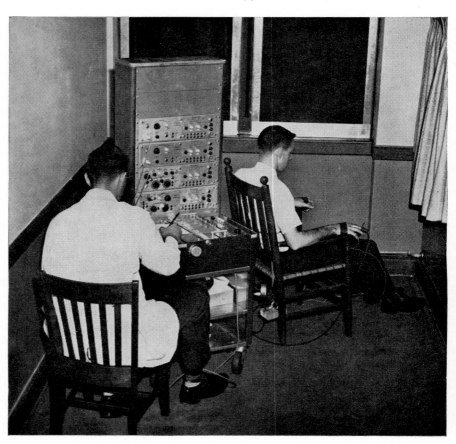

amounts. This study also explored ways of combining the three physiological measures statistically to reach a decision on each case. It was concluded, however, that the interpretation of lie detector records is not yet sufficiently objective to permit this type of treatment.

Further research on lie detection is needed along several lines. Other indices of emotional excitement should be explored and ways of improving the indices now in use investigated. Some progress has already been made in the refinement of the physiological measures employed (24; 33; 78, vol. 1, ch. 7, and vol. 2, ch. 8). For example, the use of a finger plethysmograph rather than the traditional arm cuff for measuring blood pressure permits continuous and prolonged recordings without discomfort or injury to the subject (70; 78, vol. 2, ch. 8). Other refinements of technique may decrease the frequency of ambiguous records and increase the objectivity of interpretation.

More research is also needed on ways of combining the results of different physiological measures. In this connection, the findings on autonomic response stereotypy cited in Chapter 15 are quite relevant (24, 73). These findings suggest that one person may show his maximal response to stress in increased hand sweating, another in respiratory changes, and so on. Under these conditions, the use of multiple measures (as in the typical polygraph) would seem desirable. Moreover, the weights of individual measures would vary with the individual.

One of the unanswered questions in lie detection pertains to the mechanism underlying the physiological changes and other response disturbances that occur when critical stimuli are presented (24, 84, 85). Although there has been some theoretical speculation about the nature of this mechanism, it is as yet little understood. Some controversy centers around the extent to which lying as such can be detected, as contrasted to the possession of guilty knowledge. The example cited in the opening of this section was based upon the identification of guilty knowledge. When critical and neutral items are indistinguishable to innocent respondents, consistent differentiation of responses to critical items obviously reveals guilty knowledge. Under these conditions, we would expect the maximum success with polygraphic techniques; and empirical findings do in fact support this expectation (84).

A variant of the guilty knowledge test was employed by Lykken (85) with dramatic success. In this experiment, the object was to identify each of 20 subjects by examining their galvanic skin responses to a set of 25 questions pertaining to such details as mother's first name, name of high school attended, street on which subject lived as a child, etc. Multiple-choice responses were presented for each item, in which one answer was correct for the given subject. Despite the fact that the subjects were highly motivated to mislead the experimenter, correct identification occurred in 100 per cent of the cases! For all subjects, the pattern of galvanic skin responses revealed the differential reaction elicited by the familiar alternative in each set of item responses.

Many of the practical applications of polygraphic techniques, however, are based, not on the detection of guilty knowledge, but on the detection of lying itself. Similarly, in the previously cited research by Kubis (70), most of the verbal procedures investigated were concerned with lying. For example, both guilty and innocent subjects were asked such critical questions as "Did you take the money from the coinbox?" These questions were interspersed with emotionally neutral questions ("Are you a college student?" "Do you have afternoon classes?") and emotionally toned questions unrelated to the crime ("Were you ever operated on for appendicitis?" "Is your draft status 1A?"). In this setup, the critical questions are easily recognized as such by innocent and guilty subjects alike, especially since the innocent subjects had been told that a theft of money from a coinbox was under investigation. The fact that analysis of records led to significantly more correct judgments than expected by chance suggests that lying as such *can* be detected, at least under some circumstances.

A final question on which more research is needed concerns the effectiveness of countermeasures that the subject may employ to escape detection. Results obtained to date are somewhat conflicting (70, 85). Although naïve persons would probably find it very difficult to "beat the test," with fuller understanding of lie detector principles and special training in countermeasures it may be possible for some individuals to control their physiological responses sufficiently to mislead the examiner. Such findings in turn may stimulate the development of more nearly "unbeatable" techniques.

***Stressful Interrogation.***   Unlike lie detectors, traditional procedures of interrogation in both civilian and military practice have relied upon some form of stress to elicit facts from an uncooperative witness. Both the kind and intensity of stress vary widely in different situations, as illustrated by cross-examination in courtroom procedure, the examination of witnesses by congressional investigating committees (35), "third-degree" interrogation in police investigations (79), and the questioning of prisoners of war (6, 11). In an extreme form, these stress techniques were illustrated by the so-called "brainwashing" of war prisoners by Chinese Communists during the Korean conflict. The brainwashing techniques employed to obtain false confessions and ideological conversions were similar to those used to elicit secret military information.

Stressful interrogation in any form presents many serious questions of ethics and legality. What the psychologist can contribute to the situation is some clarification of the nature of the stresses involved and their effects upon the individual. Together with psychiatrists, physiologists, and other biological scientists, psychologists have analyzed the problems of stressful interrogation in the light of available scientific knowledge (6, 11, 34, 48). To a limited extent, they have also investigated these problems more directly, as, for example, through interviewing and testing returned prisoners of war (see 6).

Although knowledge in this area is quite limited and many questions remain unanswered, there is general agreement on certain points. First, the techniques of brainwashing employed in the Korean conflict were not so novel, scientific, or mysterious as suggested by popular accounts. There is no evidence that these techniques were based on the systematic application of any specific psychological principles. The methods used did not differ fundamentally from those employed many centuries ago for coercion and persuasion. Debility, intellectual disorganization, and emotional disturbances can be induced by intense physical and psychological stresses, such as semistarvation, lack of sleep, illness, physical abuse, isolation, and sensory deprivation. Threats and acute physical discomfort eventually produce compliance in some persons.

Individuals differ in their responses to all these conditions. An important objective of psychological research was to identify the significant personal and background variables associated with such response differences, but the available data are meager. It does seem clear, however, that the disruptive effects of stress are augmented by suggestion and fear of the unknown. If the individual believes the interrogator has mysterious and powerful techniques for manipulating behavior, his resistance is further reduced. Understanding provides some measure of protection against these indirect effects of suggestion.

Still another point on which there is general agreement is that stress techniques may be so disruptive as to render the respondent incapable of accurate reporting. Drugs, excessive fatigue, severe nutritional deficiencies, infection, and other bodily disturbances may adversely affect cerebral functioning and thereby interfere with normal thought processes. Any drug that weakens the respondent's ability to withhold information, for example, is also likely to impair his ability to impart information. A victim of hallucinations is hardly a reliable informant. Even milder forms of stress, such as strong emotional excitement, may produce some confusion, loss of memory, and other thought disturbances. In these disruptive effects lies the major psychological weakness of stressful interrogation. It should be borne in mind, however, that this limitation applies chiefly to the use of stressful interrogation for fact-finding purposes rather than for propaganda, ideological conversions, false confessions, and other purposes for which it was employed in the Korean conflict.

## PSYCHOLOGICAL FACTORS IN DELINQUENCY AND CRIME

For nearly a century, anthropologists, sociologists, psychiatrists, psychologists, and other specialists have been studying the characteristics of delinquents and criminals in the effort to identify the causes of antisocial behavior (see 83; 138, chs. 8 and 9). Among the first to pursue such investigations was Lombroso (80, 81), a nineteenth-century Italian anthropologist who proposed that the criminal was a throwback to an earlier, more primitive stage of human evolution. In support of this doctrine, he gathered extensive data on physical anomalies, or "stigmata of degeneracy," that he observed in prison populations. Examples include prognathous jaw, receding chin, low forehead, flattened nose, facial asymmetry, deformities of teeth and palate, and malformations of the ears. This theory of a hereditary "criminal type" enjoyed considerable popularity until control observations revealed equal incidence of these physical defects among comparable non-criminal populations.

After the turn of the century, the emphasis shifted to mental deficiency as the major cause of crime (46, 47, 83, 128). This hypothesis was bolstered by investigations of such families as the Jukes and Kallikaks, which showed a high concentration of mental deficiency along with crime, delinquency, alcoholism, pauperism, and other social problems over many generations. Early interpretations of these familial studies stressed poor heredity, failing to take into account the extremely poor home and community environments in which each successive generation of children had been reared.

That intellectual defect cannot account for a large proportion of crimes was demonstrated by two extensive surveys of the intelligence test performance of men in state penitentiaries (100, 139). Conducted shortly after World War I, both studies found the distribution of Army Alpha scores of the penitentiary samples to be virtually identical with that of the total Army draft from the same states. As might be anticipated, there was a significant relation between intelligence and type of crime. Individuals committed for fraud obtained the highest mean scores, while those committed for sex crimes obtained the lowest. The proportion of all crimes that could be attributed to mental deficiency, however, was quite small.

Surveys of juvenile delinquents reveal a somewhat greater incidence of low intelligence. The proportion of mentally defective and borderline cases is appreciably larger than that in the general population, and the mean IQs center around 80. The deficiency is particularly apparent on verbal tests, which are highly correlated with school achievement. Several reasons have been suggested for the divergent findings regarding the intelligence of adult criminals and juvenile delinquents. The intellectually subnormal delinquent is more likely to be caught early in life, while the brighter delinquent escapes detection longer. When apprehended, mentally defective delinquents are usually sent to institutions for mental defectives, where they have no further opportunity to come into conflict with the law. Furthermore, the types of crimes committed by most juveniles are those that predominate among persons of low mental level, including physical assault, destruction of property, sex crimes, and a variety of minor offenses.

The relation between the juvenile delinquent's typical hostility toward school and his intellectual retardation is noteworthy. The intellectually backward child naturally experiences more failure and frustration in school. Such frustration tends to engender aggressive behavior. At the same time, the delinquent's antagonism toward authority and restrictions makes him a poor school learner and may in turn account for his retarded intellectual development. This is an example of the difficulty of unraveling cause-effect relations in delinquent careers.

Like intellectual defect, other pathological conditions undoubtedly account for *some* crimes, but their proportional contribution is small. A few crimes are committed by psychotics, as illustrated by the paranoid schizophrenic who shoots several strangers under the delusion that they are plotting his destruction. Similarly, the kleptomaniac, who steals articles for which he has no use, and the pyromaniac, who sets fires at random, are extreme examples of compulsive behavior. The psychopathic offender, who is impervious to socialization and unconcerned about the consequences of his actions, has been the subject of much controversy and is as yet little understood (138, ch. 12). The roles of sex perversions, drug addiction, and alcoholism in criminal behavior have been widely discussed (see, e.g., 32, chs. 9, 12, 13; 138, chs. 15–17). Certain forms of brain damage may lead to a characteristic syndrome of impulsivity and overactivity, as illustrated by delinquent children with a history of encephalitis lethargica. Although psychiatrists have written more extensively about these special types of criminal behavior, psychologists have been making increasing contributions through clinical studies and research.

Much of the research on causes and treatment of crime in general has been conducted by sociologists, although some of these investigations have dealt with distinctly psychological variables. An outstanding example is the continuing series of studies by the Gluecks (42–45), spanning a period of over thirty years. One part of this project involved periodic follow-ups of 500 youthful offenders committed to the Massachusetts Reformatory. Data were gathered retrospectively regarding their careers prior to and during incarceration, as well as directly through repeated follow-ups 5, 10, and 15 years after discharge. Among the objectives of this study was a comparison of the effectiveness of different types of penocorrectional treatments, such as probation and parole (43).

A major finding of the Glueck research pertains to the early home and community backgrounds of the offenders, which were characterized by many adverse social and psychological conditions. Parental education and socioeconomic level were typically low; economic dependency, overcrowding, and insanitary living conditions were common; and broken homes, parental neglect, and criminal influences were prevalent. These results are typical of those obtained in other studies of the early environments of delinquents. While recognizing the influence of such broad environmental factors, the Gluecks in their later work have tended to emphasize the individual's own personality traits as a major determinant of his behavior both before and after correctional treatment. An important influence contributing to the development of these traits is the nature of parent-child relations during early childhood. The role of these interpersonal factors was brought out in a later study by the Gluecks, in which 500 delinquent boys were compared with a non-delinquent group matched with them in age, general intelligence, national and ethnic origin, and residence in underprivileged neighborhoods (44). The investigators hoped thereby to help explain why some children turn to delinquency while others remain law-abiding even when reared in the same neighborhoods.

An even more direct approach to this question is provided by an earlier study by Healy and Bronner (52), in which extensive case-history data were gathered on 105 juvenile delinquents and on their non-delinquent siblings. The gross environmental variables characterizing the socioeconomic, cultural, and educational level of the family were thus automatically held constant. In comparison with their non-delinquent siblings, many more delinquent children showed strong dislike for school and for individual teachers. The delinquents manifested more discontent and emotional disturbance and more often reported feelings of rejection, insecurity, and inferiority. When non-delinquents experienced comparable emotional difficulties, there were usually counterbalancing satisfactions that made their situations more tolerable.

A limitation of most delinquency studies, even longitudinal studies such as those of the Gluecks, is that observations begin after the subjects are identified as delinquents. Retrospective studies of childhood experiences are always subject to error, even when skilled interviewers and caseworkers gather the data. Moreover, it is difficult to disentangle causal relations under these circumstances. If delinquents are backward in school, hostile toward authority, emotionally insecure, and so on, we cannot determine to what extent these reactions may result from the delinquent behavior itself, as well as from the experience of arrest and institutional commitment. One way to avoid this difficulty is to begin a longitudinal study *before* delinquent behavior occurs. This requires the gathering of data on a large sample of children, who are then followed up to see who becomes delinquent and who does not.

A few psychologists have followed this approach by surveying large samples of elementary and high school pupils by means of personality tests and rating scales, such as the Minnesota Multiphasic Personality Inventory (51; 138, ch. 10; 145), Haggerty-Olson-Wickman Behavior Rating Schedules (107, pp. 284–289), and other self-report inventories and rating scales (3). Similarly, first-

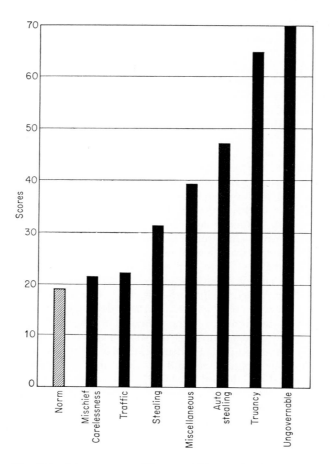

**Fig. 128**   Mean scores on Haggerty-Olson-Wickman Behavior Rating Schedules in relation to delinquency record within a six-year follow-up. (*From Olson, 107, p. 286.*)

grade public school boys in high-delinquency areas in New York City and Washington, D.C., were evaluated by use of one of the Glueck prediction tables, based on parent-child relationships (15, ch. 21; 41, pp. 1023–1051; 138, ch. 10). Despite the initial examination of large groups, the number of delinquents studied in these samples is too small to permit conclusive generalizations. Nevertheless all provide evidence that delinquency *can* be predicted from prior behavior, even as early as the first grade. Figure 128 illustrates results obtained with the Haggerty-Olson-Wickman Behavior Rating Schedules, used by teachers to report and rate the occurrence of behavior problems among schoolchildren (107, pp. 284–289). These scales were applied to approximately 3,000 children, about 1,500 of whom were in the first grade, while the remainder were enrolled in the eighth grade, junior high school, or special classes for the mentally retarded. After a lapse of six years, the names of the first- and eighth-grade children were checked against probation office and court records. The original mean problem-tendency scores of delinquents thus identified were compared with total group norms, with the results shown in Figure 128. Not only had the delinquents as a group manifested more behavior problems than did the children in general, but the mean problem-tendency score also rose with the severity of the offenses subsequently committed.

Another attempt to isolate causal factors is represented by a study of the child-rearing attitudes of mothers of delinquent and non-delinquent adolescents (92). Significant differences in the expected direction were found, although it is possible that some of these differences may represent parental reaction to earlier delinquent behavior on the part of the child. Mention should also be made of the Kvaraceus Delinquency Proneness Scale (72), which utilizes many items found to differentiate delinquent from non-delinquent groups, in the effort to detect tendencies toward delinquency in individuals. Under the innocuous title of KD Proneness Scale, this instrument presents 75 multiple-choice questions on preferences and attitudes to be filled out by the child. The same author prepared the KD Proneness Check List for use by teachers and other professional workers in rating a child with regard to both personal and environmental factors associated with delinquency (72).

In summary, it should be noted that current research on the causes of delinquency and crime has put increasing emphasis upon the individual's emotional, attitudinal, and motivational characteristics, as derived at least in part from childhood experiences. The most important single finding, however, is that crime and delinquency have, not one, but many causes. Causal factors vary among individual delinquents and criminals, a fact that strongly supports differential individual treatment. Even within a single individual, however, there is no single cause for antisocial behavior, but rather a pattern of interacting factors.

## THE PSYCHOLOGIST IN CORRECTIONAL SERVICES

At every stage in the treatment of delinquents and criminals, there is need for psychological services. Yet the utilization of such services has proceeded very slowly, and the number of psychologists so employed is still far below estimated requirements. The psychologist working in a correctional setting is typically a clinical or counseling psychologist with special experience in dealing with problems of delinquency and crime. In most situations, he functions as a member of a team which includes a psychiatrist and a social worker. In order to make effective recommendations, he needs to be familiar with penal institutions, social agencies, and other community facilities.

Psychologists may be employed on a full-time or part-time basis by courts, probation departments, parole boards, penitentiaries, reformatories, training schools for juvenile delinquents, or other penal and correctional institutions. They may also be called upon as consultants on individual cases when no psychological services are regularly available. In all these contexts, the principal activities of the psychologist consist in the application of the various clinical and counseling techniques discussed in Chapters 13 to 17. While the focus is still predominantly on diagnostic functions, therapeutic and research activities are slowly being introduced. Much of the work of psychologists in correctional settings is of an advisory nature. Thus the psychologist may provide facts and evaluations to aid a judge or a parole board in the disposition of an individual case. Or he may recommend a treatment program to be carried out by a social worker, teacher, probation officer, or other professional personnel. Although the functions of psychologists in different correctional settings have much in common, we shall examine the major features of psychological services in court systems, adult prisons, and institutions for juvenile delinquents.

*Court Psychologist.* Most court systems today have access to consultants in psychology and other relevant specialties, such as psychiatry, social work, and education (32, ch. 14; 138, ch. 11). The principal function of such specialists is to help in the understanding of the offender, so that the disposition of the case can be adapted to the characteristics of the individual as well as to the nature of the crime. Referrals for psychological evaluations of children and adults may be made prior to trial or prior to sentencing. Juvenile courts in large cities usually have their own behavior clinic, whose staff carries on these functions. Such clinics are also attached to some domestic relations courts and to a few criminal courts.

Like most clinical psychologists, court psychologists began as mental testers. Early court psychologists did little more than administer the Stanford-Binet or other intelligence tests to find the individual's "IQ." Slowly their functions have been broadening to cover a comprehensive diagnostic evaluation of the individual through a variety of testing and interviewing techniques. By these procedures, the court psychologist tries to identify the mentally defective, psychotic, brain-damaged, neurotic, or other pathological offender. He provides information regarding personal characteristics and background that helps to clarify the individual offender's motivations and attitudes and facilitates the prediction of his subsequent behavior. He also evaluates the individual's potential for education, vocational training, and job placement.

On the basis of his findings, the court psychologist may also make recommendations regarding disposition and treatment. In some court clinics, the psychologist does a limited amount of counseling and short-term psychotherapy. With children, the court clinic can serve a preventive function by prescribing remedial and therapeutic programs. Thus the youthful offender may be salvaged at an early stage without formal adjudication as a delinquent or institutional commitment. As in all clinical work with children, interviewing and counseling of parents and other significant adult associates are an integral part of the process. Remedial instruction, readjustments in school placement, recreational programs, foster home placement, and other types of environmental therapy may be arranged upon the psychologist's recommendation.

*Prison Psychologist.* Although the first organized psychological service in an American prison was established as early as 1919 (58), the number of psychologists so employed has been increasing at an incredibly slow rate. Recent estimates place the number of prison psychologists at about one for every three thousand prisoners (23; 32, p. 358). Moreover, the psychological training of those who do hold these positions is often quite inadequate. Among the major factors that have discouraged well-qualified clinical psychologists from working in such settings are poor cooperation from other institutional personnel and the difficulties of conducting psychological services in institutions not fundamentally oriented toward rehabilitation. Although there are outstanding exceptions, correctional institutions have been very slow in accepting a therapeutic point of view (23; 32, ch. 14; 138, ch. 13).

One of the chief functions of the prison psychologist is the evaluation of new admissions for purposes of classification. Diagnostic testing and interviewing for the assessment of intellectual and personality characteristics form a regular part of intake procedures. Since midcentury, however, there has been an increasing trend toward having such assessments conducted at a diagnostic center to which prisoners are sent prior to institutional assignment. Thus the choice of institution can be based in part upon the results of the diagnostic evaluation. A major purpose of classification is the assignment of the individual to appropriate work functions, educational programs, or vocational training within the institution. For this reason, the testing of adult prisoners puts considerable emphasis upon the measurement of vocational aptitudes, skills, and interests. In connection with the evaluation of parole candidates, the psychologist again conducts a comprehensive assessment of individuals with special reference to their readiness for community living and the prediction of subsequent behavior.

Prison psychologists also help in identifying individuals with severe psychopathology, who may need referral to special institutions, as well as those with milder disorders, who may be treated locally. Insofar as their work load permits it, prison psychologists carry on short-term individual or group psychotherapy with prisoners. Counseling is more generally practiced, with particular reference to vocational planning and to preparation for a return to the community, with its many adjustment problems. For the latter purpose, prison psychologists often employ group techniques, which may range from ordinary discussion meetings to psychodrama and other therapeutic methods. Psychologists may also participate in the planning and development of training programs for prisoners. In this connection reference may be made to the teaching-machine project initiated at the Draper Correctional Center, which was cited in Chapter 18 (89).

Persons committed to correctional institutions represent an excellent population for basic research on deviant behavior, as well as on other psychological problems. There are few other situations providing such large samples of adults whose time can be made available for research under controlled living conditions. Nevertheless, little basic psychological research has so far been conducted in these settings. Most of the research activities of psychologists have been limited to applied research designed to evaluate the predictive validity of diagnostic techniques or the effectiveness of rehabilitation procedures. For these purposes, follow-up studies are conducted in which psychologists usually collaborate with psychiatrists and social workers.

***The Psychologist in the Training School.***   Although the need for psychological services has been more widely recognized in institutions for juvenile delinquents than in institutions for adult prisoners, development of these services, too, has been slow. In a 1953 survey of public training schools for delinquent boys, only about one-half reported having one or more full-time psychologists on their staff; one-fifth employed no psychologists at all (123). Training standards were again low; and there were many unfilled positions.

The functions of the psychologist in the training school for juvenile delinquents are very similar to those of psychologists working in institutions for emotionally disturbed children (67; 138, ch. 14). In contrast to the work with adult prisoners, more emphasis is placed upon the diagnosis of personality difficulties. Although vocational training and counseling are an integral part of the rehabilitation program, more attention is given to psychotherapy than in adult programs. Play therapy and art therapy are especially applicable in such settings. Remedial educational programs are particularly important because of the juvenile delinquent's educational retardation and poor school adjustment. The psychologist may also make recommendations regarding milieu therapy, both with regard to total institutional organization and with regard to treatment of individual cases.

## THE PSYCHOLOGIST AS EXPERT WITNESS

As long ago as 1911, Judge Learned Hand wrote in one of his decisions:

> How long we shall continue to blunder along without the aid of unpartisan and authoritative scientific assistance in the administration of justice, no one knows; but all fair persons not conventionalized by provincial legal habits of mind ought, I should think, unite to effect some such advance (cited in 40, p. 685).

One of the means whereby scientific assistance may be made available to judges and juries is through the testimony of expert witnesses. In law, an expert in a given field is one who by virtue of his training and experience has "the power to draw inferences from the facts which a jury would not be competent to draw" (82, part I, p. 244).

Psychology is one of the most recent sciences to be recognized by the courts as providing such special training and experience. To be sure, individual psychologists have testified as experts since early in this century. This was particularly true in Germany, where such eminent psychologists as Karl Marbe, William Stern, and Kurt Bondy were called upon to testify on a variety of questions for which their training in experimental psychology qualified them (see 86, 131). Nevertheless, it is only since 1950 that psychologists have begun to make an appreciable contribution in this role. Within the decades of 1950 and 1960, American courts have been broadening and clarifying their practices regarding the admissibility of expert testimony by psychologists. In a number of cases in which psychological testimony was rejected by the trial judge, moreover, the decision was reversed by appelate courts (54, 86). These developments have been facilitated by certain advances within the profession of psychology itself, such as state certification and licensing of psychologists, specialty certification by the American Board of Examiners in Professional Psychology, standardization and evaluation of training programs, and formulation of a code of professional ethics (see Chapter 1).

In an increasing number of cases, psychologists have been appointed as expert witnesses in both Federal and state courts, either by the court itself or by the parties to the suit (82, 86). Psychologists have testified, in both civil and criminal cases, regarding many aspects of human behavior. Clinical psychologists have been called upon to assess intellectual and emotional conditions of children and adults in connection with commitment for mental deficiency or insanity, contested wills, adoption into foster homes, and determination of legal responsibility for criminal acts (see, e.g., 4, 54, 82, 86, 117, 125, 132, 141).

They have made similar contributions in accident cases where the extent of behavioral damage resulting from brain injury was to be ascertained (37, 86, 95).

Although clinical psychologists are the most likely to be called upon to testify, psychologists in other areas of specialization are also being utilized increasingly for such purposes. Consumer psychologists, for example, can be of service in cases involving trade-name and trademark infringement (see Chapter 12), misleading advertising, and other questions that pertain basically to consumer reactions or to public opinion (40; 77; 82, part I, pp. 258–272). For these purposes, relevant data can be gathered from a representative sample of the appropriate population and presented to the court with interpretations by the psychologist.

Experimental psychologists also have much to contribute, especially in the area of perception and memory. It was with perceptual and memory problems that some of the earliest court testimony by psychologists was concerned. A more recent illustration is provided by the case cited earlier in this chapter, in which a hunter was inadvertently shot by his companions (130). So far, however, the utilization of experimental psychologists as expert witnesses has been minimal. Mention should also be made of the testimony of social psychologists in connection with such matters as racial segregation, to be considered more fully in the next section (19–21, 66).

Testifying as expert witnesses is an activity in which most psychologists are still quite inexperienced. For this reason, several recent articles have set forth the pitfalls that may be encountered in such testimony (74, 87, 106, 114, 122). When the psychologist testifies for one side in a court trial, he must submit to cross-examination, in which he is called upon to defend not only the validity of his evidence but also his qualifications as an expert. This is true of any expert who testifies within the adversary system of court procedure, whatever his field of specialization. The psychologist, however, may encounter additional difficulties, arising from the lack of clarity that still characterizes the position of psychology among the learned professions and its relation to medicine.

If forewarned about these problems, the psychologist can of course function more effectively in his role as expert witness. In addition, certain impending modifications in legal procedure are designed to improve the conditions under which expert testimony is given. The Model Expert Testimony Act adopted by certain states enhances the objectivity and impartiality of the expert witness and removes him from the adversary process (144, p. 15). The act provides that each side pay one-half the fee of an expert acceptable to both and appointed by the court. Each party, moreover, is entitled to examine the expert's report in advance of the trial.

Still another way in which the expert witness may maintain his impartiality is to testify as *amicus curiae* (friend of the court). This procedure has been employed especially by groups or associations which are in a position to provide specialized information for the guidance of the court. The relevant facts and interpretations may be presented either orally, on the witness stand, or by filing a written *amicus curiae* brief. Since this practice has been followed particularly in test cases with relatively broad social implications, it will be illustrated more fully in the next section.

One recent example of the utilization of an *amicus curiae* brief, however, has a special bearing on the future role of psychologists as expert witnesses (54, 117). In a criminal case tried before the United States District Court for the District of Columbia, both psychologists and psychiatrists had testified regarding the mental condition of the defendant. At the conclusion of the trial, the judge instructed the jury to disregard the opinions of the psychologists, on the grounds that only medically trained experts are competent to give an opinion on such a question. Subsequently, in a 2:1 vote, the panel of the appellate court which heard the case held, among other things, that the trial judge had erred in excluding the expert testimony of the psychologists and ordered a rehearing *en banc* (before the full nine-man Court of Appeals). The rehearing was to be limited to the issue of "the ruling of the District Court which excluded from consideration by the jury the testimony of the psychologists concerning the existence and effects of the 'mental disease or defect'" (54, p. 627).

Because of the important implications of the ultimate decision, the American Psychological Association filed an *amicus curiae* brief explaining the training and experience of clinical psychologists and submitting that clinical psychologists are fully qualified to express expert opinion on such matters. The American Psychiatric Association filed a brief in support of the contrary argument. The final opinion of the United States Court of Appeals, handed down on June 7, 1962, sustained by a 7:2 vote the acceptibility of testimony by properly qualified psychologists in cases involving the determination and meaning of mental disease or defect as productive of criminal acts (54, p. 626). This decision should go far toward clarifying the functions of clinical psychologists as expert witnesses.

## PSYCHOLOGY IN THE DEVELOPMENT OF LAWS

Since by its very nature the law deals with human behavior, it appears obvious that psychology should have much to contribute to the formulation, revision, and interpretation of laws. Both among jurists themselves and among members of such professions as psychology, sociology, and psychiatry, there has been a steadily mounting discontent with the obsolete and prescientific concepts of human nature upon which many laws and legal practices are based.

Among the most notorious examples is the "McNaghten rule" for establishing legal sanity and criminal responsibility (15, ch. 17; 129; 138, ch. 7). Stemming from a decision handed down in the case of one Daniel McNaghten tried in a British court in 1843, this rule uses as a test of insanity the defendant's intellectual inability to differentiate between right and wrong. For over a hundred years, the McNaghten rule has been criticized as unrealistic by physicians, psychiatrists, and (more recently) psychologists. Actually this rule reflects the layman's misconception of the nature of insanity, rather than the accumulated scientific knowledge about the behavior of mentally disturbed persons. An insane person often knows that his act is wrong and forbidden by law; nevertheless he may commit it as a result of his mental disorder (129, p. 359).

Although the McNaghten rule is still widely applied in American courts, a few states have begun to replace it with more realistic practices. The trend of these innovations is in the direction of giving the expert witness more freedom in reporting on the defendant's mental condition and its relationship to his criminal act. Rather than forcing the professional expert to use concepts that fall outside his field and limiting him to a single "test of insanity," these practices permit him to utilize all the resources currently provided by his science.

There are many other areas of legal practice in which available psychological knowledge can make a substantial contribution. Among them may be mentioned laws pertaining to drug addiction, alcoholism, and sexual offenses (15, ch. 19; 32, chs. 12–13; 138, chs. 15–17). Other examples can be found in laws concerned with child development and educational matters (66) and laws dealing with civil rights and intergroup relations (111).

Granting that psychologists, along with members of other professions, ought to participate in the development of laws, we may next inquire through what channels they may do so. One approach is to assist the courts in their testing and interpretation of laws. As reported in the preceding section, a psychologist may submit relevant information, either as *amicus curiae* or as an expert witness for one of the parties to the suit. There has been an increasing tendency for courts to accept behavioral science data for consideration. One of the first instances of the extensive use of psychological data in a legal brief concerned the effects of bilingualism upon the educational development and adjustment of children (66). The case dealt with a 1943 statute prohibiting the teaching of foreign languages (i.e., other than English) to Hawaiian schoolchildren below the age of ten or before completion of the fourth grade. A survey of research on the intellectual and emotional effects of bilingualism led to the conclusion that bilingualism as such is not a handicap. Detrimental effects are attributable to improper ways of introducing the second language, poor teaching practices, and other concomitant circumstances that need not be associated with bilingualism. These findings were utilized by the lawyers in preparing an *amicus curiae* brief.

In a more recent series of cases dealing with racial discrimination in transportation, schooling, and other settings, social psychologists collaborated with other social scientists and with lawyers in the presentation of relevant data (19–21, 66). Psychological research bearing upon problems of racial segregation includes such varied topics as the test performance of different racial groups, the effect of cultural factors upon intellectual and personality development, the nature and origins of intergroup attitudes, the role of various factors in attitude change, and the effects of segregation upon the self concept and general psychological development of the individual (2, 20, 66). Particularly in cases dealing with educational segregation, psychologists have on several occasions testified as expert witnesses in state and Federal district courts. These cases culminated in the momentous decision of May 17, 1954, when the Supreme Court of the United States ruled that state laws requiring or permitting racial segregation in public education are unconstitutional. In support of its conclusion that "segregated educational facilities are inherently unequal," the Court cited materials that had been submitted by psychologists in an Appendix to the Appellants' Briefs (21, pp. 227–235).

Another major way in which psychologists can assist in the development of laws is by serving as consultants to special legislative committees concerned with the revision of laws. Both in America and elsewhere, such committees have been drawing more and more upon the advisory services of scientifically trained specialists, including psychologists (15, ch. 19; 74). In 1960, for example, the Interim Committee of the Oregon State Legislature on Revision of the Criminal Code invited representatives of the Oregon Psychological Association to attend one of its meetings and express their views on questions dealing with the McNaghten rule, the classification and treatment of prisoners (especially sex criminals), the advisability of pre-sentence investigations as aids to judges, and the role of psychology in determining whether or not a person is mentally ill (74). It might be added that, because of their concern with laws affecting the practice of psychology, state psychological associations have perforce learned a good deal about legislative machinery. These experiences should in turn help psychologists in making an effective contribution to the development of laws in general.

Psychologists may also contribute by collaborating in the research and teaching functions of law schools. As an example, mention may be made of the promising program on Law and the Behavioral Sciences, initiated in the mid-1950s at the University of Pennsylvania Law School.[3] Besides involving the participation of a psychologist in the teaching of law students, this program led to several joint reports and publications. The project has so far concentrated on summarizing and interpreting psychological knowledge pertaining to three areas in the law: evidence, criminal law, and family law. One publication, for example, provides a survey and critical evaluation of psychological studies relevant to certain aspects of censorship laws (17).

## PSYCHOLOGY IN NATIONAL AND INTERNATIONAL AFFAIRS

*Scope of Participation.* The preamble to the UNESCO Constitution declares that "since wars begin in the minds of men it is in the minds of men that the defenses of peace must be constructed" (147, p. 712). The conditions that precipitate wars and promote peace are undoubtedly numerous and complex. It would be a gross oversimplification to single out the psychological factors in the effort to explain and improve international relations. Nevertheless such factors do play a part, and their investigation should contribute toward an understanding of international problems. Psychologists may use their specialized techniques to study selected aspects of these problems, or they may collaborate with experts in political science, international law, and other relevant specialties in carrying out more comprehensive projects.

Although research oriented specifically toward international problems is of relatively recent origin, social psychologists have for some time recognized international relations as one of the many types of group relations falling within their special sphere of interest. Since 1936, the Society for the Psychological Study of Social Issues (SPSSI), a division of the American Psychological Association, has had a special committee concerned with problems of war and peace. In 1945, the same society sponsored the preparation of a volume devoted to the discussion of these problems (102). Because of the mounting international tensions and the threat of nuclear warfare, an increasing number of psychologists from different specialties are now becoming concerned with these problems.

[3] Personal communication from Dr. Julius Wishner, Dec. 10, 1962.

By the late 1950s, the participation of psychologists in this area had attained substantial proportions, with a broader base and a more systematic approach than had characterized it heretofore (118). A number of universities, both in this country and abroad, established interdisciplinary institutes for research on group relations and conflict resolution (105, pp. 89–90; 118, pp. 101–102). In 1957, *The Journal of Conflict Resolution* was founded by representatives of many social sciences, including psychologists. Colleges began to offer courses in the psychology of international relations (see, e.g., 25). *The Journal of Social Issues,* official organ of SPSSI, devoted an issue to "research approaches to the study of war and peace" (65) and another to "psychology and policy in a nuclear age" (120). Attempts to collate the rapidly growing literature in the field were made in the June, 1962, SPSSI *Newsletter* (28) and in a later book prepared under the auspices of this society (64). Several symposia in this area were held at meetings of the APA and at international congresses of psychology (105).

The spreading interest of psychologists in problems of international relations is illustrated by the establishment in 1960 of an APA Committee on Psychology in National and International Affairs and the appointment in 1962 of a full-time executive secretary of this committee, attached to the central office of the association (1). This committee has an active program under way, involving not only the coordination and facilitation of research by individual psychologists but also the establishment of contacts with government agencies and United Nations officials.

The types of contributions that psychologists can make in the area of international relations can be grouped roughly under four headings: (1) theoretical analysis of policy issues for their psychological components; (2) surveying and communicating available psychological findings on relevant topics; (3) research on problems pertaining more directly to national and international policies; and (4) application of current psychological knowledge to action programs (118; 119; 120, pp. 79–84).

**Psychological Analysis of Policy Issues.** Before the psychologist can make any contribution to international relations, he needs to analyze the issues for their psychological components and identify problems that are amenable to research. Such analyses are a necessary first step in any research program. Effective research cannot be done on anything as broad or abstract as war and peace. Not only must questions be formulated in specific terms, but the psychological aspects of the problems must also be separated from those falling in other areas.

Apart from facilitating research, such psychological analyses may serve other functions. An example is the identification of hidden assumptions about human nature that may be questionable or contrary to the trend of empirical data (127). Through teaching in political science departments, through nontechnical publications, and through personal consultations with policy makers, psychologists can engender a fuller awareness of the psychological implications of different courses of action. They can also encourage the substitution of empirically established facts about human behavior for unconfirmed assumptions and popular stereotypes.

In recent years, psychologists have published an increasing number of such theoretical analyses of international problems. Examples of the topics thus analyzed include: methods for resolving intergroup conflicts (14, 27, 62), psychological mechanisms underlying "cold-war mentality" (109, 110); and the potential psychological effects of a civilian defense program centered around fallout shelters (140). Such analyses can serve to clarify issues and to suggest questions for consideration. But it should be noted that they are better suited to raising questions than to answering them. In the field of international relations, there may have been too much "theorizing about theory," on the part of psychologists as well as other social scientists (126).

**Surveys of Available Research Findings.** A second way in which psychologists may contribute is by summarizing and integrating the research literature on relevant problems and making it available to policy makers. An example is the survey of research on tensions affecting international understanding, prepared by Klineberg (68) as part of a UNESCO project on this topic. In it are covered studies on national differences in personality, existing social stereotypes about such differences, the development and modification of attitudes, and factors making for aggression in interpersonal and intergroup behavior. A more intensive coverage of research pertaining to aggression is provided in more recent surveys devoted entirely to this topic (9, 90). Still another example is to be found in a symposium on human problems in the utilization of fallout shelters (5). Each participant in this symposium discussed implications of the available research on such related problems as submarine habitability, polar isolation, internment, isolated radar bases, and English World War II bomb shelters, as well as experimental studies of sensory deprivation (see Chapter 8).

**Research Approaches to International Problems.** The most direct contribution that psychologists can make is through research specifically designed within the framework of international problems. Both basic and applied research is needed on a wide variety of problems (62, 63, 69, 115). An example of applied research is the empirical evaluation of programs designed to improve international relations, such as student exchange, economic aid, technical assistance and education, international cultural programs, and the dissemination of information. So far little systematic information is available on the effectiveness of such programs or on the specific conditions and techniques that influence outcome, although a substantial beginning has been made in research with exchange students (22).

Research having both applied and basic implications is illustrated by field studies of intergroup hostility and conflict resolution, utilizing genuine but limited conflict situations. Intranational and factional strifes can be investigated through longitudinal field studies employing direct observation of events as well as interviews with representative samples. Examples of suitable situations include labor strikes, minority group conflicts, and intergroup clashes in countries that comprise distinct cultural subgroups (63, 69, 101, 115).

Cross-cultural attitude studies represent a third type of relevant research (59, 63, 69). Through interviews, questionnaires, and testing techniques, psychologists have investigated the images that persons have of their own nation and of other nations. Other studies have been concerned with the factors affecting national stereotypes and the conditions under which intergroup attitudes change. In one series of studies, psychologists and other social scientists in seven countries of western Europe collaborated in cross-cultural research on the response to threat (59, 121). Utilizing both opinion-survey and experimental techniques, the investigators followed the same procedures in each country in order to obtain directly comparable data.

From a different angle, field studies of human behavior in disaster situations also provide pertinent information (18, 104). Although concerned largely with such peacetime disasters as tornadoes, hurricanes, explosions, fires, and floods, this research has a direct bearing on the planning and implementation of civilian defense programs. A few experimental studies have also been conducted with subjects inhabiting simulated shelters for various periods of time (see 104). Of particular interest are three studies of responses to unanticipated air raid warnings which turned out to be false alarms (88). In each of the three localities, random samples of adults were interviewed to learn what the individual had done and felt upon hearing the warning siren. A comparison of responses in the three situations suggested certain conditions that increase the effectiveness of such warning systems.

A direct experimental approach to problems of intergroup frictions and conflict resolution is illustrated by a series of studies conducted by Sherif and his associates (see 91; 124, chs. 6 and 9). In these experiments, boys attending a specially organized summer camp underwent controlled experiences designed first to produce and later to eliminate intergroup hostility. The investigation was concerned with the conditions leading to the development of intergroup conflict; the effects of such conflicts on behavior, attitudes, and group stereotypes; and the relative effectiveness of different methods for restoring intergroup harmony. The most successful technique for overcoming hostility proved to be the introduction of a significant common goal (such as obtaining food when the food truck had broken down) that required the cooperative efforts of both groups. Participation in activities involving such "superordinate goals" tended to reduce intergroup tensions and eliminate unfavorable group stereotypes. The findings of such experiments are of course limited to the type of subjects and situations investigated. This kind of research needs to be repeated with many different groups varying in experiential backgrounds and personal characteristics, as well as with a wider variety of techniques for the reduction of intergroup tensions.

As a final example, we may consider simulation and gaming, which are being widely applied to the study of international relations (26, 29–31, 36, 49, 50, 71, 112). Diplomatical or political games are similar to the management games developed for use in management training programs (see Chapter 5). Both were antedated by military games. Game theory is a branch of decision theory in which there are two or more decision makers with typically conflicting interests. By means of mathematical models, rational solutions for such problems can be derived from the given properties of each situation. This approach has been used in the effort to develop a theory of political negotiations applicable to the type of decisions made in the Congress, the Department of State, the United Nations Security Council, and similar contexts (36, 71). It has also been applied to more specific problems, such as arms races and military deterrence (97). Of particular relevance is a series of coordinated research projects on psychological factors in strategic deterrence, conducted under the auspices of the Behavioral Sciences Group of the U.S. Naval Ordnance Test Station (53).

Simulation, it will be recalled, has been employed both in training (see

Chapter 5) and in research on man-machine systems (see Chapter 9). It involves essentially the presentation of a more or less realistic situation in a somewhat simplified and condensed form. Real subjects make the decisions on the basis of given facts, and the outcomes of these decisions are checked periodically. Simulation differs from the completely realistic situations illustrated by the previously cited Sherif experiment in that the subjects in simulation studies know they are playing roles. Typically, however, they become quite ego-involved in the game, a condition that is encouraged by the use of monetary and other kinds of rewards.

In a number of recent studies, simulation has been applied within the framework of game theory. In a continuing research program, Deutsch and his associates (26, 29, 30) have employed simulation in two-person games to study the development of trust and suspicion, behavior in interpersonal bargaining situations, and the influence of such factors as motivational orientation, the presence of threat, and different kinds of communication upon outcome. Typically, these experiments have employed "non-zero-sum games," in which both sides may gain or both may lose as a result of their combined decisions. Figure 129 illustrates the findings of one such experiment, in which the effects of threat and communication were explored. The "threat" consisted of the availability of a gate that could be closed by one participant, thereby preventing the other participant from using a road. It will be noted that the joint gain, or payoff, was highest under the condition of no threat and lowest under the condition of bilateral threat. Under the latter condition, moreover, communication had no significant effect.

Guetzkow (49, 50) describes the development and application of a political

*Fig. 129*   Mean joint payoff as a function of threat and communication. (*From Deutsch and Krauss, 30, p. 65.*)

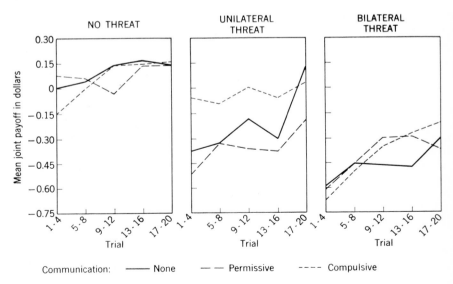

game in which each of several nations is represented by two or three persons playing specified roles. Working from given data about each nation, the subjects make a series of decisions regarding internal and external matters. Among the actions open to subjects are economic development, research programs, disarmament plans, foreign loans, alliances, and wars. Communications between nations are either written or tape-recorded, thus permitting later analyses. Known as the Inter-nation Simulation (INS), this situation has been employed for both teaching and research.

A methodologically sophisticated research project utilizing one form of Guetzkow's INS is reported by Driver (31). Its object was to investigate the effects of situational stress and of individual personality characteristics on the subjects' perception of the simulated nations. A total of 357 Middle Western high school students of both sexes participated in the different runs of the INS. Each run involved seven simulated nations, each manned by three subjects performing specified roles for a four-day period. The runs which eventuated in simulated wars were classified as providing intense stress. Peacetime runs were subdivided into the moderately stressful and the mildly stressful. The complexity of subjects' concepts of the simulated nations was evaluated in terms of differentiation, integration, and other attributes of the conceptual structure. It was pointed out that the more complex concepts permit a fuller and more balanced consideration of all relevant variables and hence facilitate effective decision making. As hypothesized, stress was found to have a curvilinear relation to the complexity of such concepts, the most complex concepts being found with intermediate degrees of stress. An independent measure of the generalized "cognitive complexity" of individual subjects was also significantly correlated with the complexity of their concepts of the simulated nations.

***Action Proposals.***   While many promising beginnings have been made in psychological research on problems of international relations, it is apparent that there is still a wide gap between such research and the solution of practical problems. Nevertheless, some psychologists, as well as other social scientists, have proposed action programs in the effort to apply what knowledge is available (see, e.g., 108, 120, 146). Although such recommendations are not based wholly upon experimentally verified facts, it is felt that the psychologist, as an expert on human behavior, has an obligation to contribute what he can to problems of such immediate urgency. Even in the absence of directly relevant data, it is argued, the informed opinion of a technically trained specialist on matters falling within his area of competence are bound to be more nearly correct than the opinions of laymen on the same matters.

When functioning in the capacity of an informed citizen, the psychologist must exercise special caution to avoid possible pitfalls (55, 119). First, he must bear in mind that the solution of complex international problems requires the collaboration of specialists in many fields. Within psychology itself, he must recognize the limits of his own competence. He must also carefully differentiate between opinions (however well informed) and facts, and he must make this distinction clear in communicating with others. Above all, it is important to separate personal beliefs and preferences from one's contribution as a scientist. To promote personal ideas under the guise of science would be both unethical and self-defeating. It is by retaining his scientific objectivity, his awareness of factors that may distort perceptions, and his research orientation toward human problems that the psychologist can make his most distinctive contribution as a psychologist. This is true in the field of international relations, as it is in every other field of applied psychology.

## SUMMARY

Although the practice of law is characteristically resistant to change, there is a growing recognition that psychology has much to offer to this field. The earliest applications of psychology to law were concerned with testimony and other courtroom procedures. Many of the findings of general experimental psychology are applicable to the evaluation of testimony. In addition, the conditions affecting the accuracy of observation and report have been investigated through Aussage tests and other controlled procedures. More recently, a limited amount of research has been conducted on the behavior of judges and juries. A major area of legal psychology is concerned with lie detection. The principal techniques explored for this purpose are free association and physiological indices of emotion, as illustrated by changes in respiration, blood pressure, and galvanic skin response. Psychologists have also given some attention to the nature and effects of certain traditional methods of stressful interrogation.

Together with members of several other professions, psychologists have investigated the characteristics of delinquents and criminals in the effort to identify the causes of antisocial behavior. Although the conditions that lead to crime are manifold, research findings have given increasing prominence to emotional and motivational factors, stemming at least in part from early childhood experiences. In the treatment of delinquents and criminals, psychological services are needed at every stage. But the number of psychologists employed in correctional services still falls far short of estimated requirements. The work of psychologists in court clinics, prisons, training schools for juvenile delinquents, and other penocorrectional institutions falls chiefly within the areas of clinical and counseling psychology. In all these settings, the emphasis is primarily on diagnostic functions, although increasing attention is being given to therapy and rehabilitation.

Since midcentury, psychologists have been called upon increasingly to testify as expert witnesses in court trials. Although clinical psychologists have most often functioned in this capacity, contributions have also been made by psychologists in other specialties, such as experimental, consumer, and social psychology. Psychologists may also aid in the development, revision, and interpretation of laws by submitting relevant research findings in court testimony, by serving as consultants to legislative committees, and by collaborating in law school teaching and research. Empirically established facts about human behavior are of basic importance in many types of laws, such as those pertaining to insanity, drug addiction, alcoholism, sexual offenses, child development and education, civil rights, and minority groups.

At a still broader level, psychologists are beginning to make contributions to national and international affairs. While recognizing that the prevention of wars and the solution of other complex international problems requires the collaborative efforts of specialists from many fields, psychologists can use their specialized knowledge, skills, and points of view to advance understanding of such problems. Their contributions include both the utilization of currently available psychological knowledge and the performance of specially designed research on many facets of international problems.

# REFERENCES

1. American Psychological Association, Committee on Psychology in National and International Affairs. Psychology in national and international affairs: A progress report. *Amer. Psychologist*, 1962, **17**, 50–52.
2. Anastasi, Anne. Psychological research and educational desegregation. *Thought*, 1960, **35**, 421–449.
3. Anderson, J. E., *et al. The prediction of adjustment over time.* Minneapolis: Univer. Minn. Press, 1961. (Inst. Child Develpm. Welf., Monogr. Ser., No. 23.)
4. Arbit, J. The psychologist as an expert witness: A case report and analysis of personal experiences previously reported in the American Psychologist. *Amer. Psychologist*, 1960, **15**, 721–724.
5. Baker, G. W., and Rohrer, J. H. (Eds.) Symposium on human problems in the utilization of fallout shelters. *Nat. Res. Coun. Publ. No.* 800, 1960. (Disaster Study No. 12.)
6. Bauer, R. A., and Schein, E. H. (Eds.) Brainwashing. *J. soc. Issues*, 1957, **13**, No. 3.
7. Benussi, V. Die Atmungssymptome in der Lüge. *Arch. ges. Psychol.*, 1914, **31**, 244–273.
8. Beran, W., *et al.* Jury behavior as a function of the prestige of the foreman and the nature of leadership. *J. publ. Law*, 1958, **7**, 419–449.
9. Berkowitz, L. *Aggression: A social psychological analysis.* New York: McGraw-Hill, 1962.
10. Berrien, F. K. Psychology and the court. In G. J. Dudycha *et al., Psychology for law enforcement officers.* Springfield, Ill.: Thomas, 1955. Ch. 8.
11. Biderman, A., and Zimmer, H. (Eds.) *The manipulation of human behavior.* New York: Wiley, 1961.
12. Binet, A. La science du témoignage. *Année psychol.*, 1905, **11**, 128–137.
13. Bingham, W. V., Moore, B. V., and Gustad, J. W. *How to interview.* (4th ed.) New York: Harper & Row, 1959.
14. Blake, R. R. Psychology and the crisis of statesmanship. *Amer. Psychologist*, 1959, **14**, 87–94.
15. Bloch, H. A. (Ed.) *Crime in America: Controversial issues in twentieth century criminology.* New York: Philos. Lib., 1961.
16. Burtt, H. E. *Legal psychology.* New York: Prentice-Hall, 1931.
17. Cairns, R. B., Paul, J. C. N., and Wishner, J. Sex censorship: The assumptions of anti-obscenity laws and the empirical evidence. *Minn. Law Rev.*, 1962, **46**, 1009–1041.
18. Chapman, D. W. (Ed.) Human behavior in disaster: A new field of social research. *J. soc. Issues*, 1954, **10**, No. 3.
19. Clark, K. B. Desegregation: An appraisal of the evidence. *J. soc. Issues*, 1953, **9**, No. 4.
20. Clark, K. B. The social scientist as an expert witness in civil rights litigation. *Soc. Probl.*, 1953, **1**, 5–10.
21. Clark, K. B. (Ed.) A symposium on desegregation in the public schools. *Soc. Probl.*, 1955, **2**, No. 4.
22. Coelho, G. V. (Ed.) Impacts of studying abroad. *J. soc. Issues*, 1962, **18**, No. 1.
23. Corsini, R. J., and Miller, G. A. Psychology in prisons, 1952. *Amer. Psychologist*, 1954, **9**, 184–185.
24. Davis, R. C. Physiological response as a means of evaluating information. In A. D. Biderman and H. Zimmer (Eds.), *The manipulation of human behavior.* New York: Wiley, 1961. Ch. 4.
25. deRivera, J. Teaching a course in the psychology of international relations. *Amer. Psychologist*, 1962, **17**, 695–699.
26. Deutsch, M. Trust and suspicion. *J. conflict Resolut.*, 1958, **2**, 265–279.

27. Deutsch, M. Psychological alternatives to war. *J. soc. Issues,* 1962, **18** (2), 97–119.
28. Deutsch, M., and Flacks, R. Psychologists and peace: II. Guide to sources of information. *SPSSI Newsletter,* June, 1962, pp. 4–6.
29. Deutsch, M., and Krauss, R. M. The effect of threat upon interpersonal bargaining. *J. abnorm. soc. Psychol.,* 1960, **61**, 181–189.
30. Deutsch, M., and Krauss, R. M. Studies of interpersonal bargaining. *J. conflict Resolut.,* 1962, **6**, 52–76.
31. Driver, M. J. Conceptual structure and group processes in an inter-nation simulation. *Educ. Test. Serv.,* RB-62-15, April, 1962. (Also unpublished doctoral dissertation, Princeton Univer., 1962.)
32. Dudycha, G. J., *et al. Psychology for law enforcement officers.* Springfield, Ill.: Thomas, 1955.
33. Ellson, D. G., *et al.* A report of research on detection of deception. *ONR Rep.,* 1952. (Contract N6 onr-18011, Office of Naval Research.)
34. Farber, I. E., Harlow, H. F., and West, L. J. Brainwashing, conditioning, and DDD. *Sociometry,* 1957, **20**, 271–285.
35. Fishman, J. A., and Morris, R. E. (Eds.) Witnesses and testimony at trials and hearings. *J. soc. Issues,* 1957, **13**, No. 2.
36. Flood, M. M. (Ed.) A symposium on game theory. *Behav. Sci.,* 1962, **7**, No. 1.
37. Frank, I. H. Psychological testimony in a courtroom. *Amer. Psychologist,* 1956, **11**, 50–51.
38. Frankel, E. The offender and the court: A statistical analysis of the sentencing of delinquents. *J. crim. Law Criminol.,* 1940, **31**, 448–456.
39. Gaudet, F. J., Harrick, G. F., and St. John, G. W. Individual differences in penitentiary sentences given by different judges. *J. appl. Psychol.,* 1934, **18**, 675–686.
40. Geiser, R. L., and Newman, R. W. Psychology and the legal process: Opinion polls as evidence. *Amer. Psychologist,* 1961, **16**, 685–690.
41. Glueck, S. (Ed.) *The problem of delinquency.* Boston: Houghton Mifflin, 1959.
42. Glueck, S., and Glueck, Eleanor. *500 criminal careers.* New York: Knopf, 1930.
43. Glueck, S., and Glueck, Eleanor. *Criminal careers in retrospect.* New York: Commonwealth Fund, 1943.
44. Glueck, S., and Glueck, Eleanor. *Unraveling juvenile delinquency.* New York: Commonwealth Fund, 1950.
45. Glueck, S., and Glueck, Eleanor. *Family environment and delinquency.* Boston: Houghton Mifflin, 1962.
46. Goddard, H. H. *The criminal imbecile.* New York: Macmillan, 1910.
47. Goring, C. *The English convict: A statistical study.* London: H.M. Stationery Office, 1913.
48. Gottschalk, L. A. The use of drugs in information-seeking interviews. In L. Uhr and J. G. Miller (Eds.), *Drugs and behavior.* New York: Wiley, 1960. Ch. 42.
49. Guetzkow, H. The use of simulation in the study of international relations. *Behav. Sci.,* 1959, **4**, 183–191.
50. Guetzkow, H., *et al. The use of simulation for teaching and research in international relations.* Englewood Cliffs, N.J.: Prentice-Hall, 1962.
51. Hathaway, S. R., and Monachesi, E. D. (Eds.) *Analyzing and predicting juvenile delinquency with the MMPI.* Minneapolis: Univer. Minn. Press, 1953.
52. Healy, W., and Bronner, Augusta F. *New light on delinquency and its treatment.* New Haven, Conn.: Yale Univer. Press, 1936.
53. Higgs, L. D., and Weinland, R. G. Project Michelson: Preliminary report, 1 February 1963. *Tech. Progr. Rep.* 309, NOTS TP 3154, March 1963.
54. Hoch, E. L., and Darley, J. G. A case at law. *Amer. Psychologist,* 1962, **17**, 623–654.
55. Holt, R. R., and Proshansky, H. Roles for psychologists in promoting peace. *SPSSI Newsletter,* June, 1962, pp. 1–4.
56. Hovland, C. I. Reconciling conflicting results derived from experimental and survey studies of attitude change. *Amer. Psychologist,* 1959, **14**, 8–17.
57. Hovland, C. I. (Ed.) *The order of presentation in persuasion.* (Yale Studies in Attitude and Communication, vol. 1.) New Haven, Conn.: Yale Univer. Press, 1957.

58. Jackson, J. D. *Prisons and penitentiaries.* In D. H. Fryer and E. R. Henry (Eds.), *Handbook of applied psychology.* New York: Holt, Rinehart and Winston, 1950. Vol. 2, pp. 573–581.
59. Jacobson, E., and Schachter, S. (Eds.) Cross-national research: A case study. *J. soc. Issues,* 1954, **10**, No. 4.
60. James, Rita M. Jurors' assessment of criminal responsibility. *Soc. Probl.,* 1959, **7**, 58–69.
61. James, Rita M. Status and competence of jurors. *Amer. J. Sociol.,* 1959, **64**, 563–570.
62. Janis, I. L., and Katz, D. The reduction of intergroup hostility: Research problems and hypotheses. *J. conflict Resolut.,* 1959, **3**, 85–100.
63. Katz, D. Current and needed psychological research in international relations. *J. soc. Issues,* 1961, **17** (3), 69–78.
64. Kelman, H. C. (Ed.) *International behavior: A social psychological analysis.* New York: Holt, Rinehart and Winston, 1965.
65. Kelman, H. C., Barth, W., and Hefner, R. (Eds.) Research approaches to the study of war and peace. *J. soc. Issues,* 1955, **11**, No. 1.
66. Kendler, Tracy S. Contributions of the psychologist to constitutional law. *Amer. Psychologist,* 1950, **5**, 505–510.
67. Klebanoff, S. G. Psychologists in institutions. In W. B. Webb (Ed.), *The profession of psychology.* New York: Holt, Rinehart and Winston, 1962. Ch. 6.
68. Klineberg, O. *Tensions affecting international understanding.* New York: Soc. Sci. Res. Coun., 1950. (SSRC Bull. No. 62.)
69. Klineberg, O. The role of the psychologist in international affairs. *J. soc. Issues, Suppl. Ser.,* 1956, No. 9, pp. 1–18.
70. Kubis, J. F. Studies in lie detection: Computer feasibility considerations. *U.S. Air Force, RADC-TR* 62–205, 1962.
71. Kuhn, H. W. (Ed.) Game theory, bargaining, and international relations. *J. conflict Resolut.,* 1962, **6**, No. 1.
72. Kvaraceus, W. C. *KD Proneness Scale and Check List: Manual of directions (revised).* New York: Harcourt, Brace & World, 1953.
73. Lacey, J. I., and Lacey, Beatrice C. Verification and extension of the principle of autonomic response stereotypy. *Amer. J. Psychol.,* 1958, **71**, 50–73.
74. Langhorne, M. C., and Hoch, E. L. Psychology in the states. *Amer. Psychologist,* 1960, **15**, 632–634.
75. Larson, J. A. The cardio-pneumo-psychogram. *J. exp. Psychol.,* 1922, **5**, 323–328.
76. Larson, J. A. *Lying and its detection.* Chicago: Univer. Chicago Press, 1932.
77. Legal status of advertising and marketing psychology experts. *J. appl. Psychol.,* 1954, **38**, 276–277.
78. Leonard, V. A. (Ed.) *Academy lectures on lie detection.* Vols. 1 and 2. Springfield, Ill.: Thomas, 1957.
79. Lindsley, D. B. The psychology of lie detection. In G. J. Dudycha *et al., Psychology for law enforcement officers.* Springfield, Ill.: Thomas, 1955. Ch. 4.
80. Lombroso, C. *Crime: Its causes and remedies.* Boston: Little, 1911.
81. Lombroso, C. *Criminal man.* New York: Putnam, 1911. (1st Italian ed., 1876.)
82. Louisell, D. W. The psychologist in today's legal world. Parts I and II. *Minn. Law Rev.,* 1955, **39**, 235–272; 1957, **41**, 731–750.
83. Lowrey, L. G. Delinquent and criminal personalities. In J. McV. Hunt (Ed.), *Personality and the behavior disorders.* New York: Ronald, 1944. Vol. 2, Ch. 26.
84. Lykken, D. T. The GSR in the detection of guilt. *J. appl. Psychol.,* 1959, **43**, 385–388.
85. Lykken, D. T. The validity of the guilty knowledge technique: The effects of faking. *J. appl. Psychol.,* 1960, **44**, 258–262.
86. McCary, J. L. The psychologist as an expert witness in court. *Amer. Psychologist,* 1956, **11**, 8–13.
87. McCary, J. L. A psychologist testifies in court. *Amer. Psychologist,* 1960, **15**, 53–57.
88. Mack, R. W., and Baker, G. W. The occasion instant: The structure of social responses to unanticipated air raid warnings. *Nat. Res. Coun. Publ. No. 945,* 1961. (Disaster Study No. 15.)
89. McKee, J. M., and Watkins, J. C. A self-instructional program for youthful offenders. Unpubl. Rep., Draper Correctional Center, Elmore, Ala., May, 1962.

90. McNeil, E. B. Psychology and aggression. *J. conflict Resolut.*, 1959, **3**, 195–293.
91. McNeil, E. B. Waging experimental war: A review. *J. conflict Resolut.*, 1962, **6**, 78–81.
92. Madoff, J. M. The attitudes of mothers of juvenile delinquents toward child rearing. *J. consult. Psychol.*, 1959, **23**, 518–520.
93. Marston, W. M. Systolic blood pressure changes in deception. *J. exp. Psychol.*, 1917, **2**, 117–163.
94. Marston, W. M. *The lie detector.* New York: Smith, 1938.
95. May, R. A psychologist as a legal witness. *Amer. Psychologist*, 1956, **11**, 50.
96. Mensh, I. N. Psychology and other professions. In W. B. Webb (Ed.), *The profession of psychology.* New York: Holt, Rinehart and Winston, 1962. Ch. 11.
97. Milburn, T. W. The concept of deterrence: Some logical and psychological considerations. *J. soc. Issues*, 1961, **17** (3), 3–11.
98. Miller, N., and Campbell, D. T. Recency and primacy in persuasion as a function of the timing of speeches and measurements. *J. abnorm. soc. Psychol.*, 1959, **59**, 1–9.
99. Münsterberg, H. *On the witness stand.* New York: McClure, 1908.
100. Murchison, C. *Criminal intelligence.* Worcester, Mass.: Clark Univer. Press, 1926.
101. Murphy, G. *In the minds of men.* New York: Basic Books, 1953.
102. Murphy, G. (Ed.) *Human nature and enduring peace.* Boston: Houghton Mifflin, 1945.
103. Muscio, B. The influence of the form of the question. *Brit. J. Psychol.*, 1915, **8**, 351–389.
104. National Academy of Sciences–National Research Council: Disaster Research Group. Field studies of disaster behavior: An inventory. *Nat. Res. Coun. Publ. No. 886*, 1961. (Disaster Study No. 14.)
105. Nielsen, G. S. (Ed.) *Psychology and international affairs: Can we contribute?* Copenhagen: Munksgaard, 1962. (Proc. 14th int. Congr. appl. Psychol., vol. 1.)
106. Olinger, L. B. The psychodiagnostician as expert witness. *J. proj. Tech.*, 1961, **25**, 81–86.
107. Olson, W. C. *Child development.* (2nd ed.) Boston: Heath, 1959.
108. Osgood, C. E. Suggestions for winning the real war with communism. *J. conflict Resolut.*, 1959, **3**, 295–325.
109. Osgood, C. E. An analysis of the cold war mentality. *J. soc. Issues*, 1961, **17** (3), 12–19.
110. Osgood, C. E. Toward international behavior appropriate to a nuclear age. In G. S. Nielsen (Ed.), *Psychology and international affairs: Can we contribute?* Copenhagen: Munksgaard, 1962. Pp. 109–132.
111. Pettigrew, T. F. Social psychology and desegregation research. *Amer. Psychologist*, 1961, **16**, 105–112.
112. Rapaport, A. Experimental games: A review. *Behav. Sci.*, 1962, **7**, 1–37.
113. Redmount, R. S. The psychological basis of evidence practices: Memory. *J. crim. Law Criminol. police Sci.*, 1959, **50**, 249–264.
114. Rice, G. P. The psychologist as expert witness. *Amer. Psychologist*, 1961, **16**, 691–692.
115. Rinde, E., and Rokkan, S. Toward an international program of research on handling of conflicts: Introduction. *J. conflict Resolut.*, 1959, **3**, 1–5.
116. Robinson, E. S. *Law and the lawyers.* New York: Macmillan, 1935.
117. Rodnick, E. H., and Hoch, E. L. . . . and justice for all. *Amer. Psychologist*, 1961, **16**, 718–719.
118. Russell, R. W. Roles for psychologists in the "maintenance of peace." *Amer. Psychologist*, 1960, **15**, 95–109.
119. Russell, R. W. Can psychologists contribute? In G. S. Nielsen (Ed.), *Psychology and international affairs: Can we contribute?* Copenhagen: Munksgaard, 1962. Pp. 48–58.
120. Russell, R. W. (Ed.) Psychology and policy in a nuclear age. *J. soc. Issues*, 1961, **17**, No. 3.
121. Schachter, S., *et al.* Cross-cultural experiments on threat and rejection. *Hum. Relat.*, 1954, **7**, 403–440.
122. Schofield, W. Psychology, law, and the expert witness. *Amer. Psychologist*, 1956, **11**, 1–7.

123. Shelley, E. L. V. Psychological services in state schools for delinquent boys. *Amer. Psychologist,* 1954, **9**, 186–187.
124. Sherif, M., and Sherif, Carolyn W. *An outline of social psychology.* (Rev. ed.) New York: Harper & Row, 1956.
125. Shoben, E. J., Jr. Psychologists and legality: A case report. *Amer. Psychologist,* 1950, **5**, 496–498.
126. Singer, J. D. Theorizing about theory in international politics. *J. conflict Resolut.,* 1960, **4**, 431–442.
127. Singer, J. D. The relevance of the behavioral sciences to the study of international relations. *Behav. Sci.,* 1961, **6**, 324–335.
128. Smith, J. O. Criminality and mental retardation. *Tr. Sch. Bull.,* 1962, **59**, 74–80.
129. Sobeloff, S. E. From McNaghten to Durham and beyond. *Psychiat. Quart.,* 1955, **29**, 357–371.
130. Sommer, R. The new look on the witness stand. *Canad. Psychologist,* 1959, **8** (4), 94–100.
131. Stern, W. The psychology of testimony. *J. abnorm. soc. Psychol.,* 1939, **34**, 3–20.
132. Stopol, M. S. A recent court experience. *Amer. Psychologist,* 1957, **12**, 42–43.
133. Strodtbeck, F. L., James, Rita M., and Hawkins, C. Social status in jury deliberations. *Amer. sociol. Rev.,* 1957, **22**, 713–719.
134. Strodtbeck, F. L., and Mann, R. D. Sex role differentiation in jury deliberations. *Sociometry,* 1956, **19**, 3–11.
135. Summers, W. G. A new psychogalvanometric technique in criminal investigation. *Psychol. Bull.,* 1937, **34**, 551–552.
136. Summers, W. G. Science can get the confession. *Fordham Law Rev.,* 1939, **8**, 334–354.
137. Thurstone, L. L., and Degan, J. W. A factorial study of the Supreme Court. *Psychometr. Lab., Univer. Chicago,* No. 64, 1951. (Also publ. in Proc. Nat. Acad. Sci., 1951, **37**, 628–635.)
138. Toch, H. (Ed.) *Legal and criminal psychology.* New York: Holt, Rinehart and Winston, 1961.
139. Tulchin, S. H. *Intelligence and crime.* Chicago: Univer. Chicago Press, 1939.
140. Waskow, A. I. (Ed.) *The shelter-centered society.* Washington: Peace Res. Inst., 1962.
141. Weitz, R. D. An expert witness. *Amer. Psychologist,* 1957, **12**, 42.
142. Weld, H. P. Legal psychology: The psychology of testimony. In F. L. Marcuse (Ed.), *Areas of psychology.* New York: Harper & Row, 1954. Pp. 119–147.
143. Weld, H. P., and Roff, M. A study of the formation of opinion based upon legal evidence. *Amer. J. Psychol.,* 1938, **51**, 609–628.
144. Wicker, W., Cureton, E. E., and Trovillo, P. V. The polygraphic truth test: A symposium. *Tenn. Law Rev.,* February, 1953, **22**, 1–64.
145. Wirt, R. D., and Briggs, P. F. Personality and environmental factors in the development of delinquency. *Psychol. Monogr.,* 1959, **73**, No. 15.
146. Wright, Q., Evan, W. M., and Deutsch, M. (Eds.) *Preventing World War III: Some proposals.* New York: Simon and Schuster, 1962.
147. *Yearbook of the United Nations,* 1946–47. New York: United Nations, 1947.

*Appendixes*

# APPENDIX A
# DIVISIONS OF THE AMERICAN
# PSYCHOLOGICAL ASSOCIATION*

1. Division of General Psychology
2. Division on the Teaching of Psychology
3. Division of Experimental Psychology
5. Division of Evaluation and Measurement
6. Division of Physiological and Comparative Psychology
7. Division on Developmental Psychology
8. Division of Personality and Social Psychology
9. The Society for the Psychological Study of Social Issues—a Division of the APA
10. Division of Psychology and the Arts
12. Division of Clinical Psychology
13. Division of Consulting Psychology
14. Division of Industrial Psychology
15. Division of Educational Psychology
16. Division of School Psychologists
17. Division of Counseling Psychology
18. Division of Psychologists in Public Service
19. Division of Military Psychology
20. Division on Maturity and Old Age
21. The Society of Engineering Psychologists—a Division of the APA
22. Division on Psychological Aspects of Disability
23. Division of Consumer Psychology
24. Division of Philosophical Psychology
25. Division for the Experimental Analysis of Behavior
26. Division of the History of Psychology

Total membership in 1966: 24,473

* Owing to reorganizations and other changes made since the introduction of a divisional structure in the APA, there are currently no divisions numbered 4 or 11.

# APPENDIX B
# MAJOR DIRECTORIES OF PSYCHOLOGISTS

Directories are published by the following organizations:

American Psychological Association, Inc.
1200 Seventeenth Street, N.W.
Washington, D.C.   20036

*Directory* lists all members of the American Psychological Association alphabetically, geographically, and by divisional affiliation. It provides personal data such as current address, education, occupational history, present occupation, fields of special interest, certification, diplomate status, etc.

American Board of Examiners in Professional Psychology, Inc.
Dr. Noble Kelley, Secretary
Southern Illinois University
Carbondale, Illinois

*Directory* lists all diplomates in clinical, counseling, and industrial psychology, together with personal data.

State Directories

By 1965, the following states had enacted legislation regarding the certification or licensing of psychologists:

| | |
|---|---|
| Alabama | Michigan |
| Arizona | Minnesota |
| Arkansas | Nevada |
| California | New Hampshire |
| Colorado | New Mexico |
| Connecticut | New York |
| Delaware | Oklahoma |
| Florida | Oregon |
| Georgia | Tennessee |
| Idaho | Utah |
| Illinois | Virginia |
| Kentucky | Washington |
| Louisiana | Wyoming |
| Maine | Canadian Provinces of Alberta, |
| Maryland | Quebec, Ontario, and Saskatchewan |

In such states, lists of certified psychologists may be obtained by writing to the appropriate agency within the state government. Information may be obtained from the local public library or from any university psychology department within the state.

Many state psychological associations also publish lists of their members, with information regarding their qualifications.

# APPENDIX C
## ETHICAL STANDARDS OF PSYCHOLOGISTS*

The psychologist believes in the dignity and worth of the individual human being. He is committed to increasing man's understanding of himself and others. While pursuing this endeavor, he protects the welfare of any person who may seek his service or of any subject, human or animal, that may be the object of his study. He does not use his professional position or relationships, nor does he knowingly permit his own services to be used by others, for purposes inconsistent with these values. While demanding for himself freedom of inquiry and communication, he accepts the responsibility this freedom confers: for competence where he claims it, for objectivity in the report of his findings, and for consideration of the best interests of his colleagues and of society.

### Specific Principles

*Principle 1. Responsibility.* The psychologist,† committed to increasing man's understanding of man, places high value on objectivity and integrity, and maintains the highest standards in the services he offers.

a. As a scientist, the psychologist believes that society will be best served when he investigates where his judgment indicates investigation is needed; he plans his research in such a way as to minimize the possibility that his findings will be misleading; and he publishes full reports of his work, never discarding without explanation data which may modify the interpretation of results.

b. As a teacher, the psychologist recognizes his primary obligation to help others acquire knowledge and skill, and to maintain high standards of scholarship.

c. As a practitioner, the psychologist knows that he bears a heavy social responsibility because his work may touch intimately the lives of others.

*Principle 2. Competence.* The maintenance of high standards of professional competence is a responsibility shared by all psychologists, in the interest of the public and of the profession as a whole.

a. Psychologists discourage the practice of psychology by unqualified persons and assist the public in identifying psychologists competent to give dependable professional service. When a psychologist or a person identifying himself as a psychologist violates ethical standards, psychologists who know firsthand of such activities attempt to rectify the situation. When such a situation cannot be dealt with informally, it is called to the attention of the appropriate local, state, or national committee on professional ethics, standards, and practices.

b. The psychologist recognizes the boundaries of his competence and the limitations of his techniques and does not offer services or use techniques that fail to meet professional standards established in particular fields. The psychologist who engages in practice assists his client in obtaining professional help for all important aspects of his problem that fall outside the boundaries of his own competence. This principle requires, for example, that provision be made for the diagnosis and treatment of relevant medical problems and for referral to or consultation with other specialists.

c. The psychologist in clinical work recognizes that his effectiveness depends in

---

* From *Amer. Psychologist*, 1963, **18**, 56–60.

† A student of psychology who assumes the role of psychologist shall be considered a psychologist for the purpose of this code of ethics.

good part upon his ability to maintain sound interpersonal relations, that temporary or more enduring aberrations in his own personality may interfere with this ability or distort his appraisals of others. Therefore he refrains from undertaking any activity in which his personal problems are likely to result in inferior professional services or harm to a client; or, if he is already engaged in such an activity when he becomes aware of his personal problems, he seeks competent professional assistance to determine whether he should continue or terminate his services to his client.

*Principle 3. Moral and Legal Standards.* The psychologist in the practice of his profession shows sensible regard for the social codes and moral expectations of the community in which he works, recognizing that violations of accepted moral and legal standards on his part may involve his clients, students, or colleagues in damaging personal conflicts, and impugn his own name and the reputation of his profession.

*Principle 4. Misrepresentation.* The psychologist avoids misrepresentation of his own professional qualifications, affiliations, and purposes, and those of the institutions and organizations with which he is associated.

a. A psychologist does not claim either directly or by implication professional qualifications that differ from his actual qualifications, nor does he misrepresent his affiliation with any institution, organization, or individual, nor lead others to assume he has affiliations that he does not have. The psychologist is responsible for correcting others who misrepresent his professional qualifications or affiliations.
b. The psychologist does not misrepresent an institution or organization with which he is affiliated by ascribing to it characteristics that it does not have.
c. A psychologist does not use his affiliation with the American Psychological Association or its Divisions for purposes that are not consonant with the stated purposes of the Association.
d. A psychologist does not associate himself with or permit his name to be used in connection with any services or products in such a way as to misrepresent them, the degree of his responsibility for them, or the nature of his affiliation.

*Principle 5. Public Statements.* Modesty, scientific caution, and due regard for the limits of present knowledge characterize all statements of psychologists who supply information to the public, either directly or indirectly.

a. Psychologists who interpret the science of psychology or the services of psychologists to clients or to the general public have an obligation to report fairly and accurately. Exaggeration, sensationalism, superficiality, and other kinds of misrepresentation are avoided.
b. When information about psychological procedures and techniques is given, care is taken to indicate that they should be used only by persons adequately trained in their use.
c. A psychologist who engages in radio or television activities does not participate in commercial announcements recommending purchase or use of a product.

*Principle 6. Confidentiality.* Safeguarding information about an individual that has been obtained by the psychologist in the course of his teaching, practice, or investigation is a primary obligation of the psychologist. Such information is not communicated to others unless certain important conditions are met.

   a. Information received in confidence is revealed only after most careful deliberation and when there is clear and imminent danger to an individual or to society, and then only to appropriate professional workers or public authorities.

   b. Information obtained in clinical or consulting relationships, or evaluative data concerning children, students, employees, and others are discussed only for professional purposes and only with persons clearly concerned with the case. Written and oral reports should present only data germane to the purposes of the evaluation; every effort should be made to avoid undue invasion of privacy.

   c. Clinical and other case materials are used in classroom teaching and writing only when the identity of the persons involved is adequately disguised.

   d. The confidentiality of professional communications about individuals is maintained. Only when the originator and other persons involved give their express permission is a confidential professional communication shown to the individual concerned. The psychologist is responsible for informing the client of the limits of the confidentiality.

   e. Only after explicit permission has been granted is the identity of research subjects published. When data have been published without permission for identification, the psychologist assumes responsibility for adequately disguising their sources.

   f. The psychologist makes provision for the maintenance of confidentiality in the preservation and ultimate disposition of confidential records.

*Principle 7. Client Welfare.* The psychologist respects the integrity and protects the welfare of the person or group with whom he is working.

   a. The psychologist in industry, education, and other situations in which conflicts of interest may arise among various parties, as between management and labor, or between the client and employer of the psychologist, defines for himself the nature and direction of his loyalties and responsibilities and keeps all parties concerned informed of these commitments.

   b. When there is a conflict among professional workers, the psychologist is concerned primarily with the welfare of any client involved and only secondarily with the interest of his own professional group.

   c. The psychologist attempts to terminate a clinical or consulting relationship when it is reasonably clear to the psychologist that the client is not benefiting from it.

   d. The psychologist who asks that an individual reveal personal information in the course of interviewing, testing, or evaluation, or who allows such information to be divulged to him, does so only after making certain that the responsible person is fully aware of the purposes of the interview, testing, or evaluation and of the ways in which the information may be used.

   e. In cases involving referral, the responsibility of the psychologist for the welfare of the client continues until this responsibility is assumed by the professional person to whom the client is referred or until the relationship with the psychologist making the referral has been terminated by mutual agreement. In situations where referral, consultation, or other changes in the conditions of the treatment are indicated and the client refuses referral, the psychologist carefully weighs the possible harm to the client, to himself, and to his profession that might ensue from continuing the relationship.

   f. The psychologist who requires the taking of psychological tests for didactic, classification, or research purposes protects the examinees by insuring that the tests and test results are used in a professional manner.

   g. When potentially disturbing subject matter is presented to students, it is discussed objectively, and efforts are made to handle constructively any difficulties that arise.

h. Care must be taken to insure an appropriate setting for clinical work to protect both client and psychologist from actual or imputed harm and the profession from censure.

*Principle 8. Client Relationship.* The psychologist informs his prospective client of the important aspects of the potential relationship that might affect the client's decision to enter the relationship.

a. Aspects of the relationship likely to affect the client's decision include the recording of an interview, the use of interview material for training purposes, and observation of an interview by other persons.
b. When the client is not competent to evaluate the situation (as in the case of a child), the person responsible for the client is informed of the circumstances which may influence the relationship.
c. The psychologist does not normally enter into a professional relationship with members of his own family, intimate friends, close associates, or others whose welfare might be jeopardized by such a dual relationship.

*Principle 9. Impersonal Services.* Psychological services for the purpose of diagnosis, treatment, or personalized advice are provided only in the context of a professional relationship, and are not given by means of public lectures or demonstrations, newspaper or magazine articles, radio or television programs, mail, or similar media.

a. The preparation of personnel reports and recommendations based on test data secured solely by mail is unethical unless such appraisals are an integral part of a continuing client relationship with a company, as a result of which the consulting psychologist has intimate knowledge of the client's personnel situation and can be assured thereby that his written appraisals will be adequate to the purpose and will be properly interpreted by the client. These reports must not be embellished with such detailed analyses of the subject's personality traits as would be appropriate only after intensive interviews with the subject. The reports must not make specific recommendations as to employment or placement of the subject which go beyond the psychologist's knowledge of the job requirements of the company. The reports must not purport to eliminate the company's need to carry on such other regular employment or personnel practices as appraisal of the work history, checking of references, and past performance in the company.

*Principle 10. Announcement of Services.* A psychologist adheres to professional rather than commercial standards in making known his availability for professional services.

a. A psychologist does not directly solicit clients for individual diagnosis or therapy.
b. Individual listings in telephone directories are limited to name, highest relevant degree, certification status, address, and telephone number. They may also include identification in a few words of the psychologist's major areas of practice; for example, child therapy, personnel selection, industrial psychology. Agency listings are equally modest.
c. Announcements of individual private practice are limited to a simple statement of the name, highest relevant degree, certification or diplomate status, address, telephone number, office hours, and a brief explanation of the types of services rendered. Announcements of agencies may list names of staff members with their qualifications. They conform in other particulars with the same standards

as individual announcements, making certain that the true nature of the organization is apparent.

d. A psychologist or agency announcing nonclinical professional services may use brochures that are descriptive of services rendered but not evaluative. They may be sent to professional persons, schools, business firms, government agencies, and other similar organizations.

e. The use in a brochure of "testimonials from satisfied users" is unacceptable. The offer of a free trial of services is unacceptable if it operates to misrepresent in any way the nature or the efficacy of the services rendered by the psychologist. Claims that a psychologist has unique skills or unique devices not available to others in the profession are made only if the special efficacy of these unique skills or devices has been demonstrated by scientifically acceptable evidence.

f. The psychologist must not encourage (nor, within his power, even allow) a client to have exaggerated ideas as to the efficacy of services rendered. Claims made to clients about the efficacy of his services must not go beyond those which the psychologist would be willing to subject to professional scrutiny through publishing his results and his claims in a professional journal.

*Principle 11. Interprofessional Relations.*   A psychologist acts with integrity in regard to colleagues in psychology and in other professions.

a. A psychologist does not normally offer professional services to a person receiving psychological assistance from another professional worker except by agreement with the other worker or after the termination of the client's relationship with the other professional worker.

b. The welfare of clients and colleagues requires that psychologists in joint practice or corporate activities make an orderly and explicit arrangement regarding the conditions of their association and its possible termination. Psychologists who serve as employers of other psychologists have an obligation to make similar appropriate arrangements.

*Principle 12. Remuneration.*   Financial arrangements in professional practice are in accord with professional standards that safeguard the best interest of the client and the profession.

a. In establishing rates for professional services, the psychologist considers carefully both the ability of the client to meet the financial burden and the charges made by other professional persons engaged in comparable work. He is willing to contribute a portion of his services to work for which he receives little or no financial return.

b. No commission or rebate or any other form of remuneration is given or received for referral of clients for professional services.

c. The psychologist in clinical or counseling practice does not use his relationships with clients to promote, for personal gain or the profit of an agency, commercial enterprises of any kind.

d. A psychologist does not accept a private fee or any other form of remuneration for professional work with a person who is entitled to his services through an institution or agency. The policies of a particular agency may make explicit provision for private work with its clients by members of its staff, and in such instances the client must be fully apprised of all policies affecting him.

*Principle 13. Test Security.*   Psychological tests and other assessment devices, the value of which depends in part on the naivete of the subject, are not reproduced or described in popular publications in ways that might invalidate the techniques.

Access to such devices is limited to persons with professional interests who will safeguard their use.

a. Sample items made up to resemble those of tests being discussed may be reproduced in popular articles and elsewhere, but scorable tests and actual test items are not reproduced except in professional publications.
b. The psychologist is responsible for the control of psychological tests and other devices and procedures used for instruction when their value might be damaged by revealing to the general public their specific contents or underlying principles.

*Principle 14. Test Interpretation.* Test scores, like test materials, are released only to persons who are qualified to interpret and use them properly.

a. Materials for reporting test scores to parents, or which are designed for self-appraisal purposes in schools, social agencies, or industry are closely supervised by qualified psychologists or counselors with provisions for referring and counseling individuals when needed.
b. Test results or other assessment data used for evaluation or classification are communicated to employers, relatives, or other appropriate persons in such a manner as to guard against misinterpretation or misuse. In the usual case, an interpretation of the test result rather than the score is communicated.
c. When test results are communicated directly to parents and students, they are accompanied by adequate interpretive aids or advice.

*Principle 15. Test Publication.* Psychological tests are offered for commercial publication only to publishers who present their tests in a professional way and distribute them only to qualified users.

a. A test manual, technical handbook, or other suitable report on the test is provided which describes the method of constructing and standardizing the test, and summarizes the validation research.
b. The populations for which the test has been developed and the purposes for which it is recommended are stated in the manual. Limitations upon the test's dependability, and aspects of its validity on which research is lacking or incomplete, are clearly stated. In particular, the manual contains a warning regarding interpretations likely to be made which have not yet been substantiated by research.
c. The catalog and manual indicate the training or professional qualifications required for sound interpretation of the test.
d. The test manual and supporting documents take into account the principles enunciated in the *Technical Recommendations for Psychological Tests and Diagnostic Techniques.*
e. Test advertisements are factual and descriptive rather than emotional and persuasive.

*Principle 16. Research Precautions.* The psychologist assumes obligations for the welfare of his research subjects, both animal and human.

a. Only when a problem is of scientific significance and it is not practicable to investigate it in any other way is the psychologist justified in exposing research subjects, whether children or adults, to physical or emotional stress as part of an investigation.
b. When a reasonable possibility of injurious aftereffects exists, research is conducted only when the subjects or their responsible agents are fully informed of this possibility and agree to participate nevertheless.

c. The psychologist seriously considers the possibility of harmful aftereffects and avoids them, or removes them as soon as permitted by the design of the experiment.
d. A psychologist using animals in research adheres to the provisions of the Rules Regarding Animals, drawn up by the Committee on Precautions and Standards in Animal Experimentation and adopted by the American Psychological Association.

*Principle 17. Publication Credit.* Credit is assigned to those who have contributed to a publication, in proportion to their contribution, and only to these.

a. Major contributions of a professional character, made by several persons to a common project, are recognized by joint authorship. The experimenter or author who has made the principal contribution to a publication is identified as the first listed.
b. Minor contributions of a professional character, extensive clerical or similar nonprofessional assistance, and other minor contributions are acknowledged in footnotes or in an introductory statement.
c. Acknowledgment through specific citations is made for unpublished as well as published material that has directly influenced the research or writing.
d. A psychologist who compiles and edits for publication the contributions of others publishes the symposium or report under the title of the committee or symposium, with his own name appearing as chairman or editor among those of the other contributors or committee members.

*Principle 18. Responsibility toward Organization.* A psychologist respects the rights and reputation of the institute or organization with which he is associated.

a. Materials prepared by a psychologist as a part of his regular work under specific direction of his organization are the property of that organization. Such materials are released for use or publication by a psychologist in accordance with policies of authorization, assignment of credit, and related matters which have been established by his organization.
b. Other material resulting incidentally from activity supported by any agency, and for which the psychologist rightly assumes individual responsibility, is published with disclaimer for any responsibility on the part of the supporting agency.

*Principle 19. Promotional Activities.* The psychologist associated with the development or promotion of psychological devices, books, or other products offered for commercial sale is responsible for ensuring that such devices, books, or products are presented in a professional and factual way.

a. Claims regarding performance, benefits, or results are supported by scientifically acceptable evidence.
b. The psychologist does not use professional journals for the commercial exploitation of psychological products, and the psychologist-editor guards against such misuse.
c. The psychologist with a financial interest in the sale or use of a psychological product is sensitive to possible conflict of interest in his promotion of such products and avoids compromise of his professional responsibilities and objectives.

# APPENDIX D
# AN EXAMPLE OF A JOB DESCRIPTION*

## Dry Cleaner (Hand)

### Job Summary
Removes dirt and spots from drapes, window shades, lamp shades, leather goods, and fabrics too delicate to be machine dry-cleaned, by scrubbing them with a solution of soap and cleaning solvent.

### Work Performed
1. Examines article to be cleaned: Observes texture and condition of fabric, and the nature of the spot, to decide how intensive a scrubbing action the material will withstand without injury; reads note attached to article to learn extent of cleaning desired by customer.
2. Cleans article: Spreads and holds article flat on scrubbing table so that scrubbing action will not tear or injure fabric; dips cup into solution of soap and cleaning solvent and pours it over spot; moistens brush of appropriate stiffness in solution and scrubs coarse fabrics with a vigorous motion in all directions; scrubs fine fabrics with a gentle motion in only one direction to avoid injury to material; scrapes hardened spots with a bone spatula; rinses article in a trough containing clean solvent to rinse out the dirt; may manipulate valves to drain and refill rinsing trough, and give article a final rinse in the clean solution. (The same kind of cleaning solvent is used for all fabrics.)
3. May assist FURNITURE WASHER to move large pieces to and from drying room.

### Equipment
Scrubbing table: A waist-high table with a wooden, stone, or metal top on which articles are scrubbed and rinsed to clean them. Usually the table is provided with a low rim around its edges and slopes gradually to a trough so that liquids will drain into the trough instead of spilling onto the floor.

### Relation to Other Jobs
Promotion to: DRY CLEANER.
Transfer from and to: FURNITURE WASHER.
Job Combination: The duties of this job may be included in those of FURNITURE WASHER or DRY-CLEANER HELPER.

### Specialized Qualifications
Many establishments hire inexperienced workers and train them in the methods characteristic of the establishment.
Ability to ascertain the strength of the various fabrics to prevent damage by excessive scrubbing, is desirable.

* From U.S. Employment Service, Job Analysis and Information Section. *Job descriptions for the cleaning, dyeing, and pressing industry.* Washington: Govt. Printing Office, 1938, p. 61.

# APPENDIX E
## TEST PUBLISHERS

Below are the names and addresses of some of the larger American publishers and distributors of psychological tests. Catalogues of current tests can be obtained from these publishers on request. Manuals and specimen sets of tests can be purchased by qualified users. For names and addresses of other test publishers, see the Publisher's Directory in the latest *Mental Measurements Yearbook*.

California Test Bureau, Del Monte Research Park, Monterey, California

Consulting Psychologists Press, Inc., 577 College Avenue, Palo Alto, California

Educational Test Bureau, 720 Washington Avenue, S.E., Minneapolis 14, Minnesota

Educational Testing Service, Cooperative Test Division, 20 Nassau Street, Princeton, New Jersey

Harcourt, Brace & World, Inc., Test Department, 757 Third Ave., New York 17, New York

Houghton Mifflin Company, 2 Park Street, Boston 7, Massachusetts

Institute for Personality and Ability Testing, 1602 Coronado Drive, Champaign, Illinois

Psychological Corporation, 304 East 45th Street, New York 17, New York

Psychological Test Specialists, Box 1441, Missoula, Montana

Psychometric Affiliates, Box 1625, Chicago 90, Illinois

Public School Publishing Company, 345 Calhoun Street, Cincinnati 19, Ohio

Science Research Associates, Inc., 259 East Erie Street, Chicago 11, Illinois

Sheridan Supply Company, P.O. Box 837, Beverly Hills, California

C. H. Stoelting Company, 424 North Homan Avenue, Chicago 24, Illinois

Western Psychological Services, Box 775, Beverly Hills, California

Numbers in **boldface** type indicate bibliography pages. The majority of references are cited in text by number only. All, however, are included in the Author Index. When looking up such a reference, find the name on the bibliography page, note the reference number, then locate it on the given text page.

# SUBJECT INDEX

200646

## DATE DUE

| NOV 15 '78 | | | |
|---|---|---|---|
| MAR 17 '80 | | | |
| DEC 1 0 '80 | | | |
| OCT 29 '90 | | | |
| MAR 0 5 1996 | | | |
| | | | |
| | | | |
| | | | |
| | | | |
| | | | |
| | | | |
| | | | |
| | | | |
| | | | |
| | | | |
| | | | |
| | | | |
| GAYLORD | | | PRINTED IN U.S.A. |